The American Search for Economic Justice

For

S M M

&

W

The
American Search
for
Economic Justice

PETER D. McCLELLAND

Basil Blackwell

Library of Congress Cataloging in Publication Data
McClelland, Peter D.
The American search for economic justice/by Peter D. McClelland.
    p. cm.
Includes bibliographical references.
ISBN 1-55786-068-8
1. Distributive justice. 2. Income distribution– –United States.
3. Capitalism– –United States– –Moral and ethical aspects. I. Title.
HB523.M37 1990
174– –dc20
                                                            89-37707
                                                                 CIP

British Library Cataloguing in Publication Data

A CIP catalogue record for this book is available from the British Library.

Typeset in 10 on 11 pt Baskerville
by TecSet Ltd, Wallington, Surrey
Printed in Great Britain by T J Press Ltd., Padstow

Contents

List of Figures

List of Tables

General Editors' Preface

Interest is growing throughout the human sciences in studies that look for an understanding beyond what can be gotten from the narrow set of methods positivist philosophy had deemed scientific. "Theory" in the human sciences need not be restricted to exercises in mathematical model building. "Empirical work" can involve more than the search for quantitative patterns in statistical data. The "philosophy of economics" can involve more than a set of methodological recipes to make the human sciences look more like physics. The "human sciences" are starting to notice that they have at least as much to learn from the humanities as they do from the sciences. Calls for a more humanistic and interpretive approach are even beginning to be heard from within the economics profession.

The *Interpretive Economics* series will be an outlet for the exciting new work in economics that exemplifies what a more interpretive approach has to offer. It is particularly interested in work that is being done on the interface of economics with fields where "more interpretive" kinds of research are already going on, such as anthropology, history, sociology, linguistics, ethics, social theory, cognitive science, and others. It will include studies that shed new light on economic subjects through the creative use of interpretive approaches.

The series will comprise three major strands under the following headings.

Interpretive Empirical Studies. Interpretive empirical studies would include, for example, historical interpretations of past events on the basis of original, archival research, or anthropological studies of current events, on the basis of participant-observation and interviewing methods. The editors are thinking of "close-up" studies of specific market processes, economic communities and institutions, and policy making. Case studies could be undertaken of the discursive processes underlying important institutions of the economy, for example, how a bank's employees make decisions about credit transactions, how management/labor relations are seen from "both" sides, etc.

History of Economic Theory. Books under this heading will study the past of economics in the light of concerns that arise in contemporary economics. The editors are especially interested in intellectual histories that are oriented toward improving our understanding of the diverse interpretive frameworks one encounters in the history of economics.

Philosophy of Economics. Here the editors are looking for studies that use interpretive strategies to study the rhetoric and interpretive frameworks of economics, as well as ethical, religious, and political issues in an economic context.

This series will not be captured under one political label. What the editors share is not policy conclusions but a certain orientation about how economics can deepen its interpretive dimension, both in its theorizing and its empirical work. They share the conviction that the interpretive approach will bring new life into economic discourse and hope that the series will be an important vehicle for the dissemination of this approach.

Arjo Klamer
Don Lavoie

Acknowledgements

For an enterprise spanning many disciplines and requiring almost a decade to complete, no brief expression of appreciation can do justice to the contributions made by so many along the way. The original inspiration can nevertheless be traced to one man. Davydd Greenwood, by his own multidisciplinary interests and by enlisting my participation in various colloquia and seminars, first stimulated my interest in the problem of American perceptions of economic justice. His support was also indispensable in acquiring a grant from the Mellon Foundation to finance the early stages of research. To that Foundation and to Davydd I am grateful for support that was decisive in launching this investigation.

Other Cornell colleagues have helped in great and small ways over the years, many by offering suggestions, references, and insights that they no doubt have long since forgotten. Among these are the members of three interdisciplinary faculty discussion groups whose wit and erudition I have been privileged to share since coming to Cornell.

For reading all or part of the manuscript and offering constructive suggestions I am indebted to Stuart M. Blumin, Urie Bronfenbrenner, Ronald G. Ehrenberg, Davydd J. Greenwood, Michael Kammen, Steven L. Kaplan, A. Gerd Korman, Isaac Kramnick, Walter F. LaFeber, David B. Lyons, Maurice F. Neufeld, Jeremy A. Rabkin, Nicholas A. Salvatore, Henry Shue, Robert J. Smith, and Cushing Strout, all of Cornell; and beyond the confines of Cornell, Barry P. Bosworth, The Brookings Institution; Martin Bronfenbrenner, Aoyama Gakuin University; Greg J. Duncan, Institute for Social Research, University of Michigan; Irwin Garfinkel and Elizabeth Uhr, Institute for Research on Poverty, University of Wisconsin; Arjo Klamer, George Washington University; and G. Daniel Little, First Presbyterian Church, Ithaca.

Two other groups should be singled out for special mention. One is the staff of Cornell's many libraries, who repeatedly gave assistance with a skill and cheerfulness quite unmatched in my experience. The other consists of all those research assistants whose diligent searching for citations and scouring of sources was indispensable for bringing this project to completion: Mica Bennett, Kathy Eagen, Robin Emanuel, Rebecca Erdman, Michelle Falk, Nina Kim, Christopher Koppenheffer, Alan Lepp, Chris Naticchia, Annette Sanford Werner, Acela Sanchez, and Neil Whoriskey.

Any project of multiple drafts and many pages inevitably taxes the patience and stamina of the one responsible for transforming written scrawl into finished typescript. To Pat Paucke I am grateful for accomplishing this task with a quiet geniality and graceful persistence that belied the mechanical frailties of a word processor given to making additions and deletions on its own. For overseeing repairs to this machine and related repairs to my morale – as well as for assistance with countless administrative details – I owe a special debt to the Economics Department's executive officer, Dan Wszolek.

The remaining debt to be acknowledged – last in order but of the first importance – is to my family who have endured with unflagging good spirits the upheavals, uncertainties and frustrations of this research, offering distractions when needed and a refuge when necessary from the toils of academia.

The political problem of mankind is to combine three things: Economic Efficiency, Social Justice, and Individual Liberty.

John Maynard Keynes, *Essays in Persuasion*, p. 344

I am certain . . . that nothing has done so much to destroy the juridical safeguards of individual freedom as the striving after this mirage of social justice.

Friedrich A. Hayek, *New Studies in Philosophy, Politics, Economics and the History of Ideas*, pp. 110–11

Introduction: The Problem

The reviewer was exasperated. The book under scrutiny – Alan Blinder's *Hard Heads, Soft Hearts* – had the subtitle *Tough-Minded Economics for a Just Society*. At issue was whether its policy proposals were both tough-minded and wrongheaded. The reviewer readily acknowledged that Blinder was "one of the brightest and most appealing"[1] of contemporary liberal economists. A dust jacket quotation from Nobel laureate Paul A. Samuelson referred to Blinder as "the golden mean 'twixt Galbraith and Friedman." For reviewer David Henderson, a former staff economist with President Reagan's Council of Economic Advisers, that mean was wide of the mark. Blinder, he conceded, was right about protectionism (against it) and right about effluent charges (for them) but completely wrong about economic justice.

[Blinder's] case [for redistributing wealth] is a familiar one: that a poor man values a dollar more than a rich man. And so, argues Blinder, it is "but a short hop" to the conclusion that government must redistribute income from rich to poor. But that's not a short hop at all – it's a huge *non sequitur*. If Blinder had two students, one with a grade-point average of A and one with an average of C, and if he were convinced that the C student valued high grades more than the A student did, would he "redistribute" grades from the A student to the C student? I doubt it. I suspect that Blinder would view any such redistribution as unjust and would argue that the A student *earned* the grade while the C student did not. Why doesn't similar logic pertain to people who earn high incomes?[2]

That economists should be writing and reviewing books about economic justice is, at first glance, rather curious. Economists themselves are quick to insist that their professional training gives them no special expertise for analyzing ethical issues. One therefore hardly expects that, in policy debates about economic justice, a small group from this particular social science should be recognized as national authorities. Yet the list of influential spokespersons for left and right within America in recent decades has become heavily weighted with economists. Milton Friedman, Friedrich Hayek, Murray Rothbard, Arthur Okun, Lester Thurow, John Kenneth Galbraith – these are but the leading members of a short list whose views are widely read and commonly cited in discussions about how the American economy does function and ought to function.

The puzzle deepens when one realizes that the arguments of all these economists concerning economic justice are fundamentally flawed. But this is to get ahead of our story. Before investigating common misunderstandings of economic justice, we would do well to investigate the basic nature of that which is misunderstood.

Economic justice has long been judged a national priority of the first importance in the United States. Most Americans would consider a just economic system an integral part of the good society, and any improvement in the actual justice of their own economic system as progress toward a better America. But what does it mean to improve the justice of an economic system? Or to sharpen the question further, what is the meaning of the phrase "economic justice"?

The search for an answer appropriately begins with distributive justice, which (as the name implies) is concerned with whether the distribution of public honors, wealth, or other rewards and penalties of society is "just."[3] The domain of economic justice is much narrower, limited as it is to questions concerning the justice of the distribution of economic goods and services. If the question is asked "Is this economic distribution just?" the questioner may be concerned with procedures leading to that distribution. For example, "Did the market system which generated these income payments function in a 'just' way?"[4] Alternatively the questioner may have in mind the actual distribution (rather than the procedures leading to that distribution) such as, for example, "Was the income distribution in the United States in 1987 a just distribution?" Ideally one would like to have it both ways: that both the procedures and the end result are judged to be just, or constitute a "just distribution justly arrived at."[5] Subsequent discussion will use "fair" as equivalent to "just," and "economic justice" as equivalent to "social justice." A case can be made that neither is strictly correct,[6] but both are common in the literature to be examined. Because our principal task will be the exploration of popular beliefs, what is commonly done will determine usage, at least for much of this work.

But what is it in popular treatments of economic justice that we should be attempting to discover? Here the philosopher seems to offer useful guidance.

The task of a theory of distributive justice is to provide the machinery in terms of which one can assess the relative merits or demerits of a distribution, the "assesment" in question being made from the moral or ethical point of view. Its objective is to establish a *principle* by which the "assessment" of alternative possible distributions can be carried out.[7]

We are therefore not looking for a set of government policies designed to make the American economic system more just. Rather, the object of our search is that which leads to the advocacy of such policies: the "principles" that provide the "machinery" for assessing distributions as just or unjust, and accordingly generate policy proposals to make the economic system, in its functioning and in its results, more just. All this sounds reasonable enough. But is it?

Among philosophers, Bernard Williams is one of the few to question the role philosophers might play in helping ordinary people to make ethical judgments.[8] In his investigation of ethics in general (as distinct from economic justice in particular), he points up two mismatches: (a) between what philosophers claim to want (universal, objective moral principles to guide ethical decision-making)[9] and what philosophers have been able to produce, and (b) between the approach to ethical questions advocated by philosophers (involving the use of the type of principles noted) and the manner in which most people actually make ethical judgments, including judgments about economic justice. Concerning the first of these, the evidence is unambiguous that the philosophers have failed to deliver the goods. No sooner is an ethical theory advanced by one philosopher than other philosophers are quick to offer trenchant criticisms, and when the dust clears what remains is not a generally accepted ethical theory but the tattered remnants of a theory.[10] What is seldom noted – or noted by philosophers – is the profound indifference of the public to these efforts at intellectual construction and subsequent tearing down. Were such indifference not so common it would be more easily seen for what it is: a remarkable absence of public attention to the efforts of some of the best minds in society to resolve problems of consummate importance to all. Which brings us to the second mismatch.

Each of us makes ethical judgments every day. We have to answer the key question put by Bernard Williams (and also by Socrates): How should one live?[11] Or as Thomas Nagel has elaborated the question: "how we should live in relation to one another is the defining question of ethics . . . ."[12] What is abundantly clear is that in finding answers, we do not limit ourselves to the procedures advocated by philosophers, and predictably so. If philosophers have not delivered what they themselves demand for making ethical judgments, and if the making of ethical judgments is an integral part of getting on with social life, then the refusal on the part of the general public to adhere to criteria and procedures advocated by philosophers in making those judgments is surely not surprising. (Put differently, the second mismatch noted above would seem inevitable, given the first mismatch.) This leaves us with a difficult puzzle: how are ethical judgments actually made by ordinary people in the course of daily living? To compress a great darkness into a single statement, the answer is not well understood – not by philosophers, and not by social scientists.

That there should be any darkness at all is puzzling. All of us, as noted, make such judgments every day. If we can make them, and do make them repeatedly, why do we have so much difficulty explaining how we make them? To explain in this context is usually to try to generalize about the nature of the decision-making process by which ethical choices are made. But that merely changes the nature of the question. Why should generalizing about ethical decision-making be so difficult?

Three related arguments, all relatively simple, suggest a least a partial answer. These same three arguments will also be found to have profound implications for the study of economic justice.

The first of these is a common topic of introductory ethics courses. At issue is whether any ethical rule – for example, "Thou shalt not kill" – can be regarded as a universal proposition. If it can, then following the rule should lead to the "right" ethical choice in every conceivable situation. This is easily shown not to be the case by imagining a situation where the rule implies a choice that appears to be wrong. In the case of the commandment just cited, suppose that your native country is about to be taken over by a foreign invader with totalitarian ambitions unless that invasion is repelled by force of arms. Or alternatively, suppose in a frontier setting that you can only save your family by killing some of the bandits who are attacking your house. These examples illustrate the general problem. Most people honor many values, and these values often come into conflict with one another in particular situations. In the above, examples were deliberately contrived in which the priority of not killing was made to conflict with the priority of preserving one's nation or one's family, but many other clashes are the stuff of daily life: telling the truth may inflict great pain; resisting tyranny may cost the lives of loved ones; welfare programs for the needy may require revenues that can only be raised by infringing on the property rights of others.

One implication of this first argument is that a hope commonly encountered in the writings of philosophers from Socrates to the present day is a vain hope: that the good society ultimately can be governed by a set of ethical truths that constitute a harmonious whole. The point is *not* that such truths are difficult to discover. Rather the set – as a set – is impossible to find because the desired intrinsic harmony is impossible to achieve. Noting the inevitability of repeated clashes among values – or among "Great Goods" as he prefers to label them – Isaiah Berlin makes a related point in more rigorous language: "The notion of the perfect whole, the ultimate solution, in which all good things coexist, seems to me to be not merely unattainable . . . but conceptually incoherent; I do not know what is meant by a harmony of this kind."[13]

A second argument follows from the one just made. If a clash among values is an inevitable component of social existence, then reaching the "right" ethical judgment frequently requires the would-be judge to make tradeoff decisions among values that conflict in a particular situation. If tradeoffs must be made, the relative importance of competing claims must be weighed. Or as Berlin illustrates the point:

. . . in concrete situations not every claim is of equal force – so much liberty and so much equality; so much for sharp moral condemnation, and so much for understanding a given human situation; so much for the full force of the law, and so much for the prerogative of mercy; for feeding the hungry, clothing the naked, healing the sick, sheltering the homeless.[14]

But how are these weights of competing claims to be determined? The search for an answer leads to the third and final argument.

Consider the problem of whether to provide a minimum income for all Americans, including the able-bodied poor. To decide whether this is the "right" ethical choice (or the best choice among those available), the decision-maker must make a number of forecasts, including the following.

1   How much money will be needed to fund such a program, what kind of tax increases will be required to raise these funds, and will such increases in those particular taxes undermine productivity by undermining the willingness to work, to save, and to invest?
2   Will the guarantee of a minimum income undermine the work ethic among prospective recipients, making them more dependent and less self-sufficient, more inclined to rely on state welfare and less willing to take responsibility for their own economic fate?
3   Does access to a generous welfare scheme such as this one disrupt the family structure of the poor, encouraging some marriages to break up and others not to form, while fostering a rise in births out of wedlock?

Notice three points. First, values commonly come in conflict with one another when ethical choices are at stake. Here the priority of charity is potentially in conflict with the desire for efficiency (or the largest possible gross national product) the self-sufficiency and self-respect of the individual, and the sanctity of the traditional two-parent family. Second, to decide the extent to which these values are in conflict, the decision-maker must make a variety of forecasts: in this instance, the forecasts required to answer the questions noted. Third, these forecasts are crucially dependent upon the context of the prospective clash. What are the specifics of the welfare scheme? To fund it, which kind of taxes will need to be raised and by how much? Will this welfare scheme, in all its specifics, affect the behavior and attitudes of different kinds of prospective recipients in detrimental ways?

From these general observations illustrated by this particular example a simple inference follows. If *a knowledge of context* is needed to make forecasts, forecasts are needed to assign weights, and weights are needed to make tradeoffs among competing values, then whenever values are in conflict, formulating general rules about the "right" choice or the "right" tradeoff *independent of the context of the clash* is extremely difficult to do. And the more common clashes are to ethical choices in daily life, the less useful general rules will be as a guide to ethical behavior.

Notice finally the kinds of forecasts required. Some may have an aura of precision: for example, estimates of dollars needed to fund a particular welfare program, or the changes in the tax structure required to generate such dollars (although both of these can also be wide of the mark, as previous federal welfare legislation has often demonstrated with a vengeance). But some forecasts cannot have any pretension to precision. Generally these are the ones that require the forecaster to gauge likely human responses (in behavior, attitudes, and values) to changes in objective circumstances associated with different choices; here, the choice between the introduction of a new welfare program and the retention of the old one. To guide such predictions we simply do not have well-established cause-and-effect generalizations linking stimulus to response as we have, say, in the natural sciences. But then how are such forecasts to be made? The answer involves bringing to bear the sum total of the forecaster's knowledge, experience, and beliefs deemed relevant – often a vast array of information, often varying markedly across individuals, and seldom capable of complete and precise enumeration by any given individual. Our difficulty in explaining how we make ethical judgments – despite the fact we make them every day – is no longer quite so puzzling. A typical explanation of choice procedures usually tries to summarize rules being employed by the chooser as, say, economic choices are summarized by the generalizations imbedded in economic theory. If the manner in which ethical choices are made does not in most instances consist of following a well-specified set of rules, but generally requires the weighing of multiple and often conflicting values in the context of a specific situation where the relevant specifics include forecasting the likely results of different possible actions on the basis of imperfect information, then explanations of this choice procedure can hardly hope to be cast in terms of simple generalizations, including generalizations describing the application of universal rules. More simply put, if context is crucial to choice, generalizations about the nature of the choice procedure are extremely difficult to make.

Because conflicts among values are inevitable and rules for resolving such conflicts are difficult to make, the process whereby one learns to make ethical judgments is not unlike the process whereby one learns to use a language. The first step consists in learning the rudiments of a vocabulary or the rudiments of a set of values (this is "good" and that is "bad"). Thereafter the choice of the "right" or "better" word or the "right" or "better" ethical action will depend crucially upon the context in which the choice is made. On a particular June morning, I confront the problem: should I tell the truth and thereby grievously hurt my closest friend? In searching for an answer, I try to identify past situations "just like" the present situation to guide my choice. The difficulty is that my previous experiences are almost never "just like" the one in question (remembering that the phrase "the situation" generally encompasses estimates of likely consequences from different courses of action). The inferential process by which past situations are judged to be "somewhat" similar to the present situation is complex, as is the adjustment process whereby dissimilarities are corrected for. My ability to make better choices over time should improve, in part because the stock of "somewhat" similar experiences will increase with age, as should my sophistication in judging similarities and correcting for differences.

Which brings us to the main point of this chapter. The advice of philosopher Nicholas Rescher quoted earlier seems to head us in the wrong direction. If our task is to gain a better understanding of distributive justice or its narrower variant, economic justice, we can hardly expect to find *the* principle or *a* principle "by which 'assessment' of alternative possible distributions can be carried out."[15] Such a quest flies in the face of points just made: in assessing alternative possible distributions, we try to honor many different values, those values often conflict, and the appropriate resolution of such a clash can seldom be specified independent of the context in which the clash occurs.

What then might constitute the right direction, or at least a more promising direction? Such a question is not easily answered. Two possibilities among many are the topics of this book. What they are and how they will be investigated are the subjects of the next chapter.

1

The Approach

A controlling premise of this book is that useful insights can be gained into both the nature and the complexity of economic justice by exploring perceptions of economic justice that have tended to dominate American culture. This exploration will proceed at two quite different levels. One focuses upon "popular" perceptions, the central thesis being that a particular set of beliefs have exerted a controlling influence on the perceptions of many Americans concerning economic justice from the time of the young republic to the present day. The other focuses upon theories and policy recommendations of influential intellectuals on the left and right, with special emphasis on those of influence in the postwar era. The writings of this latter group are generally suspect on at least four counts: (a) they tend to assume that economic justice is a relatively simple subject; (b) they approach that subject in the manner favored by philosophers, that is, they try to identify a handful of first principles from which judgments about economic justice can be inferred in any concrete situation; (c) among the principles they commonly employ are premises that directly contradict what the majority of Americans commonly believe; and (d) the conclusions reached and policies advocated by writers of both left and right are usually supported by statements of fact which, on close inspection, are often little more than educated guesses masquerading in the guise of demonstrated certainty.

A few preliminary words – and preliminary warnings – are needed concerning both kinds of perceptions to be investigated.

Terms such as "left" and "right" – or "liberal" and "conservative" – are regarded with suspicion by political scientists, their point being that such labels can be relatively devoid of meaning because a single word is used to designate a set of individuals whose views vary widely. Or put another way, "liberal" and "conservative" can imply consensus about policies preferred or philosophical premises shared or both, when no such consensus actually exists. Valid as such objections may be in other areas of belief, consensus does seems to exist concerning matters relating to economic justice – or, more cautiously, enough consensus exists within the American left and right to give those terms sufficient clarity of meaning for purposes of this study.

Many aspects of this consensus are common knowledge: the special weight in their scale of values given to freedom by modern conservatives and to equality by liberals; the asymmetry in skepticism concerning the performance of the market and the state, conservatives having much faith in the first and little in the second, while the liberal faith is just the opposite; the related concern – or absence of concern – that pursuit of the "welfare state" will bring in its wake the threat of a totalitarian government; the sharply differing views (not unrelated to the previous point) about the merits of state intervention to achieve substantial income redistribution. Other differences between the American left and right will become more clear in the course of this study. What will also become clear is that the beliefs of both camps concerning economic justice are markedly at variance with those held by the middle. Indeed, the position of either the extreme left or the extreme right, when properly understood, would destroy what is for most Americans a central tenet of their beliefs concerning economic justice, namely, that the economic system of their country is "relatively" or "reasonably" fair or just.

If the structure of beliefs of left and right within America are imperfect guides to the views of the middle concerning economic justice, those structures – judged as structures – are also less than perfect as examples of how to reason about this topic. The selection of liberal and conservative writers to be examined in this study was largely determined by two criteria: (a) they had to be generally regarded as among the intellectual leaders of their own camp, and (b) the camp they represented had to be of some importance in the American political spectrum. The first ruled out those known for the heat of their polemics but not the cogency of their arguments. The second ruled out all advocates of socialism and ideologies further to the left (including variants of Marxism and neo-Marxism), because such ideologies have never been able to muster much support within America. Typical of liberal writers to be examined are Arthur Okun, Lester Thurow, John Kenneth Galbraith and the Catholic bishops who crafted the first draft of the "U.S. Bishops' Pastoral Letter on Catholic Social Teaching and the U.S. Economy." Among the writers to be considered on the right are Milton Friedman, Irving Kristol, Friedrich Hayek, and the Lay Commission on Catholic Social Teaching and the US Economy (a collection of conservative Catholics who sought to challenge the liberal views endorsed in the first draft of the above-mentioned pastoral letter). From intellects such as these one would expect to find a breadth of vision in approach, a subtle grasp of a subject that is intrinsically complex, carefulness in the formulation of arguments, and candor in acknowledging the limits of our understanding. One finds instead a narrowness of focus in the selection of values to be honored in the pursuit of economic justice, a lack of care in defining the meaning of values thus chosen to be honored (notably "freedom" and "equality"), and a propensity to claim as demonstrated fact what is actually a tentative hypothesis made tentative by a lack of supporting evidence. Both liberals and conservatives are not totally unaware of such shortcomings, although each group tends to be more conscious of defects that mar the writings of the other camp – a standard bias in critical proclivities that Clifford Geertz has characterized as:

I have a social philosophy;
you have political opinions;
he has an ideology.[1]

Such gradations of opinion by a noted anthropologist serve to remind us that not all approaches to economic justice will be equally rigorous, particularly among Americans who are, as Albert Jay Nock put it, "the most unphilosophical of beings."[2] Henry George put it less kindly. "The average American voter . . . gives to the fundamental questions of government not much more thought than a streetcar horse does to the profits of the line."[3] What is true for the fundamental principles of government is equally true for the fundamental principles of economic justice. Which brings us to the other level of investigation of this work.

To use the phrase "popular perceptions of economic justice" is asking for trouble or, at a minimum, inviting a thundersquall of protests and confusions. Some attention must accordingly be given in these introductory remarks to (a) what the terms "popular" and "perceptions of economic justice" mean in the context of this study, and (b) the kind of evidence that will be used to document what is often not easily detected even within a given individual, let alone as an aggregate phenomenon with some claim to statistical significance.

The word "popular" has been used by social scientists and historians in many different contexts with many different meanings. Here its meaning is quite straightforward. As applied to various beliefs outlined below, "popular" simply means (a) "common" or "prevalent" among Americans, and (b) endorsed with sufficient conviction to condition the judgments and actions of those who share such beliefs. The first serves to emphasize that the beliefs in question are viewed as being shared by a wide spectrum of American society: from workers to management, from farmers to industrialists, from the prosperous to the underprivileged, from politicians to many members of the constituency they serve. To labor the point, "popular" in this work is *not* intended to designate any subset of American society, particularly any subset at the bottom of the economic or social ladder, such as "the common folk" or (least appropriate of all) "the lower class." The notion that conviction accompanies endorsement is also important. These are not beliefs articulated in public but ignored in private. They have a definite grip or purchase on the hearts and minds of the believers, shaping judgments about the justice of the American economic system and influencing decisions to endorse or oppose whatever policies are advocated in the name of making that economic system more fair or just.

If "popular" is easily defined, "perceptions of economic justice" is not. What we shall be attempting to identify are some of the principal components of a belief system, namely, some of the key premises which collectively inform and constrain the attitudes of the believer concerning economic justice. Notice what this belief system is *not*. It is not a set of premises from which one can rigorously infer conclusions about tradeoffs to be made in every concrete situation in which economic justice is at stake and values are in conflict. Instead, as we shall see, it is a set of premises that create a strong presumption (and only that) in favor of acceptance of the rewards generated by the market system as "reasonably" fair or just. What beliefs are held and why will be the subject of chapter 2. But we should not be surprised to find, as formulated by an unphilosophical people, that they feature an absence of philosophical rigor, a characteristic already evident in the appearance of "reasonably" in conjunction with "just" in the above sentence. Nor should we be surprised by recurring inconsistencies among beliefs or between beliefs popularly endorsed and actual practice. Throughout American history examples of the latter have been common, of which perhaps the first to spring to mind is the general acceptance in various regions at various times of overt discrimination or segregation or worse, despite the "self-evident truth," proclaimed at the nation's inception and thereafter repeatedly and fervently reaffirmed, that all men are created equal.[4]

We must, however, be careful to distinguish between a reprehensible inconsistency and an unavoidable dialectic. If reaching judgments about the economic justice of particular market mechanisms or particular government policies necessarily requires striking a balance among many goals, some of which conflict, the judgmental process will be fraught with tension, however self-conscious and carefully reasoned it may be. The evidence of this tension, in turn, should not be misconstrued as indicating an intrusion – latent or overt – of conflicting ideologies when it is the product of conflicting goals that are all integral parts of a given belief system. "A culture," writes Lionel Trilling, "is not a flow, nor even a confluence; the form of its existence is struggle, or at least debate – it is nothing if not a dialectic."[5] On issues relating to economic justice, Americans will be found to have a deeply cross-grained culture, honoring values seemingly destined to be in a constant state of vigorous conflict. The goals of individual self-realization are often not easily reconciled with those dictated by community needs; competitive individualism unleashed in marketplace activities can undermine a sense of fellowship and social solidarity among various members of society; the right to property can clash with notions of charity, particularly when the latter motivate demands for tax increases to fund public welfare programs. This intrinsic dialectic among competing values common to American culture – seeming to threaten continual tension in public debates – has nevertheless been muted in a major way by the very premises that form the core of the popular belief system concerning economic justice. Of which more in chapter 2.

The final problem requiring attention in these introductory remarks concerns the kind of evidence that might be used to document popular perceptions of economic justice. There is no ideal solution. Sources used in this study are primarily of two kinds. One consists of statements made in a variety of contexts by a variety of people with some claim to widespread appeal, such as speeches by politicians or theologians or other leading figures of the day directed to a broad audience; articles, books, and newspaper editorials written for the general public; preambles to union constitutions setting forth the aims of workers; and national platforms of the Populist movement setting forth the complaints and proposed remedies of the discontented. The other main source of evidence is the product of federal legislation crafted for the express purpose of improving the justice, or lessening the injustice, of the economic system. The professed objectives of most of this legislation are either to lessen or eradicate unfair practices in the market system, or alternatively to initiate or strengthen federal social welfare programs for the disadvantaged. The evidence thereby generated consists of the provisions chosen for the acts as well as the debates and hearings that preceded passage. The underlying assumption is that, in a democratic nation deeply committed to the principles and practices of representative government, federal legislation is indicative, at an aggregate level, of the tradeoff process among competing values, with the more important clashes evident in conflicts of opinion at Congressional hearings and debates, and the tradeoffs ultimately deemed acceptable evident in the terms approved by the legislature and the executive.

For both kinds of evidence – that arising through the processes of federal legislation and that arising in many other contexts – a recurring difficulty is that, while views may be strongly held and strongly voiced about particular policies, most Americans are not given to articulating the underlying thoughts that lead to those expressed opinions. Therefore the task of unearthing beliefs conditioning views on economic justice must often proceed indirectly, sometimes by assembling bits and pieces from different writers in search of a coherent whole, and sometimes by running the inferential process in reverse, beginning with expressed opinions on policies and ending with premises of a belief system that are consistent with available evidence including (a) the evidence provided by fragmentary statements about the larger belief structure of which they are a part and (b) the evidence provided by the advocacy or condemnation of particular kinds of policy proposals. Such a scouring of sources in search of relevant commentary is often usefully pursued by trying to discern popular answers to three related questions:

1   How should income[6] be distributed in America?
2   How is income actually distributed in America?
3   If the answers to the first and second differ, what should be done to narrow the gap between the actual and the ideal?

Any attempt to uncover popular perceptions of economic justice as defined above can, at best, only partially succeed. Only to the extent that the public's views about economic justice evidence a strong central tendency at any point in time can generalizations about the popularity of these views have any claim to validity. Only to the extent that this central tendency (however strong) has some stability over time can one hope to explore in a few hundred pages the history of a people's beliefs concerning economic justice.

The suggestion that such a strong central tendency exists, or has existed, or (most contentious of all) has existed for much of the nation's history is sure to be strenuously resisted by some readers. And yet the presence of a strong central tendency in American views on matters relating to economic justice has long been a commonplace among American observers: the widespread acceptance of private property and the free-market system – those twin institutional pillars of capitalism – and the widespread rejection of socialism and other ideologies of the extreme left; the hostility to egalitarian pleas for equal income shares and the ready acceptance of existing inequalities in income distribution; the belief in the chance for upward economic and social mobility, with advancement viewed as closely linked to personal effort and talent – premises that constitute the core of the American Dream – "American" indicative of widespread acceptance, "Dream" suggestive of the common hopes it captures, and the two words combined denoting a conception of possibilities peculiar to this country. (A comparable phrase for other nations – "the German Dream" or "the British Dream" – rings strangely in the ear.)

If marked central tendencies among such American beliefs are commonly acknowledged to exist, one obvious puzzle is why so much attention has been given to perspectives emphasizing diversity and change – in media accounts of New Frontiers and Reagan Revolutions (labels suggesting major shifts in what is popularly endorsed), and in historians' descriptions of the past, featuring as they so often do new movements purported to modify or transform old popular beliefs. Part of the answer is that Americans tend to be relatively uninformed about the breadth of ideologies popular in other countries, and are therefore more prone to view as significant changes what many foreigners would regard as minor movements within the same segment of the political spectrum. Americans also lack a self-conscious clarity in what they themselves believe, and thus are more amenable to claims of movement in what for them is generally ill-defined. Because consensus has tended to be so strong, major challenges from markedly different ideologies – and there have been many in this country – are seldom taken seriously, or seriously enough to force a mind-rattling inventory of what the self believes and why. An ignoring of attacks encourages a neglect of possible defenses, and thus a drift toward a lack of clarity and coherence in what is generally believed. As the metaphor of the melting pot suggests a sameness of results, so the popular response to those who defied intellectual assimilation was in keeping with that sameness: Americans generally ignored them.

Yet another reason for so much attention to diversity of beliefs is the bias of the chronicler. Media reporters are more preoccupied with finding novelty than continuity; left- and right-wing writers have a vested interest in proclaiming change when the change proclaimed is in the direction of their own views; historians often have the predilection of the antiquarian for uncovering detail in differing views rather than making judgments about the relative popularity of views uncovered.

Admittedly not all historians have refused to make such judgments, Richard Hofstadter in a modest way[7] and Louis Hartz in a grand way are among those who have documented what Hartz calls "our marvelous moral agreement."[8] Yet the extent of that agreement came as something of a surprise to me. When I first began to read nineteenth century writings and speeches of well-known figures who expressed opinions with some claim to popularity, I expected to find at least some modest central tendency, some coalescing of opinions around a common core of beliefs concerning economic justice. What took me by surprise was the extraordinary dominance of a small set of beliefs which, for large numbers of Americans, seemed to inform and constrain their judgments about the justice of their economic system throughout much of the nineteenth century.

This would change, I assumed, or at least be sharply modified in the twentieth century. The New Deal of the 1930s, the War on Poverty initiated in the 1960s, and possibly the Reagan Revolution of the 1980s would constitute turning points or watersheds in the evolution of American ideas concerning economic justice, or so the history of these periods had led me to expect. Available evidence on those ideas could also be bolstered by a crucial source not much in evidence prior to the 1930s. The very novelty of federal legislation addressing social welfare issues beginning with the Roosevelt era reinforced my expectation that dominant beliefs concerning economic justice would change as the twentieth century progressed. What I found instead was a remarkable persistence of nineteenth century premises, modified only in minor ways by the searing experience of the Great Depression and by the upheavals of the 1960s and beyond. The progress of American views on economic justice, I came to believe, has been more analogous to an ocean liner under way than a coastal schooner under sail, with an intrinsic momentum favoring original direction and a marked insensitivity to the shifting winds of intellectual fashion.

One final mismatch between what I anticipated and what I found should be noted at the outset. Consider the questions listed previously that are to be a window on American beliefs concerning economic justice, particularly the first two:

1   How should income be distributed in America?
2   How is income actually distributed in America?

As one trained in economics, I expected that the more renowned and widely read of American economists would have much to say about the mechanisms whereby income is actually distributed in America and little to say about how that income should be distributed. The exact opposite proved to be closer to the truth.

Economists typically distinguish between "positive" and "normative" economics, the first being concerned with mechanisms – or with explaining cause and effect in the economic world that is – and the second being concerned with judgments about what ought to be (including which economic policies should be pursued to further desired goals). The first (positive economics) is generally regarded as the appropriate intellectual arena of the economist *qua* economist – that expert trained in a social science whose models and theories purport to explain how the economy actually functions. By this view, then, "There is no conservative, or liberal, economics, just as there is no conservative, or liberal, chemistry."[9] Accordingly, if the general topic is economic justice and the particular concern is income distribution, what professional economists can offer is a theory (widely accepted by their American colleagues) which explains how market incentives and market mechanisms cause income to be distributed according to the contribution of each factor of production to final output. (The theory and such terms as "factor of production" will be translated into layman's terms in a later chapter.) Such experts are presumed to have no insights of special significance about the "justice" or "fairness" of the resulting distribution.[10] And yet just such experts are among the leading contributors to discussions of economic justice within America, as the previous list of liberal and conservative writers to be examined makes clear. As for the theory of income distribution widely accepted by American economists as a description of how the economy actually functions, the reader will find that there is less here than meets the eye. Developed at the turn of the century, this theory took the American economics profession by storm, and remains to the present day that profession's preferred explanation of the forces determining income distribution in a market economy – this despite the fact that little evidence from the actual economy has ever been assembled to establish its validity. The obvious puzzle is why so many economists on this side of the Atlantic have been so ready to accept a theory with so little empirical support, and moreover one that economists of Western Europe have been far more reluctant to endorse. A partial answer (but the part of interest to this study) concerns (a) the pronounced central tendency in American beliefs concerning economic justice, (b) the persistence of those beliefs over time, and (c) the close affinity of many of those beliefs with the assumptions of neoclassical economics, including the assumptions underlying marginal productivity analysis. To put a tentative hypothesis in its most controversial form, the major contributions of the American economics profession to American discussions of economic justice do not include a theory of obvious validity which explains how income in America is actually distributed, but do include writings about economic justice by some of the most widely read and widely respected liberals and conservatives in this country. Moreover, in their ready and continuing endorsement of marginal productivity theory, the American economics profession supplies some evidence – albeit indirect – of the hold upon American minds of certain premises integral to popular American beliefs concerning economic justice.

To review:

1 the general topic of our study is economic justice;
2 that topic will be explored
   (a) by investigating some of the major flaws in the theories of economic justice expounded by writers on the left and right whose ideas have dominated debate among American liberals and conservatives in the postwar era; and
   (b) by an effort to discover and document some of the major premises around which popular ideas concerning economic justice have tended to coalesce throughout much of the nation's history.

To work through details of arguments to come will require a special patience on the part of the reader. The problem is not that arguments will be difficult to follow. The problem is that the subject matter is typically considered to be understood already. Few outside an inner circle of philosophers have any sense of how difficult the study of economic justice is. Most Americans, irrespective of educational background or ideological preferences, will be willing to admit to some uncertainty in some situations when the task is to decide what should be done to make the functioning of the economic system more just. How best to help the homeless or the able-bodied poor or the underclass can raise dilemmas not easily resolved. But if many admit to puzzlement in certain concrete situations about how best to realize the goal of economic justice, most are confident that they understand the nature of the goal itself. In the vast majority of cases, that confidence is misplaced. Or to put the point more bluntly, a central theme of this book is that economic justice is commonly assumed to be a subject easily understood, and it is not.

A few cautionary words are accordingly in order at the outset for three different audiences.

The lay reader – those with little or no formal training in either philosophy or economics – should be heartened to learn that no formal training is needed to understand any of the points that lie ahead. The absence of that training, however, implies the need for extra work. If they would understand the complex issues crucial for any discussion of economic justice lurking in the seemingly innocuous word "freedom," they must bear with an extended discussion of the different possible meanings of that word. More demanding yet, if they would understand contemporary debates between liberals and conservatives concerning economic justice, they will need to know more about two key ideas that lie at the heart of many of those debates. These ideas are (a) that in the normal functioning of a competitive market, factors of production tend to be paid the value of their marginal product – a statement of fact – and the normative extension of that statement, namely (b) that factors of production *ought* to be paid the value of their marginal product. For those readers whose education has included some encounter with introductory economics, a compressed review of the relevant economic theory is provided in the text. Those without that background who desire a more extended explanation of the assumptions and causal mechanisms of the theory can find these discussed in an appendix.

Economists confront a different difficulty. Because the relevant theory is so familiar to them, as are the names and policy positions of so many of the writers to be examined, they may be tempted to assume that everything that lies ahead, or everything of consequence, is already understood. The best corrective for that temptation is to confront a question: if the criticisms outlined below demonstrate that all these works are fundamentally flawed, and if these same criticisms are already widely known and well understood, why do so many of the best minds in the economics profession still advocate such flawed positions, and why do the originators of these positions continue to be widely cited as authorities in debates concerning economic justice?

A second difficulty will be encountered by practitioners of this particular social science. The basic objectives of any social science are explanation, prediction, and control. To achieve such objectives, economists need theories and models, the second incorporating in various formal ways the cause-and-effect assertions of the first. Two kinds of challenges lie ahead for economists who take a sanguine view of their profession's record in using these tools to realize those objectives. One emphasizes how tenuous the empirical foundations are of the one theory commonly endorsed by American economists as an explanation of how income distribution is determined in any market economy, including the American economy. The other challenge questions the ability of many economic models to explain what they purport to explain. Consider the problem of unraveling the causes of economic growth, a question of fact that (as we shall see) is central to current poverty debates. The ambition of economists who would explain economic growth is not merely to list the relevant causes, but to devise a model that will indicate how much of actual growth can be attributed to each of the causes deemed relevant. The best indicator of how far economists are from realizing that ambition is the continuing wide diversity in the estimates generated by different models of the relative importance to economic growth of the same causal variable. This is *not* an argument against rigorous theory or mathematical models. It is an argument that emphasizes the degree of imperfection that pervades most of the models of the social sciences that purport to explain various aspects of human behavior, including economic behavior. What we do not model well, we generally do not understand well. The purpose of highlighting the related uncertainty is not to single out for condemnation economists who claim too much. Such highlighting is endemic to the objectives of this book. If a major theme is that economic justice is commonly assumed to be easily understood and it is not, and further, if central to understanding why economic justice is not easily understood is a confrontation with certain limitations in our knowledge about human behavior, it follows that an exploration of these limitations must be a part of this larger investigation. That economists are the main victims of such an exploration merely results from economists being a major source of factual claims about human behavior deemed relevant in discussions of economic justice.

Historians confront a different problem that may lead to a misunderstanding of one of the objectives of this study. Consider the structure of analysis to come. At its core is a comparison between (a) premises central to the analytical schemes of intellectuals on the left and right, and (b) a limited set of common themes around which popular beliefs concerning economic justice tend to coalesce. The crucial question is the extent to which the first clashes with the second. A clash cannot be demonstrated, however, until competing positions are made clear. One thesis of this work is that a small set of common themes have informed and constrained popular views concerning economic justice for better than a century. But to articulate the themes alone is not to explain the past. For any collection of individuals during any period in American history, be they midwestern farmers during the Populist revolt or dissatisfied mechanics in ante-bellum Boston, to understand what actual perceptions of economic justice were and why particular actions were advocated in the name of economic justice requires, at a minimum, the exploration of a complex struggle between some allegiance to these common themes on the one hand, and on the other, a multitude of perceptions and concerns in conflict with these themes, including perceptions of injustice, strands of radical ideologies, and concern for values often regarded as slighted or threatened by the market system. To investigate how this struggle was resolved within any group of any size is the appropriate topic of a book, but not this book. Our task is to identify whether any common themes existed, and if they did, what form they took, and whether that form changed significantly over time.

The road ahead promises to be long and, on occasion, somewhat demanding. Will the journey be worth the effort, the reader must be asking. That of course is a question that only can be answered at the end. It will depend crucially upon the extent to which the main objectives of this study are achieved. These are three in number.

The first is to explain the basic nature, and the major strengths and weaknesses, of two different approaches to economic justice, both of which have powerfully influenced the views of important constituencies in America. One has been common to the reasoning of intellectual leaders among conservatives and liberals in the postwar era. The other has been popular with large segments of the populace from the early nineteenth century to the present day. The one attempts to identify a system of universal propositions that will indicate the "right" choice, or the "just" choice, when economic justice is at stake in concrete situations. The other brings to questions of economic justice not rigorously formulated universal propositions but rather a set of vaguely articulated common themes which tend to inform (but seldom by themselves control) popular thoughts about which specific choices in a specific situation might make the functioning of the American economy more just.

The second objective follows from the first. A better understanding of the nature, strengths, and weaknesses of these two approaches to economic justice, plus some exploration of dilemmas commonly ignored by both, should pave the way for the reader to achieve a better synthesis between the best that these two approaches have to offer, and whatever knowledge, experience, and beliefs relevant to questions of economic justice the reader brings to this study at the outset. No effort at such a synthesis will be attempted by the author, but two personal evaluations will be given at the end. The first attempts to summarize, from a personal perspective, the best and worst in the various approaches to economic justice examined in this study. The second offers a set of policy proposals designed to be consistent with two priorities: (a) honoring time-honored American values relevant to any discussion of economic justice in this country, and (b) identifying what appear to be those policies most needed now to make the functioning of this country's economic system more just.

The third objective is more of a vague hope than a well-defined ambition. It is anchored in an article of faith: that American democratic institutions have been crafted, and will continue to be crafted, in such a way that the good instincts of humanity (or at least the better instincts) are drawn to the fore in the give and take of formulating policies and legislation, and that residing in the people are great reservoirs of humane instincts, ethical astuteness, and common sense to be tapped by the normal working out of the democratic processes. If that be true, then any improvement in the general understanding is worth pursuing, and any effort to move debates in more promising directions is worth attempting. The ultimate aim of such an enterprise, it should be emphasized, is not perfection. That would be to cloak in utopian garb the modest hope for movement in the right direction. But every reader should care about the direction and the movement. Or as Isaiah Berlin reminds us somewhat sternly, "Only barbarians are not curious about where they come from, how they came to be where they are, where they appear to be going, whether they wish to go there, and if so, why, and if not, why not."[11]

The last assignment of a preliminary sort is to provide some overview of terrain that lies ahead.

Chapter 2 tries to document the main premises exerting a controlling influence on popular perceptions of economic justice in the nineteenth century. The discussion then takes a curious turn, because the intellectual history of the nation took a curious turn. At the close of the nineteenth century, a new economic theory was advanced purporting to explain how income payments in a market system were determined. Its main conclusion was that all factors of production would tend to be paid the value of their marginal product. This theory and that conclusion are crucial to our investigation for several interrelated reasons. First (and least important), the theory almost immediately came to be accepted orthodoxy among the vast majority of American economists, and has remained so to the present day. Secondly, and more important, by a small revision in the wording of the above conclusion, a theoretical claim about how the economy worked, namely

factors of production are paid (or tend to be paid) the value of their marginal product

was converted into an ethical assertion about how the economy ought to work, namely

factors of production *ought to be* paid the value of their marginal product.

This latter assertion will be found to play a central role in the early stages of this study. It gave to income payments generated by the market system what the older belief system had already given to those payments: a stamp of ethical approval. The newer version, originating as it did in economic theory, differed from more popular notions primarily by offering a more rigorous explanation of what those payments were likely to be. But this harmony of viewpoint is of secondary importance because this theorizing by economists and the subsequent conversion of its main conclusion into a normative assertion were persistently ignored by the vast majority of Americans. However, such ideas were not ignored by intellectuals of the left and right. Indeed the twin assertions that factors of production (a) are paid, and (b) ought to be paid, the value of their marginal product became the battleground for leading liberals and conservatives in the modern era. In the resulting verbal charges and countercharges, both sides tended to follow the philosopher's lead, trying to infer from a handful of first principles conclusions about economic justice that could be used to guide normative judgments in any concrete situation. The main exchanges in this debate accordingly provide useful examples of how not to reason about economic justice. The route the book will follow in its early stages is the route of arguments just made. Chapter 3 explains the economic theory in layman's terms, the conversion of its main conclusion into an ethical norm, and the principal arguments of liberals against both the theory's factual conclusion and its normative extension. Conservative defenses of the market system are outlined in chapter 4, followed by a discussion in chapters 4 and 5 of the confusions of both liberals and conservatives. One primary goal of this entire section is to demonstrate how attacks on, and defenses of, the market system as that system is portrayed by marginal productivity theory are at the core of much of the theorizing about economic justice by intellectual leaders of the left and right.

At this point the discussion will again veer sharply, but in a direction less surprising because shortcomings heretofore uncovered point toward more promising avenues of investigation. Two words – "freedom" and "equality" – will have been found to play a central role in popular perceptions of economic justice and in the debates among intellectuals of the left and right. What also will have been discovered is that while "freedom" is a priority all seem to favor, this word has many possible meanings, and the policies required for a just economic society differ sharply depending upon which meaning is endorsed. In short, one obvious route to a better understanding of the general topic of economic justice as well as the nature of disagreements about that topic is a systematic exploration of the different possible meanings of "freedom" and "equality." These are accordingly the topics of chapters 6 and 7. With the resulting insights in hand, we can return in chapter 8 to the question of popular perceptions of economic justice, and whether beliefs fashioned in the nineteenth century changed significantly in the twentieth. The investigation begins with evidence gleaned from federal legislation – both the terms of acts and debates that preceded passage – as well as from popular opinion polls and other sources; these findings are then used to detect which meanings of "freedom" and "equality" seem to be consistent with that evidence; and finally, these implied meanings of freedom and equality are checked for consistency with the older beliefs of the nineteenth century.

At this juncture (the end of chapter 8), three issues will be standing in the wings demanding some attention, two of which are relatively easy to address while the other is not. The exploration of "freedom" and "equality" in the context of discussions of economic justice will have raised the question of the possible meaning of the word "rights" in those discussions. This is therefore the topic of chapter 9, in which earlier insights will be found to provide a reliable route through much confusion. The second topic demanding attention concerns not questions of value (which previously have dominated discussion) but rather questions of fact. In the interchanges between liberals and conservatives a host of factual statements will already have been encountered, most of which will have served to buttress normative assertions. Somewhat unexpectedly, almost all these can be grouped under four broad headings, each of which will be investigated in chapter 10. The main discovery there will be that what are commonly proclaimed as statements of fact are often not statements of fact at all. They are instead educated guesses based upon imperfect evidence and confident extrapolations from tentative generalizations concerning human behavior. Still not addressed but also lurking in much of previous discussion are a variety of dilemmas normally ignored in discussions of economic justice – dilemmas that inevitably must be confronted in any investigation of that topic with any claim to comprehensive coverage. Among dilemmas raised, those that seem to be among the more important are explored in chapter 11, not with the purpose of resolving them, but rather with the intention of making more clear what they are and why confronting such dilemmas must be an integral part of reaching judgments about economic justice.

The book concludes with two attempts at "summary and overview." The first tries to pull together insights garnered from this exploration of two quite different approaches to economic justice: that of intellectuals who have dominated debate among liberals and conservatives in the postwar era, and that informed and controlled by a handful of premises around which popular American beliefs have tended to coalesce for much of the nation's history. Previous chapters have illustrated repeatedly how seldom these two approaches intersect. The task of chapter 12 is accordingly to summarize the best of both, and to suggest directions in which a better synthesis might lie. The summarizing task of chapter 13 is quite different but no less predictable. If the topic is economic justice and the focus is America, two questions commonly asked are:

1 Has the United States economic system become more fair or just in recent decades?
2 What might be done to improve the justice of that system in the future?

This final chapter accordingly presents evidence relevant for answering the first, and policy options the author considers to be vital for achieving objectives implicit in the second.

Ahead would seem to lie a landscape not easily scampered through, or so many readers may conclude. Some may quite reasonably be wondering about a lack of relevant expertise, or whether they will become lost in intricate exchanges between left and right because their own views are "somewhere in the middle." For any who harbor such doubts, a few words of encouragement.

As previously noted, no formal training will be needed in either philosophy or economics. Insights from both these disciplines will be needed to understand many of the topics of later chapters, but all these insights can be converted, and have been converted, into layman's language, with technical issues and technical asides relegated to the endnotes. Those having expertise in either or both disciplines can expect on occasion to breeze through analyses that may strike them as unnecessarily elementary. But they are not the only audience for which this book is written. Questions of economic justice are too important to be confined to the experts.

That subject is one on which all readers are likely to have strong views. Liberals and conservatives are sure to be unsettled, if not provoked, in the chapters ahead by the array of criticisms directed against the leading advocates of their point of view. Those on the extreme left will be less than pleased to find their views almost completely absent from discussion because, as noted previously, those views are of little importance to the vast majority of Americans.[12] Marxists are sure to challenge the type of evidence used to detect "genuine" popular beliefs, including the reliance upon popular writers and politicians in the nineteenth century, and in the twentieth, upon the terms of federal social welfare legislation as well as the hearings and debates accompanying that legislation. At their most extreme, such writers tend to view the masses as manipulated by elites, and government legislation as indicative of the preferences of the powerful few, not the pliant many. One premise of this book is that influence runs both ways – from the top down but also from the bottom up, the views of the few not independent of what is popularly endorsed. A second and related premise is that throughout American history, on matters relating to economic justice, elites could not easily manipulate the views of the rest of the people all of the time, or even of most of the people much of the time. Other factors, it will be argued, were more important in determining those views. Finally, those who view themselves as not "extreme" but rather as members of the "moderate" left or right are unlikely to welcome the suggestion that, despite this moderation, they still have lost touch with the middle. Those in the middle, however, should be impressed by how many of the arguments and criticisms are little more than common sense. What "common sense" means is far from clear, but in this context this phrase implies nothing more than a reflexive nodding of the head because what appears on the page seems sensible enough, requiring no further justification or exploration. Indeed, when further exploration is attempted in the text, it may for this reason be resisted, but one ambition of this study is to uncover complexity in what seems eminently plausible to most for the sake of the better understanding of all. On occasion readers whose views are closely aligned with the middle may also find that arguments pertaining to economic justice, while appealing to the contemporary mind, have a certain old-fashioned quality. That is because they are old-fashioned. Or put more cautiously, many can trace their origins to the nineteenth century, as the next chapter tries to demonstrate.

2

Economic Justice in Historical Perspective

An approach to a theory of value which looks toward the behavior of actual people in actual societies living in terms of actual cultures for both its stimulus and its validation will turn us away from abstract and rather scholastic arguments in which a limited number of classical positions are stated again and again with little that is new to recommend them, to a process of ever-increasing insight into both what values are and how they work.

Clifford Geertz, *The Interpretation of Cultures*, p. 141

Introduction

To both historians and philosophers the anthropologist Clifford Geertz has clearly thrown down the gauntlet. The limitations of approaches to ethics typical of philosophy have been touched upon in chapter 1. The assignment for the present chapter is to investigate American values over time, with the hope that resulting insights will have some relevance for understanding more general ethical issues. Our inquiry will be somewhat narrow in two senses: first, because the topic to be investigated is not ethics in general but economic justice in particular; second, because the focus of that investigation will be confined to a limited number of premises of special importance to American culture for much of the nation's history. To pose the second point as a question, our particular concern is whether American popular views concerning economic justice have evidenced a strong central tendency, and, if they have, what those views are and whether they have changed much over time. Our concern is therefore not with the many but the one – not with whether a variety of beliefs concerning economic justice have existed simultaneously (obviously they have), but rather with the extent to which one set has been dominant among the many. The tasks ahead are accordingly formidable in the extreme: (a) to detect and document a central tendency despite the inability to quantify that tendency; (b) to discover some of the main premises informing and controlling the structure of popular beliefs concerning economic justice despite the intrinsic vagueness of that structure; and (c) to understand some of the determinants of why such premises became so popular despite our massive ignorance about the processes influencing individual or collective endorsement of particular moral standards.[1] On all three counts, then, this is an enterprise that can only partially succeed.

Confining our search to a single dominant set does not imply that the many not investigated were of no importance to the nation. Ideologies of the far right, for example, have served as a constant prod to recognize and honor a variety of freedoms and a variety of rights that constitute important strands in the nation's cultural fabric. Those on the far left have repeatedly been a moving force in reform movements that have made American society more humane – for example, in its treatment of women and minorities, convicts and the mentally ill, and those threatened by the harsher aspects of capitalism, including children whose lives and limbs were once daily placed in jeopardy in the mines and factories of a growing industrial power. But if the few far to the left or right would influence the many in the middle on matters relating to economic justice, their exhortations had to resonate with at least some of the premises of a belief system quite different from their own. To repeat, our task is to identify which premises had widespread appeal within American society, and some of the reasons why.

The Hypothesis

To the question "What is a fair wage?" – or the more general variant of that question "What is a fair income distribution?" – Americans have never had a single answer. Competing ideologies within a sprawling nation dominating half a continent were always predictably diffuse. But from the early years of the republic to the present day, the answer of many Americans has been informed and constrained by a small set of premises that collectively gave a moral validity to the procedures and the outcomes of the American market system. In their most simple and unqualified form, these premises are:

1 participation in the economic race is an admirable endeavor, both for the individual self-fulfillment it encourages and for the social benefits that result;
2 the economic race (by and large) is a fair race; and
3 prizes tend to be rewarded for hard work, thrift, and foresight (although luck may also play a role).

These three, in turn, seem to imply

4 that the resulting distribution of prizes (that is, incomes received) is a reasonably just distribution.

Each of these premises has a history at least as old as the nation, and the four combined quickly came to dominate discourse within the new republic whenever questions of economic justice took center stage or were lurking in the wings. Before their origins are investigated, a few words of explanation are in order concerning how each was customarily phrased and qualified.

The role of the first three premises, as premises, is easily misunderstood. Each is a mixture of facts and values. Each can be converted into a normative claim that the vast majority of Americans would endorse: participation in the economic race *ought* to be an admirable endeavor; the race *ought* to be fair; prizes *ought* to be rewarded for the exercise of meritorious virtues. The factual components of these statements are more difficult to characterize. Each obviously admits to exceptions. Prizes are sometimes the product not of industry, foresight, and thrift, but of bullying, conniving, and outright fraud. The race itself is obviously not perfectly fair for all participants, necessitating the insertion of such qualifying phrases as "by and large," which appears in the above version. The more numerous and the more serious the qualifications, the less clear is the substance of the factual claim. But while qualifications can vary in number and degree, these need not undermine the basic article of faith that each of the first three premises characterize strong tendencies inherent in the American market system. If all three tendencies could be viewed as strong, the inference could be retained that the resulting income distribution was "reasonably" just. More carefully yet, because the premises concern both the "rightness" of procedures and the "rightness" of results, market rewards could be viewed, not as a "just distribution justly arrived at," but rather as a rough approximation to that ideal.

The thesis tendered here is that, throughout most of the nation's history, popular qualifications tended to be of the sort just noted: that viewed as a distribution, American views concerning the first three premises tended to coalesce around qualifications that left unscathed the basic article of faith that each of these three characterized strong tendencies in their market system, and therefore left unscathed for most the related belief in the intrinsic justice of that system.

Two inferences follow, both of the first importance.

One concerns popular perceptions of income inequality. For most, such inequalities were not *intrinsically* offensive, because inequality *per se* was not regarded as sympotomatic of injustice. It was instead commonly regarded as a natural outcome of an economic system that had an inherent moral validity. To be sure, specific inequalities were repeatedly attacked, but almost always as the product of perceived flaws in the system. Solutions commonly advocated were therefore not to scrap the system but to find ways to remove the flaws in question. The implied article of faith was that, with lessening or removal, the intrinsic fairness of the market system would be restored, or roughly restored, or restored to a tolerable degree.

The second inference is lurking in previous points. Precisely because of the pervasive belief in the intrinsic moral validity of the market system, however grievous were the flaws that surfaced over time – and there were many as a young agricultural nation was transformed into an industrial giant – at no point in their history did large numbers of Americans entertain the possibility of scrapping the market system altogether and replacing it with some variant of socialism or communism. Indeed, given the common distrust of government intervention in economic matters dating from colonial days, even perceived flaws did not invariably generate widespread demands for government remedies. The crucial issue thus tended to be not "Are the results of the market system perfectly just?" (obviously they were not), but rather "Have imperfections reached a point where government intervention should be risked?" If any affirmative answer was given to the latter question, this same distrust of government and general acceptance of the market system created a bias for the least possible intervention to remove, not all imperfections, but those glaring imperfections obviously at odds with the system's meting out of just rewards in a just way. Or to put the point in mechanical terms as analysts sometimes did, the machine (the market system) was commonly viewed as functioning tolerably well most of the time, while the obvious repair mechanic (the government) was regarded with suspicion and accordingly called in usually as a last resort and seldom as a first resort. A little government tinkering here and there if necessary, ran a common article of faith, and all will be well – or as well as can be expected in an imperfect world.

Unlike philosophers, then, most Americans have never demanded or expected perfect justice from their economic system, just as they have not demanded rigor in the formulation of premises that influence their evaluations of that system. But if the wording of these premises has always been somewhat vague, their influence upon the hearts and minds of vast numbers of Americans has been powerful and persistent from the time they first began to dominate discourse about economic justice in the young republic.

An Admirable Race

Consider again the first premise. Long before their struggle to achieve political independence from Britain, most of the citizens of the 13 colonies were convinced that they had a right to life, liberty, and the pursuit of property. Or in the language of John Locke, they believed that they had a natural right: to acquire, protect, and dispose of property. The Declaration of Independence would shift the emphasis, keeping "life" and "liberty" in the list of fundamental rights, but dropping "property" and inserting "pursuit of happiness." But the controlling belief in the importance of the former remained, and the familiar trio of "life, liberty, and property" would resurface in the language of the fifth amendment to the Constitution when specifying what people were not to be deprived of "without due process of law." Nor should the suppression of the reference to property in the Declaration be viewed as symptomatic of uncertainty about the importance of that institution. The primary architect of the Declaration, Thomas Jefferson, even went so far as to suggest three decades after independence was achieved that "The true foundation of republican government is the equal right of every citizen, in his person and property, and in their management."[2] One argument buttressing that belief was the notion that power tended to follow property. The more widespread were property holdings in the new nation, the argument ran, the more diffused power would be, and thus the more able its citizens would be to resist encroachments on their liberty. Lincoln would even suggest as one possible definition of liberty: "for each man to do as he pleases, with himself, and with the product of his labor . . . ."[3]

The arguments in favor of the pursuit of property, however, are individually more diverse and collectively more compelling than indicated thus far. Acquiring property buttressed liberty. Pursuing property necessarily involved the pursuer in economic activity. And that involvement was endorsed by at least three different arguments, none of which had any evident linkage to issues of safeguarding liberty.

The first emphasized the relationship between economic activity and the acquisition of certain virtues. As frugality, industry, and foresight were required for economic success, so the pursuit of wealth was sure to foster (or so the argument ran) these same virtues. Others chose to emphasize different traits, but the central theme was always the same: that participation in a competitive economic system had beneficial effects on the character of the participants. "While the direct object of all trade is gain," Nathan Appleton conceded, "not the slightest prevarication or deviation from truth is allowable." Moreover, he warned, "Mercantile honor is as delicate and fragile as that of a woman. It will not bear the slightest stain." As a result, "There is no class of men with whom the Christian rule, of doing to others what we expect or require in return, is more strictly demanded than amongst merchants."[4] Emerson's perceptions were less colored than those of Appleton by success in business, but he too was willing to concede with evident admiration that "The game [the pursuit of wealth] requires coolness, right reasoning, promptness, and patience in the players."[5]

Emerson had other reasons for endorsing the game quite apart from how the game promoted virtue in the players. He too recognized the linkage between the diffusion of wealth – the output of the game – and the independence of the citizenry. "Poverty demoralizes," he cautioned, and "a man in debt is so far a slave."[6] But these concerns were somewhat secondary to more fundamental reasons for favoring man's participation in the economy. Emerson's metaphysical beliefs are not easily summarized, but those linking man, nature, and economic activity seem to incorporate the following:

1   nature was made to serve man;
2   man has an obligation not only to work, but to use his talents to best advantage;
3   man naturally searches for power, and in that search seeks command over nature; and
4   the result of such a search is the advancement of "civilization" (an amorphous concept, never carefully defined).[7]

Thus Emerson argued that to condemn man's preoccupation with material gain was to ignore the many benefits attributable to that preoccupation.

The pulpit and the press have many commonplaces denouncing the thirst for wealth; but if man should take these moralists at their word, and leave off aiming to be rich, the moralists would rush to rekindle at all hazards this love of power in the people, lest civilization should be undone.[8]

And again: "We rail at trade, but the historian of the world will see that it was the principle of liberty; that it settled America, and destroyed feudalism . . . ."[9]

The metaphysical beliefs of many Americans supported a similar endorsement, although the associated reasoning gave less play to the progress of civilization and more to man's part in the divine plan as that plan was articulated by conventional theologies of the day. The Rev. H. W. Bellows, for example, pastor of the First Congregational Society in New York City, assured his flock that they were all participants in "the great plan of Providence" in which "Nature is the clay, man the tool."[10] Many Americans tended to agree, and not a few of those with the vigorous assertiveness of the true believer. "Like artificial motors, we are created for the work we can do – for the useful and productive ideas we can stamp upon matter," wrote Thomas Ewbank, a former inventor and manufacturer.[11] Not by accident was the imagery mechanical and the emphasis upon economic tasks. Subduing and regulating the material world, the Rev. Bellows declared, was not only part of the divine plan, but precisely for that reason, the successful pursuit of economic activity was a means whereby mankind paid homage to the Creator's creative genius.

The Voice that evoked the earth continually and silently declares, "Let the earth bring forth more abundantly through created intelligence" . . . . It was left for man to find one principle here, another there, and to bring together many divinely-appointed laws of matter by his invention.[12]

Thus, to make a syllogism of the argument:

Man is best comprehended in his works;
the Creator best in man;
therefore the Creator best in the works of man.[13]

Lest the point be missed that the works in question include the results of even the most humble of economic pursuits, Bellows added:

David calls on men to praise Him with stringed instruments and organs; we might reverently add, praise Him with pictures, spades, and looms.[14]

The role of metaphysical beliefs in the popular endorsement of economic activity did not end here. If participation was admirable, so was success. Among the theological strands of influence in the nineteenth century were ideas often associated with Calvinism or Puritanism. Participation in the economy was supported by the older Puritan idea of a "calling": that each man should serve God by serving society in some useful productive occupation. But success could also be considered symptomatic of divine approval by those whose theology retained the Puritan endorsement of frugality and industry, but who did not share the older Puritan apprehensions about riches and the associated temptations of idleness, sloth, and extravagance. Whatever the wellsprings of such ideas – and they were many, of which Puritanism was just one of the more obvious – American theology, particularly American Protestant theology in almost all its popular variants, infused the laity with a glorious good conscience as they toiled and schemed to win their share in the many economic races of the new republic.

The less devout – those more concerned with personal success and less with personal salvation – also advocated frugality, industry, and prudence, and that advocacy also had a history reaching back into colonial times. The best known exponent of this viewpoint was undoubtedly Benjamin Franklin, but the popularity of *Poor Richard's almanac* merely indicated how deftly he expressed the sentiments of his time. Franklin's ethical exhortations often read like Puritan dogma watered down to aphorisms: "There are no gains without pains"; "Sloth makes all things difficult, but industry all easy"; "Never leave that till tomorrow which you can do today"; "Rather go to bed supperless, than rise in debt." The goals to be served by such behavior, however, made little reference to theology or salvation. Self-control was still the key to self-fulfillment, but fulfillment was now conceived almost exclusively in terms of acquiring material goods and services and the comforts and social standing which attended such success. "Industry gives comfort, and plenty, and respect" Franklin observed,[15] and the merits of those three were considered to be sufficiently self-evident to require no further justification.

Thus two themes with implications for the marketplace came to dominate American society in the nineteenth century. The one, anchored in theology, emphasized the place of man in the divine plan, the virtues fostered by industrious activity, and the appropriateness of man's effort to manipulate the natural world to economic ends. The other, secular in orientation, looked no further than the goal of riches and the material comforts and social standing which the possession of riches seemed to guarantee. Both endorsed a set of virtues headed by prudence, industry, and thrift, and both enthusiastically embraced participation in the economic race. Each had sufficient vitality to survive and flourish but lacked the power to obliterate the other, and thus both themes persisted, side by side, sometimes even within the consciousness of a single individual in a manner hardly calculated to meet the philosopher's demand for consistency. The new nation had its share of quasi-agnostics and apathetic Protestants preoccupied with materialistic goals. But its early history was also deeply colored by religious sentiments and religious movements: by the invention of new religions, the founding of national associations for religious purposes (such as the American Bible Society in 1816 and the American Sunday-School Union in 1817), and the deliberate insinuation of Christian moral teaching into the curricula of educational institutions ranging from one-room elementary schools to state universities. Henry James had at best a half-truth when he claimed "the field of American life is as bare of the Church as a billiard table of a centerpiece." The rest of the truth, as Howard Mumford Jones has pointed out,[16] is that the American people – or at least many of them – have always evidenced religious sensibilities that on occasion can even be susceptible to the mass revivalism of a Billy Sunday or a Billy Graham. Admittedly over time the nation's people seem to have become more secular in orientation and less devout. But – and this is the point – whichever mode of thought held sway in the new republic and beyond, the theological or the secular, the belief in the rightness of participating in the economic race never waned because it was enthusiastically endorsed by both.

Small wonder, then, that a survey of sentiments in any period of American history reveals a popular endorsement for "industry" defined as diligent economic activity. When policies for the new republic were being debated, Tench Coxe expressed the hope that the active encouragement of manufacturing would "lead us once more into the paths of virtue by restoring frugality and industry . . . ."[17] Half a century later, manufacturer and banker Nathan Appleton questioned whether, in his nation, industriousness was ever in need of restoration. With "no avenue open to wealth or power but labor," he observed, "it followed . . . that active industry should be in the highest esteem."[18] That esteem was much in evidence in the speeches of politicians and the writings of economists as well as in the everyday discourse of the common laborer. Willard Phillips noted in his 1828 *Manual of Political Economy* "the respect in which all useful industry is held in the United States," and then added a clumsy double negative: "Useful industry is so far from being any degredation, that every one has more respect for himself, and is more respected, for being usefully employed . . . ."[19] Davy Crockett put it more directly. On visiting the textile mills at Lowell, Massachusetts in the 1830s, he observed: "here everybody works, and therefore no one is degraded by it; on the contrary, those who don't work are not estimated."[20] Crockett's estimation of Lowell attitudes is confirmed by the jacket the workers designed for their literary magazine (*The Lowell Offering*): a schoolgirl near her cottage home with a beehive in the foreground, the latter "emblematical of industry and intelligence" the editors explained.[21]

For most Americans, the explanation of the symbolism was unnecessary. The culture in which they moved reminded them incessantly that industry and intelligence were appropriately directed to economic activity. Nor were contemporary observers slow to underscore the linkages between individual effort, collective prosperity, and national power. In 1847, the *Scientific American* noted that "Every American must feel a glow of enthusiasm swelling his heart as he thinks of his country's greatness, her might and power."[22] Fifty years later, as the century drew to a close, Chauncey M. Depew echoed the same enthusiasm as he reflected on the progress made possible by old-fashioned virtues: "[foresight], industry, thrift, and honesty," he asserted, had helped to make "the United States the most prosperous and wealthy nation in the world."[23]

A Fair Race

To review: participation in the economic race was popular, and the race itself was widely viewed as important: important for the well-being of the individual participants and important for the welfare of the nation. But was it a fair race? Most Americans believed that it was. More cautiously, most considered the race to be "reasonably" fair, subject to qualifications which few found deeply troubling (including the unequal treatment of blacks and women). At least three different factors encouraged such beliefs, two of which were obvious to Americans, and the third was notable for the limited attention it received.

The first of these was abundance – not just an abundance of cheap land, but an abundance of most economic factors of production captured by the phrase "natural resources": timber and minerals as well as acres of fertile soil. Unsurprisingly, the static view of society common to John Locke's day tended to give way in the New World to a more open view of human possibilities. The medieval view of trade as a zero-sum game – that one man's gain was necessarily another man's loss – also faded in a rapidly expanding market fueled by population growth and rising per capita income. Both phenomena (expanding markets and rising incomes) were something of a novelty in the Western world, or at least a novelty as sustained trends. The very notion of economic progress was alien to most Europeans, and with good reason. Their history, from the fall of Rome to the French Revolution, had offered few examples of sustained growth in real per capita income.

America's good luck was that many of the forces destined to produce industrialization and economic growth were operative almost from the beginning of this new republic. Naturally optimistic at the successful conclusion of their revoluion, Americans by and large would remain optimistic throughout the century that followed. Indeed, the optimism fairly bristled from some of the citizens. Whitman's *Passage to India*, which begins by "Singing the great achievements of the present," makes clear the special role the United States was to play in world accomplishments:

> . . . thou born America,
> For purpose vast, man's long probation fill'd.

Americans (or most of them) believed in progress – in a progressive nation, one is tempted to add, with a capital "P." "We do entertain an unfaltering belief in the permanent and continued improvement in the human race," the *North American Review* assured its readers in 1831.[24] At the opening of an agricultural fair in 1850, Henry Meigs expressed the widely shared belief that most of those improvements would be American in origin: "the freemen of our country will carry to the uttermost perfection all the arts that can be useful or agreeable to man."[25]

This faith in progress partly reflected the belief that America had a special role to play in the divine plan. "We delight to believe," theologian William

Ellery Channing wrote in 1830, "that God, in the fullness of time, has brought a new continent to light, in order that the human mind should move here with a new freedom, should frame new social institutions, should explore new paths, and reap new harvests."[26] The national motto was like the people – sanguine and self-assured. *Novus Ordo Seclorum* (A New Order of the Ages) proclaimed the Great Seal of America, and at the center of the seal was "the Eye of Providence," symbolic of a Divinity both watchful and expectant.

Such optimism could not have been sustained for long had the economic record of the nation been a disappointment. That record, however, featured exceptional growth in almost ever sector of the economy: in tobacco and cotton and wheat, in insurance and shipping, textiles and cabinetmaking, shipbuilding and shoemaking. By 1849, the *Scientific American* even presumed to announce that the Golden Age was almost assuredly at hand, and defined that age mainly in terms of material accomplishments: "The necessaries of life are as easily obtained by every person now, as ever they were, and the luxuries far easier."[27] Two years earlier, at the opening of a new railroad at Lebanon, New Hampshire, the rhetoric of Daniel Webster resonated with the same enthusiasm. "Truly this is almost a miraculous era," he told his audience. "What is before us no one can say, what is upon us no one can hardly realize. The progress of the age has almost outstripped human belief."[28] The symbols of that progress were everywhere. In the popular representations of Liberty as a maiden of classic virtue, for example, the maiden tended to be flanked by steamboats and locomotives and agricultural implements. Also somewhere in the picture was likely to be that ultimate symbol of economic success, a horn overflowing with fruits and grain. For most Americans, the economic successes of the past implied opportunities for the future, and expanding opportunities implied that many could win, not just a few, not just the very rich or very powerful or well-connected.

The American faith in the intrinsic fairness of the economic race rested on more than the belief that the available prizes were multiplying rapidly. They were also convinced (or largely convinced) that few were handicapped or received undue advantage at the starting line. They shared what Louis Hartz has called "the master assumption of American political thought . . . the reality of atomistic social freedom."[29] Mobility, both social and geographic, was the key. That economic opportunity was linked in the minds of many to a sense of geographic space may strike present-day Americans as somewhat strange. But linkage there clearly was in the new nation, feeding the hopes and ambitions of even those who never moved. Thus a Lowell textile worker, recalling her days in the mill, would write:

Those middle years of the century were full of stimulus. Vistas opened in every direction. New horizons were lifting themselves. The untrodden peaks, the unpene-trated forests, the prairies untraversed, were all around, just far enough off to give scope to the most enclosed landscape. There was boundless breathing-room for everybody. There were the hopes and the possibilities which are more to the imaginative seeker than attainment. The simple phrase "the far West" was like a talisman, rich with suggestions and beckonings.[30]

A sense of physical space was complemented by a sense of social space. This belief in the possibility of moving up the social scale was encouraged by the facts of economic opportunity which, by European standards, were nothing short of remarkable. The astonishing nature of what most Americans took for granted becomes more apparent when contrasted with European statements relating to opportunity and mobility. Arguments which seemed perfectly reasonable on one side of the Atlantic became preposterous on the other. How out of place it would have been, for example, for Americans to advocate (as many British did) that the children of the poor not be educated so they could remain in the servant class to which they belonged.[31] And who among the Founding Fathers would have dared to announce shortly after the successful termination of the American Revolution what the Manifesto of Equals proclaimed to the French in 1795: "It is scarcely six years that you have begun to breathe in expectation of independence, happiness, equality!" By French standards, the American colonists for generations had been breathing a heady mixture of economic opportunity and occupational mobility. Within the newly united states, the hurly-burly scramble to achieve material progress and social advancement was but a continuation of trends well established generations earlier. Like so many other Europeans, a French visitor in 1806 was struck by "the political equality that reigns [in America] . . . which leaves to the citizens no other distinction than that of riches, and invites them to fill their coffers by every means in their power."[32] Few Americans were embarrassed by that tendency. Most took it as symptomatic of social fluidity and equality of economic opportunity. "Wealth, in this country, may be traced back to industry and frugality," Edward Everett told his Boston audience in 1838. "The paths which lead to it are open to all; the laws which protect it are equal to all; and such is the joint operation of the law and the customs of society, that the wheel of fortune is in constant revolution, and the poor, in one generation, furnish the rich in the next."[33] Throughout the nineteenth century, most Americans regarded such rhetoric as a reasonable characterization of the world they knew. Even Karl Marx conceded that in the United States social classes were "in constant flux."[34] American writers never tired of emphasizing the theme of rapid rise and rapid turnover. Horatio Alger was just one of many to reinforce the popularity of such beliefs in his fictional accounts of the rags-to-riches progress of *Ragged Dick* and *Tattered Tom*. Politicians were constantly reviewing in their speeches the factual basis of the fiction, always with a sense of pride in past accomplishments and confidence in the future. "The hired labor of yesterday," Lincoln noted, "labors on his own account today; and will hire others to labor for him tomorrow. Advancement – improvement in condition – is the order of things in a society of equals."[35] In the same vein he observed: "When one starts poor, as most do in the race of life, free society is such that he knows he can better his condition; he knows that there is no fixed condition of labor for his whole life."[36] Most Americans – or most Americans who were male and white – believed that Lincoln was correct: that they could better their condition. And if it was not precisely accurate to claim, as Alexis de Tocqueville did, that all Americans were "born equal,"[37] that characterization was commonly accepted as a fair approximation to the truth, particularly when that phrase referred to equality of economic opportunity. To visitors from the Old World, the associated opportunities were often overwhelming. Writing of the economic and social possibilities confronting the new immigrant, the Frenchman Crèvecoeur was driven to repeated use of the exclamation mark. "From nothing to start into being; from a servant to the rank of a master; from being the slave of some despotic prince, to become a free man, invested with lands, to which every municipal blessing is annexed! What a change indeed!"[38]

Almost as an afterthought, Crèvecoeur added about such immigrants: "This great metamorphosis [in becoming an American] has a double effect, it extinguishes all his European prejudices, he forgets the mechanism of subordination, that servility of disposition which poverty had taught him; and sometimes he is apt to forget too much, often passing from one extreme to the other."[39] Many Americans were indeed quick to forget the European traditions they had left behind, and that forgetfulness raises the third and often hidden force contributing to the belief that the economic race was fair. The first was the abundance of prizes. The second was a perceived absence of barriers that suggested an exceptional degree of equality of opportunity. The third was the absence of feudalism.

The last of these, it might be argued, is appropriately subsumed under the second. The absence of feudalism – or the vestiges of feudalism – was merely one factor fostering a sense of an equal foot race in the American marketplace, or at least of a foot race featuring exceptional equality. The logic is difficult to resist, and yet a case can still be made for singling out feudalism for special mention. Precisely because it was absent, the American Revolution could not contribute to its overthrow. This meant that a host of social, legal, and political battles were never fought, and thus no bitter residue from such battles remained in the consciousness of Americans, coloring perceptions. Most first-generation immigrants, as suggested, were quick to forget the feudal legacies of Europe, and most native Americans never bothered to learn much about them. Such tendencies were not surprising in a society scarcely touched by European feudal traditions which in the Old World at their apogee penetrated every nook and cranny of economic activity: manorial monopolies of milling grain and selling wine; ordinances regulating weights and measures of basic commodities such as bread and ale; restrictions on the use of land, the sale of land, the inheritance of land; limitations on peasant mobility; and in the towns (although the phenomena were not, strictly speaking, feudal in their origins) barriers to entry, barriers to trade, and barriers to occupational mobility created by the guilds through a multitude of regulations affecting market prices and product quality and worker training. With such interference in the workings of the market came privilege, and with privilege came obvious inequalities in the economic race. On the other side of the Atlantic such multiple intrusions into the economy had never achieved an effective toehold (although not for want of trying).[40] Americans accordingly were inclined to believe their economic race had a certain intrinsic fairness, in part because of the mobility and the opportunities which pervaded the economic world they knew, and in part because of the absence of reminders in their daily lives of the kinds of advantages and handicaps that were so characteristic of Europe's economic races for much of its history.[41]

When visiting Lowell, Massachusetts, Charles Dickens felt compelled to explain to his readers some of the peculiarities he found: the pianos in the boarding houses, the tendency of mill operatives ("the young ladies") to subscribe to circulating libraries, and the presence of a periodical, *The Lowell Offering*, published locally by the workers and for the workers. Most of his British readers, Dickens believed, would "exclaim with one voice, 'How very preposterous!' On my deferentially inquiring why, they will answer, 'These things are above their station'."[42] The very word "station" implies an absence of movement and little expectation of movement, all characteristics typical of nineteenth century England. "Are we quite sure that we in England have not formed our ideas of the 'station' of working people," Dickens asked, "from accustoming ourselves to the contemplation of that class as they are, and not as they might be?"[43] The Lowell operatives had definite ideas about who they might be, and those ideas gave short shrift to any notions of social hierarchy or class-bound immobility. "I believe there is no place where there are so many advantages within the reach of the laboring class of people, as exists here," one of them wrote: "where there is so much equality, so few aristocratic distinctions, and such good fellowship, as may be found in this community."[44] The first issue of *The Lowell Offering* included on its cover "The worm on earth may look up to the star," not to imply servility, the editors insisted, but rather "the sentiment expressed . . . aspiration, and this suited us."[45] It suited most Americans. And with aspiration and little sense of social class came a self-confidence and assertiveness which many Europeans found discomforting. They were upset by the conspicious slouch-ing of Americans in public places. They were offended by the absence of servility among the working class – or among those workers who were appropriately viewed (or so they thought) as working class, but the workers apparently thought otherwise. Touring English factories in 1840, a superin-tendent of one of New York State's largest cotton mills was accosted by a British supervisor. "How do you manage to get along with republican operatives?" he demanded. "I never would superintend a factory where I could not do as I pleased with my hands. Here we can *make them behave*; they know they are in our power, where they ought to be, and they *walk straight*." Emphasizing his absence of enthusiasm for America, he added, "I have been in the United States, and I wouldn't stay there. You can't find a man, woman, or child there, that don't feel as good as his employer."[46] That latter claim would seem to be, if anything, an understatement. Large numbers of Americans felt they were as good as the next person, whether that person was an employer or anyone else. A deferential doffing of the cap was rare, as was the dropping of the eyes in the presence of wealthy citizens. Longfellow's village blacksmith

> . . . looks the whole world in the face
> For he owes not any man.

Emerson was similarly struck by assertive bearing which seemed the norm, and applauded the results: "The mechanic at his bench carries a quiet heart and assured manners, and deals on even terms with men of any condition."[47] When Noah Webster was writing his great dictionary, he borrowed verbatim Samuel Johnson's definition of "station" formulated for a British audience: "Rank: a condition in life."[48] To illustrate that particular meaning, Webster used a slightly revised wording of Johnson's example:

Johnson: I can be contented with an humbler station in the temple of virtue, than to be set on the pinnacle. *Dryden*.

Webster: He can be contented with a humble *station*.

The failure of Webster to generate a more original American example may be the result of more than just an author in a hurry. In Webster's country, that particular sense of the word "station" was unlikely to be used by literate citizens to describe the social world they knew.

The forces influencing American perceptions outlined above could and did interact. The sense of economic and social opportunity reinforced the willingness to work, and this willingness to work raised productivity. The resulting expansion in aggregate output fueled the sense of economic abundance, both actual and potential, thereby reinforcing the belief in economic opportunity and the social advancement it might bring. "There is no people on earth so ambitious as the people of America," John Adams wrote two decades after the successful completion of the Revolution. "The reason is, because the lowest can aspire as freely as the highest."[49] Contemporary manuals on political economy often repeated Adams's point. That of Willard Phillips emphasized the linkage between perceiving opportunity and enduring personal hardships for the sake of economic gain.[50] Another writer made the same argument in the negative.

If the whole population formed but one caste, from which they could neither sink nor rise by any fault or merit of their own, they would be no more inclined to labor than if they were divided into several castes. It is the *fixedness*, and not the *inequality*, of fortunes which is to be dreaded; it is the retention of them in the same families throughout many generations, which chills exertion and unnerves the right arm of toil.[51]

Prizes to the Winners

To review: throughout the nineteenth century most Americans believed that participation in the economic race was admirable and the race itself had an intrinsic fairness – marred, to be sure, by flaws, but none so egregious that a "reasonable" effort to remove them would fail to restore a "reasonable" degree of fairness to the race. But did the winners deserve their prizes? Many believed that they did. Two arguments tended to be advanced in support of that conclusion. One was the now familiar efficiency argument: if winners were not allowed to keep their prizes, the exertions of competitors would decline, and aggregate prosperity would accordingly suffer.[52]

In the nineteenth century, however, this economic argument was a distant second in popularity to the moral argument that to win in the economic race required the exercise of virtues deserving of reward (in particular, thrift, foresight, and hard work).[53] Inventor and manufacturer Thomas Ewbank asserted that "All creatures are made to labor, and their enjoyment to depend on their industry."[54] This notion that individual enjoyments were a function of industry – or at least of industriousness and related virtues – was supported by Francis Bowen, the Alford Professor of Moral Philosophy and Civil Polity at Harvard College. Writing about income inequality in America, Bowen argued that respect for the rights of property naturally tended "to an unequal distribution of the goods, I will *not* say, of fortune, but of industry and frugality."[55] Similar views were voiced by Emerson:

> Open the doors of opportunity to talent and virtue, and they will do themselves justice, and property will not be in bad hands. In a free and just commonwealth, property rushes from the idle and imbecile, to the industrious, brave, and perservering.[56]

What of the Workers?

If these beliefs were popular, and "popular" means "widely held," the implication is that many workers also shared them – an assertion that some readers may consider to be contradicted by the struggles and discontents of labor in the ante-bellum era, and by labor upheavals and populist uprisings in the period following the Civil War. So fundamental is this challenge that it must be met in some detail. Because what follows can easily be misunderstood, several points must be made clear at the outset.

At issue are three main questions: (a) whether worker views concerning economic justice tended to coalesce around a common set of premises; (b) if they did, what those premises were; and (c) what evidence might be used to detect that coalescing.

First, the matter of evidence. Given that almost every possible opinion had its supporters in nineteenth century America, a case can be made for the popularity of almost any viewpoint by selectively choosing evidence from across this broad spectrum. If the issue is what workers as a group believed, the most relevant evidence would seem to be provided when workers spoke with a collective voice, the usual forum for that expression being the trade "union" or "association." Many expressions on behalf of worker groups can be found in such documents as preambles to the constitutions of worker associations, resolutions voted at worker conventions, and memorials forwarded by worker groups to state and federal legislatures. Subsequent discussion will therefore concentrate on what was said and how it was said in documents of this sort.

The second problem to address is what "coalescing" means. Historians tend to be preoccupied with diversity, and in the many nineteenth century worker viewpoints concerning economic justice there is much to gratify such interests. The issue for this study, however, is whether the majority of these diverse views clustered around a single set of premises and, if so, whether that clustering – viewed as a distribution – is bunched or widely scattered. To do justice to describing all the variations across the distribution would be the topic of a book. The assignment here is merely to suggest the broad outlines of the central tendencies. Endorsement by workers of the premises outlined previously is not likely to take the form of worker groups reciting a litany that included these premises in their most simple form: the race is good, the race is fair, and prizes are rewarded for the exercise of meritorious behavior. As repeatedly emphasized above, all these premises were subject to qualifications, with diversity of opinion evident in the degree and kind of qualifications used. For workers (as for everyone else) the question is whether such qualifications were, in some sense, major or minor. But in what sense? Throughout the nineteenth century the single premise most under fire was the notion that the race was fair or "reasonably" fair. When that premise came under attack, the question of consummate importance is what forms these attacks took *and did not take*. If the coalescing of worker opinions around the premises outlined above was strong – or put another way, if qualifications common among workers did not lead to positions radically different from those implied by the premises in their most simple form – then these attacks on the fairness of the race should be informed *and constrained* by the premises in question.

Evidence of this kind of grip on the hearts and minds of many workers should surface in a variety of ways in documents detailing worker group opinions.

First, when the fairness of the race is under attack, other key premises should seldom be subjected to close scrutiny or vigorous challenge. Endorsement should therefore continue to be evident for the idea that participation in the economic race is good for the individual participants and for society as a whole, and – if only the race can be fairly run – prizes will reflect the exercise of such meritorious virtues as industry, frugality, and thrift.

Second, if the problem is unfairness in the market system, the solution should be construed in terms of remedying the unfairness, not scrapping the system. Statements by worker groups pertaining to the fairness issue should therefore be long on specific charges and short on general appraisals of what the American economic system was or ought to be. The implication is that with the remedying of perceived unfairness will come the restoration of a system inherently acceptable as a means for determining production and distribution within American society.

Third, if the first and second expectations are supported by the evidence, particular kinds of assertions should tend to be present, and others absent, in collective statements by worker groups concerning economic justice. Ideas expressed concerning "justice," "fairness," and "rights" in most instances should resonate with basic American values as those values have been outlined above. What should be rarely challenged and on occasion actively endorsed are the work ethic, the institution of private property, and the rights of others to a "fair" return for participating in the economic race, including the right of employers to a profit and of capital (or capitalists) to a rate of interest. Socialism and communism should accordingly be endorsed by few and rejected by many. Equally important, inequality of income should not be deemed *intrinsically* repugnant or unjust, but only particular kinds of inequality generated by particular kinds of reprehensible market behavior. Similarly, one would not expect to find widespread support for income redistribution policies whose main objective was merely greater equality of income.

These, then, are the expectations. The remaining question is the extent to which they are, and are not, supported by available evidence.

Consider first the era prior to the Civil War when the American economy was experiencing the triumphs and agonies of early industrialization, and workers caught up in the process were striving to understand its meaning and meet its threats through collective efforts. In their attempts to organize, whenever labor spoke with a collective voice on behalf of any numbers of significance – most often in the preambles, constitutions, and resolutions of newly formed associations – opinions expressed were almost invariably consistent with the premises outlined above. That claim obviously does not square with radical pronouncements that liberal historians so often celebrate:[57] about "productive" and "unproductive" labor, and how "capitalists" (among many others) belong to the latter group; about labor as the sole creator of wealth and why it thus deserves the lion's share (or the entire share) of the nation's goods and services; about the need to scrap the present competitive market system in favor of a more cooperative and egalitarian system of production and distribution as elaborated by advocates of Association, Fourierism, Agrarianism, Socialism, and Community System.[58] But such radical statements can generally be traced either to a particular individual or to small cooperative groups with a limited membership and a short life span.[59] Almost never did such statements surface (or even statements remotely like them) when labor groups spoke on behalf of large numbers of the working population. And many such statements were made on behalf of that population in the ante-bellum era: by the New-England Association of Farmers, Mechanics, and Other Working Men, the Printers' Union of New York City, the Journeymen Mechanics of the City and County of Philadelphia, The Trades' Unions of the City of New York, and the

Journeymen Cordwainers of Lynn, to cite but a few entries from a lengthy list. Labor organizations such as these typically accepted private property and rejected socialism; acknowledged employers' rights, including their right to "a just and equitable profit;" and proclaimed their intention to pursue the goals of labor by "lawful and honorable means," including the goal of "a fair day's wages for a fair day's work" so that "the laboring man can pay his debts, maintain his family, educate his children, and provide for the evening of life."[60] The market system was generally accepted, including the determination of workers' rewards by the forces of supply and demand: "We . . . are willing that demand and supply should govern the price [of labor] as it does that of all other disposable property" (Committee on behalf of the Boston Carpenters, Masons, and Stone Cutters)[61]; or again, "Wages are governed by the great law of trade – the law of supply and demand. The price of labor as well as that of any other commodity rises and falls under the operation of this law; and it is impossible to control it by any other power or law whatever" (friends of a Ten Hour Law, assembled in State Convention[62]). Admittedly worker organizations then (as now) were willing to advocate boundary conditions on the operation of those laws; for example, restrictions on the length of the workday (ten hours was the fashionable demand in ante-bellum America), or limitations on the number of apprentices per employer.[63] Their discontents and bargaining efforts tended to focus primarily upon hours, wages, and conditions of work. The problem – or much of the problem as workers saw it – was that this bargaining process was becoming undermined by employers acquiring undue power and using that power (often indiscriminately labeled "monopoly") in unfair ways: to coerce workers; to coerce other employers into rescinding wage increases granted previously; to deny employment to those who belonged to the "Union Society."[64] The preferred solution to this problem was *not* to abandon the market system and usually not to have the government intervene to break up employers' associations and thereby dissipate their power. Instead the overwhelming preference was to combat strength with strength: to fashion what John Kenneth Galbraith has termed "countervailing power" by workers combining into a single organization (the "association" or the "trades' union") and using that organization to bargain with employers, to lobby legislators, and to inform the public of the "rightness" or "fairness" of whatever workers were attempting to achieve.[65] Trade unions were thus touted as desirable new participants in conventional market processes to restore and maintain, in the language of the National Trades' Union, "a healthy equilibrium of demand and supply."[66] Or as the cordwainers of Philadelphia chose to summarize the likely results of combating strength with strength: "By these means [the formation of a Trades' Union] our interests will be supported – liberal employers will be supported – the rapacious will be checked in their evil courses – *and the blessings of our glorious free institutions, fully realized by the worthy mechanic.*"[67]

　　Such conventional objectives and conventional rhetoric were not always evident at worker gatherings. The following, for example, is a partial account of proceedings at a New York convention held in the mid-1840s:

A member from your city [Lowell] made a speech in which he said that capitalists and priests had joined hands to put down, grind and oppress the laboring man – that commerce, manufacturing and foreign emigration were killing them – that there was ten times more slavery in Lowell than on the Southern plantations – that Lowell manufactured the prostitutes of New York; and that the first thing we must do to elevate the workingmen was to collect and burn the Sunday-School books which were poisoning the minds of the young.[68]

But the convention in question was poorly attended (only 30 delegates showed up despite a call "to all those interested in the elevation of the producing classes and Industrial Reform and the extinction of slavery and servitude in all their forms") and "a great deal of dissatisfaction was expressed at the lack of interest among the workers."[69] Attendance generally was poor when announced agendas and prospective resolutions were radical in tone. Or to make the same point in a positive way, when attendance was not a problem – when large numbers of the working population came to voice their grievances and vote on possible remedies – the dominant tone was one of moderation in rhetoric used and resolutions voted. Thus, for example, labor organizations favored combating the threat of a "monopoly of knowledge" by improving access to education, particularly for children from low-income families. (It was "the duty and interest of the State to secure to all children in the community an education that will fully develop their physical, moral and intellectual powers, and render every citizen of the commonwealth worthy and capable to perform the sacred duties of a freeman"; accordingly union members were urged to "forward memorials to the legislatures of their respective states," although not with the expectation that a perfect education system "is by any means attainable in a single step.")[70] Or again, employers' reliance upon convict labor was to be resisted by a variety of conventional approaches. (Some urged further study of the problem; some called "upon the Legislature of this State [New York] to abolish the present system of contracting for mechanical labor in the State Prison" and promised labor's support at the polls for politicians favoring abolition; some urged "the operatives in the various sections of our country . . . to use all laudable means against its increase, and take such measures as are in conformity with law and good order, to eventually abolish the present system of employing convicts.")[71] The need to limit total hours labored in a given day by the passage of a Ten Hour Act workers justified by noting that a longer workday frequently resulted in "weakness, loss of health, and even life . . . [while depriving] the labourer of time to attend to his family and duties as a citizen, and [not allowing time] for mental improvement." (A longer day would be acceptable, however, if "the merchant or our employer [agreed] to pay for each and every hour over and above ten, an extra compensation in proportion to our day's work.")[72]

In sum, when workers spoke through labor organizations, moderation was the rule and shrillness the exception. To be sure, from time to time their discontents were voiced in heated terms, but almost never does one find (except from a handful of small and ephemeral organizations) outrage at the free-enterprise system as a system, or the belief expressed that the economic race intrinsic to that system was *intrinsically* unfair. Most workers seem to have endorsed what most Americans endorsed, including the work ethic, private property, and a correlation between effort and reward that made income inequality a norm to be expected, not a hateful aberration to be eradicated wherever possible. In the ante-bellum era, the major focus of their discontents with the economic race was new power that some of the other competitors had evidently gained (notably "employers" and "capitalists") – power that had sometimes been unfairly acquired and, whether fairly won or not, was giving a new and unwarranted bias to labor negotiations. The single most pressing need was to reduce or eliminate overt unfairness resulting from power mismatches: labor versus those who hired labor, particularly those who hired labor in large numbers. The preferred solution was to organize and through that organization gain added power for the workers. That gain, it was assumed, would do much to set matters right, where "right" did not imply an absence of profits for employers or of interest paid to capitalists. What "right" – or at least "better" – did imply was the restoration of greater equality in bargaining power among competing groups in a market system, where the system – as a means of determining production and distribution within society – was viewed as fundamentally sound.

The thesis that conventional beliefs informed and tempered worker perceptions concerning the justice of America's economic system appears more suspect when applied to the turbulent years following the Civil War. This was an era of violent and often vicious strikes involving state militia, Pinkerton agents, and just plain thugs hired by employers to intimidate workers; when monopoly efforts of big business precipitated trust-busting efforts by the government; when a Populist movement motivated by dissatisfactions with the economic system raged across the country with a depth of feeling and a breadth of support never seen before. This was also an era of growing fashionability of radical critiques: when a socialist party was established on a national scale, when the first socialist candidate ran for the presidency, when writers of a radical bent were widely read. The success, for example, of Edward Bellamy's *Looking Backward*, Henry George's *Progress and Poverty*, and Henry Demarest Lloyd's *Wealth Against Commonwealth* signaled a new interest in fundamental challenges to the market system, as did the popularity of Bellamy clubs.

As evidence of widespread sympathy for radical critiques, however, there is less here than meets the eye. What was true in ante-bellum America remained true in the years following the Civil War: whenever protests were voiced on behalf of significant numbers – of workers or farmers, union members or delegates to Populist conventions – the great majority of such expressions were temperate in tone and colored by conventional beliefs, including approval of private property, a commitment to the work ethic, a recognition of employers' rights, and a general acceptance of the market system. Consider the following, all typical of the post-bellum period.

Men who own capital are not our enemies. If that theory held good the workman of to-day would be the enemy of his fellow toiler on the morrow, for, after all, it is how to acquire capital and how to use it properly that we are endeavoring to learn.

Circular, May 3, 1886; Knights of Labor[73]

[For this body] its object shall be . . . To use every honorable means in our power to adjust difficulties that may arise between employers and workmen; to labor assiduously for the development of a plan of action that may be mutually beneficial to both parties; to use our influence to discountenance strikes, except when they become absolutely necessary, and to devise the best manner of supporting such organizations as may be driven to the necessity of resorting to such means to force a recognition of their rights.

Resolution, International Industrial Assembly of North America[74]

RESOLVED, that capital is an agent or means used by labor for its development, and support, and labor is an agent or means used by capital for its development and general enhancement, and that, for the well-being and productiveness of capital and labor, the best harmony of fellowship and action should at all times prevail, that "strikes" may be avoided, and the workman convinced that justice is done him, and that he is receiving an equivalent for the labor performed . . ..

RESOLVED, that we feel it to be a duty that we owe to ourselves, to society, and to our country to encourage by all means within our reach, industrial habits among our people, the learning of trades and professions by our children without regard to sex; to educate and impress them with the fact that all labor is honorable and a sure road to wealth; that habits of economy and temperance combined with industry and education, are the great safe-guard of free republican institutions, the elevator of the condition of man, the motive-power to increase trade and commerce, and to make the whole of this land the wealthiest and happiest on the face of the globe . . ..

Platform and Memorial to Congress, National Labor Union[75]

These truths we hold to be self-evident, . . . that labor and capital employed in agriculture should receive as much reward as labor and capital employed in any other pursuit; . . . and that the principal road to honor and distinction, in this country, should lead through productive industry.

Declaration of Principles, Illinois Farmers[76]

For our business interests, we desire to bring producers and consumers, farmers and manufacturers into the most direct and friendly relations possible. Hence we must dispense with a surplus of middlemen, not that we are unfriendly to them, but we do not need them. Their surplus and their exactions diminish our profits.

We wage no aggressive warfare against any other interests whatever. On the contrary, all our acts and all our efforts, so far as business is concerned, are not only for the benefit of the producer and consumer, but also for all other interests that tend to bring these two parties into speedy and economical contact. . . .

We are not enemies of railroads, navigable and irrigating canals, nor of any corporation that will advance our industrial interests, nor of any laboring classes.

In our noble Order there is no communism, no agrarianism.

We are opposed to such spirit and management of any corporation or enterprise as tends to oppress the people and rob them of their just profits. We are not enemies to capital, but we oppose the tyranny of monopolies. We long to see the antagonism between capital and labor removed by common consent, and by an enlightened statesmanship worthy of the nineteenth century.

Declaration of Purpose, National Grange[77]

Just how committed to conventional beliefs such expressions are becomes more apparent by contrasting them – all from major movements of the period – with the tone and substance of dissatisfactions voiced by a truly radical organization: the Industrial Workers of the World (IWW).

The working class and the employing class have nothing in common. There can be no peace so long as hunger and want are found among millions of working people and the few, who make up the employing class, have all the good things of life.

Between these two classes a struggle must go on until the workers of the world organize as a class, take possession of the earth and the machinery of production, and abolish the wage system. . . .

It is the historic mission of the working class to do away with capitalism. The army of production must be organized, not only for the every day struggle with capitalists, but also to carry on production when capitalism shall have been overthrown. By organizing industrially we are forming the structure of the new society within the shell of the old.

Preamble to 1911 Constitution[78]

The IWW was, however, the exception that proved the rule. Consider, for example, the *total* absence of comparable accusations and comparable ambitions in any of the national platforms framed by the Populist movement. The principal problems with the market system that movement sought to remedy were accretions in power (often unfairly won, or so most Populists believed) that were disrupting production and biasing distribution in unfair ways. The solution was not to scrap the market system or the wage system or the capitalist system. Instead, what Populists wanted was a reining in of this unfair power by government actions because private actions seemed incapable of dealing with the three problems they found most worrisome.[79] To combat the growing control of "capital and credit" by the powerful few – variously designated as "bankers and financiers," "merchant-capitalists," or "middlemen and speculators" – the Populists advocated government action to make credit more readily available (by issuing more greenbacks, "free and unlimited" coinage of silver, and the establishment of "sub-treasuries" to lend money "direct to the people at a low rate of interest").[80] To combat monopolies that tended to arise in industries with pronounced economies of scale – notably those in transportation and communication – they advocated government ownership of railroads and the telegraph and telephone systems, as well as the postal system.[81] To improve access to land by farmers and would-be settlers, they wanted the government (a) to prohibit "alien" ownership and the "monopolization of land" for speculative purposes, and (b) to reclaim lands currently owned by "railroads and other corporations in excess of their actual needs," such land then to be held "for actual settlers only." In short, nothing in the various demands of various Populist platforms constituted a fundamental challenge to the premises outlined above. At bottom, they did not want the economic race to be scrapped but merely the restoration of more fairness in that race. This is not to deny that cooperative and communal ambitions informed this movement in powerful ways.[82] This is also not to deny the depth of anger and indignation at perceived injustices in the economic system. But for the Populists, as for many other worker movements of this period, the solution for injustices perceived was the restoration of a better balance among competitors in the market system, as each dissident group defined "better balance."[83] What was expected from such a restoration was not equality of income, but merely the reduction of certain inequalities attributable to the unfair use of power.

By this interpretation, then, the limited appeal of those who favored radical solutions was not surprising. Prior to World War I, socialist party candidates for president always received less than a million votes, and dues-paying members of socialist clubs barely exceeded 100,000.[84] Other evidence is easily marshalled to indicate this absence of popular endorsement. Henry George, for example, rejected the "impulse to socialism" he found in Edward Bellamy and Henry Demarest Lloyd.[85] So too did most of George's contemporaries. Bellamy's later publishing efforts included a periodical that was short-lived and a utopian novel (*Equality*) that sold poorly. Henry Demarest Lloyd's public ownership plank was rejected by the Platform Committee at the Populist convention of 1896, and Lloyd himself was "treated as the pariah of the . . . convention, isolated and shunned."[86] Radicals and their programs for the most part have been shunned by the vast majority of Americans throughout the nation's history. The sudden burst of interest toward the end of the nineteenth century – as evidenced by the widespread sale of books by authors such as Bellamy and Lloyd – was symptomatic more of curiosity about ideas of the far left and puzzlement and distress over contemporary economic ills than of any propensity to jettison conventional beliefs and endorse radical solutions. This same blend of curiosity and uncertainty plus a heavy dose of indignation at perceived injustices led many workers whom the radicals regarded as their natural allies – the hewers of wood and drawers of water – to explore radical ideas. But for the great majority of workers, that exploration ended in rejection.[87] They were too wedded to conventional beliefs about how their economic system did function, could function, and ought to function.

To sum up: the above discussion has attempted (a) to outline the nature of some of the key premises around which popular beliefs concerning economic justice tended to coalesce, and (b) to demonstrate that this coalescing included views widely popular with workers, primarily by offering evidence that the premises in question in the majority of cases informed and constrained worker criticisms of the market system when labor spoke with a collective voice.

Enter Economic Theory

This concludes the first stage of the argument. The central question for this chapter, and the controlling question for the book, is what is a fair or just income distribution. Americans have never had a single answer, but they have had a strong and continuing predilection to regard both the procedures and the results of their market system as intrinsically fair or just. That predilection was fed by a small number of premises which, in their simplest form and expressed as normative principles, were (a) the race ought to be good for the participants and for society, (b) the race ought to be fair, and (c) merit ought to be rewarded in the marketplace. To the extent that reality was perceived to approximate these ideals (how much approximation was enough was always difficult to specify precisely), the American economic system could be regarded and was regarded as having both an intrinsic order and an intrinsic moral validity. The principles themselves were both powerful and vague. Their power was evident in the controlling influence they exercised on popular debate. Americans seldom questioned the goodness of the race, and generally believed that merit would tend to be rewarded if only the race were fair. Much of public discussion accordingly focused on the conditions required for fairness – or what was needed to remove pronounced unfairness. The vagueness of the principles was evident in the vagueness of key terms – "good" race, "fair" race, "merit," and "just" reward – and in a general absence from popular discussion of rigorous reasoning to defend the principles in question. As is also generally true of theological beliefs, most of those who endorsed the principles noted above were more atuned to the practical implications of a handful of oversimplified precepts than they were conscious of complex rationales for these precepts. But again like theological beliefs, a common article of faith among believers was that while *they* could not articulate that elaborate rationale, "the learned" could if the necessity arose (although the necessity almost never did). What did arise repeatedly in the nineteenth century were challenges to the notion that the economic race was fair, prompting repeated efforts to make the race more fair (for example, by expanding access to education) or to make it less unfair by devising means to prevent newly acquired market power (often termed "monopoly" power) from disrupting production and biasing distribution in unfair ways. To the extent that these efforts were perceived to be "reasonably" successful (perfection in the eradication of imperfections has never been a popular American demand), the common faith in the market system was restored, and with that faith came an answer to the question noted previously: What is a fair income distribution? That answer (subject to a host of qualifications, none of which was crucial) was: Whatever each participant can win in a fairly run economic race.

That conclusion could be couched in theological terms; for example, that God "assigned this earthly establishment to the charge of man," man's lot was to labor with materials provided, and the results of these labors "were to be his [the worker's] own, so that prosperity and every degree of it were to rest with himself."[88] The same ideas might be advanced as consistent with natural law and anthropological observations:

> A law of natural justice, which is recognized by savages quite as much as by civilized nations, assigns the ownership of a useful article to him by whose skill and industry that article was created. The game that is caught, the implement of the chase that is manufactured, belongs, by the consent of all, to him by whom it is caught or made.[89]

Lincoln put it more simply: "I have always thought that the man who made the corn should eat the corn."[90] Such claims applied with equal force to the product of capital. "A man has as strong a natural right to the profits which are yielded by the capital which was formed by his labor, as he has to the immediate product of his labor," argued one of the most widely read economists of Andrew Jackson's era. "To deny this, would be to deny him a right to the whole product of his labor. The claims of the honest capitalist and of the honest laborer are equally sacred, and rest, in fact, on the same foundation."[91] These views meshed neatly with another set of popular beliefs, commonly associated with the writings of John Locke, that the individual's claim to land (or property) was grounded in the wealth enhancement that resulted from the individual "mixing" his labor with the land in question.[92] A second conclusion followed from the first. Attempts to deprive the winners of their prizes (or in the language previously used, to deprive workers of "the whole product of their labor") were morally reprehensible. Madison, for example, in emphasizing the need to "break and control the violence of factions," worried that a failure to do so would lead to such "improper or wicked" projects as "the abolition of debts" or "an equal division of property."[93]

Such conclusions had a simplicity that many Americans found compelling. That simplicity, however, is deceptive. Lurking behind the premises discussed above are complexities which, when confronted, are sure to prove unsettling for those who confidently proclaim what economic justice is or ought to be – a confidence so typical in the nation's early years. Also not yet confronted is a second set of issues concerning how the American economy actually distributes income. As previously noted, if the general issue of distributive justice is to be given a policy focus in economic matters, three related questions must be addressed simultaneously.

1 What determines the actual income distribution in the economy under review (in this case, the American economy)?
2 What is a fair income distribution?
3 How does (1) diverge from (2), and how might those divergences between the actual and the ideal be narrowed or removed?

The first of these was seldom a subject of popular debate in nineteenth century America. The dominant concern of most was to remedy perceived imperfections in the market system. Just how that system (with or without flaws) functioned as a system to determine actual income payments was of little concern to most Americans. As a problem to be explained, however, it was of the first importance to economists – so much so that "Distribution" has been one of two major preoccupations of that profession since its inception. The other is "Production," and thus the three controlling questions for the discipline, as introductory textbooks never tire of emphasizing, are "What?" and "How?" (the production questions) and "For Whom?" (the distribution question).

At the close of the nineteenth century, a new economy theory was developed to answer the distribution question – a theory at once so comprehensive and compelling that to this day it remains for American economists the dominant explanation of why factors of production receive the payments that they do in a competitive economy. To this same theory the general public from first to last has maintained a monumental indifference. For purposes of this study, however, it has a special significnce for reasons outlined in chapter 1. A normative conclusion based upon that theory has become, for intellectuals on the left and right, a battleground for arguments concerning economic justice. If the subject of our inquiry is American perceptions of economic justice, we would do well to investigate ideas on that topic advanced by some of the best minds among modern defenders of liberal and conservative positions. We cannot hope to understand the major disagreements between these two warring camps, however, unless we have at least a rudimentary grasp of the distribution theory that underlies many of those disagreements.

At first glance, this new distribution theory could be construed as supporting what so many Americans believed already: that there was an intrinsic fairness to the procedures and results of a well-functioning competitive market system. This support, however, was subsequently challenged by two kinds of criticisms which, when fully elaborated, threatened nothing less than the entire fabric of the older moral argument as well as the legitimacy of the new economic theory. An elementary elaboration of this theory is accordingly the first topic of the next chapter. This is followed by a discussion of (a) how the main conclusion of the theory can be converted into a normative assertion, and (b) the arguments commonly made against both the theory and its associated normative extension.

3

Economic Justice and Marginal Productivity Theory

To determine the laws which regulate . . . distribution is the principal problem
in Political Economy . . .

David Ricardo, *Works and Correspondence*, vol. I, p. 5

Introduction

Why is income distributed within the United States the way it is? Why, for
example, should executives receive high incomes and secretaries receive low
incomes? And why should garbage collectors who perform such an unpleasant task receive so much less than professional basketball players who
obviously enjoy themselves in their work? Although such questions may
strike the layman as less than intriguing, they have been a battleground for
economic theoreticians for almost two centuries. While many European
economists regard the battle as unresolved, American economists by and
large have settled on a single answer anchored in the notion of marginal
productivity. The next section provides a brief sketch of what that notion is
and how it can be used to generate a theory of income distribution. (Readers
who wish a more extended discussion can find it in appendix D.)

Factor Payments and Marginal Productivity Theory

If fertilizer is added to a lawn, the quality of the grass should improve. If a
second worker is added for gardening, the number of weeds removed per
hour should increase. Marginal productivity theory is concerned with the
difference that additions make – fertilizer to lawn growth or another worker
to the tasks of garden care and maintenance. The core idea is that would-be
users calculate what these additions will be worth to them, and pay a price
for using the addition in question up to (but not in excess of) that calculated
value.

Consider the case of a corn farmer in a simple agrarian setting, say upstate
New York of 1850. Assume that the farmer owns 1,000 acres, has a current
workforce of three hired hands, and is wondering whether adding a fourth
will increase his farm profits. The relevant comparison is between expected
costs and expected benefits. The costs are clear enough: in this case, the
annual wage of the farm worker who might be hired. The benefit calculation

requires two steps: (a) estimating by how much total corn output will rise as the result of one more worker, and (b) estimating what that extra corn will fetch in the market when sold. If the worker is expected to add 800 bushels and corn is expected to sell for $2 a bushel, the expected benefits are 800 × $2, or $1,600. If the wage rate is $900, the extra worker is sure to be hired because profits will rise by $1,600 − $900, or by $700. Alternatively, if the wage rate is $1,800 the extra worker will not be hired, because to add him to the work force would cut farm profits by $1,800 − $1,600, or by $200. The basic comparison is always between what the extra worker costs (the wage rate) and what that worker is expected to add to farm receipts. This latter calculation is called the *value of the marginal product*: "marginal product" because it is based upon the addition to total output from adding one extra worker; "value of the marginal product" because that increment in output (in our case, 800 bushels of corn) is multiplied by its expected price to obtain a dollar value that can then be compared with the wage rate. This comparison then gives an answer to the crucial question: To hire or not to hire?

Using the core idea from this example of how hiring decisions would be made in a simple agrarian setting, economists can construct a theory of income distribution for a complex market economy. All that is required is a handful of steps, some of which are more easily followed than others. (Again, readers who have difficulty following a brief outline of these steps can find a more extended description in appendix D.)

First, if would-be employers of workers want to maximize profits, they will keep adding workers until prospective benefits from the last one hired decline to a level equal to (or just above) the cost of an extra worker, or the wage rate. To hire fewer would be to forgo net additions to profits. To hire more would be to incur a net loss insofar as incremental costs would exceed incremental benefits.

An important and somewhat unexpected conclusion follows. If all would-be employers of workers behave as just described, each user of labor should keep adding workers until, for that employer, the value of the marginal product of the last worker hired is just equal to the wage rate. What is true for each separately must be true for all combined. Thus, in equilibrium (when employers do not want to add or release workers at the prevailing wage rate), all workers will be paid the value (or approximately the value) of their marginal product *in every activity in which workers are used*.

Readers unfamiliar with the theory may object that surely some workers will be paid more and some less. This objection is met by two assumptions, both central to the theory: (a) all workers are similar in productive capability, and (b) the wage rate they are paid is set in a highly competitive market. If both assumptions hold, then no worker will accept a job that pays less than the prevailing wage, say $900, because that laborer can always earn $900 by working elsewhere. Similarly, no employer will pay more than $900 to a particular worker, because other equally productive workers are available at that wage. If the economy has two classes of workers, say "skilled" and "unskilled," and the first are much more productive than the second, then the economy will have two labor markets ("skilled" and "unskilled") and – the crucial point – in each market workers will receive (or tend to receive) a wage equal to the value for their marginal product in every form of employment, because each employer will keep hiring them until that equality is achieved (or roughly achieved).

We have reached the end of the first stage of the argument. At this point the resulting theory is simply an explanation of how different wage rates are established in competitive labor markets. To convert what is essentially a theory of wages into a theory of income distribution requires that similar reasoning be applied to the markets for other factors of production.

Economists traditionally group all factors of production under four broad headings: "land," "labor," "capital," and "enterprise." A word of explanation is required for each.

"Land" in the days of Adam Smith commonly referred to fertile acres. In a modern economy, the more accurate heading is "natural resources," indicating that the productive resources in question include stands of timber, minerals, and petroleum, as well as fertile soil available for agricultural production.

"Labor" is meant to designate a wide variety of skills, with one exception. The word "enterprise" refers to those people who pull together all the other productive factors, manage the enterprise, and take the associated risks.

"Capital" traditionally is one of the more troublesome concepts in economics, and this discussion will try to minimize that trouble by leaving many complex issues unexplored. If the subject under discussion is "factors of production," the word "capital" refers not to stocks and bonds but to "produced means of production." Examples include printing presses in publishing firms, robotic devices on Detroit assembly lines, and the buildings housing camera production in Rochester. "Produced" signals that, unlike "land," the productive factor must be created (the factory built or the printing press assembled). "Means of production" serves to distinguish these produced goods (destined to be employed in creating more goods) from consumer goods (destined to be used by their buyers to satisfy consumer wants).

With these four broad categories in hand, consider the problem of how to use a single notion – marginal productivity – to derive, not a theory of wages, but a theory explaining why each kind of factor of production has the price it does in a competitive market economy.

The case of land rent is perhaps the least complicated extension of previous reasoning. Each would-be user of land (including our corn farmer) estimates, for each additional acre that might be rented, the expected increments in costs and benefits. The cost is the rental rate of land per acre. The benefit is the expected addition to output (such as extra bushels of corn) from using one more acre, multiplied by the expected price of that output (for the corn farmer, the price of corn per bushel). For each prospective user of land, this benefit calculation (additional output multiplied by price) is the value of the marginal product of land to that user. As was true for prospective employers of labor, prospective renters of land will continue to demand additional acres until the benefit (the value of the marginal product of the last acre added) just equals, or is slightly above, the expected cost (the rental rate per acre). Here too in equilibrium – when all land users have no desire to increase or reduce the acres rented – the value of the marginal product of land should equal (or be slightly above) the rental rate *in all the many different uses to which land is put.* As was true of labor, different qualities of land will command different rental rates, with those differences reflecting differentials in the productive capabilities of the land in question. Lastly, but of the first importance to complete the theory, comparable assumptions to those made for labor are again needed to guarantee this result; namely, that (a) all would-be land users seek to maximize profits, and (b) the rental prices of different qualities of land are established in highly competitive markets.

Similar reasoning using comparable assumptions can be applied to the market for "enterprise" and the market for "capital." For the sake of getting on with the discussion (and avoiding complexities not crucial to any of the main points to follow), the details of this reasoning will not be discussed here. If they were discussed, the bottom line would again be a variant of the main conclusion previously reached: for every factor whose price is established in a competitive market, that price will roughly equal the value of the marginal product to all users of that factor.

Finally, notice two points. First, the resulting theory explains income distribution in terms of factor payments. The total income received in a year by any given individual (or any given family) according to the theory will be the sum total of payments received for the factors of production supplied by that individual (or that family) to different factor markets. Total individual (or family) income will accordingly be the sum of wages received for labor supplied to labor markets, rental payments for land supplied to land markets, and so on. Second, whether the theory in question – the marginal productivity theory of income distribution – describes well or badly the processes whereby the distribution of income is actually determined in present-day America is an issue yet to be addressed. Despite its widespread popularity among economists in this country, few have felt obliged to offer much evidence to justify that popularity. Considering the nature of most of the evidence available, such neglect is perhaps not surprising. What follows is only a brief sketch of relevant material. Readers wishing a more extended investigation can find it in appendix E.

Are Factors of Production Paid the Value of their Marginal Product?

This question rephrased might read: Does the income distribution theory widely favored by American economists explain how income is actually distributed in this country? A lot is riding on the answer. At stake is not just a popular theory but a central pillar of that elegant and complex structure, neoclassical economics.

How does one decide whether or not a theory "fits the facts"? The most obvious problems to be solved are: (a) Which facts must the theory fit? (b) How close a "fit" is close enough? One popular criterion among economists is how well a theory predicts subsequent events. For the theory under scrutiny here, the key prediction is its main conclusion: each factor of production will tend to be paid the value of its marginal product by every user of that factor. Testing that prediction against relevant evidence, however, is next to impossible. The reason is a scarcity of data. Every employer knows, or should know, what he or she pays to each factor of production (in wages, salaries, land rents, and so on). But little is known about the value of the marginal product of the factors used. Employers by and large do not have such information and show little interest in trying to collect it. Unnoticed, our agrarian example glossed over a host of practical difficulties likely to be encountered by any employer who might want information on the marginal product of the last worker hired. Bushels of corn per farm worker in a simple agrarian setting may be relatively easy to estimate. Jumbo jets per aerospace engineer or pounds of fertilizer per research chemist obviously are not. This does not augur well for the empirical validity of our theory, but this is to anticipate arguments to come.

If predictions of the theory cannot be compared with subsequent facts because the relevant facts, by and large, are unavailable,[1] the other obvious comparison is between the assumptions of the theory and evidence of how well those assumptions fit the facts.[2] The main assumptions upon which marginal productivity theory is built are:

1 prices of productive factors are established in highly competitive factor markets; and
2 users of productive factors try to maximize profits.

At first glance neither may seem to be controversial. Closer scrutiny of relevant evidence, however, suggests that both assertions are often widely at variance with the facts of American business practice.

Consider what the first assumption implies about markets for labor. If these markets can be fairly described as "highly competitive," each should feature many small-scale participants supplying or demanding labor, with their competitive behavior resulting in wages that are highly flexible, rising during boom times and falling during slack times. The evidence from many present-day labor markets challenges the above characterization at every point. For most workers wages are not highly flexible but notoriously "sticky" on the down side. They have a tendency not to fall in times of slack demand because of such inhibiting factors as the bargaining strength of unions and long-term labor contracts. The presence of unions also raises doubts about the assumption that wages are the outcome of competition among a host of small-scale participants. Frequently wages are the result not of competition among the many but collective bargaining among the few. Big unions tend to negotiate with large-scale employers, with the resulting terms critically dependent upon relative bargaining strength. In addition, large firms tend to have "internal labor markets," that is, markets which operate internal to the firm in which higher-level jobs are primarily or exclusively filled by applicants from within the company's own ranks. The world of big unions and giant firms with internal labor markets is not a marketplace well described by neoclassical theory. Nor is it one in which resulting wages can be confidently predicted using neoclassical theory. (Indeed wages under these conditions tend to be theoretically indeterminate (see appendix E).) The validity of the first assumption of marginal productivity theory at a minimum is therefore highly suspect when applied to many labor markets in this country. And more than half of all factor payments in the United States go to "labor."

The second assumption of profit maximization is, perhaps unexpectedly, also suspect. Available evidence from American firms suggests a number of mismatches between theoretical hypothesis and business reality, of which two are particularly worrisome. One concerns the goals pursued. In large corporations in which management is divorced from ownership and executive salaries can vary with firm size, the decisions of top management frequently emphasize increasing sales and growth as well as profits. The other major reservation concerns not which goals are pursued, but how they are pursued. Even if making a profit is the only goal, profit maximization is the limiting case – the end result when every decision made and action taken is the best among all those possible. As one would expect, the evidence suggests that much of the time business firms fall short of this ideal. Which decision is optimal is often far from clear for top executives confronting limited information and much uncertainty. Even when the facts are clear, the motives of firm participants can vary, and so can the productiveness of their day-to-day efforts. Or as one critic of the neoclassical portrait of the firm chose to put the point, "inertia, slothfulness, lack of concentration and attentiveness, friction between peers, and friction between those at different hierarchical levels, are ubiquitous elements in normal productive units."[3]

To all of these criticisms – concerning how factor markets work or what business executives try to maximize or how well they pursue the single goal of profits – defenders of marginal productivity theory have a single reply that amounts to one additional assumption. The associated imagery is normally Darwinian, and deliberately so. Only firms that *actually do maximize profits* will survive, runs the argument. How firms achieve that result is not important. All that matters is that maximum profits is a condition for survival. If that assumption is accepted, all of the suspect neoclassical assertions can be retrieved. One condition for maximizing profits is paying each factor of production the value of its marginal product. It follows that any firm continuing to survive must be approximating that neoclassical ideal *whether the managers of the firm do so by accident or design.* We have thus reached the final question of fact: Does the evidence suggest that the American economy features a principle of natural selection whereby firms must continue to achieve a narrowly defined goal (maximum profits) in order to continue to exist? Or are the conditions for survival far less stringent, including broad variations in profits realized, thereby permitting (among other things) broad gaps to develop between what productive factors actually are paid and what, according to marginal productivity theory, they ought to be paid?

Evidence on this point is comparatively scarce, but what there is indicates that survival is the rule and failure the exception. The annual failure rate of American business firms is of the order of 30 to 50 per 10,000 establishments (see appendix E). In a given decade, then, roughly 5 percent or less of existing business firms will be forced to close their doors (the vast majority of which will be small in scale and recently established (again see appendix E)). Clearly this is not an economy rife with Darwinian carnage. A high survival record, however, could be the result of two quite different circumstances. Achieving maximum profits could indeed be a condition of survival, with a low extinction rate indicating that the majority of firms persistently hit this narrow target. Alternatively, survival conditions could be far less stringent, with a high survival rate indicative of a considerable lack of stringency.

When two hypotheses are consistent with the same evidence, the only way to choose between them is to add more evidence. What should be added in this instance is evidence of the sort sketched above. The world in which American business managers decide and act is, by and large, a world fraught with imperfect information and uncertainty; a world in which goals vary, as do the motivations and the efforts of individual participants; a world in which wage determination is often not the product of impersonal market forces but the result of bargaining struggles, one-on-one, between a giant union and a giant enterprise. To argue that in an economic environment such as this the narrow target of maximum profits is hit by most firms most of the time is surely to strain credibility beyond all reason. To turn the point around, the tradition of a social science is that the one who asserts has an obligation to offer proof of that assertion. The task of supplying evidence in support of the contention that this particular theory captures the main forces determining income distribution in America therefore appropriately falls to the advocates of marginal productivity theory. As previously indicated, few of contemporary advocates have tried to meet that obligation. Evidence of the sort considered here (and other examples of a similar sort are legion) suggest that meeting this obligation will not be easy. Nor can this task be swept aside by the conventional reply that the theory postulates a tendency only: that its main conclusion does not guarantee equality between the two key variables (actual factor payments and the value of their marginal product to users) but only a tendency toward equality. The weaker is the tendency and the more sluggish the movement toward equality, the wider the remaining gap can be. And the wider the gap, the less the theory explains about the actual determinants of income in America. An old question therefore surfaces in a new guise: Is the actual gap between these two variables, on the average, large or small? To answer that question requires knowledge about the value of the marginal product for different factors among different users. But as pointed out at the outset of this section, little is known about such magnitudes, and that ignorance is likely to persist, given how data are assembled in contemporary business firms.

At this point the analysis teeters on the edge of uncertainty. One theory of income distribution tends to dominate within the economics profession in America; its validity as an explanation of actual income distribution turns critically upon firms achieving in the real world a close approximation to an equilibrium condition hypothesized by the theory; and even its most staunch supporters concede uncertainty about how close that approximation is. The continuing popularity of the theory is therefore something of a puzzle. Even economists who criticize its premises still seem to accept the theory, if not on the same page as their criticisms, then almost invariably in the next chapter or the next article or at the next Congressional hearing. If attacks on this particular theory's empirical validity are repeatedly made and are withering in their implications, why should it remain so popular, even among the attackers?

Part of the explanation is a lack of alternatives, or more correctly, alternatives viewed by American economists as appropriately rigorous and descriptive of the market system as they consider it to function.[4] Part of the explanation may also reflect more general influences than economists' professional norms concerning what a theory ought to be. In chapter 2, a handful of premises led to an inference that also concerned the workings of the market system. The premises concerned the merits of participating in the economic race and the absence of handicaps among participants, and the inference – loosely made, but still with widespread appeal – was that the winners deserved (or tended to deserve) whatever prizes they had won. There is a striking similarity in the imagery that lurks behind the ethical speculations of chapter 2 and the economic theorizing of the present chapter. Both portray the economic world as a vigorously competitive arena in which neither undue handicaps nor unfair advantages prevail, and in which rewards reflect what a participant has contributed to the output of the economy. The question is the extent to which the older legacy influenced the theorizing. The practices of a social science – the questions asked, the paradigms preferred, and the answers deemed satisfactory – are not entirely independent of the culture of the country in which the practices flourish. The willingness of American economists to embrace neoclassical economic theory in general and a marginal productivity theory of income distribution in particular (the latter's being very much a logical extension of the former) would seem entirely consistent with the older and simpler set of beliefs outlined in chapter 2 that have so dominated American culture from its early years as a nation.[5] Or to put the matter in a more contentious way, a central thesis of this book, yet to be developed, is that the nineteenth century beliefs outlined in chapter 2, with a minimum of modification, have continued to dominate American thoughts about economic justice throughout the twentieth century. Part of the evidence for that assertion, albeit a small part, is the acceptance of marginal productivity theory by the vast majority of American economists from the time of its first formulation down to the present day.

If the imagery of "the market" of popular economic theory and popular American culture are so similar, can a case be made for fusing both into a more comprehensive picture of what the economy is and ought to be? In particular, what arguments might be advanced for converting an economic theory about factor pricing and marginal productivity into an ethical theory about what factors ought to receive? And what is the case against that conversion? These are the questions that will control the discussion for the remainder of this chapter and throughout much of chapter 4. The answers will be found to be at the core of many of the modern disagreements between left and right concerning economic justice.

Should Factors of Production be Paid the Value of their Marginal Product?

> If it is a duty to do each according to his deserts . . . it necessarily follows that we should treat all equally well . . . who have deserved equally well of *us*, and that society should treat all equally well who have deserved equally well of *it* . . . . This is the highest abstract standard of social and distributive justice . . .
>
> John Stuart Mill, cited by John Plamenatz,
> *The English Utilitarians*, p. 225

The notion "to do to each according to his deserts," as Mill suggests, is often an integral part of the idea of distributive justice. With respect to payments made to economic factors of production, such a view implies that payments should somehow reflect merit. But how? Marginal productivity theory suggests one possible answer.

Actual payments to economic factors need have no necessary relationship to what those factors ought to be paid. Even if American markets functioned in such a way that no factor of production received the value of its marginal product, that fact by itself would not undercut the normative claim that the value of the marginal product is what all economic factors should receive. As noted in chapter 2, American thoughts on a "just" distribution during the early days of the republic tended to be influenced by a small set of premises which, in their most simple and least qualified form, implied that economic factors ought to receive whatever they could earn in the marketplace. This normative judgment rested mainly upon three related beliefs: (a) that participation in the economic race was an admirable activity, (b) that the race (by and large) was fair, and (c) that prizes tended to reward admirable traits – thrift, hard work, and foresight, to name only three, but perhaps the three most often cited. In the twentieth century these beliefs were buttressed by a particular claim of neoclassical economic theory, namely that in competitive markets factors of production tend to be paid the value of their marginal product. The older claim in its simplest form – that factors generally ought to receive whatever markets paid – could therefore be modified by this newer theoretical conclusion about what those payments were likely to be. The normative conclusion, thus revised, would read: factors of production (in general) ought to receive the value of their marginal product, a claim defined here as *"marginal productivity justice."*

This revision can be supported by two arguments implied by the economic theory, both of which seem to support the notion of marginal productivity justice. The first focuses upon the personal attributes of the causal agent. The processes of production suggest a fairly simple causal sequence. Only when a worker is added is a certain output created (such as a specific number of bushels of corn). It is therefore the worker, the argument runs, who has "caused" that particular increase in output. To shift the wording slightly, one might argue that each factor of production is "responsible" for its own marginal product, where "responsible" is used in the conventional sense of "answerable as the primary cause or agent . . . creditable or chargeable with the result."[6] Such considerations would seem to be implicit in distributional statements of the following sort.

There is no distribution of income apart from its production, with negligible exceptions . . . . What is called your income has not been distributed to you; you generated it, you produced it. There is no distribution of income separate from its production.[7]

The claim "you generated it" seems to support the inference that "you ought to receive it," where the "it" in question is either the product generated or its market value.

The implicit normative judgment, in the language of the New Testament, might be phrased: render unto Caesar what Caesar has created. This inference can be bolstered by a second line of argument which is merely an old point in a new guise. The amount that, say, a worker generates (his marginal product) will vary depending upon the worker's diligence, skill, intelligence – that same list of traits which nineteenth century Americans (unacquainted with marginal productivity theory) argued were deserving of reward. If a causal agent (the worker) creates something (marginal product) through the exercise of deserving traits (diligence, skill, etc.), then the worker ought to receive a payment equal to the value of what he creates. To put the matter in more stilted terms, if marginal product is created by the willful exercise of meritorious attributes by a causal agent, it would seem to follow that the agent in question has a "just" or "fair" claim to payment equal to the value of that marginal product.

Critics refuse to accept the inference just made, and for two quite different reasons. One attacks the underlying notion of causation as unsatisfactory because of the causes it ignores. The other questions whether markets really reward "the willful exercise of meritorious attributes," suggesting instead that rewards are often the result of accidental circumstances over which the causal agent has little or no control.

The first is easily summarized. Marginal product, the critics note, is actually joint product. A farm laborer does not create wheat without land and capital equipment any more than an automobile worker creates a Chevrolet without the aid of an assembly line. Furthermore, the size of any particular worker's marginal product will depend crucially upon the quality and quantity of cooperating factors of production. The farm worker, for example, although laboring with identical skill and diligence on two different plots, will create far more wheat on fertile alluvial soil than on infertile clay soil. One cannot therefore argue that the farm worker alone is "responsible" for the wheat created in the sense of being the *only* "cause, agent, or source of something." Even when that something is the worker's marginal product, the appropriate list of "causes" or "agents" includes all the factors of production involved in its creation, not just what the worker contributes under the heading "labor".

To acknowledge the complexity of the causal processes of production is not to discredit the claim that workers ought to be paid the value of their marginal product. That claim was ultimately anchored in the arguments of chapter 2 which, in their simplest form, made a case (although not in these terms) that factors of production generally should receive whatever they can earn in a competitive market. Marginal productivity theory merely offered an explanation of what that payment was likely to be (namely, the value of a factor's marginal product). A second type of criticism, however, is potentially devastating to the normative claim that factor rewards generated by the workings of a competitive market are rightly viewed as a just income distribution.

According to this line of argument, the role of individual volition is easily overstated in an economic world where accidental circumstances can crucially affect the earnings potential of every human actor in the system. In particular, heredity, environment, and the vicissitudes of supply and demand all affect earning power in ways quite beyond the individual's capacity to control.

Consider first heredity. Although few people other than professional scientists understand how genetic control mechanisms operate, Americans generally acknowledge the effect such mechanisms can have on the development of attributes which, in turn, are handsomely rewarded in the marketplace: for example, the good looks of a movie star, the mathematical aptitude of the computer genius, the vocal cords of an operatic singer. Genetic mechanisms may also produce blindness at birth, mental retardation, or physical deformities that impair the earning capacity of the individual afflicted. Even ardent advocates of a free-market system must therefore concede what modern biology has established: that all men are *not* created equal; that all men and women are created

with different physical potentialities that will lead to . . . different faces, different heights and bodily structures, different degrees of energy, health, immunity or susceptibility to disease, and longevity; with different intellectual . . . potentialities, gifts and deficiencies.[8]

But if attributes such as these – all the result of heredity – can have an important effect on whether the individual earns a lot or a little, then individual earnings can no longer be regarded as the exclusive product of willful acts. Chance also plays a role – in some cases, even a large role.

The most cursory study of environmental influences leads to a similar conclusion. Perhaps the most blatant example is inherited wealth, which is both an accident of birth and a crucial determinant of income received. Even if steep inheritance taxes were to abolish or substantially reduce this influence, many other causal linkages would remain between a multiplicity of factors captured by that vague word "environment" and the future earning capability of a particular individual. Earnings, for example, are partly a function of education, and education (both quality and quantity) tends to be influenced by family background. Children of wealthy parents are more likely than those from less affluent backgrounds to undertake the considerable costs of higher education. According to one postwar study of American students, those with equal ability but from the top socioeconomic quarter were roughly twice as likely to continue on to college as those from the bottom quarter.[9] Studies of the socioeconomic background of those attending college have found a similar bias in favor of the wealthy and against the poor. Even at state universities and community colleges where tuition costs were generally among the lowest available, the median family income of students attending tended to be well above the median income for the population as a whole.[10]

Family background, then, can affect schooling, and schooling can affect earning potential. But this is only one way – and possibly not even the most important way – that this accident of circumstances called one's parents can crucially affect the development of earning capabilities. Even those basic educational skills commonly associated with early schooling appear to be more influenced by family background than by type of school attended.[11] That phrase "family background" is designed to capture a host of environmental influences which range far beyond the economic earnings of the parents. Families which are not particularly wealthy can still provide their children with ready access to books, intellectual stimulation, a wealth of cultural experiences, and a broad-ranging vocabulary. But the point at this juncture is not to deny that wealth can make a difference (which obviously it often does). The point is that the influence of family background is far more pervasive than the question of wealth might suggest, and that children from a background enriched by the kind of stimuli just noted tend to have, by the time they are ready to earn a living, certain advantages which have little to do with their own volition and much to do with the luck of the parental draw.

In short, the more we learn about the influences of environment upon individuals, the more that knowledge undercuts the notion of the "self-made man" or the "self-made woman." In the cautious wording of Walter Lippmann, "however crude and clumsy our knowledge of the process, there is no doubt that a character is acquired by experience and education. Within limits that we have not measured, human nature is malleable."[12]

Notice how Lippmann's concession muddies the water if the problem is to decide why poor people are poor – a standard puzzle in all discussions of economic justice. A century ago, many viewed the answer as comparatively simple: if a man was poor, it was probably his own fault. The Reverend Russell Conwell's unsparing attitude was typical: " . . . there is not a poor person in the United States who was not made poor by his own shortcomings," although this theologian and president of Temple University did concede as something of an afterthought "or by the shortcomings of some one else."[13] Modern statements by conservatives on the present fate of the poor may sometimes appear to incorporate a similar unforgiving attitude. One popular contemporary explanation for the poverty of "the lower class," for example, is their lack of future orientation:

The lower-class forms of all problems are at bottom a single problem: the existence of an outlook and style of life which is radically present-oriented and which therefore attaches no value to work, sacrifice, [or] self-improvement . . . .[14]

Even if this explanation is correct (and many would challenge its focus on a single behavioral trait as being much too simplified), the inference does *not* immediately follow that the poor have no one to blame but themselves for their present lot. Suppose, following Lippmann's lead, one were to argue that the "environment" of poverty (a word admittedly lacking in precision) tended to foster the development of personality traits such as a lack of future orientation. Would this not undercut the notion of individual responsibility? Many liberal writers argue that it does. Michael Harrington points out that a lack of future orientation is hardly surprising if the future is perceived as being irretrievably bleak:

This pessimism is involved in a basic attitude of the poor: the fact that they do not postpone satisfactions, that they do not save. When pleasure is available, they tend to take it immediately. The smug theorist of the middle class would probably deplore this as showing a lack of traditional American virtues. Actually, it is the logical and natural pattern of behavior for one living in a part of American life without a future.[15]

James Baldwin makes the same point in language that is at once more personal and more compelling. "You find yourself in a slum and you realize at a certain point that no amount of labor, no amount of hard work, no amount of soap is going to get you out of that slum."[16] In terms of the premises noted in chapter 2, the one challenged by statements such as these is the notion of equality of opportunity: that the economic race is a fair race. One can hardly argue, as Reverend Conwell does above, that the poor are poor because of their own shortcomings if they can never enter the more rewarding races and are heavily handicapped in others.[17]

Another factor often cited as contributing to the poverty of the poor is the number of children that low-income people tend to have. But according to one line of argument, poverty and lack of opportunity cause large families, not the other way around. "The large families of the poor are an effect of their hopeless situation, in which such virtues as foresight and self-restraint show little prospect of making a difference."[18] If this hypothesis is correct, one ought to observe two tendencies.

1   Minorities who suffer additional handicaps and whose opportunities are therefore even more constrained should have even larger families than those of equally poor people not suffering such handicaps.
2   The family size of minorities should decline as family income rises.

Conservative economist Thomas Sowell is among those to note that both tendencies are evident in the United States. Mexican-Americans, Puerto Ricans and American Negroes do have, on the average, larger families than equally poor whites, and all three groups "have *fewer* children than their Anglo-Saxon counterparts, once they rise above some income or educational level."[19] Such evidence does not, of course, prove that causation runs from poverty to family size, but it is consistent with that hypothesis and poses a challenge to those who argue the reverse to provide even better evidence for their case.

In sum, a lack of future orientation may help to explain existing poverty, but those who look no further have overlooked the possibility of causal complexity linking certain conditions of poverty (especially a lack of economic opportunity) with the development of personality traits which are themselves singled out as the cause of being poor.[20] Long before the insights of behavioral psychology became the common currency of poverty debates, at least a minority of Americans recognized the interaction between harsh economic circumstances and certain personal attributes. Writing at roughly the same time that Reverend Conwell was trumpeting the case for individual responsibility, Henry George offered a different perspective on the role of personal shortcomings in a world of restricted economic opportunities:

Compel a man to drudgery for the necessities of animal existence, and he will lose the incentive to industry – the progenitor of skill – and will do only what he is forced to do. Make his condition such that it cannot be much worse, while there is little hope that anything he can do will make it much better, and he will cease to look beyond the day.[21]

Such perceptiveness was not peculiar to Henry George. If the poor, in the language of the Bible, have been always with us, so too has the insight that the condition of poverty may foster detrimental personality traits – or a lack of "virtuous" traits, to use the language of an earlier day. Writing about eighteenth century England, for example, Samuel Johnson noted: "Poverty is a great enemy to human happiness: it certainly destroys liberty; and it makes some virtues impracticable, and others extremely difficult."[22]

What is missing in Johnson and present in much of modern analysis is the influence of modern psychology and anthropology. Both disciplines have contributed to the notion of "the culture of poverty": a phrase used by liberals and conservatives alike,[23] not always with the same meaning, but usually to convey a multitude of environmental influences and their complex linkages with certain pathologies which in turn can reinforce the poverty of the poor: broken families, illegitimacy, crime, and drug addiction, to mention only the leading items in a long and disheartening list. Despite all the progress of modern psychology, we remain massively ignorant about the process – about which environmental influences matter and how. But for the purposes of this discussion these influences need not be understood completely. All that matters is the concession that environment *can* affect personality – that at least to some degree human nature is, in Lippmann's wording, "malleable." And of course the more environment and heredity influence those attributes which determine earning capabilities, the less the individual seems to be in command of his or her own economic fate, and the less individual merit seems to matter compared with accidental circumstances.

A similar point can be made about the influences of supply and demand. One possible way to distinguish the latter influences from those of heredity and environment is to borrow a dichotomy from marginal productivity analysis. According to the associated theory, the income a particular individual receives depends partly upon the quantity and quality of goods or services that individual can supply to the marketplace, and partly upon the price at which those goods or services can be sold. As a first approximation, one might think of heredity and environment as influencing the first (the quantity and quality supplied) and supply and demand as influencing the second (the market price). Genetic control mechanisms may produce a seven-foot frame, and persistent practice at a gymnasium may develop a skill for throwing a basketball through a hoop, but the market value of such skill in concert with a noticeable height advantage has changed dramatically between the 1930s and the 1980s. Such shifts in factor earnings are endemic to the workings of the market system, in which some gain and others lose for reasons quite unrelated to personal merit. The nineteenth century weaver who finds his skills depreciated by the invention of the power loom, the twentieth century insulation expert who finds his skills more in demand because OPEC has raised the price of oil, the middle-aged steel worker with specialized skills who is suddenly unemployed because the winds of competition have wreaked havoc on his industry – these are all symptomatic of a system in which rewards can shift for reasons totally beyond the individual's control. This point – like the point about the capricious role of heredity and environment – has long been a commonplace among observers of the market system. George Bernard Shaw, although he made a fortune from his own writings, readily acknowledged that "the price of ability does not depend on merit, but on supply and demand. . . . Great philosophers and poets are apt to starve because, since their wares are above the heads of the public, there is no demand and therefore no price, although the commodity offered is very scarce and precious."[24] Liberal economist Paul A. Samuelson, who also made a fortune from his writings, made the same point without the reference to great literature. Contemplating the fate of those who stood in unemployment lines, this Nobel laureate noted with perhaps a special poignancy: "There but for the grace of supply and demand go I."[25]

To sum up: the question noted at the beginning of this section was whether, in a "just" or "fair" economic system, factors of production ought to be paid the value of their marginal product. Many writers have answered in the affirmative, often building their case, at least in part, upon (a) the notion of the factor – usually the laborer – as a causal agent, and (b) the meritorious personal traits (diligence, skill, etc.)[26] exercised by that laborer while acting as a causal agent. The first point was undermined by a recognition of the complexity of the causal processes involved in most productive activities. (Marginal product tends to be joint product and thus is the result of many causes, not just the result of a single cause, such as "labor.") The second is now imperilled by the realization that market rewards are at least partly a function of heredity, environment, and the capricious forces of supply and demand. The more important such influences are, the more questionable the assertion becomes that marginal productivity payments are a reward for merit, or (in the stilted language previously used) a reward for the willful exercise of meritorious attributes by a causal agent. This is not to imply – and certainly not to argue – that individual volition plays no role whatsoever in determining who receives what. But it does underscore that, in a market system, payments received for services rendered will be, with few exceptions, the result of both individual volition and capricious circumstances. That being the case, one can only view as grossly oversimplified the popular claim that within the American economic system, each participant is "free to achieve what he [can] and rise to the level he [can] by his own wit, effort, and merit."[27] In a world in which returns are influenced by heredity, environment, and supply and demand – all forces quite beyond the individual's control – how far any participant can rise can hardly be viewed as the exclusive product of "wit, effort, and merit." Claims such as the above have evoked the occasional tongue-lashing from the left, often in terms that minimize or ignore the role of individual volition and emphasize instead capricious circumstances that can be cumulative in effect. Typical of such tirades is David Spitz's plea for equality. Provoked by the claim that economic inequality "accords with the nature of men, who differ profoundly in intelligence, talent, and virtue" and the lurking premise that merit should be and will be rewarded – that the market system tends to put "the right man in the right place" – Spitz thunders:

. . . what we find only too often is the privileged man in a privileged place. And this is where the demand for equality actually and rightly starts. The claim for equality is a protest against unjust, undeserved, and unjustified inequalities.[28]

The tone may be shrill, but the challenge is to the point: How can one justify the inequalities generated by the market system, if those inequalities reflect both personal merit and individual luck? Or to put the matter differently, if accidental circumstances (heredity, environment, and supply and demand) play a role in determining factor rewards – a role that may be large and certainly is difficult to assess – how can one claim that factors of production "ought" to receive the value of their marginal product? Conservative economists understandably feel compelled to grapple with this dilemma. They too are forced to acknowledge the role of luck.[29] (To deny it would be to disavow the obvious.) Their solution – or at least the solution preferred by most – is to shift the terms of the debate. Instead of attempting to defend the notion of merit generating its own reward, they ask a different question: Can the income distribution generated by the market system be justified with no reference whatsoever to the merits of individuals receiving income? Many believe that it can. The arguments of some of these writers will therefore be the subject of the next chapter. Notice in passing that the recognition of imperfection tends to drive the intellectuals from the battlefield. In this instance the imperfections are that (a) merit alone does not determine all rewards, and (b) the relative roles of luck and merit are impossible to determine, from which the strategic implication seems to be to give up on merit as a justification for the market system. But that retreat in the face of such flaws is not typical of popular beliefs, as we have already seen and in later chapters shall see again.

4

The Market Defended: Confusions of the Right

On the Merits of Marginal Productivity Theory

Conservative economists are generally among the staunch defenders of marginal productivity theory. Its merits, as they are quick to emphasize, are the rigor of its form, the preciseness of its implications, and its consistency with neoclassical price theory. Having seized the high ground of theoretical superiority, these defenders of the market system repel all possible alternative theories with the charge of deficiencies under these three headings (particularly a lack of rigor), and ignore the empirical mudslinging of those who suggest that the assumptions of marginal productivity theory are widely at variance with the facts – or at least with what evidence we have concerning how American business firms and factor markets function. The one response of note to these latter charges is the claim that only those firms will survive (or survive in the long run) which follow, consciously or not, the dictates of neoclassical theory, maximizing profits, and as one condition of that maximization, paying factors of production the value of their marginal product. But as pointed out in chapter 3, that is an assertion for which there is little empirical support.

The issue, then, is still in doubt, and those doubts tend to surface in the writings of conservative economists disguised as unimportant afterthoughts appended to marginal productivity theory. The traditional approach is to note that when markets "work reasonably well" or "are reasonably perfect," then factors of production will be paid (or will tend to be paid) the value of their marginal product. This is followed by a list of various market imperfections which are admitted to be more or less pervasive,[1] and that admission raises an obvious question which these writers then ignore: If imperfections are pervasive, how wide is the actual gap between what factor payments are and what, according to the predictions of marginal productivity theory, those payments ought to be? If the question is never confronted, the answer is unlikely to be found. All that can be found – or found with ease in the writings of those most committed to the neoclassical paradigm – is a conspicuous self-confidence in their explanation of how the economy works, seldom tempered by a sense of the frailty of the empirical foundations upon which their factor pricing theory rests.

On the Merits of the Market: Introduction

These same conservative economists also generally ignore a second dilemma concerning what income distribution ought to be. "Common sense, hard work and well-applied intelligence usually pay off," writes *New York Times* columnist Alan Truscott, not about success in the marketplace, but about success at the bridge table.[2] "In bridge, as in life," Truscott concedes, "the fates may kick the deserving in the teeth. Unlike chess, [bridge] is not a game of justice. Chance has a role to play . . . ." These observations are symptomatic of an American belief that a "just" or "fair" game is one in which the deserving are rewarded. The dilemma largely ignored by conservatives is that their justifications for the market system tend *not* to square with American ideas of what a "fair" or "just" outcome ought to be from economic (or any other) competition. The extent to which rewards received are correlated with merit, conservatives commonly argue, is not relevant to judging the "rightness" of the market system.

Notice in passing that the defenses articulated below give a stamp of approval to what in the previous chapter was labeled "marginal productivity justice." At first glance this statement may seem at odds with justifications about to be considered. The central proposition defended by conservative economists considered here is that the workings of the free market should not be interfered with by government action, and thus whatever distribution is generated by a free market is the one that should prevail. Whether factors are actually paid the value of their marginal product may therefore seem to be somewhat beside the point. But as noted in chapter 3, if the question is then asked what determines *how* income is actually distributed in a free market, these same economists argue what most American economists argue, namely, that factors of production are paid (or tend to be paid) the value of their marginal product. An inference is therefore lurking in opinions that lie ahead which should be made explicit from the outset. If (a) the free market should not be interfered with (the normative plea) and (b) the free market is believed to reward factors of production the value of their marginal product (the empirical assertion), then (c) any plea by such believers for leaving the free market alone would not seem far removed from an endorsement of what has been termed marginal productivity justice.

The basic problem, to review, is how to mount a defense of income distribution based upon marginal productivity without referring to the merits of those who receive the income. In broad outline, the structure of the necessary argument is simple enough, although that structure is more easily explained with the aid of several philosophical terms. From the time of Aristotle, most philosophers have distinguished between intrinsic goods and nonintrinsic goods. An intrinsic good is something valuable in and of itself (such as health); a nonintrinsic good is something valuable by virtue of its relationship to an intrinsic good. The nature of that relationship can vary, but the one of interest here concerns a nonintrinsic good that is valuable as a means to the achievement of an intrinsic good. If health is the intrinsic good, and medicine is valuable as a means to health, then medicine is what is often termed an instrumental good. (An instrumental good, in turn, is a particular type of nonintrinsic good.) These terms can be used to summarize all the arguments that lie ahead. The starting point – and the ultimate reference point – must be those values considered by a particular writer to be intrinsic goods: things valuable in and of themselves, such as the freedom of the individual. The rest of any argument then consists primarily of showing why a free-market system is a means for achieving those intrinsic goods. Or in the language previously used, the free market is usually defended as an instrumental good because of the role it is believed to play in furthering those intrinsic goods which the writer advances as the primary goals of American society. In the literature about to be considered, this structure is sometimes presented in reverse. Early in the argument the case is made for valuing the free-market system as a means for achieving desirable ends, but those ends or intrinsic goods tend to be articulated only as they arise in the discussion of the free market, and often are not assembled in one place and identified for what they are, namely, the normative assertions controlling the entire debate. But surely, the alert reader will be saying, this technique is unlikely to succeed because of points emphasized in chapter 1. If the "intrinsic goods" include many values, some of which can and do conflict, then the merits of the market as an instrumental good may become blurred insofar as in its workings it promotes certain intrinsic goods at the expense of other intrinsic goods. The tactical ploy for solving this particular problem is not difficult to anticipate: shorten the list of intrinsic goods until the potential conflicts disappear. And of course the best guarantee of no conflicts whatsoever is to shorten that list to a single intrinsic good. As extreme as this latter approach may seem, it is not too extreme for Murray Rothbard and Milton Friedman. But this last assertion anticipates arguments that still lie ahead.

The one remaining problem to be settled at the outset concerns which writers to include and exclude. The choice made here in part reflects the fashionability of the writers. Any survey of contemporary literature of the right is sure to encounter – in the text and in the footnotes – respectful references to one or more of Friedrich Hayek, Murray Rothbard, and Milton Friedman. Each offers a different defense of the market, and each defense is flawed in rather different ways. An investigation of the three combined therefore provides a useful survey of confusions typical of the right in their writings about economic justice. A number of noted conservatives not considered here are ignored primarily because their positions (and their errors) are not significantly different from those of the three about to be considered. Others are ignored because their views, while different from the three, are so imperfectly developed that they do not seem to be fertile ground for gaining fundamental insights into how to reason, and how not to reason, about topics relating to economic justice. George Stigler, for example, offers a cautious endorsement of marginal productivity justice by citing with approval the views of two writers (John Bates Clark and Thomas Nixon Carver), neither of whom offer a defense of the market that deserves to be taken seriously (see appendix F). Perhaps the most obvious name missing from the pages that follow is that of Irving Kristol, commonly regarded as one of the most thoughtful and influential of contemporary neoconservatives. Kristol's defense of the market begins in an atypical way for writers of the right – with an emphasis upon the linkage between merit and reward – but it ends in a typical way – with an emphasis upon liberty – and the arguments by which he proceeds from one position to another do not seem to follow logically, one from the other (see appendix G).

The challenge here, to repeat, is to investigate three quite different general defenses of the market system, in each case with the twin objectives of uncovering (a) the structure of that defense and (b) the more obvious flaws in that structure.

Friedrich Hayek

One of the most popular writers with American conservatives (particularly those on the extreme right) is Austrian-born Friedrich Hayek. Although an economist and Nobel laureate, Hayek approaches problems of social justice more as a philosopher than a social scientist. His efforts to solve the problem of distributive justice consist largely of trying to dismiss the question. This dismissal is in three steps.[3] First, Hayek argues that market payments to factors of production bear no clear relationship to merit; second, he points out how liberty will be imperilled if any effort is made to make factor payments correspond more closely to the merits of the recipients; and third, he defines justice in such a way that the search for social justice becomes a meaningless pursuit. In short, according to Hayek, the linking of factor payments to the merit of recipients is impossible to achieve, dangerous to try, and unnecessary to attempt.

His first point – that market payments bear no clear relationship to merit – merely echoes the concerns of the previous chapter, often in the context of similar examples. Heredity, environment, and capricious variations in supply and demand, Hayek rightly observes, all introduce an element of luck into the determination of how much income is received and by whom. (To concede that luck matters does not necessarily force abandonment of the belief that reward and merit are strongly correlated, as we shall see in a later chapter.)

His second point is really several points, many of which are as noncontroversial as the observation that luck as well as merit affects what factors of production will be paid. Any attempt to make payments correspond more closely to merit can proceed only if (a) a standard of merit can be specified, and (b) interventions in the market system can be made to achieve results more consistent with that standard. To this point, the discussion smacks of the tightly reasoned logic of the philosopher. The same might be said for

Hayek's further point that any such intervention in the workings of a free market will impair the liberty of individuals – in this case, their liberty to earn and retain (unimpaired by intervention) the rewards meted out by a free-market system. His final argument consists of an empirical assertion supported by economic reasoning that is also unexceptional: if intervention in the free market reduces incomes actually received, the receivers will have less incentive to work and to take risks, and to the extent that they respond by cutting back their labor, aggregate efficiency will suffer and total output will decline. One might reasonably ask whether output will decline by a lot or a little, and in the same spirit of elaboration, one might also ask whether the loss of liberty by some (those who have lost part of their income) is compensated, at least to some degree, by gains in liberty by others (because of the income transfers they have received). But nothing in the arguments as stated thus far seems fertile ground for controversial debate.

The same cannot be said for Hayek's more extreme version of these same points.[4] Using the criteria and the debating style of a philosopher, he tries to show that what is needed for justifiable intervention can never be achieved. The problem he chooses to address is the possibility of making payments received better reflect the merits of the income receivers. Intervention in the market to achieve that goal, he notes, requires establishing a standard for what merit is; to be acceptable (at least to Hayek), that standard must be precisely specified and universally accepted; so diverse are the views within society about what merit is that no such universally accepted standard can exist; all intervention must accordingly be based upon indefensible criteria and thus no intervention can be justified. Put more simply, the philosopher is arguing that if the standard for judging action cannot be perfect, the action (in this case, market intervention) should never be attempted.

This same bias for couching arguments in an extreme form is evident in Hayek's account of the dire consequences of any attempt by government intervention to mitigate the income distribution produced by the market system. Intervention will create demands for further intervention, he argues, and this cumulative process will almost surely lead to a totalitarian state.[5] This belief – that intervention breeds more intervention until the government controls all – is a recurring theme in the literature of the right. The fear is that, unwittingly at first perhaps, these tendencies will encourage a taste for collectivism: the ownership and control of the means of production by the people as a whole – and this "creeping collectivism," as Herbert Hoover[6] (and many others) have characterized the process, will lead to the destruction of personal liberty and representative government. This is a claim for which surprisingly little evidence has been marshalled by either its advocates or its opponents. To identify a tendency is not to prove that tendency must persist unchecked to the point of disaster. Certainly within America the expansion of political control of economic life has been a hallmark of the twentieth century, and yet the accompanying declines in personal liberty would seem at present far removed from that shackling of individual freedom associated with totalitarian states. Even Hayek concedes that since his *Road to Serfdom* first appeared in 1944, "developments . . . in Britain as well as in the rest of the Western world, have gone much less in the direction which the prevalent [circa 1944] collectivist doctrines seemed to suggest was likely."[7]

The evidence does seem to support part of Hayek's claim, but not the part that is vital to his argument. Western societies in the twentieth century have clearly evidenced a widespread tendency for democratic governments to intervene in the workings of the market system. But to claim that these observed tendencies make a future degeneration into totalitarian states inevitable (or almost inevitable) is not to argue from the facts but to urge the acceptance of what is little more than an article of faith.[8] The same evidence – including the recent history of the United States – could also be used to argue that sustained but moderate government intervention is a viable long-run possibility. The key word is "possibility." Writers of the left are no doubt sometimes too sanguine about the chances of expanded government controls *not* degenerating into tyranny. But, similarly, writers of the right are prone to overstating the dangers, and occasionally argue that probabilities which essentially remain unknown are known to them and very close to certainty.

To review: Hayek's more extreme case against the government's intervening in the market to make factor payments correspond more closely to the merit of the recipients is supported by two claims: (a) such action can never be based upon a defensible standard (since any standard for merit must be precisely specified and universally agreed to, and no such standard exists); and (b) any intervention fosters demands for more intervention that can lead to a totalitarian state. His third supporting argument is designed to show that, insofar as intervention is prompted by a concern for social justice, that intervention is pointless because the concern in question is meaningless. Here, too, one encounters the analytical methods of the skilled philosopher. To deprive the phrase "social justice" of any meaning, Hayek merely defines the word "justice" in such a way that no other conclusion is possible. Thus he argues that "justice" is a concept which "ought to be confined to the deliberate treatment of men by other men."[9] The critical word is "deliberate," and the crucial question is whether any general result (such as the income distribution of a society) is the "deliberate" design of human actors.

We are of course not wrong when we perceive that the effects on the different individuals and groups of the economic processes of a free society are not distributed according to some recognizable principle of justice. Where we go wrong is in concluding from this that they are unjust and that somebody is responsible and to be blamed for this. In a free society in which the position of the different individuals and groups is not the result of anybody's design – or could within such a society not be altered in accordance with a principle of general applicability – the differences in rewards cannot meaningfully be described as just or unjust.[10]

If Hayek is correct – that "social justice" is a meaningless concept – then American preoccupation with that term would seem symptomatic of a people who have been incapable of thinking clearly about that issue for almost two centuries. An alternative possibility is that Hayek's approach to the problem is symptomatic of Hayek's misunderstanding of deeply felt American concerns.

His argument, in outline, is that (a) the words "just" and "unjust" are appropriately applied only to the results of human action, (b) only intended results should be so judged, (c) the income distribution of a society is not the result of anybody's intentional design, and thus (d) income distribution cannot appropriately be judged as "just" or "unjust." Of these various claims, the first should arouse few objections. The results of nonhuman action, such as those produced by earthquakes or tidal waves, can be disastrous, but few would be willing to judge those results to be "unjust." The contentious claims are (b) and (c). Even abridged American dictionaries give half a dozen meanings for the word "justice," among them "fairness" and "reward or penalty as deserved." Such meanings seem to resonate with the American concerns expressed in chapter 2. Even if they did not, the framework for assessing justice urged by Hayek would seem markedly out of step with how Americans (or most of them) regard their economic system. The income distribution created by that system is admittedly not the result of any group's intentional design. Rather, it is the product of countless decisions by human actors in the marketplace (including individual actions on behalf of government policies of intervention as well as all the actions by participants in the private sector). But that fact alone does not preclude responsibility for the results. Most Americans would be quick to emphasize that (a) the original income distribution, however it was produced, can be altered by human intervention (through various government policies), and therefore (b) this possibility implies that to accept the status quo (the income distribution produced by market forces) is to endorse the status quo (since human agents, through government action, have the power to alter it). If members of a democratic society cannot escape endorsing the results, they must of necessity judge the results to see if they are "satisfactory" or can be made "better." Assessing the "justice" of the income distribution of a society would therefore seem to be not only defensible but unavoidable.

But what criteria can be used to judge income distribution and (by implication) justify government intervention to make that distribution "better"? At this juncture Hayek mounts a second defense, which is merely an old point in a new guise. Previously the argument was made that intervention in the market to make income correspond more closely to the merits of the recipients was defensible only if a standard of merit could be applied that was precisely specified and universally accepted. Those same criteria – precision in specification and universal acceptance – are lurking in Hayek's plea, noted above, that income distribution cannot be judged as "just" unless it can "be altered in accordance with a principle of general applicability." Americans as a group, however, are not inclined to aim so high. Nor are they prone to abandoning the target altogether when the defects in their aim are pointed out. Instead they seem determined to believe in the legitimacy of striving in admittedly imperfect ways toward "the good," or if not that, toward what is "generally accepted" to be better than the status quo. If pressed, they would have to admit to those frailties the philosopher abhors: their norms of what is "good" are seldom well defined, and the phrase "generally accepted," while indicating a deeply felt desire for consensus of some sort, is also lacking in precision.

But those beliefs, and that striving, seem destined to continue, and the question of the social justice of their income distribution, at least for most Americans, cannot be defined away. Nor are such people likely to be converted to agnosticism on the subject by philosophical arguments that emphasize the vagueness of their norms. The puzzle raised by Hayek is therefore not why Americans persistently pursue a norm that Hayek considers meaningless, but rather how Hayek's views could be so far out of step with those beliefs and values and judgmental processes that from the beginning of this nation have been so characteristic of its people.[11]

For all Hayek's carefully worked out arguments, then, the challenge noted at the outset of this chapter has not been dismissed and has yet to be seriously addressed. That challenge was to justify the income distribution generated by the market system without referring to the merits of the recipients. Others will follow some of Hayek's leads, particularly his emphasis on the importance of freedom, the manner in which a market system fosters freedom, and the threats to liberty from government efforts to intervene in the workings of the market system. Those arguments as they impinge upon the central concerns of this chapter will surface in more detail in subsequent sections.

Murray Rothbard

Economist and journal editor Murray Rothbard is one of the acknowledged intellectual leaders among contemporary libertarians, a group which, by American standards, is located on the far right. His views are interesting for purposes of this discussion for two reasons. First he provides a carefully reasoned defense of the income distribution generated by the market that makes no reference to the merits of recipients. Secondly, that defense proceeds from a handful of premises to a conclusion presumed to be universally applicable in any situation where the justice of the economic system is at stake. At such, it provides a classic example of how *not* to reason about economic justice. To put the second point a second way, Rothbard's approach flies in the face of key points made in earlier chapters: that to problems of economic justice we bring a multitude of values to be honored; these values can and do conflict; when conflicts arise, tradeoffs among competing values must be made; general rules for making such tradeoffs are difficult to formulate; and thus judgments about economic justice are difficult to make independent of the context of the situation in which such judgments must be made. Or, more simply put, in reaching decisions about economic justice in a concrete situation, we do not generally rely upon universal rules to determine the "right" or "just" choice.

Rothbard begins by noting what can hardly be denied: that any effort to tamper with the income distribution generated by the market would involve taking from some and giving to others. That taking, in turn, involves violating what is ordinarily regarded as a property right. This prospective violation is central to Rothbard's line of reasoning, leading to a predictable conclusion for a spokesman of the extreme right. If property rights (and only property rights) can be defended as inviolable, the question of which income distribution is "just" or "right" will have been solved. Income received from market transactions becomes the property of the receiver, the argument will run, and the right of the receiver to that property is absolute (or will be, if property rights can be demonstrated to be inviolable). All efforts at income redistribution will accordingly be indefensible, because any taking from Peter to help support Paul will infringe the property rights of Peter. If *no* redistribution is *ever* justified, the "right" income distribution must necessarily be the distribution originally created, and that amounts to a stringent endorsement of the distribution generated by the market system. Once a single premise has been granted (that property rights are inviolable), the logic of the argument is both simple and compelling. The key problem for Rothbard is therefore to construct a philosophical framework that will justify that premise.

He begins with a discussion totally divorced from economics, and develops what is ultimately a two-stage argument.[12] The first stage, grounded in philosophical considerations, lays the foundation for the second, concerned with how the economic system ought to function. The crucial link between the two is the property rights assertion previously noted. Because the key points may seem somewhat strange to many readers, a number of the statements summarizing steps in the argument are followed by quotations in which Rothbard makes the same point in his own terms.

1   The starting point is with a variant of natural-law philosophy. All phenomena, Rothbard argues, have an intrinsic nature, including man, and for each (including man) that nature is *fixed* ("man has an unchanging and an age-old, genetically determined anatomical, physiological, and psychological make-up"[13]).

2   Given that each living thing has an intrinsic nature, "goodness" is the fulfillment of what is best for that type of creature as defined by its nature ("'goodness' is therefore relative to the nature of the creature concerned"[14]). Applied to man, this argument states that "good" is defined as that which facilitates the realization of man's natural tendencies, and "bad" is that which tends to thwart those tendencies. Ethics (or "natural-law ethics") thus becomes a set of principles which best enable man to realize his intrinsic nature ("the natural law ethic states that for man, goodness or badness can be determined by what fulfills or thwarts what is best for man's nature"[15]).

3   The problem of ethics therefore becomes one of discovering (a) the nature of man and (b) those principles of conduct that best enable man to realize his intrinsic nature or natural tendencies. Both are discoverable by reason and by reason alone ("For the ends themselves are selected by the use of reason; and 'right reason' dictates to man his proper ends as well as the means for their attainment"[16]).

4   Two inferences follow. The first begins by noting that reason is objective in the sense of being unaffected by the feelings and biases of the person reasoning. Therefore, what reason discovers about man's nature and how to realize that nature should also be objective. And because what reason is trying to discover is both fixed and identical for all men (namely, man's nature), it follows that the principles of conduct best suited for the realization of that intrinsic nature have universal applicability ("natural law [can be defined] cogently and concisely as: 'Principles of human conduct that are discoverable by "reason" from the basic inclinations of human nature, and that are absolute, immutable and of universal validity for all times and places' "[17]).

5   The second inference concerns the possibility of deriving an "ought" statement from an "is" statement – a derivation many philosophers have claimed cannot be made.[18] If Rothbard's arguments thus far are accepted, such a derivation is easily achieved. The only points that need to be added are (a) to equate the realization of man's intrinsic nature to his achievement of "real" happiness, and (b) to make the achievement of "real" happiness man's only goal. The "is" then defines the "ought." Once reason has discovered what man's nature *is* and, using that discovery, has established those rules of conduct that *are* best suited for the realization of that nature, these same rules of conduct are what man *ought* to follow. They are the best guides for the achievement of that single goal of man: "real" happiness ("The natural law . . . elucidates what is best for man – what ends man should pursue that are most harmonious with, and best tend to fulfill, his nature. In a significant sense, then, natural law provides man with a 'science of happiness,' with the paths which lead to his real happiness"[19]).

The previous points can be recast within the more general framework of natural-law philosophy – or, more correctly, within the framework of a variant of natural-law doctrine dating from Thomas Aquinas. In summary form, the basic premises of this doctrine are that phenomena (including all living things) are divided into natural kinds, that each kind is distinguished by its essence or intrinsic nature, that this essence stipulates an end, and that "goodness" is necessarily linked with the fulfillment of those ends, or with the realization of that intrinsic nature. Whether God is responsible for the fixed nature of phenomena or for man's reason is, Rothbard argues, a separate issue and quite unnecessary for his case.[20] The reader is accordingly asked to accept, as it were, the Aquinas viewpoint minus the theology. The fundamental premises outlined above must be, in language previously used, truths that are self-evident. If they fail that test, all of Rothbard's other arguments collapse from the outset. If these premises are accepted, a line of reasoning can be constructed that will lead, first, to the conclusion that property rights are inviolable, and second, to a defense of marginal productivity justice. And – crucial for the purposes of this chapter – that latter defense will make no reference to the merits of the recipients of income.

Before proceeding, we should acknowledge what Rothbard acknowledges: his goal is not to develop or defend a comprehensive theory of natural law covering all aspects of human behavior. His major concern is to articulate the minimum philosophical structure needed to serve as a foundation for other arguments that he wishes to advance concerning political economy, property rights, and income distribution. The basic elements of that philosophical structure have been outlined above. The task ahead is to show how such a structure can be used to defend the income distribution generated by a market system free from government intervention.

6   As required by that structure, the starting point is to specify the "nature of man" insofar as that nature involves economic activity. To survive, Rothbard notes, man must manipulate the natural world to meet his economic needs. The more successful is that manipulation, the better off man will be in terms of economic welfare and, by implication, in his pursuit of happiness (or as Rothbard prefers to phrase it, in his pursuit of "real" happiness).

7   If man is to fulfill certain aspects of his nature through economic activity, Rothbard asserts, two different rights are crucial: the right to self-ownership, and the right to property.

(a)   Man's right to self-ownership is justified in two different ways. At one point Rothbard argues that it is a "basic axiom": a right that can be claimed by every human simply from the fact of being human ("the right to self-ownership asserts the absolute right of each man, by virtue of his (or her) being a human being, to 'own' his or her own body"[21]). At other times, and more in keeping with the line of reasoning developed previously, Rothbard argues that for man to realize his nature in the realm of economic activity, he must grapple with and transform the material world; to do that success- fully, he must be free to experiment, learn, and choose; and man cannot be expected "to learn, choose, develop his facilities, and act upon his [own] knowledge and values"[22] if he is enslaved by someone else.

(b)   As well as the right of self-ownership, man can claim (or ought to be able to claim) the right to all that he produces. Again, two quite different arguments are advanced to support this assertion. If (i) man's general goal is to achieve "real" happiness by realizing his intrinsic nature and (ii) that nature, insofar as economic activity is concerned, is bent upon maximizing economic welfare through the production of economic goods and services, then the implication seems to be that (iii) any man who is a producer will achieve greater economic welfare if he can claim as his own everything he produces. (Whether he consumes what he produces or trades it for something else is a separate issue. The only point here, Rothbard would argue, is that the right of ownership is a necessary condition for trading to proceed.) This particular line of argument Rothbard tends to make in softer language, referring not to the need of every individual to maximize his own economic welfare, but rather to man's need to "survive and flourish" or "survive and prosper."[23]

But if such reasoning seems to take the low road of self-interest as applied to economic needs, Rothbard has a high road that also leads him to the same conclusion. He begins by repeating a point made centuries earlier by John Locke: that the act of production requires man to "mix his labor" with other economic resources, and from that act of mixing comes a presumption to ownership of the results. Consider, Rothbard urges, the example of the sculptor:

He has placed the stamp of his person upon the raw material, by "mixing his labor" with the clay . . . . And the product transformed by his own energy has become the material embodiment of the sculptor's ideas and vision.[24]

The example is cleverly chosen. One factor of production (the sculptor's labor) combines with a natural resource (clay) in such a way that the result seems to be the exclusive product of the worker involved. But this would seem to base the sculptor's claim to ownership upon (a) a narrow view of causation (the statue is created by the sculptor alone) or (b) the sculptor's exercising certain traits (like "energy" and "creativity") deserving of reward.[25] If either argument is extended to all forms of economic activity, difficulties immediately become apparent. The argument from causation is unacceptably simplistic for reasons noted earlier (see pp. 59–60). The other justification for the sculptor's ownership raises what this chapter is seeking to avoid, namely, the many difficulties (outlined in the previous chapter) of arguing that income payments reward the meritorious behavior of those who receive the income. For these reasons, Rothbard's defense of property rights would seem best confined to his first line of argument, which emphasizes man's "nature," and his need, through economic activity, to "survive and flourish."

8   Once property rights are made to seem inviolable, as previously noted, the implications concerning income distribution are both simple and direct. If the producer is not entitled to the fruits of his labor, Rothbard asks, who is?[26] That question skillfully controls what will count as an acceptable answer. It confines the issue of the "rightness" of any income distribution to one of establishing property rights, and those rights, Rothbard claims, are absolute and therefore not to be violated. They also have, he argues, universal applicability:

. . . every person, at any time or place, can be covered by the basic rules: ownership of one's own self, ownership of the previously unused resources which one has occupied and transformed; and ownership of all titles derived from that basic ownership – either through voluntary exchanges or voluntary gifts. These rules – which we might call the "rules of natural ownership" – can clearly be applied, and such ownership defended, regardless of the time or place, and regardless of the economic attainments of the society.[27]

The "right" income distribution is therefore whatever distribution is generated by the actions of economic agents pursuing their own self-interest in a free market.

9   One unanswered question is how free these economic agents ought to be. Competition in the marketplace can lead to a clash of interests, and when such clashes occur, what should determine whose interests should prevail? The answer is implied by Rothbard's definition of freedom. Any man is free, he argues, who is not subject to coercion, and coercion is carefully (and narrowly) defined as physical violence or the threat of physical violence.[28] This definition then determines how rights (such as property rights) should be defined:

> When we say that one has the right to do certain things we mean this and only this, that it would be immoral for another, alone or in combination to stop him from doing this by the use of physical force or the threat thereof.[29]

Income earned is property rightfully owned. Others have no right to take it away "by the use of physical force or the threat thereof." And owners have the right to do whatever they will with that property, provided they do not imperil the "freedom" of others, that is, use physical force (or the threat of physical force) as they pursue their own economic self-interest (or try to fulfill other aspects of their "nature").

10 The remaining question of importance to this discussion is whether, as a result of the mechanisms of a free market, factors of production in Rothbard's view will tend to be paid the value of their marginal product. He begins by praising the market on several counts. By making voluntary exchange possible, it raises utility[30] (one is tempted, in Rothbard's terminology, to substitute "happiness" for "utility"); as a result, the free market is "a picture . . . of harmony and mutual benefit,"[31] and the market price is always the "just" price, partly because it is established by voluntary exchanges and partly because those exchanges are a reflection of consumer preferences.[32] As something of an aside, Rothbard also notes what will become a central point in future arguments: the free market tends to foster the most efficient use of economic resources.

> It so happens that the free-market economy, and the specialization and division of labor it implies, is by far the most productive form of economy known to man, and has been responsible for industrialization and for the modern economy on which civilization has been built. This is a fortunate utilitarian result of the free market, but it is not, to the libertarian, the *prime* reason for his support of this system. That prime reason is moral, and is rooted in the natural rights defense of private property we have developed above.[33]

The point just made suggests that Rothbard views competitive markets as functioning reasonably well, a theme he hints at repeatedly elsewhere in his writings.[34] And well-functioning markets, he states explicitly, tend to pay factors of production the value of their marginal product.[35] Thus, although Rothbard emphasizes that this particular result is not crucial to his argument about which income distribution is "right" (whatever the market generates is "right" for him), he can still be counted among the defenders of marginal productivity justice.

But is the Rothbard defense compelling? The answer depends upon one's willingness to accept all the arguments in the long line of reasoning summarized above. For most Americans, many of the separate points are extreme or simplistic or both, and the argument in its entirety is more curious than compelling. The best evidence of that is the negligible importance of the libertarian party in American politics.

This lack of popularity signals a difficulty which even Rothbard must find embarrassing. If principles of human conduct are discoverable by reason, and principles so discovered have universal applicability, why have so few Americans endorsed Rothbard's principles? One possibility is that, throughout their history, Americans have stubbornly refused to follow the dictates of their reason. Another and more likely explanation is that Rothbard's reasoning is fundamentally flawed. No political party of any consequence has ever included in its platform that property rights should never be violated. Those rights, in Rothbard's terms, have been violated repeatedly in the twentieth century, as taxation has increasingly been used to fund programs for the less advantaged members of society. Nor has this rising trend of transfer programs been significantly reversed under the more conservative administration of Dwight Eisenhower in the 1950s or even that of Ronald Reagan in the 1980s. And the many policy choices involving more tax dollars to fund more social programs for the disadvantaged have been made and implemented in a country that prides itself on the degree to which the acts of government reflect a certain consensus among the people. "The best test of truth," noted Oliver Wendell Holmes, "is the power of the thought to get itself accepted in the competition of the market."[36] In that particular competition, Rothbard, the staunch advocate of economic markets and free competition, has had a singular absence of success. The question still unanswered is why.

The main explanation would seem to be the narrowness of focus which pervades all of Rothbard's reasoning. A few examples:

1   Few Americans would be willing to equate "the good" *only* with the realizing of man's intrinsic nature, and most would want to differentiate among "natural tendencies," judging some more admirable than others, and at least a few as downright dangerous. ("Curiosity" and "social instincts," for example, are likely to be rated rather higher than "aggressiveness.")

2   Most would readily acknowledge that property rights have an important role to play within American society, but few would endorse Rothbard's claim that property rights are inviolable and *only* property rights have such a claim.[37]

3   Any effort by Americans to define freedom is sure to include what Rothbard includes, namely, the absence of physical violence and the threat of violence. But most would not be satisfied to argue that this is all there is to the concept of freedom – that any individual not subject to physical violence or the threat of violence is therefore "free."[38]

Other examples of narrow focus and extreme position could be cited.[39] But while these may be interesting to conservatives concerned with an entitlement approach to economic justice, they are of little interest outside such circles precisely because they ignore so many considerations considered by most Americans to be relevant in reaching judgments about economic justice.[40]

Extreme as they are, the arguments of Rothbard illustrate several points of importance for subsequent discussion. One is that claims about economic justice by intellectual leaders on the left and right are often derived from a philosophical framework constructed from universal propositions. A second is that this construction can be made much more easy if the many and complex concerns of humanity – concerns that range from ethics to metaphysics to the determinants of personality – are reduced to a mere handful. That handful can then be incorporated into a line of reasoning which, precisely because of its simplicity, is easy to follow and impossible to accept. The fewer are the ethical goals acknowledged, for example, the fewer are the dilemmas likely to arise because goals conflict. But that reduction of dilemmas is itself objectionable, precisely because it is achieved by ignoring much that is important – or at least much that is important to the vast majority of Americans.

The final writer to be considered in this chapter will appear to accomplish more by explaining less than Rothbard. Most of his fundamental philosophical framework will remain hidden, while the arguments about economic justice built upon that framework will be articulated with subtlety and brilliance. At the center of these arguments will be the premise that freedom is the ultimate goal. Many of the tradeoff problems that can arise when values conflict are thereby solved in a simple way: promoting the ultimate value becomes the only priority of consequence. But this simplicity of structure – precisely because of its simplicity – will again lead to unacceptable results. A second set of problems will be discovered if, for the sake of argument, one accepts freedom as the ultimate or only goal and asks what that goal, seemingly of self-evident appeal, actually means. The importance of such an exercise will become more apparent in the course of examining the views on economic justice of the one American rivalling Friedrich Hayek as an influential spokesman for the right.

Milton Friedman

Advisor to presidents, Nobel laureate, and one of the most skilled American economists in debate, Milton Friedman throughout his life has been an indefatigable defender of the market system. His strategy of argument is markedly different from that of Murray Rothbard. The latter, as noted, proceeds from the general to the particular; from philosophical foundations, carefully constructed and explained, to specific economic policies consistent with, and implied by, those foundations. Friedman focuses instead upon specific policies, and gives only imperfect glimpses of the foundations upon which his policy recommendations ultimately rest. His writings consist, by and large, of a series of examples, such as rent control, occupational licensing, and social security – each carefully chosen to illustrate his central theme that the results of the free market tend to be "good" and the results of government efforts to intervene in that market tend to be "bad."

The words "good" and "bad" make clear that Friedman's policy recommendations inevitably rest upon value judgments, and these judgments in turn are determined by criteria which are part of a larger philosophical framework. Just what that framework is, as already indicated, is far from clear. What Friedman chooses to make explicit is the following.

1   Beginning with the premise of the dignity of the individual, he infers from this that the individual is the "ultimate entity" of any society, and individual freedom is the "ultimate goal."[41]
2   This ultimate goal, he cautions, is "a rare and delicate plant," continually threatened by any concentration of power.[42]
3   If concentration of power is the central problem, diffusion of power is the obvious solution. And if the government is the most likely source of power concentration, two policy conclusions would seem to follow which Friedman argues are imbedded in the American Constitution:

   (a) the scope of government must be limited; and
   (b) government power must be dispersed, from the federal government to the states or (better yet) to the localities, at least wherever possible.[43]

As simple as these arguments may seem, they are crafted with consummate care. The value judgments stated at the outset resonate powerfully with the basic beliefs of almost all Americans. The logical inferences seem irresistible, or almost so. If individual freedom is to be preserved, surely the coercive powers of the state must be curbed, and what more obvious way to pursue that goal than by giving to government a minimum of power and dispersing that minimum as widely as possible? Hidden from view, however, are a host of philosophical puzzles which, once confronted, will shatter the seeming simplicity of the argument. Why this is so will be discussed below. The task at this juncture is to show how Friedman uses these three points to develop a defense of the market system in general, and marginal productivity justice in particular.

4   The ultimate goal, to repeat, is individual freedom. The economic system best suited for pursuing that goal, Friedman argues, is competitive capitalism (or the "free enterprise exchange economy"[44]), and for two quite different reasons.

   (a)   The economic freedom of the market is "a component of freedom broadly understood."[45] Thus the market (or the freedom it makes possible) is an "intrinsic" good: something valuable in and of itself. Further, as the phrase "free private enterprise exchange economy" implies, exchange is voluntary. Friedman therefore argues (as does Rothbard) that all those engaged in this system of exchange must expect to increase their "utility" or "economic welfare" from participation. (Otherwise, they presumably would opt for not giving in exchange whatever they actually did trade.) The merits of such a system are often illustrated by an analogy with political democracy: consumers "vote" with the dollars they have to spend, the market system responds to the preferences these votes reveal, and the resulting production and distribution of economic goods and services reflects a "democratic" response to the wishes of the people. ("[The market] is, in political terms, a system of proportional representation. Each man can vote, as it were, for the color of tie he wants and get it; he does not have to see what color the majority wants and then, if he is in the minority, submit."[46])

   (b)   While the freedom that the market makes possible is an "intrinsic" good, the market system itself is an "instrumental" good because of the role it plays in combating coercive power, particularly the coercive power of the state. In part, this results because of what the market removes from state control. The fewer are the decisions about production and distribution made by government officials, the less power those officials have. The market not only allocates economic decision-making to private individuals, but the result of that allocation is the creation of foci of economic power in the private sector which, although tending to be widely dispersed,[47] are appropriately viewed as part of a system of checks and balances constraining the potential for abuse of power where power tends to be most concentrated, namely, in the government. The owners of private property, the argument runs, are more independent and less vulnerable to any coercion, including efforts at coercion by the government. And those who have amassed sufficient private property can serve as patrons, helping to finance novel experiments or unpopular ideas (including the publication of ideas and the initiation of novel schemes not favored by those in positions of political power).

In sum, for Friedman, competitive capitalism or the free-enterprise exchange economy is both an intrinsic and an instrumental good: both "a system of economic freedom" and "a necessary condition for political freedom."[48]

5   The market also functions as an instrumental good by promoting efficiency and economic growth. Friedman is quick to emphasize what Rothbard emphasizes: that these particular economic benefits are "a happy by-product" of a system whose major importance derives from the role it plays in promoting individual freedom.[49] Secondary though such achievements are, Friedman never tires of offering examples to support his claim that no other economic system can match competitive capitalism in its efficient use of economic resources. This is a "static" claim, concerned as it is with getting the largest possible pie from a fixed bundle of resources and a given technology. Friedman also makes a "dynamic" claim concerning the growth of the pie. Competitive capitalism, he argues, has been central to the achievement of sustained economic growth (or a sustained rise in real per capita income), in part because of the creative energy it releases, in part because of the experimentation and risk-taking it encourages.[50]

6   The willingness of economic actors to experiment or take risks depends, of course, upon the rewards offered for success. This raises again the two questions that dominate this inquiry. (a) In a free market system, what determines how much factors of production will be paid (a question of fact)? (b) How much ought factors of production be paid (a question of values)?

Friedman answers the first question in a predictable way for a noted advocate of neoclassical price theory. Factors of production (in a competitive market) tend to be paid the value of their marginal product.[51]

But is this what factors should receive? Friedman acknowledges (indeed labors) the important role of luck as one influence determining income payments, and is quick to concede the implication noted previously: "payment in accordance with product" cannot be viewed as rewarding only meritorious behavior.[52] He nevertheless defends the resulting distribution system by emphasizing the importance of individual freedom while adopting an agnostic posture with respect to other "social values" (his term). The argument is in three steps.

1   Suppose the desirable goal for all factor payments is to achieve an income distribution that is "fair," and "fairness" is linked to rewarding merit. If the market does not reward merit – or more cautiously, does not reward *only* merit – then, Friedman notes, some distribution scheme other than that generated by the market must be implemented.

2   If some other distribution scheme is to be implemented, some administrative organization must be given the responsibility of establishing what "fairness" is, and then reallocating the income payments generated by

the market in accordance with those criteria. This would be wrong-headed, Friedman argues, on two counts.[53] First, it would give to some authority control over a vast range of economic matters; with that control would come a concentration of power; and with this concentration of power (as with any concentration of power) would come the likelihood of abuses that would imperil Friedman's primary goal of individual freedom. Secondly, the criteria needed are impossible to identify, because "it is difficult, if not impossible, to define precisely" what "fairness" is.[54] "Fairness," Friedman argues, is "not an objectively determined concept" but rather "is in the eye of the beholder."[55] If definitions of fairness vary depending upon who is doing the defining, it follows that society can never redistribute income according to a universal standard for fairness. Consequently, the standards that will determine any reallocation of market income, Friedman argues, will simply be the personal preferences of those charged with administering the redistribution program.

3   The goal of "fairness" in income distribution is therefore not only dangerous to pursue, but impossible to achieve (a position quite similar to Hayek's). This being so, argues Friedman, the preferable solution – or at least the lesser of two evils – is to accept the income distribution produced by the market system. And since Friedman believes that the market (if left alone) will tend to pay factors of production the value of their marginal product, he too is ultimately a defender of marginal productivity justice. The word "justice," Friedman might object, is misleading: the distribution in question has no claim to being "fair," but the income distribution of the market is nevertheless "right," because any effort to tamper with it would be "wrong."

The Friedman defense of the market system tends to evoke a markedly different response from that produced by the arguments of Murray Rothbard. Precisely because Friedman's reasoning appears more simple and less dependent upon questionable philosophical assumptions, his position seems less vulnerable to attack. Part of that simplicity derives from Friedman's emphasizing a single goal – individual freedom – and this in turn ensures the reader will encounter few of the dilemmas that normally arise when ethical goals conflict. The problem of how to reconcile equity of distribution with property rights is thus easily resolved by Friedman:

I find it hard . . . to see any justification for graduated taxation solely to redistribute income. This seems a clear case of using coercion to take from some in order to give to others and thus to conflict head-on with individual freedom.[56]

One curious feature of Friedman's position is the manner in which optimism and pessimism are combined. Humanity can never be trusted to use power with wisdom and discretion, but it can always be relied upon to use individual freedom in a manner that will promote – or at least not undermine – the "good" or "virtuous" society. In the pursuit of self-realization, however, why should the "selves" thereby realized always tend to be acceptable and even admirable, rather than decadent and perhaps even deplorable? If the nastier tendencies of mankind are pursued by many, or even by a significant few, the results might be a society more distinguished for its viciousness than its virtue. The puzzle is why Friedman should ignore such possibilities while emphasizing how dangerous and destructive humanity can be when given any power. As fellow conservative Irving Kristol has pointed out, lurking beneath the surface of Friedman's arguments is "much hidden metaphysics" (and, in Kristol's view, "of a dubious kind" – a proposition to which the discussion will return later on[57]). The main difficulty with Friedman's position, however, lies elsewhere.

Again the problem begins with a curious blending of sharply differing beliefs – in this case, beliefs about ethical values, where Friedman's position is a mixture of assurance and agnosticism. About the value of individual freedom he has no doubts whatsoever. This is for him the ultimate goal and the only ultimate goal: a claim that makes the reader wonder what other goals have been dismissed. Economic freedom, Friedman argues, "is freedom to use the resources we possess in accordance with our own values,"[58] but which of *those* values are "right" or "wrong" or "better" or "worse" is a question he never addresses. Often he writes as if individual values were like consumer preferences: varying widely across individuals and none with any special claim to rightness or universality. For example, as previously noted, "fairness" (or fairness in income distribution) he characterizes as being "in the eye of the beholder."[59] But if this is true for "fairness," might it also be true for other values? And worst of all for Friedman's position, might it also be true for "freedom"?

Consider the following example. Suppose that certain individuals living in poverty cannot afford to pay for the training needed to gain a better job or, because of malnutrition, cannot benefit from schooling as much as other students. If a welfare program could pay for their training or solve that malnutrition, these people would be "more free" to pursue self-realization in general and economic advancement in particular. A redistribution of income from rich to poor might therefore actually *increase* freedom (or the "net" freedom in society) – the gains of the poor more than offsetting the losses of the rich, the latter losing some of their freedom because of tax payments that took away some of their property. Friedman would be quick to point out that different definitions of freedom are being used to make a net calculation that is highly suspect. Freedom *from* coercion, he could rightly point out, is not the same thing as freedom *to* seek economic advancement. But to note the importance of such distinctions is to concede the central point: that Friedman's arguments about the "rightness" or "justice" of the market system can only be intelligently assessed if the meaning of the word central to those arguments ("freedom") is made clear. Further, as the different possible definitions of freedom are examined, a variety of other social goals will necessarily be confronted (such as "equality"), and that confrontation should help to clarify which of these goals are important and to what degree. The end result of such a labor will not be the discovery of a standard for economic justice that will command universal assent. But it should remove many of the confusions that currently surround the acrimonious exchanges between left and right within America as to what a standard of economic justice ought to be. More importantly, it should also make clear (or at least more clear) what the key points of disagreement really are. This exploration of philosophical issues is therefore the main assignment of chapters 6 and 7.

Before it is attempted, some further effort is required to clarify confusions of the left that are similar in kind to those of the right discussed above. Two of these are of particular interest for this study. One involves a question of fact: whether marginal productivity theory is an apt description of how the American economy actually functions. The position of most liberal economists to be examined below is similar to that of conservative economists explored above, namely, a mixture of acceptance and qualifications that undermine acceptance, with no systematic attempt to resolve that evident tension. The other main confusion involves questions of value. Intellectual leaders of the left, like a number of their counterparts on the right, often search for a universal decision rule to resolve particular problems of economic justice. For the left, a key problem is income redistribution, and the rule they seek specifies the optimal manner in which income should be redistributed, irrespective of the context in which redistribution issues arise. These are accordingly the main concerns of chapter 5.

5

Redistribution Defended: Confusions of the Left

The Road Behind

To this point much of the inquiry has been directed to determining answers to three related questions.

1　How is income actually distributed in America?
2　How should it be distributed?
3　If the actual distribution diverges from the ideal, what might be done to lessen or remove the gap between the two?

Within America of the nineteenth century, a small set of premises, variously qualified, came to exert a controlling influence on answers claiming widespread popularity. Whether baldly stated or carefully hedged with qualifications, these premises – that the race was admirable and reasonably fair, and that the system of rewards tended to reflect the exercise of meritorious virtues – collectively created a strong presumption in favor of acceptance of the market system as the means of determining production and distribution within society. This is not to deny the pervasiveness of claims concerning monopolistic practices and exploited workers, particularly as industrialization took hold, work became more mechanized, and the size of business firms increased. But if those firms were thought to be behaving like monopolists, the solution commonly advocated was to halt the monopolistic practices by fostering competition or by government regulation. The key role most citizens therefore assigned to government was to spot the cheaters – those who sought to handicap their competition or to gain an unfair advantage for themselves – and restore greater equality among competitors in a race viewed as being both intrinsically admirable and intrinsically fair. At no time were large segments of the population willing to question the merits of the market system itself (as opposed to tinkering with the system's flaws to make it function better). The limited success of socialism and communism in America, even under the worst of industrial crises, is perhaps the most compelling proof of that.

Toward the close of the nineteenth century, a new economic theory was expounded that, from that time to the present, has been the predominant explanation among American economists as to what determines income distribution within a market system. The new theory seemed to reinforce the old idea that market payments were reasonably fair or just, in part by linking factor payments to the value of what that factor actually created (the factor's marginal product), and in part by demonstrating that this creation and those payments were a function of such admirable traits as industriousness, intelligence, and skill. This fusion of old and new, in turn, suggested that factors of production *ought* to receive the value of their marginal product – a normative claim we have labeled "marginal productivity justice."

These factual claims and normative implications of marginal productivity theory have, from their inception to the present, largely been ignored by the general public. They have, however, been at the center of controversies about economic justice among intellectuals on the left and right, particularly in the modern era. Two kinds of potentially devastating attacks were developed against this dual claim about what income distribution was and what it ought to be. The first attack challenged the validity of marginal productivity theory as an explanation of the forces determining factor payments within the American economy. The focus of the attack was the evident gap – of chasm-like proportions some asserted – between the key assumptions of the theory and the factual evidence concerning how American business firms and labor markets actually functioned. The second attack was largely independent of the first and sought to challenge the normative claim that factors of production *ought* to receive the value of their marginal product. Its primary targets were two assertions with a long history of widespread acceptance in America, namely, that the economic race is fair (or "reasonably" so) and that rewards tend to reflect the willful exercise of meritorious attributes exercised by a causal agent. In the terminology of economic theory, the causal agents are the factors of production. But the income payments they receive, runs the argument, cannot be viewed as a reward for personal merit (or even primarily personal merit) if such accidental circumstances as heredity, environment, and supply and demand also play a significant role in determining how much those factors will be paid.

Defenders of the income distribution generated by the market acknowledged that both luck and merit played a role in determining prizes won, and accordingly felt compelled to abandon any reference to the linkage of reward to merit in their defense of market payments. Rebuttals of this particular attack have therefore emphasized the sanctity of property rights and the role that the market plays in buttressing individual freedom. The more inviolable are those property rights – or the more individual freedom is made to dominate society's goals – the weaker is the case for meddling with the market, including meddling with the factor payments generated by that market (which, as income received and now owned, take on the sanctity of property rights).

At least three major issues have yet to be resolved. One is whether *any* philosophical framework comprised of universal propositions can identify, for every situation, those choices that necessarily lead to an income distribution that is "right" or "fair" or "just." The framework of Rothbard, although clearly specified, had limited appeal, and the arguments of Friedman are largely unsupported by a well-articulated philosophical foundation. A second puzzle was raised by Friedman but left unresolved. If freedom is a goal – or a "major" goal or (stronger yet) the "ultimate" goal – how should that concept be defined? Definitions of freedom vary widely, as do the policy implications of trying to achieve what is implied by different definitions. Finally – and almost forgotten in the twists and turns of philosophical inquiry – one crucial question of economic fact is still waiting for an answer: What actually determines (as opposed to what ought to determine) income distribution in America today? The answer popular with American economists – that factors of production tend to be paid the value of their marginal product – has also been an answer under fire as grievously defective. The question still unresolved is whether its defenders can success-fully repel the accusations, or if not, whether the attackers, after demolishing one explanation of what determines income payments, can supply another.

The Left and the Merits of Marginal Productivity Theory

As noted in the previous chapter, one question of fact that conservative economists tend to avoid is whether factors of production in the American economy actually are paid (or tend to be paid) the value of their marginal product. Many economists of the left suggest that factors do tend to receive such payments, and make that point with the same mixture of assertiveness and uncertainty that typifies the writings of economists of the right. The early chapters of their textbooks outline marginal productivity theory as if it were an apt description of how the economy functions. Later pages (often in the same chapter explaining the theory) then note the standard qualifications of how the assumptions of the theory diverge widely from the facts: markets are often imperfect; producers tend not to maximize profits (or only profits); collective bargaining introduces uncertainty into wage determination; few if any employers either know or want to estimate what the value of a factor's marginal product is – all these are typical of concessions that make the reader wonder just how valid marginal productivity theory is. Having raised that question, however, these liberal economists seem no more inclined to address it systematically than are economists of the right.[1]

A second approach of liberal economists, and one particularly popular with those well known for their writings about income distribution and economic justice, is to emphasize the frailities of marginal productivity theory from the outset. Their catalog of defects, often detailed with an air of indignation, bears a marked resemblance to that list of flaws conceded without fanfare in the textbooks of the advocates of marginal productivity theory.[2] The problem that these critics raise and fail to solve is how the income distribution of a market system should be explained if *not* by this particular economic theory. Having delivered blows aimed at demolishing marginal productivity analysis, these same liberal economists proceed to resurrect a similar intellectual structure, not boldly, but with subtlety, hedged about with qualifications and bolted down with footnotes. More simply put (and in its most blatant form), these attacks on marginal productivity theory seem to be accompanied by a persistent allegiance to what the attacker would destroy.[3] Why this curious behavior? Why, to change the imagery, should liberal economists chop so vigorously at the very theoretical limb on which they themselves seem prone to sit? To seek an answer would lead the discussion into murky regions that need not concern us here: the sources and nature of the criteria that most American economists insist a theory must fulfill; why neoclassical theory is judged to meet such criteria so well and alternatives to meet them so badly; and how acceptance of marginal productivity theory is inextricably intertwined with allegiance to the neoclassical paradigm of how a market works. Commenting on the last point, Edward Nell (a severe critic) noted in a survey of income distribution theory: "To reject neoclassical distribution theory [that is, marginal productivity theory] would entail reconstructing large parts of the theory of the firm, and of long-run supply generally. It would signal the break-up of the neoclassical paradigm."[4] For the vast majority of American economists, both liberal and conservative, such a break-up is unthinkable. Neither side is therefore willing to abandon what each is willing to concede is a most imperfect theory of how American factor markets actually work. As to how imperfect that theory is, both camps at their best think not so much about that question as in the vicinity of that question.

The Left on the Merits of Redistribution

The same difficulty of formulating precise alternatives for what they criticize seems to be typical of liberal economists' approach to what income distribution *ought* to be (as opposed to what determines actual distribution).[5] As was true of our review of confusions of the right, a similar review of confusions of the left raises the difficult question of who to include and who to ignore. The decision rule here is the same as that used in the previous chapter. Those investigated represent the main approaches by the more notable writers to a single problem; in this case, the problem of defending income redistribution and specifying how that goal should be pursued. Here, as in the previous chapter, those ignored generally take positions not significantly different from those investigated, or alternatively, take positions that are different but their views remain too ill-defined to provide fertile ground for gaining insights into how to reason, and how not to reason, about topics relating to economic justice.

Irving Kristol tells the story of how, as editor of *The Public Interest*, he invited a number of liberal writers well known for criticizing American income as "too unequal" to specify what, in their view, was a fair income distribution.[6] That invitation did not elicit a single reply. The puzzle is why.

Liberal economists (including presumably those contacted by Kristol) deny that freedom is the *only* ultimate goal. Another crucial priority for them – for many, the most important priority – is equality. Applied to economic matters, this concern for equality leads inevitably to a questioning of the existing inequalities in American income distribution. Liberals thus tend to be committed to making incomes more equal (if not completely equal), and insist upon a justification for existing inequalities. Mindful of the role chance plays in determining market payments, they are not inclined to endorse the notion that marginal productivity payments are fair or just. Arthur Okun, one of the most thoughtful of these writers, unequivocally declares that, for him,

> . . . incomes that match productivity have no ethical appeal. Equality in the distribution of incomes (allowing for voluntary leisure as a form of income) as well as in the distribution of rights would be my *ethical* preference. Abstracting from the costs and the consequences, I would prefer more equality of income to less and would like complete equality best of all. This preference is a simple extension of the humanistic basis for equal rights. To extend the domain of rights and give every citizen an equal share of the national income would give added recognition to the moral worth of every citizen, to the mutual respect of citizens for one another, and to the equivalent value of membership in the society for all.[7]

But what are "the costs and consequences" that make Okun (and most other liberal economists) reject the liberal preference for a markedly more equal income distribution? One cost noticeably absent from their concerns – or at least from their primary concerns – is the threatened loss of freedom. Okun reduces this concern to one of unimportance by turning Murray Rothbard's priorities upside down. Property rights are downgraded, and this downgrading is then used to dismiss freedom as a priority of great concern in discussions of how to make the economy more just.

To begin where Okun and other liberals begin, income inequalities generated by the market system are regarded as being primarily (or exclusively) the product of luck, and accordingly existing income inequalities are viewed as being "unlovely" (the muted adjective) or "outrageously unjust" (the outright condemnation). To make the economy more just therefore requires making incomes more equal. The question is how. The two most obvious solutions are (a) to keep the market system while redistributing income through taxes and transfers, or alternatively (b) to scrap the market system in favor of some variant of socialism. In his discussion of these two options Okun dismisses any threatened loss of freedom in four quick steps.[8]

1 For either option (income redistribution or socialism) the only freedom loss of consequence Okun acknowledges is that associated with the loss of private property.
2 Any creation of private property, he notes, involves both gains and losses of freedom: "The plus is the enhanced scope of the owner through exclusive powers over the asset: the minus is the restriction the keep-off sign imposes on nonowners."[9]
3 Accordingly, any loss of property would similarly involve both losses and gains in freedom.
4 The losses in freedom that would accompany a shift from capitalism to socialism Okun does not find worrisome because "Any realistic version of

American socialism that I can visualize would not encroach dangerously on the rights that are precious to me."[10]

The implication is that all those with preferences similar to Okun should be similarly unconcerned about any threatened loss of freedom. The implicit inference seems to be that many should share those preferences.

If the reasoning is accepted and the preferences are shared, one problem has been solved, and accordingly a second problem can now take center stage. If pursuit of greater income equality through the policies noted does not imperil freedom in important ways, the threatened tension between gaining more equality at the cost of less freedom becomes trivial. Okun's book, subtitled *The Big Tradeoff*, is thus not about the tradeoff between freedom and equality. It is instead, as its title proclaims, about *Equality and Efficiency* – or more carefully, about equality *versus* efficiency, and how to strike an appropriate balance between two goals that often conflict. Notice that the end result will be one more example of the philosopher's method applied to resolving problems of economic justice. The set of values is reduced to two (equality and efficiency), the possibility of conflict between those two is acknowledged, and the challenge is accordingly viewed as being one of specifying general rules for making tradeoff decisions in any concrete situation where the two conflict.

Of the two main options noted (income redistribution with a market system or replacing a market system with socialism), liberal economists of a moderate stripe tend to favor the first and reject the second,[11] with that rejection usually based primarily upon the expectation that losses in efficiency would outweigh gains in equality. The main preoccupation of these writers accordingly becomes one of specifiying that income redistribution within a market system for which the expected costs associated with lost efficiency do not exceed the expected gains from increased equality.

The mechanisms that make the tradeoff between these two goals inescapable (or inescapable as income redistribution proceeds beyond some point) are easily grasped without recourse to rigorous economic theorizing: to tax income as a prelude to transferring funds from rich to poor reduces the rewards for economic activity; any reduction in rewards tends to impair incentives; as economic incentives become impaired, economic effort will decline; as effort declines, so will output, and accordingly so will the amount of GNP available for distribution.[12] The mechanisms and conclusion of this line of reasoning are generally accepted by American economists, both left and right.[13] The standard way to make the point is with the imagery of a pie: the more the government intervenes to make the (after-tax) slices more equal, the more likely is the overall size of the pie to shrink.

Economists of the left and right also agree that shrinkage is an undesirable result, or to put the matter as a positive priority, both sides agree that economic efficiency and economic growth are highly desirable. The distinction between the latter two might be expressed as follows: economic efficiency consists in getting the largest possible pie for a given supply of resources and a given technology; economic growth consists in expanding the size of the feasible pie, partly by expanding supplies of inputs such as capital and partly by improving technology.[14] Although both left and right approve of efficiency and growth, their reasons for approval tend to differ. Concerning available supplies of economic goods and services, each side affirms that "more" is preferable to "less" because an expanding GNP tends to enhance economic welfare, and improvements in economic welfare are "associated with" (but not tightly correlated with nor identical to) improvements in general welfare.[15] Here, however, the similarity in their reasoning ends.

Not surprisingly, conservative economists tend to defend both priorities (efficiency and growth) because of perceived linkages to freedom in general and economic freedom in particular. To impair efficiency by impairing economic rewards is to undercut a payments scheme (paying factors the value of their marginal product) that is an integral part of the market system, and that system, in turn, is highly valued both for the economic freedom it makes possible and the political and social freedom it promotes (see pp. 82–5). Economic growth (expanding the size of the feasible pie) increases the size of the property-owning middle class and thus the prospects that individual rights will be respected.[16] As for maintaining the nation's freedom in the rough-and-tumble of international competition, the better the nation's record of economic growth, the more likely it is to have the resources and the strength to survive and flourish.[17] Finally, these writers of the right point out, sometimes as an aside and sometimes as a major point, economic growth has been a most effective way of raising the income levels of the poor.[18]

Liberal economists also acknowledge the beneficial impact of economic growth upon poverty, often choosing, like conservatives, to make that point by citing the metaphor made famous by John F. Kennedy: a rising tide lifts all boats. But for liberals the point is linked to larger concerns about equality. Economic growth, they emphasize, is desirable in part because an expanding GNP improves the political feasibility of introducing welfare schemes that redistribute income. The supporting imagery tends to shift from rising tides to growing pies. The theorizing about behavior reduces to the observation that less resistance is encountered if what is redistributed is part of the increment of a growing pie rather than part of a (previously received) slice from a fixed pie. A member of President Kennedy's Council of Economic Advisors argued the same point by using yet another metaphor: "the great and good society . . . takes root far more readily in the garden of growth than in the desert of stagnation. . . . Prosperity extends economic freedom more deeply, creating jobs and enabling a President to battle the tyranny of poverty for some without wrenching resources away from others."[19]

The tradeoff emphasized by liberals is therefore *not* between equality and freedom (as conservatives would have it) but between equality and efficiency (or more correctly, efficiency plus economic growth). The obvious problem is to specify at what point the gains of one are outweighed by the losses of the other. Possible solutions would seem logically to divide into three different categories.

The first consists essentially of ignoring the tradeoff and pursuing the goal of equality by whatever means are judged to be consistent with that goal. Such is the approach of philosopher John Rawls. On matters of distributive justice, he argues:

All social primary goods – liberty and opportunity, *income and wealth*, and the bases of self-respect – are to be distributed equally unless an unequal distribution of any or all of these goods is to the advantage of the least favored.[20]

"The least favored," in the context of income distribution, are obviously the poor. The implication of Rawls's position is that *any* redistribution of income is to be desired as long as that redistribution makes the lowest income group better off.[21]

Most liberal economists would consider such a tradeoff unacceptable. One notable exception endorsing Rawls's position is the first draft of the Catholic bishops' Pastoral Letter on the US economy. Although not stated in identical terms, the bishops seemed to accept the Rawlsian view of what should determine acceptance or rejection of policies designed to redistribute income.[22] The second draft of this Pastoral Letter, appearing a year after the first, took a markedly different position, with all the key wording of the first draft softened or removed. The presumption in the revised edition is no longer against income inequality per se, but only against "extreme inequality." The needs of the poor are "of the highest priority," but are no longer the only priority, and (unlike the first draft) no reference is made to Rawls's work or his criterion for distributive justice, even in the footnotes.[23]

Liberal economists have also tended to reject the Rawlsian position on income distribution. Many would accept *some* loss in GNP if the effect were to make the poorest members of society better off. But none (or none with any significant national reputation) would accept that *any* loss in total output is justified, provided the position of the poor is improved by *any* small amount. Liberal economists are almost uniformly sympathetic to the notion that society should guarantee some economic minimum – an income "floor" beneath which no member of society should be allowed to fall. But while they favor a minimum, they resist the Rawlsian notion that the best society is one that tries to *maximize* the minimum. Their reasons include all those previously noted that make liberal economists favor efficiency and economic growth. Many also make the further point that American preferences are evidently not in tune with the choices Rawls would make. If asked to choose (with no advanced knowledge as to their likely position on the income scale) between one of two societies – one in which income averaged $20,000 and the poorest were guaranteed $15,000, and one in which the average income was twice as great but the poorest received only $14,000 – the expectation of most economists is that the vast majority of Americans would reject the first (the Rawlsian choice) and choose the second.[24]

A second approach to trading off equality and efficiency is to argue that existing income inequality should be reduced *until* losses begin to be encountered in efficiency. The implicit assumption is that the present level of unequal rewards in the marketplace is more pronounced than necessary to evoke the same energy, thrift, and creativity from all participants. Following this line of reasoning, John Kenneth Galbraith claims that the salaries of executives tend to exceed by a wide margin the monetary reward needed to elicit their talents, and accordingly he argues these salaries should be reduced.[25] Lester Thurow pursues similar thoughts to a more general policy conclusion. The market for fully employed white males, Thurow argues, is not distorted (or unduly distorted) by problems of discrimination, lack of skills, or unemployment.[26] Further, the earnings distribution generated in this market is relatively unaffected by inherited wealth.[27] And most important from the standpoint of preserving efficiency, this existing distribution evokes (from fully employed white males) the effort presently observed and, for that reason, can be presumed to have sufficient dispersion of reward to evoke from others similar effort for similar work.[28] With no loss in efficiency, Thurow therefore argues, society could seek to achieve as its "general equity goal . . . a distribution of earnings for everyone that is no more unequal than that which *now* exists for fully employed white males."[29] Extended to the whole population, that distribution, he calculates, would reduce the present dispersion of incomes in America by 40 percent.[30] The key empirical assertion is that a redistribution of this magnitude would not affect incentives. But even if it did, the Thurow approach is easily modified to allow for such contingencies. The policy rule remains the same: redistribute income to achieve more equality until incentives begin to be impaired, and then stop. The insight – and the associated policy recommendation – is at least as old as John Stuart Mill, who argued:

Experience has shown that a large proportion of the results of labour and abstinence [saving] may be taken away by fixed taxation, without impairing . . . the qualities from which a great production and an abundant capital take their rise.[31]

To review: for liberal economists, equality in some general sense tends to be an important priority – for some, the most important priority of all. This concern applied to economic matters tends to make them favor less income inequality (although not necessarily total income equality). In pursuing that priority of less inequality they quickly confront a tradeoff with efficiency. Of the three logical alternatives for grappling with this tradeoff, the first – to ignore efficiency and concentrate only on helping the poor – has little popular appeal. The second alternative, more palatable to many, is to reduce observed inequalities in income until efficiency costs begin to be encountered. The third approach pursues the tradeoff that the second carefully avoids. *Some* loss in efficiency is to be tolerated, the argument runs, provided that the resulting gains in terms of improved income equality offset these costs. When stated in this way, the obvious problem is one of estimating gains and losses so the two can be compared.

Many left-wing writers respond to this comparison requirement with a noticeable absence of precision. Their arguments reduce to little more than advocating "somewhat less" for the rich and "somewhat more" for the poor.[32] Nor do their supporting arguments usually include any speculation about how much efficiency loss would be acceptable in pursuit of greater income equality, and how much loss would be too much.

Arthur Okun's work is an outstanding exception to this general lack of clarity. In a book that conservative Irving Kristol acclaimed as "the best there is" and as a "thoughtful, candid, and lucid statement of the moderate egalitarian position,"[33] Okun explores the equality–efficiency tradeoff by using the analogy of a leaky bucket to explain the problem of output losses that may accompany income transfers.[34] Consider the problem of shifting money from rich to poor, he asks us to imagine, by carrying money in a leaky bucket. The greater is the leak, the less money reaches the poor (that is, the greater the loss in efficiency). If all the money taken from the rich (by taxes) can be given to the poor (say, through welfare payments), efficiency is unimpaired. If 10 percent of the money leaks out, then for every $1,000 taken from the rich, the poor will receive only $900 (and, by implication, GNP will be reduced by $100). The advantage of Okun's example is that it enables the crucial question to be framed with some precision: How much leakage should be tolerated in pursuit of greater income equality (or less inequality) before the transfering process should stop? The philosopher John Rawls seems to favor any transfer with any amount of leakage, provided that some quantity remains (however small) to reach the least advantaged members of society. Lester Thurow prefers a watertight container, and resists income transfers that would involve any noticeable leakage. Arthur Okun tries to specify a more desirable point between these two extremes. But what point? Okun's training as an economist suggests an obvious framework for pursuing the answer. The problem is accordingly cast in terms of finding that point where the extra losses in efficiency would just equal the extra gains in terms of greater income equality. Until that point is reached, income should be transferred from rich to poor; when that point is reached, the transferring should stop. The difficulty – as obvious as it is insoluble – is that the quantities for calculating gains and losses cannot be computed and compared. Losses in efficiency might be calculated in dollar terms as GNP forgone, but the gains from the resulting improvement in equality (or reduction in income inequality) resist any effort to be quantified (never mind quantified and then converted into some dollar equivalent for the purposes of comparison with efficiency losses). What therefore began as a seemingly rigorous exercise collapses into a subjective judgment: in Okun's case, the judgment that he would tolerate a leakage of 60 percent, but no more, provided the income was being taken from the very rich and given to the very poor.[35] (If the income transfers were to be made from the less wealthy to the less poor, he would prefer a significantly smaller leakage.)[36]

This tradeoff puzzle arose because greater income equality (or less income inequality) was judged to be a positive good by liberal economists. Other left-wing writers sometimes focus less on efficiency and more on the fulfilling of other criteria as they try to specify what income distribution (or income redistribution) ought to be, but their specifications (like Okun's) are fraught with imprecision. A few examples:

1 Income should be distributed according to conscientious effort.[37]
2 "What [a man] has a right to demand, and what it concerns his fellow-men to see that he gets, is enough to enable him to perform his work."[38]
3 Each individual has a right "to an adequate supply of good things" which implies "equal access to what is needed for the purposes of life. . . . Fair or equitable distribution as a complete operation requires the agency of public authority, first in reaching agreement as to the kinds of things that are essential to living well and second in determining the precise allotments to be made to families or to individuals."[39]

Imprecision would thus seem endemic to liberal efforts to specify what a more desirable income distribution ought to be. But that imprecision, as we shall see, is only a small part of a larger complex of problems.

The Road Ahead

All of the previous discussion points in a similar direction. Two kinds of issues have been raised and not yet seriously considered. One concerns the philosophical foundations of liberals and conservatives. What underlying premises can prompt these two groups from the same culture to arrive at such differing views about the importance of such fundamental American values as freedom and equality? The answer apparently must be pursued by an examination of both terms: their various definitions, which meanings are preferred by whom, and why. These are therefore the topics of chapters 6 and 7. The second avenue of inquiry still awaiting exploration concerns not questions of philosophy and related issues of values, but questions of fact: the evidence from history and from our knowledge of human behavior that can be brought to bear to bolster conservative and liberal opinions about what income distribution policies ought to be. Or phrased as a question, what evidence can each side offer to justify their claims about the likely consequences of pursuing different income distribution policies? Later chapters will accordingly investigate their answers with the hope of establishing, not the facts of the case, but rather what we do and do not know about key factual assertions in dispute.

   Nowhere on the path ahead will any consideration be given to one factual question previously raised: What economic mechanisms produce the American income distribution actually observed? That puzzle is abandoned here because much of what economists can offer for its resolution has already been considered. Their dominant explanation – marginal productivity theory – would seem to enjoy a curious popularity despite its evident state of intellectual disrepair: roundly criticized for assumptions judged by many to be wildly at variance with actual conditions in American factor markets, and yet widely accepted by the American economics community (and usually even by its critics) as an explanation of what determines factor payments in any market economy, including the American economy. With cessation of this particular inquiry, however, we must admit to having found no convincing answer to the first question posed at the outset of this chapter: what determines income distribution in the world that is (as opposed to what income distribution should approximate in the world that ought to be)?

Finally, a path to be avoided (as opposed to examined and then abandoned for want of promising leads) is the well-traveled road of *ad hominem* attacks. Both left and right at their worst are equally adept at disparaging the motives of the other side: the left, by such accounts, concerned with reallocating power to the government to foist their own elitist notions on the public or satisfy their lust for power or line their own pockets and those of their supporters;[40] the right, viewed from the same low ground, concerned with rationalizing their own privileged position in society, indifferent to the lot of those less fortunate than themselves and viewing government as something to be minimized unless manipulated for their own selfish ends.[41] The worth of an idea, Oscar Wilde maintained, has nothing to do with the worth of the person expounding it. Wilde had perhaps a vested interest in making that point, but the point surely is well taken. Among both liberals and conservatives can be found intelligent and thoughtful proponents deeply concerned with the fate of American society. In the discussion that lies ahead, attention will therefore be given only to the best arguments that each side can muster to support its views on what constitutes an appropriate or just income distribution. To investigate the further question about what motivated a particular remark would necessarily involve speculation that is little more than that – speculation – and of no particular relevance for this discussion.

6

On Freedom

Ideological Foundations

What is that bedrock ideal – or one bedrock ideal – exerting a controlling influence on almost all American discussions of social justice? The answer is neither surprising nor profound, although the readiness with which it comes to mind is merely a commentary on how a creed completely alien to other cultures has come to dominate our own. Generations of Americans have made the point in speeches and sermons, poetry and prose, but perhaps the testimony of David Lilienthal will serve for all:

> I believe in – and I conceive the Constitution of the United States to rest, as does religion, upon – the fundamental proposition of the integrity of the individual; and that all Government and all private institutions must be designed to promote and protect and defend the integrity and the dignity of the individual; that that is the essential meaning of the Constitution and the Bill of Rights, as it is essentially the meaning of religion.[1]

The integrity and dignity of the individual: this is a common article of faith shared by Americans from colonial times to the present, a strand that runs powerfully – one might even say, majestically – through all the cultural norms and institutions of the nation. (That strand, of course, is not without its frayed and wizened parts, as the treatment of women and minorities has demonstrated in the past.)

Whether such a belief is typical of all religions, as Lilienthal claims, might be debated. But certainly that belief is consistent with, and derives support from, the two major religions of America: Christianity and Judaism. Both are intensely individualistic theologies. Both regard each person as precious because each is believed to be created in the image of God and capable of salvation. A secular tradition with a distinguished history also points to similar conclusions about the sanctity of the individual. At the heart of this latter argument is the belief that each person is deserving of respect as a rational moral agent. The ethical implications are well summarized by Kant's famous injunction: "treat each man as an end in himself, and never as a means only."

If the integrity and dignity of the individual is a controlling article of faith, logic suggests that the development of each individual's capabilities is necessarily one of the primary objectives of society. More cautiously, society should be so structured as to foster the maximum possible self-development or "self-actualization" for the individual members who comprise it. But how?

Part of the answer is obvious, and part is not. Indeed, the investigation of the less obvious part will lead the discussion into some of the most contentious issues dividing liberals and conservatives on matters of economic justice. But first, to the obvious.

Freedom From

From Individualism to Freedom from Coercion

The key to self-development or self-actualization is clear enough: the individual must be free to exercise his or her choice across a range of alternatives. The best society – or at least the better society – is therefore one that makes available more options while leaving the individual free to choose among them. But what does "being free" mean in this context? As harmless as that question may appear, it promises complex puzzles for the rest of this chapter and the remainder of the book. But at least part of the answer, as already indicated, is neither complex nor puzzling. If one is to be free to choose, one cannot be the slave of another, so institutions such as slavery are necessarily ruled out. (In the American case, that ruling was rather long in coming.) More generally, whatever the notion of freedom should include, it must surely include the absence of physical violence and the threat of physical violence. "Life, liberty, and the pursuit of happiness" becomes an empty promise without the expectation of being free is this restricted sense. Thus "being free" must obviously include the absence of coercion. But what should and should not be counted as coercion?

Puzzles in Defining Coercion

Unnoticed, the discussion has progressed a long way along a single path. Defining "freedom" is a notoriously complicated task because the word has been used to convey so many different ideas. (Isaiah Berlin claims to have counted more than 200).[2] Subsequent discussion will consider only two – although two with a formidable history and (as we shall see) capable of many interpretations: "freedom from" and "freedom to."[3] This narrowness of focus is defensible only because these two usages have dominated – and still dominate – American discussions of economic justice.[4] Questions of defining "freedom *to*" will be taken up later in this chapter. The issue here is how to define "freedom *from*" – or, as that idea has already been expanded to read, "freedom from coercion." But what, to repeat, should be counted as coercion?

The phrase "absence of coercion" suggests a human agent as the source of prospective constraints. Thus

a man is said to be free to the extent that he can choose his own goals or course of conduct, can choose between alternatives available to him, and is not compelled to act as he would not himself choose to act, or prevented from acting as he would otherwise choose to act, by the will of another man, of the state, or of any other authority.[5]

Nonhuman agencies also limit human actions but, when they do, we would not characterize being subject to that limitation as being coerced. Gravity restricts my ability to make a leap of 30 feet, but I would hardly describe that restriction as being "coerced" by gravity. People coerce people; gravity does not.

A number of definitional difficulties are lurking in the wings, but all will be temporarily ignored for the sake of clarifying the inferences that follow from a simple definition of coercion. That definition states that a man is "free" as long as he acts of his own volition and is not coerced in what he does by others, "coercion" here referring to his being deliberately forced or restrained by another person.[6] The inferences that follow from this definition of freedom concern the appropriate role in society of (a) the government, (b) private property, and (c) the free market. All three kinds of inference are characteristic of conservative reasoning within America. But lest the point be lost, what makes these inferences possible is a definition of freedom which, as we shall see later on, is limited in a very special way.

Implied Role of Government

If society is to be the arena in which the individual pursues self-realization, several problems must be solved. The efforts of person A to achieve self-realization may clash with those of B, and when they do, an orderly system is needed to resolve disputes. Moreover – although perhaps not appropriately viewed as part of the human search for self-fulfillment – the nastier propensities of man to injure man must clearly be held in check if society is not to degenerate into anarchy. The Ten Commandments' singling out of killing and stealing for special mention is merely one indication of dangerous proclivities with a long history. That history and those proclivities were much on the minds of the Founding Fathers as they tried to frame a nation. "Why has government been instituted at all?" asked Alexander Hamilton, and then provided his own answer: "Because the passions of men will not conform to the dictates of reason and justice without constraint."[7] Jefferson agreed. "To close the circle of felicities," he wrote in wording quaint to modern ears, Americans required "a wise and frugal government, which shall restrain men from injuring one another . . . ."[8] Therefore to preserve order at home (and to fend off foreign powers with aggressive tendencies) a government had to be established that would institute a rule of law, ideally – at least in the American tradition – including equality before the law. The resulting rules were nothing less than an indispensable fabric of society: rules of behavior that were known, enforced by the state, and applied in a manner judged to be just (or reasonably so) by most of its citizens.

By such means one problem can be solved (restraining dangerous human tendencies), but only by creating a second. The establishment of a government and the rule of law enables the citizens of the resulting state to be more free in the sense of not being subject to "the inconstant, uncertain, unknown, Arbitrary Will of another man" as Locke chose to put it.[9] But who – or what – will assure that these same citizens will not be subject to the arbitrary will of those controlling the government? These state officials are also subject to the same pernicious human tendencies that necessitated establishing a government and the rule of law in the first place. Worse, with government comes a concentration of power, and thus the possibility for using that power in undesirable ways, including those that would impair the freedom of citizens bent upon pursuing their own self-realization.[9]

The fear of power, particularly power in the hands of government officials, is an oft-repeated theme in American history. It was also a central concern – perhaps *the* central concern – underlying the upheavals that culminated in the founding of the republic.[10] Human frailties being what they are, the architects of the 1787 Constitution argued, those with power will seek to advance their own interests, and those with too much power will almost surely try to dominate, to oppress, to exploit. But if any concentration of power was sure to be a problem, its diffusion was the obvious solution – a diffusion carefully crafted in a system of checks and balances. "Power must be opposed to power," John Adams urged, "force to force, strength to strength, interest to interest . . . ."[11] And so it was, and so it still is today. The executive and the different branches of the legislature, for example, can check each other by the mutual privilege of rejecting what the other has originated. An independent judiciary, precisely because it is independent, can restrain the actions of the executive and the legislative branches. The primary role of the courts in this connection is that of policeman, ruling (upon request) when power encroachments appear to violate the law, particularly that most fundamental of laws, the Constitution.

This summary of the origin and purpose of checks and balances merely repeats what most American students learn in a high school civics course. The rationale for such mechanisms is as old as the nation and as revered as the flag. To the question of how to control potential abuses of power by government officials, however, conservative Americans bring further thoughts that by no means share a similar popularity.[12]

Their main thought can be simply put. If the establishment of government is unavoidable but the resulting concentration of power is always dangerous, the best defense against such dangers would seem to be to minimize the role that any government can play in society. This "night-watchman state," as it is sometimes called, has, as that name implies, a policeman function but little else. Adam Smith was among the first to advocate such ideas, but he understood that there was more to running a state than patrolling a store. The desirable functions of any government he specified as follows:

> . . . the sovereign has only three duties to attend to . . . first, the duty of protecting the society from the violence and invasion of other independent societies; secondly, the duty of protecting, as far as possible, every member of the society from the injustice or oppression of every other member of it, or the duty of establishing an exact administration of justice; and, thirdly, the duty of erecting and maintaining certain public works and certain public institutions, which it can never be for the interest of

any individual, or small number of individuals, to erect and maintain; because the profit could never repay the expense to any individual or small number of individuals, though it may frequently do much more than repay it to a great society.[13]

Although Smith's ideas were framed two centuries ago in a society that had barely begun to industrialize, his list of appropriate government functions is still widely endorsed by present-day conservatives. Milton Friedman declares that the list "is not easy to improve on."[14] The election rhetoric of Ronald Reagan reveals a similar preference: "I've always thought that the best thing government can do is nothing."[15] The controlling notion, from Smith to Reagan, is that the best possible government is the one that governs least.[16] *Laissez faire* – literally "let [people] do [as they please]" – is a reaffirmation of an ideal more than a characterization of any period in America's past; an ideal that would minimize the role of government and maximize the freedom of the individual. But if individuals are to make the best use of that freedom, conservatives argue, a "night-watchman state" must still be complemented by those two indispensable institutions of capitalism: private property and a free-enterprise economy.

Implied Role of Property

The arguments for private property, like those for checks and balances, are part of popular American beliefs concerning how society should be structured, and are not just the preoccupation of a conservative few. The defense of property is also constructed around the same three themes developed thus far: desire for individual freedom, fear of coercion, and the goal of self-development.

To be free, the argument runs, the individual must have the power to resist coercive acts by other individuals and by the state; private property gives such power; thus, private property is a crucial institution for the preservation of individual freedom.[17] The insight is simple and compelling, and has a long history in Britain and America. In the eighteenth century, Edmund Burke considered the instinct for private ownership of property to be "one of the securities against injustice and despotism implanted in our nature."[18] Alexander Hamilton put the case in a negative way: "a power over a man's subsistence amounts to a power over his will."[19] The inference is that to the extent a man has power over his own subsistence, he is more free, and the achievement of such power would seem to be conditional upon granting to each citizen the right to acquire, hold, and transfer property.

As simple as the point may seem, its ramifications are many and diverse. Private property, for example, enables individuals to earn their living unaided by the state. This follows in an obvious way if the flow of income from property owned provides the owner with a satisfactory living. It follows in a slightly less obvious way if private property leads to the establishment of a multiplicity of private firms that in turn give employment to many owning little, thereby enabling even those with negligible property holdings to make a living independent of the state. The widespread diffusion of property and the associated diffusion of job alternatives across a multiplicity of firms also helps the laborer to avoid threatened coercion within a given firm by moving on, while the knowledge of that potential movement serves to inhibit coercive tendencies of employers who would retain their labor force.

Private property also bolsters other freedoms, including freedom of speech. Opinions critical of the government, or those unpopular in other ways, are difficult to publicize if the state owns all the media. But if the institution of private property includes private ownership of newspapers and radio and television stations, those with contentious ideas they want to publicize can acquire their own media outlet or buy advertising space on radio or in newspapers owned by others, or lacking the resources to do either, they can still hope to gain the sponsorship of those who have resources and share their views. Consistent with this view, *Time* magazine, in a 1986 article entitled "Freedom first," noted "the chaotic abundance of free ideas" that was not unrelated to the presence of 9,144 newspapers, 11,328 periodicals, 9,824 radio stations, and 941 commercial television stations in America.[20]

The justification for private property is not confined to noting how it bolsters individual freedom and helps to fend off coercion by private citizens or public bureaucrats. Once acquired, property expands the alternatives available to the owner, and thus furthers the pursuit of self-development. Here property is synonymous with wealth, and the alternatives are all those for which the control of economic resources can make a difference. The poet can buy time to compose; the would-be lawyer can purchase a law school education; the entrepreneur can use resources that he owns to develop and exercise his creative capabilities in the marketplace. If property serves humanity in part as wealth, however, one question immediately arises: What institutions other than private property are well suited to increasing the available supply of wealth? The answer – perhaps quickest to the lips of conservatives (but by no means to theirs alone) – is "the market system," or, as many conservatives would prefer to characterize it, "the free-exchange economy."

Before turning to this topic, we should note what is special in the conservative treatment of private property. That institution, as suggested, enjoys almost universal popularity within America. What sets the conservative approach to the institution apart is primarily their treatment of property rights. Clearly, if property is to fulfill the functions noted previously, the individual's claim to what he "owns" must be a right secured by law. But what are the appropriate limitations on this right? The fewer the limitations, the closer one approximates the position of conservatives such as Murray Rothbard who argues that property rights are inviolable.[21] Rothbard's reasons for so arguing have been discussed in chapter 4 and need not be repeated here. What should be noted, however, and will be considered in more detail below, is how this claim – the inviolable nature of property rights – meshes neatly with the desire for the minimal state. The more inviolable are property rights, the less the state is entitled to take from Peter to fund its welfare programs designed to aid Paul. At the extreme, as the word "inviolable" implies, the state would have no right to effect any property transfers in pursuit of welfare goals. And that, in turn, would halt what many conservatives consider to be the paramount threat to individual freedom in the twentieth century: the rise of what they term "the welfare state."

These same themes will be encountered in the section that follows: the widespread popularity of an institution within America, with the conservative endorsement differing only in detail, but those details will be crucial to limiting the role of the government to that of a "night-watchman state."

Implied Role of the Market

"The institution of property," noted John Stuart Mill, "when limited to its essential elements, consists in the recognition, in each person, of a right to the exclusive disposal of what he or she have [sic] produced by their own exertions, or received either by gifts of fair agreement, without force or fraud, from those who produced it."[22] The words "received" and "disposal" imply that the institution of private property is normally accompanied by some arena in which property claims can be acquired and traded. The need for such an arena also becomes unavoidable if the state is not to be the means whereby all economic activity is directed and controlled. The device used in capitalistic systems to generate and direct production and distribution is the market – or more correctly, a host of interrelated markets whose existence is presumed to be captured by such phrases as "the free-exchange economy" or "the free-enterprise system" or simply "the market." As was true for private property, the justification for the market will focus upon three goals: the desire for freedom, the related desire to avoid coercion, and the goal of individual self-development.

First and foremost for conservatives, the market dramatically reduces the power of the state by removing from state control the vast bulk of economic decisions within society. Because those decisions are decentralized and in private hands, economic power is thereby diffused throughout the market system. And the more power is diffused – any power – the fewer are the chances for abuse of power through coercive acts. Further, as private fortunes accumulate, those fortunes provide independent foci of power that will act as a check upon the power of the state.[23]

The market's other principal virtue is that it provides an arena for the exercise of individual freedom. Because all exchanges in a market are voluntarily made, the presumption is that all parties to a transaction expect to gain. Otherwise, the question is always asked: Why would they voluntarily participate? The freedoms that the free-exchange economy provides include freedom for consumers to choose among competing goods and services, freedom for producers to introduce new products and new methods of production, and freedom for individuals seeking work to choose among a range of possible occupations. To the extent that participation in the economic system is part of the road to self-development, these freedoms of the marketplace enhance the possibilities for personal growth. Or in the impassioned wording of conservative Michael Novak, the market system "frees the intelligence, imagination, and enterprise of individuals to explore the possibilities in world process, which [Adam Smith] conceived of . . . as a universe of emergent probabilities."[24]

The conservative endorsement of the market does not end here. The arguments tend to repeat those made in chapter 4. In summary form, they are as follows.

1   The point made above about the market system reducing the coercive powers of the state is made again, but in somewhat stronger terms. Economic freedom, grounded in the twin institutions of private property and a free market, is now portrayed as "crucial" to political freedom,[25] or – more strongly put – as a "necessary condition" for political freedom.[26]

2   If (a) individual self-realization is the ultimate goal of society, (b) the freedom of the individual is indispensable for the pursuit of that goal, and (c) the market system is indispensable for political and economic freedom, it follows that the income distribution generated by the free market is the "right" distribution, because that distribution is an integral part of an institution (the market) that no society devoted to such goals can do without. Whether that income distribution can also be labeled as "fair" or "just" (as distinct from "right") will depend upon the extent to which the arguments of chapter 2, originating in the nineteenth century, are still found persuasive by present-day conservatives.

3   Freedom is the main benefit the market brings in its wake, but an added bonus is improved usage of economic resources. (Conservatives are quick to emphasize that this is *only* a bonus, and not indispensable to their case for arguing the merits of the market.) The compelling imagery is of a self-adjusting mechanism that efficiently processes vast amounts of information, conveys the results of that processing through the signals of changing prices, and thereby generates a kind of order that is both spontaneous and beneficial to society as a whole. In the much-quoted metaphor made popular by Adam Smith, each individual, although pursuing only his own economic self-interest, will be "led by an invisible hand to promote an end which was no part of his intention."[27] That end is the maximum "annual revenue of society" as Smith put it, or in modern terminology, the maximum national income or national output.[28] This assertion usually involves not one empirical claim but two: that the free-market system maximizes efficiency (getting the biggest pie from available resources and technology) and maximizes economic growth (getting the largest possible increase in the potential size of the pie over time). The extent to which the evidence supports each claim will be discussed in chapter 10.

The final point to be stressed here about *all* conservative claims for the market is that this institution is conceived as being part of a larger system of political economy composed primarily of a free-exchange economy, private property, and the minimal state. All three are advocated because of the role they are presumed to play in maximizing the freedom of the individual.[29] But the merits of that claim turn crucially upon how freedom is defined. Even if one follows the conservative lead and defines freedom as the absence of coercion, one might, surprisingly, still argue that the institutions favored by conservatives are the worst possible for enhancing individual freedom.

Expanded Notions of Coercion

"Marxist socialism," writes Marxist sociologist Charles Anderson, "is concerned with individual liberation and human creativity."[30] So too, one might remark with some surprise, are Milton Friedman and Friedrich Hayek. The puzzle deepens when one discovers that Marxists usually define freedom in much the same way as conservatives do. For the extreme left, as for the extreme right, the goal is individual freedom, freedom is defined as the absence of coercion, and coercion is defined (by arch-conservative Hayek, but in a manner not likely to offend most proponents of either the extreme left or the extreme right) as

such control of the environment or circumstances of a person by another that, in order to avoid greater evil, he is forced to act not according to a coherent plan of his own but to serve the ends of another.[31]

Despite this evident similarity of goals and similarity in their definitions of freedom and coercion, radical economists such as Samuel Bowles and Herbert Gintis affirm in no uncertain terms what Hayek and Friedman would surely deny, namely, that "the U.S. economy is a formally totalitarian system in which the actions of the vast majority (workers) are controlled by a small minority (owners and managers)."[32] If the disagreement between radicals and conservatives is not how coercion should be defined, it must be about how coercion works in the American economy.

Bowles and Gintis identify those who, according to their view, are doing the coercing: the owners and managers of business firms. To coerce requires power, and this group, according to the radical view, gains power by a variety of means which tend to be cumulative in effect. The "free" market favors the strong and scheming who first gain wealth, then use that wealth to control the government, and then use wealth plus government control to gain more wealth, more power, and more control. The details of this process need not concern us here. In outline form, the argument runs roughly as follows. Business units tend to combine into larger units, thereby acquiring more economic power. The wealth such power generates is used to manipulate the government into passing legislation that benefits business interests while assisting business in "the taming of labor."[33] This taming of the work force by policy measures is reinforced by economic conditions that restrict the alternatives available to workers, thereby increasing worker insecurity and thus their vulnerability to the power of employers. Further – and perhaps worst of all – the elites who control the corporate structure are also not above using racism and sexism to keep wages down and to keep the work force divided against itself.[34] Even public education is portrayed as serving the private interests of the corporate elite. "Schools attempt to meet the needs of monopoly capitalist organizations," writes Marxist Martin Carnoy, "by teaching lower-class children to be better workers and middle-class ones to be better managers in the corporate economy, and by reproducing the social relations of production in the schools to inculcate children with values and norms which reinforce the prevailing economic structures."[35] The "freedom" of the free-enterprise society, by this view, is therefore nothing more than "freedom for the strong [and] oppression for the weak."[36] Bowles and Gintis summarize the somber implications for the entire structure of society:

> Capitalist production, in our view, is not simply a technical process; it is also a social process. Workers are neither machines nor commodities but, rather, active human beings who participate in production with the aim of satisfying their personal and social needs. The central problem of the employer is to erect a set of social relationships and organizational forms, both within the enterprise and, if possible, in society at large, that will channel these aims into the production and expropriation of surplus value.[37]

Marx was more blunt. The modern state, he claimed, is "nothing more than the form of organization which the bourgeois necessarily adopt both for internal and external purposes, for the mutual guarantee of their property and interests."[38]

But surely, conservatives will object, this is a gross distortion of the facts. If the government is the tool of the business class, for example, how can one explain the passage in America of acts to protect the workers' right to unionize, to mitigate cyclical unemployment with countercyclical policies, or to alleviate poverty by such welfare programs as food stamps and Aid to Families with Dependent Children? Radical economists have a ready reply. Such legislative acts, they claim, also reflect the interests of the business elites, in this instance their interest in maintaining social peace and preventing political upheavals. Thus, by this account, the welfare measures of the so-called welfare state are designed "to ameliorate the most blatant injustices of capitalist development . . . so that corporate capitalism can continue to function with no signifcant shift in economic control and power."[39]

By this line of argument, *any* evidence that seems to contradict the radical view of government as the tool of business can be reinterpreted to be consistent with that view. All seemingly contradictory legislation is simply attributed to the elite's desire for social peace. This in turn raises a knotty philosophical problem about the worth of a hypothesis which, precisely because it is consistent with *any* evidence, cannot be falsified by contradictory evidence. Fortunately, those philosophical issues are not of great importance here. What is important, and cannot be overemphasized, is the negligible appeal that the Marxist description of society has for most Americans. The nation they believe they know and the political and economic reality they experience daily strike the vast majority as markedly different from a world in which

. . . the ruling class requires inequality in order to exercise its power and accumulate its profits. It requires mass insecurity, scarcity, and uneven privilege in order to maintain labor force control, to keep the masses sweating uncomplainingly and apathetically. Capitalism needs dirty workers, a hierarchy of education and status, a stratification system in which people know their place and the dedicated servant is elevated to the feet of the powerful.[40]

Perhaps such conditions may exist in some countries of the Old World, Americans are inclined to remark. But certainly not in this republic of the New World. The reasons for American decisiveness – for their adamant rejection of Marxian theories and Marxian descriptions as applicable to their country – are ultimately as vast and complex as American culture itself. Some of those reasons have been touched upon in the themes of chapter 2. Some will be encountered in chapters 7 and 8. Whatever the reasons, the rejection of extreme left ideology by citizens of the United States is as striking as it is pervasive. But that rejection does not assure the dominance of the right. Another and very different effort to expand the notion of freedom will ultimately prove far more troublesome for conservatives. The first effort, by the extreme left, accepted the conservative definition of freedom as the absence of coercion, and attempted to broaden the notion of coercion. As the backbone for a popular ideology, that effort fails, at least within this country. A second effort, mounted by moderates of the left, will challenge conservatives where they are most vulnerable, namely, in their attempt to limit the definition of freedom to the absence of coercion. Freedom, the argument runs, is a much broader idea than this.

Freedom To

The conservative's "first concern," writes Senator Barry Goldwater, is "*Are we maximizing freedom?*"[41] But what is it that is to be maximized? What, for example, was Franklin Roosevelt referring to in his fireside chat of 1934 when he told his listeners, "I prefer and I am sure you prefer that broader definition of liberty under which we are moving forward to greater freedom, to greater security for the average man than he has ever known before in the history of America"?[42] This "broader" definition begins where conservatives begin: whatever freedom means, it surely means the absence of coercion by other individuals. But can the word – or should the word – be used to imply more than this?

Attempts to broaden the definition of freedom from "freedom *from*" to "freedom *to*" are generally viewed as originating, at least in the English-speaking world, with a change in usage initiated by British reformers in the late nineteenth century.[43] For these people, British workers at the bottom of the economic ladder, however much unrestrained by the coercive acts of others, were still not properly described as "free." Their poverty and their lack of education appeared so extreme as to make a mockery of the idea of their being free to pursue self-development, whatever self-development might mean. Similar sentiments can be found in America in the twentieth century, for example in Franklin Roosevelt's championing the need for every citizen to achieve "freedom from want."[44] The word "from" appended after "freedom" in this instance is deceptive. What is at issue is not the absence of coercion, but the presence of a possibility. One of the more partisan explanations of what that possibility was or ought to be was given by Congressman Estes Kefauver the year following Roosevelt's death. The bill before the House was the Full Employment Act of 1945 (subsequently passed in 1946, and thus subsequently known as the Full Employment Act of 1946). What had Kefauver exasperated was the prospect that an act assuring all Americans of the right to work would not be passed.[45] "Let me ask you," he railed at his colleagues who opposed the bill:

how can the Government assure freedom without seeing to it that every individual has the opportunity to earn a living? If a man has no job, how can he enjoy freedom of political participation, freedom from fear, freedom of competition, freedom to health, education, recreation and security, freedom of social and economic democracy, freedom to make the most of himself? How can a man on the dole exercise that initiative and self-reliance which is declared to be a major objective of this committee bill? Without the right to work, a man is not free.[46]

Drained of its antagonism, this statement makes a simple point: freedom *from* want implies an income, the necessity of earning an income implies a job, and thus freedom *from* want implies freedom *to* work; that is, to seek and find gainful employment, the latter being commonly viewed in America as part of the route to self-development, both for the activity it provides and for the possibilities that are placed in reach once income has been earned.

We began our inquiry into what "freedom" means in American discussions of economic justice by defining freedom as the absence of coercion. Now to this first idea has been added a second which, in Locke's phrasing, involves "the power a man has to do or forbear doing any particular action."[47] On the face of it, this seems reasonable enough. To pursue my own self-development I must be "free" to choose among alternatives; to be free in this sense, I must not only be uncoerced by others, but have "the means or power to achieve the objectives I choose of my own volition."[48] If I am starving or illiterate, being uncoerced is hardly synonymous with being free to choose, or so the argument runs. That argument, however, is neither as simple nor as self-evident as it may first appear. I do not have "the means or power" to walk across the Atlantic, but for that reason can I be described as being "not free"? Once the notion of being free means more than being not coerced – once freedom also means having "the power or means" to achieve objectives – the obvious question is where to draw the line. Which "powers" are integral to this notion of "being free" and which are not? On the matter of crossing the Atlantic, I am evidently not free in the sense of not having the "power or means" to walk upon water, but no one would speak of that limitation as equivalent to my being "unfree."

Again, the narrow focus of this study will allow us to avoid a host of philosophical complexities.[49] Our concern is with the meaning of economic justice to Americans. The relevant issue here, then, is the appropriate meaning of freedom in the realm of economic choice or, more narrowly yet, the appropriate meaning as Americans use that word. "Freedom *to*," we have established, implies "having the power or means" to pursue particular objectives. For Americans concerned with economic choices, the crucial power is the power to compete in the economic race. The plea for freedom in its broader sense of "freedom to" thus in this context tends to narrow quickly to the plea for no competitor in the economic race to have an unfair advantage or handicap at the starting line or on the racecourse. In short, the effort to define "freedom to" in the realm of economic justice leads inevitably to the idea of equality of opportunity. But that phrase immediately raises the kind of puzzles we were attempting to resolve for the word "freedom." To review our progress with those puzzles: (a) the word "freedom" has a multiplicity of meanings; (b) our concern was how the word should be defined and used in discussions of economic justice; (c) for those discussions, the definition that comes most readily to mind – and the one preferred by conservatives – is an absence of coercion; (d) the efforts of the extreme left to expand the meaning of "freedom" by expanding the idea of coercion was found to have negligible appeal for most Americans; but (e) another effort originating on the left to expand the notion of freedom has had considerably more appeal in this country, namely, defining freedom to include "the power or means" to achieve economic objectives; and finally (f) this second type of broader definition quickly leads the discussion from issues of freedom of economic choice to issues of equality of opportunity. The suspect word now – suspect in the sense of sure to cause difficulties – is "equality." Questions similar to those raised for "freedom" must now be raised for it. In particular:

1   How should equality be defined?
2   What are the ideological foundations underlying the American usage of that word?
3   How does the general idea of equality relate to the particular usage of that word in the phrase "equality of opportunity"?

The haste to get on with the discussion of equality should not obscure our limited success to date in defining freedom. We have been grappling with that problem because earlier discussions made it clear that "freedom" is a value of the first importance to most Americans, but what it is that is so highly valued was not clear because the word itself has many possible meanings. The obvious part of any definition of freedom is easily identified. At a minimum, freedom means the absence of coercion by others. But is that all? Advocates of the extreme right would answer "yes" with alacrity and conviction. But many others would be more hesitant and less sure. What is it that has not been included – and should be included – in the American notion of what freedom means when applied to economic choices? To clarify why this is inevitably a central question for any discussion of economic justice has been one key objective of all the preceding chapters. A search for the answer will require the remainder of this book. But at least we now seem headed in the right direction.

7

On Equality

Ideological Foundations: Old Ideas in a New Perspective

"The heart of the doctrine of equality," asserts Isaiah Berlin, and the formula that has colored much of liberal and democratic thought, is "Every man to count for one and no one to count for more than one."[1] This doctrine would seem to have a profound affinity with the ideological foundations discussed at the start of the previous chapter. "Respect for the worth and dignity of the individual" seems to mesh easily with the notion that each individual should count for one, and none should count for more than one.[2] The theological and secular ideas bolstering the first, for example, can also be used to support the second. The belief in the worth of the individual, as previously noted, can be buttressed by the Judeo-Christian belief in the sacredness of each individual, or by the humanist belief that each individual is deserving of respect as a rational moral agent.[3] But either belief could also be used to support what Berlin claims lies at the heart of the doctrine of equality. Indeed, to argue the worth and dignity of the individual while denying that each should count for one and no one for more than one would strike most Americans as most peculiar.[4]

The previous chapter began with the first of these central tenets of American ideology (the dignity and worth of the individual) and then noted how this belief implied that an essential goal for any society was the self-development of the individuals who comprised it. The challenge for that chapter accordingly became to specify the freedom necessary to pursue that goal. A similar challenge must be confronted in this chapter, but amended in several important ways. As before, the main assignment will be to specify the implications of a slippery concept – in this case equality – for the pursuit of economic justice. But that pursuit must now attempt to be consistent with two central tenets of American ideology, not one. The first, involving the fundamental worth of the individual, has been explored above. The second, until now, has been totally ignored.

Ideological Foundations: New Additions

A story said to be a favorite of Ronald Reagan's concerns a bomber shot down over the English Channel during World War II. As the disabled plane plummets toward the sea, the yarn runs, the crew begins to bail out, but a young tailgunner is so badly wounded that he cannot jump. Confronted with the impossibility of one of his men abandoning the aircraft, the captain quietly announces to the wounded youth: "That's all right son. We'll just ride this one down together."[5]

The story illustrates a second powerful theme in American ideology. The first was individualism and self-realization. Crashing in a crippled bomber, however, is not a recommended route to self-development. The key word in the story is "together" – a word that, in the context of the present study, encompasses two ideas. One is community. The good society for most Americans consists of something more than a collection of individuals preoccupied with their own self-development. The second idea is charity, or generosity, or kindliness toward one's fellow human beings. The ideas of community and charity can readily be linked, but they need not be. Hitler's SS troops had a sense of community, but that community was not particularly noted for its charitable instincts, even toward fellow storm troopers. For Americans, however, the two ideas tend to mix and run together, with the good citizen presumed to have both a sense of social solidarity and a compassion toward others. The underlying concepts may ultimately be vague, but the power of their appeal is not. Mario Cuomo illustrated both the difficulty of defining the concern and the passion this strand of ideology can evoke when he exhorted graduating Harvard seniors not to retreat "from the sense of the common good, from caring about each other, from the central thread of western culture and American history – from intelligent compassion."[6] Similar sentiments and similar endorsements are to be found in the major religions of America. Community as an ideal is central to both Christianity and Judaism. And charity, while a dominant theme of the New Testament, is a recurring theme in the Old, as evidenced by Cain's question: "Am I my brother's keeper?" Many Americans would impulsively answer in the affirmative, or perhaps more thoughtfully and with greater candor, "Yes, in some sense."

One of our tasks will be to specify more clearly the meaning of that qualifying phrase "in some sense." Another and related task will be to explore the extent to which our two themes are complementary or in conflict: individualism and self-development on the one hand, and on the other, community plus charity. Some might argue that the second has always been subservient to the first, but that is to attribute to individualism a dominance that obscures a host of conflicts, tensions, and uneasy compromises throughout American history. Community and charity, as a composite theme, have long pervaded the ideology of the nation with a vigor and ubiquity that challenges any notion that such ideals are secondary or derivative. The examples are legion: from John Winthrop's 1630 charge to the faithful, "if thy brother be in want and thou canst help him, thou needst not make doubt what thou shouldst doe,"[7] to Jimmy Stewart's discovery in the final scene of the movie *It's a Wonderful Life* that he could count on the generosity and communal instincts of his neighbors, to F. Scott Fitzgerald's simple statement: America is "a willingness of the heart."[8] That willingness is almost invariably sensed by foreign visitors and singled out for special mention, whether the visitor be Alexis de Tocqueville in the nineteenth century[9] or

Helmut Kohl in the twentieth.[10] Foreigners who come not for a temporary visit but to stay are often similarly impressed, and even sometimes over-whelmed, by American generosity. The experience of television personality Sara Bermudez has been replicated throughout the nation's history, al-though details may vary. "One thing I'll always remember about coming to America is how kind people were. When our neighbors saw we had nothing, they began to bring us things. One woman brought a chair; another brought an old television set. It made the first months livable."[11] Congressional and state legislators seeking to bolster their arguments in the hearings and debates accompanying social legislation of the last half-century have repea-tedly evoked these ideals of charity, community, and collective generosity – have repeatedly argued that a particular piece of legislation should be enacted because it would require the government to do what private citizens so often do by instinct: lend a hand to those in need.[12] At the risk of laboring the point, consider the Statue of Liberty in New York Harbor with, by international standards, its eccentric plea: "Give me your tired, your poor, your huddled masses yearning to breathe free." How out of place a similar statue similarly inscribed would seem in the harbors of Hamburg or Le Havre or Genoa or, perhaps least probable of all, in Tokyo Bay. And yet Americans in their recent celebration of the statue gave no indication that for their current ideology the symbolism of the statue is in any way out of date. That symbolism incorporates not only the promise of freedom but a gesture of generosity: give me your poor, the message reads implicitly, because I have something to give them. A concern for giving to others is every bit as American as is a preoccupation with freedom and self-realization. Historian Richard Hofstadter is therefore right to emphasize the importance of the theme of individualism in American beliefs, but wrong to conclude that this is the only theme of note; that what the people favor is "a democracy of cupidity rather than a democracy of fraternity."[13] Americans tend to favor *both* individualism and community, *both* aggressive self-development through the pursuit of economic self-interest *and* charitable concern for the econo-mically disadvantaged. How else can one explain, when international disaster strikes – earthquakes or famines or plagues – the outpouring from America of food and medical supplies and trained personnel? Rarely are these American responses matched or even approximated by other countries, even after allowance is made for relative per capita income and total population. If Americans, unlike the French, have never explicitly endorsed *fraternité* along with *liberté* and *egalité* in their national motto, their sense of collective responsibility and collective generosity – of communial obligations and the imperative of charity toward their fellow human beings – has long been a dominant characteristic of their principles and their practice. A second powerful theme of community and charity accordingly cuts right across the first of rugged individualism. The result is inevitably a cross-grained culture, a condition no doubt typical of many cultures, but within America the lines of conflict run particularly deep. The people who praise freedom of the individual are also uncommonly comfortable with collective activity that often has as one priority the collective good, or at least the good of those beyond the immediate sphere of self. "We love a crowd," observed Jacques Barzun of his fellow countrymen: "we work and play in gangs, we go from the church social to the committee room. Gertrude Stein was right to say that the true America was a camp meeting."[14]

But what, one might reasonably ask, has all this to do with equality? To review a point made earlier, the task ahead is to explore the meaning of a concept (equality) as it applies to a particular American ideal (economic justice) while struggling to strike a balance between (a) whatever implications are derived in this intellectual endeavor and (b) honoring two basic tenets of American ideology that frequently conflict: the dignity and worth of the individual, and community plus charity toward others. The next order of business is to gain a sharper sense of what the word equality implies for economic activity.

Equality and Economic Justice: General Observations

Consider again Isaiah Berlin's thesis that at the heart of the idea of equality is the formula: each to count for one and no one to count for more than one. Once accepted as a premise, this formula creates a strong presumption in favor of equal treatment; for example, for equality before the law, or for "one man, one vote" in the election of government representatives. As Berlin points out, moreover, equal treatment seems to require no justification, whereas unequal treatment does.[15] If we are asked to divide a cake among ten people, a division of one-tenth to each seems to require no explanation, whereas any other division (say, twice as much to one as to the other nine) does seem to demand a justification. Acceptable reasons for an unequal division can often be given; in this case, one might defend the larger share of cake to the one on the grounds that person is suffering from malnutrition whereas the other nine are not. Similarly, an unequal allocation of authority to a military commander or to an orchestra conductor might be justified by appealing to other goals such as the defense of the nation or the playing of a symphony – goals, the argument would run, that are likely to be achieved with far greater success if such an unequal division of authority is made. But once Berlin's formula is accepted, the controlling premise is that human beings should be treated "in a uniform and identical manner, unless there is a sufficient reason not to do so."[16] The potential stumbling block for those who would defend particular inequalities is therefore whether their "sufficient reasons" are also deemed sufficient by those who are inclined to challenge the inequalities that the first group would defend. Or put more generally and as a question, what should and should not count as a sufficient reason? And what criteria can be used to answer such a question?

A similar set of questions arises if one begins, not with Berlin's thoughts on equality, but with Aristotle's thoughts on justice. The latter argued that justice consists of treating equals equally and unequals unequally according to some relevant criteria.[17] Once again a strong presumption is created in favor of equality of treatment. Inequality requires justification, and that justification requires "relevant criteria." The question immediately arises as to which criteria are appropriately viewed as relevant. In deciding who qualifies to vote in American elections, for example, sex is not a relevant criterion (although it once was), whereas the age of the prospective voter is considered to be relevant (voters must be 18). What counts as relevant can of course change over time, and inequalities of treatment acceptable in one age may be considered indefensible in another, as illustrated by changing American attitudes toward a female's right to vote. But whatever the particular reasons that might be given to justify inequality of treatment in a particular instance, two general points would seem above dispute.

1 Any departure from treating human beings in a uniform and identical way seems to demand a justification using "relevant criteria" or (Berlin's phrase) "sufficient reasons."
2 This compulsion to justify inequality seems to follow naturally once one accepts the general principle: each to count for one and no one to count for more than one.

Equality of Results

The foregoing arguments have a number of implications for debates within America concerning what income distribution ought to be. First, any departure from equality of income shares seems to require justification. Second, those justifications consist of offering "sufficient reasons" or "relevant criteria" for existing income inequalities. Third, those who argue for equal income shares, or for "equality of results" as this income distribution is often termed, do so by trying to show that the arguments defending income inequality rest upon reasons that are not "sufficient" or upon criteria that are not "relevant." Rarely do these defenders of equality present any compelling reasons why their goal of equality is the one to be desired. Instead, as indicated, they tend to settle for attacking the reasons given by others in support of inequality.[18] Their main attacks have been outlined previously. In summary form, these tend to consist of a number of denials and one key assertion: the denials attempt to refute the claims that the economic race is fair or that equality of opportunity exists or that income payments reflect personal merit; and the assertion consists in the claim that income received is primarily or exclusively the product of luck, or of luck plus the coercive power made possible through wealth initially acquired by luck. In short, the advocates of equality would undercut all of the principal beliefs outlined in chapter 2.

Much has sometimes been made by advocates of the left that perfect equality of income has rarely been advocated by any writer or group of note. While that claim is correct, it should not obscure the fact that advocates of greater income equality almost invariably begin with perfect equality as their ideal, and then qualify that ideal to allow for other goals to be achieved; for example, the goal of maintaining efficiency in production by preserving some inequalities in factor payments as a reward for effort, or alternatively the goal of meeting "needs" by adjusting income payments made to allow for the differing needs of the recipients.[19] The Marxian formula "from each according to capacity to each according to need" is but a variant of the latter.

As already suggested, arguments defending income equality as a goal are rarely given, but if they were, what form might such arguments take? How, for example, might Henry Simons or Arthur Okun defend the claim that *any* income inequality is "unlovely"?[20] To have persuasive force for most Americans, their defense must ultimately be anchored in at least some of the basic beliefs cited earlier, particularly those affirming (a) the worth of the individual, (b) the importance of charity and community, and (c) the principle each to count for one and none to count for more than one. Several of these are evident, explicitly and implicitly, in Okun's explanation of why an equal distribution of income is his "ethical" preference:

This preference is a simple extension of the humanistic basis for equal rights. To extend the domain of rights and give every citizen an equal share of the national income would give added recognition to the moral worth of every citizen, to the mutual respect of citizens for one another, and to the equivalent value of membership in the society for all.[21]

Conservatives attack such claims primarily by focusing upon the threats to freedom (as they define that word to mean the absence of coercion). Here too the main arguments can be anticipated from all that has gone before. Writers of the right tend to emphasize two points: (a) to take income away from any individual impairs that individual's freedom and violates his or her property rights (the emphasis on the latter tending to increase the more inviolable those property rights are claimed to be); and (b) greater income equality requires a major policy of income redistribution, to implement that policy the government must be given increased powers, and this increased centralization of power – like any increase of power at the center – poses major threats to the freedom of the individual.

In the resulting interchange between left and right, both sides tend to gloss over a central point. The priority of income equality and the related claim that inequality is "unlovely" have *never* had widespread appeal within America. The main reason for that limited appeal is the continuing belief of most Americans in ideas and ideals that tend to coalesce around a small set of premises outlined in chapter 2. (To review them in their simplest form: the race is good and reasonably fair, and prizes tend to be rewarded for the exercise of meritorious traits such as industry, thrift, and foresight.) American resistance to a policy of extensive income redistribution is thus *not* anchored exclusively in conservative concerns that such a policy would threaten individual freedom. Or put in terms of mistaken perceptions of the left, most Americans have *not* been persuaded that the ideas of chapter 2 in support of income inequality have become outmoded or obsolete.

The continuing force of those reasons can be seen in the continuing popularity of such childhood fables as *The Little Red Hen*. Consider again the problem of how to divide a cake among ten individuals. As the problem was initially presented, the answer seemed obvious enough: give an equal share to each individual unless compelling reasons exist to do otherwise. What was missing in that example was any consideration of production. How was the cake created in the first place, and does *that* answer affect our judgment concerning a just or fair distribution of the cake?[22] The story of *The Little Red Hen* reverses the sequence, with its emphasis upon production first and distribution second. Despite the pleas of the hen for help, she was forced to do all the work herself: growing the wheat, transporting it to the miller, and baking the flour thus created into bread. When the question of distribution arose, the other barnyard animals who had contributed nothing to production all pleaded for a share, but the moral of the tale was that such pleas were legitimately ignored. In terms of the general framework developed earlier, the general presumption is *still* in favor of equality of treatment unless "sufficient reasons" can be given for unequal treatment. But here the production efforts of the hen and the refusal of the other animals to aid that process are portrayed as sufficient reasons for abandoning equality in the division of the output.

In a simplified form, *The Little Red Hen* repeats many of the themes of chapter 2. The widespread popularity of those themes, to be sure, is not to be demonstrated by reference to a single children's tale. But the popularity of such themes would seem everywhere apparent, and what is strikingly absent is widespread condemnation of income inequality as *intrinsically* "wrong" or "unfair." Also strikingly absent is widespread support, now or in the past, for a policy of massive income redistribution. Even liberals who wish American ideals were otherwise admit that "the tolerance of the masses for economic inequality is puzzling."[23] Those masses are tolerant because their belief system gives to observed inequalities a legitimacy that encourages acceptance. Nor are they sympathetic to pleas for a significant redistribution of the economic pie. George McGovern discovered this during his 1972 presidential campaign when he announced to a gathering of workers in a rubber factory his plan to raise inheritance taxes so drastically that the rich would have little to bequeath to their families. To McGovern's surprise, he was roundly booed.[24] Most legislators understand the sentiments behind the boos, even if McGovern did not. In all of the Congressional hearings and debates for all the major pieces of social legislation in this century, one almost never finds overt endorsement of income redistribution as a goal. Instead one finds the arguments favoring passage of a given act – for food stamps, or medical care, or Aid to Families with Dependent Children – couched in terms of helping those who cannot help themselves, with these appeals (as we shall see in chapter 8) closely linked to the ethical precept of collective generosity, and largely divorced from any notion that prevailing income inequalities are intrinsically offensive or unjust. Liberal economist Arthur Okun, although displeased by what Americans accept, characterizes their acceptance of inequality in incomes with an unswerving honesty typical of the man:

. . . people show surprisingly little resentment toward the extremely wealthy. While they express some concern about inequalities of opportunity and discriminatory treatment, most view those aspects as flaws rather than fundamental defects of the system.[25]

Three implications follow. First, liberals like Okun who view income inequality as intrinsically unlovely would seem to be profoundly out of step with popular American beliefs.[26] Second, conservatives have somewhat missed the mark in defending the inequalities of income generated by the market as necessary for the preservation of individual freedom. The belief system supporting those inequalities is far more comprehensive and complex than that. Third, if we would understand what the words "freedom" and "equality" mean to most Americans when applied to issues of economic justice, we must broach such issues having firmly in hand much of the intellectual baggage accumulated in previous chapters. Premises and assumptions have been piled one upon the other. The interconnected beliefs of chapter 2 must now be brought to bear in concert with such basic goals as respect for the dignity and worth of the individual and the preservation and enhancement of the community's sense of community, including the related priority of charitable instincts toward its less fortunate members. Finally, we must bring to issues that lie ahead two ideas that have been reasonably well defined, and one that still remains unclear:

1 "freedom from," now defined as "freedom from coercion";
2 "freedom to," expanded to mean having "the power or means" to pursue desirable goals, but just which "powers" or "means" are desirable for all participants to have in economic matters is still not clear; and finally,
3 "equality," expanded in two ways, the first specifying the heart of the idea (each to count for one and no one to count for more than one), and the second elaborating what the first implies if justice, including economic justice, is to prevail (all people should be treated in a uniform and identical manner, unless there is sufficient reason not to do so).

With the rejection of income equality or "equality of results" as an ideal, and the resurrection of the premises and assumptions of chapter 2, our task has at least become more clearly specified. The controlling imagery is again that of an economic race, and the issue becomes one of specifying those conditions that will ensure the race is fair and the prizes are distributed in a manner that most Americans would acknowledge to be reasonably just. But for most Americans of the modern era, what do the words "freedom" and "equality" mean when applied to the notion of an economic race? And what do the meanings chosen then imply about the belief system that is determining these choices? These will be the central questions of chapter 8.

8

Equality and Freedom in the Economic Race: The Modern Perspective

Introduction

The discussion now returns to themes first raised in chapter 2. The hypothesis tendered there was that throughout most of the nineteenth century a handful of premises powerfully influenced American thoughts concerning economic justice. Stated in their most simple form, these were:

1 participation in the economic race is an admirable endeavor, both for the individual self-fulfillment it encourages and for the social benefits that result;
2 the economic race (by and large) is a fair race; and
3 prizes tend to be awarded for hard work, thrift, and foresight (although luck may also play a role).

These three, in turn, seem to imply:

4 that the resulting distribution of prizes (that is, incomes received) is a reasonably just distribution.

The thesis is not that all these premises in the form just stated were believed by most of the people most of the time. Rather, the argument is that popular views strongly coalesced around such premises. What "coalescing" implies is that qualifications commonly made tended to be relatively minor. When defects were perceived in the workings of the market – as frequently they were – the dominant response was thus to search for remedies for the specific defects, not to re-evaluate the merits of the entire system, and certainly not to contemplate scrapping the system in favor of some alternative such as socialism. Such a response was indicative of a popular faith that the system, as a system, worked tolerably well in the sense that (while obviously less than perfect) it had an intrinsic order and an intrinsic moral validity. Or put another way, the overwhelming tendency to search for flaw-specific remedies indicated a faith that once specific remedies were found, the intrinsic tendencies of the system would restore a system inherently acceptable to much of American society as a means for determining production and distribution within the country.

The controlling quest for the present chapter is the extent to which the influence of these nineteenth century premises persisted into the twentieth century. The search for an answer will be somewhat indirect. As noted in the previous two chapters, the words "freedom" and "equality" can mean different things to different people. More importantly for our purposes, the meanings chosen for each in the context of defining a "fair" or "just" economic race sheds significant light on the chooser's views concerning economic justice. Accordingly, the approach of the present chapter is to try to identify the meanings popularly given to "freedom" and "equality" as those words applied to desirable conditions for participants at three positions in the economic race: at the starting line, on the course, and beyond the finish line. Relevant evidence will include federal legislation designed to make the race more fair (both the terms of the acts and views expressed in debates and hearings that preceded passage), as well as other evidence indicating views widely shared, such as the results of public opinion polls. To anticipate what still lies far ahead, what will emerge from a search of this sort is evidence that suggests a striking continuity across almost two centuries of American history: that the same premises which informed and constrained popular views in powerful ways in the previous century continued to do so right down to the present day.

A few cautionary words should be added about what will *not* be attempted. Our concern is with perceptions, not with facts, and factual evidence is therefore relevant only insofar as it sheds light upon popular perceptions. What follows accordingly is not a comprehensive history of twentieth century social welfare legislation or antitrust legislation. We shall instead use bits and pieces from that history to detect which defects in the market system the legislation sought to remedy, and what perceptions of those defects indicate about the kinds of freedom and equality believed to be appropriate for an economic race. Similarly, we shall not be interested in explanations of facts advanced by social scientists: why, for example, differentials in male–female wages and in white–nonwhite wages still persist or whether a rise in the minimum wage causes unemployment or how family background affects school performance and subsequent earnings. We shall, however, be concerned with what public efforts to combat discrimination or improve public education tell us about popular views concerning how an economic race should and should not be run.

At the Starting Line

The ideal that appeals to most Americans is to get each would-be competitor to the starting line of the economic race with an equal chance to compete. This ideal encompasses a number of subsidiary goals, of which two are particularly crucial. One involves the notion of "freedom *to*"; here, "freedom to compete" in the sense of having whatever "powers or means" are indispensable for entering the race. This in turn implies that, prior to approaching the starting line, each entrant has been able to develop his or her capabilities. Most American discussions on how that development should take place have focused upon public education, of which more in a moment. The second subsidiary goal imbedded in the ideal noted above is that of equality. All would-be competitors should have an equal chance. Policies and institutions designed to help them develop their capacities prior to entering the race should therefore treat each one in a uniform and identical manner, unless (Berlin's phrase again) there is sufficient reason not to do so.

"If you're so smart, why ain't you rich?": this quip, so popular in America, and sounding so out of place in many European settings, is indicative of how ingrained the belief in equality of opportunity is on this side of the Atlantic. The clear implication is that if you are smart and you want to be rich, you can become rich. Achieving perfect equality of opportunity, however, is an elusive ideal. As repeatedly discussed in previous chapters, the capacities that competitors bring to the starting line are profoundly affected by the accidents of heredity and the luck of the parental draw. Those coming with a superabundance of brain cells or coming from an enriched family background are likely to have an edge on those who are less gifted or from broken homes. How then can perfect equality be achieved for all competitors at the starting line? The American response to this conundrum has been typically pragmatic. By and large they have tended to address only those defects in equality that admit to being modified by public policy, and have refused to be diverted from this ambition by unsolvable dilemmas that any search for ultimate perfection would entail.

The dominant policy approach, as previously indicated, has been the provision of a public education that is free and equal for all.[1] The first half of that twin objective is well defined and the second half is not. No subtlety surrounds the meaning of making education "free," an idea that dates in American history from seventeenth century efforts in the Massachusetts Bay Colony. Increasingly popular and progressively implemented in the nineteenth century, the goal of a free education in the twentieth century has come to be regarded not so much as a priority to be pursued as a right that every child and parent can demand. If much is demanded, much must be spent. One measure of the importance of this priority in present-day America is that this country leads all advanced industrial nations in per capita spending on schooling.[2]

But if education is to be free, what does it mean to claim that educational opportunities should be "equal"? This latter priority is not well defined, and the search for definition is a theme of long standing in America. To make education free is, of course, a considerable help. Competing in the economic race requires skills, acquisition of skills requires education, and education costs money. Free education therefore assures that such training is available to the children of rich and poor alike. Or to put the argument in the negative and in R. H. Tawney's unsettling way: "The idea that differences of educational opportunity among children should depend upon differences of wealth among parents is a barbarity."[3]

Education freely provided by the government is an obvious step toward making educational opportunities "equal," but what else is required? To search for the answer is to become embroiled in a variety of hotly debated issues, of which three would seem particularly crucial to the concept of equality at the starting line. Each of the three can be put as a question for which American society has no agreed-upon answer.

As Presently Provided by the Public Schools, What Does Equal Education Mean?

The very phrasing of the question brings to mind "separate but equal," and the Supreme Court's decision in 1954 that "separate" was intrinsically "not equal." As the court explained at the time:

> To separate [Negro children] from others of similar age and qualifications solely because of their race generates a feeling of inferiority as to their status in the community that may affect their hearts and minds in a way unlikely ever to be undone . . . . We conclude that in the field of public education the doctrine of "separate but equal" has no place. Separate educational facilities are inherently unequal.[4]

In what is ultimately a complex argument for a major shift in American education policy, one idea tends to dominate: that peer group interaction at school affects the attitudes and achievements of the students, and thus society has an obligation to try to modify any peer grouping within the public school system that has serious detrimental effects upon the children. "Detrimental effects" is admittedly a vague phrase that begs many questions. John Dewey was equally vague but perhaps equally to the point:

> . . . it is the office of the school environment . . . to see to it that each individual gets an opportunity to escape from the limitations of the social group in which he was born, and to come into living contact with a broader environment.[5]

But should society's efforts to provide a "broader environment" in the classroom include the forced reallocation of peer groups across schools by such devices as forced busing? To that question, and to many others like it, Americans have no answer that commands widespread support. All (or almost all) agree in principle that every disadvantaged group should be provided with an "equal education," but the different camps are poles apart concerning what "equal" ought to mean in this context.

That disagreement ranges far beyond the appropriate educational facilities for minorities. Independent of race, creed, or ethnic background, students vary enormously in the mental capabilities they bring to the classroom. What does "equal treatment" mean when applied to the very clever and the very slow? Does it imply that schools should strive for equality of results, devoting more of their personnel and programs to raising the performance of the slow? Or does "treating equals equally" imply "treating equally gifted students equally," in which case the more gifted might receive more of available resources because developing their exceptional talents might require exceptional teachers and costly programs? Egalitarians are inclined to favor the first, but the second approach also has its supporters in America. A variant of the thinking that leads naturally to endorsement of the second approach was evident in Senator John Tower's challenge to the egalitarian premises of Sargent Shriver:

Have we not perhaps been too much concerned with the democratization of our society rather than developing the intellectual potential of the child in our schools to the extent that we felt that everybody is entitled to the same sort of education, the same sort of approach to education? Would we perhaps be better off if we followed the British plan of weeding them out at a certain age and taking those who perhaps are not competent to do the preparatory work and putting them in vocational school and training them for industry?[6]

Some readers will cringe at the Senator's suggestion. Others will be inclined to give it an approving nod. That diversity of response merely illustrates that the issue of what "equality" should mean in American education is still largely unresolved.

Should Free Universal Education be Expanded to Age Groups Other Than Those Now Served?

Should children of pre-school age have access to free day care deliberately designed to improve their education (perhaps similar in kind to that presently available to a limited number of disadvantaged children through Head Start programs)? Many liberals argue that they should. Those arguments usually emphasize the growing need associated with increased female participation in the labor force and the rise of single-parent families, and the evidence that the learning environment the child experiences prior to kindergarten is crucial to that child's performance later on. Critics have a range of rebuttals that tend to stress parental responsibility for these early years, as well as questioning the alleged merits of such a scheme. Whatever the merits of each side's position, the prospects for a massive expansion of free educational services in this direction at present seem remote, to judge by the almost total absence of serious discussion of that possibility in the legislative bodies of this country.

Another possible extension of free education would be in the direction of training beyond high school. Americans have resisted any simple extension, but in recent decades they have struggled to find a compromise reflecting egalitarian concerns and the greater need for greater skills to compete successfully in an economic race becoming ever more complex. In the immediate post-Sputnik era, the surge in support for higher education had little to do with fostering equality of opportunity and much to do with catching up with the Russians. Accordingly, public funds tended to be used to encourage the most talented of high school graduates to continue on to college. Beginning in the 1960s, however, increasing emphasis was given to equality of opportunity, culminating with the Basic Educational Opportunity Grants in 1972 designed to remove financial barriers to higher education for lower-income students. This system has subsequently been modified by further legislation to expand the coverage or expand the grants or, in recent years, to cut back both,[7] but the rationale for the initial legislation would now seem generally accepted: *some* public effort should be made through grants and loans to give capable students from low-income backgrounds more equal access to institutions of higher learning.[8]

What Should be Done About the Failures?

When used in the context of public education, "failure" tends to be a contentious word, referring to student problems of many kinds with many causes. The concern here is with extreme failure: those youths who have acquired so little through formal schooling that they may be permanently handicapped in the economic race, or worse, not even qualify for the starting line. Despite America's commitment to equal education that is available to all without charge, such failures do exist, and in numbers that are troubling. "We have a vast army of underprivileged dropouts, " observed a Congressman in the mid-1960s: "unskilled dreamers and blank human cartridges who must be reschooled, retrained, and retrieved."[9] Willard Wirtz, Secretary of Labor under President Johnson, made the same point with imagery less subtle but more compelling: "We are throwing 250,000 to 300,000 young Americans on the scrap heap every year."[10] To suggest that significant numbers of American youth have been relegated to an economic scrap heap may strike some readers as a gross exaggeration. The evidence nevertheless supports the contention that not all those who experience a public education gain the most basic skills required to compete successfully in even the most unskilled labor markets of the country. According to a 1983 report of the National Commission on Excellence in Education, for example, 13 percent of all American seventeen-year-olds could be considered functionally illiterate.

But if the educational system is clearly failing some, who is responsible for that failure? The answers tend to vary in predictable ways. Liberals are inclined to emphasize events beyond the individual's control. The system has failed the students more than the students have failed the system, their argument runs, and thus the government has an obligation to give remedial training to those who have been badly served by conventional public education. (Cast in Aristotelian terms, this amounts to the charge that public education has treated unequals equally, and thus the results are not only unsatisfactory but also unjust.) At the opposite extreme are conservatives who tend to stress the individual's responsibility or that of the family for the individual's success or failure in gaining a satisfactory education. They also usually warn against an excess of paternalistic programs that threaten to sap the vigor and initiative of participating youth.

Whoever is responsible for such unequivocal failures, both left and right agree that the nation's economic needs are badly served by such a defective preparation of part of its labor force. That point was made by the Chicago *Sun-Times* in language that had such general appeal the editorial in question was read into the *Congressional Record*. "Our industrial society demands that every person be able to play a useful part in it," the paper's reasoning ran. "The unskilled must be taught, the ignorant must be educated. The very affluence that America enjoys depends on the optimum use of all hands."[11] One Congressman sharpened the general concern to a single point: give those with deficient skills remedial training, he argued, to make them "taxpayers instead of tax eaters."[12]

For economic reasons such as these, but also because of a genuine concern for the fate of those confronted with the prospect of a "scrap heap," the federal government introduced a variety of remedial training programs beginning in the 1960s, most notably the Manpower Development and Training Act (1962), the Economic Opportunity Act (1964), the Comprehensive Employment and Training Act (1973), and the Job Training Partnership Act (1982). Their general objective, as outlined in one of the earliest acts, was

to eliminate the paradox of poverty in the midst of plenty in this Nation by opening to everyone the opportunity for education and training, the opportunity to work, and the opportunity to live in decency and dignity.[13]

That the federal legislation just quoted should claim as one of its objectives the elimination (rather than the reduction) of poverty is one measure of the optimism and naiveté that infused the early years of President Johnson's War on Poverty. Subsequent experience would temper both.

All of these programs are designed to provide training primarily for the disadvantaged: minorities, welfare recipients, and low-income groups. The mechanisms used to provide that training are mainly of two kinds: (a) classroom training and other institutional training for specific occupations,[14] and (b) on-the-job training programs that pay a subsidy to employers for hiring disadvantaged workers. (The subsidy is sometimes given merely for providing a job, and sometimes given with the express understanding that the employer will provide a job *plus* training.) The record of these latter programs aimed at eliciting training within the private sector is easily summarized. The impact of on-the-job training has been negligible, because the participation of employers has been negligible. The impact of public sector efforts is more difficult to assess. Evidence of the success of individual programs is mixed and much debated.[15] Even staunch supporters usually concede that no program has had a startling success, and that each program even at its best has made some difference to some of the participants some of the time. What is clear to supporters and critics alike is that the problem of curing poverty in general or of remedying defective skills in particular are far less tractable and less well understood than was originally believed when manpower training programs were first initiated. What is also clear, although neither left nor right seems inclined to emphasize the point, is that the American public and their elected representatives have yet to take manpower training problems seriously. The limited nature of initiatives tried, their limited success, and the poverty of new proposals presently under serious review would all seem convincing proof of that. Surveying the unsatisfactory record of the past, liberal critic Robert Kuttner is among the many who remain disheartened.

In a society that supposedly prizes the work ethic, the policymakers never got around to devising . . . a comprehensive approach to training . . . . The manpower programs of the 1960's and 1970's had confused, diverse goals, and although some of them did train people, they were never part of a coherent system or strategy.[16]

In sum, if the question is the one noted at the outset – What should be done about the failures? – the answer of American society as measured by initiatives and accomplishments is (at least to date): Not much.

What then can be said by way of overview about the American vision of desirable equality and freedom at the starting line? Has that vision changed? The fundamental tenets dictating the appropriate role of government in fostering equality at the starting line would *not* seem to have been modified significantly during the past three decades, despite the many initiatives, much celebrated, to make the race more equal. The overarching goal remains equality of opportunity, but the policy focus, from first to last, has been to give would-be competitors the training necessary to compete, primarily by providing what has long been provided in this country: free public education from kindergarten through high school. Marginal changes have been made: a Head Start program for a limited number of disadvantaged children prior to their entering the public school system; a modest expansion in financial support available to students from low-income families who wish to attend college; limited increases in remedial training programs for the most disadvantaged and the least skilled. The evidence indicates now what it has always indicated in the past: all competitors are *not* equal at the starting line. Some remain so handicapped that their very participation is in doubt. Yet how to help the handicapped become more willing and more able to compete is also in doubt, and those doubts have multiplied since the buoyant years of new initiatives and high expectations of the Kennedy–Johnson era. Causal forces are now less clear, and consequently so are possible solutions. "Family background," "neighborhood environment," "the culture of poverty": these typify the phrases used to capture influences crucial to the formation of attitudes and to the acquisition of skills needed to compete successfully in the economic race. All are vague, and that vagueness is a commentary on our understanding.

The prospects for America's "underclass," as they are sometimes called, do not appear encouraging. Policies initiated to help them better prepare for the economic race have, at best, affected a limited number in a limited way. This record of the past three decades in turn suggests that America lacks the consensus needed to launch a massive program to improve equality at the starting line. It also seems to lack the knowledge where and how to begin such an undertaking should that ever become a national priority of the first importance. The prevalence of handicaps among the underclass seems destined to increase, particularly as the skills required for many facets of the economic race become more demanding and more difficult to acquire. Should society do no more for this underclass in the future than it has done in the past, the human costs will rise, but other costs, quite apart from humanitarian concerns, might plague American society. President Kennedy warned in his inaugural address that "If a free society cannot help the many who are poor, it cannot save the few who are rich."[17] Writing of another time and place, Winston Churchill expressed the same concerns in darker terms:

If we [carry] on in the old happy-go-lucky way – the richer classes ever growing in wealth and in number, and the very poor remaining plunged or plunging ever deeper in helpless, hopeless misery – then I think there is nothing before us but savage strife between class and class, with the increasing disorganisation, with increasing waste of human strength and human virtue . . . .[18]

To draw a parallel between Britain at the beginning of the twentieth century and America of today is admittedly strained, if not deeply suspect. And yet, as the Churchill observation suggests, the reality of social and economic immobility, when combined with thwarted hopes, can make for social instability. A striking difference between the United States and Britain – for all the accusations of the left – is that the former still has a social structure noted for its mobility, and that mobility, as noted previously, undercuts the very concept of class. But as the phrase "underclass" implies, some in America have little mobility, are losing some of what they have, and accordingly are becoming progressively locked into the lowest echelons of the economy and of society. Or in the language of the Congressman cited above, many of these would-be entrants in the economic race approach the starting line as "unskilled dreamers and blank cartridges." The likely fate for many down the racecourse is therefore just what Secretary of Labor Willard Wirtz claimed it would be almost thirty years ago: "the scrap heap."[19]

On the Course

As we have seen, a single idea seems to dominate the American approach to the starting line: equals should be treated equally, and in this context, equal treatment is viewed (at least as an ideal) as giving all would-be competitors equal access to equal educational facilities, with equality of access presumed to be achieved by making those facilities free.

Once competitors break past the starting line, the problem becomes one of assuring fairness on the course. But in an economic race, what does "fairness" mean? No single answer commands general acceptance in America. Instead, various answers have been proposed to solve a range of problems. The latter are primarily of three kinds, and can be conveniently grouped under the three headings already developed:

1 "freedom from," expanded to the now familiar "freedom from coercion";
2 "equality," which in the context of a racecourse implies that all competitors should be treated in an identical manner unless there is sufficient reason not to do so; and finally
3 "freedom to," here meaning "freedom to compete" or, more suggestively, "having the power or means to compete."

To anticipate a division of opinion still to be examined, we would expect conservatives to be preoccupied with the first, given their emphasis on freedom as a goal and their insistence on defining that goal as the absence of coercion. Liberals willingly acknowledge the importance of limiting coercion on the racecourse, but also emphasize achieving priorities (2) and (3). The sharpest disagreements tend to arise concerning the meaning and importance of "freedom to compete". Examining these disagreements should therefore have the added benefit of sharpening our sense of some of the unresolved problems still lurking in that troublesome word "freedom."

Freedom from Coercion

The American image of an ideal racecourse is very similar to Adam Smith's image of an ideal market: many small-scale competitors vying with one another for economic success, all responding to market signals in the form of changing prices, and none large enough to affect those prices directly. Most crucial under the last heading is that no competitor has the monopoly power within a given market to dictate prices to consumers or dictate wages to workers.[20]

As Adam Smith well knew, producers have a chronic propensity to seek monopoly power,[21] and thus public policies must be devised to inhibit the formation of monopolies and break up any that are formed or, failing that, to restrict their ability to operate "to the detriment of the public interest," as the Justice Department likes to characterize the negative effects. Examples of detrimental practices are only too apparent in American history, most of them aimed at eliminating competition by such suspect procedures as the clandestine buying up of other firms (Rockefeller while establishing Standard Oil), vicious price wars (National Cash Register in its early years), or even outright violence (the fur wars of J. J. Astor in the trans-Mississippi West). The many charges against monopolies and their owners, by and large, tend to reduce to the double accusation of gaining power by restricting competition and using the resulting power to coerce others – most notably, to force price concessions from buyers or wage concessions from workers.

American indignation at such practices has a long history. There is something particularly un-American in advantages gained through contrived inhibitions on competition, something that gives a special force to Theodore Roosevelt's phrase "malefactors of great wealth,"[22] and to Franklin Roosevelt's language of condemnation when he scored monopolies for crushing initiative and opportunity "in the cogs of a great machine," using "economic tyranny" to transform "free enterprise" into "privileged enterprise."[23] By any standard of fairness in the economic race – or any standard that Americans are likely to endorse – this clearly will not do.[24] If monopoly power is the problem, the solution is to remove it, or failing that, to regulate it, or as a last resort, to bolster the power of those who must compete with those who are already powerful.

All three solutions have been attempted in the past, each with a record of uneven success. Major federal efforts to regulate monopoly date from the establishment of the Interstate Commerce Commission in 1887. Those to restrict monopoly formation and monopoly practices date from the Sherman Antitrust Act passed three years later. The third approach – adding to the bargaining power of the less powerful – was most in evidence in the 1930s when two acts were passed (the Norris–La Guardia Act in 1932 and the Wagner Act in 1935) to strengthen labor's hand in its dealings with management in general and large corporations in particular. Following World War II, the pendulum swung back the other way, with the two most important acts (the Taft–Hartley Act of 1947 and the Landrum–Griffin Act of 1959) designed to inhibit coercive union practices directed at employers or employees.

Given their preference for the minimal state, conservatives, although they oppose monopoly and coercion, are uneasy about any government attempts to mitigate abuses of monopoly power. They emphasize the tendency of bureaucratic behavior to go awry and for legislated regulations to make a bad situation worse. They are also quick to point out that charges of inhibiting competition and exploiting monopoly power in protected markets can be leveled against certain union practices as well as certain practices of management. Not infrequently a conservative's bias – insofar as any government action is advocated – is to focus more on union abuses than on management abuses, with this tendency more in evidence the further to the right the writer is.[25]

Liberals are inclined to be much less fearful of big government and of large-scale government intervention to rectify perceived defects in the market system. They are accordingly more prone to favor dismemberment of the more flagrant monopolies plus regulations to control, inhibit, or eradicate monopolistic practices where those practices are less flagrant and enforced dismemberment appears impractical or unwarranted. Liberals also tend to be more sensitive to any mismatch of power that works to labor's disadvantage, and thus are more inclined to favor government intervention to rectify the mismatch. Perhaps the best known exponent of this viewpoint is economist John Kenneth Galbraith, whose conceptual framework of "countervailing power," as the name implies, favors strengthening the weak to compete more successfully with the strong.[26]

In this push and pull between left and right, one might expect organized labor to endorse wholeheartedly the policies and premises of the liberals, and yet schisms of the first importance exist between American liberals and American labor. The testimony of United Automobile Workers (UAW) President Walter Reuther offers a clue to where one of the most important schisms lies, and therefore deserves to be quoted in some detail.

This increasing imbalance in the distribution of wealth has been in part a consequence of the fact that those in our economy who possess a large measure of freedom to appropriate more than their fair share of the fruits of economic growth have been persistently abusing that freedom – particularly the major corporations which dominate whole industries, and which have and use the power to set the prices of their products, and consequently their profits, at a level of their own choosing without being subjected to the pressures of competitive market forces. The abuse of this power has been reflected in the fact that dividends, which go largely to a relatively few wealthy individuals, together with undistributed profits and depreciation allowances retained in corporate treasuries have increased in the past 10 years far faster than the incomes of those whose work produces corporate wealth.[27]

In the Sherlock Holmes adventure involving the death of a horse trainer, a crucial clue was the failure of a dog to bark. The most significant aspect of Reuther's testimony would also seem to be what is *not* expressed. The UAW President reminds us that the ultimate issue is not market power but income distribution. And yet while addressing this subject in hearings conducted by one of America's most prestigious legislative bodies, he makes no reference, explicitly or implicitly, to those premises and ideals so central to the liberal position on economic justice: that income inequality is intrinsically "unlovely"; that existing inequalities are little related to merit and effort and determined primarily by luck; that a more just income would accordingly be a less unequal division; and thus that a high priority of government policy should be income redistribution. When challenged in the hearings on this final point, Reuther stated flatly, "I am not advocating sharing the wealth," adding that the American labor movement supported the free-enterprise system and believed that system "should be the core of our economic efforts."[28] The only change of consequence this labor leader wanted in that system was less "abuse of power" by management and the reinstatement of "the pressures of competitive market forces." After that, labor would willingly take its chances in the economic race – and, the implication seemed to be, reap its just reward. In short, Reuther's testimony offers further evidence for a central thesis of this book: that the premises and ideals of the nineteenth century, as elaborated in chapter 2, have persisted into the twentieth century; these ideas still have powerful and widespread appeal; and that appeal is the central reason why liberal arguments about income inequality's being intrinsically "unjust" or "unfair" remain largely unheeded by most Americans, including the majority of the American work force.

Equal Treatment of Competitors

"Discrimination" suggests that equals are not being treated equally. Whatever reasons might be given for unequal treatment, the presumption is that such reasons are not "sufficient," and accordingly such behavior is considered to be unjust. For the participants in the American economic race, the most common charge of discrimination applies to situations where would-be competitors are excluded from certain jobs, or if not excluded, do not receive "equal pay for equal work." While the treatment of women and minorities in this way is abhorrent to most Americans, such censure is a relatively recent phenomenon, at least by the time-scale of the historian. In attacking prejudices that still exist, present-day reformers tend to forget how far and how fast American society has progressed under this heading: the flagrant discrimination against women in the work force in every era but our own; the exclusion of Negroes from many labor unions prior to World War II; the fighting of World War II with a military force deliberately divided along racial lines. What counts as "sufficient reason" for differential treatment of human beings can evidently vary widely over time. Happily, the American trend of recent years has been toward treating all competitors in the economic race more equally. The major legislative impetus for this change came in the 1960s with the pasage of the Equal Pay Act (1963) and the Civil Rights Act (1964). But what might be accomplished – or ideally should be accomplished – under these and other acts still remains in doubt.

Three policy options tend to dominate debate. The first is negative in thrust, designed to prevent what most now acknowledge is morally reprehensible: discrimination against existing or prospective workers for reasons related solely to the worker's race, age, sex, or ethnic background. The second and third have a more positive ambition, as the title "affirmative action" suggests. The major problem that they address is how to institute remedies for past wrongs; in particular, the disadvantages now suffered by certain groups because of discriminatory practices of the past. Two main types of policies have been proposed, one far more controversial than the other. One seeks to aid the previously disadvantaged by outreach and recruitment. A Justice Department official explains what he terms this "original, undefiled" meaning of affirmative action: "outreach and recruitment intended to expand the applicant pool to include greater numbers of qualified members of minorities and women, from which non-discriminatory employment decisions are made."[29] More simply put, the aim of such a policy is to get the previously disadvantaged into the competition on more equal terms, but after that they are on their own. The other type of affirmative action seeks to give these groups a deliberate edge in the competition by "numerical objectives for hiring" usually in the form of quotas, or more generally, through "race- and gender-preferential employment policies."[30] The obvious dilemma posed by this approach (which has no easy resolution) is that the very act of discriminating in favor of one group – those who obtain jobs because quotas are enforced – discriminates against another group – those excluded from the jobs in question by the enforcement of the quotas.

The appeal of each of these three policy options to the left and right is not difficult to predict. All would agree that discrimination in the marketplace is wrong, although some conservatives resist the notion that government intervention can successfully combat it.[31] The more extreme is the intervention, the less likely is it to be supported by those who advocate a minimal state and a free market. Liberals are more inclined to favor preferential treatment for the disadvantaged. In justifying this unequal treatment for unequals, they tend to cite as a "sufficient reason" the many unfair practices of the past that have tended to make for handicapped competitors in the present.

Which kinds of intervention will be allowed or encouraged in the future will depend upon a complex interaction among three groups: legislators who frame the relevant acts, court officials who interpret the acts, and the public at large, whose moral stance on these issues, although influenced by a host of factors including legislative acts and court interpretations, still remains the great engine that gives the driving thrust to change.

Freedom to Compete

"Freedom to compete" implies "having the power or means to compete." Invariably some competitors are knocked out of the economic race through no fault of their own: the construction worker temporarily laid off because the national economy is experiencing a recession; the steel worker permanently laid off because the firm employing him was forced to close by international competition. Does society in general or the government in particular have an obligation to help such people, and if so, how?

One way to help is to try to prevent the unemployment from arising in the first place. Two kinds of government policies have been advocated in this context, one designed to mitigate short-run swings in general economic activity, and the other designed to address long-run or secular problems in particular sectors of the economy experiencing particular difficulties *not* related (or not primarily related) to a short-run recession in the economy at large.

The first of these involves the use of countercyclical fiscal and monetary tools made fashionable by Keynesian economics. To mitigate nationwide slumps and thus to mitigate the unemployment caused by slumps, Keynesians argue, fiscal and monetary policies should be implemented to stimulate demand; that is, the federal government should institute some combination of tax cuts and spending increases (thereby putting more money into the hands of the public to spend), and monetary authorities should increase the money supply to lower interest rates to stimulate the kind of spending that tends to rise when interest rates fall, such as investment in plant and equipment and housing purchases. Such policies have recently come under heavy attack in Washington, particularly from monetarists. The dispute between these two warring camps (Keynesians and monetarists) is not easily summarized, but the main bone of contention is whether national authorities can intervene with the right policies at the right time to smooth out – or at least dampen – swings in aggregate economic activity typical of a capitalist economy, making recessions less deep and booms less excessive (and thus less inflationary). Keynesians claim (a) the economy is intrinsically unstable (that is, prone to swing between boom and bust), (b) policymakers have the tools to mitigate this instability and sufficient knowledge to use those tools successfully, and thus (c) fiscal and monetary policies should be used to "fine tune" the economy, as it is sometimes called. Monetarists deny both (a) and (b), and thus argue against (c). Who is right – or, more cautiously, which side has a better understanding of how the economy actually functions – is still unclear, as evidenced by the fact that both factions have vigorous and prestigious advocates and neither side shows any sign of winning the debate. However that debate is finally resolved, the bias of monetary authorities at present remains basically Keynesian; that is, Federal Reserve officials seem inclined to continue to try to implement countercyclical policies to smooth out economic fluctuations. The prospects for the continued use of counter-cyclical fiscal policy is more in doubt, at least in the short run. The need to cut the federal deficit in recent years has tended to overwhelm any discussion of using tax cuts and spending increases to combat the likely negative effects of a looming recession. And the more the Congress moves to a position of accepting a balanced budget as the norm, particularly a norm mandated by law, the less capable it will be of using variations in taxes and spending to create either surpluses or deficits to offset either booms or recessions in aggregate economic activity.

A different policy option, widely discussed in the early 1980s and then virtually dismissed, concerns selective long-run policies to stimulate growth and combat unemployment. "Industrial policy" was a popular phrase in the early Reagan years, with almost as many meanings as writers on the topic. The problem at the heart of the debate was obvious enough: the sagging growth rate in American productivity. What was not obvious was why American productivity growth had slowed down, beginning in the early 1970s and persisting into the 1980s. Different causes were emphasized by different analysts who accordingly advocated different solutions. Foremost among the remedies suggested were export–import controls, subsidies for research and development, and tax incentives or low-cost loans. Each remedy was to be targeted for selected industries, some to shore up those in decline and some to stimulate those showing promise of becoming leading sectors of the future. "Industrial policy" and "reindustrialization" were topics of a spirited debate, particularly in the 1984 Presidential election. But since that time those topics have tended to disappear from the front pages of the press, the back rooms of Congress, and the academic journals devoted to policy issues. One reason for this quick demise in popularity is that economists on both the left and right quickly converged to a consensus that industrial policies of the sort suggested had little to recommend them. Their agreement reflected, in part, the widely held belief that the government could not do a better job than the free market in identifying winners and phasing out losers. As the topics of industrial policy faded as a focus of debate, so too did the prospects of any coherent and concerted government action to address the particular concerns of this section: the lessening of unemploy-ment caused by layoffs in declining industries, or the helping of laid-off workers to retrain and find new jobs.

To review: the prospects remain limited in the extreme for government policies designed to help back into the economic race those knocked out through no fault of their own. Countercyclical monetary policy seems likely to persist, but the use of fiscal policy to mitigate the effects of business cycles seems destined to decline. The use of "industrial policies" to combat the worst effects of secular decline in particular industries, which never seemed a serious possibility when those policies were much discussed, is even less likely now that such issues are seldom discussed.

The list of possible aid for the involuntarily unemployed within America does not end here. Unemployment insurance payments ease the economic strain of being out of work and can make the search for an alternative job more feasible to the extent that time and money are needed for the search. The government has also made modest efforts to help retrain some of the unemployed and to assemble and make available information on job opportunities within the locality, the region, or the state. One additional proposal, more controversial than those discussed to date, is to make the government the employer of last resort for those who cannot find a job elsewhere. Although advocated by many liberals,[32] this policy seems to have little chance of mustering widespread support, at least barring economic calamity and attendant social dislocation of the sort experienced in the 1930s.

The government's role in fostering freedom to compete is thus viewed by most Americans as appropriately restricted to one of modest intervention in the market to help those knocked out of the economic race to get back into it, or to prevent some (but by no means all) from being knocked out in the first place. Countercyclical monetary policy is crafted, in part, to lessen unemployment in recessions; unemployment insurance payments ease the financial pinch of being out of work and of searching for a new job; limited job training programs help a few of those in need of new skills to acquire them; job information sources aid the search for new employment. But beyond this limited government assistance, the individual is generally viewed as being responsible for finding a job, and if laid off, for finding another. If old skills are becoming obsolete and new ones are required, the individual must identify which skills are in demand and how best to acquire them. If an assembly line is shut down temporarily or a plant is closed permanently or the national economy experiences widespread decline, those who lose their jobs as a result must look primarily to their own resources to find alternative employment. In short, the dominant premise seems to be that on the racecourse most of the participants *are* free to compete, or "reasonably" free in the sense of having "the power or means to compete." The best evidence of that is the widespread acceptance of government intervention that is subdued in scope and limited in kind.

Beyond the Finish Line

Prizes to the Winners

The handful of premises that dominated nineteenth century American views concerning economic justice appear to have preserved much of their dominant role in the present century. Part of the evidence for that assertion is the support for one or more of these premises that tends to surface in media polls or academic surveys directed to issues of economic justice (see appendix A). But much of the relevant evidence concerns what tends to be muted or missing in America: the negligible support for socialism or communism, even for the more moderate varieties of such beliefs; the absence of widely respected and widely read polemical attacks upon existing income inequalities as intrinsically unjust; the almost total lack of any reference to "class" or "class consciousness" or to income redistribution as a priority of importance in the debates of the legislative bodies of the country, whether federal, state, or local. The government policies examined in the first two sections of this chapter share a common set of goals: to make the economic race as fair as possible in the sense of maximizing the equality of competitors at the starting line, and preserving that equality on the course while inhibiting coercion by the powerful. They also share a common premise about the appropriate role of government in the pursuit of these goals: that only modest intervention is generally required, not to achieve the goals, but to achieve an approximation to them generally acceptable to the citizens. The implicit premise, made explicit in the themes of chapter 2, is that with minor exceptions the individual is responsible and should be responsible for acquiring the skills and knowledge indispensable for entering the race, for achieving success in competition on the course, and thus for the amount of payments received for races run. The government's appropriate role is that of attentive policeman and infrequent Samaritan, stepping in to penalize coercive behavior or occasionally to give aid to competitors who seem unduly handicapped at the starting line or unduly penalized on the course through no fault of their own. But the government is not in the business of modifying the racecourse in a major way, only in attempting to maintain "fair" competition in a race primarily structured by the market system. Above all, the government is not in the business of supplying a substitute racecourse of its own.

The confidence with which Americans adhere to such ideas appears to have changed at least marginally in recent decades. By European standards, disputes within the United States concerning economic justice still reflect an ideological spectrum that is remarkable for its narrowness and for the similarity of controlling premises of the major competing schools of thought. But beneath this somewhat homogeneous surface are undercurrents of uncertainty. Americans of the present generation seem less inclined to trumpet the claim that equality of opportunity pervades their economic system, less inclined to insist that virtue earns its just reward within the marketplace, less inclined to glorify the strenuous life of economic enterprise as furthering the public good or leading to the self-fulfillment of competitors. This lessening of general confidence, if lessening there has been, should not be misinterpreted as signaling a shattering, or even an impending shattering, of the heretofore strong coalescing of popular ideas around the premises of chapter 2 and their key conclusion: that (by and large and subject to qualifications that may be on the increase) the race is fair, the race is good, and the winners deserve the prizes they have won.

A Maximum on Winnings?

Even if winners in general deserve their prizes, two modifications in the distribution of rewards might be deemed appropriate. One would place a maximum on the winnings of the most successful. The other would provide a minimum for all members of society, irrespective of their participation or performance in the race. Both might be justified by the now familiar argument that existing income inequality is unjust, and accordingly income should be redistributed from rich to poor. As emphasized repeatedly above, however, this line of reasoning has never had much appeal to most Americans. But other arguments can be found and have been used to justify a maximum on winnings and a minimum for all.

A maximum might be enforced either directly by a steeply progressive income tax that becomes virtually a 100 percent tax beyond some designated income level, or somewhat indirectly by a steeply progressive inheritance tax designed to prevent the passing on of accumulated wealth. Each can be used to reinforce the restrictions on high incomes effected by the other. Income is the annual flow that over time, if saved, will generate a stock of wealth. A steeply progressive income tax will therefore limit wealth accumulation; a stiff inheritance tax will sharply reduce the annual income generated by funds inherited.

Arguments can be marshaled in defense of such taxation policies that have little or nothing to do with the belief that existing income inequalities are intrinsically unjust. One argument concerns the premises of chapter 2 and a particular condition that supporters of a maximum would claim is necessary for fairness in the race. The offspring of the wealthy, the argument runs, acquire an unfair advantage at the starting line and on the course if they start out with a fortune. Moreover, their possession of a fortune, at least at the outset, is quite unrelated to any personal effort or achievement on their part, and for that reason cannot be justified as a reward for meritorious behavior in the competition of the marketplace. While this argument might be used to support the case for a stiff inheritance tax, it has no obvious implication for debates about the merits of a steeply progressive income tax.

Another line of reasoning in support of a maximum on winnings can be used as a justification for both kinds of taxation. Great wealth bestows upon its owner the potential for great power, this latter argument runs, and such power may be used to subvert a representative government, making it more responsive to the needs and interests of the wealthy. As Jack London put the point, affluence means influence. Or as the Medici family of sixteenth century Florence elaborated the point: money to get power, power to protect the money. If successful and widely prevalent, such political machinations by the opulent few would constitute nothing less than the subversion of a government ostensibly of the people, for the people, and by the people. In any society with serious claims to representative government – in which each is supposed to count for one and none to count for more than one, in which "one man, one vote" is presumed to be a shared goal and an accomplished fact – such bending of the governmental processes to the will of the wealthy clearly will not do.

Perhaps somewhat curiously, only writers of the extreme left within America make much of this threat or openly acknowledge the importance of placing a maximum upon winnings. More moderate liberals seldom endorse such a policy, and many explicitly reject it.[33] As one would expect, conservatives from moderate to extreme give short shrift to any suggestion that a maximum should be enforced on income earned or wealth passed on to heirs. What is less predictable but no less striking is the short shrift such ideas get from most Americans. Certainly George McGovern was surprised, as previously noted, to discover the hostility of American workers to his suggestion for sharply raising the inheritance tax to be paid by the wealthy. Another instance of similar sentiments concerning what taxation should *not* attempt to accomplish was the limitation generally accepted for the recent debates concerning tax reform. The main issue was whether marginal rates should be lowered by a little or a lot, and the most extreme liberal position of any popularity in Congress consisted in arguing for preserving the progressive tax structure as it was. Even the isolated few who argued for higher rates on higher incomes were not inclined to argue that the appropriate tax rate was 100 percent above some designated maximum.[34]

The evidence would therefore seem to indicate that most Americans do not favor any taxation policies designed to place a maximum on what competitors in the economic race can win, or having won, can pass on to their heirs. From that resistance one can only infer a considerable indifference to the threats discussed above in terms of great wealth imperiling the fairness of the economic race or the functioning of representative government. But if Americans have collectively remained unresponsive to suggestions for a ceiling upon incomes earned, they appear in recent years to have softened their position on the merits of a floor. That appearance, however, is deceiving.

A Minimum for All?

The payment of welfare benefits to certain categories of citizens can be traced at least as far as back as the constitution of ancient Athens.[35] But the goal of guaranteeing that no citizen will slip below some minimum income precisely specified in monetary terms is a decidedly modern notion, and predictably so. Pre-modern societies simply did not have the bureaucratic machinery to identify the income of each and therefore single out those whose incomes fell below a certain minimum. Per capita GNP in earlier societies also tended to be so low and so closely tied to fluctuations in agrarian output (which could fluctuate enormously) that they lacked the economic resources to ensure that large segments of the population would not starve when famine struck.

Within America, only since the Great Depression of the 1930s has much attention been given to providing what Ronald Reagan would label "a safety net for the truly needy," and liberal Michael Harrington prefers to relabel "a floor under misery."[36] Beneath these similar sounding phrases are profound differences concerning who should be helped and how, as we shall shortly see. The first order of business, however, is to identify the justifications that can be given for providing a minimum for all, irrespective of whether that minimum is high or low.

Two main kinds of arguments have been advanced, each consistent with themes developed earlier. The first begins with the familiar premise of the worth and dignity of the individual, and notes the inconsistency between honoring that ideal and allowing the least well off members of society to live in grinding poverty. "Starvation and dignity do not mix well," Arthur Okun reminds us,[37] if the point needs laboring and surely it should not. The second argument begins with the twin themes of charity and community, and emphasizes the obligation of those who are well off to take care of those who are less fortunate. Judeo-Christian beliefs reinforce both lines of reasoning, particularly the second. Both the Old and the New Testament hammer repeatedly at the theme of caring for the destitute, and both portray a woeful fate for the "haves" who have a lot and give not to the poor.

With themes such as these that resonate so well with American beliefs and ideals, the history of this country's social legislation presents something of a puzzle. Measured by international norms, America is justly famous for the generosity of its people, and is accordingly the most likely candidate among industrial nations to lead in the devising of modern legislation to protect the vulnerable, aid the temporarily unemployed, and care for the lame, the halt, and the blind. Instead of being a pioneer, however, the United States is usually among the last of modernizing nations to follow the lead of others in passing laws providing for worker safety and workmen's compensation, and instituting welfare programs for the poor such as health care, family allowances, and old-age pensions (table 8.1). Why should the country known internationally for its willingness of the heart be so unwilling to make available for its own disadvantaged citizens the benefits that other advanced industrial societies have provided for theirs?[38]

The answer is complex, but at least part of that answer would seem to be related to arguments developed previously. The more a people embrace the beliefs of chapter 2, particularly those that emphasize equality of opportunity, the more those people are inclined to view the individual as responsible for his own economic fate. According to such a view the poor are not regarded as being invariably responsible for their own poverty, but they are viewed as being, as the lawyers would have it, *prima facie* responsible: guilty of precipitating their own destitution through personal choices and personal shortcomings unless specific evidence can be marshaled to the contrary. Part of the natural tension between the desire to honor the worth and dignity of the individual on the one hand, and on the other to honor community needs and the priority of charitable treatment of the less fortunate is thereby mitigated. *If* economic need is the result of bad luck, the importance of lending a hand is generally conceded. But if the need is the result of perceived personal weaknesses of the needy, the hand is likely to be withheld. The more a society, its legislatures, and its courts presume that the latter is the case because equality of opportunity is presumed to be the rule, the less responsive all three will be to pleas for the state to help the least well off members of society. American tardiness in the passage of social legislation, by this interpretation, is not symptomatic of uncharitable instincts. Rather,

Equality and Freedom in the Economic Race

Table 8.1 Dates of initial passage of social welfare legislation for selected industrial countries[a]

Program legislated	Date of first comprehensive legislation					
	USA	UK	France	Germany	Sweden	Denmark
Accident insurance (workmen's compensation)	1908	1906	1898	1884	1916	1898
Health insurance	1965	1911	1930	1883	1891	1892
Pension insurance (old-age pension)	1935	1908	1905	1889	1913	1891/2
Unemployment insurance	1935	1911	1958	1927	1934	1907
Aid for dependent children	1935	1921	1904	1923	1917	1888
Family allowances	–[b]	1945	1932	1954	1947	1950

[a] Identifying the first act designed to address a particular problem, such as health insurance, sometimes involves difficult judgments concerning which of several acts directed to the same purpose is appropriately regarded as first. Where such decisions had to be made, the act chosen was the one that seemed to have the best claim to being the first effort to give comprehensive coverage.
[b] No act passed.

Sources: Peter Flora and Arnold J. Heidenheimer (eds), *The Development of Welfare States in Europe and America* (New Brunswick, NJ: Transaction Books, 1981), p. 59 (France), p. 129 (Sweden); Orla Jensen, *Social Welfare in Denmark* (Copenhagen: Det Danske Selskab, 1961), pp. 35, 39, 45, 82, 100 (Denmark); Peter A. Kohler and Hans F. Zacker, *The Evolution of Social Insurance 1881–1981* (New York: St. Martin's Press, 1982), pp. 26, 45, 50, 66, 121 (Germany), pp. 111, 114, 120, 122 (France), pp. 151, 153, 185, 189, 220 (UK); James Leiby, *A History of Social Welfare and Social Work in the United States* (New York: Columbia University Press, 1978), pp. 205, 232, 305 (USA); Ernst Marcussen, *Social Welfare in Denmark* (Copenhagen: Det Danske Selskab, 1980), p. 17 (Denmark); Gaston V. Rimlinger, *Welfare Policy and Industrialization in Europe, America, and Russia* (New York: Wiley, 1971), p. 216 (USA); Social Welfare Board, *Social Sweden* (Stockholm: Gernandts Boktryckeri, 1952), pp. 140, 141, 158, 168, 175, 213 (Sweden)

popular beliefs of Americans as that country modernized tended to minimize the urgency of devising state welfare schemes because of the associated confidence that the American economic system would give to most individuals the chance to avoid poverty through their own efforts in the marketplace.

However widely held such views were within this country in the early years of industrialization, one would expect the facts of the 1930s to constitute an unwelcome shock forcing reassessment. With over 20 percent of the population dependent upon federally sponsored job programs, with over 30 percent of the people receiving aid or social insurance at some point in the Great Depression, with one-third of the nation, according to its president, ill-fed, ill-housed, and ill-clad, the idea was hardly credible that all or even most were personally responsible for the economic hardships they were suffering. The more the focus shifted in explanations for why the poor were poor from individual responsibility to the capricious role of fortune, from the failings of the individual to the failings of the system, the more reasonable pleas became for the government to take countermeasures. "I assert," declared Franklin Roosevelt, "that modern society, acting through its Government, owes the definite obligation to prevent the starvation or the dire want of any of its fellow men and women who try to maintain themselves but cannot."[39] If they have tried and they have failed through no fault of their own, the reasoning runs, they are deserving of a hand. What is striking is how little the facts of the Depression and arguments like those of Roosevelt modified American beliefs concerning why poverty occurred and what the state should do about it. This puzzling phenomenon will be examined in more detail below. It becomes even more puzzling when one realizes that rational risk-aversion by itself should also have been prompting a more dramatic shift in attitudes than evidently took place.

Risk-aversion arguments in support of social welfare legislation emphasize the self-interest of all in acquiring insurance against the worst effects of economic misfortune: temporary unemployment or permanent disability, poverty at any age, or poverty in old age. The appeal of such insurance obviously depends upon some belief that those to be insured are not total masters of their own economic fate; that accidental circumstances rather than personal shortcomings can lead to poverty. Insuring against such a contingency therefore becomes a matter of rational self-interest. Again to quote Roosevelt:

The establishment of sound means toward a greater future economic security of the American people is dictated by a prudent consideration of the hazards involved in our national life. No one can guarantee this country against the dangers of future depressions, but we can reduce those dangers. We can eliminate many of the factors that cause economic depressions, and we can provide the means of mitigating their results.[40]

A different kind of risk-aversion argument could also be made in favor of some kind of safety net for the poor. All those who are well off have a vested interest in preventing poverty so grinding and widespread as to trigger upheavals that would prejudice the institutions and governing procedures vital for the preservation of democracy and the free-market system, not to mention the property and privileges of the wealthy. The argument is often advanced in concert with humanitarian pleas, often by the most civic-minded. A Catholic bishop, for example, pleading the case for the Full Employment Act in 1945, reminded Congress: "A nation that is ill-housed, ill-fed, and ill-clothed in any considerable part is a fertile ground for the curse of totalitarianism."[41] The drawbacks of that curse were much on the minds of Americans in 1945. In the same year, for the same act, a rabbi added his voice of support, noting with a special poignancy the ancient saying: "Where there is no bread there is no law."[42]

Again notice the linkage of this plea to notions of individual responsibility. If the arguments stressing the need for social stability are not to offend most

Americans, one accompanying premise must be that the needy whose unrest might disrupt the social fabric are in need chiefly through no fault of their own. This is readily apparent if one imagines trying to advance the opposite argument: that the poor are poor because they are profligate, lazy, and short-sighted, but nevertheless should be given state aid to keep their discontents from building to the point of imperiling the social stability of the nation. For Americans wedded to beliefs in individualism, equal opportunity, and merit earning its just reward, that line of reasoning, however compelling on pragmatic grounds, is sure to leave a stench in every nostril.

Notice finally that any argument challenging the notion of each individual's responsibility for his or her own economic fate, pushed to the extreme, would undermine all of the belief system advanced in chapter 2. Despite the searing experience of the Great Depression, despite the new directions evident in the New Deal, no such undermining took place – not in the 1930s, and not in the decades that followed, as the social legislation of the period made abundantly clear.

The 1930s were years of crisis for the American economic system, challenging accepted notions that the system functioned reasonably well, and even bringing into question venerable articles of faith on how it ought to function. The worst depression of the century raised in the starkest of terms the inconsistency between a belief system emphasizing individual responsibility and the facts of millions out of work through no fault of their own. Some government intervention in the market system seemed urgently required, if not to put the system right, at least to alleviate some of the suffering its defects were producing. Those defects were so pronounced and so long lasting, and the quandaries they raised for the belief system outlined in chapter 2 were so obvious, that one might reasonably expect the Great Depression to precipitate a wholesale re-examination by Americans of how an economy ought to function. That expectation, however, is not supported by the facts, or put more cautiously, by the terms included in, or omitted from, social legislation of the 1930s.

The first act of any consequence was not passed until the middle of the decade. Before then, federal programs for providing welfare relief or insurance protection that were comprehensive in coverage and national in scope were virtually nonexistent. State efforts under these same headings consisted, at best, of a few states offering a little to a small number of beneficiaries. (For example, only one state, Wisconsin, had an unemployment insurance law, and that was passed in 1932.) The federal government's Social Security Act of 1935, as its name implied, attempted to alleviate economic insecurity by providing (a) a federal system of old-age insurance, (b) a state system of unemployment insurance, and (c) specific welfare grants for selected categories of the poor. Radical as such provisions appeared at the time, on close inspection they were, in the main, little more than efforts to address new problems with old thinking, with the latter little changed in the process.

The problem of poverty in old age was not solved in the obvious way, namely, by providing a guaranteed minimum income for all citizens over a certain age. This smacked too much of the dole for most Americans, and outright relief for most remained a suspect category, unwelcome and unwanted despite the severity of the Depression. The federal program introduced was commonly regarded as a contributory insurance scheme[43] financed by private sector contributions through payroll taxes paid by employers and employees. The compulsory nature of the program was commonly justified because of perceived limitations of the market: private pension schemes could not successfully be devised to cope with a labor force on the move from job to job and region to region. The government's role, aside from making participation mandatory, was generally viewed as little more than that of a piggy-bank, retaining deposits and making payments. These payments were to go to workers after they retired, and were to reflect their previous contributions. The resulting pension scheme was thus not a dole available to all, but rather a contributory insurance program available to those who worked and paid in now to gain retirement benefits later. Only those who worked could participate, and those who contributed more were to receive more. (When the plan began in 1940, only 20 percent of workers qualified.) In short, the initial structure of the plan was eminently consistent with such old-fashioned beliefs as thrift and work had merit and should generate rewards, and further that those rewards should vary with the sacrifices and the contributions of the beneficiaries. Certainly nothing in this new pension scheme of the 1930s signaled a new belief that those who worked and earned had an obligation to give welfare relief to those less fortunate than themselves. (Notice how all these policies would become indefensible if market rewards were a function of luck alone, and all income inequalities – in the language of the left – were intrinsically "unlovely.")

The same was true of the unemployment insurance plan adopted. Here, too, financing was to be through private sector contributions – in this case, those of employers through a payroll tax. Here, too, benefits were to be paid only to those who had previously worked, and were again linked to previous earnings (commonly half-pay for sixteen weeks). No effort was made to assure that the resulting income flow for those out of work would guarantee a minimum subsistence (a priority often reflected in comparable European legislation). The controlling priority was to provide not welfare for those in need but short-term insurance for those temporarily without jobs.

The third main provision of the Social Security Act did address the needs of the truly needy, but defined that category in the narrowest of terms. Federal grants were to be made to states to reimburse them for part of the cost of aid to selected categories of the indigent: the aged, the blind, and children deprived of the support of a parent (the last of these being labeled Aid to Dependent Children (ADC)). What was not provided, and was not even acknowledged as a desirable target for future legislation, was a minimum income level for all who qualified as the least well off members of society. The two insurance schemes were designed for those who worked. The welfare supplements were directed to selected groups incapable of working. As for the poverty of the able-bodied, that problem was seen as caused primarily by a shortage of jobs. The preferred solution was to provide temporary jobs through federal programs: the Federal Emergency Relief Administration (FERA), the Civil Works Administration (CWA), the Civilian Conservation Corps (CCC). Welfare for the majority of the poor was regarded as a last resort and generally distrusted, especially if given to the able-bodied. "The lessons of history," declared Franklin Roosevelt in 1935, "show conclusively that continued dependence upon relief induces a spiritual and moral disintegration fundamentally destructive to the national fibre. To dole out relief in this way is to administer a narcotic, a subtle destroyer of the human spirit."[44] Accordingly, even the author of the New Deal was reluctant to offer welfare deals. "The Federal Government," he announced in the same speech, "must and shall quit this business of relief."[45] The public tended to agree. Opinion polls of the time indicated an overwhelming preference for work relief over outright welfare payments. As the decade progressed, those polls also evidenced a growing sense that the able-bodied could find work if they tried.[46]

Admittedly in the Depression decade new ideas were in the air, often revolutionary ideas that sought to undercut, modify, or supplant the premises outlined in chapter 2. But if the premises and values that remained dominant within America are to be gauged not by opinions voiced, but by policies proposed and by legislation enacted, the old beliefs concerning how an economy ought to function dating from the nineteenth century survived the trauma of the 1930s unchanged to a remarkable degree.

They remained relatively unchanged in the first two decades following World War II. Here, too, the terms of social legislation passed provide compelling evidence of continuity. From 1945 to the mid-1960s, the main terms of the original Social Security Act were amended in minor ways; for example, disability insurance was added in 1956, and ADC benefits were expanded to include a grant for the mother as well as for the children. On matters economic, optimism was the dominant mood, and poverty a topic seldom raised and rarely studied by those influencing national policy. Economic growth would alleviate poverty and reduce joblessness, ran a common article of faith. The able-bodied accordingly continued to be viewed, in the main, as masters of their own economic fate. Welfare continued to be regarded with a jaundiced eye, and thus pleas to institute a national minimum income for all were rarely heard and generally ignored whenever voiced. Work was available, work was desirable, and effort would tend to earn its just reward: these were beliefs that still colored American thinking about how their economy did function and ought to function.

This continuity was evident not only in the terms of legislation passed, but in the hearings and debates that preceded passage. The philosophy underlying the pension scheme of 1935 was still very much the philosophy controlling proposed amendments to the Social Security Act in the postwar era (although tempered now in minor ways by welfare considerations). In 1950, for example, Democratic Senator James E. Murray, one of the architects of earlier revisions, pointed out the need to preserve a system linking benefits to contributions: "Just as we must have a variable wage structure to encourage individuals to make their maximum contribution to national productivity, we must have a variable benefit structure in our social insurance programs."[47] Senator Herbert Lehmann agreed. It would, he claimed, be "un-American . . . to provide the same old-age benefit payment for the man who has contributed for 20 years and for the man who has contributed for 4 years."[48] More than a decade later, a White House Conference on Aging under President Kennedy expressed related sentiments with a similar appeal to traditional values: "so far as Government intervention is necessary to protect the increasing number of aged persons in our population, it is better than such intervention implement to the fullest extent possible the principle of a self-reliant contributory contract between the whole people and their Government . . . than the principle of needs-tested relief to dependent individuals."[49]

This image of untroubled continuity appears to shatter in the upheavals of the later 1960s. Antiwar demonstrations, campus protests, and ghetto riots are but a few of the symptoms singled out by those who sense a social revolution in this period. The record of social welfare legislation also seems at first glance to imply a sharp break with the past. Poverty, long neglected as a national priority, became a target of the first importance with Lyndon Johnson's announcement of a "War on Poverty" in 1964. In subsequent years spending on welfare programs shot up at unprecedented rates to reach unprecedented levels (table 8.2). Perhaps even more remarkable, when Democrat Johnson left the White House his Republican successor announced plans to grapple with a priority no administration had previously dared to broach: a national minimum income for all Americans.

As signs of revolutionary times, however, each of these three developments signify less than first impressions might suggest.

Social legislation introduced during the Johnson years was, in the main, an extension of conventional premises and values to long-standing problems now given a new importance. Old-age benefits were modified to provide Americans beyond a certain age with some minimum benefit, but the core philosophy of the program was still that of a contributory insurance scheme. The continuing belief in that philosophy was also much in evidence in the terms of a new health program for the aged, Medicare. Like the pension program of social security, this too was to be contributory, financed by a social security tax on wages. This too could be supplemented by private plans (in this case, private health care plans). Finally, and perhaps most crucially, Medicare was commonly portrayed as an insurance scheme for contributors, not as a welfare scheme for needy who were too old. "This is not a giveaway program," declared Congressman John H. Dent at the time of passage: "It is an insurance program, much of which is voluntary."[50] Others in the Congress were quick to make the same point:

. . . the majority of the Senate and the majority of the House of Representatives . . . have indicated they clearly favor the plan in this bill, which provides limited

Table 8.2 United States: selected welfare expenditure under public programs, 1966, 1975, and 1983[a] (billions of dollars)

	Current dollars				Constant dollars (1967 = 100)			
	Total expenditure			Change	Total expenditure			Change
	1966	1975	1983	1966–83	1966	1975	1983	1966–83
Social insurance (non-income-tested)								
1. Old-age insurance[b]	20.3	78.4	224.7	204.4	21.2	50.5	75.9	54.7
2. Medicare	–[d]	14.8	56.9	56.9	–	9.5	19.2	19.2
3. Unemployment insurance[c]	2.7	13.8	25.3	22.6	2.8	8.9	8.5	5.7
4. Total (items 1–3)	23.0	107.0	306.9	283.9	24.0	68.9	103.6	79.6
Benefits for persons with limited income								
5. Medicaid	1.7	13.5	36.3	34.6	1.8	8.7	12.3	10.5
6. Aid to Families with Dependent Children (AFDC)	2.3	9.3	15.4	13.1	2.4	6.0	5.2	2.8
7. Supplemental Security Income (SSI)	–	6.1	10.8	10.8	–	3.9	3.6	3.6
8. Food stamps	–	4.7	11.7	11.7	–	3.0	4.0	4.0
9. Housing benefits	0.3	3.2	9.1	8.8	0.3	2.1	3.1	2.8
10. Total (items 5–9)	4.3	36.8	83.3	79.0	4.5	23.7	28.2	23.7
Total of above (items 1–3 plus 5–9)	27.3	143.8	390.2	362.9	28.5	92.6	131.8	103.3

Constant dollar calculations made by deflating current expenditures by the consumer price index (CPI–U series) in US Department of Commerce, *Business Statistics 1984* (Washington, DC: US Government Printing Office, 1985), pp. 24, 169, using as deflator the annual average for 12 months ending with Federal Government's fiscal year end for years noted (see footnote a).

[a] Through 1976, the fiscal year ended June 30 for the Federal Government; beginning in 1977, its fiscal year ended September 30.

[b] Entered as "Old-age, survivors, disability, health."

[c] "Unemployment insurance and employment services."

[d] Benefit payments began July 1, 1966.

Sources: Social welfare expenditure data from US Department of Commerce, *Statistical Abstract of the United States: 1986* (Washington, DC: US Government Printing Office, 1986), pp. 355, 357; ibid, 1977, pp. 318, 319, 348; ibid., 1969, p. 275;

medical care for the aged, regardless of need, financed by social security taxes on wages, regardless of ability of wage earners to pay them.[51]

Poverty was attacked directly by new legislative programs, but the terms of the new acts were notable for their consistency with old American beliefs. Outright welfare for the able-bodied continued to be distrusted, and the work ethic continued to have a dominating influence in the design of antipoverty programs, as did the associated beliefs in self-reliance and individual responsibility. The War on Poverty focused upon providing "doors, not floors,"[52] giving to those at the bottom of the income distribution an opportunity to escape, not a dole that might encourage them to remain where they were. The Manpower Development and Training Act of 1962 foreshadowed many training programs to come, all with same objective: to give the able-bodied poor the skills they lacked which, once acquired, would enable them to get a job, become self-sufficient, and, it was hoped, compete for ever larger prizes in an economic race still regarded as it had been regarded for better than a century – a reasonably fair race, open to all (or almost all), that tended to reward such virtues as diligence, foresight, and thrift.[53] The "doors, not floors" theme was trumpeted repeatedly by those who led the War on Poverty, as illustrated by the following.

Lyndon Johnson: "We want to offer the forgotten fifth of our people opportunity, not doles."[54]

Sargent Shriver, director of the Office of Economic Opportunity: "I'm not at all interested in running a handout program . . . or a 'something for nothing' program."[55]

Willard Wirtz, Labor Secretary under Johnson: society owes "everyone the opportunity to work," but a guaranteed annual income for all Americans is the "wrong answer . . . . I don't believe that the world owes me a living and I don't believe it owes anybody else a living."[56]

The popularity of these themes with most Americans was evident in public opinion polls at the time, which indicated a persistence of other conventional beliefs, including a distrust of welfare, a desire to limit outright relief to those who were incapable of work, and a reluctance to give welfare to the able-bodied unless combined with some kind of work or training (*see* appendix A). A phrase gaining common currency – "the culture of poverty" – incorporated complex ideas about the forces causing poverty, ideas which, if pursued, could have undermined, or at least substantially modified, the notion that most able-bodied individuals were personally responsible for their own economic fate. More commonly, however, that phrase was used to reinforce unflattering stereotypes of the poor, and those stereotypes often portrayed the poor as being poor because of personal shortcomings.

The puzzle then becomes why social spending increased so dramatically in the years following Johnson's declaration of a War on Poverty. Why with American beliefs so little changed was their government now prepared to spend so much? Part of the answer becomes more apparent if total spending is disaggregated into several broad categories. Those in table 8.2 encompass roughly two-thirds of all welfare payments and better than 90 percent of all social insurance payments (as of 1983). What is striking is how much of what is labeled "Social welfare spending" went for insurance schemes not directed primarily at the poor. By one estimate, such programs in this period benefited roughly four times as many nonpoor as poor.[57] These same social insurance programs dominated in the rise of dollars spent. Consider, for example, the total increase in spending between 1966 and 1983, when dollars spent are corrected for inflation (or current dollars are converted to constant dollar terms). The rise in total spending on the three insurance programs noted (old age, unemployment, and health) was over three times the rise in spending on the five welfare programs listed. If instead the focus is shifted to the change between 1975 and 1983, the increase in annual spending on the nation's three most important insurance schemes was almost eight times that for the five major welfare schemes. The inescapable conclusion is that, following the opening salvos of the War on Poverty, as inflation worsened and economic growth slowed Americans were willing to protect and strengthen social insurance schemes whose benefits went primarily to the nonpoor, but were not equally willing to protect or augment welfare programs designed to aid the economically disadvantaged.[58] When dollar totals are corrected for inflation, expenditure on both Aid to Families with Dependent Children (AFDC) and Supplemental Security Income (SSI) actually declined between 1975 and 1983. The decline is even more dramatic in the average AFDC monthly payment per family, which in constant dollar terms fell by one-third between 1970 and 1983.[59]

The dollars spent on welfare programs after 1964, as novel as they were in American history, were relatively unimpressive by international norms. In the early 1960s, before the War on Poverty had begun, the United States ranked fifteenth out of eighteen industrial nations in percentage of total national product spent on welfare, surpassing only Australia, Greece, and Japan.[60] By the mid-1970s, a similar ranking indicated the United States had passed only one additional country (New Zealand) to rank fourteenth.[61] A question raised earlier is raised again: Why should Americans, known internationally for their generosity, be so ungenerous by international standards to the least advantaged members of their own society? Again, a significant part of the answer would seem to involve the persistent popularity of a set of premises that undercuts the urgency of responding to the poverty of the able-bodied, partly because of the economic opportunities those able-bodied are assumed to have, and partly because exploiting such opportunities is deemed desirable in a society that still places great emphasis upon the work ethic. More simply put, Americans have been less inclined to fashion state aid for the needy because they have believed that the able-bodied needy can and should do more for themselves.

The pervasiveness of such beliefs does not, however, seem to square with a federal initiative, launched by a Republican president, to provide all American families with a guaranteed minimum income. In the summer of 1969, Richard Nixon unveiled his Family Assistance Plan (FAP), a program designed to provide a family allowance that amounted to a guaranteed minimum income.[62] If the scheme itself was novel as a federal initiative, most of its terms reflected conventional thinking; in particular, the provision requiring the able-bodied to accept "suitable" training or work to qualify for subsidies, and the rigging of incentives to encourage those on relief to seek jobs and earn income in the private sector.[63] Efforts to pass the plan quickly bogged down in legislative haggling. Ultimately the proposal was abandoned, in part because of the resistance of special interest groups, in part because of the public's considerable indifference to the plan.[64] It is the latter that is especially noteworthy for purposes of this discussion. As one proponent of FAP conceded: "If it had been put to a referendum, the public would have murdered it."[65] A national minimum for all families was evidently not an idea whose time had come: not in 1969 when Richard Nixon initially proposed it, and not in the years following when advocates time and again fought to resurrect and pass some variant of the plan and just as frequently lost. The absence of public support was evident in pressure not felt in Congress and in public opinion polls of the 1970s. Americans were willing to grant a limited minimum income to selected categories of the needy who were clearly not able-bodied: to the aged and disabled by passing SSI in 1972, and to those who qualified for AFDC through amendments passed in 1979. What they would not grant in principle and would not endorse in practice was the right of the able-bodied poor to a guaranteed minimum income.

In sum, the record of social legislation of the 1960s and beyond does not appear to signal any major shift in American attitudes toward the poor. The War on Poverty emphasized doors not floors for the able-bodied poor – training to gain the skills to gain a better job, but not a "dole" to meet the economic needs of this particular category of the needy. Moreover, as previously noted, the achievement of all these training programs combined was modest in the extreme. As for the dramatic increase in dollars spent for social welfare programs after 1965, somewhat surprisingly this also is consistent with the continuing dominance of old attitudes. Most of that spending went for non-means-tested programs, and thus most of the dollars spent found their way into the pockets of the nonpoor. As for welfare programs specifically designed to help the least advantaged members of society, the rise in actual spending paled in comparison with increases for social insurance schemes. Most striking of all, when corrected for inflation, the annual spending for several of the major welfare programs actually declined when inflation worsened in the 1970s.

This is not a record of a people suddenly evidencing a new determination to do more for the poor. It is instead a record more notable for its consistency with past trends and previous attitudes. If the span of time is broadened to include changes in welfare programs and welfare priorities throughout the twentieth century, against the backdrop of this larger canvas the record is still notably devoid of watersheds or revolutions. Admittedly with the New Deal and especially with the legislation of 1935 came a new variant of an old idea. The obligation of "the community" to provide some kind of safety net to protect against economic disaster – an idea in evidence since colonial days – was now shifted to a significant degree from the local to the federal level. But what was provided in 1935 and the years beyond were primarily two kinds of safeguards: insurance schemes whose benefits were linked to contributions irrespective of the income level of the beneficiary, and specific welfare programs targeted at particular categories of the impoverished incapable of work. One novelty added to this list by the War on Poverty was the notion of remedial training programs for the poor who were able-bodied but unskilled. While the idea was new, the record of implementation was not indicative of a collective determination to make the ideal a reality for most of those in need.

Small wonder, then, that after scanning the history of America's welfare programs, James Patterson should conclude that the War on Poverty "eventually sputtered into a skirmish."[66] Small wonder also that this same historian should be struck by the continuity in the philosophical premises exercising a controlling influence on American approaches to problems of poverty since the beginning of the twentieth century.

Inhospitable opinions about the poor . . . were among the most durable features of America's experience with poverty and welfare since 1900. . . . In the . . . world of 1980, middle-class Americans continued to denigrate many of the poor and to hope that the need for welfare might soon wither away. On this level of popular opinion, the "social philosophy" of Americans had not changed much in eighty years.[67]

Americans' "social philosophy" about poverty is, however, a derivative philosophy. Why the poor are poor and how they should be treated is but one set of issues to be decided within the larger framework of economic justice, and that larger framework is composed mainly of beliefs concerning how the economy actually functions compared with how it ought to function. The premises outlined in chapter 2 – with their emphasis upon the work ethic, the availability of opportunities, and thus the individual's responsibility for success or failure in the marketplace – are easily meshed with a considerable indifference to the poor, or put more strongly, tend to encourage and legitimate such indifference. The argument would run (with minor qualifications) that participants in the economy by and large have the opportunity to succeed and should strive to succeed because of the associated benefits to the individual and to society; thus, those who fail miserably (with a few exceptions, such as the disabled) have no one to blame but themselves.

The argument was almost never put this bluntly. But the welfare programs put in place during the present century – the legislation passed, the agencies created, and the money spent – are in the main consistent with a reproachful attitude toward the able-bodied poor. That consistency, in turn, gives further credence to a central thesis of this book concerning the persistence of certain nineteenth century views on economic justice, with only minor modifications, down to the present day.

Conclusion

The points just made could be viewed as running a logical sequence backwards. The usual direction for inference to proceed is from principles to practice. To resolve questions of economic justice, for example, the starting point is usually a framework of general beliefs and values concerning (a) how the economy functions and (b) how it ought to function, from which can be inferred the appropriate treatment for the poor. These derivative notions on appropriate treatment can then be used to judge which policies should be implemented to help the poor. A critical problem for this chapter, and for the entire book, is to identify some of the main characteristics of the general framework that dominates American thinking about issues of economic justice at any point in time. The search for evidence has proceeded here by running the above inferential process in reverse. Observed actions – in this case, legislative acts passed and opinions expressed at the time of passage – are used to infer underlying premises: here, the controlling influence of premises that coalesce around the sort outlined in chapter 2. That inference is not deductive but inductive: the observed acts can be shown to be consistent with the premises; that consistency makes the hypothesis that these premises exerted a controlling influence more probable; and the more evidence that can be marshaled of this sort, the more probable the hypothesis becomes. But to demonstrate that a hypothesis is probable is not to prove that it is true. It is merely to demonstrate it is probable.

The general challenge, to review, has been to detect meanings commonly given to two words (freedom and equality) as those words applied to desirable properties of an economic race, and to check these meanings for consistency with premises widely shared in the nineteenth century about how an economy did function and ought to function. What emerged, rather unexpectedly, is the evident influence of premises not markedly different from those outlined in chapter 2. The movement in such fundamental notions seems more analogous to an ocean liner leaving port than a coastal schooner under sail. With a Titanic-like momentum for original direction, such premises have been remarkably unaffected by new findings and new fashions in the intellectual community, and by wide swings in the performance of the economy. Because discussion has been somewhat diffuse and has ranged well beyond points of central importance, a summary of those points would seem in order under headings that, by now, are only too predictable.

Freedom From

Much of government legislation passed to regulate the American economy has as its objective inhibiting coercive acts, and as such indicates how the idea of "freedom from" – here expanded in the conventional way to mean "freedom from coercion" – is linked to the idea of a fair economic race. As is always true with questions concerning "freedom from," the crucial issue is how coercion should be defined. In the framing and implementation of American laws aimed at inhibiting unfair behavior in the marketplace, one senses a certain lack of breadth and subtlety in the underlying definition of coercion. The main defect that these laws seek to remedy is not the existence of monopoly, but the misuse of monopoly power. Thus, high rates of return which might be considered symptomatic of monopoly profits are not, per se, grounds for litigation as they are, for example, in Britain. The issue in American law is always the behavior used to secure and maintain whatever monopoly power has been acquired. Reprehensible behavior punishable in the courts is generally concerned with inhibiting the workings of competitive forces by such practices as price discrimination, collusion to fix prices, predatory pricing to drive out competition, and boycotts or the use of collective power to impair normal market transactions. Perhaps the key word in all of the above is "normal." The list of reprehensible actions is relatively short, and the focus of the list is relatively narrow. The implication is that in the absence of coercive acts by monopolists aimed at inhibiting competition in product or factor markets in unfair ways, those markets function with tolerable fairness for most of the participants most of the time. The undertone is one of confidence: confidence in the market system that is deeply rooted and, when challenged by evidence of failure, is never deeply shaken. The controlling premise seems to be that the machine works wonderfully well, and when it sputters or churns in unexpected ways, a minimum amount of government tinkering will almost surely set it right.

Equality

That aspect of equality that tends to dominate American thoughts about fairness in the marketplace is equality of opportunity. Efforts to assure this kind of equality have mainly been of two types, both designed to get competitors to the starting line with the minimum skills needed for the race. One is broadly based and reasonably effective. Free public education gives to all children, irrespective of parental income, the opportunity to gain basic skills and aptitudes that are indispensable for would-be participants in a market economy. (The extent to which this same priority requires making free or low-cost education available beyond high school is still a subject of debate.) For those who, despite a public school education, are grievously deficient in basic skills, a second approach has been tried that is neither broadly based nor distinguished for its successes. Remedial training programs for the disadvantaged, both public and private, have failed collectively to make a major dent in a problem that is both widespread and growing.

Here, too, one senses American confidence; in this case, confidence that with a system of free public education, equality of opportunity will tend to prevail at the starting line. Beyond this assistance by the state, the premise seems to be, responsibility for preparation for the race lies with the family and the child. How else can one explain the widespread tolerance for so little effort to institute remedial programs, and for the limited success of programs tried?

Beyond the starting line, American efforts to assure equality of opportunity in the economic race are aimed mainly at inhibiting coercion of competitors, either through monopolistic practices or discrimination. The actions of monopolists that are declared illegal have been discussed in the previous section. The prevention of discrimination seems to be a priority that has risen in importance during the twentieth century, and expanded to cover more categories (from race to sex to age). But this expansion, like the development of antimonopoly laws, is generally regarded as a minor interference with a system that needs but little interference to assure intrinsic fairness for all who would compete.

Freedom To

American attitudes under this final heading can be inferred from attitudes evident under the previous two. In the context of an economic race, the freedom at stake is the freedom to compete, where "freedom" means "having the power or means" to compete. With minor exceptions, Americans generally believe that competitors tend to have that kind of freedom. The exceptions are those noted above: at the starting line, all would-be participants should be provided with a free public education to gain the minimum skills needed for the race; on the racecourse, the government should act to minimize coercion by monopolists and discriminatory practices by all. The confidence evident previously is evident again, and unsurprisingly so. If Americans believe that little is required to assure equality at the starting line beyond a free public school education, and if they believe further that undue coercion and discriminatory practices are not commonly encountered on the racecourse, they are likely to be confident that the vast majority of would-be competitors do have "the power or means to compete." To believe the first two assertions and not the third would make sense only if some skills were needed at the starting line beyond those provided by a public education, or some power was needed for survival on the course despite efforts of the state (presumed to be largely successful) to prevent coercion by monopolists and discrimination by all.

This, then, is the economic world in which so many Americans have believed and still believe: a world in which equality of opportunity tends to prevail, in which the marketplace is relatively free from coercion, in which competitors by and large have the power or means to compete and thus are free to compete. These views, in turn, are integrated with other time-honored beliefs concerning how the economy ought to function, all of which are qualified in minor ways but not in ways that undermine to any noticeable degree the granite-like structure anchoring most judgments about economic justice: that the economic race (in the main) is an admirable enterprise, fairly run (or tolerably so) and awarding prizes in a manner reasonably consistent with prevailing norms concerning what is just or fair.

The final point can be put in the form of an "if–then" statement. If the above hypothesis is correct – that the influence of premises much akin to those fashioned in the nineteenth century as outlined in chapter 2 has persisted, largely unchanged, down to the present day – then a number of puzzles become considerably less puzzling. These include:

1 why a nation known internationally for the generosity of its people was so slow to introduce social legislation in the twentieth century;
2 why America presently ranks near the top among western industrial nations in per capita expenditure on schooling, and near the bottom in per capita expenditure on social welfare programs;
3 why most Americans still maintain the old distinction between the "deserving " and the "undeserving" poor, with that distinction turning crucially upon the individual's ability to work;
4 why the American labor movement, unlike those in so many other industrial countries, is so hostile to steep inheritance taxes being imposed on the wealthy, and is unwilling to endorse income redistribution as a government policy of the first importance;
5 why a people so deeply committed to the idea of equality of opportunity have made so little effort to provide remedial training for those badly trained in their system of free public schools; and finally,
6 why, despite an Employment Act guaranteeing a "right" to seek and find employment for all those wanting to work, most Americans are still unwilling, when jobs are scarce, to have the government become the employer of last resort.

The last of these statements includes the word "right," a word that, like freedom and equality, is central to any discussion of economic justice. Like freedom and equality, it has also been the source of much confusion. Many of these confusions can, however, be easily resolved with the aid of themes developed in this and the previous two chapters.

9

On Rights

Introduction

Senator Robert Taft was puzzled. The 1945 debate over the Full Employment Act was becoming heated on the floor of the Senate, but the implications of the proposed legislation were far from clear. The version passed by the House had read in part:

All Americans able to work and seeking work have the right to useful, remunerative, regular and full-time employment, and it is the policy of the United States to assure the existence at all times of sufficient employment opportunities to enable all Americans who have finished their schooling and who do not have full-time housekeeping responsibilities freely to exercise this right . . . .[1]

This section of the bill had been amended by the Senate, the clause

All Americans able to work and seeking work have the *right* to useful, remunerative, regular, and full-time employment . . .

having been revised to read

All Americans able to work and desiring to work are *entitled to an opportunity* for useful, remunerative, regular, and full-time employment . . . .

The difficulty was that the word "right" still seemed to be lurking in the word "entitled." Did this mean, Senator Taft wanted to know, that the legislation "intended to confer a legal right on a man to get a job"?

Mr Taft: Does the Senator mean to say that a man who cannot get employment otherwise can go to the Federal Government and say, "Give me a job"?

Mr Wagner: No.

Mr Taft: It is not a legal right the Senator is proposing to confer?

Mr Wagner: No; it is not a legal right in the sense that he can sue.

Mr Taft: Then what is it exactly? What is the right a man has? Wherever the word "right," or the word "entitled," so far as that is concerned, is used in the Constitution or statutes, it confers a legal right. What kind of a right does this confer if it does not confer a legal right?[2]

Taft was not the only member of Congress puzzled by the wording and apprehensive about its implications. In hearings held by the House of

Representatives, witnesses repeatedly emphasized that a right implied a duty.[3] If the proposed act was guaranteeing the "right" to a job – or the "right" to an opportunity for employment – whose duty was it to assure that this right would be fulfilled? And if it was the Government's duty, which seemed to be the implication of the legislation as written, did this mean that the Government must become the employer of last resort of those who could not find employment in the private sector? That was not a happy prospect, at least not for Senator Taft and many others in the Congress equally unsure just what it was that they were being asked to authorize.

Few words are more likely to generate more confusion in discussions of economic justice than the word "right." Partly this is because the word is so heavily charged with normative implications. The basic cause of confusion, however, is that we use the word "right" in so many different senses. The best evidence of that is perhaps the many meanings and the many associated puzzles, largely unresolved, that are invariably encountered in even the briefest of philosophical reviews of how the word has been used and continues to be used.[4] Some of these complexities can be avoided because of the narrow focus of this work. As was true for those troublesome words "freedom" and "equality," our concern is only with possible meanings of "right" as the word is used in discussions of economic justice. The first order of business is therefore not to decide which duties the Government is implicitly accepting when it guarantees the right to the opportunity for employment. Rather, the issue is what the claim itself means. What *is* being asserted when the claim is made that all Americans have a "right," whatever may be the particular right at issue?

Rights Narrowly Defined

The point that many made in debating the Full Employment Act – that a right implies a duty – is also often made in philosophical discourse. In the somewhat arid language of that discipline, to say that "X has a right to $10 from Y" is equivalent (or so the argument runs) to saying "Y has a duty to pay X $10 if X so chooses."[5] A moral right (Y ought to pay up if requested) can be converted to a legal right if Y's refusal to pay when requested can lead to an actionable case in the courts. The difficulty with defining rights in this narrow way is that we often use the word "right" when no clear duty is implied. The right to make a will, for example, seems to imply no clear duty for anyone else beyond the maker of the will. Thus, although a "right" may imply a duty, either moral or legal or both, it need not always do so.

The preoccupation with individual rights is a comparatively modern phenomenon. During the past 300 years, particularly in the West, that topic has been catapulted into prominence in political and philosophical debates, but the linkage that dominated these debates, especially in the early years, was not between rights and duties, but rather between rights and freedom, where the freedom at issue was usually the absence of coercion. Between the Middle Ages and the Enlightenment, between the writing of *Summa Theologica* by Thomas Aquinas (1267–73) and *The Theory of Moral Sentiments* by Adam Smith (1759), within the western world, particularly the English-speaking parts of that world, a profound shift occurred in prevailing views about the appropriate role of the individual in society. Medieval philosophers tended to regard problems of political ethics as problems not so much of rights as of duties: the duty of the individual to his lord, to his king, to his church, and to his God. By the seventeenth century, however, in countries such as England under the influence of writers such as John Locke, a new emphasis was given to the rights of individuals. The task of philosophers and others concerned with such matters accordingly became one of identifying these rights, explaining their origins, and, above all, specifying how these rights could be crafted to protect the individual against coercive acts, especially arbitrary coercive acts by the State. Thus in the eighteenth century, Adam Smith would argue:

Among equals each individual is naturally, and antecedent to the institution of civil government, regarded as having a right both to defend himself from injuries, and to extract a certain degree of punishment for those which have been done to him.[6]

By the nineteenth century, Herbert Spencer would ask rhetorically, "What . . . do they [the people] want a government for?" and then supply the answer:

. . . simply to defend the natural rights of man – to protect person and property – to prevent the aggressions of the powerful upon the weak – in a word, to administer justice.[7]

This strand of reasoning has persisted to the present day. Reviewing American progress from the perspective of an ultraconservative, Ayn Rand reiterates with a special vigor the traditional conservative point that the main threat to individual rights is not other individuals but the government itself:

The Declaration of Independence laid down the principle that "to secure these rights [the unalienable rights listed in the Declaration], governments are instituted among men." This provided the only valid justification of a government and defined its only proper purpose: to protect man's rights by protecting him from physical violence. Thus the government's function was changed from the role of ruler to the role of servant. The government was set to protect man from criminals – and the Constitution was written to protect man from the government. The Bill of Rights was not directed against private citizens, but against the government – as an explicit declaration that individual rights supersede any public or social power.[8]

The above citations should not be taken to imply that these priorities and this line of reasoning appeal only to conservatives, past and present. Within America, that appeal has always been widespread. At the outset of the new republic, rights were deliberately designed to carve out areas of freedom for the individual. The freedom at issue was the absence of coercion, and the primary threat was commonly viewed as the possible abuses of power by the State. The great bulwark was the right to "Life, Liberty, and Property" (Locke's trinity), the third as noted previously regarded as indispensable for the other two.

In addition to these three, certain rights were written into law to guarantee that various individual activities could proceed free from interference, particularly interference by the State, such as the right to freedom of speech, to freedom of worship, and to assemble peacefully. Other rights were instituted partly or primarily to make the government more responsive to the will of the people and thus less inclined to abuse its powers. The right to vote, to petition the government, and to hold public office all give to those not in power avenues of correction should those in power begin to abuse their position of trust. The line of demarcation between these two types of rights is ultimately blurred. The right to vote and to hold office, for example, would count for less if not accompanied by the right to freedom of speech and freedom to assemble peacefully.

Given a first set of rights that carve out domains of freedom for the individual, a second set of rights must be devised to legitimate intrusion into those individual domains of freedom when special circumstances warrant. Consider, for example, David Hume's "three fundamental laws of nature, that of the stability of possession, of its transference by consent, and of the performance of promises."[9] All three are protected in America by legally enforceable rights. Note, however, that enforcement of the right of A to receive repayment of a loan (the performance of a promise) may require intruding on the rights of B through legal action forcing repayment, thereby compelling a property transfer from B to A. Rules for such intrusion would seem indispensable for the effective operation of any society and for the efficient operation of any market. Notice also that the burden of proof within America tends to rest with those who advocate intrusion. Any proposed rule or action that would impair the individual's domain of freedom by coercive interference is generally regarded as *prima facie* objectionable until a persuasive case can be made to the contrary.

Rights Broadly Defined

To review: in the rise to prominence of individual rights in the value systems of Americans – first as colonists and then as citizens of a new republic – the linkage of foremost importance was that between rights and freedom, where the latter tended to be narrowly construed as the absence of coercion. In the late nineteenth century and beyond, efforts were made to broaden the concept of freedom, from "freedom from" to "freedom to," and with those efforts came an expanded meaning for the word "right" when used to indicate a claim to these new freedoms. If freedom could now mean "having the power or means" to do X, then to claim a "right" to this kind of freedom was to assert a claim to whatever "power or means" was at issue. This kind of freedom, and these kinds of rights, are usually advocated *not* to protect the individual from coercion (the older linkage between freedom and rights) but rather to enable the individual to pursue self-development or self-realization. Sometimes this distinction is characterized as the difference between negative rights (the older priority) and positive rights (the newer priority).

In the twentieth century, positive rights have become a commonplace of both popular discourse and political rhetoric. A case in point is Franklin Roosevelt's message to Congress in 1944, which read in part:

In our day these economic truths have become accepted as self-evident. We have accepted, so to speak, a second Bill of Rights under which a new basis of security and prosperity can be established for all – regardless of station, race, or creed. Among these are:
The right to a useful and remunerative job in the industries or shops or farms or mines of the Nation;
The right to earn enough to provide adequate food and clothing and recreation;
The right of every farmer to raise and sell his products at a return which will give him and his family a decent living;
The right of every businessman, large and small, to trade in an atmosphere of freedom from unfair competition and domination by monopolies at home or abroad;
The right of every family to a decent home;
The right to adequate medical care and the opportunity to achieve and enjoy good health;
The right to adequate protection from the economic fears of old age, sickness, accident, and unemployment;
The right to a good education.[10]

Only one of these rights is related to the absence of coercion (the fourth in Roosevelt's list). The rest are aimed at self-development, either by providing the necessary minimum conditions for the pursuit of that development, or by providing an enabling environment in which that development can be pursued more effectively. Similar lists of similar rights have been fashioned by others who have tried to specify at least some of the requirements if modern society is to approximate the good society. Article 25 of the United Nations Universal Declaration of Human Rights reads in part:

Everyone has the right to a standard of living adequate for the health and well-being of himself and of his family, including food, clothing, housing and medical care and necessary social services, and the right to security in the event of unemployment, sickness, disability, widowhood, old age or other lack of livelihood in circumstances beyond his control.[11]

Pope John XXIII, in his encyclical "Peace on Earth," advocates many of the same economic rights, with a similar emphasis upon "a standard of living in keeping with human dignity."[12]

Advocacy of a minimum standard of living for all tends to take one of two forms. Either one can specify certain economic goods and services that are part of that minimum – for example, the minimum amount of food, clothing, shelter, and medical care that all citizens should have – or one can simply designate some dollar amount as the income floor below which no citizen should have to subsist (leaving to the individual the task of allocating those dollars across expenditure categories). Whichever form this advocacy takes, the justifications tend to emphasize that anything lower than the minimum is inconsistent with human dignity, and the related belief that only with such a minimum will individuals have the necessary economic "power or means" to pursue their own self-development.

Attempts to provide all citizens with a minimum standard of living can proceed through a system of transfer payments (such as a universal system of family allowances) or through efforts to assure that all able-bodied adults can find the work that will pay an income equal to, or greater than, the amount designated as the minimum income floor. Which brings us back to Senator Taft's puzzle raised at the beginning of this chapter. Whichever approach is designated as a "right" – the right to a minimum income or to a job that will allow that minimum to be earned – what is the government agreeing to when it announces that goals such as these are now "rights"?

The first point to note is that Americans in the modern era have given widespread support to the idea that all those desiring work have the right to the opportunity to acquire a job, and have given little support to the notion that all citizens, including the able-bodied poor, have a right to some minimum income. Thus America remains a notable exception to the general tendency of advanced industrial nations in the West to provide a system of family allowances for all citizens.

The second point is that Americans tend to justify the right to a job, or the right to the opportunity for a job, in terms of the freedom required for self-development and self-fulfillment. One supporter of the 1946 Full Employment Act spoke for many when he challenged those in Congress who argued that the function of the Government was to assure the freedom of the individual but not the right of that individual to work.

Let me ask you, how can the Government assure freedom without seeing to it that every individual has the opportunity to earn a living? If a man has no job, how can he enjoy freedom of political participation, freedom from fear, freedom of competition, freedom to health, education, recreation and security, freedom of social and economic democracy, freedom to make the most of himself? How can a man on the dole exercise that initiative and self-reliance which is declared to be a major objective of this committee bill? Without the right to work, a man is not free.[13]

The third point is perhaps the most important. The word "right" is often used in a general and somewhat vague way to advocate a moral priority or a canon which, the argument runs, *should* be used to evaluate and criticize social or economic or political arrangements. Thus, for example, the Preamble to the United Nations Universal Declaration of Human Rights notes that the list of rights about to be presented is merely "a common standard of achievement for all people." How these standards should be pursued – and what actions governments should take to facilitate that pursuit – is deliberately left up in the air. Rights in this sense are therefore targets to be aimed at, not duties that are legally enforceable.

This evidently was the sense in which the word "right" was being used by many Congressional supporters of the Full Employment Act of 1946. Republican Senator Wayne Morse was among those who tried to make this clear.

[This bill] says that it is the obligation of the Government to assure that everyone will have a chance to earn a living. It definitely does not say . . . that we will assure jobs for some and doles for others. It says in plain language, which I think the common people of this country can understand, that we will do whatever is necessary to assure full employment.[14]

Senator Taft evidently grasped the meaning and endorsed the priority.

When we talk about the right to work, we do not mean the absolute right. All we mean is that the Government ought to adopt a policy which will create a condition in which everyone who wants a job will find one somewhere.[15]

Which policies the government should adopt to assure this right therefore became the crucial issue, and one on which many were divided and not a few confused. Some argued for a minimum of intrusion by the government into the workings of the private market system. Accordingly, they favored the pursuit of full employment through policies that minimized government regulations and government interference in the market. At the opposite end of the political spectrum were those who favored an extremely active role for government, including the role of employer of last resort for those who could not find jobs in the private sector. Between the far right and far left was a large middle quite unsure what policies should be followed if the goal was full employment and the associated right was the opportunity for employment. Policy guidelines in the bill itself were of little help, couched as they were in the vaguest of terms, that vagueness being yet another symptom of Congressional uncertainty.[16]

Given that Keynesian thinking in the main had yet to penetrate the corridors of Congress, even those who intuitively favored countercyclical measures to combat unemployment when the economy faltered lacked the analytical framework to back up those intuitions.[17] In Congressional hearings on the bill, a Catholic priest reminded the senators of what should have been obvious to all: "We have devoted comparatively little thought to implementing this right."[18]

The right in question – "to the opportunity for employment" – at the time of passage of the Full Employment Act was therefore little more than a target to be aimed at using policies that remained largely undefined. In the decades that followed, those policies gradually took shape, particularly countercyclical Keynesian policies beginning in the Kennedy–Johnson years. But if the means to achieve the end were becoming more clear, the end itself remained little more than a target.

This is not always the case with rights that initially are advocated as a norm or canon to evaluate and criticize social, economic, or political arrangements. The right to a free public education, for example, which in most states of the young republic was simply a target, has now become a legally enforceable duty of the government that every parent and child can demand. The legal system can be marshaled to enforce many other rights that were unknown a century ago and are now taken for granted, such as the right of employees to bargain collectively and to strike. In recent years America has added to this list such diverse rights as the right of a homeless family to emergency shelter, the right of Medicare patients to challenge their discharge from a hospital if they think they are being sent home prematurely, and the right of nursing home patients to inspect their medical records and to receive advance notice before being transferred to another facility.

American conservatives, as one would expect, fear that rights initially accepted as targets will, over time, be converted into legally enforceable duties of the government. The more duties that the government has, the larger will its role become and thus the more power it will have and the more likely the government will be to intrude upon individual freedoms. In its extreme form, this concern about growing government duties and government powers emphasizes the likelihood of the modern welfare state's becoming a totalitarian state. Such apprehensions in muted form are evident in the chidings of George Will.

My friend and fellow columnist Joseph Sobran asks, "Why is it that every time somebody asserts a new right, all of us wind up less free than we were before?" He notes that many new "rights" are not protections against power but claims against the freedoms of fellow citizens.[19]

The apprehensions of Edmund Fuller are perhaps less muted because he is more fearful of the trend.

A threat lurks in a current confusion of "rights" with "entitlements," as to housing, jobs, and vacations. Rights in this sense are perfectly compatible with the most despotic of totalitarianisms. . . . The time could come when the social entitlements will be widely perceived as more important than the constitutional rights, which will mean that the essential institutional prerequisites of liberal democracy have eroded away.[20]

Many conservatives are not only fearful that such an erosion will take place, but incensed because behind the mechanism of erosion is a forced transfer of property that offends their moral sensibilities. "If you claim a 'right' to 'an income sufficient to live in dignity,' whether you are willing to work or not," writes Henry Hazlitt, "what you are really claiming is a right to part of somebody else's earned income. What you are asserting is that this other person has a duty to earn more than he needs or wants to live on, so that the surplus may be seized from him and turned over to you to live on. This is an absolutely immoral proposition."[21] The further to the right the conservative, the more likely he or she is to consider property rights inviolable – a view that adds to Hazlitt's general condemnation a particular focus for moral indignation.

What conservatives deplore, liberals not infrequently embrace, and the tendency of rights as targets to become duties of the government provides a case in point. Those on the left tend to reject as exaggerated or unjustified conservative fears concerning threats to freedom, particularly the fear that the welfare state will degenerate into the totalitarian state. More entitlements are generally preferred to less by the left, particularly economic entitlements, and accordingly most liberals have a list of rights they advocate, sometimes as targets only, sometimes with the hope that these targets will quickly become legally enforceable duties of the government. The language used to press the claim to legitimacy of such rights is often couched in terms that resonate with older norms and older legislative landmarks. Thus the right to a minimum income is commended as "an absolute constitutional right,"[22] the right to health, education, and work are advanced as part of "An Economic Bill of Rights,"[23] or the rights established by the Full Employment Act of 1946, modest as they were, are deliberately magnified by labeling that act "the nation's economic Magna Carta."[24] One variant of this strategy is to link the right being advocated to the unalienable rights expounded by the Declaration of Indepedence. David Spitz illustrates the technique in one of its more compelling forms.

Given this equal right to life, it follows that all men are equally entitled to whatever is necessary to sustain and protect life. At a minimum, this means that no man can legitimately be denied adequate food, clothing, housing, medical care, etc.[25]

Reduced to a syllogism, this argument seems to read:

1 all men have an unalienable right to life,
2 a necessary condition for life is the minimum income needed to sustain life, and thus,
3 all men have an unalienable right to a minimum income.

Americans generally accept the first, and few of any intelligence would challenge the second. The third, however, has consistently been rejected throughout the twentieth century. "The American system," most Americans argue, "owes no man a living." What it does owe, they concede, is what the Full Employment Act of 1946 was attempting to guarantee: the right to the opportunity for employment. This employment, in turn, is their answer to the third part of the Spitz syllogism: if a minimum income is needed to sustain life, let that income be earned through employment, at least by all those capable of employment.

Such ideas are recurring themes in the hearings and debates that preceded passage of the Full Employment Act. Other recurring themes that touched upon related ideas included the following.

1   Employment and the income thereby acquired are vital for assuring all three unalienable rights, not just one: for life, liberty, and the pursuit of happiness, not just for the first of these cherished priorities of the republic.
2   The market system, for all its faults, works tolerably well in providing employment for those who wish to work.
3   Thus the role of the government in attempting to assure employment opportunities should be that of fostering possibilities in the private sector, not that of employer of last resort (or worse, of first resort).

If the government has a duty to try to assure able-bodied citizens that jobs will be available, the legislators argued, those citizens also have a duty to become and remain self-reliant, in part by getting the training needed for work, seeking out work, and performing satisfactorily in the place of work. Values mattered, argued Democratic Senator George Radcliffe – values that must not be undermined by any misinterpretation of an act that guaranteed the "right" to an opportunity for employment.

I certainly would not want to see anything said or done which would lessen the initiative of a young man to feel that he has to earn what he is going to get, and not that it is going to be handed to him. . . . I am just hoping that no one will give the impression that it [the Full Employment Act] is going to lessen the need of the individual to try to fit himself for work and to see to it that he continues to be qualified to do the work, and that he continues to be resourceful and active in trying to find it, that he continues to find it essential to make a good impression as he works, and that both by this temperament and by his work, and in all other ways, he continues to show a qualification for it.[26]

Contemporary liberals might protest that all these views – the faith in the market system and the distrust of government intervention, the emphasis upon the work ethic and the individual's responsibility for his own economic fate – smack of nineteenth century beliefs little modified by twentieth century insights into how forces beyond the individual's control can shape the possibilities which in turn heavily influence what the individual can earn. To voice that complaint, however, is merely to reiterate, albeit unintentionally, a central thesis of this book: that key premises in American beliefs concerning economic justice continue to coalesce around a small set of premises fashioned in an earlier era – premises that down to the present day have remained remarkably unscathed by evolving knowledge in psychology, genetics, and economics, to mention only three disciplines whose findings have some bearing upon issues of economic justice. How older views might be modified by modern insights is a topic of chapter 11. Before that perplexing task is attempted, however, several stands of intellectual brushwood should be cleared away, or at least thinned out to some degree.

10

Four Questions of Fact

Introduction and Summary

What is a fair income distribution? That question has been somewhat lost in the last four chapters, preoccupied as they were with defining terms and identifying attitudes toward those terms. The terms examined – freedom, equality, and rights – are central to most debates concerning economic justice. Until such terms are carefully defined, or at least until the range of meaning of each term has been explored, we cannot hope to understand the various answers given to the central question of this book. Or as the philosophers remind us in their implacable way, we cannot begin to understand what we are talking about unless we take some pains to clarify the meaning of words that will be central to our discussion.

Also central to discussions about economic justice are certain questions of fact about which competing ideological camps make competing claims. Most of these – or most of the more important ones – can be grouped under four broad headings. Phrased as questions and put in their most simple form, these are:

1   Does pursuit of the welfare state lead to totalitarianism?
2   Is the free-market system vital for the achievement of economic growth?
3   Would tax levies needed to finance expanded welfare programs seriously impair industriousness and thrift?
4   Do existing American welfare programs increase the dependency of the poor and disrupt family structure?

This opening section has two objectives. The first is to show how these questions are connected, and why the four as a set lie at the heart of so many of the debates between the American left and right. The second is to give some sense of the indeterminacy that inevitably accompanies the answers to every one of these questions.

To demonstrate that indeterminacy is endemic to answers will not be easy. In the popular literature, answers not infrequently ring with certainty: William F. Buckley, Jr, is convinced that American society "is marching toward totalitarianism";[1] the Lay Commission on Catholic Social Teaching and the US Economy declares that the causes of economic growth "are not only knowable but known";[2] Senator Daniel Patrick Moynihan is certain that government welfare programs do not have a catastrophic effect on the behavior of the poor, while Charles Murray is just as certain of the opposite.[3]

Examples could be multiplied of conflicting claims made by competing camps, suggesting that at least one side has its facts wrong. Another possibility is that both sides are claiming as established fact what is not established fact at all. Which brings us to the central message of this chapter. Given the present limitations of our knowledge, certain kinds of factual questions about human behavior and human society cannot be answered in any definitive way. But why, the reader may be asking, is such a message central to discussions of economic justice.

Recall the point noted at the beginning of this book: that economic justice is commonly assumed to be an easy subject, and it is not. Recall further that to make choices in concrete situations designed to make any economic system more just – or less unjust – requires forecasting the effects of different possible choices and comparing the results. Because much of our knowledge of human behavior is lacking in precision, many of these forecasts are necessarily shrouded in uncertainty. And that uncertainty, in turn, is one reason why deciding what is just is difficult, and one reason why economic justice is a complex topic.

The main exposition problem for the present chapter is this. While the list of questions to be examined is short, explaining why uncertainty invariably accompanies the answer to each one requires a careful sifting through relevant evidence, which some readers may find wearing if not downright tiresome. And yet without that sifting, the claim about endemic uncertainty will remain unsubstantiated. The obvious compromise is to summarize first and sift second, leaving to the reader the choice between a brief overview of problems concerning methods and evidence, or a more detailed accounting of what has been claimed by whom, the evidence for those claims, and the tentative nature of that evidence.

Does Pursuit of the Welfare State Lead to Totalitarianism?

This question – not always framed in such a simple way – captures a major concern of conservatives in the postwar era. At bottom, their fear is that ever increasing government power will erode individual liberties. That erosion, by this view, is likely to be cumulative. The central mechanisms precipitating such a process are believed to be (a) the tendency of power to corrupt the behavior of those who have it, including fostering a desire for more power, (b) the tendency of the public, through ignorance and indifference, not to resist in satisfactory ways these increasing demands for power on the part of state officials, and (c) the cumulative interaction between insatiable demands and ineffective resistance that sooner or later will produce some variant of the totalitarian state. In the period between the two World Wars, this fear was usually focused on the rising popularity of socialism in Europe. Socialism meant central planning, central planning meant more power in the hands of state officials, and this increased power could well have disastrous implications for individual liberties, or so the argument ran. As the popularity of socialism in recent years has waned in Western Europe, the preoccupation of many conservatives has shifted from the threats of socialism to the threats accompanying the rising popularity of the welfare state. With that increased popularity will come a rise in government power and government intervention in the economy, runs the argument, and this power and that intervention is likely to culminate in a catastrophic loss of individual freedoms, at bottom because of mechanisms of the sort outlined above. That the welfare state will lead to the totalitarian state is variously portrayed as somewhat likely, highly likely, or almost certain. Should such forecasts become widely accepted in America – particularly those forecasts in which the probability is portrayed as close to one – popular support for welfare programs would be largely undermined, if not totally shattered. Few would be willing to endorse new or expanded programs for the disadvantaged if the likely cost of implementing such programs would ultimately be a catastrophic loss in individual liberties for all. The question of whether the related risks are high or low is therefore far from trivial.

The little evidence there is makes the estimation of relevant probabilities a highly subjective enterprise. What can be said with certainty is that present evidence does not support the claim that socialist programs, or welfare programs, whenever implemented *inexorably* lead to a totalitarian form of government. Both kinds of policies have been pursued by many countries in Western Europe without that calamitous result, at least to date. Such a pursuit evidently can also be reversed. In recent years, as the drawbacks of socialism have become more clear, the electorates of many Western European countries have supported a move away from state ownership of various means of production. Less state ownership and more private market activity may also be the end result of current upheavals in the Soviet Union and Communist China, although whether a major reversal is in the wind in either country is, for the moment, impossible to say. Closer to home, the progressive intrusion of government into the American economy has been a hallmark of the twentieth century. In 1900, for example, government budgets (federal, state, and local) took less than a tenth of gross national product; today they take more than a third. Further, a large part of this rise can be attributed to increasing state expenditures for welfare programs. Such programs are not, however, commonly viewed as bringing in their wake a disastrous loss of personal freedom, either as a condition of the present or as a likely prospect for the future. In short, nothing in the record of increased government incursions into the economy in pursuit of socialist objectives or welfare objectives – and nothing in popular perceptions of that record – suggest that either of these pursuits, once begun, does lead with any certainty, or even with a high probability, to a form of government deserving to be labeled totalitarian.

This is not to say that such a result is necessarily ruled out in the future. Nor is the argument that losses in individual liberties are necessarily trivial as welfare policies of the state expand. Rather, the argument is that those who claim such losses are likely to be catastrophic, and estimate that likelihood to be very high or close to one, have no hard evidence to justify such estimates. They have instead a deep concern for freedom, a deep distrust of government, and apprehensions about mechanisms that may be set in motion by expansion of welfare policies. The intensity of that concern and distrust, in turn, may help to explain why their apprehensions are sometimes cloaked in the unwarranted guise of confident forecasts.

Three Questions and a Catholic Debate

In the autumn of 1984, a group of bishops representing the more liberal wing of the Catholic hierarchy published the first draft of a pastoral letter on "Catholic social teaching and the U.S. economy."[4] Even before the draft appeared in print it was challenged by a short treatise written and published by 29 prominent Catholic conservatives, including William Simon, Michael Novak, and Clare Boothe Luce.[5] At the heart of the controversy between liberal bishops and conservative laity was how to help the poor. And at the core of this disagreement over means were three questions of fact. This was not surprising. The same three questions tend to surface in any extended debate about the plight of the disadvantaged in America, and whether welfare programs should be regarded in the first instance as part of the solution or part of the problem.

Conservatives in recent decades have mounted two distinct attacks against expansion of what they term "the welfare state." The first, as noted previously, focuses upon the threats to individual freedom presumed to accompany any concerted effort to implement welfare programs by the state. The second attack emphasizes those ways in which welfare programs may hurt the very people they are designed to help. The argument, roughly summarized, is (a) that the single best way to help the poor is to foster economic growth ("a rising tide lifts all boats" being one popular metaphor in this context), (b) the free-market system is vital for the achievement of economic growth, and (c) that system will be undermined by extensive welfare programs, in part because tax hikes needed to pay for greater welfare benefits will undermine industriousness and thrift. At this point the imagery of the argument often shifts from rising tides to shrinking pies, the crucial claim being that increased welfare benefits will end up giving the poor a larger slice of a smaller pie, with that portion going to the disadvantaged probably declining in absolute size. Not only will the poor end up with less total income, conservatives generally conclude this argument, but the very receipt of welfare – at least as that receipt is structured in America – will undermine the character of the poor and disrupt the structure of their families. This three-part argument – that welfare policies tend to (a) inhibit growth, (b) reduce the incomes of the poor, and (c) undermine both character and family stability among recipients – depends for its validity on the answers to three factual questions. These are accordingly the topics that lie ahead. In each case the important issue is the extent to which the question being asked admits to a decisive answer.

Is the Free Market Vital for the Achievement of Economic Growth?

Part of this question is clear, but part is not, and that lack of clarity should be underscored at the outset. Economic growth is generally defined by economists as a sustained rise in real per capita income. This is admittedly a summary statistic for a complex process, but it has the virtue of a measure that is both simple and operational. The difficulty is with the phrase "the free-market system."

At their most extreme, conservatives are prone to argue that the choice of an economic system reduces to *either* "the free-market system" (alternatively called "capitalism" or "the free-enterprise system") *or* some variant of a centrally planned system, "socialism" being the most obvious contender. In many countries, however, the two kinds of systems are mixed to varying degrees. Government policy can include state ownership of a few means of production or many, with private competitive markets determining production and distribution of many goods and services or a few. The choice at issue, therefore, is not between one of two mutually exclusive entities (a "socialist" or a "market" system), but between having a little more of one and little less of the other. Even if the preference is for exclusive reliance upon private markets, the choice of "system" includes a vast array of possibilities. "The free-market system" is a tidy phrase for a sprawling reality, namely, all the different possible combinations of laws and customs, institutions and practices that have prevailed at different times and different places as a system guiding and constraining economic activity. The choice of a "market system" is thus not unlike the choice of a "legal system": just what is being chosen is not clear until more details are given.

The first problem, then, is to define what "the free-market system" means. The second is to explain why such a system – however defined – is "vital" for the achievement of economic growth. Two observations complicate the search for a decisive answer. The first is that economic growth has been achieved in such nonmarket countries as the Soviet Union and Communist China. The use of a market system is therefore clearly not a necessary condition for economic growth. (If it were, presumably those countries would not have experienced any growth.) This complicates evaluation. The question now becomes: *How much more* growth would have been produced by a free-market system in country A (which lacked that system), or alternatively *how much less* growth would have been recorded in the absence of a market system in country B (which does have some variant of that system)? To answer a question beginning "How much more . . ." or "How much less . . ." in economics generally requires a model. The purpose of a model of economic growth, for example, would be (a) to incorporate in a formal way the major cause-and-effect mechanisms producing growth, and (b) to show how much of total growth can be attributed to each cause included in the model. Which brings us to the second observation complicating the search for certainty.

Growth models of economics commonly do not include any of the laws and customs and institutions that comprise "the free-market system." If they are not included, the model cannot tell us how important they are for achieving economic growth.[6] Economists might reply that such models are still useful for analyzing changes in growth in situations where the market system is relatively constant over time. But even in these more simple cases, the record of growth models does not inspire confidence in their ability to identify in any decisive way the *relative* importance of the different factors contributing to increases and decreases in the rate of growth. The best evidence for that assertion is the wide disagreement that persists among economists concerning how much different causal factors actually have contributed to recorded growth in different situations. Consider, for example, one of the most pressing of recent American growth problems – the dramatic slowdown in the rate of growth in labor productivity beginning in the 1970s. The most obvious of suspected causes is the slowdown in capital formation. And yet economists' estimates of the contribution of the second (reduced capital formation) to the observed reduction in the first (growth in labor productivity) range from zero to 50 percent. This does not suggest a social science with a solid understanding of the reality it would explain. Economists themselves on occasion have underscored that point. At a recent meeting of the American Economics Association, for example, Henry Aaron noted in the prestigious Richard T. Ely Lecture:

We economists . . . are not sure we have identified all the causes, and we can't agree on what actions would spur labor productivity at reasonable cost. We do not know whether the high growth of the [postwar] quarter century was an aberration or established a new norm. We do not know whether the inferior recent performance of the United States is caused by transitory events that will naturally correct or by deep and recalcitrant problems.[7]

In sum: discussions of the contribution of the free-market system to economic growth are fraught with uncertainty for two quite different reasons. One is that the cause in question – "the market system" – often lacks clarity of definition because that phrase covers such diverse possible realities. The second is our limited understanding of what produces economic growth. Even in those situations in which the various elements of the market system remain substantially unchanged, economists evidence wide disagreement concerning the contribution made to growth by other causal factors more easily incorporated into growth models.

Would Tax Levies needed to Finance Expanded Welfare Programs Seriously Impair Industriousness and Thrift?

This question logically divides into three subquestions:

1   How much money would the new welfare programs require?
2   What kinds of taxes would be used to raise that money, and by how much would each tax be increased?
3   Would this magnitude of increase in these kinds of taxes seriously undermine the willingness to work and to save?

Most of the relevant research – and most of the numerical debates – have been focused on question (3). The major findings of that research, again roughly summarized, are as follows.

1   No clear relationship of any pronounced magnitude has been established between changes in after-tax income and changes in the American labor supply. More simply put, variations in taxes paid do not seem to cause any marked changes in the aggregate willingness to work in this country.

2   American savings rates are, by international standards, exceptionally low, but why they are low is another unresolved dispute among economists. Here, too, lurking in the wings are various models assigning markedly different importance to different factors suspected of causing variations in the savings rate of individuals. Among the unresolved issues in this larger debate is the importance of the particular causal mechanism at issue here. We simply do not know whether a reduction in after-tax returns on money saved will raise or lower the willingness to save, as well as whether the change thereby precipitated in savings will be large or small.

The implication of this uncertainty for welfare debates is clear enough. Those who claim that the higher taxes needed to finance more welfare will "seriously" undermine these particular causes of economic growth have an obligation to provide what the experts acknowledge they have yet to find: unambiguous evidence that higher taxes lower savings and work effort by significant amounts.

Do Existing Welfare Programs Increase the Dependency of the Poor and Disrupt Family Structure?

This question might be compressed to read: Do welfare programs end up hurting the very people they are supposed to help? One source of puzzlement is a disturbing trend. Despite the expansion in welfare programs and welfare spending after President Johnson's War on Poverty was initiated in the mid-1960s, the percentage of poor in America failed to decline substantially in the later Johnson years and throughout the 1970s, before showing signs of drifting upward in the 1980s. The upward drift critics of the Reagan Administration are quick to attribute to Reagan policies. But even *before* 1980, the War on Poverty as conducted by earlier presidents failed to make a substantial dent in the percentage of Americans who were poor. The obvious puzzle is whether this limited success reflects fundamental flaws in welfare programs.

Many Americans, particularly those on the right, have argued that receipt of welfare increases the chances of recipients remaining poor, in part by undermining their sense of independence and self-sufficiency, and thus undermining their willingness to train for a job, seek a job, and hold a job, and in part by encouraging behavior that leads to the break-up of established two-parent families and lower rates of marriage, thereby fostering the rise of single-parent families more prone to poverty. Each criticism amounts to a claim about established facts, with welfare the cause and altered behavior the effect. The challenge – not easily met – is to discover evidence and tests that will support or refute such claims in a convincing manner.

Defenders of existing welfare programs are quick to emphasize what the evidence makes abundantly clear: that the majority of those who receive welfare in America are poor for only a brief period (usually two years or less), and consequently receive welfare assistance for only a brief period. The obvious implication is that welfare is not like heroin; the slightest use does *not* invariably create dependency. Critics respond by noting that for a subset of welfare recipients, the record is markedly different. Roughly one-sixth of those who are poor remain poor for eight years or more, and for many of these, receiving welfare has become a way of life. Nor are these long-term welfare users randomly distributed throughout the population. They tend instead to be heavily concentrated among those with some or all of the following characteristics: (a) young, nonwhite, and an unwed mother, (b) a high school dropout, and (c) did not have any work experience before receiving welfare payments through Aid to Families with Dependent Children (AFDC). Thus, for example, mothers receiving AFDC who are under 30, nonwhite, unmarried, and high school dropouts receive welfare on the average for a decade. Such evidence points up the relationship between being a single parent and being poor. But is the receipt of welfare the cause of both?

Much of available evidence helps to rule out simple, direct cause-and-effect relationships. There is no evidence, for example, that as welfare benefits rise and fall so too do the number of births out of wedlock. Nor is there any simple relationship in recent decades between rising welfare payments and the observed drop in labor force participation among young black males, ages 16–24, for the most obvious of reasons: such males commonly qualify for very little welfare. This does not, however, rule out the possibility of complex and indirect relationships between welfare expansion and altered behavior.

The waters begin to get muddied when one consults the experts about important questions that are easy to pose but impossible to answer in any decisive way, or so the experts say. These include the following.

1   For welfare recipients already working, will higher welfare benefits cause hours worked to fall by a little or a lot?
2   Do higher welfare benefits encourage two-parent families to break up and other potential two-parent families not to form?
3   Are children of long-term welfare users more likely to depend upon welfare after they themselves reach maturity and establish their own households?

The reasons why available evidence has failed to yield decisive answers to these and other similar questions are not easily summarized, buried as they are in a welter of disputes about imperfect data, mis-specified models, and ambiguity in test results (particularly the results of the Negative Income Tax Experiments conducted between 1968 and 1978). The bottom line of these highly technical debates is nevertheless easily stated: in no case for the questions noted are the charges linking welfare to destructive behavior proved, or more cautiously, proved beyond a reasonable doubt as the best of the experts characterize their doubts.

Critics of welfare, as one might expect, are reluctant to accept the indecisiveness of such conclusions. Those given to guarded statements emphasize that the main charges linking welfare to increased dependency and disrupted family structure have not been proved *or disproved*. Those less cautious, such as Charles Murray and George Gilder, reject the doubts and trumpet the negative results of welfare as established fact.

The arguments of Charles Murray illustrate the tenor of such claims and the flaws in their presumption to decisiveness. The general approach is to link welfare programs to changed behavior in a hypothesis that has many complex and circuitous cause-and-effect mechanisms, often by processes and with time-lags that are ill-defined. Charles Murray, for example, has a complex "threshold" model. Below the threshold, not much happened; above the threshold, many undesirable things happened. This threshold was crossed, argues Murray, in the 1960s. The major changes precipitating the crossover were (a) the existence of more generous welfare benefits, (b) a change in attitude toward the receipt of welfare encouraged by welfare workers, (c) a rising sense among the poor they were largely not responsible for their own poverty and had little control of their own economic destiny (again, a shift in attitude encouraged by distributors of welfare), (d) a reduction in popular disapproval of births out of wedlock, encouraged by "educational reformers" who advocated less punitive treatment of unwed pregnant girls in schools, and finally (e) another attitudinal shift within urban ghettos placing less stigma and more respectability on male reliance for income upon criminal activity and/or females receiving welfare support. The results of this constellation of factors, the argument continues, included the undermining of male authority within established families, a declining sense of responsibility of males toward their family and their offspring and the need to become economically self-sufficient, and an increasing unwillingness on the part of females to regard such males as desirable husbands, with an associated increase in the willingness of females to have children out of wedlock and retain those children in a single-parent family dependent upon welfare. The resulting diffusion of attitudinal shifts is best described by Murray.

To simplify a rich argument: The existence of an extensive welfare system permits the woman to put less pressure on the man to behave responsibly, which facilitates irresponsible behavior on his part, which in turn leads the woman to put less reliance on the man, which exacerbates his sense of superfluity and his search for alternative definitions of manliness. When welfare recipients are concentrated, as they are in the inner city, these dynamics create problems that extend far beyond the recipients of welfare. Community values and expectations of male behavior are changed, and with them the behavior of young men and women who never touch an AFDC check.[8]

The argument, as its author notes, is "rich" in the sense of hypothesizing a multitude of causal processes, beginning with changes in welfare (but not these alone) and ending with altered behavior, particularly among those who are young, nonwhite, and living in urban ghettos. The difficulty is that such a complex hypothesis, precisely because of its complexity, is impossible to test in any decisive way. If it cannot be tested decisively, it hardly warrants being advanced with the sort of conviction typically found in Murray's writings.

We have therefore reached an impasse. Defenders of welfare note that the evidence does not support a simple cause-and-effect relationship between more welfare and less willingness to work or more family break-ups or more births out of wedlock. Critics of welfare are inclined to reply that much of this evidence is beside the point because the relevant causal mechanisms are neither simple nor direct. But lacking any convincing method to demonstrate the correctness of their own views about the destructive effects of welfare on individual behavior, these same critics are in much the same position as the defenders of welfare, namely, case not proved.

And yet the human tendency is to crave certainty – to find *the* explanation for the puzzle – and by such norms there is something deeply dissatisfying about previous analysis: not just the uncertainty that pervades the summing up of findings for the fourth question examined above, but the agnostic tone that suffuses all the summary judgments about the other three. Why should conclusions, confidently stated and generally accepted, be so scarce throughout the literature that examines questions such as these? The answer is not difficult to find, although it is frequently ignored by even the most thoughtful writers on the topics of this chapter.

The Missing Overview

Each of the four questions noted at the outset of this chapter has been stated incorrectly. As originally posed, they read:

1 Does pursuit of the welfare state lead to totalitarianism?
2 Is the free-market system vital for the achievement of economic growth?
3 Would tax levies needed to finance expanded welfare programs seriously impair industriousness and thrift?
4 Do existing American welfare programs increase the dependency of the poor and disrupt family structure?

The first question illustrates the general problem. As presently worded it is far too vague. The facts of the case concern causes, the causes are particular policies (and not a vague entity labeled "the welfare state"), and one cannot systematically investigate the facts until the terms of the policies are made clear under such headings as old-age insurance, health insurance, family allowances, and so on. The effect of ultimate concern is "totalitarianism," but that is also much too vague. What must be specified in detail is how particular government actions (passage of particular kinds of welfare legislation) will undermine certain freedoms, and how this undermining makes more probable subsequent changes that would ultimately culminate in the totalitarian state. The first question should therefore be revised to read something like:

1A What is the increase in the probability of a totalitarian state in the future if this welfare legislation (now specified in detail) is enacted by the government?

The second question suffers from a similar vagueness. The effect is clear enough. Or put more cautiously, "economic growth" can be gauged by the measure fashionable with economists: changes in real per capita income or (the output side) changes in gross national product per capita. The problem is the cause. "The free-market system," as noted, is not a well-defined entity with a given set of characteristics across time and space. That phrase instead is designed to capture a multiplicity of customs and laws and institutions, with the collective package of free-market characteristics of the economic system showing wide variation among different societies. Variation implies the possibility of more or less. One is therefore not choosing to have or not have a discrete entity ("the" market system). The issue is one of addition and subtraction. The problem is to determine the impact on long-run economic growth from, say, introducing a specified set of business laws and commercial institutions and repealing certain onerous government regulations – and this is only to begin the list. The second question in revised form would therefore read something like:

2A What will be the increase in the growth rate of real per capita income in the future if these particular ("pro-free-market") changes are made in a country's customs, laws, and institutions?

Compared with the first two questions, the third is not nearly so defective as it stands. One only needs to fill in the details of the tax legislation contemplated (who will pay more, and how much more) and then estimate the likely impact of these tax changes on two aggregate measures: total labor supply in the economy and total savings. Revised in this way, the third question might read:

3A If a given piece of tax legislation becomes law (again, with details specified), what would the impact be on the country's labor supply and supply of savings?

The fourth question is more like the first two. The cause ("existing American welfare programs") must be spelled out in detail. The assignment is not merely one of elaborating the terms of particular pieces of legislation. The charge commonly made is that changes in the welfare system since the 1960s have precipitated or encouraged destructive behavior among the poor. What therefore must be identified are the changes that mattered, and all the cause-and-effect sequences from these changes to modifications in behavior; in particular, (a) the propensity to rely upon welfare, (b) the willingness to marry and to dissolve marriages, and (c) the willingness to have a child out of wedlock. For each of the behavioral tendencies noted, question (4) would have to be reworded. For the last of these, for example, the question might now read:

4A How much of the total increase in births out of wedlock can be explained by a particular (post-1960) package of changes in the American welfare system?

Now to the central message of this chapter. The reader is urged to reread each of the revised questions (the A versions) in haste and as a sequence. What will be apparent is that all the questions have the same general form: by how much will effect B change when cause A changes – or expressed in the past tense, how much of the observed change in B (growth in per capita income or change in aggregate savings or increase in illegitimate births) can be attributed to the observed changes in A (laws and institutions affecting market behavior or the tax structure or the structure of the welfare system)?

Questions of this general form are typically asked in the natural sciences, and have been for hundreds of years. This form of inquiry received a special impetus in the seventeenth century when Galileo first articulated one of the more profound insights of the past thousand years: that the natural world is subject to laws that can be expressed in mathematical form discoverable by mankind through scientific inquiry. Scientists trying to answer questions of the sort noted accordingly tend first to search for the mathematics that best describes the interactions in the natural world, and then use that mathematics to assess the difference that changes in A make to changes in B: by how much, for example, the orbit of a satellite will be changed by an additional thousand pounds of rocket thrust, or by how much the tensile strength of steel will be changed by the addition of 0.1 percent more carbon to a molten mass of metal in an open hearth furnace.

The purpose of this brief excursion into the natural sciences is to make two points. First, questions of a particular form are typical of the sciences. Second, the scientist's search for answers generally involves trying to discover regularities in the natural world that can be expressed in mathematical form. To return to the main line of the argument, we are at last confronted by a dilemma that should have been obvious from the start: all four questions of fact examined in this chapter are of the same general form popular in the natural sciences, but each of the four requires explaining or predicting human behavior, not natural events. Can we bring to their resolution an article of faith similar to that articulated by Galileo for the natural sciences: that human behavior is also subject to laws that can be expressed in mathematical form discoverable by mankind through the research techniques of the social scientist? That is ultimately an empirical question. The answer is to be found by asking, for all the social sciences combined: How many widely accepted generalizations have been found that can be expressed in mathematical form? Or to narrow the focus to our particular concern, how many generally accepted laws of human behavior can be identified of the form: To change cause A by this much will change human behavior in the following way and to the following degree? The previous brief foray into methodological issues was designed to make a single point – and a crucial point it is. If the world of human behavior has not been found – at least to date – to be subject to the laws of mathematics knowable by mankind, or to very many of such laws, how can we hope to calculate with any accuracy the *quantitative* impact of a given cause on a given effect? We can indeed, and with some confidence, list some of the causes of some relevance to explaining certain kinds of human behavior. But our search – the search dictated by the form of the questions of fact examined in this chapter – is not to find causes of some influence, but to assess how influential a particular cause was or is likely to be.

Again notice what the argument is not. This is not an argument against theoretical speculation or model building in the social sciences. The argument concerns what valid claims to knowledge can be made on the basis of existing theories and models. We are inclined to believe that on the average and over the long haul, our predictions about human behavior will be more accurate if based upon educated guesses rather than upon outright guesses. The inputs for the former include all of the knowledge, experience, and beliefs deemed relevant. But this knowledge invariably includes a lot about tendencies and very little about the magnitudes produced by those tendencies. We know a lot, and are learning more, about certain human propensities: about the tendency of power to corrupt; about the tendency of investment spending to respond to different tax incentives; about the tendency of long-term reliance upon welfare to erode the sense of personal control and self-worth of the recipients; about the tendency of children with low weight at birth to later work below their mental capacity; about the tendency of family background to influence performance in the classroom.[9] But we still know relatively little about the magnitudes involved; for example, by how much investment will increase if depreciation rates allowable for tax purposes are increased by 25 percent; by how much employment among the able-bodied poor will rise in response to a workfare program combining the carrot of access to job training with the stick of benefit denial to those unwilling to enroll in such training; by how much teenage births out of wedlock will fall if these mothers, to receive welfare, must continue living at home with their own parent or guardian.

The lack of knowledge about such magnitudes does not necessarily silence the call to public action. In the realm of the blind, the one-eyed man can often offer useful guidance, and knowledge of tendencies alone may be enough to fashion public policies with a reasonable chance of making a poor situation better. As noted at the beginning of this section, however, a sharp sense of the limitations of this knowledge is critical. To restate the central difficulty in its most general form, if we shift from asking which causes matter to asking how much each matters, the answer calls for an assessment of what the effect would be with and without the cause in question; to guide that assessment (at least for the kind of causes considered in this chapter) there are no widely accepted mathematical models that capture with precision the interactions being analyzed; and without that guidance, assessments can be little more than the roughest of judgment calls which, being rough, are always open to dispute. In short, uncertainty pervades our analyses of particular kinds of human behavior for the same reason that uncertainty pervades most analyses of human behavior: understanding of that behavior is imperfect, and one of the more telling signs of that imperfection is the social scientist's inability to duplicate the kinds of quantitative evaluation of contributing causes so typical of the natural sciences.

At least the dilemma is now clear: questions of fact that pervade discussions of economic justice often seem to call for more precision in our understanding than we evidently have, or even than most experts have. But this is not the only dilemma frequently ignored in discussions of this sort. Others have in common with the one just noted that each must be confronted in any systematic examination of economic justice with a claim to comprehensive coverage of the topic. These will accordingly be the topics of the next chapter. Some readers will wish to move on to that discussion. Others wanting more detailed investigations of points summarized above can find them in the remaining sections of the present chapter.

Does Pursuit of the Welfare State Lead to Totalitarianism?

This question is difficult to compress into a single sentence because no simple phrasing, including that above, adequately captures the many different kinds of state intervention in economic life that are the source of concern. The question as posed is merely an extreme variant of this general concern which tries to trace out, and warn against, the threats to individual liberty from increasing government involvement in the market economy (issues to which the discussion will return in the next chapter). The variant noted, extreme as it is, might not be worth singling out for special study if it were not so fashionable in the literature.

In the 1920s and 1930s in both America and Europe a wide range of commentators warned against the threats to freedom lurking in "collectivist" goals, particularly the goal of socialism. Their argument, somewhat oversimplified, is as follows: (a) socialism requires extensive planning; (b) such planning requires massive interference in the market economy; (c) that interference invariably places increased power and control in the hands of bureaucrats; (d) the appetite of bureaucrats for more power and the indifference of the people to incremental infringements on their liberties (particularly infringements in the name of social justice) will assure a continual drift toward more state planning and more bureaucratic power and control; until (e) the end result is a totalitarian state. The appalling infringements of liberty lurking in the final point threaten to be even more appalling because of new control techniques made possible by modern technology. George Orwell's *Nineteen Eighty-Four* sketches some of those possibilities, albeit in exaggerated terms to some, but not absurdly exaggerated in the judgment of many conservatives whose reasoning runs much as described above.

Steps (a) through (c) in that reasoning would seem above dispute. The argument becomes more controversial in step (d), particularly the assertion that bureaucrats can be counted on to seek and misuse power. At bottom that claim is merely a particular instance of Lord Acton's general observation that all power tends to corrupt and absolute power corrupts absolutely. In his apprehensions about such tendencies, Lord Acton was hardly alone. "In all bureaucracies there are three implacable spirits," warned Herbert Hoover:

self-perpetuation, expansion and an incessant demand for power. These are human urges and are supported by a conviction, sometimes justified, that they know what is good for us. Nevertheless these spirits are potent and possess a dictatorial complex. . . . Power is the father of impatience with human faults, and impatience breeds arrogance. In their mass action, they become veritable exponents of political tyranny.[10]

The persons most feared by many in this scenario, as Herbert Hoover intimates, are not evil men with tyrannical intentions, but rather well-intentioned individuals with mistaken views about what is desirable and what is possible. In Britain of three centuries ago, Adam Smith cautioned the public to beware of would-be leaders with high ideals, benevolent intentions, and extravagant ambitions. This "man of system," as Smith called him,

is often so enamoured with the supposed beauty of his own ideal plan of government, that he cannot suffer the smallest deviation from any part of it. He goes on to establish it completely and in all its parts, without any regard either to the great interests or to the strong prejudices which may oppose it: he seems to imagine that he can arrange the different members of a great society with as much ease as the hand arranges different pieces upon a chess-board; he does not consider that the pieces upon the chess-board have no other principle of motion besides that which the hand impresses upon them; but that, in the great chess-board of human society, every single piece has a principle of motion of its own, altogether different from that which the legislature might choose to impress upon it.[11]

In this country in this century, Louis Brandeis was among those apprehensive about the implications of such human frailties:

Experience should teach us to be most on our guard to protect liberty when the government's purposes are beneficient. Men born to freedom are naturally alert to repel invasion of their liberty by evil-minded rulers. The greatest dangers to liberty lurk in insidious encroachment by men of zeal, well-meaning but without understanding.[12]

But must such encroachments ultimately culminate in tyranny? Will the tendency of the modern state (and the modern bureaucrat) to intervene in the economy inevitably maneuver an unwilling public down the road to the totalitarian state? Three kinds of answers are commonly given by those who fear the threats to liberty that accompany a more intrusive and more powerful government. The answers vary, depending upon the probability assigned. They are, respectively, that all the tendencies described (a) may lead, (b) will probably lead, or (c) will certainly lead to the establishment of the totalitarian state.

Time and again some variant of the first or the second has been voiced in American debates that accompanied the passage of social legislation. The Full Employment Act of 1946, for example, was opposed by those who saw it as giving to all who wanted jobs a government guarantee that jobs would be available. To make good on that guarantee, they argued, would require such massive government intervention in the economy and such a host of bureaucratic controls that the net result would threaten many individual liberties, the functioning of the market system, and possibly even American democracy itself.[13] Such concerns, in turn, help to explain why defining the word "right" (the "right" to a job or to the opportunity for employment) figured so prominently in Congressional hearings and debates. The Economic Opportunity Act of 1964 faced similar problems, although the associated apprehensions tended to be less vehement and more focused. The object of particular scorn was the bureaucratic chief who would direct the proposed programs, a post opponents were wont to label "federal poverty czar." "The American people," Congressman John Ashbrook warned his colleagues, "have consistently rejected the concept of czarism. Concentration of unlimited power within the grasp of a single individual is anathema to us all, and properly so."[14] Many objected that to characterize the prospective head of the poverty program in this way was to exaggerate the powers of that office. Others noted that, exaggerated or not, one bureaucratic czar does not a totalitarian state make. The latter objection, however, is somewhat beside the point if the issue is whether the previous reasoning has empirical validity. The causal processes postulated there are cumulative, and thus what matters is not how much power is given to any single bureaucrat, but whether the end result of giving more power to many bureaucrats will lead to a tyrannical form of government. A number of conservative writers consider the likelihood of the latter prospect to be highly probable or, stronger yet, virtually certain.[15] "For at least the past forty years," George Stigler wrote in 1975, "the conservatives have been in high alarm at the encroachments on liberty by the state. It would be possible to amass a volume of ominous predictions – and not by silly people – on the disappearance of individual freedom and responsibility."[16] In support of that contention, however, conservatives usually offer little evidence, and on occasion none at all – an omission that many on the right tend to gloss over, and a few such as Stigler boldly highlight as a gaping hole in right-wing arguments.[17] Considering the stakes involved, this failure to document the facts behind such dire forecasts is, to say the least, more than a little odd.

The evidence is overwhelming that in the twentieth century democratic governments have had a tendency to intrude into the workings of the economy. Starting prior to industrialization with minuscule budgets by modern standards (or at least minuscule in peacetime), governments of advanced industrial nations have taken an ever larger share of gross national product as these countries have advanced, until their budgets in most cases now equal from a third to a half of total GNP.[18] In the case of the United States, the sum of all government spending (federal, state, and local) – less than 8 percent of GNP at the beginning of this century – is now more than 33 percent, with no evident tendency to decline despite the announced intention of a conservative president in the 1980s to institute a fiscal revolution.[19] Some of this increase reflects the rising importance of peacetime military spending, but a significant proportion of the present American budget (and that of other advanced industrial nations) is now allocated for social welfare programs of the sort discussed in chapter 8.

Alarmed by such trends, conservatives are inclined to view the modern era as "the century of galloping government."[20] The issue, however, is not whether government is galloping but the direction it is going. One of the more ominous forecasts, and certainly one of the most frequently cited by American conservatives, is that of Austrian Friedrich Hayek, as expounded in his early work *The Road to Serfdom*. As the title makes clear, the expectation is that these trends in government intrusion will have calamitous implications for personal liberties. What is not clear is why intrusion will lead to tyranny, or "almost surely" lead to tyranny. Little evidence is offered by Hayek and by others proffering similar forecasts in support of a contention which, if true, must be of the utmost importance to every citizen of every democracy.

One hotly debated topic among academicians (and little noted elsewhere) is whether Hayek was arguing from historical evidence when predicting that collectivist programs, particularly socialism, would lead to a totalitarian state.[21] In an effort to insinuate his own opinions into this discussion, Hayek offered a clarifying statement that seemed less decisive than his original position. In the 1944 foreword to *The Road to Serfdom* he summarized his forecast thus:

What I have argued in this book, and what the British experience convinces me even more to be true, is that the unforeseen but inevitable consequences of socialist planning create a state of affairs in which, if the policy is to be pursued, totalitarian forces will get the upper hand.[22]

Three decades later, he offered second thoughts in a revised preface indicating his displeasure at being misunderstood.

It has frequently been alleged that I have contended that any movement in the direction of socialism is bound to lead to totalitarianism. Even though this danger exists, this is not what the book says. What it contains is a warning that unless we mend the principles of our policy, some very unpleasant consequences will follow which most of those who advocate these policies do not want.[23]

The unpleasant consequence that Hayek has in mind, as the first of these two quotations makes clear, is the totalitarian state. The only question is how the probability of that occurrence is modified by the qualifying phrase "unless we mend the principles of our policy."

None of this is particularly interesting to the general public. What is of interest – indeed, of critical importance – is not what Hayek said, but what evidence exists to support the contention that "collectivist" goals and associated policies can lead to a tyrannical form of government. The evidence since World War II has forced even Hayek to modify his position. In advanced industrial nations with democratic governments and democratic institutions, enthusiasm has waned for socialist policies, particularly the taking over of some of the means of production by the state. Equally important, in those nations that experimented with such policies in earlier years, experimentation was not accompanied by any evidence of a galloping toward, or even a slow trot toward, a totalitarian form of government. Confronted with these developments, Hayek was forced to concede the collapse in the postwar era of the socialist movement in the West, or at least of "hot socialism" in the sense of "that organized movement toward a deliberate organization of economic life by the state as the chief owner of the means of production."[24]

Although Hayek's position has changed, his pessimism has not. Collectivist ambitions are still rife in Western democracies, he insists. These ambitions are now merely redirected into a concerted drive to achieve "social justice" in the "welfare state." This widespread pursuit of social justice, Hayek's amended reasoning runs, will also tend to "drive us toward a totalitarian order," and primarily for the same reasons: such a pursuit invariably requires massive government intervention in the economy; this intervention necessarily gives increasing power and control to bureaucrats; and that transfer of power and control, through mechanisms previously outlined, will lead to the same result as was feared for governments that dabbled in socialism, namely, the tyranny of the totalitarian state.[25] "I have . . . never felt so pessimistic about the chances of preserving a functioning market economy as I do at this moment," Hayek wrote in 1973, "and this means also of the prospects of preserving a free political order."[26]

The issue of evidence, however, is still unresolved. Do the facts of the recent past suggest that such undesirable consequences are likely (or highly probable or almost certain) from any concerted effort by democratic governments to implement welfare policies in the name of social justice? As already intimated, few conservatives including Hayek supply much evidence on this point. In Hayek's case one could even argue that one of his few discussions of factual trends tends to undermine his own position. The disillusionment with socialism in the postwar era Hayek attributes primarily to the growing realization that socialist forms of production are less efficient, do not necessarily lead to greater social justice, and imperil important individual liberties.[27] This amounts to an admission that a movement (socialism) portrayed as having cumulative effects leading in only one direction (down the road to serfdom) could be halted in its tracks, and even reversed. Moreover, that halting is attributed to the public's ability (a) to assess the strengths and weaknesses of programs as they evolved and (b) to force a radical revision of government policies when their assessments indicated that such redirection seemed warranted. This is not the image of an ill-informed and passive electorate, trapped and helpless on the slippery slope to tyranny contrived by others. It is instead an image of the corrective processes of democracy working more or less as one would hope they would work.

Most Americans remain unpersuaded that the mechanisms for suppressing freedom described by Hayek and others are as all-embracing or as implacable as these writers on the right would have them believe. The causal processes involved are complex and do not always operate to force a change in one direction only. Totalitarianism has arisen without the total destruction of the free market in such countries as Nazi Germany and Fascist Italy. Repressive regimes can become more repressive, as was the case in Russia under Stalin, but the suppression of liberty, including economic liberty, has on occasion been relaxed in such countries as Hungary and Czechoslovakia. To most Americans, the examples cited seem far removed from their own experience. They tend to minimize the odds of their encountering such massive threats to liberty. Nor are they apprehensive, by and large, about the threats to freedom lurking in examples from their own past. Despite the rapid rise within their own country of government budgets and bureaucracies and regulations, they do not feel their freedoms have been impaired in any major way. Even conservatives concede, often with a sense of frustration, this pervasive sense in present-day America of freedoms relatively unimpaired.[28] Some, like William F. Buckley, Jr, admit to feeling relatively free themselves, although in Buckley's case that concession must be extracted from a double negative. "Even though I myself take the gloomy view that our society is marching toward totalitarianism," he writes, "I should not go so far as to say that America is not now, as societies go, free. . . . "[29] If America is not now not free, it follows (as societies go) that it is relatively free, despite the massive rise of government intrusion into the economy in the twentieth century.

If the focus is shifted from what Americans believe to what would be reasonable to believe given the available evidence, the one conclusion that appears defensible is that the threats of future tyranny lurking in the present tendencies of democratic governments to pursue "social justice" through welfare programs are largely unknown. This in turn implies that forecasts about such threats, often clothed in the garb of certainty, are in fact little more than educated guesses. The question must then be asked why so many conservatives are willing to make decisive forecasts on a topic about which decisive knowledge is noticeably absent. Why this propensity, in the colorful language of conservative economist Herbert Stein, to wave "the bloody red shirt of the totalitarian takeover"?[30] Part of the answer undoubtedly is that the belief is strongly held, however uncertain the evidence. Given the frightful nature of the tyrannical form of government feared, the human tendency is to overstate the likelihood of catastrophe becoming a reality.

Conservatives also stand to gain immense political advantage if the totali-tarian takeover can be portrayed as almost sure to follow in the wake of the government policies that conservatives oppose. Advocates of the minimum or night-watchman state would surely win large numbers of Americans to their cause if those Americans could be convinced that any government expansion beyond the minimum would lead inevitably to a totalitarian state. The very willingness of Americans to tolerate government expansion, and their sense that such expansion in the past has not substantially undermined important freedoms, are but two of many signs that the dire forecasts of conservatives, however certain and dogmatic they may be, are not taken seriously by the majority in this country.

One final point: *nothing* in this highlighting of a lack of evidence and a corresponding lack of certainty in associated forecasts should be construed as undermining in the least the basic conservative concern that expanding the government's domain involves a loss of liberty. Which liberties are lost, and which losses should be a source of general concern, are complex topics to which the discussion will return in the next chapter.

The Catholic Lay Commission versus the Bishops

Conservatives have a second line of defense to repel those who advocate the implementation of policies associated with "the welfare state." Their primary defense, as noted, is to emphasize how such policies threaten individual freedom. But quite separate from these objections is a second line of argument that emphasizes, somewhat unexpectedly, the need to help the poor.

In outline form, this latter reasoning consists of two premises and one inference:

1 the free-market system is crucial for the achievement of economic growth;
2 economic growth is the key to improving the lot of the poor; thus,
3 the preservation of the free-market system is crucial for improving the lot of the poor.

Two supplementary arguments are usually added, both calculated to discredit alternative schemes for helping the poor by following the usual liberal prescription of raising taxes to fund welfare programs designed to benefit the least advantaged members of society. These are:

4 the large tax increases needed to fund large welfare programs will stifle incentives to work and to save, and thus seriously hamper economic growth; and
5 a system of extensive welfare benefits will do the poor more harm than good by undermining their self-sufficiency, encouraging dependency, and disrupting their family structure.

These five arguments (particularly (1) through (3)) have been central to the recent clash between conservative and liberal factions within the Catholic

Church. What brought this clash to the attention of the American public was the determination of a handful of bishops to have their theological colleagues approve and circulate a pastoral letter "meant to provide guidance for members of the Catholic Church as they seek to form their consciences about economic matters."[31] The extent to which the composing of the first draft was controlled by a liberal faction among the bishops is a matter of debate, but there could be no debate about the liberal tenor of the policy recommendations endorsed by the first draft: progressivity in the income tax structure, public service employment programs, increases in the minimum wage, expanded job-training programs, and increased welfare payments to provide a minimum floor for all who are needy.

Catholic conservatives were not slow to recognize an ominous challenge. If the sentiments of the first draft became the sentiments of the final draft, the hierarchy of the Catholic Church would be giving "guidance" to the faithful that amounted to an endorsement of liberal policies that conservatives oppose. Even before the bishops' first draft was made public, a rebuttal was published entitled *Toward the Future*, a document prepared by a small number of conservative catholics headed by William Simon and Michael Novak.[32] The lengthy name Simon and his colleagues chose for themselves signaled their concerns while acknowledging their subordinate status within the Catholic hierarchy: The Lay Commission on Catholic Social Teaching and the US Economy.

The strategic problem for this 29-member group was to mount a counterattack in such a way that the majority of American bishops would be deflected from the liberal tenor of the first draft and ultimately endorse a revised pastoral letter on the economy more in keeping with conservative priorities.[33] Arguments of the sort outlined above clearly would not do. To accuse bishops (however liberal) of advocating policies favorable to a totalitarian takeover was not likely to be well received by a church hierarchy accustomed to deference from the laity, and certainly not accustomed to no-holds-barred debates with the laity even on matters economic. The retreat of the Lay Commission to the second line of defense cited above was therefore to be expected. Beginning with a posture of deferential dissent, they noted their common agreement with the bishops concerning theological premises relevant to the debate. The Lay Commission also stressed the sharing of a common goal, although the language and the emphasis differed slightly. For the bishops, "The fulfillment of the basic needs of the poor is of the highest priority."[34] In guarded language, the Lay Commission emphasized their agreement: "We share with our bishops the full intention of raising up every single person on earth from the tyranny of poverty."[35] If helping the poor was not acknowledged as being "of the highest priority." what was acknowledged was that "One measure of a good society is how well it cares for the weakest and most vulnerable of its members."[36]

The disagreement, then, appears to be primarily over means, not ends. Central to the disagreement were three empirical assertions, each of which is an integral part of the line of reasoning developed at the outset of this section. Rephrased as questions, these are:

1   Is the free-market system crucial for the achievement of economic growth?
2   Do tax increases needed to fund extensive welfare programs so undermine incentives to work and to save that the economic performance of the economy is seriously impaired?
3   Does the mixed bag of policies that constitute current welfare programs in America do the poor more harm than good by undermining their self-reliance, fostering dependency, and disrupting family structures?

These three will be the focus of attention for the remainder of this chapter. In the following discussion of conservative positions, those of the Lay Commission will often be given special prominence for reasons already indicated.

Is the Free-market System Vital for the Achievement of Economic Growth?

The question as phrased suggests a naive understanding of two complicated issues.

The first concerns the meaning of the phrase "the free-market system." The above wording implies that this is a well-defined entity. The reality behind the phrase, however, is a sprawling complex of institutions and laws, customs and practices, that can vary enormously across time and space. By ignoring this complexity and this variability, those who assume the entity is well defined can portray society's choice of economic systems as consisting of one of two options: *either* the free-market system *or* some other system (often "socialism"). This is a mistaken view of available options on several counts. In a democratic country where socialists compete with free-market advocates for the public's ear and the popular vote, the choices for structuring the economic system invariably include a little more of one and a little less of the other, and not just the two extremes of "pure" socialism or "pure" free-market system (whatever "pure" might mean). Popular debates in Western European countries where the two systems have been deliberately mixed have therefore turned upon such incremental choices as which firms or industries should be state controlled, and which goods and services should be left to the private sector to produce; which product and factor markets should be relatively free of government regulations, and which should be interfered with to promote such priorities as increased worker security or a lessening of monopoly power and monopoly profits. Even casual acquaintance with American attitudes and American history suggests that much of what has just been discussed is somewhat beside the point. In the decades following World War II, socialism in the sense of widespread government ownership of the means of production has never been a serious contender in the political arena prompting widespread public debate. If "a lot more socialism" is not a feasible political option in America – if the "mix" of free-market system and socialism in this country presently features a lot of the first and little of the second – what do American conservatives want to change in that complex of laws and institutions which are part of "the free-market system" as presently constituted in their country? More specifically, what undesirable changes in that market system do they consider likely to be generated by further movement in America toward that much feared leviathan, the welfare state? To these questions the discussion will return shortly. The point to get clear at the outset is that a single phrase ("the free-market system") encompasses a vast array of options, and among those options, widespread government ownership of the means of production, although a serious possibility in many Western European countries, is not a serious possibility in the United States, given the widespread and pronounced bias of Americans against that option.

If the free-market system is not a well-defined entity, economic growth is not a well-understood process.

Recall the distinction made previously between efficiency (getting the largest pie possible from available factors of production and existing technology) and economic growth (expanding the feasible size of the pie by expanding factor supplies and/or improving technology). Debates concerning the merits of the free-market system frequently confuse the two, and not infrequently mix together the causes responsible for each. Neoclassical economics has a well-articulated theory explaining how, under certain assumptions, a competitive economy will be the most efficient economy. The assumptions in question frequently have been challenged as being widely at variance with the facts of the American economy.[37] That challenge, however, need not concern us here, because the focus of subsequent discussion is growth, not efficiency. The central issue, to repeat, is how best to help the poor, and it has been economic growth during the past two centuries that, for the first time in human history, has lifted a large proportion of the population out of grinding poverty in a handful of countries now designated as advanced industrial nations – a nomenclature unthinkable in George Washington's day, and an economic accomplishment beyond the imaginative reach of even the most visionary of Washington's contemporaries. The puzzle here is what caused this truly extraordinary process.

Conventional economic theory offers a number of models that purport to explain the processes of economic growth. Such models reflect the priorities of the social scientist. The economist does not simply want a list of causes "crucial" or "important" for the achievement of economic growth. What is desired is some measure of the relative contribution of each of the causes suspected of being important to the growth process actually observed, and the indispensable device for this is a model of the economic growth in question.

Consider one of the conventional models frequently employed in this context. Suppose one believes that, for a given country, the growth of total output O is a function of four causal variables: labor inputs L, capital inputs K, land or natural resource inputs R, and a catch-all variable A to indicate how total factor productivity is changing over time because of such developments as improvements in technology. Then the causal assertion just made can be rewritten as

$$O = f(A,L,K,R).$$

The trick is to translate this general causal assertion into a precise mathematical model. The form that translation often takes in economic analysis is log-linear; that is, the above general expression is given the precise form

$$\log O = \log A + x \log L + y \log K + z \log R.$$

This function usually appears in the literature in its nonlogarithmic form, or as

$$O = AL^x K^y R^z.$$

The first equation is simply the logarithmic transformation of the second.

The reader concerned lest the discussion degenerate into mathematical manipulations and (even worse) partial derivatives has nothing to fear. All that matters for our purposes is a handful of points easily grasped with no reference at all to mathematics. First, consider the meaning of x in either of the above equations. This is one of the key parameters of the model: it indicates the *quantitative* change in total output O that will take place for a given change in labor inputs L, with other relevant causal variables held constant (here A, K, and R). Thus, if

$$x = 0.6,$$

this indicates that a 10 percent increase in labor inputs will result in a 6 percent increase in total output. (Why the numerical relationship is between proportional changes in an input and proportional changes in output need not detain us.)[38] Second, recall that our task was to identify the importance of "the free-market system" as a contributing factor to economic growth. One might therefore define

$$M = \text{free-market system},$$

and rewrite the above equation as

$$O = AM^w L^x K^y R^z.$$

The reader will protest that this will not do. Such a mathematical formula attempts to capture in a single symbol M what is in fact a multiplicity of variables, namely, all the different possible institutions and laws and customs and practices that comprise "the free-market system." Which brings us to the third point. Models need precisely defined variables, "the free-market system" is not a precisely defined variable, and thus the tendency of contemporary economic growth models to ignore this causal factor is hardly surprising. Finally, and somewhat more surprising, even for historical periods during which the many variables relevant for growth buried in the phrase "the free-market system" did not change much (and thus ignoring such changes would not seem a major omission of growth models), these growth models still have an undistinguished record as explanatory tools for the growth observed. Consider, for example, one of the most obvious of contemporary American growth problems – its tendency in the past decade or so to slow down – and the most obvious of all causal factors accounting for that slowdown – the decline in capital investment. The best estimates of the most respected economists of how much of decline in the first (growth) can be attributed to a decline in the second (capital formation) range from zero to 50 percent.[39] That range in turn is symptomatic of how limited our understanding is of the processes which cause economic growth. Or to put the matter differently and more starkly, economists simply do not have models that are widely acknowledged to give a precise assessment of the relative importance of different causes of economic growth, even when that growth occurs in countries experiencing little change in such complex variables as their market system, political institutions, or cultural norms.

This latter judgment resolves our search for a credible growth model, but unsatisfactorily so. The human tendency is to distrust agnosticism, and in this instance the normal instinct is to insist that *something* can be said: that *some* assessment of the relative importance of different causes contributing to observed growth must be possible, if not by using mathematical models, then by some combination of intuition and empirical observation. Consider, for example, Communist China and the Soviet Union. Both countries do not have distinguished growth records. Both countries employ an economic system far removed from capitalism. Surely these two observations are not unrelated. The difficulty is that both countries have experienced some growth, and so the question becomes: How much *more* growth would each have experienced if their present economic systems had been replaced by some variant of a free-market system. And to answer questions that begin "How much more . . . " requires, for reasons previously noted, a model of the process in question (in this case, the process of growth), and satisfactory models of growth incorporating variables such as "the free-market system" are scarce to the point of being nonexistent. Our intuition tells us that the absence of certain freedoms and certain market institutions does inhibit economic activity and thus also inhibits the possibilities for growth "a great deal." But to translate that suspected importance into a precise quantity of demonstrated validity requires a model of demonstrated validity. And this the economics profession has not been able to provide. Moreover, empirical observation harnessed to "intuition" and cut loose from theoretical models of the causal processes at work is all too often an unreliable guide to the truth. The economist can, for example, calculate the annual rate of growth of each country in Western Europe since World War II, note that this growth was much faster when the size of the government sector was much smaller, and conclude that the recent slowdown in economic growth "reveals the devastating effects of the public-sector boom in Europe."[40] But similar data and similar reasoning can lead to the opposite conclusion. For example, in the United States during the period 1892–1929, federal expenditures averaged about 4.5 percent of gross national product and output per worker-hour rose at an average rate of 1.5 percent per annum; in the period 1948–85, federal expenditure averaged about 20 percent of gross national product and output per worker-hour rose by 2.3 percent per annum.[41] The obvious inference is that greater government intervention in the economy caused a surge in worker productivity. This second inference, of course, is no more justified than the first. To make an accurate assessment of the role of government in the growth process, one must know for the period under review – either America throughout the twentieth century or Western European countries in the postwar era – what all the variables are that affect the growth process (including those related to government activity), how these variables changed during the time period in question, and how those changes affected economic growth. And to achieve that (by now the conclusion is predictable if still unwelcome), one needs a model.

The Lay Commission on Catholic Social Teaching and the US Economy has therefore set for itself a demanding task. Despite a lack of credible growth models, it wants to demonstrate the relative importance to economic growth of a causal factor not easily defined, namely, the free-market system.

The Commission begins by postulating three causal relationships that would seem above dispute. These are:

1 for economic growth to be achieved, certain human abilities need to be channeled into economic activity, such as inventiveness, prudence, and foresight;[42]
2 this channeling of abilities is encouraged by an economic system that features ease of access for would-be participants and rewards for productive participation;[43] and
3 such ease of access and such rewards are characteristics of a free-market economy based upon such institutions as private property, patent and copyright protection, and competitive markets (both factor markets and product markets) with few barriers to entry.[44]

Beginning with these three assertions, the Lay Commission then infers:

4 that among the causes of wealth, "institutions of political economy . . . are of decisive importance";[45]
5 that capitalism (with its associated institutions of political economy) "seems to be a necessary, but not a sufficient, condition for . . . economic development";[46] and accordingly,
6 "If the United States is not, today, a 'Third World nation', it is above all because of the fundamental ordering of its institutions."[47]

The inference in (5) is clearly incorrect. Countries that are not based upon capitalism, such as Russia and China, have also experienced *some* economic development, so capitalism can hardly be a necessary condition for such development.

The inference in (6) is but a particular instance of the generalization stated in point (4). "Decisive" implies "of great importance"; to make that kind of assessment one needs to be able to estimate what growth would have been minus capitalist or free-market institutions; and to make such estimates one needs the kind of growth model that the economics profession has yet to supply. This particular judgment of "decisive" importance is therefore nothing more than an educated guess by the Lay Commission. A similar lack of sophistication is evident in the Commission's claim that the causes of the wealth of nations "are not only knowable but known."[48] What is known are many of the causes (although not necessarily all the causes) that make a difference to the growth process. What is not known is how much of a difference each cause makes.[49]

Of the many clashes between the Catholic bishops and the Lay Commission, the analysis to this juncture has much to do with their disagreements on how to help the peoples of less developed nations, but little to do with their differences over how best to improve the economic lot of poor people within the United States. The solution for American poverty can hardly be to introduce free-market institutions into a country that already has those institutions. Something else must be required if the needy in America are to be helped. Not surprisingly, the bishops and the Lay Commission have sharply differing views about what is needed most. Their disagreement is perhaps most readily brought into better focus by asking two related questions:

1 Which policies are advocated by the Catholic bishops to help the American poor that Catholic conservatives would view as an expansion of the welfare state?
2 Why are these policies regarded by the Lay Commission as likely to impair economic growth, and therefore likely to impair the lot of the poor by slowing down the rise in the tide that otherwise should lift all boats?

Policies advocated by the Catholic bishops include the following:[50]

(a) expanded welfare benefits, including a minimum income for all needy people;
(b) expanded job-training and apprenticeship programs;
(c) direct public-service employment programs;
(d) a generous rise in the minimum wage.

These are but a subset of a lengthy list of policy recommendations designed to help the poor, but they indicate the kind of economic strategies favored by the Catholic clergy. The Lay Commission's main concerns about such strategies warrant quoting in some detail:

. . . again and again, the final draft [of the bishops' pastoral letter] turns to the state to "direct" economic activism, to create jobs, to play a determining role in foreign aid assistance, and the like ... [W]e are not opposed to an activist state, but wise activism means counting costs as well as benefits. A wise citizenry properly hunts out government programs and activities that erect barriers to and introduce biases against productive activity. For example, welfare programs giving direct payments to individuals may, among their effects, subsidize nonparticipation, raise the cost of working against the cost of not working, raise the cost of employing people, and alter the sense of social responsibility and personal dignity. An unwise tax system may penalize saving and productivity-advancing activities.[51]

The costs of state activism that particularly concern the Lay Commission are those associated with expanded welfare programs and the taxes needed to pay for those programs. "Productive activity" is the key phrase, here used to signal apprehensions about both efficiency and growth. If productive activity suffers, the implicit argument runs, the resulting reduction in total output may be so severe that the American poor will receive (thanks to "state welfare policies") a larger share of a smaller pie so reduced in size that the absolute amount received is not as great as what would have been received (a smaller share of a bigger pie) if the policies in question had never been implemented. Here too the issues, at bottom, are questions of fact, and the questions turn upon relative magnitudes.

1   Would the taxes needed to finance expanded welfare programs impair industriousness and thrift by a little or a lot?
2   Would the proposed expansion in welfare programs discourage working and encourage dependency by a little or a lot?

If the likely effects under both headings are pronounced, then efforts to help the poor by expanding welfare policies within America are likely to be counterproductive. But are such effects likely to be so large?

Would Tax Levies Needed to Finance Expanded Welfare Programs Seriously Impair Industriousness and Thrift?

The Elements of the Problem

This question logically divides into three subquestions.

1   What is the estimated cost of the proposed expansion in welfare?
2   What kind of tax increases will be required to finance those expanded welfare costs?
3   How are such tax increases likely to affect the performance of the economy?

Much of popular discussion in recent years has ignored (1) and (2), while focusing upon (3), revising that question to read:

3A   Would a significant tax increase above present levels have a major adverse effect upon the performance of the economy?

This latter version of the question can be turned around to ask whether a significant tax cut would have a large beneficial impact upon the economy – a question that lies at the heart of supply-side economics. The emphasis upon supply is all-important. Deficient demand is the primary focus of Keynesian economics, which also argues that a tax cut will benefit an economy provided that economy has idle resources. The underlying cause-and-effect mechanism is a thrice-told tale of introductory economics courses. Roughly summarized, the argument is that tax cuts increase after-tax incomes, thus stimulating a rise in consumer spending; this increased spending constitutes demand for more goods and services; and business firms respond by expanding output, thereby re-employing heretofore idle resources (unemployed workers and excess plant capacity), which in turn helps to move the economy out of recession and back toward full employment.[52] Using again the imagery of a pie, one can say that the Keynesian problem arises when the economy does not create the largest pie possible because of idle resources, and the Keynesian solution is to expand demand (in this case by tax cuts) in order to get resources re-employed, thus enabling the achievement of a pie size closer to the maximum that can be created when all factors of production are fully employed.

Supply-side economics tells a different story. The main concern is *not* how to get the largest possible pie from presently available technology and the existing supply of factors of production. Rather, it is how to expand the feasible size of the pie over time. The reader will recognize the old problem of economic growth in a new guise. The novelty is that the causal mechanism of initial concern is a change in taxes. Conventional growth problems re-emerge because the empirical issue, at bottom, is how a tax change (increase or decrease) will affect all those variables that in turn affect economic growth.

The complaint that high taxes are stifling economic activity is not peculiar to the modern world. In ancient Rome under Diocletian, "taxation rose to such heights that men lost incentive to work or earn, and an erosive contest began between lawyers finding devices to evade taxes and lawyers formulating laws to prevent evasion."[53] The tales of Robin Hood also suggest a somewhat burdensome tax structure under King John, although the incentive effect on Robin's men was not so much to give up work as to reallocate their energies to extra-legal endeavors and their base of operations to Sherwood Forest. In recent years within America, this old concern about burdensome taxes has resurfaced with a new vigor and a new cogency as part of what has become known as "supply-side economics." The leading advocates of this school of thought have been a small group of economists and a few influential members of Congress. Their principal argument is that taxes affect the incentive to work, save, and invest, and these three activities, in turn, affect the course of economic growth. That such arguments should capture popular attention in the late 1970s was not surprising. As previously noted, American productivity growth had been flagging since the early 1970s, and economists could offer no generally accepted explanation for this slowdown. Supply-side advocates claimed to have diagnosed contributing causes of the first importance, and accordingly advanced a set of policy proposals that they believed would make a decisive contribution to reviving the growth performance of the economy.

At the core of this diagnosis were a handful of insights at least as old as the investigations of Adam Smith into the causes of the wealth of nations.[54] The growth of society's total output depends in part upon the supply of labor and capital, the argument runs, and the supply of capital depends crucially upon the willingness to save and invest. Supply-side advocates and many conservatives not closely allied with that school of thought hammered out repeated variations on a single theme: the supply of labor and capital is crucially affected by the tax structure; thus high taxes impede growth and lowering taxes will stimulate growth.[55] The central question in subsequent disputes became: Stimulate by how much?[56]

The reader should be warned that these disputes remain essentially unresolved, although the American economics profession can be fairly viewed as split between a large majority whose opinions cluster around one set of judgments, and a small minority whose opinions are quite different from the majority's views. What follows, then, is an attempt to summarize majority opinion, with the caveat that in no case do the views in question constitute unanimous opinion. In a profession not known for its unanimity, however, some consensus about the relative size of certain empirical relationships is not a trifling achievement.

Taxes and Work

Supply-side advocate Congressman Jack Kemp once asked a college audience what would happen if the government took baseball player Reggie Jackson's salary and redistributed it equally among all members of Jackson's team. From the back of the lecture hall a youthful voice called out: "He'd hit singles!"[57] From this example Kemp draws the inference that all work is responsive to how much government demands intrude upon the individual's income, rising when taxes fall, and falling when taxes rise. The difficulty is that Kemp's analysis ignores half the relevant causal mechanism. A tax cut, he rightly points out, raises the reward for working and therefore creates an incentive to work more. The same tax cut, however, makes it possible to achieve a particular level of after-tax income by working less. The first effect encourages a substitution of work for leisure, while the second effect encourages a substitution of leisure for work.[58] What the net effect of a tax cut will be on the willingness to work is therefore not a question of theory but a question of fact. The freedom of laborers to vary their work effort in response to tax changes is admittedly constrained by contracts that designate fixed hours of work. Variations are nevertheless possible, particularly for the self-employed, but also for others by such devices as increasing or decreasing part-time work, varying the intensity of work (especially if pay is determined by piece rates), varying the length of time unemployed, and accelerating or delaying the time of retirement.

Evidence on the responsiveness of the labor supply to tax changes comes primarily from three sources: (a) surveys of professional and high-income persons; (b) econometric analysis of available data on work effort and after-tax income; and (c) income-support experiments (in America, primarily the negative income tax experiments with low-income persons).

Examination of (c) will be taken up in a later section. The evidence from (a) and (b) all points to a similar conclusion.[59] Cautiously expressed by conservative William Simon, that conclusion is that "Statistical studies have failed to establish a definite negative relationship between taxes and labor supply."[60] Translated into a positive statement by Brookings expert Barry Bosworth, this implies that "the net effect on labor supply of a proportionate change in tax rates is relatively small."[61] Such statements constitute a summary judgment of a range of findings, of which three are particularly noteworthy. Surveys of professional and high-income earners indicate little responsiveness of work effort to variations in after-tax income (that is, to tax disincentives).[62] These findings, in turn, challenge a traditional conservative assertion that the work of the gifted few – which they view as crucial for economic growth – will be gravely impaired by high marginal tax rates. For the general work force (that is, those outside high-income brackets), the evidence suggests different conclusions for men and women. The labor supply of adult males seems markedly unresponsive to changes in marginal tax rates. However, the labor supply of females, particularly married females, does show some sensitivity to variations in after-tax income. The summary judgments of Simon and Bosworth cited previously therefore amount to the assertion that two notable insensitivities (of high-income earners and adult males in general) plus one sensitivity of some significance (of adult females) aggregate to a considerable insensitivity for the labor force as a whole. Or to quote from one of many efforts to aggregate these net effects more precisely: "a 1 percent rise in the after-tax wage rate would increase hours of work by 0.15 percent."[63]

One cannot hope to fashion empirical support for the factual assertions of supply-side economics from evidence such as this. More importantly for our purposes, these findings present a challenge to those conservatives who argue that the best way to help the poor is to stimulate growth, and a tax hike to fund welfare expansion will seriously impair growth possibilities. This latter claim is obviously not supported by the evidence just cited concerning the unresponsiveness of the aggregate labor supply to changes in the tax rate. These conservatives therefore face two options: either they must present evidence of their own demonstrating that the consensus concerning the insensitivity of the labor supply to tax changes is incorrect, or they must build the case for censuring tax hikes as detrimental to economic growth by citing other cause-and-effect mechanisms that link tax changes to variables crucial to the growth process. Two variables often cited are saving and investment. Each contributes to growth, and each is claimed to be responsive to tax changes. Here, too, the key question is a question of fact: Is that responsiveness large or small?

Taxes and Saving

"To accumulate capital, we must reward the saver and encourage him to save," writes conservative Howard Kershner.

Machines and industrial equipment could conquer poverty the world over, but vast amounts of capital must be accumulated to supply them. Whoever contributes to the fund of capital required for the financing of industry, is like the fourth son, a benefactor to the human race. He is the hero of the productive society.[64]

The economic mechanisms underlying these heroics are relatively un-complicated. In any given time period (say a year), the economic system can create two kinds of outputs: those destined for consumption by consumers (for example, dresses, haircuts, and tomatoes), and those destined to be used in the productive system to create more goods next year (for example, Kershner's "machines and industrial equipment," but also industrial plants). This latter kind of output augments the nation's stock of capital, where "capital" refers to "produced means of production," and the stock is the amount of such goods in existence at any point in time. (Notice that "capital" here is a physical concept, quite different from the other common meaning of "capital" that refers to financial assets such as stocks and bonds.) The amount of total output, or total gross national product, that can be created in any given year is determined by available technology and the existing supply of factors of production. The latter, as noted in chapter 3, are commonly lumped by economists under four broad headings: "land" or "natural resources," "labor," "enterprise" (which can be viewed as a special kind of labor), and "capital" – the last of these, as pointed out above, referring to the currently existing stock of produced means of production.

Two conclusions follow. First, the more capital produced this year and added to the present stock of capital, the larger will be total possible output next year.[65] The more chemical factories we build and equip this year, for example, the more chemicals we can produce next year. Secondly, the more resources used to produce consumer goods and services, the fewer resources will be available to produce capital goods (assuming that the economy is operating at full employment). Thus if capital goods are to be produced this year, consumers must be persuaded to "abstain" from using all the available resources to create consumer goods. This in essence is the reason why "real abstaining from consumption" or "real saving" is essential if annual increments are to be added to the nation's capital stock. These increments are usually labeled "annual investment," where the investment in question refers not to the purchases of stocks and bonds but to the use of dollars to buy the resources needed to build new plant and new machinery. (The three general categories of such "investment" are (a) plant and equipment, (b) residential construction, and (c) changes in inventories, where the last of these can be positive or negative in any given year.)

Some clarification is required to link "real" saving to dollars saved. "Real saving" (or "abstaining from the use of real resources to create consumer goods and services") has its financial counterpart in dollars saved from incomes received. Consider the following oversimplified example. If $100 million worth of goods is created this year, an equivalent amount ($100 million) will be paid out to those who helped create that output, these income receipts generally taking the form of wages and salaries, rents, interest payments, and profits. If households receive $100 million in income and spend only $70 million on consumer goods, they have, in a real sense, "abstained" from using up through their consumer demands $30 million worth of goods – or looked at from the input side, consumers have *not* demanded the services of $30 million worth of resources that can create $30 million worth of output. Shifting from "real" saving to dollars actually saved – in this case the difference between income of $100 million and consumption spending of $70 million – one can imagine this $30 million in saved dollars being supplied to financial markets either directly through the purchase of stocks and bonds, or indirectly by depositing the money saved in banks which in turn funnel those dollars into financial markets through such devices as increased loans or bank purchases of securities. With this example in hand, one can more easily see the essence of what in reality can be a tangled causal mechanism: the more dollars saved, the more dollars supplied to financial markets; the more dollars supplied, the lower will be the interest rate or the cost of borrowing; and the lower the interest rate, the more would-be investors will be encouraged to undertake new projects that will add to the nation's capital stock, such as building new cement factories or replacing old computers with new computers. In sum, increased savings lowers borrowing costs which in turn stimulates more investment or more additions to the nation's supply of produced means of production, and these additions will enable greater output in the future, or greater economic growth. And lest it be forgotten, the last of these – increased economic growth – was the objective that provoked this discussion in the first place. The question at issue here – which may also have been forgotten in the above tracing out of relevant economic mechanisms – is whether a tax change, by having a large impact upon the willingness to save, will have a large impact upon economic growth through mechanisms of the sort just described.[66]

To pose the first part of this cause-and-effect sequence as a question: Will a tax cut significantly affect savings? Unfortunately, even the direction of the impact is not certain. The point made in the previous section about a tax cut producing two opposite effects upon the willingness to work needs to be made again, and for similar reasons. Certainly a tax cut, by raising the after-tax return on savings, will create an incentive to consume less and save more to take advantage of this higher return on every dollar saved. But this same higher return means that to achieve a given standard of living later on (in part through income earned on accumulated savings), the saver now does not need to save as much to generate the same prospective income flow in the future. Again the issue cannot be resolved by theorizing about cause-and-effect relationships, but only by appealing to the facts.[67]

The facts, at first glance, suggest a marked insensitivity of American savings rates to any stimuli, including tax changes. From the early 1950s to the present, the gross private saving rate in this country has remained remarkably stable, all variations being within the narrow range of 16–18 percent of gross national product.[68] More systematic studies of data on aggregate amounts saved and after-tax returns on savings force yet another retreat from certainty. Various studies offer conflicting claims about the sensitivity of savings to available returns on saving, with all claims heavily dependent upon imperfect data, the assumptions made, and the periods chosen to test for this sensitivity. With no claim decisive and all open to legitimate objections, the one clear implication of this cacophony of opinion was well summarized at the conclusion of a comprehensive survey of the main empirical investigations: "Assertions that an increase in the return to capital will or will not raise the overall private saving rate must be based on personal beliefs, because the existing empirical evidence must be judged as inconclusive."[69]

A road that at the outset gleamed in the light of confident opinion has once again become obscured by the mist of unresolved scholarly debate. And once again conservatives who claim that welfare expansion is an unsatisfactory way to help the poor because the associated tax hikes will seriously impair economic growth must look elsewhere if claims about related mechanisms of importance are to gain convincing support from a systematic investigation of the facts.

Taxes and Investment

"Don't tax you, and don't tax me; tax that guy behind the tree," runs a Washington quip attributed to Senator Russell Long. American businessmen have long argued that if the government wants more investment in productive forms of capital, it should tax them less. Their case, however, needs more justification than the simple observation that lower taxes should stimulate greater spending on investment projects.

For those who would stimulate investment to stimulate capital formation to increase economic growth, the first question is what determines investment decisions. The answer in general terms is quite straightforward: primarily the expected earnings on investments made.[70] Earnings in turn are a function of receipts and costs. Costs might be changed indirectly through tax policies of the sort outlined in the previous section (provided a cut in general taxes would stimulate more saving, thus lowering interest rates to would-be investors). More direct mechanisms are available for stimulating investment through changes in tax policies, of which the three most important in America are changes in the corporate tax rate, investment tax credits, and the amount of depreciation write-off allowable for tax purposes. A change in any of these three has an unambiguous effect on costs, and accordingly should have an unambiguous effect upon the willingness to invest. The question (yet again) is whether that effect is large or small.

Not surprisingly, the first stumbling block in searching for an answer is the complexity of the tax code. Investment tax credits, for example, are designed to permit the deduction from federal income tax liabilities of a portion of certain types of capital expenditures. How that simple ambition can lead to tax code intricacies is suggested by even the briefest of descriptions of one of the first acts to include investment tax credits.

In 1962 businesses purchasing new durable equipment (and up to $50,000 a year of eligible used property) with service lives of eight or more years could claim a 7 percent tax credit; equipment with six- to seven-year service lives qualified for two-thirds of the 7 percent credit; and equipment with four- to five-year service lives qualified for one-third of the 7 percent credit. The total tax credit generally could not exceed the first $25,000 of the business's tax liability plus one-fourth of the tax liability in excess of $25,000.[71]

Whether such an act stimulated investors to invest, it undoubtedly prompted many to seek the counsel of a tax lawyer. Variations in the amount of depreciation allowable for tax purposes can also pose a labyrinth of possibilities and prompt a similar demand for expert aid. Consider the following summary of some of the provisions of the first tax act introduced by the Reagan Administration.

The Economic Recovery Tax Act of 1981 introduced the "accelerated cost recovery system" (ACRS) which allowed businesses to use a tax life of either three years or five years for most equipment. Structures, which formerly could have had tax lives greater than 30 years, could be depreciated over 15 years under ACRS. The 1981 law also allowed investors to use 150 percent declining-balance schedules for equipment and 175 percent declining-balance schedules for structures.[72]

With measured language Brookings expert Barry Bosworth seemed to be laboring the obvious when he noted: "effective tax rates are highly variable by type of capital asset, method of financing, and owner."[73] In a less guarded moment the same expert conceded: "It's too damn complicated to take all the provisions, net them against one another and find out what they're doing."[74] To cite but one example, machinery might receive investment tax credits and fast write-offs through accelerated depreciation allowances, while buildings receive no credits and slower write-offs. Suppose, however, the buildings are financed through mortgages, whereas the machinery is paid for out of current cash balances. If mortgage interest is tax-deductible, the combined effect of all these tax provisions could still favor buildings over machinery.

Once the dollar value of new tax breaks has been calculated for each type of investment – no small task, as already indicated – the other major issue is how large a stimulus such prospective dollar saving is likely to give to various categories of investment. The responsiveness of investment to changing tax costs depends crucially upon a question of fact, namely the ease or difficulty with which capital can be substituted for labor in the production process. If a new building can be designed with or without costly robot devices installed on the assembly line, a tax break significantly lowering the cost of capital might prompt a decision in favor of the technologically more advanced technique. Put more generally, if would-be investors in plant and equipment can choose from a range of production processes that use different combinations of labor and capital, a tax change reducing the cost of capital (relative to the cost of labor) can lead to more capital-intensive methods of production. But is this theoretical possibility an actual characteristic of the United States economy? The economics profession is yet again divided about an empirical relationship – in this case, the ease of substitution of capital for labor in production – with expert estimates of this substitutability ranging all the way from "negligible" to "appreciable."[75]

With so much uncertainty about key empirical issues – about the prospective dollar savings of any given tax change and about the economy's ability to respond to any given tax change by substituting capital for labor – one is not surprised to find continuing disagreement over whether business investment responded by a little or a lot to the kinds of tax breaks instituted in the early years of the Reagan Administration "to get the economy moving again" as the President often characterized the objective behind his 1981 tax changes.[76] For purposes of this discussion, the difficulties lurking in these disagreements can be side-stepped simply by noting the small size of tax cuts likely to be instituted for this purpose. The 1981 Reagan legislation, for example, in the various tax breaks crafted to stimulate investment in plant and equipment gave up tax revenues of the order of $20–$25 billion.[77] If the issue is the one posed at the beginning of this section – whether welfare expansion will necessitate tax hikes that will so impair economic growth that the poor will end up being worse off than before – and if the tax *reductions* needed to stimulate investment are of the order of $10–$30 billion, then surely a government determined to do both can do both: cut taxes to stimulate investment while simultaneously raising other sorts of taxes (such as consumption or expenditure taxes) not likely to slow growth but sure to cover whatever revenue shortfalls would otherwise result from the combination of revenue needs produced by (a) expanded welfare programs and (b) cuts of the sort just mentioned in particular categories of business taxes. Or to put the obligation where the obligation would seem to belong, conservatives who claim welfare expansion will have bad effects on economic growth because the requisite tax hikes will have bad effects on business investment must offer some supporting evidence that the tax breaks needed by business to stimulate capital formation would be impossible to implement because of the expanded revenue needs of an expanded welfare state.

Conclusion

Conservatives might object that this last point misses the essential point: if welfare expands, *some* tax increases will be inescapable, and these increases, whatever form they take, will be sure to have a negative effect upon the growth potential of the American economy. The main cause-and-effect mechanisms linking higher taxes to less growth have been outlined above. The question of importance, to repeat, is not whether higher taxes will have some negative effect on growth, but whether those negative effects will be large or small. Nothing in the previous discussion *proves* that the conservative position is wrong. But given the noticeable lack of evidence of large effects, either in terms of significant cutbacks in labor supplied or savings undertaken in response to tax increases of the past, the obligation to supply contrary and convincing evidence would seem in this instance also to rest with the conservatives. Until such evidence is forthcoming, their condemnation of welfare expansion because of the supposed deleterious effects on economic growth would seem to be little more than an unsubstantiated article of faith. Conservatives, however, have other reasons for opposing welfare expansion quite unrelated to issues of economic growth. Among these, perhaps the most important is the claim that increased welfare programs of the past – by themselves and not because of indirect effects associated with higher taxes – have had a detrimental impact upon the poor. Examining the nature of this charge is therefore the final topic of this chapter.

Do Existing American Welfare Programs Increase the Dependency of the Poor and Disrupt Family Structure?

The Charges

In his 1986 State of the Union address, President Reagan noted that "After hundreds of billions of dollars in poverty programs, the plight of the poor grows more painful." How could this be?

Many conservatives believe that they have, if not the answer, at least a large part of the answer. The welfare programs initiated or expanded in the Johnson era have, they argue, made the poor worse off, in part by undermining self-reliance and making the poor more dependent upon state handouts, in part by disrupting the stability of poor families. Not so, liberals tend to respond: welfare is the solution for the poor, not the cause of their problems. Even the Catholic Church has not remained aloof from the associated debates. Seeking to move their church to the center of the controversy, a group of bishops crafted the first draft of what would ultimately become the Church's Pastoral Letter on "Catholic social teaching and the U.S. economy." The main problem, argued these bishops, was not too much welfare but too little, along with many other defects in the capitalist system that worked to the disadvantage of the underprivileged.

The challenge to Catholic conservatives could not have been more boldly thrown down. The restraint in their response – at times bordering on immoderate moderation (at least by the customary standards of conservative rhetoric) – is therefore somewhat odd. On the subject of welfare and the poor, the tendency of the Lay Commission on Catholic Social Teaching (all notable conservatives) was to scrutinize the positive and circumnavigate the negative. The key to helping the economically disadvantaged, they stressed repeatedly, was to help the able-bodied to become self-reliant through job-training programs and employment.[78] The negative effects of welfare were rarely alluded to, and then usually in phrases drained of decisiveness. For example, "welfare programs giving direct payments to individuals *may*, among their effects, subsidize nonparticipation, raise the cost of working against the cost of not working, raise the cost of employing people, and alter the sense of social responsibility and personal dignity."[79] The word "dependency" admittedly does appear with some frequency in the Lay Commission's discussion of welfare, but usually as something to be avoided more than a behavioral trait welfare programs invariably encourage.[80] Discussions about family structure are similarly circumspect. The one statement that addresses directly the linkage between the proliferation of welfare programs and changing family structure among the poor does note that the first has had a negative effect upon the second.[81] What the related negative mechanisms are, and whether their effect has been large or small, are nevertheless topics on which the Lay Commission remains noticeably silent.

Other conservatives have been neither silent nor circumspect. On the linkage between welfare payments and behavior of the poor, many on the right have argued that such payments "foster" or "encourage" an undesirable dependency among recipients, particularly able-bodied recipients.[82] A few claim to find in welfare not just a cause of some importance but the dominant explanation for the problem. "The cause of pauperism," Murray Rothbard flatly states, "is relief."[83] That judgment is echoed by George Gilder, who adds that relief is also the cause of the erosion of family structure among the poor:

> . . . the fruits of the Great Society can now be seen as unmitigated tragedy. The focus of all these programs was the ghetto, and that is their test. The results are now clear: the destruction of the black family in the slums and the perpetuation and intensification of poverty . . . [created] a wreckage of broken and dependent families – cradles of crime and despair – that should ever remain on the conscience of American liberalism. The fact that these families now have more income than before only disguises the terrible fact that most of them have lost all hope of self-sufficiency or family life.[84]

Few conservatives would put the charge concerning family structure quite so baldly. But many believe that the present welfare system has "fostered" or "encouraged" the decline of the family among the poor, or at least among a subset of the poor.[85] Extremists on the right are, unsurprisingly, more extreme. The latter do not shrink from pursuing the implications of their more radical diagnoses to more radical policy proposals. If welfare is the cause of increased dependency and the disintegration of families among the poor, the solution is to emasculate or scrap the present welfare system. "The crucial goal" for any welfare system, writes George Gilder, "should be to restrict the system as much as possible, by making it unattractive and even a bit demeaning. . . . In order to succeed, the poor need most of all the spur of their poverty."[86] Charles Murray is equally scathing in his condemnation of the system and equally unsparing in the remedies he advocates. Scrap "the entire federal welfare and income-support structure for working-age persons," he counsels, and "leave the working-aged person with no recourse whatsoever except the job market, family members, friends, and public or private locally funded services. It is the Alexandrian solution: cut the knot, for there is no way to untie it."[87]

Confronted with such draconian proposals, many readers may question the factual analysis, intelligence, or compassion of those who propose them. (Liberal critics have not been slow to suggest deficiencies under all three headings.) Dismissal of such arguments, however, is not a simple matter of marshalling a few *ad hominem* remarks. Whether the positions of conservative writers such as Gilder and Murray can be taken seriously or dismissed as preposterous depends crucially upon whether convincing evidence can be found to support their two main cause-and-effect assertions: (a) the present welfare system has created a debilitating dependency among the poor, and (b) the same system has seriously undermined family structure among the poor. The discussion therefore moves from the simplicity of declarative statements to the perplexing topic of whether "the facts of the case" support those declarations.

The Evidence on Dependency

How to give relief to the poor without fostering dependency among recipients is a problem reaching far back in Anglo-Saxon history to Elizabethan poor laws and beyond. On this side of the Atlantic, associated policy debates tended to give a predictable emphasis to the importance of the work ethic and to encouraging economic self-sufficiency among the populace. The puzzles of what to give and how to give it are as old as the young republic, and the answers from that time to the present have generally been crafted to be consistent with a philosophical framework that has changed little in 200 years. This continuity in perspective is evident in the following.

In the dispensation of public charity the most important rules are, 1st, to provide for the support of such only as cannot support themselves; 2d, to dispense the funds in the most economical manner, so that as great relief as possible may be afforded out of a given amount of means; 3d, to supply employment to the poor whereby they may, as far as practicable, defray the expense of their own support; 4th, to govern and support them in a manner the most favorable to the improvement of their morals and habits; and, 5th, not to make their situation so comfortable as to render it desirable, and preferable to working at wages, nor so uncomfortable and irksome as to render it a place of punishment, or charitable penitentiary.

With minor changes in the language, such sentiments might appear in a contemporary editorial advocating "workfare" for those who receive Aid to Families with Dependent Children (AFDC). The recommendations actually date from Andrew Jackson's era, appearing in an 1828 *Manual on Political Economy*.[88] The argument then and now is that a safety net must protect the "truly needy" from the worst ravages of poverty, but that the net must not become a hammock for the able-bodied.

Since the War on Poverty was launched in the mid-1960s, a handful of trends have developed that, for critics of that war, suggest something is very wrong with America's present welfare system. Consider poverty. Before the Johnson initiatives were enacted into law, the aggregate poverty rate within America was falling rapidly. Shortly after these initiatives began, that decline leveled off, and thereafter the poverty rate remained on something of a plateau during the 1970s before showing signs of rising in the early 1980s (see figure 10.1). In the same period that poverty was failing to decline, welfare expenditures were rising rapidly, as was the percentage of poor families reached by welfare programs (see table 10.1 and figure 10.2).[89] Were these trends symptomatic of a growing welfare dependency among the poor?

Noting little more than the above correlation between poverty rates and welfare payments, less thoughtful critics on the right concluded that dependency was on the rise and welfare was to blame, and there they let the matter rest. A more systematic assessment of these charges requires more detailed knowledge about what the programs were and who qualified for benefits.

Subsequent discussion will focus on means-tested programs only. Table 10.1 indicates which programs were most important and how the outlays for those programs changed over time. Of the various projects of varying importance – what Milton Friedman characterizes as "a ragbag of well over 100 federal programs that have been enacted to help the poor"[90] – three dominate in terms of total dollars spent: AFDC, Food Stamps, and Medicaid. Their targets for assistance are primarily those poor who are aged, disabled, or living in single-parent families.

AFDC began in 1935 as Aid to Dependent Children (ADC), the original title making clear the original concern: to provide state aid to children deprived of the care and support of a parent. Assumptions in the 1930s concerning the likely causes of that deprivation tended to emphasize (a) the role of the husband as breadwinner for the family, (b) the loss of his earning power through death or disability, and (c) the need for the mother to remain home with the children rather than seeking employment herself. All these assumptions were challenged by developments in the years following World War II. Perhaps the single most dramatic development in the labor force was the rising participation of women, both married and single. The changing relative importance of reasons for fathers being absent from AFDC families also suggested the need for rethinking old ideas. By 1961, two out of three families receiving AFDC were eligible because the father was "absent from

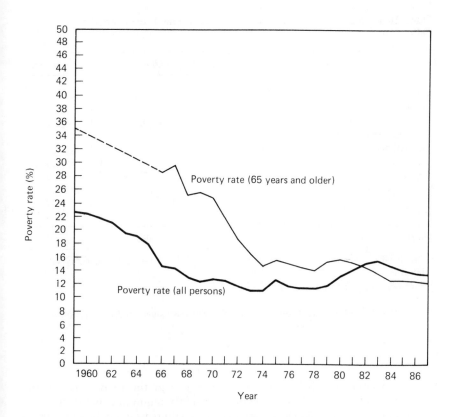

Figure 10.1 US Poverty rate, 1959–1987.
Sources: US Department of Commerce, "Money income and poverty status of families and persons in the United States: 1985," *Current Population Reports*, Series P-60, no. 154, August 1986, p. 22; ibid., no. 163, February 1989; "Characteristics of the population below the poverty level: 1981," *Current Population Reports*, Series P-60, no. 138, March 1983, p. 7; "Characteristics of the low-income population: 1972," *Current Population Reports*, Series P-60, no. 91, December 1973, p. 16.

home"[91] rather than being deceased or disabled. By the 1970s that ratio became three out of four; by the 1980s, nine out of ten. If more women were working, ran a newly fashionable argument, and fathers were "voluntarily absent," then a new priority of AFDC should be "to help families become self-supporting rather than dependent upon welfare checks."[92] One possibility consistent with that priority was to impose work requirements (as they were in 1967) with the hope of promoting re-entry of recipients into the work

Table 10.1 United States: expenditures on low-income benefit programs,
1960–1980[a]

| | Total expenditure | | | | | Increase |
	1960	1965	1970	1975	1980	1965–80
AFDC	5.3	6.7	8.1	7.3	7.3	0.6
SSI	3.7	4.3	3.6	6.8	6.4	2.1
Low-income home energy assistance	–	–	–	–	1.8	1.8
Earned income tax credit	–	–	–	–	1.3	1.3
Housing assistance	0.4	0.5	0.9	3.0	5.4	4.9
Food and nutrition assistance	0.6	0.7	1.9	9.4	13.9	13.2
Medicaid	–	0.7	5.3	9.7	14.0	13.3
Total[b]	10.0	12.9	19.8	36.1	50.1	37.2

[a] For fiscal years ending in year shown, current dollar totals deflated by GNP
deflator.
[b] Numbers may not add due to rounding.

Source: John C. Weicher, "The 'safety net' and the 'fairness' issue," *AEI Economist* (August
1984), p. 2

force.[93] Another possibility, much in evidence in the early years of the
Reagan Administration, was to tighten eligibility requirements to trim from
the welfare rolls those AFDC recipients who could reasonably be expected to
be economically self-sufficient without such aid.[94]

The history of AFDC since the War on Poverty began in terms of family
payments and family use are two stories quickly told. The percentage of poor
families relying upon this means of welfare support shot up in the 1960s,
leveled off by the late 1970s, and declined somewhat in the 1980s, in part
because of the stiffer eligibility requirements mentioned above (see figure
10.2). The pattern of payments per family, when corrected for inflation,
shows the expected and the unexpected (see figure 10.3). Even before
Johnson's War on Poverty was initiated, these benefits were rising rapidly.
Not surprisingly, they continued to rise after the war began. What is rather
less expected is the savage cuts in real benefit levels that took place in the
1970s as inflation far outpaced any change in dollar grants – so much so that
by the early 1980s the benefit level per family (about $312 per month in 1983
dollars) was not significantly different from what it had been in 1955,[95] ten
years before the War on Poverty began. Current AFDC benefits, when
combined with Food Stamps, yield an income that on the average is roughly
three-quarters of the income level officially designated as the dividing line

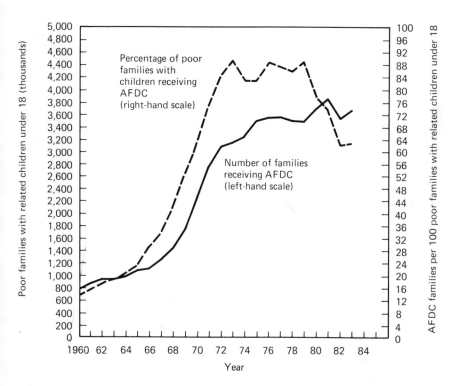

Figure 10.2 Families receiving aid to dependent children (AFDC), 1960–1983.
Sources: US Congress, House, Committee on Ways and Means, *Children in Poverty*, 99th Cong., 1st sess., May 22, 1985, p. 192.

between being poor and not being poor. This average (three-quarters of the poverty income level) obscures a wide variation in benefits actually paid across the country. Within guidelines established by the federal government each state establishes its own rules for eligibility and benefit levels. The result is a study in complexity and inequality,[96] in which the same single-parent family of one adult and two children would receive in Mississippi one-sixth of the welfare aid received in New York. When Food Stamps are added to AFDC benefits, the variation is less marked, but the family noted would receive in combined aid less than half the official poverty income level in Alabama, Mississippi, and Tennessee, and slightly more than 100 percent of that level in Alaska and New York. (See appendix B, table B.4.)

At bottom, the arithmetic of the previous comparison consists in noting than when one number that varies a lot (AFDC benefits) is added to a second number based on national, not state, standards (Food Stamp benefits) the

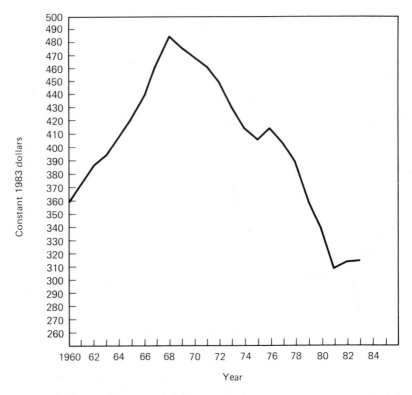

Figure 10.3 Aid to Families with Dependent Children (AFDC): average monthly payment per family in constant 1983 dollars, 1960–1983.
Sources: US Congress, House, Committee on Ways and Means, *Children in Poverty*, 99th Cong., 1st sess., May 22, 1985, pp. 190–1.

combined total will vary less. As this arithmetic implies, compared with AFDC, the Food Stamp program is a model of simplicity. Established in 1964 by the Food Stamp Act, it evolved during the first decade of operation into a national program that provided modest benefits to the poor in the form of vouchers redeemable for food. Few restrictions are presently placed on eligibility beyond demonstrating limited income and assets (plus the requirement of continuing to seek work if one is able to work).[97] The end result is the closest approximation America has to a universally available guaranteed income, although the guarantee is relatively small (as of 1985, $70 per person per month) and the aid in question is usable only for food.

The other main in-kind benefit available to the poor in this country is Medicaid. This program, like Food Stamps, traces its origins to the Johnson era, with the first important legislation passed in 1965. That same legislation authorized a second program, Medicare, whose similar sounding name guaranteed confusion between the two ever since. Medi*care* offers a national health insurance program for the aged (mainly for Social Security beneficiaries) administered by the federal Social Security Administration.[98] Medi*caid*, as the suffix "aid" implies, offers in-kind medical benefits to the poor – primarily the aged not covered by Medicare, the permanently disabled, and those living in single-parent families. (AFDC recipients are automatically eligible for Medicaid.) In design, the program resembles AFDC. The federal government establishes guidelines, and within those guidelines the states set up their own eligibility rules and benefit levels. As originally conceived, for example, each state had to provide five basic services, but could choose which, if any, of 17 other optional services to provide.[99] With discretion this broad, the end result was a wide variation in services rendered across the different states, with those variations largely unrelated to the cost of living or the cost of medical care.[100]

In sum, at the heart of America's approach to aiding the poor are three programs dispensing most of the benefits: two offering in-kind benefits (food and medical care) and one offering cash assistance (AFDC); one offering minimal aid with a minimum of eligibility requirements beyond being poor (Food Stamps) and two with wide variability in eligibility requirements and benefits available. All three typically are available to those poor living in single-parent families. Given the dominance of women in the latter group – less than 2 percent of single-parent families qualify for AFDC because "Mother is absent, not father"[101] – the collective package of welfare aid that includes AFDC can therefore be viewed as directed first and foremost at mothers with dependent children.

"Welfare dependency" might be encouraged by these or any other welfare programs in two different ways. Or put another way, the word "dependency" as used in the literature on poverty can have two quite different meanings. One simply indicates that when transfer programs make more leisure possible, many of those eligible will choose to work less and make up at least part of the lost income through available welfare schemes. Alternatively, the very receipt of welfare over a sustained period of time may change the attitudes of the recipients, undermining their ambition and commitment to the work ethic, and eroding their sense of self-reliance, their sense of personal responsibility, and their belief that they have some control over their own economic fate. This shift in attitudes some have characterized in terms familiar to psychologists as "learned helplessness."[102] In colloquial language more familiar to Americans, the get-up-and-go of recipients is portrayed as being undermined, "partly" or "largely" because of attitudinal shifts that are claimed to accompany sustained reliance upon state transfer payments as a source of income. The key distinction between these two kinds of dependency thus turns on whether preferences are viewed as fixed and independent of welfare, with recipients making conventional work–leisure choices in the context of new options made available by welfare; or alternatively whether preferences themselves are viewed as being molded by the receipt of welfare, so that future choices become ever more biased in favor of continued reliance upon state aid.[103] The latter type of dependency is generally regarded in the literature as having especially pernicious effects, especially upon young adults, including the closing off of avenues of self-improvement because of the role employment plays in acquiring skills, gaining knowledge of the job market, and building up a record of employment that future employers often weigh heavily in deciding among job applicants.

Whether the American welfare system – particularly the system as developed and expanded since the mid-1960s – has fostered either or both of these kinds of dependency among recipients is a hotly contested issue. Debates about relevant evidence have tended to focus mainly upon four issues: (a) labor force participation, (b) work effort, (c) duration of reliance upon welfare, and (d) intergeneration transfer of dependency.

Labor force participation A number of conservative critics, particularly Charles Murray,[104] have made much of the tendency of young black males to withdraw from the labor force since the War on Poverty began. As table 10.2 indicates, the labor force participation rates for both black and white males have tended to decline in recent decades, but Murray has a point: the most striking difference between the races is that while the participation rates for white male youths (ages 16–24) have been rising, those for blacks have been declining sharply.[105] Linking this difference in behavior to the expansion of welfare payments, however, is not a simple matter. The decline in teenage participation rates of black males began long before the War on Poverty began (again, see table 10.2). The youths in question, if poor, would normally be eligible only for Food Stamps which, as noted previously, are a modest supplement to income but no substitute for earned income. Finally, other factors have been suggested to explain this decline – in particular, rising school enrollment and falling demand for labor in inner cities – although how much of the total decline in participation rates can be attributed to such factors is very much an unresolved dispute.[106] However that dispute might be resolved, other evidence suggests that something is desperately wrong in many of the urban ghettos of America: a world in which crime is viewed by many young men as an acceptable alternative to regular employment,[107] in which too many of the youths, in the words of one liberal observer, evidence "hostility, poor work habits, passivity, low self-confidence, alcoholism [and] drug addiction."[108] But is expanded welfare to be blamed for any of this? That blame, as just demonstrated, cannot be attributed in a simple way for the simple reason that most of the male youths in question do not qualify for much welfare. It might still be attributed in a complex way by arguing that cultural values have shifted since the 1960s, and the War on Poverty and its aftermath contributed decisively to that shift. As we shall see, such arguments compromise the core of Charles Murray's case for condemning welfare, but that condemnation is particularly concerned with deterioration in family structures, and thus the topic is more appropriately considered below.

Table 10.2 Male civilian labor force participation rates by age and race.[a] 1955–1980

| Age | Race | Total participation rate | | | | | | Change 1965–80 |
		1955	1960	1965	1970	1975	1980	
16–17	White	48.0	46.0	44.6	48.9	51.8	53.6	9.0
	Black	48.2	45.6	39.3	34.8	30.1	31.9	−7.4
18–19	White	71.7	69.0	65.8	67.4	72.8	74.1	8.3
	Black	75.7	71.2	66.7	61.8	57.5	56.3	−10.4
20–24	White	85.6	87.8	85.3	83.3	85.5	87.1	1.8
	Black	89.7	90.4	89.8	83.5	78.4	78.9	−10.9
25–34	White	97.8	97.7	97.4	96.7	95.8	95.9	−1.5
	Black	95.8	96.2	95.7	93.7	91.4	90.4	−5.3
35–44	White	98.3	97.9	97.7	97.3	96.4	96.2	−1.5
	Black	96.2	95.5	94.2	92.2	90.0	89.7	−4.5
45–54	White	96.7	96.1	95.9	94.9	92.9	92.2	−3.7
	Black	94.2	92.3	92.0	88.2	84.6	83.9	−8.1
55–64	White	88.4	87.2	85.2	83.3	76.5	73.3	−11.9
	Black	83.1	82.5	78.8	79.2	68.7	63.5	−15.3
Total, 16	White	85.4	83.4	80.8	80.0	78.7	78.3	−2.5
and over	Black	85.0	83.0	79.6	76.5	71.5	70.8	−8.8

[a] "Black" refers to "Black and Other."

Source: *Employment and Training Report of the President*, transmitted to the Congress, 1981, table A-5, pp. 127–8

Work effort   The discussion now shifts its focus from black male youths to female heads of single-parent families. These are among the most important recipients of welfare in America, and it is their behavior that has been particularly studied in empirical investigations to be examined below. As to why females and not males, the answer has been previously given: over 98 percent of all single-parent families receiving AFDC are headed by women.

Perhaps unexpectedly, welfare programs usually impose what amounts to a high rate of taxation upon the recipients of aid. Understanding the nature of this tax is crucial to understanding why welfare programs may discourage the work effort of those who receive welfare.

Consider the typical AFDC recipient: probably a mother with several children and the father absent from the household. If she decides to work to supplement the income received from welfare payments, the more dollars earned from employment, the more her welfare payments will be reduced. A gap is thereby created between gross receipts from working and net receipts, or earned income minus (a) expenses incurred by working and (b) welfare dollars lost. For those on welfare, these prospective reductions in welfare benefits operate much like a government tax on extra income earned. Most

Americans are only too familiar with the disincentive effects of taxes taken out of earnings. Few who have not experienced welfare, however, have any sense of how rapidly welfare aid falls off as employment earnings rise – or put differently, how high the "effective" tax rate is on the earnings of welfare recipients.[109]

Those receiving Food Stamps, for example, lose $30 in benefits for every $100 of monthly income earned.[110] Those receiving AFDC lose, on the average, 50–60 cents in AFDC benefits for every dollar earned. High as these rates are, they understate the problem. When *all* welfare programs are combined and the question is asked by how much does *total* welfare fall as income from work increases, depending upon the state of residence the answer varies from 70 to 90 cents per dollar received from working for the first $1,000 in earnings.[111] Readers unfamiliar with welfare may find such high rates straining credibility. They can find further confirmation in appendix B (table B.7), in which average rates are calculated for an "average state" (Pennsylvania) by a leading expert on taxation. The rates in that example will be found to range as high as 98 percent.

As part of the tax reform debates of the early 1980s, the Reagan Administration and many others trumpeted the claim that a 50 percent tax rate was too high, that such rates for the nation's highest income earners seriously impaired their willingness to work. How unsurprising it therefore is that many should ask whether rates of 70–90 percent discourage the work effort of those at the bottom of the economic ladder. The interesting issue is not whether such high rates have *any* disincentive effect – obviously they do – but rather whether that disincentive effect is large or small. To answer the latter type of question requires an estimate of exceptional precision. What must be gauged, for each category of welfare recipient deemed relevant, is an average behavioral response; in this case, the average reduction in time worked for each "significant" increase in welfare (for example, for each extra $50 in benefits). This measure should then predict behavior in both directions: work effort cuts when welfare expands, and work effort expansion when welfare is cut. Efforts to gauge this behavioral response have produced a range of estimates that vary widely and show no signs of converging to a narrow range. The inevitable result is an ongoing debate that is often technical, sometimes heated, and, for the moment, unresolved.

If the question is whether increased welfare causes a complete withdrawal from the work force, the data indicate no wide swings in the willingness to be employed on the part of those who are poor, female, and heads of single-parent families – or more narrowly yet, on the part of mothers who are AFDC recipients (see tables 10.3 and 10.4). Despite the wide swings in AFDC benefits per family – sharply up in the 1960s and sharply down in the 1970s – women with low incomes and dependent children have not responded by moving in markedly greater numbers into, or out of, the labor force. Nor are the high rates of nonparticipation in the labor force suggested by tables 10.3 and 10.4 surprising. Many of the mothers in question have

Table 10.3 Percentage of household heads who did not work at all during the year, 1959–1984

	1959	1966	1970	1980	1984
In poor families					
All households	30.5	39.7	44.0	49.6	50.6
Female-headed households	57.1	52.7	56.6	61.5	62.5

Source: James Gwartney and Richard Stroup, "Transfers, equality, and the limits of public policy," *Cato Journal*, VI (Spring–Summer 1986), p. 129

Table 10.4 Work effort of mothers receiving Aid to Families with Dependent Children, 1967–1979[a]

	1967	1969	1971	1973	1975	1977	1979
Percentage of AFDC mothers							
Working full or part time	13.3	13.5	13.9	16.1	16.1	13.8	14.2
Looking for work	5.9	5.4	5.3	11.5	9.0	10.6	10.0
Total	19.2	18.9	19.2	27.6	25.1	24.4	24.2

[a] Labor force participation figures are for the month when the survey was done.

Source: Lawrence M. Mead, *Beyond Entitlement* (New York: Free Press, 1986), p. 75

young children to care for, face prospective day care costs that are relatively high for low-income families, and lack the skills to earn enough to afford these and other expenses associated with gainful employment.

The question noted previously, however, has yet to be addressed directly. For welfare recipients already working, will higher welfare benefits cause hours worked to fall by a little or a lot?

Some critics of the welfare system argue the case for "a lot,"[112] usually by citing evidence from Negative Income Tax (NIT) experiments, conducted during the late 1960s and 1970s at four sites across the country.[113] Each experiment (a) took a sample of the low-income population, (b) gave a generous benefit to each family irrespective of whether members were "voluntarily" or "involuntarily" unemployed, and (c) rewarded extra work by cutting benefits less than the amount of extra income earned to provide appropriate work incentives.[114] The results suggested that while hours worked by males did not change much in response to welfare, those of females did, including those females who were heads of single-parent families. The results of the Seattle–Denver experiment, generally regarded as the most sophisticated of the four, were summarized by the director of that study as follows:

On the average we found that the experiments caused a reduction in annual hours of work of about 5 percent for the male heads of families, about 22 percent for wives and 11 percent for female heads of families.[115]

Two of these numbers (11 and 22 percent) look impressive and suggest a significant response in hours worked to changes in state aid. Those wishing to discount such results have counterattacked on two fronts.

The first challenge is to question the relevance of NIT experiments for predicting or explaining the behavior of actual welfare recipients. The NIT experiments, the argument runs, were too narrow in geographic coverage, offered benefits far above those typically available to welfare recipients, and included in the test group the wrong group – those heretofore working regularly and not receiving welfare rather than "typical" welfare recipients.[116] Moreover, the argument continues, the findings of the four experiments diverged so widely from each other that any effort to collapse these findings into a single average is highly suspect. The disincentive effects for husbands, for example, ranged from 1 to 8 percent, whereas for wives they ranged from zero to 55 percent.[117] From dispersions such as these, assert the critics, no obvious inferences can be drawn concerning by how much *actual* work will fall for *actual* recipients of welfare when welfare benefits are increased.

The second challenge to NIT results is to note how the associated claims of "significant" responsiveness in work effort to changing welfare payments are inconsistent with another body of evidence. In 1981, the Omnibus Budget Reconciliation Act (OBRA) resulted in many AFDC recipients having their welfare benefits sharply curtailed or terminated. For those heretofore receiving such aid (mainly female heads of single-parent families) the effect was not unlike running the NIT experiment in reverse. In the NIT case, state aid was increased to see by how much work effort would decline. Now actual aid was being cut, and the empirical issue of particular interest was by how much work effort would increase. The answer, roughly summarized, was "not much." Female heads of single-parent families did not work significantly more hours if they were already working, and those not working previously showed no marked inclination after cuts in benefits to join the work force.[118]

In sum, two competing bodies of evidence suggest that two quite different adjectives can legitimately be used to characterize the responsiveness of work effort to welfare changes on the part of female heads of single-parent families: the NIT experiments are consistent with the claim of "significant" responsiveness; the observations of behavior following the 1981 cuts in AFDC benefits are consistent with a "relatively insignificant" responsiveness. Other evidence shows no sign of resolving this debate. One can therefore do little more than reiterate the opinions of two experts following a comprehensive review of the literature – the review now somewhat dated, but the opinion not: "the research findings are too varied, too uncertain, and themselves too colored with judgment to serve as more than a rough guide to policy choices."[119]

Duration If the controlling question is one of welfare dependency, one empirical issue to explore is the length of time that recipients of state aid remain on welfare. As is true for investigations of work effort, writers on duration tend to be split into two camps, one telling an optimistic story and the other a discouraging story. Compared with the previous conflict, the notable difference is that the two stories about duration are consistent with one other for the simple reason that they concern two different groups of welfare recipients.

The optimists tend to emphasize what none can deny: that a massive body of evidence indicates most of those who receive welfare do so for only a brief period of time.[120] Most often cited in this context are the findings from the University of Michigan Panel Study of Income Dynamics (PSID), which followed the economic fortunes of some 5,000 families for a decade (1969–78).[121] The evidence thereby assembled suggested two unexpected conclusions:

1   within a given decade, roughly one-quarter of all Americans can expect to be poor at some point, but most will be poor for only a year or two, and
2   between one-half and two-thirds of all welfare spells last for no more than one or two years.[122]

If the first is correct, the second is not surprising. If poverty (as officially measured) for most is a short-term phenomenon, presumably their reliance upon welfare will also be short-term. The other main point featured in the optimistic story is that when welfare is received, in many cases it is combined with income from other sources, including income from working. All of these findings point to one conclusion: that for most Americans, a spell on welfare is *not* analogous to dabbling in heroin – users do not quickly form a habit difficult to break. Or in the wording of two of the experts who emphasize this conclusion, "The patterns of welfare receipt . . . clearly allay the concern that any brush with the welfare system necessarily leads to dependence."[123]

And yet, retort the pessimists, the same body of evidence cited by the optimists makes abundantly clear that all is not well with the American welfare system. If many rely on welfare for only a short time, what of the few who use it for a long time? Although most who become poor remain poor only for a year or two, roughly one-sixth will be poor for eight years or more.[124] Many of the latter group come to depend on welfare for sustained periods of time. Half of those receiving AFDC at any point in time, for example, are in the midst of a welfare spell that will last eight years or longer.[125] Moreover, these long-term users are not randomly distributed throughout the population. A limited set of characteristics describes most members of this group, of which the following seem to be especially important: (a) young, nonwhite, and an unwed mother; (b) a high school dropout; and (c) did not have work experience before first receiving AFDC. Thus, for example, mothers receiving AFDC who are under 30, nonwhite, unmarried, and high school dropouts remain on welfare, on the average, for a decade.[126] Or to cite a second example, half of AFDC expenditures go to households in which the mother had her first child as a teenager.

This is the group that has become the focus of study by conservatives, particularly Charles Murray. To explore the characteristics of this cohort of welfare recipients, Murray used the data of the University of Michigan Panel Study to investigate (in that sample) how long women who were under 25 when they first received welfare remained on welfare. What he found was that only 3 percent were on welfare for a year or less, whereas 70 percent used welfare for five years or more, and one-third used it for ten years or more.[127]

None of this evidence on long-term use proves long-term welfare dependency in the sense of preferences being remolded by receipt of state aid.[128] But a mounting body of evidence is consistent with the hypothesis that reliance upon welfare has become a way of life for a small subset of welfare users. Other troubling evidence has surfaced about the disintegration of the family as a viable institution for many in this cohort. But that topic – and that evidence – are more appropriately considered in a later section.

Intergenerational dependency   Are children of long-term welfare recipients more likely to depend upon welfare after they themselves reach maturity and establish their own households? In theory, such transmission of welfare dependence (if there is transmission) could take place irrespective of whether the child is raised by one parent or two. In practice in America, as noted previously, the long-term users of welfare, particularly AFDC, are dominated by female heads of single-parent families.

The phrase "culture of poverty," popularized by Oscar Lewis and others in the 1960s, suggests the possibility that children raised in a poor household in a poor neighborhood are likely to acquire attitudes or behavioral traits that increase the chances they will be poor themselves after they become adults.[129] This somewhat vague and general concern is narrowed for purposes of this discussion in two ways: (a) the cause at issue (or at least the proximate cause of paramount concern) is not the "culture of poverty" but rather the long-term reliance upon welfare on the part of parents, and (b) the effect to be investigated is whether children of such parents themselves become long-term users of welfare after they become adults. If they do, such evidence is consistent with the controversial hypothesis that poverty and welfare dependence tend to persist "from one generation to the next because they foster the development of deviant values in parents, who in turn pass the deviant values on to their children, preparing them only for a similar life of welfare dependency."[130] To stand that inference on its head, if the hypothesis just cited is correct, one would expect a marked difference in welfare dependence among the offspring of long-terms welfare users. If that difference is not observed, serious doubts arise concerning the validity of the hypothesis.

By and large, that difference is not observed. Any conclusion must, however, be tempered by a sense of how sparse the relevant evidence is. Efforts to gather such evidence date largely from the 1960s, and the time elapsed since then is still too short to permit the amassing of comprehensive studies covering several generations in succession. The most promising source of information is the Panel Study of Michigan's Survey Research Center which was initiated in 1968. Evidence from that source and other data all point to a similar conclusion: that children who grow up in families dependent upon welfare are not themselves more likely than other children to become welfare users when they reach maturity.[131]

To repeat one point and add another, these findings are inconsistent with the hypothesis of intergenerational dependency, but they cannot be taken as conclusive proof that this hypothesis is wrong. As Edward Gramlich recently reminded those particularly concerned with studies of intergenerational dependency, "there are many difficulties with such analyses" and the results "need further scrutiny."[132] One topic for that scrutiny (albeit only one of many) is the linkage between poverty, dropping out of high school, and family structure. Those raised in single-parent families headed by females are more likely to drop out of high school,[133] and those who drop out of high school are more likely to be poor and thus future users of welfare.[134] A more formidable question standing in the wings is whether the recent startling rise in single-parent families can itself be attributed to welfare policies of the 1960s and beyond. But that is to raise the central issue of the next section.

The Evidence on Family Structure

In a subject rife with controversy, the one conclusion no one resists is that the family in America is an institution under pressure. Falling marriage rates and rising divorce rates, the growing importance of births out of wedlock and of single-parent families – all these signal in unmistakable terms a decline in the allegiance of the population to one of the country's most time-honored institutions (see figures 10.4–10.6).[135] But to what extent can these developments be attributed to the postwar expansion of America's welfare system, particularly those changes put in place as part of Lyndon Johnson's War on Poverty?

Some conservatives, as previously noted, single out welfare programs as the primary cause, denouncing the results with a vehemence uncommon in twentieth century welfare debates. Stripped to their essentials (and in the process losing many nuances) most of the accusations that "the welfare system" has disrupted the family structure of the poor reduce to one of three charges. (A fourth charge by Charles Murray will be taken up later.)

The most innocuous (or least distasteful) of the three is the claim that income support made possible by all welfare programs combined has reduced the economic pressures on those with limited income to endure an undesirable marriage, or to remarry quickly because of a perceived need for economic security.[136]

A second and quite different charge links the increased availability of welfare to the startling rise in illegitimate births, much in evidence in the United States since the mid-1960s. (Again, see figure 10.5.) One variant of this argument is that females with limited income prospects deliberately have a child to collect the welfare available to heads of single-parent families.[137] A second variant, and the one more commonly argued, is that few deliberately

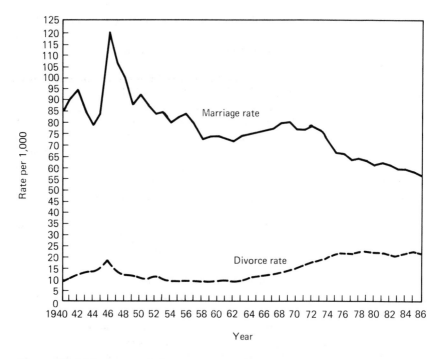

Figure 10.4 Marriage and divorce rates per 1,000 women 18 years and over, 1940–1986.

Sources: US Department of Health and Human Services, *Monthly Vital Statistics Report*, vol. XXXV, no. 1, supplement, May 2, 1986, p. 5; no. 6, supplement, September 25, 1986, pp. 5, 7; vol. XXXVIII, no. 2, supplement, June 6, 1989, p. 4; no. 3, supplement 2, June 13, 1989, p. 9.

become pregnant in order to qualify for welfare, but once pregnant, the unwed female is under much less pressure to become married or to have an abortion because of the prospective income available through welfare. Similarly, the argument concludes, once the child is born, the female is under less pressure to consider putting the baby up for adoption.

A third charge is directed at a single program: Aid to Families with Dependent Children. The eligibility requirements of this program, claim the critics, discourage the formation of families and encourage the breaking up of those already formed. Federal law restricts AFDC to needy children in single-parent families unless the second parent is incapacitated, under-employed, or unemployed. In practice, state restrictions in implementing this law have prevented two-parent families from collecting AFDC benefits in about half the states.[138] How little is received by two-parent families is indicated by the fact that approximately 10 percent of those families

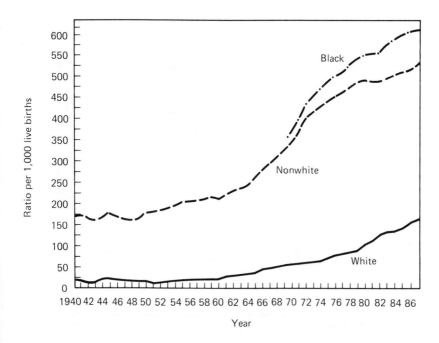

Figure 10.5 Births to unmarried women, 1940–1987 (ratio per 1,000 live births):
data for 1940–80, "estimated"; data for 1981–4, "reported/inferred"; data for
"Black," not available prior to 1969.

Sources: US Department of Health and Human Services, *Vital Statistics of the United States, 1982*
(Hyattsville, MD: National Center for Health Statistics, 1986), vol. I, *Natality*, table 1–31, p.
53, and *Monthly Vital Statistics Report*, vol. XXXIV, no. 6, supplement, September 20, 1985,
table 16, p. 30; vol XXXV, no. 4, supplement, July 18, 1986, table 16, p. 30; vol XXXVI,
no. 4; supplement, July 17, 1987, table 18, p. 31; vol. XXXVII, no. 3, supplement, July 12,
1988, *table 18*, p. 32; vol. XXXVIII, no. 3, supplement, June 29, 1989, table 18, p. 32.

qualifying for AFDC are deemed eligible because the father is "incapacitated" or "unemployed." The remaining 90 percent are families with only
one parent, and out of every 100 of these single-parent families, 98 are
headed by a female.[139] Small wonder then, conclude the critics, that the
female-headed single-parent family has rocketed into prominence in the
postwar era.

Buried in this last assertion is a cause-and-effect hypothesis, AFDC being
the cause and family disruption among recipients being the effect. Debates
among the experts about the validity of that statement or any other linking
welfare availability to the disturbing trends shown in figures 10.4–10.6 are
directed mainly to the question of whether available evidence squares with
the cause-and-effect mechanisms hypothesized by the critics of welfare. Here

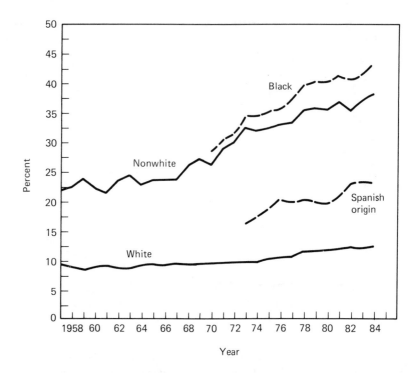

Figure 10.6 Percentage of families with female head, 1957–1984.
Sources: US Department of Commerce, *Statistical Abstract of the United States, 1958*, p. 47; *1959*, p. 43; *1960*, p. 43; *1961*, p. 39; *1962*, p. 43; *1963*, p. 42; *1964*, p. 37; *1965*, p. 37; *1966*, p. 37; *1967*, p. 38; *1969*, p. 36; *1970*, p. 36; *1971*, p. 37; *1972*, p. 38; *1973*, p. 40; *1974*, p. 40; *1976*, p. 40; *1977*, p. 43; *1978*, p. 46; *1979*, p. 47; *1980*, p. 48; *1981*, p. 43; *1982/83*, p. 46; *1984*, p. 48; *1985*, p. 41; *1986*, p. 40; William Julius Wilson and Kathryn M. Neckerman, "Poverty and family structure: the widening gap between evidence and public policy issues," in Sheldon H. Danziger and Daniel H. Weinberg (eds), *Fighting Poverty* (Cambridge, MA: Harvard University Press, 1986), p. 235; US Department of Commerce, *Current Population Reports*, Series P-20, table 1 in no. 371, no. 381, no. 388, no. 398.

too the limitations of evidence and existing explanatory models leave most of the major debates unambiguously unresolved.

Evidence from the negative income tax experiments   If the hypothesis is that more welfare increases the likelihood of families breaking up, one of the most obvious sources of evidence to check is that provided by the NIT experiments described earlier. Participants in those experiments received financial aid well above that typically available through regular welfare programs. If the hypothesis noted is correct, more of those families receiving such aid should break up – or "more" relative to those in the control group of the experiment who received no aid. Such an empirical investigation sounds simple enough, but how the observed results should be interpreted is still a topic in dispute.[140] The evidence of the NIT experiments, some argue, convincingly demonstrates that income maintenance payments to intact families increased the likelihood of marital dissolution. Others remain unconvinced, challenging this interpretation with a list of reservations that bears a marked resemblance to the list of reservations used to challenge the claim that NIT results demonstrated welfare "seriously" impairs work effort. The effect of NIT on family structure remains inconclusive, insist the skeptics, who note (among other reservations) that (a) the evidence on the propensity of families to break up is inconsistent across different experimental sites (splits did not increase at one site and at another increases in cash assistance seemed to decrease family dissolution), (b) family dissolution propensities differed significantly by race across different sites, and (c) the experiment as designed failed to distinguish between the effects of cash assistance and the effects of counseling and training, with the latter (counseling and training) singled out by some as the key to explaining much of the increase in marriage dissolutions when increases were observed.[141]

Few advocates of either viewpoint bother to point out that the NIT experiments were actually designed to test a different hypothesis; namely, that when state aid increases, marriage dissolutions will *decrease* (not increase), the major premise being that greater certainty of income among low-income families will alleviate marital tensions associated with economic insecurity. The evidence as described above clearly does not support *that* hypothesis. But to find evidence inconsistent with one claim – that more aid helps family stability – is not always equivalent to demonstrating the correctness of the opposite claim, as the reservations noted previously make clear. The same point was made more diplomatically by a former assistant secretary of the Department of Health, Education, and Welfare: "the hypothesis that noncategorical welfare would increase family stability remains unsupported by empirical research. The contrary hypothesis has received official, if premature, support."[142] In sum, if the question is whether welfare helps or hurts family stability, and the body of examined evidence is confined to that provided by the NIT experiments, the one defensible conclusion would seem to be: case not proved.

Other evidence   The other main source of evidence that has been analyzed for clues to the effects of welfare upon family structure is that provided by the observed behavior of AFDC recipients as AFDC payments have varied. As pointed out above, the real dollar benefits available through this program vary widely across states at any point in time, and over time have risen and then fallen sharply since the War on Poverty began. Casual observation of these trends has prompted some observers to conclude that any linking of welfare to the difficulties of the American family does not square with the most obvious of facts. For example, the percentage of single-parent families rose in the 1970s as did the percentage of births out of wedlock, while the real

value of AFDC payments fell (see figures 10.3, 10.5, and 10.6); thus, the rise
in the first two can hardly be the result of expansion of the third since welfare
was not expanding but contracting, or so runs an argument based upon a
casual scanning of the facts. Less casual and more scientific are the studies of
behavior of AFDC recipients by David Ellwood and Mary Jo Bane, who pool
cross-section and time series data to test whether any systematic relationship
exists between variations in AFDC benefits on the one hand and changes in
illegitimacy rates and changes in divorce and separation rates on the
other.[143] Their major findings are that changes in AFDC benefit levels
(a) have no measurable impact upon births to unmarried women, (b) have
only a modest effect upon divorce and separation rates (primarily among
young married mothers), and (c) have only a modest effect upon "female
headship rates," or the rate of formation of single-parent families headed by
females. Ellwood and Bane do find that the level of welfare payments has had
a significant impact upon the living arrangements of single mothers: young
mothers not living with a husband are much more likely to live independently than at the home of their parents when AFDC benefits are high.

Overall their findings imply that welfare has not played a major role as a
cause of recent trends in rising family dissolutions and rising illegitimacy
rates – a conclusion many have been quick to infer from the Ellwood–Bane
study and others have been quick to repeat in the professional and popular
literature.[144] Reinforcement for such views can be found in many other
studies that reach similar conclusions about a similar lack of importance of
the present welfare system in any explanation of existing pressures on the
American family. (A minority of studies, often using the same data, have
reached the opposite conclusion.[145]) If this finding of the unimportance of
welfare is accepted, the charges of conservatives such as George Gilder and
Charles Murray can only be regarded as incorrect or, at the very least,
grossly overstated. The War on Poverty cannot be accused of creating "a
wreckage of broken and dependent families" (Gilder's claim),[146] nor can one
reasonably expect that scrapping existing welfare programs "would
drastically reduce births to single teenage girls [and] reverse the trendline in
the breakup of poor families" (Murray's policy solution).[147] If welfare has
not been a major cause, scrapping welfare is unlikely to be an effective cure.
Murray, however, still believes otherwise.

*Challenging the evidence by changing the hypothesis: the rejoinder of Charles
Murray*   Built into the above analysis, and probably unnoticed, is a seemingly uncontroversial hypothesis about how the cause in question (welfare)
affects two variables (family dissolutions and illegitimate births). The
relationship hypothesized is one of direct incremental interaction: that a little
more of one will cause a little more of the other. One of the easiest ways to
challenge all of the above findings about the seeming unimportance of
welfare is to assert that the causal processes at work are markedly different
from the one just described. Suppose instead that welfare has an impact only
when a certain threshold is achieved, and then the impact persists as long as

welfare remains above that designated level. Below this threshold, welfare – whatever its level or fluctuations might be – has little impact upon family stability or births out of wedlock. Once this threshold is crossed, however, it has a "major" or "decisive" effect upon these two. Moreover – and this is the central point – as long as welfare continues above this threshold, its decisive impact continues, *whether the dollar value of (above-threshold) welfare rises or falls.* To demonstrate that illegitimate births have continued to rise despite the recent fall in welfare payments is therefore to prove nothing about the irrelevance of the second as a cause of the first. To assert that such a demonstration does prove the absence of cause and effect is equivalent (or so the argument would run) to asserting that if matches will still light in a submarine when the oxygen level falls by 5 percent, then oxygen must be irrelevant for ignition. If welfare payments remain above the threshold level, concludes this argument – even if actual benefit payments decline – their impact upon illegitimate births persists, and this impact is of the first importance. To put the matter more bluntly, the findings of Ellwood and Bane are irrelevant because they are predicated upon a cause and effect relationship that is irrelevant. Or so Charles Murray would have us believe.

For Murray, the welfare threshold was crossed in the 1960s. The crossing is portrayed as a complex phenomenon involving not just more dollars for welfare recipients, but also a shift in a variety of attitudes encouraged by those dispensing welfare. The effects of this threshold crossing are also portrayed in complex terms, but the end result can be stated simply: a disruption of the family among those the welfare programs were designed to help.

In spelling out the nature of this disruption, Charles Murray begins where George Gilder begins – with the notion that generous welfare payments undermine male authority in the family, impairing the husband's sense of self-worth and his sense of responsibility toward his family and his off-spring.[148] The attitude of unmarried males is also changed for the worse. A new option is now available to them: reliance for income support upon a female who is herself supported by the (now generous) welfare system. As this option gains in social acceptability, community allegiance to the family as an institution wanes. "Getting a woman to support you confers status. Conversely, the status formerly associated with 'being a good provider' disappears . . . ."[149] The last step in this reasoning Murray describes as follows.

To simplify a rich argument: The existence of an extensive welfare system permits the woman to put less pressure on the man to behave responsibly, which facilitates irresponsible behavior on his part, which in turn leads the woman to put less reliance on the man, which exacerbates his sense of superfluity and his search for alternative definitions of manliness. When welfare recipients are concentrated, as they are in the inner city, these dynamics create problems that extend far beyond the recipients of welfare. Community values and expectations of male behavior are changed, and with them the behavior of young men and women who never touch an AFDC check.[150]

To a picture already bleak Murray adds further causal interactions he claims have made a bad situation worse. These include:

1 the "concentrated efforts" of "educational reformers" to stop schools treating unwed pregnant girls in punitive ways;
2 the rising crime rate in inner city ghettos, and the associated decline in the willingness of women to rely upon men prone to illegal activity; and
3 the rise in the popularity of a set of attitudes or beliefs, encouraged by welfare programs and welfare workers, that the poor are largely not responsible for their own poverty and have little control over their own economic destiny (a message, Murray concludes with more than a little disenchantment, that has been "conveyed most loudly and emphatically to black youths").[151]

The combined results, Murray concludes, are both unwelcome and unsurprising.

The environment in which a young poor person grew up changed in several mutually consistent and interacting ways during the 1960s. The changes in welfare *and* changes in the risks attached to crime *and* changes in the educational environment reinforced each other. Together, they changed the incentive structure facing young people and they changed status rewards associated with behaviors that make escape from poverty possible.[152]

Or again:

The hypothesis is that the effect of the social reforms of the 1960s on a specific problem such as illegitimacy springs not only from discrete changes in incentives and status rewards, but also from a larger effect on the formation of character among poor young people, and especially black poor young people.[153]

The ensuing battle between conservative Murray and his liberal critics remains unresolved, and predictably so. The ultimate defense against empirical assault is an untestable hypothesis, and at bottom that is what Murray has advanced. No evidence comes readily to mind which, if discovered, would be glaringly inconsistent with his thesis.[154] The absence of a discontinuous jump in illegitimacy rates and family breakups once the welfare threshold was crossed in the 1960s, for example, is perfectly consistent with the impact mechanisms he postulates, given that these mechanisms require time for attitudes to be remolded and observed behavior subsequently to change.[155] What therefore seemed at the outset of this section to be a straightforward question of fact has now become a contest between at least two competing hypotheses about human behavior, with no clear way of resolving that competition. If it cannot be resolved, what might be said about conflicting claims still being trumpeted from the battlefield?

Hypotheses and evidence reviewed   What do we know, and what do we not know that we wish we did know?

Under the first heading – what we know – the evidence is unequivocal that the family in America is an institution in considerable difficulties. Three related findings are both striking and worrisome.

1 Postwar trends in aggregate measures – marriage rates, divorce rates, percentage of single-parent families, percentage of births out of wedlock – all demonstrate that pressures on the family, while not new, have become far more pronounced in recent decades.
2 Although all racial and ethnic groups appear to have been affected by these trends, the effects are particularly evident among the black population. Thus, between those Bureau of the Census categories "White" and "Black" is a gap of significant magnitude in whatever indicator one might choose as symptomatic of these pressures: percentage of families headed by women, percentage of unwed teenage mothers receiving welfare, percentage of children living in "mother-only" families (see tables 10.5 and 10.6).[156]
3 Among the black population, these pressures have had little impact upon some while for others the impact has been little short of devastating. In the latter group are large numbers of young people living impoverished lives in urban ghettos. Many of the males are high school dropouts

Table 10.5 United States: racial differences in marital and family status, 1960–1984

	White	Black
Percentage of women 15–44 living with husband		
1960	69	52[a]
1970	61	42
1980	55	30
1984	55	28
Percentage of families with children under 18 maintained by a woman		
1960	6	24[a]
1970	9	33
1980	14	48
1984	15	50
Percentage of children under age 18 in mother-only families		
1960	6	20[a]
1970	8	29
1980	14	44
1984	15	50

[a] Data for 1960 for "Nonwhites"; not available for "Blacks" separately.

Source: Reynolds Farley, "Assessing black progress: employment, occupation, earnings, income, poverty," *Economic Outlook USA*, X (Third Quarter 1986), p. 19

Table 10.6 Poverty and public assistance participation of mothers aged 16–19 by race and marital status, 1984–1985

	Percentage in each marital status, 1985	*Percentage with incomes at or below poverty, 1984*	*Percentage who received public assistance,*[a] *1984–5*
Total: 559,926		32.0	30.0
Never married	50.0	34.6	44.6
Married	44.3	29.7	11.5
Divorced or separated	5.8	28.1	46.5
Whites: 374,943		26.5	20.7
Never married	30.3	27.5	35.7
Married	62.1	26.2	10.6
Divorced or separated	7.7	24.7	43.1
Nonwhites:[b] 184,983		43.4	49.0
Never married	89.7	39.4	50.7
Married	8.2	83.5	24.5
Divorced or separated	2.0	53.8	72.5

[a] Public assistance includes AFDC, SSI, and General Assistance.
[b] Hispanics are included in white and nonwhite categories. Blacks comprise 97 percent of nonwhites.

Source: Sheldon H. Danziger, "Breaking the chains," University of Wisconsin Institute for Research on Poverty Discussion Paper 825–86, table 2. Data from the 1985 Current Population Survey Extract, analysis prepared by IRP

lacking marketable skills, with high unemployment rates and a limited history of participation in the labor force, for whom crime both threatens daily existence and provides dubious options as a source of income. Many of the females are also high school dropouts, similarly short on basic marketable skills, who had their first child as a teenager but still lack a husband, and rely on welfare as a major source of income. Whatever may be the causes of their present plight, the future prospects for most of these young people are unremittingly bleak, with little chance of moving to a less perilous environment, little chance of remedying deficiencies in basic skills, little chance of grasping for a higher rung on the economic ladder. The United States therefore seems to be developing what many Americans would claim has never truly existed in the past: an "underclass," immobile and at the bottom, with the growing popularity of that term indicative of a growing acknowledgement of the problem.

What is to be done? One can hardly offer remedies – or offer them with confidence – until the causes of the problem have been determined. The difficulty, as developed at length above, is that the search for causes is still shrouded in the smoke of unresolved debates. Experts remain passionately divided on most of the key issues, including whether welfare should be regarded as a large part of the problem or a large part of the solution. What has been settled to the satisfaction of most is that no simple direct relationship exists between welfare as a cause and family dissolutions and illegitimate births as effects. This does not of course rule out complex and indirect relationships of the sort hypothesized by Charles Murray. In more technical language, to demonstrate an absence of statistical significance is not to prove that no relationship exists among the variables included in the model of causation being tested. All that has been demonstrated by the test is that the relationship (if there is one) is not of the sort hypothesized by that particular model. Moreover, the fashionable tools for statistical testing (such as those of conventional regression analysis) are ill-suited for detecting complex relationships with many interactions (from cause to effect to cause) and many circuitous and delayed interactions (from cause A to B to C to D to the effect of particular concern.)[157] For testing a hypothesis such as Murray's, with many of the variables difficult to quantify and many of the interactions purported to occur in discrete jumps vaguely specified, such tools are likely to be no more helpful to the would-be analyst than a pickax is to a brain surgeon. Whether other tools and other methods of analysis will be devised to help gauge the validity of such a complicated hypothesis is yet another unresolved question in this debate.

If old tools have yielded few definitive insights and new tools have not yet been devised to shed more light upon these issues, the most defensible position is obviously one of caution. The most careful of informed discussants therefore argue that the reaching of conclusions (or conclusions that are relatively trustworthy) is premature because of "incomplete data" or "inadequate model specification" or "our incomplete understanding" of the causes and effects at issue.[158] Their position, which seems unassailable, makes all the more surprising the confidence and zeal with which other discussants in the same debate argue their position. As pointed out above, George Gilder and Charles Murray are not given to couching their condemnation of the welfare system in language that suggests gray areas of uncertainty. But they are not alone.[159] On the other side of the debate, Senator Daniel Patrick Moynihan appears as confident that the welfare system had no detrimental effects as Charles Murray is confident it did. After castigating Murray for reaching conclusions unsupported by the evidence, Moynihan himself concludes:

Government did not transform the behavior of those in greatest difficulty; it pretty much left them be. Behavior that was already more than sufficiently self-destructive simply went forward, with the consequences growing more pronounced – which is the normal progression of self-destructive behavior.[160]

From political scientist Glenn Loury came a rapier-like thrust that went to the heart of the issue: "We must ask the Senator, as he asks Charles Murray: How does he know?"[161] What Moynihan knows is that studies, such as the much-cited work of Ellwood and Bane, find no statistical evidence that government welfare transforms behavior in simple and direct ways. What Moynihan does not know (and neither does Charles Murray) is whether complex interactions of the sort hypothesized by Murray were actually at work as causal mechanisms of some significance, or of great significance, in the 1960s and later decades. Or to put the same point in more general terms, to make a decisive claim about the absence of an influence is to claim more than the current evidence will support.

As for the underlying reasons why uncertainty seems inescapable for all the analysts of these problems – and for all the analysts of other problems raised in previous sections of this chapter – the reader is referred to "The missing overview" at the end of the opening section.

11

Dilemmas Few Confront

Introduction

Writing a book on a sprawling topic such as this one is a bit like trying to organize furniture in a newly acquired house. Each chapter (like each room) begins in disarray, and ends – or so one hopes – with a semblance of order and decorum, in part by shunting extraneous material somewhere else. In the end, of course, one has the task of straightening up the final room, with the uncomfortable realization that the remaining furniture and bric-a-brac must either be integrated into the room's decor or thrown out. The present chapter for our study of economic justice is, in a sense, that final room. Admittedly two others follow, but their task is merely to summarize all that has gone before and then formulate a few policy recommendations in the light of that summary. The topics about to be considered here, in placement but not in significance, are appropriately regarded as a residual. They are intellectual furniture that had no obvious place in earlier rooms, but because of their importance must be retained somewhere in the house. Judged as a collection, they therefore lack a certain unity and coherence. The reader accordingly may sense the absence of a unifying theme. That is because there is none – or none beyond (a) each topic is concerned with economic justice, (b) all highlight various complexities endemic to discussions of economic justice, and (c) each constitutes a dilemma not easily resolved and commonly ignored.

Merit, Luck, and Social Justice

So, then, to every man his chance –
To every man, regardless of his birth,
His shining, golden opportunity –
To every man the right to live,
To work, to be himself,
And to become
Whatever thing his manhood and his vision
Can combine to make him –
This, seeker,
Is the promise of America

Thomas Wolfe

The left and right within America have lost touch with the middle. To foreign observers, this may seem unsurprising. In any spectrum of ideology, the two extremes, precisely because they are extreme, are expected to be different from the center. The difficulty is that, within America, most liberals and conservatives do not consider their views to be that far removed from those of the majority of the population. One of the important differences – perhaps the most important difference of all – is that both left and right as they expound on economic justice tend to dismiss what is still, for most Americans, an integral part of their notion of economic justice, namely, that in the marketplace merit is rewarded and ought to be rewarded.

Throughout English and American history, one idea with immense appeal has been that human actors through their actions bring upon themselves their just deserts. Adam Smith begins Part II of *The Theory of Moral Sentiments* with the observation:

There is another set of qualities ascribed to the actions and conduct of mankind, distinct from their propriety or impropriety, their decency or ungracefulness, and which are the objects of a distinct species of approbation and disapprobation. These are Merit and Demerit, the qualities of deserving reward, and of deserving punishment.[1]

As Smith points out, one common definition of merit *is*, "deserving of reward." How reasonable it seems, therefore, to run this definition backwards in discussions about how an economic system ought to function. Income payments are the rewards, and these ought to be received, runs an appealing argument, for the exercise of merit – or in more stilted language, for praiseworthy qualities of conduct. The conduct most Americans are inclined to praise in the marketplace is that which is productive, and the qualities singled out as admirable virtues leading to such results are diligence, thrift, foresight, and the like. (The reasons for the fusion of the two in the popular imagination – the exercise of virtuous traits and the results of greater output – have been discussed at length in earlier chapters.)

Liberals are inclined to dismiss such arguments as naive, singling out particularly the role of luck as a determinant of market rewards. The prizes in the economic race, they never tire of emphasizing, are a function of a multitude of factors all beyond the individual's control: that bag and baggage of causal forces lumped under the three broad headings of (a) heredity, (b) environment, and (c) the operation of supply and demand in a market economy. If luck as well as individual volition determines rewards, and none can say how much is contributed by each, the role of merit as a determinant of incomes actually received becomes obscure. Some liberals go further and claim in essence that luck determines all (or almost all). Accordingly the American Dream about which Thomas Wolfe writes so eloquently at the outset of this section is, for these writers, nothing more than a myth.[2] Equality of opportunity does not exist, they argue, and prizes in the economic race have nothing to do with meritorious behavior and everything to do with luck and that special brand of luck called "privilege": having the right parents and the right connections. If individual volition and meritorious behavior have no effect upon outcomes in the market, recipients of incomes would seem to have no moral claim to what they have received. When moral justification for observed income inequalities is lacking, the condemnation of the economic system by egalitarians is sure to follow. And so it does. Michael Harrington aptly summarizes the opinions of many on the extreme left when he denounces capitalism as "outrageously unjust."[3] The final step in this reasoning commonly advanced by the extreme left is to note that if the economic system under capitalism is unjust, the way to make that system more just is to get rid of a number of capitalist institutions, or better yet, scrap the entire system in favor of another, with the preferred choice usually being some variant of socialism.

Conservatives balk long before that bottom line, but they do accept the initial premise: that the role of merit in determining market rewards is unclear because the role of luck is impossible to deny and difficult to assess. Having accepted that premise, they feel obliged to build their defense of the market system upon foundations that omit any reference to merit earning its just reward. The nature of that foundation has been explored above, particularly in chapter 4, and need not be reviewed here. What is worth underlining, however, is the evident scorn with which so many conservatives dismiss the notion of social justice and related ideas linking market rewards to meritorious behavior. Friedrich Hayek is perhaps best known on the right for this disdain, but he is not alone. Thomas Sowell concedes that other conservatives "do not discuss it [social justice], even as something to be rebutted." In what Sowell labels the "constrained vision" (a vision appealing to conservative Sowell), the concept of social justice is "beneath contempt."[4] This is an astonishing admission about a concept so integral to the belief system of so many Americans. Conservatives willingly admit that popularity.[5] Some conservatives, particularly those better known for the style of their polemics than the rigor of their reasoning, on occasion even write as if they harbored some suspicions – or more than this, harbored the expectation – that rewards in the marketplace are in some way linked to merit.[6] But those acknowledged as intellectual leaders on the right by the right generally reject such ideas out of hand. (The outstanding exception, as discussed in appendix G, is Irving Kristol.)

This unanimity of liberals and conservatives concerning the futility of discussing merit in discussions of how an economic system ought to function raises the obvious question of why so many Americans cling to what so many intellectuals have relegated to the ideological scrap heap. Part of the answer is the intellectual's bias for rigor – a bias encountered repeatedly in earlier chapters, and one that does not always lead in fruitful directions if the topic under scrutiny relates to economic justice. The question might be put more positively. Suppose one's notion of economic justice included the idea that merit in the marketplace should be and is rewarded, but had to admit that luck also influenced rewards and, further, that the relative importance of the two – luck and merit – can seldom if ever be discerned. If these beliefs and this admission are to be in some way reconciled, what additional arguments might be offered? For solving this dilemma, as previously pointed out, one turns to left and right in vain.

Two requirements come readily to mind. One would want *some* correlation – preferably a *strong* correlation – between meritorious actions and subsequent market rewards. The difficult problem is luck. What might "fairness" mean in a system in which luck influences the outcomes? One tempting mental dodge is to set aside the problem. "Luck never just *happens*," Grandfather Frog assures his listeners in the Thornton Burgess children's tale of life at the Smiling Pool. "What people call bad luck is just the result of their own foolishness or carelessness or both, and what people call good luck is just the result of their own wisdom and carefulness and common sense."[7] Grandfather Frog's claim to the contrary – and the claim is a common theme in children's literature – some rewards and penalties are clearly the result of accidental circumstances beyond the individual's control. If the influence of luck cannot be avoided, what would make that influence "fair," or at the very least, not "outrageously unjust"? The notion of equality of opportunity suggests one possible answer. Luck should not affect any identifiable group in a disproportionate way. Or put as a positive premise, luck should be a random event equally likely to strike rich and poor, and equally likely to affect any other grouping of society that one feels is relevant for discussions of economic justice. The more this ideal is approximated (the random influence of luck across different groups), the more the result would seem consistent with conventional American thoughts about equality of opportunity, particularly insofar as those thoughts are bolstered by a belief that market rewards, although random with respect to luck, are decidedly nonrandom with respect to meritorious behavior.

This revised conceptual framework could be regarded as an effort to salvage a workable notion of economic justice (including merit receiving some reward) in an imperfect and uncertain world. If luck is random in the economic system while merit remains strongly correlated with reward, then on the average, those engaged in meritorious activity should receive some compensation for their efforts. Consider, for example, rewards to farmers. Rainful affects grain yields, but so too does the diligence of the farmer. The first could be considered the result of luck, with the "fairness" in the luck consisting in the "randomness" of its incidence; that is, good or bad rainfall within a given region is no more likely to be experienced by the wealthy farmer than by the poor one. As to the role of diligence in a world where rainfall also influences results, the premise is that, on the average, farmers who work hard will do better than those who do not. How much better is difficult to say, and some who work hard may actually do worse because of other accidental circumstances (flooding or tornados, for example). The article of faith assures nothing for the individual but does hold out a hope for statistical aggregates: that collectively and over time, the hard working in agriculture will have more to show for their efforts than will those who are less industrious. The end result is far from perfect, and the associated norms of fairness are far from precise, but this may be the best that can be hoped for by those who cling to notions of merit receiving some reward in an economic system fraught with capricious influences.

The fairness of this merit-cum-luck version of a fair market system might be further bolstered by a variety of policies, for example, those designed to strengthen the correlation between merit and reward, as well as those designed to minimize the nonrandomness of luck across different income groups. One might also, in the name of fairness, want to mitigate the worst effects of bad luck in the market, however randomly that bad luck is distributed across participants.

It could be argued that a predilection for premises akin to those outlined above helps to explain why the American middle tends to accept what left and right reject, namely, the notion that economic justice should include the idea of merit earning its just reward, and that in the American market as it presently functions, merit does tend to be rewarded despite the evident role of luck. For many who espouse such beliefs no doubt the associated premises remain vague or ill-formed. As a people Americans are not inclined to agonize about the degree of rigor in their ethical reasoning, including that reasoning concerned with enhancing the justice of their economic system. Much of social legislation promoted in this century might nevertheless be viewed as motivated, at least in part, by a desire to make rewards become more closely correlated with merit, or to make the influence of luck more random across income groups, or to mitigate the worst effects of economic misfortune, particularly when those effects have their impact on the least advantaged members of society. Laws prohibiting discrimination and laws promoting equality of opportunity are all consistent with one or more of these priorities, as are efforts to develop unemployment insurance, workmen's compensation, and protection against the economic catastrophe that can accompany catastrophic illness.[8]

Whatever their motivation, Americans of the modern era have remained doggedly determined in their efforts to refine their laws in the name of promoting a more just economic system, and have refused to be deflected from that ambition by the finely spun arguments of either left or right. They remain monumentally indifferent, for example, to an argument of the extreme right that (a) equality of opportunity can never be perfect unless family influence is abolished, (b) the family is a social institution that should never be abolished, and thus (c) the pursuit of equality of opportunity is a pointless endeavour.[9] Even if perfection is unattainable, the majority of Americans evidently believe that there is no reason not to attempt to address egregious imperfections which can be readily identified and usefully improved by government action. A similar plea for another kind of perfection by the extreme right is similarly dismissed. Friedrich Hayek is among those who have argued that (a) any government action in the name of social justice must be based upon a set of values precisely specified and universally agreed to, (b) no such set of values exists, and therefore (c) no state action in pursuit of social justice can ever be justified. Americans are generally content to aim much lower, searching for some workable consensus on what is "better" and "worse," and for some means that appears to have a reasonable chance of achieving the "better" without incurring unreasonable costs. The previous sentence is a paragon of vagueness, with words like "better" and "worse" and "reasonable chance." Such vagueness may offend the advocates of rigor, but it seldom deters most of the citizenry from getting on with the business not of devising the perfect society, but rather of making small changes in a machine they view as working tolerably well when the need for change is evident to the many and the means for change are reasonably well identified. This is not a society which, in its fumblings toward improvement, is likely to win the admiration of either Friedrich Hayek or John Rawls. It is a society that seems to embrace the priority of improvement and recognize that fumbling will be the rule, not the exception, on the road to progress.

To sum up: unlike many leading writers among liberals and conservatives, the vast majority of Americans have been able to acknowledge the role of luck and still cling to the notion that their society can claim a reasonable measure of economic justice. Merit, they believe, still influences reward and the American Dream of which Thomas Wolfe writes in the passage cited at the outset still resonates powerfully in the popular imagination. Intellectuals on the left may dismiss the dream as a myth, but politicians on the left are generally inclined to endorse it. Witness the ringing affirmation by Governor Mario Cuomo: "You will rise or fall on your merits as a person and the quality of your work. All else is distraction."[10] Admittedly the dream lacks clarity, colored as it is by indefinite hopes and elusive ideals. Admittedly reality has never quite matched the dream, however defined, with some mismatches more embarrassing than others: slavery in the nineteenth century, for example, and discrimination in the present century. But the influence of luck on actual outcomes has never seriously imperilled the dream nor been a source of marked embarrassment as long as the belief persists that reward and merit are strongly linked and luck is reasonably random, all phrases comfortably vague. The race is admittedly not entirely fair – a point that Americans are usually willing to concede – but the odds for most are not that bad. And where the odds seem unfairly stacked against competitors suffering from misfortunes not of their own making, most seem to favor state action to attempt to improve those odds. The Economic Opportunity Act of 1964 offers a case in point. President Johnson's endorsement emphasized an ambition which the Act's title had already made clear: "It is a struggle to give people a chance. It is an effort to allow them to develop and use their capacities, as we have been allowed to develop and use ours, so that they can share, as others share, in the promise of this Nation."[11]

Such beliefs and such ambitions are not trivial for the nation. Only if the processes of the economic system are viewed as reasonably fair can the outcomes of that system be regarded as morally defensible. And to view the American brand of capitalism as morally defensible, or reasonably so, is crucially important for most citizens of this country. If that impression were destroyed – if the majority came to believe that their economic system was intrinsically unjust – then part of the glue that holds the fabric of society together in its present form would also be destroyed. "Isn't the most valuable thing we have," asked Congressman Gossett of Treasury Secretary Vinson, "the personal initiative, pride and confidence of the everyday average American citizen in his belief that he can earn by virtue of his own character and resources?"[12] One suspects that the everyday average citizen – or most of them – would nod their heads, not with the reluctance of hesitant believers but with a punctuated snap suggesting certainty and pride.

Despite the role of luck, then, most Americans regard their economic system as reasonably just and the associated income distribution as morally defensible, or reasonably so. One as yet unexamined difficulty is that crucial to this defense, as noted, is the linking of merit and reward, and modern insights of psychology and biology threaten to so expand the notion of luck that the notion of individual merit becomes problematic. It is to some of the problems that are created for notions of economic justice by this expanded notion of luck that the discussion now turns.

Environment, Personality, and Individual Responsibility

Environment and Personality

The belief that heredity can affect personality in pervasive ways is a very modern notion. We now know that genes or genetic malfunction can cause certain diseases, such as hemophilia or muscular dystrophy. Many also believe that genes create "predispositions" to react to certain environmental stimuli in certain ways, raising the possibility that in the future such behavior as aggressiveness and criminal tendencies may be linked to factors of heredity. For the moment, however, "predisposition" would seem to be a word that helps disguise our ignorance about what remains largely unknown or, at best, dimly understood. The role of heredity in personality formation is accordingly a story to be written largely in the future.

The notion that environment can affect personality in major ways is very old. Aristotle complained that "The wealthy are insolent and arrogant, being mentally affected by the acquisition of wealth . . . ."[13] Horace noted the effect on character of being at the other end of the economic spectrum, where poverty "makes men both do and put up with anything and desert the hard road of virtue." "The roots of depraved desires must be eradicated," he advised, "and characters that are too soft must be shaped in sterner pursuits."[14] In the modern era, development economics has helped to publicize behavioral tendencies that its practitioners have labeled the "demonstration effect"; that is, desires and satisfactions are conditioned by the goods and services others are seen to be enjoying. Similar insights were common in the nineteenth century. Marx wrote that "if a palace arises beside [a] little house" the owner of the house "will feel more and more uncomfortable, dissatisfied and cramped within its four walls."[15] Emily Dickinson generalized the propensity, and suggested more subtle possibilities:

Had I not seen the Sun
I could have borne the shade
But Light a newer Wilderness
My wilderness has made –[16]

However frequently made and commonly endorsed such observations were in times gone by, no generation before our own has had its thinking quite so colored by the notion that environment can and does affect personality in a multitude of ways. Partly this reflects the growing influence of modern psychology, for which insights such as that of Emily Dickinson can be the stuff of which entire subdisciplines are made. But even those unfamiliar with the discipline and subdisciplines – those who have never heard or read the pronouncements of psychiatrists of psychologists – almost invariably include in their own daily discourse a host of references suggesting that environment affects character and competence. The key words in the previous statement – "environment," "character," and "competence" – are noticeably vague. Under the first are commonly included the "influence" (another vague word) of family, school and church, peer group values, professional standards, and cultural norms. The "character and competence" of particular concern in discussions of economic performance usually include all the items on that list of old-fashioned virtues spelled out in previous chapters: prudence, diligence, and thrift, and such related ideas as commitment to the work ethic and the desire to strive and to excel. The public has also come to recognize the possibility that if environment can affect personality, manipulations of the environment might be used for good or ill to manipulate the character of the citizenry. Extreme variants of this strategy have been popularized in such fictional works as Huxley's *Brave New World* and Orwell's *Nineteen Eighty-Four*. The facts occasionally surfacing from totalitarian regimes also suggest that such manipulations have, regrettably, much to recommend them for a dictatorial regime. But one does not need to look abroad to find examples of environmental influences warping personality. The now popular phrase "culture of poverty" suggests a possibility closer to home. One might, for example, begin with Senator Moynihan's observation that the quality of family life "is decisive in determining not only if a person has the capacity to love another individual but in the larger social sense whether he is capable of loving his fellow men collectively."[17] Then read Ken Auletta's account of Mickey, convicted at the age of 12 of battering in the skull of an elderly woman when she resisted his attempt to steal her purse.

His mother is a heroin addict. His father comes by the house "sometimes," according to his mother. Mick-Mick [as he's called] is one of seven children his mother had with three different men. "The children drove me to use drugs," she says. Her children and her two sisters' children – in all about 20, including Mickey – live with their grandmother on Willard Street. . . . Grandmother says she couldn't always keep track of Mickey. "He'd be gone for days," she said. "He liked to go downtown and be around the hustlers and the pimps . . . ." Mickey's lawyer, Dennis O'Keefe, agrees: "His problem is that he finds himself involved with older kids. He is easily led by his peers . . . . He has no inner drive of his own. He goes along with the crowd. . . . This kid was without any acceptable role model of what he should become. With all the kids in the house, his grandmother couldn't control them. He was cut adrift to mingle among kids, roam the street. His male model was older kids. For them, street robberies or anything else is acceptable."[18]

Few would be surprised at Mickey's limited capacity for "loving his fellow men collectively" (Moynihan's phrase). That lack of surprise, in turn, seems to reflect acceptance of the notion that environments such as this are not well suited to fostering capacities such as those.

Liberals and conservatives have both endorsed this common notion that environment has *some* effect on personality. The extent of their endorsement, however, differs markedly, as do the purposes for which they use environment–personality arguments.

The right, at bottom, is reluctant to use any of these arguments, and with good reason. Their emphasis has always been on the individual's responsibility to be self-reliant and pursue self-fulfillment, and as we shall see, just what responsibility means becomes progressively less clear as the domain of environmental influences expands.

Conservatives nevertheless cannot resist employing environment–personality arguments when such arguments support other claims important to policy positions they support. Recall, for example, what is for most conservatives the foremost item on their agenda: resistance to the expansion of the welfare state, that *bête noire* that liberals threaten to impose upon an unwary public, or so the right would have that public believe. Part of the conservative argument against expansion turns on the dangerous human propensities unleashed when power becomes concentrated in the hands of state officials, including welfare officials. Often quoted in this context is Lord Acton's assertion that all power tends to corrupt and absolute power corrupts absolutely – about as unambiguous a linkage as can be made between environment and the effects on personality that environment can produce. A similar linkage is evident in another conservative attack upon the welfare state. The bottom line – in this case, Charles Murray's – is that for the good of the poor the programs of the welfare state should be abandoned. The premises leading to that policy recommendation are all those professed by Murray linking a changed welfare environment in the 1960s to the development of undesirable personality traits, including those traits associated with increased dependency[19] and increased family disruption among the poor. As for secondary effects from dependency to the development of further undesirable traits, conservative Irving Kristol has rephrased Lord Acton's dictum to read: "dependency tends to corrupt and absolute dependency corrupts absolutely."[20]

On rare occasions and usually as something of an aside conservative writers will acknowledge the existence of far more pervasive and complex causal mechanisms running from environment to personality; for example, Thomas Sowell's observations on the importance of cultural norms as a determinant of economic success,[21] Friedrich Hayek's concern that "extensive government control produces . . . a psychological change, an alteration in the character of the people",[22] Irving Kristol's plea (unexpected from a conservative but evidently not from a neoconservative) that the state take some responsibility "for helping to shape the preferences that people exercise in a free market – to 'elevate' them, if you will."[23]

Even if many conservatives find unappealing such broader visions of how social setting can affect the character of society's members, they clearly support the narrower environment–behavior arguments of the sort advanced by Murray and Lord Acton. And to concede the legitimacy of such arguments is to open the way for a line of reasoning that, when pushed to the limit, can threaten many cherished conservative beliefs. Of this, more in a moment.

Liberals are more willing – one might even say, more determined – to endorse a vast array of possible mechanisms linking environmental stimuli to personality traits. In part this endorsement helps them make their case that economic rewards are heavily influenced by luck: the more the character and competence of income receivers are a function of environment, the less individual volition matters and thus the weaker the case for personal merit as a determinant of rewards. Thus, the weaker is the case of those who claim observed income inequalities are morally defensible, and the stronger is the case for those who press egalitarian claims.[24] Accordingly, the list of environment–personality mechanisms endorsed by liberals is forever under pressure to expand. For example, poverty (not welfare) is singled out as the environment that creates social pathologies – alcoholism, drug addiction, loss of self-esteem, and the like. These personality traits are, in turn, often portrayed as being transmitted from one generation to the next in what is variously called a "web" of poverty or "vicious cycle" (or "vicious circle") of poverty. Michael Harrington, long an exponent of such views, writes with an indignant melancholy about how, "because of the sheer, grinding, dirty experience of being poor, the personality, the spirit, is impaired."[25] The same reasoning can be expanded to incorporate the effects of racism: racism leads to poverty, the argument runs, and poverty leads to the development of traits which racists then cite to justify their bigotry. This action and reaction Gunnar Myrdal termed "the principle of cumulation": "White prejudice and discrimination keep the Negro low in standards of living, health, education, manners and morals. This, in its turn, gives support to white prejudice. White prejudice and Negro standards thus mutually 'cause' each other."[26] The hypothesized causation can be expanded further, with grinding poverty now portrayed as undermining the stability of the family, and the resulting broken homes opening the way for nonfamily influences as imperilling to personality as those that came to dominate the life of "Mickey" described above in such harrowing detail.

The web of interactions hypothesized between personality and social setting need not stop here. At the limit, "environment" (whatever that vague word means) threatens to determine almost all personality traits in a world in which individual volition has all but disappeared. This is the world as usually portrayed by socialism, a world in which "ideologies are highly malleable" and "human nature will be in the end what we want it to be."[27] And if, as most socialists believe, (a) mankind is intrinsically good and (b) capitalism as an environment is responsible for bringing to the fore most of the presently observed nasty traits of humanity, it follows that (c) abolishing capitalism will create the possibility of restructuring society and its institutions so that the better traits of humanity will flourish in a "better" environment. Just what that environment should be is often less than clear, but the line of reasoning and the utopian hope have a long history, running back through the writings of Marx and Rousseau. As repeatedly emphasized above, most American liberals resist such extreme left-of-center arguments, but they do not resist the central premise on which the arguments are built: that environment is a factor of the first importance in determining the character and competence of participants in the economic race. With that concession, liberals, like conservatives, have opened the way to a line of reasoning which, if pushed to the limit, could threaten cherished liberal beliefs. But like the right, the left seems largely unaware of the threats their concessions have unleashed.

Freedom and Volition

The discussion must now turn, for the last time, to a question raised long ago that has yet to be resolved: What does the word "freedom" mean in the context of discussions of economic justice? In chapter 6 a sharp distinction was drawn between negative and positive freedom – between "freedom *from*," meaning "freedom from coercion," and "freedom *to*," meaning "having the power or means to do X." Some have argued with considerable vehemence that this distinction is false – that a correct grasp of what freedom really means will make distinctions like the one just noted disappear. To anticipate the route that lies ahead, the task is to link the claim that environment affects personality to the problem of defining freedom, and once that problem has been addressed, to show that the means chosen to resolve it will affect the chooser's notion of individual volition and the related notion of individual responsibility.

The distinction between "freedom *from*" and "freedom *to*" can be attacked on several counts. The first begins by noting that, as the word freedom is commonly used, one speaks of being free *from* certain constraints – say, the chains of the slave – in order *to* do something – perhaps become employed and earn a living. The absence of constraints (freedom from) is thus commonly linked to some purpose (freedom to) that the person arguing the case for freedom has in mind. Admittedly the slave may simply hate his chains and wish to be free of such constraints without any specific thoughts about what he wants to do once the chains have been removed.[28] Typically, however, complaints against constraints are made in tandem with expressed desires of what might be done if only those constraints did not exist.

If only positive factors are counted as contraints, then a pauper might be free of constraints to his (actual or possible) desire to buy a Cadillac. But of course he is not free *to* buy a Cadillac. Similarly, if constraints are restricted to external factors, then the chronic alcoholic and the extremely ill man in a fever or coma are both free from constraints to go about their business; but of course, neither is free *to* do so. . . . A constraint is something – anything – that prevents one from doing something. Therefore, if nothing prevents me *from* doing X, I am free *to* do X; conversely, if I am free *to* do X, then nothing prevents me *from* doing X. "Freedom to" and "freedom from" are in this way logically linked, and there can be no special "positive" freedom *to* which is not also a freedom *from*.[29]

A second type of argument leads to a similar blurring of the distinction between "freedom to" and "freedom from," although it is little more than a logical extension of the first. The crucial word in the statement just quoted is "constraint." One detects a certain verbal sleight of hand in the second sentence. The phrasing "if constraints are restricted to external [to the individual] factors," particularly in the context of alcoholism, seems to suggest that *of course* the definition of "constraint" should not be so constrained. And that is the key problem: What should count as a "constraint"? Consider the conventional definition of coercion: the "deliberate forceful interference in the affairs of human beings by other human beings,"[30] where "forceful interference" refers to the use of violence or the threat of violence. If one begins with this definition, but wants to expand the concept of freedom, one obvious possibility is to include under "constraints" those limitations on individual choice which work indirectly by affecting "environment." Thus, environment affects personality, the argument runs, and the effects in question act as "constraints" on the choices available to the individual affected. Given such a definition of constraint, one would treat as similar cases (a) the constraints on individual choice enforced by prison walls and (b) the constraints on individual choice resulting from "an environment of poverty" (or "the culture of poverty") which so affect the character and competence of individuals as to seriously impair their ability to obtain or hold a job. Such symmetry of treatment would seem to be implicit in the following: "Often poverty, illness, ignorance, and other 'internal and negative constraints' are themselves the indirect results of deliberately imposed and modifiable social arrangements [the environment of consequence]. In such cases, we have every right to refer to them as restrictions on political liberty"[31] – or just as reasonably, on "economic" liberty. To labor the implied argument: "ignorance" is a constraint, albeit one internal to the person who is ignorant; this constraint is the "indirect result" of "social arrangements"; "social arrangements" tend to be deliberately imposed or at least can be modified by human action; thus the ignorant are "coerced" by the "social arrangements" in question. If they are "coerced," they are not free, and if their lack of freedom is attributable to social arrangements capable of being modified by human action, that modification should be implemented in keeping with the time-honored American priority of maximizing the freedom of each individual wherever possible.

Conservatives will not be slow to recognize the threatened liberal blitzkrieg. If, as Milton Friedman and so many others on the right are wont to insist, the ultimate goal of society is individual freedom and the main responsibility of government is to promote that goal, and further if the accepted definition of freedom must now include the absence of a vast array of constraints internal to the individual, then the government must take on responsibilities sure to push it untold leagues beyond the boundaries of the night-watchman or minimal state. Conservatives have also not been slow to carve out a defensive position along predictable lines. If the threat, at bottom, is the linking of the notion of freedom to the idea of constraints internal to the individual, it is most easily repelled by insisting that coercion and constraint are concepts that, in discussions about freedom, should be limited to factors external to the individual. More carefully yet, the solution is to insist not only that external factors, and only external factors, be counted as constraints, but also that only the "immediate" or "first-round" effects of such constraints be counted. Thus violence in the ghetto, when encountered, qualifies as a constraint. But if this violence and the threat of violence, as part of an inner city environment, fosters personality traits in ghetto youths that inhibit their ability to obtain and hold jobs, these latter inhibitions do *not* count as constraints deserving of government attention in the name of fostering individual freedom, however clear the causal nexus is between environment and personality, and however much the resulting personality traits act as real constraints on individual choice. Thus conservative Thomas Sowell notes that in the "constrained vision" popular with the right, "freedom is a process characteristic – the absence of externally imposed impediments."[32] The key word is "externally." Sowell explains by quoting Thomas Hobbes.

A man was not free if chained or restricted by prison walls, and water was not free if hemmed in by river banks or by the walls of a container. But where the lack of movement was due to *internal* causes – a man "fastened to his bed by sicknesse" or a stone that "lyeth still" – that was not considered by Hobbes to be a lack of freedom. The same concept of freedom continues to characterize the constrained vision today. Freedom to Hayek means "freedom from coercion, freedom from the arbitrary power of other men," but *not* release from the restrictions or compulsions of "circumstances."[33]

On what grounds can such a division be justified? How can one causal chain count (from violence external to the individual to resulting constraints on individual choice) and one causal chain be downgraded to irrelevance (from violence to environment to personality traits to constraints on individual choice)? Conservatives can hardly deny the existence of the latter type of causal mechanism, since their own writings, as previously noted, feature assertions concerning the effects of environment on personality. If barriers internal to the individual can inhibit choice as effectively as prison walls, and if both kinds of barriers – external and internal – are ultimately the creation of other human beings, why should only one count as "coercion" and thus only one be the appropriate domain of public policy if the objective is to promote the freedom of the individual? Notice the implied "constrained vision" of equality of opportunity is unsophisticated in the extreme, stripped as it is of any reference to twentieth century insights concerning the determinants of personality. Equality of opportunity presumably exists when would-be competitors in the economic race are equally free from constraints, and such equality is evidently assured, or so the argument runs, if all are equally unconstrained by violence or the threat of violence, *and only that.* This in turn makes clear that left and right cannot be viewed as sharing the same ideal of equality of opportunity. Both endorse the same phrase which, in its connotations, is not the same at all, because left and right have markedly different definitions of freedom, and those definitions crucially condition their views about what is required to achieve equality of opportunity. Put another way, there are a number of logical relationships among three ideas: (1) freedom, (2) equality of opportunity, and (3) the effects that environment are acknowledged to have on personality. The importance given to the third critically affects the definition of the first, and the first, once defined, implies boundary conditions for the second.

Conservatives will be quick to defend their ignoring of the third in their definition of the first on several counts, of which two would seem to be much to the point.

Perhaps the more telling of the two begins with the traditional conservative emphasis on the limits of human knowledge. True, conservatives will admit, environment has *some* effect on personality, and *some* of those effects no doubt act as constraints on individual choice. But given our massive ignorance about the processes in question, we are at a loss to identify with any precision which environmental influences affect which type of person, to what degree, and by which processes. We can recognize chains and prison walls and anticipate with tolerable accuracy the constraints they will impose upon individual choice. But we have trouble identifying internal barriers to the exercise of choice, where they come from, and how public policy might help to remove or lessen such barriers. If the causes are this poorly understood, concludes the argument, attempts to remedy the adverse effects of environment on personality by government action are likely to be little more than shots in the dark.[34]

Moreover, conservatives might add, bringing to bear a second argument as predictable from this quarter as the first, repeated shooting in the dark is not without its dangers, not just because the targets may be missed and damage accidentally done, but because authorizing a central authority to take repeated shots is to concentrate more power in the hands of government officials, and such increases in concentrated power are always dangerous. Conservatives must concede that this last assertion itself constitutes a claim to know the effects of an environment (power concentration) on personality (a tendency to foster corruption). But that influence, they would insist, is well documented throughout history and accordingly "reasonably well understood." The latter expression is admittedly somewhat vague, but that vagueness seldom tempers the zeal with which conservatives advance this particular article of faith.

Most Americans would seem receptive to both arguments, at least to some degree. They distrust meddling with environment in the name of personality modification, and they have a distrust of large-scale government incursions into the economy because they recognize that, whatever the announced purposes might be, expansion can bring threats to individual liberty. They will, however, make exceptions. Their staunch support of free public education would seem a case in point. It is central to their notion of equality of opportunity, and that notion, as noted, is crucially dependent upon how freedom is defined. A policy of free public education can be defended using two definitions of freedom, but not a third. One could argue that free education for all helps to remove the "internal" constraints of being uneducated in a society in which the economic system requires certain minimum skills including literacy to qualify for the competition for most jobs. Or one could argue that such a policy is necessary to pursue the goal of freedom, meaning "freedom to," which in this context means having the minimum requisite "power or means" to compete in the economy. Both claims would seem, at bottom, to come to the same thing. (What one treats as a requisite "power or means" the other treats, when it is absent, as a constraint.) But one could not argue the case for free public education to promote freedom if that word is restricted in meaning to "being uncoerced" and coercion is defined to mean nothing more than violence or the threat of violence.

Which brings us to the central point. Each time a policy is chosen to remove impediments in the name of freedom, that choice potentially expands the definition of freedom that the chooser is willing to endorse. Or to reverse the decision-making process, defining freedom is a demanding task of consummate importance, because that definition will imply acceptance or rejection of a vast array of possible social policies. "Ethical systems," argues philosopher Harald Ofstad, "may determine the sense of 'freedom' we select as relevant."[35] The determinants, one suspects, tend to be far more comprehensive than this. The act of defining freedom – that is, of carefully giving content to that word – is for most an ongoing process, and in that process the preferred definition at any point in time reflects the influences on the definer of a vast array of knowledge, experience, and beliefs. No hint of this complexity is evident in Milton Friedman's plea that promoting individual freedom should be the touchstone by which to judge the rightness or wrongness of government actions. The hesistancy that comes from grappling with perplexing definitional problems is nowhere in evidence in the decisive summary offered by Irving Kristol at the end of a chapter entitled "What is 'social justice'?": "In sum, the distribution of income under liberal capitalism is 'fair' if, and only if, you think that liberty is, or ought to be, the most important political value. If not, then not."[36] What both writers of the right present as a readily intelligible goal of seemingly self-evident appeal can now be seen for what it is: a single word ("liberty" or "freedom") which, in discussions of economic justice, encompasses a vast array of judgments. Given that arrays can and do differ markedly across individuals, the word itself is almost meaningless until the associated judgments are made clear. The dilemma is this: What judgments should it encompass?

Some of the possibilities have been discussed above. Neglected to this point are judgments relating to individual volition. Those judgments, however, are intimately connected with others already considered under the heading of defining freedom. The final assignment of this section is to make this connection clear.

"The only freedom which deserves the name," writes John Stuart Mill, "is that of pursuing our own good in our own way, so long as we do not attempt to deprive others of theirs or impede their efforts to obtain it."[37] To pursue "our own good in our own way" implies that, in some sense, the pursuer is in charge of his choices. But in what sense? The tempting answer is simply to point out that choices should be the product of individual volition, where volition is defined in the conventional way as "exercise of the will" or "determination by the will." Here too we must be wary of assuming that a definition solves our problems, when all it does is point the way to where the important problems can be found. One such problem concerns the question of how individual freedom should be defined. Prison walls impair the exercise of the will. So too, it could be argued, do personality traits produced by an environment that fosters illiteracy or antisocial attitudes. Somewhat curiously, the more encompassing one makes the notion of freedom – the more constraints whose absence is included as part of that definition – the narrower becomes the domain of individual volition. As the latter shrinks, this retrenchment raises obvious questions about related notions of individual responsibility. It also makes problematic an assertion accepted until now without question: that any democratic system worthy of that name accepts as one of its most hallowed goals the promotion of self-development or self-fulfillment among its citizenry. But what is the meaning of the "self" in "self-development" in a world where environmental influences can affect the character and competence of the selves that seek fulfillment?

Volition, Responsibility, and Self-Realization

Few concepts play a more important role in American discussions of economic justice than individual responsibility. Time and again in earlier sections of this book, particularly those concerned with remedies for poverty, the analysis has encountered the priority of individual responsibility and, with the implicit assumption that the meaning of the term was clear, moved on. This lack of scrutiny, for reasons just now raised, will obviously no longer do.

Consider those circumstances under which an individual might *not* be judged "responsible" for his or her actions. Suppose, for example, Cain "goes berserk" and kills Abel, but the action is later traced to a tumor on the brain. The tumor is removed, and Cain's homicidal tendencies disappear. Under these circumstances, was Cain "responsible" for the death of Abel? From the standpoint of causation, the case is quite straightforward. The knife was driven by Cain into the chest of Abel, and this put a stop to the latter's bodily functions. But was Cain "morally responsible" for Abel's death? Most would be inclined to answer "No." If pressed to explain why, they would undoubtedly claim that, in some sense, Cain was "not in charge" of his actions: that the knife attack was not the result of volition, or – in language previously used – the result of "the exercise of the will." If Cain did not freely choose to kill Abel but was compelled by forces beyond his control, then, runs the argument, Cain is not morally responsible for Abel's death.[38]

The example helps to illustrate the association commonly made between presuming that individuals are free to choose and subjecting the choices that they make to moral evaluation. If individuals are free to choose, they tend to be held accountable for their actions. More rigorously, a person is commonly regarded "as morally responsible for some act or occurrence x if and only if he is believed (1) to have done x, or to have brought x about; and (2) to have done it or brought it about freely."[39] The reference to freedom in the foregoing statement makes clear where the problem lies (or at least the problem of particular concern for this discussion). The broader the definition of freedom, as previously noted, the narrower the boundaries become on individual volition; thus, the smaller becomes the arena of willful choice, and the fewer are the actions for which the individual can be held morally responsible. Defining freedom is therefore an even more important task than previously indicated. The associated dilemma to be considered here is how to decide the appropriate arena for willful choice and therefore identify the actions appropriately subjected to moral evaluation.

At first glance conservatives appear to favor a limited definition, restricting freedom to the absence of coercion and limiting coercion to violence or the threat of violence. But they have already muddied their own waters by noting that environment can affect personality in ways that affect resulting individual choices. Consider, for example, Charles Murray's evident moral indignation at choices made in the modern urban ghetto.

It is not a question of denying that environment affects behavior. Of course it does. But people still make choices. Large numbers of poor men impregnate women and *choose* not to take responsibility for the resulting child. Knowing their men may well behave irresponsibly, large numbers of poor women who cannot afford to take care of a child on their own nonetheless *choose* not to practice birth control, *choose* not to have abortions, and *choose* not to put the child up for adoption.[40]

Murray's concern is to restructure incentives to encourage different choices from those observed. Our concern is to make sense out of the claim that individuals are morally responsible for their actions in a world in which, in Murray's words, "of course" environment affects behavior.

Conservatives seem generally unaware of this dilemma, and of the related problem of making sense of the goal of self-realization. Their usual argument, somewhat oversimplified, is that in a "capitalist" system featuring democratic government and a free-exchange economy the individual tends to be "free" to pursue self-realization (freedom meaning nothing more than the absence of coercion), and because of that freedom, the individual is responsible for whatever success he or she realizes in pursuit of economic goals in particular and self-realization in general.

But the notion of the "self" that is seeking self-realization becomes problematic once one acknowledges that the character of the self can be influenced in major ways by environment, including influences that help to define the goals that the self wants to pursue. The usual conservative solution is to deny the problem. Consider the following, all typical of conservative pronouncements on the subject.

The Conservative realizes . . . that man's development, in both its spiritual and material aspects, is not something that can be directed by outside forces. Every man, for his individual good and for the good of his society, is responsible for his *own* development.[41]

The principal affirmation of modern liberalism [i.e. neoconservatism] is that every individual is a person of many parts, a person who assembles himself or herself. Every individual can be a self-constituting creature, manufacturing himself by choosing purposes and values by whatever principle he wishes from the universe of possibilities. . . . The great American novel *The Great Gatsby* is about a work of art: Gatsby's creation of his "self."[42]

The principle of equality of opportunity derives from a fundamental tenet of classic liberalism: that the individual . . . is the basic unit of society, and that the purpose of societal arrangements is to allow the individual the freedom to fulfill his own purposes – by his labor to gain property, by exchange to satisfy his wants, by upward mobility to achieve a place commensurate with his talents.[43]

The market is an opportunity, an open place. It allows us our liberty of conscience. What we make of it defines our character and prepares us to meet our Judge. Unlike our fellow Catholics whose liberties are cramped by command societies, we are left by the open market with no excuses, our liberties intact.[44]

The ideal of the "self-made person" is lurking in all these assertions – not just "self-made" in the narrow sense of achieving a particular rung on the ladder of success, but in a more profound sense that whatever one is, and whatever person one is striving to become, the "self" is the architect of being and becoming. Given all we know about how that mulitiplicity of factors lumped under the one word "environment" can affect the complexity we attempt to capture with the one word "personality," we cannot assume that the "self" one would realize springs full-blown from the head of the would-be self-realizer as an act of will uninfluenced by family background, social setting, or cultural norms. To fabricate an oversimplified example, suppose that a teenager in prewar Germany fell under the spell of Nazi propaganda, and for that reason decided that the life of a storm trooper was the arena in which he could best pursue self-realization. Even if he rises in those ranks and accordingly believes he has succeeded in his own terms, our evaluation of that success is tempered by the realization that the terms were not entirely his own – that had the same youth been raised in, say, a small town in America during the same time period, the self he would have chosen to pursue would probably have been significantly different. The self, then, is not appropriately regarded as the sole architect of consequence in a one-man enterprise, choosing both the goals and the route to self-realization. The self is, at best, a collaborator – one contributor among a vast constellation of causal forces, many not easily identified, and all (or almost all) impossible to assess in terms of their separate contributions to the self that is or the self that one is seeking to achieve. This does not make irrelevant the goal of self-realization. But it does highlight that the concept underlying that goal is not as simple or as unproblematic as conservative rhetoric might lead us to believe.

In thinking through the problems that environmental influences create for the concepts basic to discussions of economic justice, liberals tend to avoid one additional problem that their own rhetoric helps to create. They usually are aware of the logical connections emphasized thus far: that defining freedom broadly (as they tend to do) narrows the boundaries of individual volition, and the narrower those boundaries, the narrower is the domain of freely chosen actions for which individuals can be held morally responsible. Indeed, a pervasive theme in writings of the left is that the causes of failure, particularly economic failure, are to be found in factors primarily beyond the individual's control. From this liberals tend to infer that the economically disadvantaged are more victims of "the system" (i.e. forces external to the individual) than they are victims of their own shortcomings. The poor, by this account and in the wording of an old-fashioned song, are more to be pitied than censured, including the able-bodied poor. In short, liberals understand a line of reasoning that begins by broadening the definition of freedom and ends with a reluctance to make negative moral judgments.

What liberals generally fail to realize is that this line of reasoning, writ large and publicized, can itself become part of a larger environment influencing the economically disadvantaged in destructive ways. The more popular the view becomes that the poor are not responsible for their poverty, the more that idea is likely to be incorporated into the belief system of the poor. Whatever the truth of such a view, the belief in that view can have destructive influences if the believer happens to be among the worst-off members of society. As those in poverty become convinced that they have little or no mastery over their own economic fate, they tend to lose self-confidence and self-respect, lose a sense of self-reliance, and lose a sense of responsibility *as the belief in question implies they should.* Conservatives have not infrequently hammered at this theme, but on occasion, so too have liberals. "Independence of mind or strength of character," Friedrich Hayek notes, "is rarely found among those who cannot be confident that they will make their way by their own effort."[45] *Washington Post* columnist William Raspberry makes a similar point but in the negative: "There is no more crippling an attitude than to think of yourself primarily as a victim."[46] Such insights are not, however, peculiar to the right or to the modern era. At the turn of the century integrationist Booker T. Washington and black national-ist Marcus Garvey emphasized self-help and self-reliance, believing "that a sense of 'victimization' can retard a person's ability to help himself, can become an excuse to surrender to frustration and adversity, can become another form of dependency."[47] To believe that one has *some* control over one's fate, according to contemporary psychologists, is crucial for mental health. More than this, some psychology experts claim experiments indicate that

the higher a person's desire for control, the more persistently he would tackle difficult challenges. Moreover, such people set higher goals for themselves and went about achieving them in a more realistic fashion than did those with a lower need for control.[48]

Lincoln made a similar point in simpler language in discussing the causes of American prosperity.

There is something back of these [the Constitution and the Union], entwining itself more closely about the human heart. That something is the principle of "Liberty to all" – the principle that clears the *path* for all – gives *hope* to all – and, by consequence, *enterprize*, and *industry* to all.[49]

This, then, is a dilemma for liberals. The more "the heart," in Lincoln's phrase, becomes entwined with tendrils of despair – the more the poor become convinced that they are not masters of their own fate and accordingly lose hope – the more likely they are to become lethargic when employed, acquiescent in the face of failure, and preoccupied with present gratifications over future possibilities. In short, the more likely are the poor to develop those personality traits that reduce the probability of their ever climbing out of poverty. The more liberals emphasize their theme of "victimization," the more they contribute to this process. This is not to suggest the abandonment of that theme. But it does highlight that emphasizing such a theme is not without its costs. Above all, it throws into sharp relief a puzzle neglected by left and right alike: how to recognize publicly the influence of factors beyond the individual's control in explanations of why the poor are poor while minimizing the detrimental effects of that recognition and that publicity upon the attitudes of the least advantaged members of society.

What, then, can usefully be said about volition, responsibility, and self-realization? Philosophers will recognize that the discussion is dangerously close to that pit of conundrums associated with free will, including the extent to which "the will" itself is determined. In that direction lies perplexity and lack of resolution. We might therefore do well to adopt the standard American posture of shoulder-shrugging pragmatism, and redirect our thoughts to those assumptions and approaches that might prove useful for the sake of getting on with the business at hand, which is to explore dilemmas associated with the pursuit of economic justice, although now conducted against a broader backdrop that includes thoughts about the nature of the good society.

The first thought, which is an old thought in discussions of free will, is that we might as well assume we have some freedom of the will – or in language previously used, some volition in economic and other matters – in part because we can never know with any certainty how free we are and thus can only decide the issue by assumption, and in part because to assume an absence of freedom is to court disaster. If freedom of choice, in some larger sense, is assumed not to exist, then moral evaluation would be grievously undercut for reasons developed earlier. And with that undercutting would necessarily come a sharply revised attitude toward our fellow human beings, including the homage given to that fundamental American value: the dignity and worth of the individual. Such homage depends to a significant degree on our belief that each individual is a rational moral agent, and that belief would disappear if agents were perceived as having no freedom of choice and thus no responsibility for choosing well or badly. Americans view other Americans as centers of choice, evaluation, and decision. Not by accident did the young republic "conceived in liberty" have ingrained in its early cultural norms the right of each to "pursue happiness" *and* to take responsibility for the results. To challenge the premise that individuals are free in the sense of having some domain for the exercise of volition is to threaten an entire culture with devastation of unknown proportions and unforeseeable results. This same premise about individual freedom that helps to hold together American society in its present form also serves to legitimate the hopes of individuals bent upon self-fulfillment. Consider the implications for such hopes if the premise is denied and the opposite asserted: that what each does is entirely determined by forces external to the self. The implications for self-respect and a sense of personal responsibility would be shattering.

The reader may surmise that this line of reasoning, if pursued, could lead to a repetition of points made in previous paragraphs, and so it would. The question at issue is the personality transformations likely to result if individuals become convinced they have no mastery over their own fate. The impact on the personality of the poor of becoming convinced they have little mastery over their own economic fate is but a special instance of the general problem. One implication of the present discussion for the previous discussion is just a variant of a point made earlier: that to convince the poor they have little mastery over their own economic fate can have catastrophic implications for the welfare of the poor. If they do not believe they are free to make choices that make a difference to their own economic well-being, they are unlikely to become willing and vigorous participants in efforts to improve their lot, and without that participation any effort, however comprehensive, is unlikely to realize significant success. The Reverend Jesse Jackson put the case more simply and more harshly: "nobody can save us from us for us but us."[50] This is not to argue that forces external to the poor are irrelevant in any explanation of their plight. But it is to argue that however much "the system" is to blame for the problems of the poor, the poor themselves must be primary actors in any attempted solution that would make a major difference to the disadvantaged. And for that participation to be forthcoming, the poor must embrace the assumption noted earlier: that they have a domain of volition in economic matters – that they have freedom to make choices that matter and the responsibility to make those choices wisely.

This discussion began not with the plight of the poor, but with general problems of volition and responsibility. A graceful route from the particular back to the general has been provided by the reflections of liberal Ken Auletta, as he puzzles over why some members of minority groups within America are so desperately disadvantaged.

A society cannot subject some of its people to the things blacks have been subjected to over long periods of time without certain abnormalities manifesting themself. Take what the Jews were put through with the Holocaust. That was a relatively short period of time. Yet I've read accounts of abnormal behavior when people got out of the concentration camps. It caused pathological behavior. So, yes, American society has a responsibility for the pathological behavior of some blacks. And yet, even though I believe society is responsible, . . . individual responsibility also comes into play. That's where I get in trouble. Where do you draw the line?[51]

Where indeed, not just for the few demonstrating pathological behavior, but for all of humanity? At stake are all of our notions about how free the self is to pursue self-development, to make willful choices that make a difference to one's destiny, to be held accountable for choices made because they were the product of the will and freely made, and to be honored as a rational moral agent because of that accountability. Also at stake is a derivative notion central to American beliefs about economic justice and the manner in which merit is linked to reward as their economic system presently functions. Those rewards can only be viewed as the product of the willful exercise of meritorious virtues if individuals are viewed as being free to exercise their will.

The general question that Auletta raises is the extent to which any human action is the product of volition, and thus the results of that action are the responsibility of the actor. The particular variant of that question raised in the first section of this chapter is the extent to which economic behavior and associated rewards can be attributed to individual volition as distinct from forces external to the individual. Given how little we know and are likely to know about the relevant importance of the causes at work – "volition" and "other" – any drawing of the line between the two is invariably somewhat arbitrary. A case can nevertheless be made for biasing that arbitrary choice in favor of volition. Philosophers might argue, in their detached way, that we should assume we are free to choose just in case we are. The student of political economy would argue for assuming a maximum of free choice because to assume the opposite would threaten to bring in its wake all the undesirable consequences for the individual and for society discussed above (and many others not discussed). The shoulder-shrugging pragmatist would probably assert that assuming freedom of choice is the way to bet not only for the sake of sanity but, equally important, for getting on with the business of life. To liberals and conservatives who emphasize that luck plays a large role in determining rewards in the free-market system, the pragmatic individual is inclined to retort that surely the role of luck does not preclude volition from also being of *some* relevance, and as long as he retains this article of faith, he is willing to believe that the willful exercise of meritorious virtues also influences who wins which prizes in economic races typical of a capitalist system.

Finally, and more vaguely yet, many would argue that the domain of volition can be expanded, although that too must ultimately be an article of faith. In the narrow realm of economic behavior, the belief in expansion may be linked to increased options made possible by all those policies designed to make the economic race more "free," where freedom here concerns the absence of coercion and the presence of the power or means to compete. Such notions about freedom are of course far removed from more general puzzles about volition and free will. The domain of volition in this larger sense may also be viewed as expanding for the individual over time, although these thoughts too are invariably ill-defined. The very act of struggling with adversity, the argument runs, and in that struggle having a sense (whether well founded or not) of volition being exercised to overcome adversity bolsters the confidence of the actor in a manner that may make constraints external to the self less constraining in the future. The domain of volition may also be expanded by puzzling over problems of free will. The more aware the individual becomes that attributes of self and goals the self wishes to pursue can be influenced by factors external to the self – family rearing practices, peer group pressures, cultural norms, and the like – the more likely that individual is to identify some of those influences affecting him or her, and that very act of identification raises the possibility of lessening their effects and thus expanding the realm of individual volition. Such articles of faith – and ultimately all premises about the domain of volition must be articles of faith – are evident in the personal aspirations and general advice of poet and teacher Paul Mariani:

Listen to what Joseph Brodsky has said in a recent interview. "Basically," he reminds us, "one writes not about what surrounds or happens to one; it's a very Marxist attitude that the actual living conditions determine the operation of the conscious-

ness. Obviously, it's true, but only up to a certain point, after which the consciousness, or conscience, starts to determine the nature of the living conditions, or the
attitude towards them, anyhow.

When we were young, the world shaped or misshaped us as it saw – or did not
see – fit. But as we get older, we learn to shape our world according to our own best
lights. Eventually it is up to us to do what we can to make sure that time chisels us as
we would want, so that the myth we leave behind us is one to which we can add our
signature."[52]

Mariani's belief that we can contribute to the chiseling of self in some
larger sense may also be a myth. We can never know for certain. But this
much is clear. Within America, that belief, whether myth or not, runs
powerfully through the country's culture from its inception to the present.
Further, the pervasiveness of that belief brings in its wake a host of benefits
compared with what American society would be if most of its citizens
believed the opposite. Finally, precisely because of those benefits, encouraging a belief on the part of every citizen in the maximum domain for
individual volition – or the maximum that seems credible – has much to
recommend it.

Environment and Values: The Role of the Market and the State

Environment and Values

The previous section began by acknowledging that environment can affect
personality, and noted that this insight when pursued can make problematic
certain concepts and ideas central to our thoughts about economic justice,
including the domain of individual volition and the associated domain of
individual responsibility, as well as the meaning of the "self" that seeks
self-fulfillment. The present section begins with the same general insight –
that environment affects character and competence, attitudes and aptitudes – but pursues this thought in a different direction. To anticipate the
road ahead: environment can also affect values; for those living in a capitalist
economy the free-market system constitutes an environment of considerable
importance, raising the question of whether, as an environment, it has
desirable or undesirable effects upon time-honored American values; and if
some of those effects are deemed undesirable, the additional question raised
is whether public action should be contemplated to help remedy these
perceived deficiencies in the private sector.

The word "value" and its plural are made to serve a multitude of purposes
and accordingly have a multitude of meanings. For purposes of getting on
with this particular discussion, we shall simply borrow in a rough-and-ready
way the meaning commonly assigned to the word "values" in the social
sciences: "Values serve as criteria for selection in action. When most explicit
and fully conceptualized, values become criteria for judgment, preference,
and choice."[53] If the self, however defined, is affected by environment (a
point already made), and if the criteria chosen to guide "judgment,
preference, and choice" are integral to any definition of the self (consider the

problem of describing your best friend with no reference whatsoever to the "values" that friend seems to honor), then one obvious question is the extent to which values are influenced by environment. The origin, evolution, and transmission of values are topics at best only dimly understood, and thus the role environment plays in this process is also, at best, only dimly understood. But *some* environmental influence on values would seem inevitable. Few would claim that the values they hold have been totally unaffected by family upbringing, peer group pressures, and cultural norms, to mention only three of the more obvious influences.

Whatever the various sources of influence, the end result within America has been a topic of concern. In the writings of all who diagnose contemporary difficulties of this country – from liberal to conservative, from social scientist to theologian – a recurring theme is what has often been labeled "a crisis in values." Just as the word "values" has a multiplicity of meanings, so the phrase "crisis of values" is used to designate a multiplicity of difficulties. All touch upon the fading allegiance to time-honored American values, and the implications for society if values commonly honored in the past become typically ignored in the future. Such concerns were evident in a recent *Time* cover story on ethics entitled "What's wrong?" with the subtitle: "Hypocrisy, betrayal and greed unsettle the nation's soul." At the core of that article was a single question: "Put bluntly, has the mindless materialism of the '80's left in its wake a values vacuum?"[54] *Fortune* magazine evidences similar concerns. Although not known for its critical stance toward business, that periodical has featured in the recent past such articles as "The decline and fall of business ethics" and, as a cover story, "The money society."[55] According to the latter, "under the blazing sun of money, all other values shine palely," with the tendency in business to acclaim "but one breed of hero: He's the honcho with the condo and the limo and the Miro and lots and lots of dough."[56] This does not bode well for the capitalist society whose free-market system is supposed to develop and reinforce the virtuous traits of participants for all the reasons developed at length in chapter 2. Complaints about a crisis in values, however, have ranged far beyond behavior in the business world. Also cited in this context are the scandals, indictments, and convictions that pervade, among other realms, politics and religion, college and professional sports, educational institutions, day care centers, and charitable organizations. *Time* magazine may have the major thrust of the causation wrong: the existence of a vacuum in values may be primarily responsible for the rise of a "mindless materialism," rather than the other way around. Whichever way causation runs, the web of interactions leading to the perceived decline in allegiance to traditional American values is undoubtedly vast and labyrinthine. But in that maze of interactions, surely the market must have some role to play as an environment of importance to its participants. Thus the defects in American society decried by those who cite "a crisis in values" – the phrase for some a call to arms and for others an admission of despair – raises the question of whether the environment of the market system is at least partly responsible for the problem.

Oddly enough, the latter possibility tends to be neglected in much of the literature on this topic. The common foci of attention are family, church, and school, with the last of these in recent years singled out for special attention. The schools have a special role to play in molding the values of those being educated, or so runs an argument emphasized by (among others) President Reagan, his Secretary of Education, the Supreme Court, and former Securities and Exchange Commission chairman, John Shad, who recently promised $30 million to improve the teaching of ethics at Harvard Business School. A revision of school curricula, however, or of school environments generally is likely to be little more than a small step toward regeneration of particular values that can easily be swamped by other influences. As James Baldwin put the matter for those in urban ghettos, "you can't hope to invest a child with a morality in school which is going to be destroyed on the streets of Harlem . . . ."[57] Just as the effect of the educational system on the values of a child can be sharply modified by other influences in the child's environment, so the values that the child carries into adulthood can be sharply modified when the individual, to earn a living, becomes immersed in the market system. Is this latter modification likely to be for good or ill?

Values Promoted by the Market

Supporters and detractors of the market tend to divide along predictable lines, with conservatives emphasizing the good effect it has on values and liberals emphasizing the bad effects.

Those wishing to make the case for good effects usually do little more than repeat all of the arguments made in chapter 2 linking economic activity to the development of such virtuous traits as industry, honesty, frugality, sobriety, and prudence. As for reasons why such linkages exist, modern explanations tend to echo older explanations, such as the following which dates from the eighteenth century.

Commerce attaches [men] one to another through mutual utility. Through commerce the moral and physical passions are superseded by interest. . . . Commerce has a special character which distinguishes it from all other professions. It affects the feelings of men so strongly that it makes him who was proud and haughty suddenly turn supple, bending and serviceable. Through commerce, man learns to deliberate, to be honest, to acquire manners, to be prudent and reserved in both talk and action. Sensing the necessity to be wise and honest in order to succeed, he flees vice, or at least his demeanor exhibits decency and seriousness so as not to arouse any adverse judgment on the part of present and future acquaintances; he would not dare make a spectacle of himself for fear of damaging his credit standing and thus society may well avoid a scandal which it might otherwise have to deplore.[58]

Present-day versions detailing similar mechanisms often seem less telling and more truncated by comparison. For example,

. . . the thrust of the capitalist system is to favor those who keep their contracts and to hamper those who do not. Sanctity of contract is one of the most important elements in the cement which binds a civilized society together, and it tends to arise naturally in a society where private property is respected. At the same time it has an elevating effect on men's character.[59]

Or again,

Capitalism is based on self-interest and self-esteem; it holds integrity and trustworthiness as cardinal virtues and makes them pay off in the marketplace, thus demanding that men survive by means of virtues, not of vices.[60]

Conservatives generally applaud the competitive struggle endemic to the market system, again for reasons fashioned in an earlier era – in this case, reasons emphasizing self-fulfillment of the individual and material progress of society. The powerful metaphor crafted and polished in the nineteenth century remains the controlling metaphor today: the market is a race, with an associated system of rewards and penalities that encourages all to have their reach exceed their grasp, to strive to reach the limits of their capabilities (or at least their economic capabilities). Conservative Michael Novak makes this traditional point by reference to Latin roots: "To compete – *com* + *petere*, 'to seek together although against each other' – is not a vice. It is . . . an indispensable element in natural and spiritual growth."[61]

Liberals are not convinced. They see the striving that the market engenders and the values fostered by that striving as highly suspect. The article of faith advanced in chapter 2 has therefore now become a question of fact: Does the free-market system as it presently functions in America encourage or discourage admirable human traits? According to the critics, the main traits encouraged are aggressiveness and greed. The competition that conservatives applaud most liberals regard as making for a commercial world red in tooth and claw. The ethos of the market system, they claim, celebrates personal advancement, encourages acquisitive appetites, and rewards uncompassionate aggressiveness. The general point, more softly put by Robert Heilbroner, is "that the drive to make money, even when it does not reach grotesque limits, brings out an unlovely side of human nature."[62]

The battle is thus joined, and the central issue is whether the principles and practices of the business world tend to bring out the better or worse side of the participants – or (a slightly different question) whether they tend to strengthen or weaken allegiance to time-honored American values. In the charge and counter-charge of those embroiled in this debate, both sides have tried to take and hold the theological high ground. Each stands to gain immense support from the general public if they can demonstrate the consistency (if conservatives) or inconsistency (if liberals) between religious precepts and market practice. But both sides have tended to gloss over their sharply differing views concerning the meaning of such terms as "charity" and the practical implications of such precepts as the Golden Rule. What follows is the briefest of considerations of complicated issues widely ignored despite their evident centrality to discussions of economic justice in America.

Precisely because it is brief, subsequent discussion will often exaggerate differences and simplify positions in an effort to suggest the skeletal framework of the debate. (Those given to denouncing oversimplications for being oversimplified should perhaps re-read the previous sentence before proceeding on.)

A useful starting point is the Golden Rule: Do unto others as you would have them do unto you. The wording serves to focus questions of ethical behavior on personal desires. The second half of the rule consists of deciding what is best for number one, while the first half urges the extension of a similar consideration to others. With liberals and conservatives having such differing views about what is best for the self, one would expect them to disagree about the nature of desirable behavior toward others implied by the Golden Rule.

At the center of conservative concerns are conventional conservative ideas: in this case, the desire for freedom and an emphasis on the limitations of our knowledge concerning the preferences of others. What they want above all else for self – and thus by implication for others – is the maximum freedom or maximum "space" in which to pursue self-fulfillment as the self chooses to define that goal. Thus,

The individual citizen, generally speaking, wishes nothing better than to be left in peace to see his family prosper.[63]

Or again,

This is the key to the commandment to love our neighbor. What we want above all for ourselves, and which therefore we must accord to our neighbor, is freedom to pursue our own purposes. . . . As a corollary to this freedom we want others to respect our individuality, independence, and status as responsible human beings. . . .This is the fundamental morality which capitalism requires and which it nurtures.[64]

Freedom is defined in the traditional conservative way as the absence of coercion, and coercion is defined as violence or the threat of violence. Interpreted this way, the Golden Rule comes close to being converted into what has sometimes been called the Silver Rule: here, "Do no coerce others as you would have them not coerce you," or in the more archaic wording of ancient times, "Hurt not others in ways that you yourself find hurtful" (Buddhism), or alternatively, "What is hateful to you, do not to your fellowmen" (Judaism).[65] The reluctance of conservatives to give the Golden Rule a more positive thrust – to shift from merely not hurting humanity to trying to actively help humanity – is justified by a presumption of ignorance about what others value and prefer.

This same emphasis on ignorance shapes the conservative meaning of "love" to give more emphasis to distinctiveness and distance than to similarities and sharing.

When we first love we feel that we know the other. We see our face mirrored there. As our love deepens, it is the separateness, the unique creation that bears upon us, and we begin to sense the weight and mystery and wonder and preciousness of another's being – no longer an extension of ourselves.[66]

The result is more a sense of admiration than a sense of closeness or bonding: "To love . . . is to *value*; love, properly, is the consequence and expression of admiration . . . ."[67] The traditional conservative priority of *laissez faire* thus seems to color conservative notions about the nature of love and the practical implications of the Golden Rule.

For liberals committed to egalitarian ideals, such a framework is clearly unacceptable. In part this is because, compared with conservative beliefs, they believe individuals have less freedom to control their economic fate and more knowledge concerning the internal landscape of their fellow man. If individuals are less free, they are (for reasons previously noted) less to blame for misfortunes suffered. The extreme variant of this line of reasoning implies that society consists of individuals who are intrinsically equal, but unequally blessed with economic goods because of capricious circumstances. Thus individuals, mindful of that equality and the role of capriciousness in determining who gets what, are bound together in a fellowship emphasizing mutual sympathy and mutual obligations. Recall Arthur Okun's rationale cited earlier for preferring equality of income:

Abstracting from the costs and the consequences, I would prefer more equality of income to less and would like complete equality best of all. This preference is a simple extension of the humanistic basis for equal rights. To extend the domain of rights and give every citizen an equal share of the national income would give added recognition to the moral worth of every citizen, to the mutual respect of citizens for one another, and to the equivalent value of membership in the society for all.[68]

The imagery emphasized by the left is of "a cooperative, humane society of equals,"[69] in which each has sufficient knowledge of the others to recognize similarities and to find in those similarities justification for believing in the innate goodness of man – the recognition and the belief both crucial for developing a spirit of fellowship, or stronger yet, of brotherhood.

The spirit of fellowship consists in realizing and responding to human persons in the light of these samenesses: the sameness in capacity for spiritual greatness and the sameness in capacity for misery and happiness. Respect for the dignity of a human individual is first and foremost respect for his capacity for spiritual greatness and concern for his welfare. All else grows out of this respect and concern.[70]

In a community grounded in such fellowship, the meaning of charity and the practical implications of the Golden Rule are rather different from that advocated by conservatives. Liberals tend to emphasize "liking" and "sharing," with sharing closely intertwined with the notion of what it means to be kind. To better understand the implications of such words for such a community, one might be tempted to pursue the possible relationships between "liking" and "being kind" on the one hand, and the ideal of "charity" on the other, particularly as that ideal evolved in Christian teaching. The Greek word *agapē* does not translate well into either "love" or "charity," as the latter words tend to be used in present-day America. "Considerateness" is perhaps closer to the mark, as is Michael Novak's paraphrasing of Thomas Aquinas: "to will the good of the other as the other."[71] But this raises the problem of identifying what *is* "the good" for the other, and what role personal preferences can and should play in that identification. We have thus circled back to where we began: with the Golden Rule and the puzzle of what the self wants, which, according to this rule, will determine what should be extended to others.

An alternative route to understanding the meaning of liking and sharing to liberals is to investigate the reasons they advance for liking our fellow man – reasons, as noted previously, that emphasize similarities, and among those similarities, qualities deserving of respect and reverence. To these reasons could be added the normal human craving for social warmth: that to like others and be liked in return gives a communal texture to existence that otherwise threatens to become insular and empty. For egalitarians, the word "fellowship" and its stronger variant "brotherhood" imply a sense of bonding with others[72] (not distance and distinctiveness) and a related obligation of the fortunate to share their economic goods with the unfortunate, the latter policy seemingly implied by this notion of fellowship in conjunction with a belief system emphasizing luck and not volition as the key determinant of economic success or failure. Consider for example the familial obligations implied by "brotherhood," and how the sense of obligation to help a brother can be affected by one's assessment of the causes of the brother's difficulties. Suppose we discover that one of our own brothers is in dire financial straits, and to pay off a debt coming due he will have to sell a large number of assets – say, his stereo equipment, his only car, and a favorite guitar. Our willingness to volunteer financial help is noticeably different if those debts resulted (a) from medical expenses incurred from being struck by a hit-and-run driver, as opposed to (b) from placing repeated and unsuccessful bets with a bookie. The example merely illustrates that our sense of obligation to share our worldly goods with those in need depends crucially upon our perceptions of the extent to which the needy are or are not responsible for being in dire economic straits. Thus, the more one views the rewards of the market as the product of circumstances beyond the individual's control, the more appealing the case becomes for the economically advantaged sharing wth the less fortunate.

The priorities of "liking" and "sharing" liberals tend to view as being threatened by the competitive atmosphere of the free market. The reward system featured in that competition, they argue, fosters acquisitiveness and aggressiveness and indifference to the fate of others. "Look out for number one" and "the devil take the hindmost" are not shibboleths signaling a community preoccupied with fellowship and brotherhood, kindness and sharing. They indicate instead, according to market critics, a community in which there is "no other nexus between man and man [except] naked self-interest,"[73] in which "there is not much love or hate," but rather "a superficial friendliness" behind which "is distance and indifference."[74] Jack Kemp, whose sentiments are far removed from liberal ideology, nevertheless provides a telling sketch of some of the effects on attitudes and values that can develop in an environment of incessant and combative confrontation: "When every day you wake up with the feeling somebody is going to try to take a piece out of your hide before the sun goes down, you stop trusting people; fellowship and charity vanish. We become a nation of loners."[75] The economist's image of the ideal market thus clashes with the liberal's image of the ideal community. However well the single-minded pursuit of economic self-interest by all members serves to promote Pareto efficiency and economic growth, these same attributes do little to promote bonds of affection and a sense of mutual obligation for the well-being of all. Instead of the out-stretched hand of fellowship, the interpersonal relations of the competitive market system, argue liberals, are better characterized by the boxer's crouch.

Conservatives are not lacking for rebuttals. One traditional defense is to insist that liberals are utopian, their ideals impossible to achieve or even to approximate if one sees human beings for what they are and recognizes the considerable limitations on the best they can become. "A capitalist order," writes Irving Kristol, "begins with the assumption that the world is full of other people, moved by their own interests and their own passions, and that the best we can reasonably hope for is a society of civil concord, not a community of mutual love."[76] Notice the shift in the terms of the debate – from emphasizing the intrinsic goodness of humanity to emphasizing human frailties and the implications of those frailties for the best that the human community can hope to be. Milton Friedman takes the argument a step further.

Interviewer: How would you answer those who claim that capitalism cannot foster a just and orderly society, since it's based on the emotion of greed?

Friedman: What kind of society isn't structured on greed? As a friend of mine says, the one thing you can absolutely depend on every other person to do is to put his interests ahead of yours. Now, his interests may not be greedy in a narrow, selfish sense. Some people's self-interest is to save the world. Some people's self-interest is to do good for others. Florence Nightingale pursued her own self-interest through charitable activities. Rockefeller pursued his self-interest in setting up the Rockefeller Founda-tion. But for most people, most of the time, self-interest is greed. So the problem of social organization is how to set up an arrangement under which greed will do the least harm. It seems to me that the great virtue of capitalism is that it's that kind of system.[77]

In short, the trick in structuring society is to devise a system in which the less desirable attributes of humanity are held in check. To hope for more – to believe that a better community can be fashioned characterized by liking and sharing, fellowship and brotherhood – is to refuse to face the harsh realities of human limitations, or so conservatives such as Kristol and Friedman avow.

Another kind of argument has also been used by right-of-center writers to criticize the liberal critique of the market system as destructive of human values. It begins by acknowledging that a competitive economic system does discourage certain kinds of behavior and attitudes while fostering others, but argues that the gains are worth the costs. Recall the primary importance that conservatives give to individual freedom. That freedom can be promoted, or so runs the argument, in a community in which distance and indifference are typical of human interactions. Those who crave " 'social space' within which civil and political liberty can flower"[78] and personal space in which the unconventional can flourish may welcome distance and indifference in social relations because they make tolerance and nonintervention more probable. Michael Novak is one of the few to confront this tradeoff and argue that liberal community ideals in practice would tend to undermine the individual's sense of freedom. American society, he acknowledges, quickly became more mobile and less settled than Old World settlements from which so many immigrants came, and this mobility and the constant uprooting it implies have disrupted "close human associations" and increased the typical American's sense of separateness and loneliness.[79] But the challenge of that increased isolation can act as a stimulus to individual development in which group norms play a lesser role and attitudes and aptitudes that are unconventional have a greater chance to flourish. Where "group instinct" is too strong, Novak contends, "many are too 'other-directed,' too quick to take their signals from their associates."[80] The plea for rugged individualism is thereby used to challenge the ideal community of liberals as inhibiting to personal development. "In our sentimental age," Novak begins a key argument (the beginning already signaling disparagement to come),

there is a tendency to desire a different sort of community, less a community of the spirit and the inner life than a community of sentiment, emotional support, and often expressed intimacy. Such communities are no doubt precious, but they are also often dubious, cloying, and imprisoning. Community is not a simple reality. The much celebrated "loss of community" is not, correspondingly, all loss.[81]

What has been lessened is a sense of the "cooperative and fraternal" texture to existence in a community in which the members "may not have much emotional attachment to each other, spend much time looking into each other's eyes for moral support, or be particularly intimate with one another."[82] What has been created instead is "a community of colleagueship, task-oriented, goal-directed, freely entered into and freely left" in which the competition of the marketplace translates into "the competitive urging of each other to new heights of development . . . ."[83] The end result, Novak admits, is not the only form of community, but "it is a noble one."[84]

In sum, the ideal community that liberals advocate these writers of the right would discredit either as being impossible to approximate and thus useless to pursue, or alternatively, as being dangerous to pursue because any close approximation would inhibit personal freedom[85] and stunt personal development. The alternative notion of community that conservatives favor features a maximum of personal freedom and a minimum of social bonds insofar as those bonds threaten to imperil that freedom. Although informing most of the literature of the right, these priorities are perhaps most clearly evident in the writings of the extreme right. For example,

Civilization is the progress toward a society of privacy. The savage's whole existence is public, ruled by the laws of his tribe. Civilization is the process of setting man free from men.[86]

To challenge the merits of such views and counter conservative denigration of their own ideals, liberals might argue (as conservative George Will has argued) that the nation already "has acquired political values and practices which involve a disproportionate individualism and an inadequate sense of human beings as social creatures."[87] The accompanying and ongoing debate between left and right is not likely to be resolved, involving as it does the kinds of issues touched on above, including the ideals appropriately incorporated into words like "charity" and "community" and the practical implications of the Golden Rule. Those issues were initially broached within the context of the market system as an environment influencing values, and the question of whether that influence was good or bad. To this point the discussion has provided nothing beyond an oversimplified sketch of disagreements between liberals and conservatives about which influences should count as good or bad. The "badness" of some recent market developments, however, is not a topic of dispute, because those developments suggest a declining allegiance to traditional American values honored by both left and right. It is to this evidence of recent and disturbing trends that the discussion now turns. The question at issue is whether, by the norms embraced by most Americans across the political spectrum, the present behavior of many participants in the market suggests that something is deeply wrong.

Complaints about unethical behavior in the business community are as old as business itself. Thus, current grumblings about declining values and ruthless behavior in the American economy follow in a long tradition of denunciations by observers of American business practices, no doubt first expressed when the first colonist sought to turn a quick profit or went looking for a bargain. Present-day accusations nevertheless seem to be especially strident and pervasive. They emphasize particularly the preoccupation of individuals with making money and of corporations with making profits and the undesirable effects of both.

According to one recent poll of company managers, "about 75 percent . . . report feeling pressured to satisfy corporate goals."[88] The goal that tends to dominate – indeed, to supersede and squelch all other goals according to the critics – is making a profit. Symptomatic of that tendency, the eight publicized goals of a nationally known company were known to employees as "profits and the seven dwarfs" according to a business executive who made that revelation to this writer with the understanding the company would not be named. Similar complaints made more publicly are not difficult to find. "Today, greed is in," a chief executive of the Champion International Company told *The New York Times*. "We are told greed and intolerance are good for the country and for the company."[89] Another business leader writes: "I have been in business for almost 40 years and I cannot recall a period in which greed and corruption appeared as prevalent as they are today."[90] William Woodside, executive committee chairman of Primerica Corporation, makes a similar point in softer language, noting that for the new crop of corporate managers "it has become positively un-American to look at anything except their own bottom line."[91] The greater is the preoccupation with that bottom line, the less companies are inclined to give to charity, and Woodside's point would seem consistent with the decline in corporate giving in recent years. As to the rationale for gifts still made, Texas oilman T. Boone Pickens no doubt speaks for many of the modern generation when he insists: "Company giving has to be related to the company's interests"[92]

The modern corporation's preoccupation with profits, runs the modern complaint, tends to be accompanied in the business world by the individual's preoccupation with making money. By this interpretation, the gospel of wealth is in danger of being collapsed into the single commandment: Enrich thyself. College students of the present generation, encouraged "to do their own thing," are more inclined than previously to view "their thing" as making money. A 1967 poll of college freshmen found that 40 percent wanted "to be very well off financially" while 80 percent considered "developing a meaningful philosophy of life" a crucial objective. By 1986, the numbers had been reversed, roughly 40 percent still concerned with the meaning of the good life and 80 percent wanting to be rich.[93] The priorities of business school students, as one would expect, are not significantly different. Complains one Harvard teacher about would-be MBAs, "MBAs aren't interested in ethics. They're obsessed with getting jobs and competing with each other."[94]

The graduates of high schools, colleges, or graduate programs who enter the business world willing to honor few goals beyond personal advancement and personal riches will not be hard pressed to find others similarly inclined, or so much of recent evidence from that world suggests. Part of this evidence is the rising complaint voiced by corporate leaders about the decline in company loyalty, a perception that employee polls suggest is not without foundation.[95] In a competitive world with narrowly construed objectives and ruthless firings in the name of profit, the absence of steadfast loyalty among some of those not fired toward the company would seem to be a predictable development. As loyalty to the larger organization wanes, the attention to the goals of self tends to take on increased importance, as does the willingness to pursue such goals at the expense of the employer or fellow employees. "Me Inc." is one name given to this attitude by a president of a career-counseling firm.[96] Another analyst engaged in career counseling adds: "People have learned you owe allegiance only to your own career. It's the Paladin mentality – 'Have Gun, Will Travel'."[97] The portrait of the modern employee (particularly the modern executive) as a mercenary is a recurring theme in contemporary criticisms of the business world. A veteran of the investment banking community, Felix Rohatyn, acknowledges that "the big business community views all investment bankers as a bunch of samurais who will do anything for money."[98] But investment bankers are not the only ones so characterized. Maury Klein, historian and biographer of Jay Gould, would apply the tar from this particular brush liberally throughout the business world. "What we're living in now," he suggests, "is an age of Hessians."[99]

Hessian behavior suggests that the morals and deportment of the mercenary are tending to pervade a competitive arena in which ruthlessness is becoming all too common and personal trust is becoming progressively more rare. The increasing willingness to accept bluffing, bullying and conniving as a way of life is suggested by the titles of popular books: *Winning Through Intimidation, Winning at Confrontation, Winning with Deception and Bluff, Techniques of Harrassment*, and *How to Steal a Business*. These are not the titles of manuals the upstanding businessman of earlier generations would have been anxious to have discovered on his desk. As ruthlessness in competition has led to questionable ethical practices – or practices that many who honor older American norms would question – wheelings and dealings in the moral borderlands have not infrequently led to transgressions of the law. Only partly in jest did Securities and Exchange Commissioner Joseph Grundfest begin his 1987 graduation address to students of the University of Southern California by noting: "It's a privilege to address this distinguished gathering of unindicted business-school graduates, their unindicted faculty, family and friends."[100] Scandals, indictments, and convictions of the great and the small have been a regular feature in the business press in recent years – from the payment of a $100 million Securities and Exchange Commission penalty (the largest ever) by Ivan Boesky, to the conviction of two tow-truck operators in New Jersey for pouring oil on a freeway ramp to cause accidents and boost their business; from E. F. Hutton being ordered to pay in excess of $6 million in fines and restitution to banks for illegal overdrafting, to the discovery that a defense contractor with $11 billion in annual sales to the government was charging $1,118.26 for a plastic cap on the leg of a stool. Nor is such questionable behavior limited to the intemperate strivings of the heretofore underprivileged. "Some of those we're bringing cases against are Baker Scholars, Rhodes Scholars, Phi Beta Kappas," lamented the outgoing chairman of the Securities and Exchange Commission (and a former vice-chairman of the recently fined investment firm of E. F. Hutton). "It's the cream of the crop, and that's what is so shocking and causes concern."[101]

When allegiance to what were previously accepted values tends to wane and unprincipled behavior is more in season, a decline in personal trust is sure to follow. Complains one business school dean who is also a private investor: "I can't do transactions on the telephone any more because people do not keep their word."[102] From the other end of the telephone, the president of an investment banking business admits: "I used to think that I could tell good guys from bad guys, and wouldn't deal with people I thought dishonest or unethical. But I've learned that I can't tell the difference. They look alike."[103]

A handful of anecdotes and the results from a few polls are hardly conclusive evidence that a crisis in values does exist in the business community or America at large. Whether the morality of the average business person is better or worse now than it was in, say, the era of Jay Gould and John D. Rockefeller is impossible to say. It is also beside the point. What is to the point – and has been emphasized in the foregoing analysis – is that whether or not a crisis exists, and if it does, its extent and nature and the contributing role of the market system, are all topics that can be debated on several levels. At one extreme are subtle disputes about which ideals should be incorporated into the meaning of such words as "charity" and "community," and about the practical implications of the Golden Rule. At the other extreme are few debates about what is good or bad, or which values should dominate a value system. Instead discussion centers on business practices that clearly contravene time-honored American values that neither left nor right are prone to challenge (such as honesty, loyalty, and honoring the confidentiality of clients). The major topics in dispute accordingly are the extent to which such behavior is typical of the American business world and whether, typical or not, such behavior is primarily a symptom of a larger set of societal problems encapsulated in the phrase "crisis in values," or alternatively, whether questionable behavior in the market system has been a major contributing factor to that crisis. The more flawed business behavior is perceived to be, and the more those flaws are seen as contributing to undesirable trends in society at large, the more one is inclined to ask about this aspect of the market system what is generally asked whenever that system seems to be functioning in defective ways: Should the state take action to rectify, modify, or counteract such defects? Both left and right within America are inclined to answer "No," but for reasons that are quite different.

Should the State Promote Values?

An overview of pro and con   A republican government, noted the Founding Fathers, "presupposes the existence" of admirable qualities in its citizens, but how these qualities should be fostered and whether the government should play a role in that process were topics left largely up in the air.[104] They are still up in the air today. "If we believe that moral excellence should be encouraged, why should we not use government to promote it?" asks a former student of Friedrich Hayek, and then supplies the answer:

. . . what we understand by moral excellence is logically inconsistent with making laws to produce it. For it is a kind of excellence that does not consist in a set of goals which everyone ought to pursue, or a pattern to which all men should conform. It consists in each man's ability to make a coherent, self-sufficient life for himself in his own way among other men, while meticulously respecting the efforts of others to do the same.[105]

Such an argument, at bottom, would discredit the question by denying the problem. If values, at least to some degree, are influenced by environment – and surely they are – then one obvious question to ask is how the government affects that environment, and whether government actions should be deliberately tailored to have a good effect. Liberals and conservatives alike will be quick to point out problems lurking in the phrase "a good effect." Which values to promote and the means to use in that promotion, they will rightly insist, have always been contentious issues.

One obvious device for promoting values, and probably the least contentious, is through the leadership provided by leading government officials. Their personal examples and public exhortations can and do make a difference by encouraging respect for certain norms of behavior. "Aristotle said that people in government exercise a teaching function," ethicist Sissela Bok reminds us. "Among other things, we see what they do and think that is how we should act. Unfortunately, when they do things that are underhanded or dishonest, that teaches us too."[106] The lessons taught by the Reagan Administration, for example, have been singled out for comment under both headings. For conservative supporters, the "Reagan revolution" included a resurgence of attention to old ideals, with the President acting "as the most prominent and influential moral traffic cop in the country."[107] Critics are less enthusiastic about the moral tone they sense in the vicinity of the Potomac. They note that at least seven special counsels have been appointed to investigate charges of wrongdoing among administration officials and more than 100 Reagan appointees have come under some cloud of impropriety. Concerning the many under that cloud, a national magazine joined liberals in pointing out that "Many of the allegations were relatively minor, but the accumulation of cases produces a portrait of impropriety on a grand scale."[108]

Whether the Reagan leadership on balance has strengthened or weakened the public's allegiance to traditional American values is not the issue here. The point is that leading figures in this or any other administration give moral leadership, whether positive or negative, precisely because of their perceived importance and high visibility in an era of extensive – one might even say, exhaustive – media coverage of the smallest detail of personal behavior or personal utterances by the powerful and the famous. Under this heading, then, the state does exercise an inevitable effect on values through the public personalities of those elected or appointed to high office.

Laws can also be used to shape community values. This smacks, however, of an effort to legislate morality, a process many argue vehemently against in a long-standing debate that is usually more murky than deep. "By the legislation of morality," writes George Will, one of the few conservatives to advocate such activity, "I mean the enactment of laws and implementation of policies that proscribe, mandate, regulate, or subsidize behavior that will, over time, have the predictable effect of nurturing, bolstering or altering habits, dispositions and values on a broad scale."[109] Will rests his case for government activity in this area on a variant of the argument made above: that values can be affected by environment; the values of the citizenry are a matter of importance to society; thus the government has a responsibility to influence those values favorably. Or as Will puts the matter, "If a human being is, except for a few strong forms of animal spirits, a *tabula rasa*, then an urgent task of citizenship is to see that the civic system does some careful writing on the blank slate."[110]

Most liberals and conservatives are less ready to endorse such arguments. One reason is the tension between (a) their desire for a place of special importance in society for those values they value most, and (b) their recognition of the right of others to *reject* those values because that right of rejection seems to be implied by such venerated American rights as the right to free speech, the right to privacy, and the right to the pursuit of happiness, with such pursuit conditioned by values the individual chooses for himself. This point is sometimes made more simply by those who argue that liberals and conservatives (like most Americans) want to have it both ways. The legality of sodomy illustrates the problem. Do such traditional American rights as those just cited imply that individuals should have freedom of choice in sexual matters, provided those choices are exercised in private? Indicative of the lack of national consensus on this particular issue, 26 states have "decriminalized" sodomy since 1961, while 24 still have statutes imposing prison terms ranging from 30 days (Arizona) to 20 years (Georgia and Rhode Island).[111] Recently the Supreme Court, in a sharply disputed 5–4 decision, upheld the Georgia law. The public appeared to be as divided as the Court but, unlike the justices, many were willing to endorse both sides of the argument simultaneously. A poll of adult males taken shortly after the Court's decision found that 72 percent agreed that sexual practices are "up to the individual to decide for himself or herself," while 51 percent "would allow federal or state authorities to limit or outlaw . . . acts of anal sex."[112] One therefore senses in the sodomy case a traditional American tension between conflicting desires to honor individual freedom and to honor certain values by having laws that punish behavior considered to contravene those values.

There is a second and more subtle tension in the views of liberals and conservatives toward using laws to promote certain values. At first glance, the tension in question may appear to be anything but subtle. The argument that the government should not attempt to legislate morality is, on the face of it, preposterous for the simple reason that the government cannot avoid doing so. Many of its laws endorse, support, or enforce values by their very terms. That being so, the only question is which values will be imbedded in state legislation. George Will accordingly scolds Ronald Reagan for suggesting that "the taxing power of the government . . . must not be used to regulate the economy or bring about social change." As Will points out, laws that affect property are laws that can and do affect behavior, and those effects can include fostering industriousness and thrift – effects that Ronald Reagan himself announced were among the desired results of his proposed tax legislation. "Tax deductions and tax exemptions are not alternatives to social programs," writes Will. "They are social programs. And unlike many such, they often achieve their intended effects. They alter behavior on a large scale for the advancement of chosen goals."[113] Most liberals and conservatives are nevertheless reluctant to acknowledge the promotion of values as a general responsibility of the government. Although that promotion may be imbedded in certain kinds of legislation (such as tax laws and social welfare programs), both left and right apparently prefer to debate which values to imbed and how to imbed them within the context of specific laws designed for specific purposes. In such discussions, liberals tend to argue for laws promoting egalitarian values, including a more equal sharing of the community's resources. Conservatives tend to resist such sharing for all the reasons previously developed, arguing instead for laws protecting property and promoting individual freedom, including the promotion of more competition and less regulation in the marketplace.

Each camp will admit that not all values in their own value systems are appropriately imbedded in, or endorsed by, government legislation. Each considers certain values to be "a matter of personal preference," a phrase designed to signal that what is preferred may vary widely (for example, whether to abstain from alcohol), and no particular preference should be regarded as superior to any other (or at least superior enough to warrant public endorsement in government laws.)[114] To oversimplify what is ultimately a complex hierarchy, one can think of both conservatives and liberals as having a two-tier system of ethics, with one set comprising values that are "right" for the community as a whole (such as "industriousness" and "thrift," which tax legislation may seek to promote), and the other set comprising values appropriately left to the individual to decide (such as the values determining the appropriateness of a particular sexual act between consenting adults in the 26 states that have no laws against sodomy). In this distinction between values to be publicly endorsed and values to be privately chosen lurks a tension between claiming to know what is right and acknowledging, for some domains of personal behavior, the relevance of ethical relativism. The manner in which this tension manifests itself, however, tends to take a different form in the writings of the left and right.

Liberals, relativism, and the activist state   As Democrats are sometimes identified as the party of moral license, so liberalism in its modern form is sometimes identified as the ideology with a permissive view about appropriate personal values. Ronald Dworkin makes the point with greater precision: "[liberalism] supposes that government must be neutral on what might be called the question of the good life"; that is, "political decisions must be, as far as possible, independent of any particular conception of the good life, or of what gives value to life."[115] Dworkin defends this neutrality with a simple argument anchored in a single premise: "Since the citizens of a society differ in their conceptions [of the good life], the government does not treat them as equals if it prefers one conception to another . . . ."[116] The case can be put in a positive way by noting that the priority of equal treatment in a society of differing views implies that the government must strive for neutrality in the sense of not favoring one particular viewpoint about "the good life" over any other.

Liberal economists seem similarly reluctant to pass judgment about differences in personal preferences about "what gives value to life." In many cases one senses an inclination to argue by analogy from economic theory: consumers have preferences for economic goods and services, these are revealed through choices made in the marketplace, and the more the economic system enables the diverse preferences of the many to be met, the better it is presumed to function; similarly, the analogous argument might run, individuals have ethical preferences, these find expression in words and deeds, and the more the social system enables the diverse preferences of the many to find expression, the better it is presumed to be functioning. Shadows of this kind of reasoning seem to flit between the lines in the analysis of liberal economist Lester Thurow. "Individuals and society may simply have a taste for equality or inequality," he writes, "just as they have a taste for paintings."[117] Thurow then discusses how this "taste for equality" can change as per capita income rises, but always in a context that treats ethical preferences in much the same way as economists treat consumer preferences: they vary among individuals, can shift over time, and no one set of preferences is intrinsically superior to any other.[118]

Statements such as these have on occasion been cited by critics of the left who claim to detect a basic inconsistency between (a) arguing for active government intervention to promote social goals, and (b) arguing for ethical neutrality in government policies because no one conception of the good life is superior to any other. This charge of inconsistency misses the point just made. Liberals (and conservatives) can be regarded in a rough-and-ready way as having a two-tier value system. For those on the left, some values are simply "right" – such as equality[119] – and accordingly should be promoted by state legislation.[120] Other values are appropriately decided by each individual – such as those affecting sexual behavior in private between consenting adults – and no particular opinion concerning these latter values ought to be considered intrinsically superior to any other. To the charge of inconsistency just noted, liberals might therefore reply that their critics have failed to understand a crucial distinction in the way liberals regard different kinds of values.

To acknowledge this distinction, however, is to suggest a vulnerability on a different front. If some values are simply a matter of personal preference, and no one set of such values in superior to any other, why should all values not be treated this way, including the liberal's preference for equality? The shadow now threatening to cloud discussion is that of ethical relativism: the view that all moral claims are subjective in the sense that "there are no objectively sound procedures for justifying one moral code or one set of moral judgments as against another code or set of moral judgments."[121] In drawing the distinction noted and thereby acknowledging the existence of values of the second sort (those that are nothing more than personal preferences), liberals must confront an old challenge in ethical discourse: how to legitimate the special moral force they claim for values of the first sort (such as equality). As old and common as that problem is, liberals raise it with a special force because their division between the two sets of values traditionally gives exceptional length to those that are appropriately the domain of individual choice and (as Dworkin implied earlier) not the appropriate subject for community endorsement or enforcement.

This generous division in favor of individual preferences, which from one vantage point encourages tolerance and cultural diversity, from another threatens cultural uncertainty. At the extreme, to tolerate everything is to honor nothing. Or to put the argument in a less extreme form, the fewer values acknowledged as appropriately venerated by the community and supported by government policy, the less guidance citizens receive from established cultural norms. With few publicly recognized values, public discourse concerning national priorities will be in danger of becoming impoverished and confused. "If making value judgments is a private business, or such judgments have no objective validity," asks Stephen Hart, "how are we to argue with each other about what values ought to inform public decisions?"[122] Consider, for example, the recent pleas within America to give more attention to the teaching of values in the education system. The more an attitude of ethical relativism pervades society, the more problematic becomes the question of which values to teach. Moreover, that attitude, if it pervades the student body, may undercut or defeat any effort to discuss value questions in the classroom. Illustrative of this latter situation is the classroom dilemma described by California's Superintendent of Public Instruction.

I have a friend who teaches a class in 19th-century English literature to freshmen at U. C. Berkeley. The theory of the course was to use literature as a way of saying to young people, "Here are some standards of personal and ethical behavior, moral ideas that you should at least look at in deciding how you want to live your life." Her problem . . . was that those students would not accept the validity of any outside standard. They had gone through a high school education so ingrained in the philosophy of ethical relativism that they could not even agree that you should look at some standard in, for example, "Pride and Prejudice," for some help in deciding what true nobility is.[123]

Schools can hardly meet the call to "instill" or "inculcate" a sense of values in their students if the social world in which the students move runs counter to the veneration of any values. Similarly, those concerned with "the decline and fall of business ethics," to borrow a recent title from a business magazine, cannot hope to give old-fashioned norms like keeping promises and truthfulness a renewed place of importance unless participants in the business community generally accept, as a general principle, that *some* values are *not* just a matter of personal preference but a matter of public concern, and as such deserving of all the affirmation and advocacy that business leadership can muster.

One final point: nothing in the previous discussion should be construed as an argument in favor of intolerance. Rather, the argument is that, where values are concerned, tolerance of differences and diversity has its costs, and such tolerance in an extreme form can threaten costs which are similarly extreme. Finally, if such a tradeoff is inescapable between more tolerance and the costs of increased tolerance, one should beware of trying to have it both ways. The more one gives special homage to certain values, the less forbearing one becomes of behavior inconsistent with those values. Liberals can readily grasp the point if asked to choose between public enforcement of laws against discrimination and tolerance of racist attitudes. Opposition to discrimination, they would insist, is not merely one option among many in interpersonal relations among different races to be decided "as a matter of individual preference." Liberals nevertheless frequently evidence less certainty about public promotion of other values, such as those associated with the preservation and strengthening of the family. One cannot hope to venerate the traditional two-parent family as an institution in the nation's culture and instill that sense of veneration in successive generations while simultaneously treating such issues as births out of wedlock and lesbian households as nothing more than different individual preferences for different lifestyles. The question can be sharpened by citing the reaction of a San Francisco psychologist to the recent Supreme Court decision to uphold Georgia's law against sodomy: "The primary problem with the [Court's] decision is the psychological damage it does. It is not good for people to be told they're bad, especially when they're not."[124] For liberals concerned with the declining allegiance to the family as an institution within America the question becomes: If values associated with the preservation of the family are to be publicly endorsed, which forms of behavior inconsistent with those values must be publicly condemned, including, on occasion, condemnation written into law? In a similar vein one cannot argue that what counts as pornography is strictly in the eye of the beholder (or is merely a matter of personal preference) and simultaneously decry the rising popularity of certain sexual practices as symptomatic of a bad trend in national norms. If "bad" is to have any meaning in public discussions of national norms, the values relating to the behavior in question cannot be regarded as the exclusive province of individual preferences. To labor a point worth laboring, time-honored values imbedded in the nation's culture cannot be regarded as nothing more than options for the individual to consider. That point was made in the caustic commentary of TV personality Ted Koppel to the graduating seniors of Duke University:

We have actually convinced ourselves that slogans will save us. Shoot up if you must, but use a clean needle. Enjoy sex whenever and with whomever you wish, but wear a condom. No! The answer is no. Not because it isn't cool or smart or because you might end up in jail or dying in an AIDS ward, but no because it's wrong, because we have spent 5,000 years as a race of rational human beings, trying to drag ourselves out of the primeval slime by searching for truth and moral absolutes. In its purest form, truth is not a polite tap on the shoulder. It is a howling reproach. What Moses brought down from Mount Sinai were not the Ten Suggestions.[125]

At issue here is *not* what is right and wrong in sexual behavior, but how defining what is right and wrong in public terms is crucial to the shaping of a culture and the progress of a nation. Only with an acknowledged set of national values can we have the requisite criteria for judging whether the nation is or is not making progress. The more extensive and detailed that list of nationality approved values, the more the culture takes on shape to guide behavior of the citizens, but the less that culture will be known for tolerance and diversity. Governor Mario Cuomo was therefore broaching a complicated issue involving delicate tradeoffs when he made the seemingly banal statement to an Indianapolis audience: "it is again within our power to choose the kind of America we want."[126] In choosing the kind of America desired, Americans must answer the question: What kind of people are we? The more Democrats and liberals heed Cuomo's call and give shape to that answer, the less tolerant they must be of values and behavior inconsistent with that answer. And that is a dilemma most left-of-center writers seem unwilling to confront. Conservatives face a somewhat similar dilemma, although it tends to surface in their writings in a different guise.

Conservatives, spontaneous order, and the minimal state The notion of "spontaneous order," as his supporters are quick to insist, is central to Friedrich Hayek's ideas about how the good society ought to function and the appropriate role for government in that society.[127] If "order" is to be "spontaneous," and spontaneous implies an absence of contrived efforts by state planners, the reader can anticipate why such arguments often play a central role in buttressing the conservative case for the minimal state.

The first order of business is to clarify what "spontaneous order" means. One of the more useful summaries is provided by Hayek when he in turn quotes Michael Polanyi.

When order is achieved among human beings by allowing them to interact with each other on their own initiative – subject only to the laws which uniformly apply to all of them – we have a system of spontaneous order in society. We may then say that the efforts of these individuals are co-ordinated by exercising their individual initiative and that this self-co-ordination justifies this liberty on public grounds. The actions of such individuals are said to be free, for they are not determined by any *specific* command, whether of a superior or a public authority; the compulsion to which they are subject is impersonal and general.[128]

Often cited as a prime example of spontaneous order is the order achieved by the free-market system. Individual participants are free to pursue their own economic self-interest, subject only to general rules (such as the laws of contract) that apply to all. The incentives, or the rewards and penalties of the system, are provided by prices established in competitive markets. These prices, in turn, constitute a decentralized information system, comprehensive in coverage and responsive to the changing preferences of the many participants in the market. No system of government planning of the economy can serve the citizens as well, the argument concludes, for several reasons. First, the free-market system, as its name implies, leaves individuals more free to exercise economic choices (and the role of a potentially coercive state is accordingly minimized, at least in the realm of economic activity). Secondly, the price system of a competitive market incorporates a myriad of information that far exceeds what any central authority can possibly acquire and incorporate into its economic planning. Thirdly, in large measure because of this information-gathering function of market prices, the free market tends to facilitate more efficient use of society's economic resources compared with the usage likely to result from any planned alternative. Thus the concept of spontaneous order when applied to a market system leads to the same bottom line as that reached by Adam Smith with his metaphor of the "invisible hand," and for the same reason. Although individuals tend to pursue only their own private interests – here, economic self-interest – the end results will be socially beneficial – in this case, all the benefits that accompany the larger gross national product made possible through more efficient resource utilization. This conclusion which Adam Smith expressed in a rough-and-ready way has since been rigorously demonstrated by neoclassical economics. The conclusion has also been attacked by neoclassical critics as too dependent upon assumptions widely at variance with economic reality. Neither the demonstration nor the criticisms need concern us here.[129] What is at issue is whether the notion of spontaneous order – however well it may describe the functioning of a free-market system – can be used to describe the rules and institutions that comprise the very fabric of a society that is both capitalist and democratic.

The following sketch will not do justice to all the complexities of Hayek's conceptual framework, nor will it try to show, as others have, the possible areas of confusion, ambiguity, and inconsistency in that framework. As will be apparent shortly, the two major problems to be examined below are endemic to any notion of spontaneous order when applied to the rules and institutions of society, however complex and carefully qualified the associated conceptual framework may be.

Hayek begins with the noncontroversial observation that many of the long-established institutions in Western capitalist societies have tended to evolve gradually over time with little or no conscious planning, and that, despite this lack of planning, in their present form they serve a variety of useful social purposes. Language and English common law are cases in point. From thoughts about institutions, Hayek proceeds to thoughts about "rules," which are essentially observed patterns of behavior.[130] Rules may be "articulated" or "non-articulated." "A non-articulated rule is a descriptive rule, a pattern of regularised behaviour which has not been specifically expressed in language, while articulated rules are formalized normative rules that do not merely describe behaviour but govern that behaviour in terms of setting appropriate standards."[131] More simply put, some rules can be (and are) put into words and others are not, but both describe how we behave as social creatures and influence the judgments that we make about acceptable and unacceptable behavior.

The importance of such rules to the functioning of society is explained by Hayek using concepts and beliefs that resonate powerfully with traditional conservative notions about freedom and human nature. He begins with the standard conservative premise about the nature of humanity, namely, that human beings have certain traits that are innate and not easily changed, and that some of these traits, when unconstrained by social rules, lead to nasty social behavior – or as Hayek would have it, lead to self-centered behavior giving vent to "man's more primitive and ferocious instincts."[132] The trick to achieving "order" in society is therefore to devise rules that constrain these dangerous propensities and, where possible, channel the associated energy into useful social enterprises. To return to our previous example of the competitive market, its rules – or its "traditions and institutions"[133] – and the associated incentive system of rewards and penalties help to channel the economic self-interest of participants in a manner well-suited to making efficient use of society's economic resources.

But how do such rules evolve, and why are the rules produced by spontaneous evolution to be preferred to those that a central authority might deliberately put in place to achieve specific ends?

Here too conservatives are inclined to use the example of the market to answer questions such as these. The multitude of rules that make the market system possible (that is, all the rules embodied in its institutions and traditions) develop gradually over time in response to changing needs as economies become more integrated and sophisticated. Evolution of rules is thus explained in Darwinian terms: new challenges evoke experimental responses by the few; the more successful responses will be adopted by the many; and old rules will accordingly give way to new rules that better serve the needs of the majority of market participants. The total fabric of rules at any point in time is therefore appropriately viewed as incorporating the collective wisdom of a host of past experiments. That fabric is also superior to any alternative set of rules that a central authority might contrive for reasons noted previously that emphasize the freedom of the individual[134] and the knowledge limitations of central planners.

This Darwinian notion of superior rules evolving over time Hayek would apply to all the rules that govern society, not just to those that govern the operation of a competitive market system. Consider the evolution of rules specifying what counts as moral behavior. At the core of Hayek's arguments concerning this complex process is a line of reasoning with a compelling simplicity.[135] Given humanity's innate tendencies for aggressive acts toward one another, rules are necessary if some measure of individual freedom is to be achieved, freedom being defined in the traditional conservative way as the absence of coercion. With such freedom, individuals can pursue their own purposes, and when purposes clash, the rules provide a framework for the resolution of conflicting interests. Humans can accordingly plan with greater certainty, and better planning implies better results (at least on the average and over the long haul). These advantages suggest that over time better rules – including better moral rules – will be devised in response to the challenges of an evolving society, where "better" implies more freedom (or less coercion) and more certainty in planning. The collection of rules at any point in time can therefore claim "an inbred wisdom," embodying "more inherited knowledge and experience than any individual could be capable of ascertaining himself."[136] Hayek sums up the matter this way:

> Where the elements of such an order are intelligent human beings whom we wish to use their individual capacities as successfully as possible in the pursuit of their own ends, the chief requirement for its establishment is that each know which of the circumstances in his environment he can count on. This need for protection against unpredictable interference is . . . the essential condition of individual freedom, and to secure it is the main function of law.[137]

Or again:

> These "tools" which man has evolved and which constitute such an important part of his adaptation to his environment include much more than material implements. They consist in a large measure of forms of conduct which he habitually follows without knowing why; they consist of what we call "traditions" and "institutions," which he uses because they are available to him as a product of cumulative growth without ever having been designed by any one mind.[138]

Despite the evident appeal to common sense, this reasoning glosses over a multitude of complicated problems, of which two are particularly relevant for topics discussed in this section.

The first problem can be put as a question: If rules evolve and individuals accordingly are made more free to pursue their own purposes, why should this evolution and those pursuits be consistent with "the good society," or at least with progress toward a better society? Consider the evolution process sketched above. Are "good" rules likely to triumph over "bad" rules? The survival of the fittest assures nothing in the first instance beyond the survival of the survivors. The tempting inference is that survivors are always superior, but one has reservations about letting a garden run wild so the roses can fight it out with the weeds. The principle of natural selection that Hayek applies is quintessentially Darwinian. The key to group survival is adopting superior rules. Rules are judged to be superior for the individual when, as previously noted, they facilitate (a) greater freedom to pursue one's own purpose, and (b) greater certainty in planning that accompanies that pursuit, enabling individuals on the average to be more successful in their pursuits. This greater average success implies that the group adopting such rules will also be more successful, although the mechanisms assuring their success remain somewhat vague in Hayek's writing.[139] Repeatedly he refers to the capacities of such groups to survive and flourish. Sometimes he adds that flourishing may include attracting new adherents to the group. At other times flourishing is linked to the ability to outcompete other groups, presumably in the struggle for geographic supremacy or other forms of dominance. The increase in material welfare resulting from greater freedom and better planning could also contribute to a fall in the death rate and a rise in the rate of natural increase of the group. Whatever the relevant mechanisms, the multiplication of numbers remains the central assertion. But why is this a "good" development? To be sure, however one defines progress for humanity, survival is a necessary condition, but hardly a sufficient condition.[140] In defining the good society or what constitutes progress toward the better society Americans are inclined to aim a bit higher than mere multiplication of numbers. The "goodness" or the "better-ness" that accompanies Hayek's Darwinian processes therefore turns crucially upon the type of society likely to evolve as new rules permit more individuals greater freedom and greater success in pursuing their own purposes. At first glance this appears to be an achievement of self-evident merit, but as Edmund Burke pointed out long ago: "The effect of liberty to individuals is, that they may do what they please: We ought to see what it will please them to do, before we risk congratulations . . . ."[141] The question of what it will please humanity to do becomes all the more urgent if one believes, as conservatives like Hayek believe, that humanity has innate and dangerous propensities that must be constrained by social rules.[142] To raise a possibility raised by neoconservative Irving Kristol, might a " 'free society' in Hayek's sense [give] birth in massive numbers to 'free spirits', emptied of moral substance but still driven by primordial moral aspirations"?[143] If the collective achievement resulting from the freeing of humanity to pursue their own purposes is nothing more than "the mere aggregation of selfish aims,"[144] what claim has such a society to "goodness"?

The typical conservative response is to ignore the problem. Some merely reiterate that freedom is the ultimate goal, and thus the best society is the one assuring individuals the maximum freedom to pursue their own goals ("freedom" being defined in the conventional conservative way as the absence of coercion).[145] Hayek himself offers little beyond noting the importance of survival,[146] of which more below. Milton Friedman is confident that the end results of greater freedom will be good, but leaves up in the air what "goodness" means as well as the reasons for his confidence.[147]

This lack of resolution raises again a problem raised in chapter 4 concerning Friedman's "hidden metaphysics." That phrase belongs to Irving Kristol, as does one of the more succinct summaries of the problem.

The idea of bourgeois virtue has been eliminated from Friedman's conception of bourgeois society, and has been replaced by the idea of individual liberty. The assumption is that, in "the nature of things," the latter will certainly lead to the former. There is much hidden metaphysics here, and of a dubious kind.[148]

What is hidden are all the reasons for believing that humanity – despite its darker side – will use its freedom to pursue objectives that will aggregate into a tendency toward "progress" or toward a "better" society, however "progress" or "better" might be defined. The assumption hiding Friedman's "metaphysics" is thus a philosophical premise, not an empirical conclusion. The reasons for suspecting that the hidden metaphysics are "of a dubious kind," as Kristol puts it, relate at least in part to (a) the belief that humanity has a darker side, (b) the evidence that freedom to pursue individual purposes does not always lead to admirable results, and (c) the suspicion – at least on the part of Kristol – that at the moment humanity is not even headed in the right direction.

. . . when [Hayek] turns to a direct contemplation of present-day society, he too has to fall back on a faith in the ultimate benefits of "self-realization" – a phrase he uses as infrequently as possible, but which he is nevertheless forced to use at crucial instances. And what if the "self" that is "realized" under the condition of liberal capitalism is a self that despises liberal capitalism, and uses its liberty to subvert and abolish a free society? To this question, Hayek – like Friedman – has no answer. And yet this is *the* question we now confront, as our society relentlessly breeds more and more such selves, whose private vices in no way provide public benefits to a bourgeois order.[149]

Kristol's doubts can be thrown into sharper focus by asking: What evidence from contemporary American society can be marshalled that is *not* consistent with Friedman's article of faith that individuals freely pursuing their own purposes will invariably move society in an admirable direction? If such examples can be found, their inconsistency with Friedman's article of faith then lends legitimacy to the doubts of those who wonder when spontaneous forces praised by writers such as Friedman and Hayek might *not* lead society in the right direction, and when they do not, what might be done about it.

The rapid rise in recent years of litigation in America – now called by some a "lawsuit crisis" – makes one reluctant to believe that major new directions and devices developed in response to new opportunities in a free-market system will *always* be for the better. So too do developments associated with the recent merger mania, in which, as one expert summarizes the process: "Companies have been bought simply to be broken up, . . . [and] not for any larger, constructive purpose."[150] Or consider the spontaneous order that has emerged in big-time college sports, as described by the Chancellor of the University of California at Berkeley.

We have gotten caught in an "athletics arms race." We try to win in order to cover costs. But we have to spend more to win. To get an edge over the competition, we increase the scale and intensity of our programs. We recruit harder. We demand more from our athletes and build more lavish facilities. The spiral continues. Our quest for more revenues often results in a distortion of our priorities and values. We begin to lose sight of our responsibilities to our students and institutions. . . . By getting a bowl bid or making it to the Final Four, a college can earn a million dollars. When college teams are given a profit incentive, people are constantly tempted to cheat in order to win.[151]

A few final points. The above examples – including the recent explosion of litigation and unproductive mergers and the frenzied competition that bedevils big-time college sports – are not advanced as an argument for state intervention, but to suggest that the evolving results of spontaneous order may not always be "desirable" as most Americans use that word. Perhaps more unsettling yet, identifying what words like "desirable" or "good" mean to Hayek is not easy because his entire analysis continually hovers on the brink of ethical relativism. Which brings us to the second major problem. The first is how one can be sure that the processes of spontaneous order and cultural evolution as expounded by Hayek will lead to good results and toward a better society. The second is whether the conceptual framework of spontaneous order and cultural evolution makes problematic the meaning of words like "good" and "better."

Recall the difficulty posed by ethical relativism: the view that all moral claims are subjective in the sense that there are no objectively sound procedures for justifying one moral code as against another. What "objectively sound procedures" can Hayek advance for preferring one set of moral rules over another? Clearly he is on delicate ground. Central to his analytical framework is the notion of cultural evolution whereby new sets of moral rules repeatedly replace older ones. With a framework of ongoing replacement, the question naturally arises how any one set can be judged as "good," or as "better" than the rest. Hayek tries to supply an answer, although grudgingly and without fanfare. Considering his answer, the absence of fanfare is not surprising. Essentially he converts the Darwinian mechanism of his evolutionary process into an ethical norm. If (a) the moral rules that have prevailed are "simply those which favor the practices that assist the multiplication of mankind"[152] and (b) this principle of natural selection is to be converted into a standard of objective goodness, then (c) the only standard possible is the survival and multiplication of the human race. Thus Hayek writes:

Our morals, the morals which have prevailed, the morals of private property and honesty, are simply those which favor the practices that assist the multiplication of mankind. The economic calculus is a calculus of life: it guides us to do the sort of things that secure the most rapid increase in mankind. In a sense, I am prepared to defend this contention by saying that life has no other purpose than itself, by which I mean that we have been so adjusted that our actions contribute to produce more human beings than there existed before.[153]

Most of humanity – and certainly most Americans – would be reluctant to endorse the notion that "life has no other purpose than itself." They want something more,[154] and thus the issue for Hayek supporters who would broaden his appeal is whether they can find within his framework some justification for expanding the notion of "good" beyond mere replication of the species.

Thomas Sowell is one of those who tries. What he tries is the second of two possibilities, Hayek having taken the first. The processes of spontaneous order and cultural evolution as expounded by Hayek produce two unambiguous benefits for humanity: (a) survival and multiplication on the part of members of groups who adopt superior traditions and institutions (or superior "rules"); and (b) better preference realization by members of these groups as they pursue their own purposes in their own way, aided by the increased freedom and superior planning made possible by these superior rules. Hayek's ultimate emphasis is on the first; Sowell focuses on the second. That focus is perhaps predictable, not only because it is the most obvious possibility for expanding Hayek's notion of what "good" means using Hayek's framework, but also because Sowell, as a neoclassical economist, is inclined to view as a good achievement preference realization by consumers seeking economic goods and services, and greater preference realization by more consumers as a better achievement. Now preference realization is to be writ large (well beyond the realm of realizing desires for economic goods and services) but the economist's normative bias is retained; that is, preference realization is assumed to be a good thing, and the more preference realization the better. Within a larger intellectual arena Sowell now argues that "social processes" in general (and not just the market system) "are to be judged by their ability to extract the most social benefit from man's limited potentialities at the lowest cost."[155] The crucial question, of course, is what is to count as social benefit. To Hayek's point about survival and multiplication Sowell adds "material and psychic well-being,"[156] with the latter, on close inspection, constituting little more than the greatest pleasure and least pain – or greatest net pleasure – for the greatest number. Repeatedly Sowell writes of "the revealed preference of the many" and the merits of a system that allows the greatest gratification of those preferences. Thus:

Man, as conceived in the constrained vision, could never have planned and achieved even the current level of material and psychic well-being, which is seen as the product of evolved systemic interactions drawing on the experiences and adjusting to the preferences (revealed in behavior rather than words) of vast numbers of people over vast regions of time. The constrained vision sees future progress as a continuation of such systemic interactions – and as threatened by attempts to substitute individually excogitated social schemes for these evolved patterns.[157]

Although not particularly attracted to this constrained vision himself, conservative George Will concedes its popularity among members of the American right, and puts his finger squarely on its central normative claim: "The social good is, by definition, the aggregate of whatever effects individuals produce through voluntary arrangements."[158] Small wonder that another conservative unenthusiastic about such a definition should observe: "the sum floats free."[159]

Sowell's effort to find an expanded meaning of "good" consistent with Hayek's framework thus yields a particular variant of utilitarianism (hedonistic), whose central normative principle can be loosely characterized as "the greatest good for the greatest number," where "good" now refers to preference realization.[160] That variant is therefore vulnerable to all the objections customarily raised against hedonistic utilitarianism. Admittedly the core principle appeals strongly to our generalized sense of benevolence: that the welfare of all should count and not just the welfare of self. For those on the right, Sowell's approach also appeals because of its consistency with the traditional conservative emphasis on our limited knowledge of what is good for others and the corollary that each is the best judge of what is best for self.[161] But the principles of either system (hedonistic utilitarianism or Sowell's variant of it) in some cases will imply that one should advocate certain types of action that the ordinary man or the average citizen or the typical American will consider to be wrong. To take a classic example, suppose that five lives can be saved only by killing one innocent victim and publicly touting the execution as legitimate punishment. Most people would instinctively regard such action as "wrong," however consistent the results of that action are with the greatest good or greatest happiness or greatest preference realization of the greatest number. Or consider two societies in which the aggregate preference realization is essentially the same, the one comprised of industrious family-oriented citizens with a healthy respect for all forms of life, and the other comprised of indolent citizens largely indifferent to children and given to bear-baiting and other forms of animal torture. Although the aggregate of preference realization in the two may be equivalent, most Americans would not be willing to judge both societies as equally good. In short, Sowell's variant of hedonistic utilitarianism (like all variants) can easily be shown to be incomplete as a system of descriptive ethics.[162] Or put another way, for the majority of Americans the priority of preference realization simply will not do as the *only* objective standard by which to justify a moral code or moral judgments, and neither will the priority of survival and multiplication of the human species. Here, too, the right has once again lost contact with the middle, although that loss of contact is seldom blatantly apparent, because the basic ethical priorities of right-wing writers such as Hayek are seldom baldly stated. Notice finally how old problems resurface in points just made. Many values matter, those values can and do conflict, and thus tradeoff problems must often be faced in concrete situations. This set of problems cannot be resolved by dismissing all values except one (such as multiplication of the species or maximizing preference realization). Such a dismissal is invariably objectionable for the most obvious of reasons: the importance of the values that such an approach would relegate to unimportance.[163]

Conclusion

At the heart of issues raised in this chapter are two kinds of questions:

1 those concerned with causation (what affects what and how); and
2 those concerned with values (particularly what does "good" mean in the phrase "the good society," what constitutes human progress, and in trying to answer questions like the two just cited, what objectively sound procedures can be used for justifying one set of moral judgments as against another).

The first kind of question arose in the effort to disentangle the causes of rewards received in the marketplace – an effort necessitated by the need to identify the relative importance of individual volition and luck as determinants of rewards. This effort to disentangle causes raised again the puzzle of how personality is affected by the many causal mechanisms included under the two broad headings of heredity and environment. Under both headings our ignorance is massive, but we know enough from the insights of modern psychology and biology to realize that the list of possible mechanisms is formidable, as is their possible importance in determining the character and competence of participants in any economic race. The greater the role that such mechanisms are assumed to play, the less certain we become about where to draw the line between marketplace results attributable to factors beyond the individual's control, and results attributable to volition or to the willful exercise of meritorious virtues. The same set of puzzles making for uncertainty in the drawing of that line also makes somewhat problematic a number of ideas central to the notion of economic justice, including the meaning of the "self" that pursues self-realization, and the extent to which economic actors are responsible for their actions and thus to be held morally accountable for them. The more all of these issues were examined, the more the concept of freedom was seen to be central to associated puzzles, as defining freedom was central to any proffered solution. If nothing else, we have learned to be wary of those who treat freedom as a self-evident goal of self-evident worth. The works of both left and right within America are laced with summary dismissals of this complex topic of consummate importance: complex, because the concept of freedom is inextricably intertwined with dilemmas that have no easy resolution; important, because giving that concept content, or defining what freedom means in the realm of economic behavior, will crucially affect one's willingness to endorse or condemn a host of policy proposals advanced in the name of making the American economic system more just. Last, but hardly least, we found that the task of defining freedom for the thoughtful citizen invariably must be a tentative and ongoing enterprise because our understanding of cause-and-effect processes that ultimately determine how free we are is both imperfect and evolving.

The second kind of problem encountered in this chapter, as noted, concerned values; that is, how we use words like "ought" and "should" and what we mean by "good." These arose initially in the discussion of what many Americans have termed "a crisis in values" – a phrase that naturally raises questions about which values are now viewed in decline and why that decline should be regarded as a bad thing. Discussion was briefly diverted to cause-and-effect questions – how the market as an environment might alter the values of participants in undesirable ways – but the question of what should count as undesirable quickly swung the focus back to value issues. What was discovered was that left and right tend to have markedly different views about what should count, because even when they began with the premises of Christianity, they often disagreed about the meaning of crucial words like "charity" and the practical implications of the Golden Rule. Those disagreements, in turn, were anchored to a significant degree in differing views about the nature of man – both the extent to which his innate characteristics were good or bad, and the extent to which one can know the internal landscape of another. What is desirable or good – in human interactions and in the evolution of society – presumably should be conditioned by what is feasible. Those on the right, at bottom, believe our knowledge of each other is severely limited (which sets constraints upon the most that human fellowship can be) and that certain human traits are both innate and dangerous (which sets limits upon what society can become). The left is more sanguine on both counts, and therefore more inclined to believe in a community characterized by greater liking and sharing, as opposed to one where distance and distinctiveness dominate human interactions. Believing that they know their fellow man much better than their counterparts on the right, the left is more willing to use knowledge of humanity presumed to be extensive to fashion and guide policy interventions designed to make others better off. For them, the Golden Rule is as an exhortation to activity. For the right, the same rule implies primarily a hands-off policy in order to extend to others that which the self wants most: freedom in the form of an absence of coercion to pursue one's own purposes within a reasonably well-defined social space featuring a minimum of unwanted incursions by others.

It could be argued that the foregoing description overdraws and oversimplifies what is in fact a subtle and complex array of differences, and so it does. One purpose of this chapter has been to indicate the location and suggest the barest possible outline of terrains generally ignored in discussions of economic justice – terrains which, were they to be carefully explored, would each be the appropriate topic of a book.

The other major purpose has been to emphasize the legitimacy of questions too seldom encountered in discussions of economic justice, or which, when encountered, are commonly dismissed. To review what by now is perhaps too obvious a list, these include:

1 How can both luck and merit earning its just reward be combined in the notion of economic justice?
2 How should the ongoing discoveries of psychology and biology modify our views about luck, about volition, and about the appropriate meaning of freedom in the context of an economic race?
3 How should the concept of equality of opportunity be revised in the light of answers given to the first two questions, and which policy proposals should be considered to achieve a closer approximation to that revised concept?
4 In defining economic justice and giving shape to American culture, which values should the nation honor, and how should efforts to honor those values be pursued?

Questions such as these are challenges for the future. The remaining tasks here are two. The first is to summarize the best and worst – or better and worse – ideas concerning economic justice of the many writers and many different perceptions examined in this book. This is accordingly the topic of chapter 12. The other remaining task is some brief assessment of accomplishments and failures of the present, with the intention of identifying those policies most needed now to make the economic system of America more fair or just. During the twentieth century, struggling to achieve that goal has become an important priority in this country, particularly since the Great Depression. The final chapter will examine some of the evidence of how much has been done, and how much remains to be done, to achieve a better approximation to a just economic system in a nation proudly referred to by its Founding Fathers as "the republic": a name suggesting in the eighteenth century both a daring political experiment and unprecedented possibilities for many of its people.

12

Summing Up: A Personal Perspective

Introduction

As noted in the first chapter, this is a book about perceptions of economic justice and about economic justice itself, the first to be used as a means for achieving a better understanding of the second. The time has come to review the major insights gained. Any such review is invariably colored by the values, understanding, and beliefs of the reviewer. What follows, then, is not a definitive overview of what American ideas are or ought to be concerning economic justice, but my own summary thoughts about those ideas after studying the views of the American left, right, and center for better than a decade.

The Disorderliness of the Enterprise

One central insight – perhaps *the* central insight – is that the topic of economic justice is intrinsically messy. Usually we can recognize the judgments for what they are when we have to make them: judgments that involve the fairness or justice of the economic system. The difficulty is that the premises or principles upon which such judgments are based are usually vague in form and can change over time. For example, one value to be honored in deciding what is "just" is the freedom of participants in a competitive market system. But "freedom" is seldom a carefully defined concept. In part this is because the boundaries of that concept are difficult to specify (except by those who favor only the narrowest possible kind of freedom based upon the narrowest possible meaning of coercion). In part this lack of clarity results from the tendency of those ill-defined boundaries to shift over time as our views on values and human nature change with increased knowledge, more experience, and advancing age.

A second reason for the intrinsic messiness of our subject matter is that however well defined the principles may be underlying our judgments about economic justice, those principles attempt to incorporate the many values that we honor, those values can and often do conflict, and for the resolution of such conflicts the context of the clash is all-important. Freedom often clashes with equality, and equality with efficiency, to cite but two of the more obvious conflicts that have repeatedly arisen in previous discussions. If the question is posed: "Do you want to help the poor?" our first instinct is to answer "Of course." But as we delve into the specifics of the problem to be solved and the policies being advocated, we begin to realize that our answer must be crucially dependent upon context: Which poor? At what cost? Using which kind of policies? With what likely effects? When values clash (as generally happens in welfare debates), weights must be assigned to competing claims; these weights can change depending on the context; and thus general rules for resolving such conflicts are difficult to formulate. Were this not the case – if universal propositions could be framed spelling out, for all possible situations, which values should be honored and how, including what to do when values clash – then philosophers presumably would have found a number of such propositions after so many bright minds have labored so long to discover them. One certainty where uncertainty abounds is that this ambition to discover universal propositions has not been realized. That failure, as Isaiah Berlin suggested in the first chapter of this book, may reflect not the limitations of the minds at work, but the intrinsic nature of the subject under scrutiny. If Berlin is right – and I believe he is – then economic justice is destined to remain an intrinsically messy subject. And until that messiness is recognized as inevitable, much ink will be spilled – or word processor printouts deposited in wastebaskets – because of the vain hope that rigorous reasoning alone can provide universal propositions about what is, and what is not, a fair or just economic system.

Economic Justice and Conflicting Values

If the topic of economic justice is intrinsically messy in the sense described above, the procedures whereby clashes among values are resolved take on a special importance in a well-functioning democracy. A particular policy problem arises involving economic justice – not vague and general but anchored in specifics: Should the tax structure be made less progressive? Should "workfare" be used to aid the able-bodied poor? The question then becomes: How can values that clash be successfully incorporated into efforts to resolve such problems? A partial answer involves several points, none of them surprising.

First, a tradition must exist of publicly acknowledging the obvious: that we do have many values, not one "primary" value or one "ultimate" value that dominates all others in every situation. This can easily be demonstrated – and is repeatedly demonstrated in philosophical works – by taking a single value with strong appeal (say "the greatest good for the greatest number") and fabricating an example in which other values conflict with the one in such a way that we become uncomfortable with the claim that honoring the one will always lead to the "right" decision. If that one value is "the greatest good for the greatest number," we are led to question its primacy in every conceivable situation by imagining (for example) a situation in which five lives can be saved if an innocent man is falsely accused of a heinous crime and subsequently executed. The point, as philosophers usually choose to make it, is that *any* ethical system based upon the primacy of a single value fails as a system of descriptive ethics: it is not an accurate portrayal of our inner landscape of ethical sensibilities.

The second point is that many of the values that we honor privately must have a place in public discourse. If they do not, public interchanges on policy issues will not reflect important ethical concerns of the debaters. More importantly, some values must be recognized to have a special claim to shaping the outcome of debate. If the opposite were true – if all values were regarded as a matter of individual preference only, and no value had any claim to public support – then policy debates would be cut loose from any moral moorings and quickly become undirected if not incoherent. Put another way, to decide the "right" policy among those proposed to make the economic system more just requires some consensus about what "right" means.

In searching for that consensus, Americans do not insist that all values be precisely specified and universally accepted. Thus, for example, they do not consider as fatuous or naive such statements as : "It is the social consensus or the public sentiment which in the last resort is our only test of justice in taxation, as of justice in other human relations."[1] The search for "social consensus" to determine "justice" would not strike most as a preposterous ambition. The key to finding such consensus is the presence of value sets that overlap. Not all citizens share the same set or give the same weights to values when they clash. But if democratic procedures are to function effectively, overlapping must be the rule and wide divergences the exception, thereby allowing (a) a majority to coalesce and endorse one policy among many possibilities and (b) the minority opposed (or most of them) not to become so outraged by choices made that their faith in democratic procedures becomes imperilled or destroyed. Within America, this overlapping would seem to have been assured by a strong central tendency in values popularly endorsed, particularly those values relevant for decisions about economic justice.

Overlapping value sets, per se, of course do not assure the best of policy debates. Another key requirement is that the procedures of a democracy be crafted in such a way that the best in those value sets be drawn to the fore (and the darker side of humanity suppressed) in reasoned debate among intelligent and informed people with good intentions and common sense – or allowing for human frailties, among people who can claim these attributes to a "reasonable" degree. Without a common faith in the latter, the moral worth of legislators and the moral validity of legislation would be subject to a questioning that would ultimately strike at the heart of democracy itself. Americans generally have believed that their political system and its participants have approximated this ideal, not in any exact way, but in a manner deemed close enough to warrant a continuing allegiance to demo- cratic procedures that still runs powerfully through the population.

Criticisms of Left and Right

Given that most Americans honor many values, a summary judgment on the appeal of left and right to the majority in the middle would seem easily compressed into a single sentence: their strengths are what they emphasize;

their weaknesses, what they ignore. That judgment, however, is much too simple on several counts.

Consider first liberal writers of the modern era. Their strengths include an emphasis on the dignity and worth of the individual, and the need to honor that dignity with humane policies for the disadvantaged. Such policies should be crafted, runs their customary argument, with an eye to striking a balance between equality and efficiency, the two priorities of the first importance to most liberals, and not without importance to most Americans.

One obvious weakness of these same writers (or most of them) is their tendency to give scant attention to losses in freedom that can accompany an expanded role for government in the economy. In part this reflects a faith that government intervention will usually make a bad situation better. What is missing from such analyses and sorely needed is a greater symmetry of skepticism in assessing the performance of the market and the state: a symmetry that acknowledges the possibility government intervention may well make a bad situation worse. As Tom Hayden now concedes, "the problems of bureaucracy should be seen as massive and troubling from *any* ideological perspective."[2] These troubles involve much more than the efficiency of the bureaucracy. In this context conservatives surely have a point: that every increase in the power of the government can threaten losses in liberty. Nor should a threatened loss be easily dismissed because the loss in question appears "relatively minor." Small increments can ultimately lead to disastrous results, as the histories of many nations have sadly demonstrated. The greatest single cause of violent deaths in the twentieth century has not been international and civil wars, but rather totalitarian regimes turning upon their own people.[3] Such a possibility seems far-fetched to most Americans, and rightly so. But the general tendency behind such a worse-case scenario remains of the first importance. In the assessment of every policy proposal that increases power at the center, we should proceed with excruciating care, making explicit which freedoms will be lost and which might be lost or imperilled if tendencies encouraged by the present policy become pronounced. If the tragic lessons of the past have taught us nothing else, they surely should have driven home the message that freedom involves multiple aspects of civil life; throughout human history a widespread sharing of many freedoms has been the exception not the rule; and America is unlikely to remain a leading example among exceptions if its citizens take a cavalier attitude to marginal losses in freedom. This is *not* to argue that when values clash in policy decisions, the preservation or enhancement of freedom must always dominate the rest. It is to argue that any sacrifice of freedom for the sake of promoting other values should be made grudgingly, and with a sense of whether freedoms previously lost should give added weight to freedoms at stake in the present clash of values.

The problems of modern liberalism in America run much deeper than a propensity to undervalue freedom when that priority conflicts with other values liberals hold dear. At bottom, writers of the left appear to believe what most Americans do not believe: that income inequality is intrinsically "unlovely" or (stronger yet) inrinsically "unjust." Time and again liberals express surprise at the tolerance for inequality of the American population. And time and again surveys of that population confirm this tolerance. (Black and feminist leaders in the United States, for example, support a greater income disparity than do *conservative* party leaders and business executives in Sweden.[4]) Puzzled by the phenomenon, American liberals tend to explain its persistence by citing simple causes, and hope for its eradication by uncomplicated changes in perceptions. For example: "The constituency for equality is weak because public policies continue to isolate the poor"; thus, "Would that ordinary people might simply grow indignant at the gross inequalities of American society and organize for progressive change."[5] What many of these left-wing writers seem incapable of understanding is how, for many Americans, a network of beliefs concerning economic justice intertwine and reinforce each other, and lead to a tolerance for income inequality. The beliefs in question have a long history and include all those enumerated in chapter 2: that participation in the economic race is good for the participants and for society, that the race is reasonably fair, and that merit tends to be rewarded. Interwoven with these beliefs are other premises and values giving their combined strength added force: a high value placed on work, on being self-sufficient, on seeking part of self-fulfillment through marketplace activities; a faith that the economic race features a "reasonable" degree of equality of opportunity which, combined with a "reasonable" degree of fairness on the course, assures that a linkage will be preserved between merit and reward. Americans have few delusions about the perfection of their economic system, as evidenced by the recurring use of "reasonable" in the above. But the approximation to perfection, although commonly acknowledged to be "rough," has commonly been viewed as close enough to give that economic system, for most Americans, an intrinsic order and an intrinsic moral validity. The fusion of these two – order and moral validity – in the popular imagination means that what liberals would attack in the perceptions of Americans is something more complex and more enduring than a misguided tolerance for income inequality. At their most naive, such attacks are reminiscent of a woodsman hacking at a redwood with a penknife, ever expectant of imminent collapse.

Should these attacks succeed and collapse become accomplished fact – should liberals ever manage to convince the majority of Americans that their economic system is intrinsically unjust, that the economic race is intrinsically unfair, that as a determinant of rewards, luck is all or almost all and accordingly all particpants in the race have little or no control over their own economic fate – the impact on American beliefs would be nothing less than shattering. Yet in their attacks (explicit and implicit) upon American beliefs, most liberals evidence little awareness of the havoc they would wreak upon the believers. Commonly such writers readily concede a certain intellectual disarray in their own camp, that disarray requiring not just new policies and programs but a refashioning of "a progressive vision" for society.[6] If that new vision incorporates old liberal ideas that have previously assured a profound mismatch of beliefs between the left and the middle in America, it is unlikely to precipitate a stampede to the liberal cause.

There is a third difficulty of modern liberalism in America that is at least as fundamental as the two raised thus far. The first was a slighting of many values important to Americans (including freedom) in the liberal preoccupation with equality and efficiency. The second was a mismatch in beliefs concerning how the economic system does function and ought to function. The third concerns neither values nor facts, but the method chosen to resolve the many problems relating to economic justice. The method favored by intellectuals on the left is a variant of the method favored by philosophers for addressing ethical questions. In summary form as practised by the left, this method consists of shrinking the set of values to be honored to a few, and then searching for universal rules that indicate how that honoring should be accomplished in every situation involving economic justice. Consider for the final time the approach to economic justice of Arthur Okun, one of the most thoughtful of postwar American writers of the left. The values he would honor are two: equality and efficiency. The difficulty is that these two are often in conflict. The problem Okun therefore sets himself to solve is to discover a rule for resolving such conflicts that can then be applied in any situation in which these two values clash. The key flaw in this approach is *not* that what begins as a search for an objective rule collapses into a subjective judgment about which tradeoff (equality versus efficiency) is optimal. A more fundamental difficulty is Okun's assumption that questions of economic justice can be resolved and should be resolved by identifying a universal decision rule that can be applied to concrete cases independent of the context of the case. To labor points made previously, if (a) we honor many values, (b) these can and do conflict, and (c) rules for resolving such conflicts generally cannot be specified independent of the context of the clash, then the search for a universal decision rule for resolving clashes is a vain search. Okun thus assured the failure of his enterprise once he chose his method of attack.

Conservatives do not seem in such a state of intellectual disarray as the contemporary American left. Certainly in the literature of the right one finds more assurance and less self-doubt, and few if any jeremiads. And yet the same three problems of the left addressed above are also present in the writings of the right, albeit in a slightly different form.

Here too one encounters a reduction in the set of values commonly honored by Americans. At their most extreme, conservatives reduce that set to the single value "freedom," with the inevitable result that the accompanying analytical framework fails as a system of descriptive ethics: it simply does not honor a multiplicity of values honored by many of the people of this nation.

As was also true of liberals, the premises that conservatives bring to analyzing the economic justice of the market would undercut the claim that merit is strongly correlated with reward. For most Americans, the belief in that correlation is central to whatever moral validity the market system has for them, and such an undercutting would threaten this validity if those in the middle took to heart the arguments of either left or right.

Conservatives also share with their counterparts on the left a preference for a suspect method for approaching issues of economic justice. This method attempts to seek out and identify universal propositions that will determine ethical choices in concrete situations. For many conservatives (particularly the extreme members of this camp) this search is often greatly simplified by reducing all the values in their analytical scheme to a single value, freedom. Any problems that might arise because values can conflict are accordingly avoided once freedom is acknowledged as the "only" good or the "ultimate" good. If this latter premise is accepted, the search for universal propositions narrows to finding those that will assure the maximizing of a single value. But as simple as that task may seem, it can become complex depending upon how freedom is defined. If that definition is expanded beyond the narrowest possible – if freedom means something more than the absence of violence and the threat of violence – then deciding what to maximize and how to maximize it can become assignments of excruciating complexity, as much as this book has tried to demonstrate.

One final charge can be leveled against both liberals and conservatives. As noted above, both shrink the values to be honored in their analytical schemes to a small set of those commonly honored by Americans. That conservatives tend to throw out more than liberals and on occasion end up with a single value is perhaps less striking than the large percentage of the total thrown out by both. Were the majority in the middle to follow the lead of either camp, what would be lost would be not just a list of values honored, but also a certain richness in American culture that is associated with multiple clashes among many values. More simply put, American culture would be less interesting because, to quote again the point of Lionel Trilling cited in chapter 1, "A culture is not a flow, not even a confluence; the form of its existence is struggle, or at least debate – it is nothing if not a dialectic."[7]

Whither goes the Middle?

A major thesis of this work is that the majority of Americans have brought to questions of economic justice a set of interconnected beliefs – limited in number and vague in phrasing – which, from the early years of the republic to the present, have only changed in minor ways. Many of these beliefs have been attacked, particularly by the left, as myths. Among those singled out for special scorn are such assertions as (a) merit is strongly correlated with reward, (b) the race is "reasonably" fair, and the related assertion (c) that a "reasonable" degree of equality of opportunity exists for most would-be participants. But is the charge of being "mythical" so damning?

All cultures bear testimony to a common drive of different peoples to make sense out of reality by filtering perceptions of the world through various belief systems that give an order to that reality. (Among the many reasons for this propensity, perceived order gives confidence to forecasts, and confidence in forecasts gives a sense of more mastery and less vulnerability in the struggle to control one's destiny.) More than this, these same perceptions, where possible, are linked to the values of the perceiver. The end result is an effort to find congruence – or some congruence – between the world that is and the world that ought to be. Thus, within a celebrated and sweeping framework, anthropologist Clifford Geertz notes the search for congruence between "ethos" and "world view," where

> A people's ethos is the tone, character, and quality of their life, its moral and aesthetic style and mood; it is the underlying attitude toward themselves and their world that life reflects. Their world view is their picture of the way things in sheer actuality are, their concept of nature, of self, of society. It contains their most comprehensive ideas of order.[8]

In a more modest and partial framework, this book has tried to track the search for congruence between the "is" and the "ought" in some of the beliefs influencing American judgments about economic justice. Here, as in the more wide-ranging analytical framework of the anthropologist, this search would seek to impose order on reality, and give to that perceived order – in this case, the workings of the economy – a moral validity. In this instance that validity stems from a perceived fairness in procedures (derived from beliefs about the fairness of the race) and from a perceived fairness in results (derived primarily from beliefs linking reward to merit in a race that is both "good" and "fair"). The ultimate expression of this moral validity is the one encountered in chapter 1: a just distribution, justly arrived at – now qualified by words such as "reasonably" in front of "just" to acknowledge what can hardly be denied (and is so disturbing to radicals on the left): the evident gap between perfection and reality, between what ought to be and what evidently is. The discovery of this gap leads to the charge of myth and to a call for jettisoning what is "obviously false." But those reactions to this gap would seem to overlook a number of points that can change the focus of evaluation of belief systems in general, and of this handful of beliefs in particular.

First, every belief system surely includes premises that diverge from reality. Can the beliefs of a communist, socialist or facist, for example, boast unfailing accuracy? Given the wide divergences among the three, surely some must be at variance with the truth. Put more cautiously, no belief system comes readily to mind that includes *no* divergence whatsoever between what is believed to be and the world that actually is. Perhaps the easiest way – and certainly the most personal way – to verify that assertion is to re-read Geertz's definitions of "ethos" and "world view," sort out personal beliefs under both headings, and ask whether those beliefs, in all their parts, are absolutely accurate as a portrait of reality.

Second, precisely because the beliefs outlined here concerning economic justice establish some congruence between the perceived order of an economic system and the norms of the perceiver (with that congruence giving moral validity to the economic system), the grip or purchase of such beliefs on the hearts and minds of believers tends to be formidable in the extreme. This is not, then, a structure to be readily overthrown by tirades against "mistaken perceptions" or the "falseness" of the beliefs in question. Economists have a saying: you can only beat a theory with a theory. The implication is that once a social scientist becomes committed to a theory, that commitment cannot be destroyed by criticism alone, but only by criticism plus another theory that seems to offer a better explanation of reality. Put differently and generalized, humans (including economists) do not seem prone to abandon a set of structured beliefs for a vacuum. Criticism of the "lack of realism" in any belief system (including those concerned with economic justice) is thus by itself unlikely to precipitate an abandonment of that system.

Third, the demise of an intricate and widely endorsed belief system can have far-reaching implications, many of which are difficult to anticipate. Consider, for example, George Bernard Shaw's condemnation of the mythical aspects of democracy: "I hold with Adolf Hitler, that our political democracy is a lie. Its 'waning' means presumably its being found out. The faster it 'wanes' in this sense the better I shall be pleased."[9] As subsequent events would demonstrate to Shaw and others, the costs of demise can come high (even when touted as consistent with the search for truth). Those who call for the dismissal of a belief system with no thought about likely alternatives are therefore not unlike judges in a beauty contest, anxious to give first prize to the second candidate on the strength of seeing only the first candidate.

Fourth, if belief systems invariably include assertions that diverge from the truth, a case can be made for asking, of a given system, not "Is it true?" but "How has it served?" Many of the questions appropriately raised under this latter heading have been enumerated by Walter Lippmann in a slightly different context. For Lippman, "it" in the following is a creed; for us, a belief system. The questions nevertheless seem equally to the point for both: "Where has it helped [those who believed], where hindered? What needs did it answer? What energies did it transmute? And what part of mankind did it neglect? Where did it begin to do violence to human nature?"[10]

Answering such questions can be a tall order. For the beliefs outlined above concerning economic justice, a few effects are relatively clear, but many are not. The faith they have encouraged in the "rightness" of the market system has reinforced the American propensity to minimize government powers – in this case, the powers that would come with widespread government intervention in the market system. The conclusion that (subject to a host of minor qualifications) the workings of the market system naturally tend to generate a reasonable approximation to "a just distribution, justly arrived at" has all but removed from American public debates what frequently has a central place in comparable European debates; namely, how the existing income distribution should be modified through government redistribution policies so that the end result (the new pattern of redistributed income) better approximates a "just" pattern. Another contrast with Euro-

pean perceptions and policy debates is equally striking. The American belief
that their economic system includes – indeed, features – a "reasonable"
degree of equality of opportunity for most would-be participants has
encouraged a certain narrowness in American perceptions of "the truly
needy" or "the deserving poor," and this narrowness, in turn, has slowed the
pace and tempered the generosity of welfare legislation.

Other links from this set of beliefs to various attributes of American society
are easily identified, but their net effect is difficult to gauge. One is struck, for
example, by the coincidence in time between (a) the dominance of the beliefs
in question, and (b) the extraordinary achievements of this nation in terms of
freedoms enjoyed and economic progress made by the vast majority of its
citizens. Multiple strands of causation run between the two. The beliefs did
much to unleash and channel creative energies into economic activity.
Advancing gross national product per capita did much to reinforce a belief in
the possibility of economic progress for the many and not just for a few. A
faith that market opportunities were widespread – that many had, if not an
"equal" chance, a "reasonably good" chance for advancement – would not
have long persisted if perceptions had not been continually supported by
accomplished fact – if not personal advancement, then the advancement of
friends and relations, of children and their children. If multiple causal
strands run in both directions – from beliefs to economic reality and back
the other way – how can one assess the effect of all these strands combined?
That question requires a confrontation with a counterfactual: What would
America have been throughout its history if the dominant beliefs concerning
economic justice had been substantially different from those beliefs that
actually held sway? Put this way, the question gives a better sense of the
magnitude of the enterprise required if an answer is to be forthcoming. Once
that magnitude is confronted, the typical reaction is to dismiss the question
as unsolvable. And with that dismissal goes any chance of resolving in any
comprehensive way the question noted at the start: How did this particular
set of beliefs serve?

Have we therefore reached an impasse? I think not. A number of previous
observations point in the same direction. These include (a) the compelling
power of the small set of beliefs that for generations has dominated American
views concerning economic justice, (b) the invulnerability of this set to
attacks that only criticize the mismatch between beliefs and reality, (c) the
difficulty of supplanting one set of beliefs with another, and (d) the caution
that one should bring to the prospect of supplanting one belief system with
another, because the effects of such a change are likely to be vast and difficult
to gauge. But if supplanting is both difficult and dangerous, achieving
marginal modifications may be neither. The task of the would-be reformer
might therefore usefully be narrowed to asking which marginal changes in
the belief system presently dominant in America are most in need of being
made, and how such changes might be achieved.

But where to begin? Walter Lippmann may have a point: perhaps "human
nature in all its profounder aspects [has changed] very little in the few

generations since our Western wisdom has come to be recorded."[11] Our understanding of human nature nevertheless can change, has changed, and continues to change. And many of those changes have implications for beliefs concerning economic justice.

At the core of American beliefs about the justice of their economic system is the premise that the race is reasonably fair, with fairness viewed as largely a matter of assuring the freedom and equality of participants both at the starting line and on the course. The meaning of both terms (freedom and equality) can change as our understanding of human nature changes, and with these alterations can come new priorities and policies in the name of either freedom or equality. Admittedly many improvements in the fairness of the race – both those accomplished in the past and those yet to be addressed at present – require no overhaul of intellectual framework but simply facing up to the practical implications of old priorities. The reining in of the unfair use of undue power, the attack on discriminatory practices in the market-place – these can be undertaken, and have been undertaken, because of a recognized inconsistency between certain economic behavior and long-standing notions of freedom and equality as those notions pertain to desirable conditions for fairness in an economic race. No doubt much remains to be done, but debates concerning where to begin and how to proceed are not confounded by a lack of understanding of the concepts (mainly "freedom" and "equality") that such endeavors try to honor.[12]

The same may not be true for improving fairness at the starting line. The master priority remains equality of opportunity – a priority encountered whether discussion begins with trying to identify requisite freedom or requisite equality at the starting line. If the question is how to insure the freedom of would-be participants in the economic race, pursuit of the answer will quickly lead to questions of "freedom to," namely, how to assure that all who reach the starting line have "the power or means to compete." Without that power or those means, the opportunity to compete is minimal, and that is the fundamental opportunity at stake in the phrase "equality of opportu-nity." Alternatively, one can begin with the priority of equal treatment (treat each person in a uniform and identical manner, unless there is a sufficient reason not to do so), and ask: If conditions at the starting line are to be fair, what is it that should be made available to all? In short, in the phrase "equality of opportunity," notions about freedom define what is necessary for opportunity, and notions about equality define who should have access to that opportunity.

These general considerations leave unanswered which "power or means" are necessary to compete, and what role the state should play in helping would-be participants to gain such power or means.

Of the many different roles the state might play, Americans have directed much of their legislative energies and much of their money to only one, namely, providing "free and equal" public educational facilities for all children. Notice parenthetically the implications of this priority for the definition of freedom imbedded in public policy. If part of the rationale for providing such facilities is to give would-be competitors in the economy the "power or means to compete," then (at least in this instance) the public has acknowledged the government's responsibility for promoting the freedom of participants, where the "freedom" in question clearly refers to "freedom to." That acknowledgment in turn flies in the face of conservative pleas to restrict the government's promotion of freedom in the marketplace to inhibiting the use of coercion. But if government policy has moved beyond the confines of promoting freedom narrowly defined to promoting freedom broadly defined – if a recognized responsibility of the state is to promote the acquisition of "the power or means to compete" – where should one draw the line? How much is the minimum required of government under this heading, and how much is too much? Not questions easily answered, the reader may be saying, and with good reason.

A large part of the difficulty of knowing where to draw the line reflects both improvements in, and continuing limitations on, our understanding of human behavior. Because we know more, we have a sense that old boundaries may need to be redefined. Because we are conscious of how limited our understanding is, we are unsure where those new boundaries should be. What we do know beyond a shadow of a doubt is that heredity and environment affect character and competence, including the attributes that make a difference to success in the economic race. What usually remains in doubt is the precise nature of these effects. Under those two vague headings "heredity" and "environment" we have a long list of causes "of some influence." But we have few models (or few of generally recognized validity) tracing out the mechanisms and the magnitudes of the influences in question. Small wonder, then, despite all the advances in psychology, novelists still write of "the opacity of people." The associated uncertainties raise problems that have surfaced and resurfaced throughout this work. What is the role of luck as a determinant of market rewards? What external influences affect the self that seeks self-realization, including influences that affect how the goal of self-realization is defined? When choices must be made among competing policy proposals to improve the justice of the economic system, how can we forecast the likely impact of each of the choices advocated on all of those who will be affected by that choice?

Beyond providing public educational facilities, then, what the government should do to promote greater equality at the starting line is far from clear because the likely impact of different policy options on the character and competence of those likely to participate in prospective programs is far from clear. One approach to equalizing "power or means" of would-be competitors is not likely to find much favor in this country. Most Americans would vigorously oppose any policy for reining in the swift. They do not want, for example, abandonment of programs for the gifted in public schools or the outlawing of elitist schools or (most unthinkable of all) the removal of advantages gained through family upbringing by the forced removal of children from their parents. Each of these policies involves a clash of values, and in that clash other values outweigh the importance of fostering greater equality of opportunity.

What most Americans would be willing to endorse, at least as a general priority, is helping the slow become more swift before they reach the starting line. This endorsement nevertheless is usually tempered by two considerations. One is the traditional American distrust of government. More government programs imply more power in the hands of state officials, with all the potential for abuses that such an increased power concentration brings. The other major reservation is whether any policies implemented in the name of aiding disadvantaged children will have the effects desired. If the relevant mechanisms influencing character and competence are many and complex and poorly understood, how can we be sure that we will get value for dollars spent? Indeed, how can we be sure that new policy proposals to help the disadvantaged child will not have unanticipated effects that hinder more than help?

At the limit, such reservations imply that nothing should be done, or nothing more than presently is being done to foster equality of opportunity through conventional educational programs. The problem with this strategy is that those programs are clearly failing large numbers of the nation's children. Put more cautiously, despite those programs, many would-be competitors now reach the starting line with grievously deficint skills, and once eligible for the race, many remain marginal competitors or on the sidelines with little hope for economic opportunity or reward. As these numbers grow, the popular belief in a fair race becomes more suspect, and rightly so. The cost of throwing in the towel – of settling for the status quo in government policies to aid would-be competitors gain the power or means to compete – is therefore far greater than opportunities forgone by disadvantaged individuals and aggregate output lost because fewer and less skilled participants enter the labor force. Beyond some point, the growing presence of handicapped and nonparticipants in the race is sure to challenge basic American beliefs about the justice of their economic system. That growing presence will also make progressively more suspect a basic premise of democracy: that all (or most) adults can meet successfully the challenges of responsible citizenship. Alienated youth, work force dropouts, and the functionally illiterate are not the stuff of which great modern democracies are made. Last but hardly least, a nation whose culture features the promise of advancement and includes among its citizens large and growing numbers who perceive themselves as having little chance for sharing in the promise will inevitably confront problems of growing social instability.

A special urgency therefore accompanies the call to do *something* to remedy deficiencies in the character and competence so many bring at present to the starting line. While the limits of our understanding of human nature admittedly complicate the devising of appropriate policies, I believe we know enough to devise policies with a reasonable chance for reasonable success. The choice of what to try, however, depends in part upon which defects under equality of opportunity are most glaring in America, and which have been significantly improved in recent decades. Which brings us to the final topics of this book. The first assignment of the last chapter is to review progress made to date; the second, to suggest policy changes which, in my view, are among those needed most for progress in the future.

13

The American Dream and Present-day America

Introduction

John Gunther once remarked that America had the rare distinction of being "deliberately founded on a good idea."[1] However true the claim that the country's foundation was anchored in a single admirable goal, a number of such goals were imbedded in its culture from the outset. Among them are two emphasized in this book; the one focusing upon the individual, and the other upon society; the one honoring the dignity and worth of the individual, and emphasizing the importance of individual freedoms for the pursuit of individual goals, and the other blending thoughts about community with the priority of charity, and thereby emphasizing the obligation of all not only to make a contribution to collective goals but also to give a helping hand to the other fellow when he is down. Admittedly these are not goals peculiar to America, but the blending and the combined emphasis are peculiarly American. A nation known for its generosity and the gregariousness of its people would also be known for its rugged individualism. As Lincoln emphasized, conceived in liberty (not in fraternity), it would grant to each individual the right to pursue self-fulfillment and the freedoms to make the exercising of that right a realistic possibility. And yet, as Lincoln phrased the other ambition, "all American citizens are brothers of a common country, and should dwell together in the bonds of fraternal feeling."[2] "America the Beautiful" – both a patriotic hymn and a national prayer – puts the case more strongly, entreating the Divinity to

> . . . crown thy good with brotherhood
> From sea to shining sea!

The exclamation mark is suggestive of the self-assurance of the people. The linkage of "good" with "brotherhood" signals that for most Americans the good society is marked – or more than marked, "crowned" – by a communal sense among its citizens that is more than civility, more than cooperative congeniality, and ideally approximates the many complex notions of fellowship implicit in a single word: "brotherhood."

The priorities of individualism are not easily meshed with those of brotherhood. Ambitions tailored in the first person singular can often clash with obligations cast in the third person plural. The challenge is thus to combine in a single culture two themes that forever threaten to be mutually inconsistent. Part of the effort at combining consists of national norms emphasizing that self-development should include the building of bonds with other individuals as well as honoring obligations to the larger community. Most Americans are unwilling to regard the "successful individual" as one who merely achieves fulfillment of ambitions designed to satisfy the self, independent of the communal setting in which the self seeks self-fulfillment. The laudatory labels "good citizen" or "great American" are not commonly bestowed upon those known for their preoccupation with looking out for number one, however much such individuals have succeeded in their own terms. Thus many Americans are somewhat uneasy about "the loner," admiring the implied strength of character but distrusting – indeed, often resenting – the implied unsociable demeanor.[3] In the pursuit of rugged individualism, then, one can, by American norms, have too much of a good thing, although where to draw the line is never clear. While the pursuit of happiness is a cherished right of each individual, Americans generally want the pursuer to view that goal as intimately linked with achieving fellowhip with others and furthering community priorities.

Such a linkage is not easily made when the pursuits in question concern the realization of personal ambitions in a competitive market system. Michael Novak's point made earlier bears repeating here: that "to compete" reflects the fusion of two ideas: *com* + *petere*, "to seek together although against each other."[4] "Community" also involves two ideas. Its Latin root *communis* is composed of *com*, meaning "together," and *munis*, meaning "ready to be of service." One does not easily combine the notion of service with the imagery of an economic race in which all competitors, at bottom, are "against each other." Conservatives traditionally try to fuse the two ideas (competition and service) by emphasizing that (subject to certain assumptions) if each competitor pursues self-interest the result will be the largest possible gross national product which in turn will serve the material needs of all. But achieving Pareto efficiency is not the same thing as furthering fellowship or brotherhood. Giving participants access to the largest possible pile of bones in what is essentially a dogfight is not the imagery of an economic system that appeals to most Americans. And if the metaphor is changed – from scrapping in a dogfight to running in a race – the revised imagery may seem to have an evident consistency with the one major priority of assertive individualism but still lacks a self-evident consistency with the other major priority of brotherhood.

To be sure, some of the obligations implied by the word "brotherhood" can be assumed to arise rarely if one adds the premise of equality of opportunity to the metaphor of an economic race. The need to lend a hand to those who are disadvantaged through no fault of their own becomes less likely if one believes the economy is so structured that most can help themselves. Americans commonly believe that these particular obligations of brotherhood arise for only a comparatively small set (usually designated as "the deserving poor" or "the truly needy") precisely because the belief in equality of opportunity is so firmly imbedded in American culture. It constitutes the core of the American Dream, and that core in turn holds a central place in most belief systems about what constitutes a fair or just economic system.

From these thoughts about the nature of the dream and the nature of economic justice one can infer at least one appropriate empirical test of the extent to which the American economic system conforms to American goals, namely, the extent to which all participants in the economic race do have some semblance of equality of opportunity, both at the starting line and on the course. The gap between the actual and the ideal cannot be precisely quantified or even roughly quantified by any single aggregate measure. The best that one can do is to assemble evidence suggesting where the gap has narrowed and where it yet remains unconscionably wide. What follows accordingly might be viewed as two sets of snapshots for inclusion in two impressionistic guides to America, the one emphasizing achievements of the past and the other failures of the present, and both providing images that must be reckoned with in any broader assessment of the fairness of the market system of America when measured against the norms of economic justice that have long dominated the culture of its people.

Glimpses of Success

In the late spring of 1985, Atlanta Mayor Andrew Young recalled the circumstances of his own graduation while addressing the graduates of Boston College in Chestnut Hill, Massachusetts.

As I drove back to my hometown in New Orleans [after graduation], I passed through the state of Georgia and I was afraid to stop, for Georgia was perhaps the worst place in the United States in those days for a young black man to be alone at night. And if anybody had ever said, "Son, you better slow down in Georgia, you're going to represent Georgia in the Congress of the United States; you're going to be an Ambassador to the United Nations, named by an ex-Governor of Georgia who's going to be President of the United States; and then you will come back to be mayor of the city of Atlanta" – the only thing I could have done would be to recommend them to the nearest mental institution.[5]

That same June day, a few miles distant from Boston College on the Wellesley campus, Geraldine Ferraro was telling other graduating seniors a different personal story which, in a larger sense, was part of the same story.

When I applied to law school, a university official asked if I was "serious" – because, after all, I was taking a man's place. No professor could be caught dead today saying to a female student that she was taking the place of a man. First of all, that professor could be a woman. In fact, if she were at Wellesley, you can bet her department chair would be a woman. More important, the greatest achievement of the women's movement has been to transform our expectations. Today in America, women can be whatever they want to be. We can walk in space and help our children take their first steps on earth. We can run a corporation and work as wives and mothers. We can be doctors, and we can bake cookies at home with our six-year-old future scientists.[6]

Ferraro and Young speak for a generation whose opportunities within America have changed dramatically in the decades just passed. The country can never claim at any time to have offered to women and to various minorities an equality of opportunity comparable to that available to white males. But in the course of the twentieth century, and most particularly since World War II, the strides made have been truly of the seven-league variety in narrowing a disconcerting gap too long evident in the country's approximation to this avowed ideal. Hard evidence assembled from the economic system – whether culled from information on who participates in which activities or from data on rewards received – makes clear that the economic race in contemporary America bears little resemblance to that of fifty years ago, and is virtually unrecognizable by standards commonly accepted in the nineteenth century. Examples are legion. A few are noted below.

(1)   Perhaps the single most dramatic development in the labor market in the twentieth century has been the increasing participation of women and their progressive diffusion through a range of occupations previously dominated by men. When President McKinley lectured a Buffalo audience in 1901 on the merits of participating in "business life [which] is ever a sharp struggle for success"[7] women did not have the right to vote, had little access to higher education, and in the business world had almost no chance to compete or to succeed. When Theodore Roosevelt succeeded McKinley (and when Harding succeeded Wilson) only one out of every five women of working age participated in the labor force compared with two out of three today.[8] (For President McKinley, the low rate of female labor force participation relative to that of other industrial nations was a credit to "American civilization."[9])

With the increasing participation of women in the market economy has come their increasing presence in occupations previously regarded as primarily or exclusively the appropriate domain of working males. A woman serving in a top corporate position, for example – viewed as an aberration in the 1930s and a curiosity in the 1950s – has become a commonplace today. Women now receive one-third of MBA degrees conferred and hold one-third of executive, administrative, and management jobs. At the top of the corporate ladder, half of all major American business firms have women on their boards of directors.[10] Nor are women any longer a tenuous appendage at the margins of the business world of men. Between the mid-1970s and the mid-1980s females went into business for themselves at a rate three times that of men while the number of self-employed women grew by 74 percent.[11] By 1986 when the White House held a Conference on Small Business, one-third of the delegates were women – a ratio which, while falling short of parity, would have seemed preposterous in McKinley's day, or Franklin Roosevelt's, or even John F. Kennedy's. Observed Mary Farrar, owner of

Hallmark Construction since 1978: "Ten years ago, people were very surprised to meet a woman who owned a construction company. Today, however, women are losing their touch at surprising people."[12]

(2)   Only one out of four bachelor's degrees were awarded to women when the present century began. Now women receive roughly one out of two as one would expect the law of averages to dictate in any society with pretensions to equality of opportunity in educational possibilities. The rise of females to a place of prominence in professional graduate programs in recent years has been meteoric. As recently as 1960, women received only 0.8 percent of the degrees granted in dentistry, 2.5 percent of those in law, and 5.5 percent of those in medicine. Now they receive roughly one-fifth of the dentistry degrees, one-quarter of the medical degrees, and one-third of the law degrees.[13] Again two points are clear: perfect equality between the sexes has not yet been achieved, but the rate of improvement in opportunities for women in the present generation is astonishing by the standards of any previous generation. Compared with their exclusion from so much in President McKinley's day, American women now confront a prodigious array of educational and occupational possibilities. The odds of a female succeeding in many vocations may still not equal that for males, but for the first time in American history those odds are not discouragingly long for the talented and determined. The hopeful implications for young women planning their careers have been pointed out many times in many ways. Debi Coleman, chief financial officer of Apple Computer, made the point as well as any: "Don't waste time and energy on trying to predict your future. Concentrate on inventing it."[14]

When the Declaration of Independence was originally drafted and signed, few noticed an obvious omission in its dedication to the proposition that all men were created equal. Only in 1848 at the first modern woman's rights convention in America was a public effort made to revise the wording to read: "all men and women are created equal." Evidence from recent decades of the sort just cited makes clear that promises of possibilities implicit in that revised wording are finally being extended to the other half of the nation's population.

(3)   In 1944, on the heels of a depression and in the middle of a great war, Swedish economist Gunnar Myrdal published a study of the American Negro entitled *An American Dilemma*, which concluded, with good reason, that the economic condition of most blacks in this country was "pathological."[15] Among adult black workers, men typically earned far more than women,[16] and yet three-quarters of these men lived in poverty with little hope of economic advancement for themselves or their children. Of black adult males in the work force, 80 percent had no more than elementary schooling, and only one in twelve had graduated from high school. (Only one in a hundred had a college degree.) Compared with the average for all white males, blacks

earned only 43 percent as much. Compared with comparably educated whites, blacks earned only half as much.[17]

By 1980, every single numerical comparison cited above had changed radically and for the better. The poverty rate for black males had fallen from three in four to one in five. Average years of schooling had doubled to a level only slightly behind that of white males. The majority of adult black men in the work force were now high school graduates and almost one-third had some college training. Compared with the earnings of white males, those for black men averaged 73 percent overall, while for comparably educated whites and blacks the average gap in earnings had shrunk in half, from 50 percent to 25 percent. As wage differentials narrowed and the country experienced sustained economic growth raising the average income level of the entire population, the unsurprising result was a spectacular rise in the black middle class – by one estimate, from 22 percent of all black males in 1940 to 68 percent in 1980.[18]

(4)   Even more striking during this same period was the economic progress of black females. As recently as 1960, their earnings averaged only 60 percent of those for white females. Now this gap in average earnings has all but disappeared, and at a time when white females have been making progress of their own in narrowing the pay differentials between men and women.[19]

(5)   With the gap in average earnings narrowing between blacks and whites for both males and females, one would expect some improvement in the relative position of two-parent black families. As the poverty line is presently defined, three out of four intact black families were poor in 1940, with family incomes, on the average, only two-fifths of the average for two-parent white families. By 1980, only 15 percent of intact black families were officially classified as poor, while their incomes now averaged four-fifths of that received by two-parent white families.[20]

(6)   Fragmentary though it is, the above evidence leaves little doubt that a staggering transformation has taken place in the relative position of blacks in American society in the past half-century. Other evidence is readily available supporting the same conclusion, including the following.

(a)   When Jackie Robinson joined the Brooklyn Dodgers in 1947, he became the first black player in major league baseball. Three years later, Chuck Cooper joined the Boston Celtics to become the first black player in the National Basketball Association. Now blacks comprise 25 percent of the players in major league baseball, 55 percent of players in the National Football League, and 75 percent of players in the National Basketball Association.[21]

(b)   When Gunnar Myrdal's study of American blacks was published in 1944, this country was fighting a global war with a segregated armed service. In 1948, that segregation was abolished. Now, according to one recent study of the armed services, "Blacks occupy more management

positions in the military than they do in business, education, journalism, government, or any other significant sector of American society."[22]
(c) As recently as 1963, one-third of all employed black women were domestic servants. Now "private household workers" account for less than 5 percent of all black women in the work force.[23]
(d) During the 1960s, for the first time since Reconstruction a concerted effort was made by the federal government to strengthen the economic and political rights of blacks by passage of the Civil Rights Act (1964), the Voting Rights Act (1965), and the Fair Housing Act (1968). By 1970, the total number of elected black officials in America was more than five times what it had been in 1964. In the 15 years after 1970, that total would increase again, this time by a multiple of four.[24]

"There is nothing mysterious about the foundations of a healthy and strong democracy," Franklin Roosevelt told Congress in 1941.

The basic things expected by our people of their political and economic systems are simple. They are:
Equality of opportunity for youth and for others.
Jobs for those who can work.
Security for those who need it.
The ending of special privilege for the few.
The preservation of civil liberties for all.
The enjoyment of the fruits of scientific progress in a wider and constantly rising standard of living.[25]

One of the puzzles of America is why, from first beginnings to the present, the foundations have remained so strong while the opportunities for so many, even in Roosevelt's day, not only were egregiously unequal, but were easily seen to be egregiously unequal. Inequality has been decreasing in recent decades, and at a rate that even Roosevelt would have found surprising. One measure of this progress is that a former vice-presidential candidate addressing Wellesley seniors in 1985 should be a woman. Another is that a black pastor of Thomasville, Georgia, who ultimately became ambassador to the United Nations and then mayor of Atlanta should look back upon his own career with amazement.

Glimpses of Failure

If much has been done to make the hopes implicit in the American Dream seem more realistic for those who, in earlier generations, had much less reason to hope, a gap remains between reality and the ideal so broad for some that the dream is little more than myth. Admittedly the economic race within America has never been completely fair. Granted further than no range of policy proposals, however radical and far-reaching, could restructure opportunities so that all would be, in some sense, equal at the starting line and on the course. Nevertheless, the evidence is easily assembled to demonstrate that the presently existing degree of inequality for some would-be competitors in the race is still woefully unfair.

(1)   Despite the growing participation of women in the labor force, and despite their rapid diffusion in many occupations previously dominated by men, females still earn on the average less than two-thirds the average earned by males.[26] Women graduating from high school, for example, tend to earn about 63 percent of what comparably educated males earn. A female with a college degree can typically expect to be paid slightly less than a male high school graduate with comparable work experience.[27] The obvious question is why such divergences should persist, despite the Equal Pay Act of 1963 outlawing gender discrimination in payments made to workers, despite Title VII of the 1964 Civil Rights Act outlawing gender discrimination in hiring and promotion, despite all efforts at affirmative action, and despite the courts repeated use of the equal protection clause of the Fourteenth Amendment to strike down gender discrimination in a wide range of occupations. One answer advanced by advocates of women's rights is that, for all the recent spate of laws and favorable court decisions, the earnings and occupational possibilities for women are still constrained by "sex discrimination, the old boys' network and the massive stereotyping of women's work."[28] Without some qualification, such statements are open to the charge of being too simplistic. The crucial question is not "Do women still suffer from discrimination in the work place?" but rather "How much of the observed gap between males and females in average wages or average earnings can be attributed to factors other than sex discrimination, such as differences in education, training, or work experience?" The discussions of chapter 10 should have made the reader wary of questions of the form: "How much of effect B can be attributed to cause A?" In this instance, that wariness would seem well advised. Various studies give various estimates, and the estimates differ markedly. On one point, however, most experts are agreed. However much of the observed earnings gap is estimated to be explained by economic factors (such as differentials in training and work experience), all major studies demonstrate that much of this gap – often as much as 50 percent – cannot be explained by *any* observed differences in economic variables of the sort that affect how much a person earns. The persistence of this unexplained gap, to phrase the matter cautiously, is consistent with the hypothesis that sex discrimination still persists and still has a significant effect on the relative earnings of women in the marketplace.[29]

(2)   However much of this persistent gap can ultimately be attributed to discrimination, one of the proximate causes of women earning less than men is the continuing high concentration of women in occupations that traditionally are among the lowest paid. Seventy percent of all women employed full time are in occupations in which over three-quarters of the employees are female and the prospects for high earnings are generally low or negligible.[30]

Women still comprise 99 percent of dental assistants but only 7 percent of dentists, 98 percent of secretaries but only 18 percent of lawyers and judges, 84 percent of elementary school teachers but only 35 percent of college teachers, 95 percent of registered nurses but only 17 percent of physicians, 93 percent of bank tellers but only 36 percent of financial managers, 98 percent of receptionists but only 11 percent of architects, 89 percent of telephone operators but only 8 percent of electrical and electronic engineers.[31] Among the highest paying jobs, females are usually under-represented, and generally by a wide margin. Only two of America's top 1,000 corporations, for example, have a female chief executive officer.[32] For women choosing a political career, their representation in high office is also still the exception, not the rule. Women comprise only 5 percent of the members of Congress, and 16 percent of the members of state legislatures.[33]

A tension becomes apparent if one juxtaposes Debi Coleman's advice to American women of how best to pursue the American Dream – "Don't waste time and energy on trying to predict your future. Concentrate on inventing it" – and Thomas Wolfe's characterization of that dream quoted near the beginning of chapter 11.

> So, then, to every man his chance –
> To every man, regardless of his birth,
> His shining, golden opportunity –
> To every man the right to live,
> To work, to be himself,
> And to become
> Whatever thing his manhood and his vision
> Can combine to make him –
> This, seeker,
> Is the promise of America.

Perhaps unnoticed when first read in chapter 11 but now impossible to miss in the context of the present discussion is the masculine focus of Wolfe's lyrical portrayal of possibilities in this country. One indication of progress in career possibilities since Wolfe's day is how out of date his characterization of the dream now seems when measured against contemporary American norms about the appropriate role of women in society. Those same norms, however, invariably highlight progress not yet made. The above evidence merely serves as a reminder that myth still colors pronouncements like that of Geraldine Ferraro to the 1985 graduating class of Wellesley College: "Today in America, women can be whatever they want to be."

(3) The improvement in the relative position of blacks within America during the postwar era is indicated by the narrowing differential between whites and blacks in a variety of measures, including average wages, average family income, and average years of schooling. The remaining gaps in the same measures, however, are indicative of progress yet to be made. By any collection of aggregate measures of average welfare, blacks are still a

Table 13.1 Family composition, mean real income, and incidence of poverty by race, 1967–1984

		1967	1973	1979	1984
Composition of families with children (percentage of total)					
White:	two parents	90.9	87.4	83.0	80.2
	single parent–male	1.3	2.3	2.3	3.3
	single parent–female	7.8	14.7	14.7	16.5
		100.0	100.0	100.0	100.0
Black:	two parents	66.1	57.3	48.3	44.1
	single parent–male	3.1	3.0	3.8	4.1
	single parent–black	30.8	39.7	47.9	51.8
		100.0	100.0	100.0	100.0
Mean real income of families with children (in constant 1984 dollars)					
White:	two parents	30,963	36,276	35,976	34,954
	single parent–female	15,836	15,853	16,016	14,611
Black:	two parents	21,121	27,040	28,645	28,096
	single parent–female	10,819	11,619	11,710	10,522
Incidence of poverty among persons living in families with children (percent)					
White:	two parents	7.7	5.2	6.1	9.4
	single parent–female	34.2	36.2	32.9	40.7
Black:	two parents	31.3	18.7	15.5	19.3
	single parent–female	67.6	61.1	57.1	60.5

Sources: "The changing economic circumstances of children: families losing ground," *Focus*, University of Wisconsin Institute for Research on Poverty, IX (Spring 1986), p. 7; Sheldon Danziger and Peter Gottschalk, "How have families with children been faring?" University of Wisconsin Institute for Research on Poverty Discussion Paper 801–86, January 1986, pp. 10, 24

disadvantaged minority in this country (see table 13.1). The infant mortality rate among blacks is still twice that of whites. Approximately one out of three black persons is officially classified as poor, as are two out of every five black children. While the gap in average income between black and white two-parent families has continued to narrow in recent years, the black–white differential for all families combined has been getting slightly wider. The main explanation for what seems, at first glance, a statistical inconsistency is the much more rapid rise of single-parent families among the black population, from one-fifth of all black families in the early 1960s to over half by the late 1980s. The income and earnings record of this latter group relative to national averages has been abysmal. Compared with the average income of two-parent *black* families, for example, female-headed black families have, on the average, less than 40 percent of the income and are three times as likely to fall below the official poverty line (see appendix C, table C.2). Most disturbing of all is the large representation of blacks among what has become known as "the underclass": those with low incomes and few skills who often rely upon welfare to exist and show every sign of being locked into their present destitute condition for life.

(4)   The gap in years of schooling between blacks and whites, as previously noted, has narrowed substantially, but the average performance of black students still remains well below that of white students. According to one recent study, for example, 17-year-old blacks on the average read at the same level as 13-year-old whites.[34] Differentials in the performance of black and white students who take Scholastic Aptitude Tests (SATs) have narrowed in the past decade, but the remaining gap between the two groups is so wide and the rate of narrowing so slow that, at the present rate, roughly similar performances are not likely to be recorded for another half century.[35] The continuance of even the present slow rate of closing is far from certain. Among the factors limiting improvement in the future is the present high concentration of black students in inner city schools often characterized by low levels of performance, high dropout rates, and an environment in and out of school inimical to learning. These same urban schools often have few if any white students, with the result that in the next generation, many black youths living in inner cities will face the prospect of a "separate but equal" education of the sort the Brown decision roundly condemned in 1954.

(5)   All the evidence from American labor markets indicates that on the average blacks are still at a competitive disadvantage relative to whites. Thirty years ago the unemployment rate for black males was roughly twice that for white males. It is still roughly twice as high today, and so is the unemployment rate of black females relative to that of white females.[36] Wages of black male workers still average only three-quarters of those paid to white males, and this gap of 25 percent has shown no tendency to narrow in the past ten years.[37] Further, much of this gap (from two-fifths to two-thirds) cannot be explained by any observed differences in such economic factors as education, training, and work experience.[38] How much can be attributed to the persistence of racial discrimination in labor markets is a much debated issue among labor market experts. What can be stated without fear of contradiction has been stated with the utmost caution in a recent Rand Corporation study of the wages and earnings record of the black population over forty years: "race is still an important predictor of a man's income."[39]

(6)   In discussions of the disadvantaged in America, much of the attention of the media tends to be focused upon the black population, although other

minorities are not significantly better off, and some are worse off. American Indians, for example, have similar income levels by family type (two-parent or single-parent),[40] and are more likely than blacks to suffer poor health. They are also more likely to face limited employment opportunities because government policies of the past have resulted in many Indian families being located in the more isolated regions of the United States.[41] Hispanics are commonly regarded as being, on the average, better off than blacks, and by various measures they are. Their poverty rates are lower and their average family incomes are higher. If aggregate measures are broken down by family type, however – from "all families" to "two-parent" and "single-parent" – the average poverty rates and income levels for Hispanic families become roughly identical to those of blacks. The main reason measures of economic welfare for all families combined place Hispanics somewhat ahead of blacks is that a far higher percentage of Hispanic families are "two-parent" as opposed to "single-parent" (see appendix C, table C.2). If the Hispanic population is disaggregated into principal subgroups, Puerto Ricans appear to be one of the worst-off minorities in America. Compared with single-parent *black* families, for example, single-parent Puerto Rican families on the average receive only two-thirds as much income and have a poverty rate that is almost 25 percent higher.[42]

(7)   Examples to this point might be mistakenly interpreted to imply that destitution and opportunities foreclosed is an economic fate experienced primarily by minorities in America. That fate is also experienced by many whites, with perhaps the most telling symptoms of that fate to be found among the homeless and the hungry.

(8)   No one knows the extent of hunger and malnutrition in America. The Harvard-based Physician Task Force on Hunger has estimated that up to 20 million in this country may be hungry for at least several days each month; President Reagan's Task Force on Food Assistance acknowledged hunger exists but insisted that an aggregate measure of its extent was impossible to make. If no agreement exists on the magnitude of the problem at any point in time, no consensus is likely to emerge on whether hunger is getting worse or getting better over time. Evidence from at least 75 local and regional studies nevertheless repeatedly makes the same unwelcome point: the problem is serious, and thousands upon thousands are involved.[43] Much of this evidence comes from those associated with emergency food programs: soup kitchens, food pantries, school lunch programs, and the like. Their data on rising demand for their services and their stories of human privation and suffering document as no single measure of nationwide malnutrition could how far removed are most of the lives of the hungry from any of the possibilities implied by the American Dream. Consider only the evidence uncovered by the Physician Task Force in its ten-month survey of four broad areas of the country, ranging from hospitals in Chicago to huts in the hills of Tennessee.[44] The two groups it found to be particularly hard hit were children and the

elderly. Among children, the most common symptoms of malnutrition were poor health and stunted growth. That summary phrase – "poor health and stunted growth" – is somehow less than satisfactory as a description of what food privation can mean to the young people of the nation. The evidence behind the phrase includes the following:

(a) children in Tennessee mountain country living on biscuits, butter, and neck bones;
(b) babies in Mississippi with no access to milk;
(c) children digging for food in dumpsters outside apartment buildings in St. Louis;
(d) children in Texas living on rice, beans and potatoes;
(e) anemic babies in North Carolina's Madison County;
(f) deficiencies among Memphis preschoolers in vitamins A, B_1, B_2, C, and iron so widespread that the Chief of Nutrition and Metabolism at a local hospital spoke of "epidemic levels of marginal undernutrition";[45]
(g) nine-year-olds in rural Mississippi with the stature of six-year-olds;
(h) stunted children in the Midwest in the heart of the nation's food producing region;
(i) kwashiokor and marasmus, normally associated with famines like that of Ethiopia, in hospitals in Chicago and on Indian reservations of the southwest.

The experience recounted by an Albuquerque school principal while administering a federally funded school lunch program is typical of the anguish and the frustration of the hundreds trying to help thousands.

"Today two little boys came to see me after lunch to say they were still hungry. It's against federal regulations to give a child more than one meal. But I looked down at their 22-inch waists and told them to get in line again." Another staff member . . . told us [members of The Physician Task Force] that many Albuquerque teachers have begun preparing sacks of food on Fridays for some of the children because they know the parents have little to give them at home. Their efforts seem to help some, as they note fewer bellyaches on Monday mornings when the children return.[46]

(9)　No one knows how many people are homeless in America. Estimates range from a low of 250,000 to a high of 3 million, but all are little more than educated guesses. What cannot be denied is that a problem most Americans associate with Third World cities can now be found in the streets and alleys of most of America's larger cities: homeless people by the thousands, living lives of threadbare destitution and sleeping where they can. Whenever those not poor themselves encounter pictures of the homeless in the media or actual bodies in the street the typical reaction is to turn away, but not before at least subconsciously conceding some variant of John Cardinal O'Connor's thought: "There is something terribly wrong."[47] A few, like Boston's Mayor Raymond Flynn, react with less puzzlement and more indignation, viewing the widespread urban presence of the homeless in a country known for its wealth as a "national scandal."[48] Particular surveys of particular cities indicate that the problem is widespread and may be getting worse. A 25-city survey in 1986, for example, revealed that in all but one of the urban centers surveyed the number of homeless people needing shelter had increased in the past 12 months. In New York City the number of homeless given shelter has more than doubled since 1983. Nor are these people exclusively adults who are maladjusted or mentally ill. A 47-city study found that, for the first time among the homeless, families with children comprised the largest segment.[49] The homeless given shelter in New York City include some 9,000 children and their families in 63 hotels, often crammed six or seven to a room. What the impact upon the personality of the young and homeless sheltered in hotels will be from living most of their early years in an environment distinguished for its absence of security and presence of criminal elements is a subject many find troubling. One forecast from a psychologist who has been studying the children of homeless families is that such young people are likely to become "alienated adults, unable to forge relationships and tending toward anger, criminality and poor educational achievement."[50] At The Prince George on East 28th Street, a psychologist working with the homeless children housed in that hotel responded to a reporter's question with an observation now a commonplace among investigators of such disadvantaged youth, but a commonplace worth repeating: "They are the future, as all kids are, and it's scary."[51]

American journalist Tom Wolfe is known for the jaunty style and satirical wit with which he has described various aspects of American life, from stock-car racing in the South to the Pop art market in Manhattan to *The Right Stuff* as Wolfe viewed the stuff of which astronauts are made. His deftness at crafting memorable characterizations is not always matched by accuracy of observation. On the extent to which reality approximates the American Dream, he must be counted among the optimists. "After all," he wrote in 1965, "this is a nation that, except for a hard core of winos at the bottom and a hard crust of aristocrats at the top, has been going gloriously middle class for two decades, as far as the breezeways stretch."[52] As a lighthearted aside in *The Kandy-Kolored Tangerine-Flake Streamlined Baby*, that observation is likely to provoke a smile. Following on the heels of examples like those just cited, the same remark seems painfully wide of the mark. The magnitude by which Wolfe misses the mark brings to the fore a policy question that has been standing in the wings, both in this section and throughout the book: What should be done to make at least some of the more glaring inequalities in the economic race less pronounced, particularly for those who are among the most handicapped in that race as it is presently run?

Personal Reflections on Policy Options

To this point, the major concern has been what Americans believe, not what they ought to believe, and what they have done in the name of economic justice, not what they ought to do. The focus of this section is quite different, offering as it does a few thoughts of my own about policy options that should be considered if the American market system is to become more fair or just. Their inclusion here is motivated mainly by a sense that, given the importance of the problems and the length of time I have spent studying the views of others, I have some obligation to offer whatever thoughts I have – or at least whatever policy recommendations I have that are somewhat at variance with those dominating contemporary popular debate. I also feel I owe the reader at least a few personal reflections on how the fairness of the American economic system might be improved after our mutual slogging through such an extended consideration of concepts and beliefs relating to issues of economic justice.

Much of contemporary discussion about how best to help the disadvantaged in the United States concerns which remedial policies for able-bodied adults will improve their skills and their sense of self-reliance, and thus strengthen their willingness and their ability to participate in the economic race. The media has touted "the new consensus" between left and right concerning the merits of combining a number of old ideas under the heading of "workfare." That word is used to designate a range of policy options, but the core ideas behind the options are usually quite similar, namely, that receipt of welfare by the able-bodied should be linked to work (hence the name "workfare"), primarily through schemes emphasizing a mutual obligation – of the recipient to become economically self-sufficient, and of the state to provide the means for that transition, such as education, training, and placement services.[53]

Appealing as these ideas are – and all would seem consistent with conventional American beliefs about economic justice – to me the current preoccupation with helping disadvantaged adults smacks of trying to remedy a recurring break in the dam by building better levees downstream. If the problems of disadvantaged adults are not unrelated to problems they encountered before becoming adults, then policies need to be designed not only to remedy skill and attitudinal deficiencies among the present generation, but also to reduce the flow from childhood into adulthood of those similarly disadvantaged in the next generation. Two related thoughts have similar policy implications. Foreign policy experts have long argued that America must deal with all Russian problems simultaneously and as parts of an interrelated whole. The same point can be made with equal force about domestic programs designed to help the disadvantaged: all the related problems must be treated simultaneously and as parts of an interconnected whole. Part of that interconnectedness is the relationship between the disadvantaged children of today and those likely to become disadvantaged adults in the future. If the goal is to reduce the numbers in the second group, remedies must be found to reduce handicaps among the first group. A second thought, similarly self-evident, points in a similar direction. In the current outpouring of articles and books on welfare reform, I am struck by the limited attention given to helping that disadvantaged minority in America least capable of helping themselves, namely, the children of the poor.

However much one views the poor as partly or primarily responsible for their own destitution, that viewpoint surely is of limited relevance for this group. However much one believes that American norms should include, in F. Scott Fitzgerald's graceful phrasing, "a willingness of the heart," that willingness would seem appropriately directed to helping those children living in poverty whose handicaps are many and whose means of self-help are few.

The following thoughts have no claim to comprehensive coverage of the topic. They are advanced with the hope of giving a more prominent place in future welfare discussions to a subject now too often slighted, and one of crucial importance to any plan with any claim to lessening those inequalities of opportunity most flagrantly at odds with American beliefs about what constitutes a just economic system or a fair economic race.

Children presently comprise 30 percent of the American population but more than 40 percent of America's poor. After reaching a low point in 1969, the percentage of children below the official poverty line gradually rose in the 1970s and then shot upward in the 1980s. Today, approximately one American child in five lives in poverty.[54] (Among Hispanics, the ratio is almost two in five; among blacks, almost two in four.[55]) Poverty rates of this magnitude among the youngest members of society far exceed those in other advanced industrial nations. Of the five included in table 13.2, for example, the American poverty rate for children is 60 percent higher than Britain's, 80 percent higher than Canada's and more than double that of any of the other three countries. All comparisons, moreover, are for the period 1979–81 (the US data are for 1979), after which, as previously noted, the rate of childhood poverty in the United States increased substantially. Nor can this relatively poor American showing be blamed entirely on the rapid rise in recent years of single-parent families. Two of the countries with less than half the American childhood poverty rate actually have a higher percentage of one-parent families (Norway and Sweden). More importantly, the unfavorable position of America does not change if poverty rates for children are disaggregated by family type. Whether calculated for one-parent or two-parent families, the percentage of poor children in this country is far higher than in any of the others noted (see table 13.3). Of the many handicaps poor children in America are likely to experience, three seem particularly widespread and particularly unfair.

(1)   First and perhaps foremost is a shortage of the basic necessities of life, including food, clothing, shelter, and medical care. The prevalence of children among the malnourished and the homeless has been indicated above. The child who comes to school hungry is also likely to come to school in threadbare clothing and ill-fitting shoes. The extent to which poor families have access to adequate medical care is a subject about which little is known. What is known is that the well-off and better educated tend to have better health than the poor and less educated.[56] We also know that only about half

Table 13.2 Absolute and relative poverty rates among children, adults, and the elderly in six nations[a]

Country	Children (%) Absolute	Children (%) Relative	Working-age adults (%) Absolute	Working-age adults (%) Relative	Elderly (%) Absolute	Elderly (%) Relative
United States	17.1	22.4	10.1	13.4	16.1	23.9
United Kingdom	10.7	9.3	6.9	5.7	37.0	29.2
Canada	9.6	15.5	7.5	10.7	4.8	17.2
West Germany	8.2	4.9	6.5	4.5	15.4	11.1
Norway	7.6	4.8	7.1	5.4	18.7	5.6
Sweden	5.1	5.0	6.7	6.7	2.1	0.8

[a] Absolute poverty is defined as the percentage of persons of each type with disposable incomes below the official US poverty line, converted to appropriate national currency using OECD estimates of purchasing power parity. Relative poverty is defined as the percentage of persons of each type living in families with adjusted incomes below half of national median income (income adjusted to reflect differences in family size). Data are for either 1979 or 1981.

Source: Timothy Smeeding, Barbara Doyle Torrey, and Martin Rein, "Patterns of income and poverty: the economic status of the young and the old in six countries," Paper presented at the Conference on the Well-Being of Children and Aged, The Urban Institute, February 1987; reproduced in Gary Burtless, "Inequality in America: where do we stand?" *Brookings Review*, V (Summer 1987), p. 14

of the poor are covered by Medicaid, and that roughly 11 million children are not covered by any health insurance.[57] Parents already hard pressed to afford such basic necessities as shelter and food are likely to be even more hard pressed to afford satisfactory medical care in a world of spiraling medical costs.

(2)   Even less affordable for the nation's impoverished is professional group day care. The cost of full-time preschool care at a licensed group facility according to even the lowest estimates ranges from $2,000 to $3,000 a year per child.[58] For a single-parent family of three living at the poverty line, such a charge would constitute a quarter to a third of total family income. What is commonly forgotten is that some 40 percent of those officially classified as poor have incomes that are less than half of the poverty line,[59] and for these people the above charges would amount to one-half to two-thirds of total family income.

(3)   The relationship between being raised in poverty, doing poorly at school, and becoming an adult with defective skills is not well understood. Certainly among those with defective skills are many who were raised in poor families.[60] We do know that a child from a poor family is more likely to drop out of school.[61] What we do not know – or at best, only dimly understand – is

Table 13.3 Low income[a] rates of the young by family type for selected countries

	Family type			
Country	One-parent families[b]	Two-parent families[c]	Other families[d]	All types of families
Canada	51.2	13.2	13.0	16.8
Germany	30.5	3.3	10.2	6.3
Norway	13.7	3.7	10.7	5.6
Sweden	9.8	5.5	2.5	5.2
United Kingdom	36.4	9.2	6.2	10.4
United States	60.0	16.6	20.6	24.1

[a] Low income is defined as children living in a given type of family with adjusted net after-tax income less than half of the median for all families as a percentage of all children of each type. Children are persons age 17 or younger.
[b] Children in one-parent families live with only one natural parent and no other adults in the family.
[c] Children in two-parent families live in units with only two parents and no other adults.
[d] Children in other families may live with adults other than one parent alone or two parents alone, for example with grandparents, in extended family situations, or in foster homes.

Source: Timothy Smeeding, Barbara Doyle Torrey, and Martin Rein, "Comparative well-being of children and elderly," *Contemporary Policy Issues*, V (April 1987), p. 68.

how disruption of family structure affects both the income of the family and the character and competence of children raised in such families. More than half of all poor children in America live in single-parent families headed by a female.[62] Whatever the advantages captured by the vague phrase "enriched family background," a large number of those advantages are likely to be absent if the family is headed by a single parent who (a) lacks basic educational skills, (b) has few marketable skills, and (c) is a teenager. As the percentage of single-parent families continues to grow and the percentage of out-of-wedlock births to teenagers continues to rise (the latter often resulting in the mother dropping out of high school), the odds are increasing that a child raised in poverty at best will receive only limited family enrichment at home, and at worst will be the victim of a bleached out family environment. Across that spectrum of possibilities from best to worst, in the words of the president of the National Urban League, "too many . . . kids simply don't get the parenting and supervision that build self-esteem and self-confidence."[63] Such parenting may include not just an absence of enrichment but the presence of abuse. By one estimate, children in single-parent families are twice as likely to suffer child abuse as children in two-parent families.[64] If the single parent is a teenager, the incidence of child abuse is even higher – a finding not surprising among mothers who themselves are in an age cohort less likely to have the skills and the patience for parenting.

"The test of our progress," Franklin Roosevelt told a nation struggling through the Great Depression, "is not whether we add more to the abundance of those who have much; it is whether we provide enough for those who have too little."[65] A similar criterion is surely not irrelevant for a nation that has achieved unprecedented affluence since Roosevelt's day. As to who should be counted as having too little, and who to help because of a limited ability to help themselves, the children of the poor deserve a special place in both the first group and the second. Federal policy recognizes that special claim to aid in programs designed to help the young and disadvantaged have better access to the basic necessities of life, to professional day care, and to remedial educational and training programs designed to remedy deficient skills. Under all three headings, however, the record of accomplishments is primarily one of too little now, and less likely in the future.

(1) *Basic necessities.* Most readers will not be surprised to learn that after two terms with a Republican president determined to trim federal spending, total spending to aid children of the poor has been reduced. What they may not anticipate is the magnitude of the cuts made. In recent years, the percentage of the poor receiving food stamps has fallen, while nearly a million children from low-income families have been dropped from federally funded school lunch programs.[66] Approximately half of the poor qualify for Medicaid at present. A decade ago, two-thirds qualified. This decline is attributable mainly to two factors: (a) most poor people gain access to Medicaid by qualifying for Aid to Families with Dependent Children (AFDC), and (b) AFDC eligibility requirements have been tightened substantially in recent years. Restricted access of the poor to adequate medical care in all likelihood will become even more pronounced in the future if current trends in health care persist, including the increasing importance of profit-motivated hospitals in the private sector.[67] The outlook for low-cost housing is equally discouraging. Many older units of public housing are falling into disrepair or being demolished, while the number of new units financed by the federal government has plummeted. Under the Reagan Administration, the housing budget was slashed by 75 percent. In the no-nonsense language of a recent survey of the problem: "In the absence of revolutionary change in Washington's attitude toward housing, do not look to the federal government for a comprehensive or enduring solution to the housing problems of the poor."[68]

As access of the poor to such in-kind benefits as food and medical care has declined, so has the value of the cash benefits they have received through welfare payments. For families dependent upon AFDC, the nation's most important cash assistance program, the real value of dollars received has fallen by one-third since the early 1970s, mainly because inflation has continually outpaced any legislated changes in benefits. With this decline has come a declining share of federal outlays for entitlement programs. In 1973, poor families with children received 22.5 percent of cash transfer payments. By 1984, that share had fallen by one-quarter to 16.8 percent.[69] As less has been given, fewer have been lifted out of poverty. In 1979, for example, almost one out of every five families with children who were poor was raised above the official poverty line by federal cash assistance programs. By 1986, that ratio had fallen to one in nine. If noncash benefits are also included (such as food stamps and medical care), the recent drop in the proportion lifted out of poverty by federal assistance is even more pronounced.[70]

(2) *Day care.* The United States lags behind almost every other industrial country in day care. It has no national policy for widespread provision of this service or for monitoring the services provided by the private sector. A handful of states do commit substantial resources to child care programs, but the majority do little or nothing and many are cutting back on the little they provide. As of 1986, for example, 23 states were providing fewer children with day care than in 1981. Whether care facilities are public or private, located in a home or in a professional group center, the care provided is often "of distressingly poor quality."[71] Even at the best of professional centers, low pay and high turnover are the rule. As a group, day care employees are among the worst paid workers in the nation. (As one expert dryly noted, "It says something about our society's values that we pay animal caretakers more than people who care for our children."[72])

The absence of government support for this service and of public concern for the quality of service provided is curious, given Americans' concern with children and child-rearing practices and the pressing need for day care services by working women in general and poor families in particular.

Roughly one out of every two mothers with preschool children now works. Of those who work, only about 15 percent currently rely upon group day care, this restricted usage unsurprising given the high cost and limited availability of such care (see appendix C, table C.4). Nor have business firms done much to alleviate the problem. Of the nation's 6 million employers, fewer than 1 in 1,000 provide any sort of child care assistance.[73] Neither public nor business sector, then, shows any sign of addressing in any concerted way a problem that has invariably accompanied one of the most dramatic developments in American labor markets in the twentieth century: the rising participation of women. Secretary of Labor William Brock is just one of many disconcerted by this minor response to a major challenge: "It's just incredible that we have seen the feminization of the workforce with no more adaptation than we have had . . . ."[74]

The discussion to this point has focused only upon the government response to growing day care needs on the part of working mothers. For mothers of low-income families with preschool children, ages three to five, the federal government does provide funds for a day care and child development program called Head Start. Because of funding limitations, however, this program serves only one out of every six preschool children from poor families who are eligible for the program.[75] The prospects for substantial increases in federal funding for this or any other day care program for the poor are not encouraging. Much of contemporary debate has centered upon the need to append day care support to workfare legislation designed to get able-bodied mothers back into the work force. Proposals likely to receive Congressional approval seem unlikely to make a large dent in a national problem. That of Daniel Patrick Moynihan, for example, is estimated to add 1 percent to current welfare expenditures in order to help an additional 2 percent of welfare recipients. This hardly seems to warrant the rallying cry: "Pray God, this time, we don't let the children down."[76]

(3) *Remedial education and training programs.* A recent study of 3,600 young adults found that 20 percent read below the eighth-grade level, although to read instruction manuals for most American jobs requires reading ability at the high school level.[77] A 1987 California study of welfare recipients found that more than a third needed remedial education of the most basic sort.[78] Half of the adults in federal and state correctional facilities have little or no ability to read or write.[79] To fill 2,000 job openings New York Telephone had to interview 90,000 candidates, of whom 84 percent failed the qualifying examination which required less than a high school education to pass.[80]

These are but a few examples from mounting evidence that the public school system in this country is not having uniform success in turning out young adults adequately prepared for the demands of responsible citizenship and the needs of industry. If a gap is developing between the skills some have and the skills they need to join the work force with any chance for advancement, the obvious question is whether the state should provide remedial programs to make a bad situation better. Beginning in the 1960s, the federal government launched a number of programs designed to provide work experience and training (classroom and on-the-job) to make the less employable more employable, targeted primarily on minorities, welfare recipients, and low-income youths.[81] In the 1980s under the Reagan Administration, some of these initiatives were discontinued (such as CETA), some survived (notably the Job Corps and the Work Incentive program), and one major new initiative was launched under the Job Training Partnership Act (JTPA). The details of these programs, old and new, terminated and ongoing, need not concern us here. What matters are three general points. First, in the 1980s funding for all programs combined has been slashed. (Between 1981 and 1986, for example, total federal support for five major programs was cut by two-thirds.[82]) Secondly, this decline in funding is unlikely to be offset by any increase in effectiveness of new initiatives. The Job Training Partnership Act, for example, offers to those in need of remedial education and training no stipends and limited assistance for a relatively short period of time. Like so many of its predecessors, it seems likely to earn the summary judgment of "investing too little and hoping for too much."[83] The third point is implicit in the previous sentence. The record of accomplishments, past and present, is modest in the extreme relative to the magnitude of the problems prompting all these remedial programs. Whether those who participated in particular programs benefited by a lot or a little is a hotly debated issue.[84] What is generally admitted by all sides, however, is that participants in these various programs are but a small percentage of those needing help, and the general problem of skill deficiencies among youths and young adults is not merely unsolved, but has yet to be seriously addressed. From the 1960s to the present, this kind of negative summary judgment has been echoed in various evaluations of different training programs. That of a National Academy of Sciences panel in 1985 makes the usual point in the usual way:

The employment and training system is trying in large part to do what the education system should be doing but, for some significant segment of the youth population, apparently fails to do. Yet the employment and training system has not attained stability of funding, professionalization of staff, and delineation of authority, in short, institutionalization of the sort that has given the educational system its accepted place in the mainstream of American life. As a result, in most communities, organizations involved in employment and training are considered marginal.[85]

A director of a "second chance" training program in the Southwest put the matter more bluntly:

If we really wanted to serve hard-core unemployed youth, we'd have to do a lot more than we've been willing to do. You wouldn't be looking for a payoff in less than three years, possibly four years. A reasonably stable nineteen to twenty-year-old with some work experience, we can brush him up and send him out on a job. But the others? We don't want to make the investment, so we forget about them.[86]

America evidently has a productivity problem; not the one commonly featured in the media concerning the relationship between inputs and outputs in American business firms, but the one linking such inputs as public education and child-rearing practices to the output of young adults ready to face the challenges of responsible citizenship and productive employment. Suppose one were to tackle this latter productivity problem, not with the tentativeness of the politician, but with the dash and determination typical of the American business community at its best. To minimize constraints on brainstorming at the outset, let us put aside all questions of costs, to be taken up only when a general strategy has been drawn up that has some chance of success. The touchstone for success is the extent to which we can achieve two related goals: (a) to improve equality of opportunity for children of the poor, and (b) to improve the relationship between the number of children raised in this country and the number who ultimately become valuable additions to the citizenry and the work force. The scope of our initial planning should be consistent with two observations. If in the transformation of a helpless infant into a responsible and productive adult every childhood year is an important year, our strategy should try to encompass as many of those years as possible.

Secondly, large-scale and complex problems generally call for large-scale and multifaceted solutions. Our bias at the outset should therefore be for the broad brush and the big canvas. With these few guidelines and the general charge to design a set of interrelated policies to further the goals noted, what policy options might be worth exploring under the three headings controlling discussion thus far: basic necessities, day care, and remedial education and training?

(1) *Basic necessities.* As the opening salvos of the War on Poverty were fired in 1964, Attorney General Robert Kennedy could be found among the vanguard. "We must dedicate ourselves," he told Congress in that year, "to see that no child is hungry because there is no food in the house; that no child is cold because he has no warm clothing; that none will need a doctor and not be able to afford one . . . ."[87] Despite the passage of a quarter-century, despite a War on Poverty in the interim, and despite an affluent society becoming more affluent, the nation has not begun to approximate this ideal. And it could. The problems are easily identified and solutions are not difficult to find.

The problem, at bottom, is insufficient parental income. In some instances this is compounded by parental expenditure decisions that result in children already wanting for basic necessities receiving even less. The economist's solution is to allocate more funds to the parent and let that person decide how best to use the money to meet the family's needs. But if one cannot trust all of the parents all of the time to use discretionary funds in the best interests of their own offspring – and one cannot (although how pervasive such tendencies are is impossible to say) – an alternative solution is a system of in-kind benefits delivered directly to the child. The means for delivery is readily at hand for children of school age, namely, the school itself. (Problems relating to preschool children will be taken up in the next section.) Food requirements could be met by expanding the current school food programs to include two meals a day designed to meet the minimum nutritional needs of each child. Participation could be voluntary with charges on a sliding scale (from free to full cost) depending upon parental income. Medical and dental care could be made available to all children by schools providing medical and dental check-ups, with any care deemed necessary provided through local medical and dental facilities. Here too charges could be levied on a sliding scale depending upon family income. Another in-kind benefit that could be delivered in a similar way is clothing. All schools would have mandatory school uniforms – an appalling thought to most Americans until they realize that many European schools presently have such a requirement, thereby guaranteeing what the majority of children seem to want in attire, namely, the assurance that their own clothes will be in step with what all the other children are wearing. To soften the community's sense of totalitarian intervention, uniform design might be the subject of a school-wide or district-wide contest, with final selection determined by a panel of teachers, parents, and students. The uniforms themselves (including shoes, overcoats, and raincoats) could be provided either directly through the school or indirectly through designated merchants, with charges again on a sliding scale depending upon family income. In sum, if the problem is to deliver the basic necessities to the children of the poor, for school-age children one possible solution for many necessities is to use the public school system to ensure delivery. The resulting scheme, however generous and comprehensive in design, could never guarantee perfect equality of access to all the basic necessities of life. But a system surely could be crafted that would put an end (at least when schools were in session) to the widespread presence in our society of school-age children who are ill-clothed and ill-nourished, with little or no access to adequate medical and dental care.

(2)   *Day care.* "Conservatives," notes conservative George Will,

> are . . . fond of the metaphor of a footrace: All citizens should be roughly equal at the starting line of the race of life. But much that we have learned and continue to learn – and we are learning a lot – about early-childhood development suggests that "equality of opportunity" is a much more complicated matter than most conservatives can comfortably acknowledge. Prenatal care, . . . infant stimulation, childhood nutrition and especially home environment – all these and other influences affect the competence of a young "runner" as he or she approaches the academic hurdles that so heavily influence social outcomes in America. There is, of course, vast scope for intelligent disagreement as to what can and should be done to make "equality of opportunity" more than an airy abstraction. But surely it is indisputable that "equality of opportunity" can be enhanced by various forms of state action.[88]

The question for this section is whether, for the sake of enhancing equality of opportunity, state action should include government involvement in the provision of day care, and if so, what kind of care should be provided and under what conditions. Here too the search for policy options is usefully constrained by several general observations. First, in a world in which so many mothers work, the need for high quality affordable day care reaches far beyond the particular needs of low-income families. Second, the care needed includes both full-time day care for preschool children and after-school care for school-age children. Third, to meet the second kind of need, the schools themselves offer a physical structure that tends to be underutilized at precisely the right time, namely, after the regular school day is over. Fourth, children from deprived family backgrounds, if they are to become less deprived and more successful in the public school system, need more than custodial care. Fifth and last, many parents of disadvantaged children – particularly those who are young and single parents – need both day care for their children and help in developing their parenting skills. The general problem raised by George Will's observations might thus be brought into a sharper focus by the question: What state-sponsored revisions in the present system of day care in America might be devised to respond to the needs and possibilities raised by these five observations?

For preschool children   One theme to be repeated throughout this and subsequent policy sections is that, whatever the problem, a variety of solutions have already been attempted. In many cases, the challenge is therefore not to reinvent the wheel but rather to find among solutions tried some combination which (perhaps with modification) has a reasonable chance of success. Consider the set of needs that should be met by any preschool day care program for disadvantaged children. For the children these include custodial care, enrichment programs emphasizing language development, social skills, and readiness for formal schooling, and better access to such basic necessities as food and medical care. (Many low-income children suffer from untreated vision and hearing problems as well as anemia, all of which, if left untreated can affect subsequent performance in major ways.[89]) In addition, parents of disadvantaged children often need assistance in developing their parenting skills. The Head Start program at present provides services that include the following:[90]

educational programs tailored to the child's individual needs, with the goal of fostering the child's intellectual, social and emotional growth (including being introduced to the concepts of words and numbers);
comprehensive health care, including medical, dental, and nutritional services (beginning with a comprehensive examination to identify such physical handicaps as impaired vision or hearing);
a minimum of one hot meal and snack each day to meet at least one-third of the child's daily nutritional needs;
involvement of parents in parent education, program planning and operating activities.

As it presently functions, the Head Start program is thus one possible starting point from which to build a more comprehensive approach to preschool day care. Ideally this program would be modified in at least four major ways, two of which are relatively easy to design while the other two are not.

First, funding would have to be significantly expanded in order to reach the majority of eligible children. (As previously noted, Head Start now serves only one-sixth of the children living in poverty.)

Second, this expansion should include a special effort to reach children of teenage mothers who are single parents with low incomes. Of every six babies born in the United States, one is the child of a teenage mother. Less than half of teenage mothers graduate from high school, and over half of present welfare expenditure goes to families in which the mother first became a parent as a teenager.[91] Children of such mothers are therefore likely to be particularly disadvantaged. But day care programs for the children should be combined with efforts to encourage teenage mothers to stay in school, or if they have dropped out, to enroll in training and educational programs, of which more below.

Third, attention to the disadvantaged should not obscure the more general need for high quality, accessible, and affordable day care for preschool children of working parents. To meet this need would require a plan to expand in a major way funding support for group care facilities. Part of that plan should include ways in which this general expansion can be combined with enlargement of day care programs of the Head Start sort for disadvantaged children. For those who resist such a broad approach to a national need, consider the following. If part of the intellectual and social development of school-age children is appropriately viewed as a public responsibility to be met primarily through the public school system, should not similar development in younger children – also crucial for ultimate success – not be acknowledged as a public responsibility and thus a public priority? If the public school system, in meeting its mandate, mixes children from all backgrounds, should not a similar mixing be part of a comprehensive day care program for preschool children? Finally, on the sensitive subject of funding, if quality preschool day care is prohibitively expensive for most families, and if free public day care is politically not feasible, is a viable compromise yet again a sliding scale of charges depending upon family income?

Fourth, if the government is to become involved in the widespread provision of preschool day care, it must set standards for services to be rendered and monitor the results. If quality is to be high (as opposed to the low quality all too typical of many contemporary day care facilities), standards must be high. If standards are high, salaries must be significantly raised above present levels. In a competitive market system, high quality is generally not available at a low price, and the persistence of salaries at their current low levels will attract only the unskilled, the mediocre, and a handful of the particularly dedicated. The basic rationale for improvement would seem self-evident: early childhood years are crucial to formation of character and competence; a comprehensive day care system for all children of working parents should try to influence that development in the most constructive way; and a low quality system cannot be expected to produce high quality results.

For school-age children   This topic is one of the most neglected in the current literature. Again consider the needs: of children of working parents who, at a minimum, require custodial care; of disadvantaged children who need custodial care plus programs designed to help compensate for some of their disadvantages; and of parents (particularly those of disadvantaged children) who often need ongoing help with parenting skills. The school itself is one place where many of these needs could be met when school is out – after school, on weekends, and even during the summer. To discover how such needs might best be met one can again begin by surveying successful experiments throughout the country. In Los Angeles County, for example, state funds are already used to meet a range of after-school child care needs. ("The school district provides the sites, janitorial services and liability insurance, the city provides parks, summer staff and transportation, the local United Way has organized the project and developed scholarships for those who could not afford the fees. It serves children from kindergarten to 8th grade every day until 6 p.m. at a cost of $40 a month per family."[92])

The choice of specifics should be conditioned by several general objectives. After-school programs ideally should feature a mix of children from many backgrounds for the same reasons that a mix is preferred during the regular school day. Such programs should also include a mix of activities, from recreational to academic, from athletics to computer-assisted instruction, from enrichment for the gifted to remedial assistance for the slow. With the right mix, schools would begin to be considered "the place to be" when school is out, by children because of the intrinsic interest of the programs, and by parents because of valuable opportunities provided for their child's development. At every stage of planning, implementation, and review, every effort should be made to involve the widest possible spectrum of the community: teachers and parents, obviously, but also those whose voluntary participation could strengthen programs – youth service agencies, community organizations, and members of the business and academic communities. Developing effective outreach, while never easy, would be less difficult if a massive government assault of the sort envisioned here were launched in concert with a national publicity campaign emphasizing the single theme: children are everybody's business. The overarching conceptual framework for such an assault would be one in which the child's development, from earliest years to adulthood, is regarded as one continuous process in need of continuous and informed nurturing, with special nurturing for those from disadvantaged backgrounds. Thus preschool programs should lead naturally into after-school programs which should blend into vocational education and training programs, of which more in a moment. At every stage, programs should develop and strengthen attitudes and skills needed for success as an adult, including such general traits as self-reliance and a sense of self-worth, plus particular traits needed in the work place, including good work habits, a mastery of basic skills, and problem-solving ability. Last but hardly least, care for children, including disadvantaged children, should be designed to complement ongoing programs for disadvantaged parents. Success at school is crucially dependent upon the home environment which, in turn, is crucially dependent upon the attitudes and abilities of the parent. At the core of the more successful programs must therefore be a sense of mutual responsibility and personal opportunity. The responsibility in question is for the child's development, to be shared by the child, the parent, and every other contributor to that development. The opportunities for parents must include the chance not merely to improve parenting skills, but also to participate in education and training programs to raise their skills, improve their earning capability, and strengthen their own sense of self-worth. Which raises the third part of what is basically a three-part strategy.

(3)   *Remedial education and training.* The title suggests failure. Adults have emerged from the public school system with skills that are deficient relative to the demands of society and the work place. The best long-run solution is to

improve the public education system so that remedial difficulties are identified quickly and corrected long before the child leaves school. Part of the correction process envisioned here consists of the ongoing monitoring and ongoing assistance made possible by an integrated system of day care programs for preschool children and after-school programs (as well as in-school programs) for school-age children. But these two lead naturally to a third.

At some point between the onset of puberty and exodus from school, the needs of developing youth, particularly those not going on to college, include vocational training in the broadest sense of that term. Development of character and competence, previously fostered by an integrated set of in-school and after-school programs, must now be fostered by programs providing in-school vocational training, after-school apprenticeships and part-time jobs, and summer internships and training programs. The constructive use of summer vacations would seem to be particularly important. The time available runs to months, and free time can be the enemy of disadvantaged youths living in neighborhoods dominated by teenage gangs, drug dealers, and others given to criminal activity. "To put the issue starkly," write two experts on the dropout problem in America,

more affluent youngsters attend camps that provide educational enrichment, visit museums, go to concerts, have parental encouragement/demands for summer reading and may travel widely with their families in the United States and abroad. Poor youngsters often hang out on the streets of their ravaged neighborhoods.[93]

If useful vocational training and guidance are to be provided – both in school and out of school through school-sponsored programs – the cooperation and active participation of members of the local business community is sure to be a necessary condition for success. This involvement must include much more than making available a handful of jobs for a few students. Ideally it should include working with teachers and parents to set realistic goals, design programs to meet these goals, and monitor the results. A simple exhortation is unlikely to evoke widespread participation from business people whose primary concerns are often personal success and company profits. But neither is widespread participation a preposterous ambition. Over 80 million Americans were engaged in volunteer work in 1985, giving on the average three-and-a-half hours of their time each week.[94] One task is therefore to design an ongoing publicity campaign that will help to redirect some of this energy, expertise, and good will into school programs, including vocational training programs.

The programs in question should include in-school lectures on state-of-the-art technology and on-the-job training featuring state-of-the-art equipment so that students will be challenged to master advanced skills rather than merely settling for a minimum grasp of the basics. Above all, these programs must be tailored so that student participants can see a prospective pay-off from their own efforts to improve their vocational skills. To decide which features to include in which programs one can again turn to examples provided by successful programs. Possibly the best known is the Boston COMPACT, which combines education and labor market programs to facilitate the transition from school to work. Designed as a joint project of the schools, social service agencies, and the business community, the Boston COMPACT emphasizes the mutual obligations of all participants; sets specific targets in terms of annual improvements in school attendance, dropout rates, and college and job placements; and provides (among other features) access to summer jobs, job placement services, and assistance for pursuing further education.[95] Other successful programs with similar object-ives are not difficult to find. For example, the Summer Training and Education Program (STEP) of Public/Private Ventures "takes in-school youth, ages 14 and 15, who are at risk of dropping out, and provides paid summer jobs, 90 hours of intensive competency-based academic skills remediation, and (to combat teen pregnancy) family/life skills planning."[96] Common elements for success include useful training opportunities ("useful" as defined by both the students and the business community), acceptance of mutual responsibility for success by all participants, and realistic goals with continual monitoring of results.

Two final points. Until now, nothing has been said about remedial education and training for high school dropouts and others with defective skills. This cohort of the disadvantaged would seem to need both remedial help, and – once such help has been received – the same opportunities to improve their skills in vocational training programs as students still in high school. The programs for vocational training previously outlined might therefore be regarded as the second tier of a two-tier system, with remedial education and training the first tier leading ultimately to greater economic opportunity. Secondly, assistance for vocational training need not end here. Extensive financial support through loans and grants is presently available to low-income students continuing on to college.[97] Similar assistance should be available for those wishing to pursue vocational training at accredited schools. In this way a third tier could be added to a two-tier system for vocational training managed through the public schools. As the education system presently functions, it discriminates in favor of those bound for college in terms of both curricula emphasized in high schools and the financial support available for pursuing education beyond high school. Equality of opportunity would seem to require a tailoring of both – school curricula and financial aid for training beyond high schools – to serve more adequately the needs of two constituencies, not one: those bound for college, and those not.

In 1947 George Marshall outlined to a Harvard audience the main elements of what would become known as the Marshall Plan for Europe. "Our policy," he declared, "is directed . . . against hunger, poverty, despera-tion, and chaos."[98] What has been outlined above is, in a sense, a kind of Marshall Plan for the children of America, with special emphasis on children

from disadvantaged backgrounds.[99] Such a massive restructuring of the
American education system – from broadening preschool day care to putting
in place a range of after-school and summer programs to revamping the
approach of high schools to vocational training – is sure to evoke a host of
objections, of which four are likely to be voiced with particular vigor.

(1)   *The care of children, particularly preschool children, is the responsibility of the
parents and best provided by the parents.* In earlier generations this objection
would have been difficult to meet, both because of the factual setting (few
mothers worked) and because of community norms emphasizing that the
appropriate place for women was in the home caring for young children. The
factual setting has now changed, and so have the norms. The prevalence of
working mothers has been detailed above, as has the associated need for day
care facilities for both preschool and school-age children. Also detailed above
is some of the evidence indicating the erosion of the family as an American
institution. To review only two of those findings: one out of four children is
now born into a family without married parents, and only two out of five
children will reach the age of eighteen with both natural parents in the home.
For centuries the family has been an institution of singular importance to the
education and development of children. If that institution in this country is
now under pressure and consequently offering less enrichment to many
children, the question is whether state initiatives should be devised to help to
compensate for some of that loss. This is what the above set of proposals tries
to do by providing help for parents to become better parents and special aid
for disadvantaged children through a range of programs covering most of the
childhood years.

(2)   *Education is a local responsibility, not a federal responsibility.* The American
education system as it presently functions is a product of local, state, and
federal initiatives and programs ranging from state standards for local
schools to federal funding for school lunch programs. The programs proposed above could be put in place by a simple extension of various functions
currently provided by the different levels of government in this tripartite
system.

(3)   *Whatever is implemented will not begin to solve the problem.* Lost all too often in
the litany of failed educational experiments are the examples of success.
Many such examples can be found among recently launched programs in
various localities. The near total absence of specific details in all the general
proposals made above may strike the reader as a major flaw. This is
intentional. To borrow an analogy from another time of national stress: the
challenge as of December 8, 1941, was not for Washington politicians and
bureaucrats to design a fighter plane with performance characteristics better
able to compete with the Japanese Zero that had just wreaked such havoc at
Pearl Harbor. The challenge for government at every level was to provide the

leadership, incentives, and opportunities so that American engineering capabilities would be channeled into solving that problem. Similarly, the way to create a better system for the education and development of American children is not for the government itself to draft the blueprint. Here too the key to success is channeling the creative energies of those most capable of identifying and developing possible improvements. This admittedly will require the active participation of the government – providing funds, providing leadership in a nationwide publicity campaign, rewarding excellence, and facilitating the interchange of information on successes and failures. (For the last of these, for example, the federal government should take the lead in sponsoring an annual conference at which all those charged with devising educational innovations can hear from the best and brightest about past experiments that have and have not worked.) If in three years Americans could develop a fighter plane the equal of any in the world, within a decade they should be able to discover ways of modifying educational opportunities available to the nation's children so that more of those children will be better prepared for the opportunities and responsibilities of adulthood.

This redesigning must incorporate powerful incentives, both positive and negative. Sprinkled throughout this country are the gifted few with the talent and creativity for developing educational improvements of the sort envisioned here. At present such people are among the most valuable and most underutilized resources in the nation. The first task is to find them, channel their energies, and reward them for successful innovations, including national recognition as well as financial compensation. But the appropriate role of incentives is far more general than this. For potential high school dropouts, for example, the prospective rewards for pursuing educational opportunities, including vocational training, must be superior – and must be seen by the students to be superior – to those available from alternatives that include reliance upon welfare and/or criminal activities. (A survey of inner city black male youths living in poverty areas in Boston, Chicago, and Philadelphia found that 71 percent who were not employed and not in school thought they could easily obtain a minimum-wage job, but still preferred "alternative opportunities."[100]) For the young and able, receipt of welfare might be tied to efforts by the recipient to upgrade his or her education and job skills. The state might offer to many children what philanthropist Eugene Lang offered to 61 sixth-graders of a Harlem school with dramatic results: the promise of financial aid for all those who finished high school and wished to continue on to college. (Governor Mario Cuomo has proposed just such a scheme in the form of "Liberty Scholarships" for low-income children of New York.[101]) With altered incentives and opportunities should come revised attitudes about personal options and personal responsibilities. However much "the system" is to blame for initial disadvantages, these are unlikely to be overcome in any decisive manner unless the disadvantaged child (aided and encouraged by the parent) comes to believe in the opportunities and accepts the responsibility for the personal initiative necessary to exploit those opportunities.

(4) *Such programs would cost too much*, or the more sophisticated variant, *their benefits would never exceed their costs.* Of all the criticisms sure to have widespread appeal, this one is the most compelling and the least likely to be turned aside by an abbreviated argument. It can nevertheless be challenged by an extended argument in four parts.

Before these are considered, two seemingly important matters can be brushed aside as having limited relevance. One is the present federal deficit. Large government expenditures of the sort contemplated here are out of the question, runs the argument, as long as the dominant fiscal priority in Washington is to shrink the federal deficit. But the deficit is shrinking, and barring unexpected catastrophes in the economy or the Congress, it will have largely disappeared in the next few years. That rate of disappearance may even accelerate if Soviet arms agreements permit some cutbacks (even of a marginal nature) in military spending. The initial discussion and planning stage for a set of programs as broad as those advocated above is sure to take several years. To dismiss such programs as fiscally not feasible is therefore to shelve a long-range plan because of short-run problems that, with the exercise of any fiscal sense, should be well on the way to being resolved by the time such plans would begin to have significant expenditure implications.

A second plea that, on first hearing, sounds equally appealing can also be ignored. The topic is not fiscal feasibility but method of assessment. In venturing a number of proposals of their own, the National Governors' Association urged an approach now popular in Washington, namely, "to translate the 'investment in human resources' rhetoric into a credible, durable dollars-and-cents case that such policies are in the long-term national interest."[102] Many efforts have been made to subject previous education and training programs to this "dollar-and-cents" test, actual costs and prospective benefits all being translated into monetary terms to show whether benefits have exceeded, or are likely to exceed, costs. The difficulty is that while most costs are known, likely benefits are hard to gauge. To calculate the dollar value of benefits for a program such as Head Start or the Job Corps, one must estimate what the earnings capability and welfare dependency and criminal activity of participants would have been if they had not participated. All benefit estimates must therefore be based upon assumptions about participant behavior in a world that never was (the world minus the program in question), and as such are open to question and have been questioned.[103] For programs of the sort advocated above, therefore, the plea to quantify all costs and benefits, however reasonable it may seem, is actually a call to cloak with an aura of precision the results of thought processes that are speculative in the extreme.

Clearly prospective costs will not be trivial. And as Senator Everett Dirksen was fond of point out, a billion here and a billion there, and the first thing you know, you are talking real money. How can one hope to demonstrate that for such large expenditures, prospective benefits will be larger still? One possibility is a general discussion of the benefits involved, with the hope that once the kinds of benefits are made clear, a case for further exploration of the programs will have gained some credibility.

As indicated above, most of the likely benefits can be grouped under four broad headings.

The first of these involves not so much achieving benefits narrowly defined as achieving consistency (or a better consistency) with a time-honored American ideal. At issue is the extent to which the reality confronting the children of the nation is at variance with the goal of equality of opportunity. Nineteenth century educator Horace Mann viewed education in America as "the great equalizer." However relevant that viewpoint was in the nineteenth century, it is far more relevant today. The above proposals in essence are designed to broaden the concept of public education and to put in place programs consistent with that broader definition. Although designed for all children, those that would particularly benefit are children from disadvantaged backgrounds. These in turn encompass far more than a handful of minority youths living in urban ghettos. Only 7 percent of the nation's poor live in large cities in poverty areas, defined as areas in which 40 percent or more of the residents are officially classified as poor.[104] Of the more than 12 million children in this country whose families are poor, three in five are white.

The second set of benefits – and probably the first to come to mind – relate to prospective improvements in the functioning of the economy. Better educated workers should lead to higher productivity, lower unemployment, fewer adults dependent upon welfare, and lower expenditures for crime prevention. While the direction from cause to effect is relatively clear – from program implementation to a better educated labor force to a particular economic gain – the magnitude of prospective gains is not. What then might usefully be said about economic benefits that would result from an integrated set of programs designed to expand educational opportunities at every level of the education process, beginning with day care for preschool children and ending with vocational training for high school graduates?

We do not know the likely improvement in the skills of the least skilled workers, but we do know that defective skills mean higher costs and lower profits for American business firms. A few examples:[105]

a steel-mill worker who misordered $1 million in parts because of his incapacity to read instructions;
an insurance clerk who paid a claimant $2,200 instead of $22 because she did not understand decimals;
a feed-lot worker who fed poison to a pen of cattle because he misread the label.

These costs of productivity forgone and outright losses help to explain why business firms are currently allocating billions of dollars to education and training programs, a significant proportion of which is being used to fund remedial programs for overcoming employee deficiencies in such basic skills as reading, writing, and arithmetic. (A 1985 survey of Fortune 1000 companies for example, found that about half were involved in basic skills instruction.[106]) The loss in national output from defective labor skills, whatever its present magnitude, is likely to become larger in the future. Current forecasts call for a much higher rate of growth in high-skill jobs than low-skill jobs in the next decade at a time when new additions to the labor force will include twice as many minority workers as white male workers, largely because of racial differences in birth rates.[107] Productivity at home and competitiveness abroad will therefore depend upon the education system turning out a higher average quality of student than in the past.

If children become better educated, we do not know how many fewer adults will be unemployed, but we do know that unemployment is expensive. Beginning in 1975, the nation has compiled one of the worst unemployment records of the twentieth century, with the annual rate in most years averaging 7 percent or more. Part of the explanation is rising structural unemployment, which in turn is partly attributable to a growing mismatch between skills demanded in the work place and those offered by the least skilled youths emerging from the educational system. If an upgraded labor force could reduce the unemployment rate by one percentage point, with those who otherwise would not find work now earning little better than the minimum wage (the latter an assumption likely to prove much too low), the prospective annual increment to gross national product would be of the order of $10 billion.

If children confronted better educational opportunities, we do not know how many fewer teenagers would drop out of high school, but we do know that dropouts are expensive. Compared with high school graduates, dropouts are far less likely to seek work; if they seek work, they are far less likely to find it; and if they seek work and find it, they are almost sure to earn much less.[108]

If children became better educated, we do not know how many fewer adults would depend upon welfare, but we do know that welfare is expensive. If better education while in school would raise the earnings of the least skilled to a level only one dollar an hour above the minimum wage, over time the result would be the near total disappearance of Americans (now numbering two million) who work full time and yet have incomes below the poverty line.[109]

If the least advantaged become better educated, we do not know how many youths would be diverted from criminal activity, but we do know that crime prevention is expensive. The nation's federal and state prisons are already loaded beyond capacity, and despite that overloading, the cost of imprisoning a male adult for one year is not significantly different from the cost of sending a student to Harvard for a year.[110]

All the above arguments can be compressed into a single counterfactual speculation. Consider two Americas as of the year 2000, one in which the present education system with all its attendant limitations and failures persists largely unchanged, and one in which educational opportunities have been dramatically improved by a set of comprehensive and integrated programs of the sort envisioned here. The question of net economic benefits then becomes: Which of the two is likely to have the larger gross national product (or gross national product per capita)? One answer from those who presume they know the answer has occasionally been cast as an invitation to explore an unattractive option: "If you think education is too expensive, try ignorance."[111]

The third set of benefits concerns not the quality of the work force needed for a market economy but the quality of citizens needed for a democracy. The linkages between the intellectual training of the youth, the character of adult citizens, and the welfare of the community are recurring themes among all those who have speculated about the importance of education – from Aristotle to Erasmus, from Diogenes to Disraeli. The Founding Fathers of a new nation, as one would expect, were given to similar speculations. For John Adams, the improvements in humanity made possible "by early education and constant discipline" were "truly sublime and astonishing."[112] His collegue Jefferson, an unyielding advocate of more accessible schooling, understood the obvious. If the fate of the republic depended in part upon talented leadership and an informed electorate, an education system must be devised to develop both. If "we hope to avail the state of those talents which nature has sown as liberally among the poor as the rich, but which perish without use if not sought for and cultivated,"[113] then education must be accessible to rich and poor alike. If "the people themselves" are the only "safe depository of the ultimate powers of the society," then they must be "enlightened enough to exercise their control with a wholesome discretion . . . ."[114] The latter point was made in less archaic language in the Texas Declaration of Independence: "it is an axiom, in political science, that unless a people are educated and enlightened it is idle to expect the continuance of civil liberty, or the capacity for self-government."[115]

Here too the problem of judging likely benefits from an expanded education system of the sort proposed above can be put as a counterfactual. Imagine two Americas in the twenty-first century; one in which the present possibilities for disadvantaged children persist substantially unchanged, with all the associated implications for a significant segment of the adult population having limited literacy, few marketable skills, little sense of opportunity and thus little sense of personal responsibility; and the other in which that disadvantaged segment has been significantly reduced by improved educational opportunities. The questions then become how large a shrinkage is likely to be achieved, and what benefits will follow for the functioning of a democracy. Phrased this way, the inescapable vagueness in resulting forecasts becomes clear. But to run the argument in reverse, what is also clear (or reasonably so) is that the larger this segment of the population becomes who are neither educated nor enlightened, the more tenuous become the very foundations of democracy.

The final set of benefits might be viewed as an extension of points just made. Those lacking the education and the opportunities to become responsible citizens, because of their own sense of having negligible opportunities in a land of opportunity, are likely to become alienated and a source of "social unrest" – a vague phrase meant to cover everything from increased ghetto crime rates to rioting or rebellion. Often quoted in this context (and indeed, quoted in a previous chapter) is John Kennedy's observation that "If a free society cannot help the many who are poor, it cannot save the few who are rich."[116] But this particular insight is an old one linking poverty, exclusion from opportunities, and social instability. In the depths of the Great Depression, one of Chicago's more successful bankers resorted to the conventional imagery of a social ladder to make the conventional point in language not that different from Kennedy's: "I have come to the conclusion that unless we make certain that people in the lower scale of income have their feet upon the ladder there is no security for us who are at the top."[117]

The American Dream has always been part myth. For two centuries, however, the reality of economic and social developments has constantly provided instances for the many to suggest they too may get their feet upon the ladder. And once upon that ladder, most have believed that upward movement is crucially dependent upon personal effort and talent as well as upon luck. If the dream is now shattered for large segments of society, one can surely expect unrest among the ruins. Or put another way, a shattering of the belief in the American Dream in the minds of a significant segment of the population is not only unkind, unfair, and un-American. It is downright dangerous. Perhaps the final word, and final warning, should be that of Langston Hughes:[118]

> What happens to a dream deferred?
> Does it dry up
> like a raisin in the sun?
> Or fester like a sore –
> And then run?
> Does it stink like rotten meat?
> Or crust and sugar over –
> like a syrupy sweet?
>
> Maybe it just sags
> like a heavy load.
>
> *Or does it explode?*

Conclusion

In 1987, a year marked by bicentennial celebrations of the signing of the Constitution, "to celebrate the community we really are" public television presented a collection of musical segments from previous programs, entitling the resulting one-hour special "Of Thee We Sing." The settings for the segments ranged across America, from a baptist church in the Midwest to a Las Vegas concert, from children dancing on a Broadway stage to members of the East Hampton High School Band parading down main street. The songs touched on many themes at many levels. Singers included profes-sionals and amateurs, the famous and the unknown: folk artists pleading social causes and gospel singers affirming their faith; Metropolitan Opera stars performing in a public park, and the audience itself providing the chorus for a "sing-it-yourself" performance of Handel's *Messiah*; Diana Ross urging night club patrons to "Reach out and touch somebody's hand," and war veterans, arms linked, singing "Homeward Bound." The finale of the one-hour special, in keeping with its title "Of Thee We Sing," featured the folk trio Peter, Paul, and Mary singing with a concert hall audience "This Land Is Your Land." As the opening chorus ended and the first verse began, the singers faded from the television screen and in their stead were shown, with changes paced to match the music, a variety of scenes of Americans working and at play. Some featured isolation and individual accomplish-ment: solitary figures painting or fishing, on horseback or in a kayak, feeding cattle or sweeping a storefront sidewalk. Others featured communal inter-action: a mounted policeman giving directions to a motorist, children playing on a beach, veterans embracing at the Washington Vietnam Memorial. These same two themes – the communal and the individual – are echoed in the words of Woody Guthrie's song of praise to his native land. Each verse begins with an assertion about self:

I roamed and rambled, and followed my footsteps . . . ;

but each culminates with a declaration deliberately in the plural:

This land was made for you and me.

America's is a deeply cross-grained culture.

Appendix A

American Opinion Polls and Economic Justice

Opinion polls are both an important and imperfect source of evidence on popular opinions concerning economic justice. Their importance stems largely from their claim to comprehensiveness, a claim anchored largely in the size of a given sample and efforts made to adhere to the canons of random selection. Their defects are legion, of which two are particularly troubling for this study. First, the questions asked are seldom those that one would wish if the task is to discover public views on such matters as the fairness of the economic race and the appropriateness of any given income distribution. Secondly, responses reported are often crucially dependent upon the wording of the question asked – a common problem in opinion polls, but one raising special difficulties in matters of economic justice, as will be discussed below.

A cursory review of opinion polls taken in this country from the 1930s to the present suggests widespread support for the following:

1 a belief in the work ethic, in the merits of competition to foster excellence and personal self-development, and in the capitalist or free enterprise system;
2 a belief that the economic race is reasonably fair, and that the rewards won in the form of incomes earned reflect to a significant degree the exercise of talent and diligence by the competitors;
3 a belief that inequalities in income payments are needed to preserve incentives, combined with a reluctance to endorse any major effort to redistribute income to achieve *markedly* greater equality; and finally,
4 a belief that the able-bodied poor are, to a significant degree, responsible for their own economic fate, and thus assistance for these poor should be confined primarily to training and/or work relief and should not feature much in the way of cash payments or "the dole," the latter generally condemned as fostering indolence and dependency.

A more careful sifting of poll results indicates that popular endorsement is somewhat qualified (if not somewhat confused) for some of these ideas, but not for all.

Most Americans seem to have few, if any, significant doubts about the merits of the work ethic, competition, and the free enterprise system.[1] Most Americans also seem to be relatively confident that the economic race is reasonably fair, and that the prizes won in terms of incomes received reflect the exercise of talent and hard work.[2] Popular judgments about the "fairness" of the present income distribution and the related issue of the desirability of income redistribution seem to be heavily dependent upon the wording chosen in the question asked. For example, Americans seem to be reluctant to label any existing income distribution as "exactly right," and often admit to reservations about their own rate of pay. In one survey on the latter subject, only 28 percent claimed they were "fairly paid," and a further 40 percent felt they were either "slightly" or "somewhat" overpaid or underpaid.[3] On the subject of income distribution in general, if the question asked is phrased in vague and general terms a majority seem inclined to support the notion that the government should do "something" to "reduce the gap" between rich and poor.[4] What should be done and by how much the gap should be reduced, however, are issues about which there is far less agreement. When the proposal has been phrased in terms of "taking money from those who have much and giving money to those who have little," about one-third or more have rejected the idea outright and roughly another quarter were willing to endorse the idea only with the added proviso "if it doesn't go too far." (How far is too far is of course the crucial issue.) If instead the question concerned the policy of deliberate redistribution "by heavy taxes on the rich," a majority of those polled rejected the idea outright.[5] Even stronger negative reactions have been consistently recorded to any suggestion that the government place a ceiling on the amount an individual should be allowed to earn.[6]

In sum, evidence from popular polls suggests that while Americans generally concede that income distribution within their society cannot be viewed as "perfectly" fair, and while they will endorse the notion, vaguely phrased, that "something" should be done to make it "more" fair, a majority still resist any policy proposal deliberately designed to effect a "major" redistribution from rich to poor, or (what amounts to the same thing) they tend to oppose any "major" effort to make observed results from the economic race more equal.

Attitudes toward the poor vary, depending upon who is assumed to be in that set: the able-bodied, or those who are incapable of work, or both.

Concerning the able-bodied poor, Americans tend to endorse a set of ideas consistent with the work ethic and the presumed existence of "equality of opportunity," or at least "reasonably accessible" opportunities. Accordingly, policy proposals that evoke widespread support emphasize helping the able-bodied to help themselves, primarily by making available to them jobs, or training, or both, to help such individuals become economically self-sufficient. Aid in the form of cash assistance (or "the dole" or simply "welfare") is generally resisted if not condemned outright.[7] The popularity of the belief that the able-bodied poor do not deserve, and should not be given, cash assistance helps to explain the general endorsement of the view that "welfare cheating" is widespread.[8] If (a) many of those receiving welfare payments are believed to be able-bodied and (b) such assistance for the able-bodied tends to be regarded as inappropriate, then (c) the temptation is to view able-bodied recipients as "cheaters," and such payments – presumed to be widespread – as indicative of widespread welfare cheating.

Quite different attitudes are much in evidence if poll results concern the poor who are "truly needy," with that phrase usually applied to those who are not able-bodied and thus are not capable of work. For these people, the vast majority of Americans readily endorse the notion that the government has a responsibility to offer some provision precisely because such people are judged to be incapable of providing for themselves.[9]

Poll results such as those cited are merely part of a vast array of evidence indicating that Americans have preserved from colonial times to the present the distinction between the "deserving poor" and the "undeserving poor," with this distinction turning largely upon the ability to work. If polls of the public fail to make clear which of these two is the subject of a question, however, the answers can often seem to be contradictory. Proposals to expand "welfare" are a case in point. Unclear who the beneficiaries of expansion are to be, and suspicious about the prevalence of "welfare cheaters" partly for the reasons noted, most Americans when asked have not favored "welfare expansion."[10] If instead the question is phrased to suggest the beneficiaries will be the "truly needy" (and only or primarily the "truly needy"), then Americans are far more disposed to endorse expansion.[11] Similar confusions are evident in poll results attempting to determine popular views about why the poor are poor. For reasons previously cited, most Americans are inclined to view the able-bodied poor as largely responsible for their own economic fate. (If they are able-bodied, the dominant view seems to be, opportunities for work are sufficiently available for these poor, "by applying themselves," to solve or at least greatly reduce their own poverty.) The "truly needy," in contrast, are widely regarded (almost by definition, it could be argued) as not responsible for their own economic deprivation. Crucial as this distinction is, most opinion polls fail to make clear which category of "the poor" is the subject of inquiry. A common way to phrase the question is:

Which is more often to blame if a person is poor?

with the possible responses limited to (a) lack of effort, (b) circumstances (by implication, beyond the individual's control), and (c) both. Confronted with this vagueness and these choices, roughly one-third of those polled opted for each of the choices noted.[12] Had the question been rephrased to refer unambiguously to "the truly needy," these results almost surely would have been dramatically different. As for the able-bodied poor, other responses to other polls do suggest that a majority of Americans regard such people as bearing a large share of the responsibility for their own poverty.[13]

All of the above citations refer to polls of "the general public." Evidence of support for similar ideas among more narrowly defined constituencies can be found in a variety of sources.[14]

Appendix B

Supplementary Tables for Chapter 10

Table B.1 Aid to Families with Dependent Children: average monthly number of recipients and average monthly payment, 1936–1983

	Average monthly number of recipients (thousand)			Average monthly payment (constant 1983 dollars)	
Calendar year	Families	Total	Children	Per family	Per recipient
1936	147	534	361	202.41	55.73
1940	349	1,182	840	227.21	67.00
1945	259	907	656	266.73	76.12
1950	644	2,205	1,637	295.21	73.01
1955	612	2,214	1,673	313.17	86.54
1960	787	3,005	2,314	355.76	93.36
1961	869	3,354	2,587	369.57	95.71
1962	931	3,676	2,818	383.05	96.96
1963	947	3,876	2,909	391.11	95.54
1964	992	4,118	3,091	407.55	98.19
1965	1,039	4,329	3,256	420.60	100.92
1966	1,088	4,513	3,411	438.48	105.67
1967	1,217	5,014	3,771	463.09	112.41
1968	1,410	5,705	4,275	482.28	119.19
1969	1,698	6,706	4,985	475.29	120.34
1970	2,208	8,466	6,214	469.87	122.57
1971	2,762	10,241	7,434	460.42	124.18
1972	3,049	10,947	7,905	449.79	125.27
1973	3,148	10,949	7,902	428.01	123.06
1974	3,230	10,864	7,822	412.69	122.67
1975	3,498	11,346	8,095	406.21	125.23
1976	3,579	11,304	8,001	413.21	130.82
1977	3,588	11,050	7,773	404.89	131.48
1978	3,522	10,570	7,402	387.72	129.19
1979	3,509	10,312	7,179	360.80	122.78
1980	3,712	10,774	7,419	338.58	116.66
1981	3,835	11,079	7,527	308.96	106.96
1982	3,542	10,358	6,903	312.77	106.93
1983	3,671	10,737	7,106	312.88	107.20

Source: US Congress, House, Committee on Ways and Means, *Children in Poverty*, 99th Cong., 1st sess., May 22, 1985, pp. 190–91

Table B.2 Families receiving Aid to Families with Dependent Children and poor families, 1960–1983

	AFDC families (thousands)	Poor families with related children under 18 (thousands)	AFDC families per 100 poor families with related children under 18
1960	787	5,328	14.8
1961	869	5,500	15.8
1962	931	5,460	17.1
1963	947	4,991	19.0
1964	992	4,771	20.8
1965	1,039	4,379	23.7
1966	1,088	3,734	29.1
1967	1,217	3,586	33.9
1968	1,410	3,347	42.1
1969	1,698	3,226	52.6
1970	2,208	3,491	63.2
1971	2,762	3,682	75.0
1972	3,049	3,621	84.2
1973	3,148	3,520	89.4
1974	3,230	3,875	83.4
1975	3,498	4,172	83.8
1976	3,579	4,060	88.2
1977	3,588	4,082	87.9
1978	3,522	4,060	86.7
1979	3,509	3,955	88.7
1980	3,712	4,822	77.0
1981	3,835	5,191	73.9
1982	3,542	5,712	62.0
1983	3,679	5,849	62.9

Source: US Congress, House, Committee on Ways and Means, *Children in Poverty*, 99th Cong., 1st sess., May 22, 1985, pp. 192

Table B.3 United States: percentage of families with female head, 1957–1984

	White	All other		Spanish origin
		Total	*Black*	*Spanish origin*
1957	8.9	21.9		
1958	8.6	22.4		
1959	8.4	23.6		
1960	8.7	22.4	21.7	
1961	8.9	21.6		
1962	8.6	23.2		
1963	8.5	24.4		
1964	8.9	22.7		
1965	9.0	23.7	24.9	
1966	8.9	23.7		
1967	9.1	23.7		
1968	8.9	26.4		
1969	8.9	27.3		
1970	9.0	26.8	28.3	
1971	9.4	28.9	30.6	
1972	9.4	30.1	31.8	
1973	9.6	32.8	34.6	16.7
1974	9.9	31.8	34.0	17.4
1975	10.5	32.4	35.3	18.8
1976	10.8	33.0	35.9	20.9
1977	10.9	33.9	37.1	20.0
1978	11.5	36.0	39.2	20.3
1979	11.6	36.8	40.5	19.8
1980	11.6	36.6	40.2	19.2
1981	11.9	37.1	41.7	21.8
1982	12.4	35.9	40.6	22.7
1983	12.2	37.1	41.9	22.8
1984	12.6	38.4	43.1	22.7

Sources: US Department of Commerce, *Statistical Abstract of the United States, 1958*, p. 47; *1959*, p. 43; *1960*, p. 43; *1961*, p. 39; *1962*, p. 43; *1963*, p. 42; *1964*, p. 37; *1965*, p. 37; *1966*, p. 37; *1967*, p. 38; *1969*, p. 36; *1970*, p. 36; *1971*, p. 37; *1972*, p. 38; *1973*, p. 40; *1974*, p. 40; *1976*, p. 40; *1977*, p. 43; *1978*, p. 46; *1979*, p. 47; *1980*, p. 48; *1981*, p. 43; *1982/83*, p. 46; *1984*, p. 48; *1985*, p. 41; *1986*, p. 40; William Julius Wilson and Kathryn M. Neckerman, "Poverty and family structure: the widening gap between evidence and public policy issues," in Sheldon H. Danziger and Daniel H. Weinberg (eds), *Fighting Poverty* (Cambridge, MA: Harvard University Press, 1986), p. 235; US Department of Commerce, *Current Population Reports*, Series P–20, table 1 in no. 371, no. 381, no. 388, no. 398

Table B.4 Maximum monthly potential benefits, Aid to Families with Dependent Children and food stamps – one-parent family of three persons, January 1984

State	Maximum AFDC grant ($)	Food stamp benefits ($)	Combined benefits ($)	Combined benefits as percent of esimated 1983 poverty threshold (%)
Alabama	118	199	317	48
Alaska	696	196	892	108
Arizona	233	193	426	64
Arkansas	164	199	363	55
California	526	105	631	95
Colorado	336	162	498	75
Connecticut	529	104	633	96
Delaware	287	177	464	70
District of Columbia	299	173	472	71
Florida	231	193	424	64
Georgia	202	199	401	61
Hawaii	468	234	702	92
Idaho	305	171	476	72
Illinois	302	172	474	72
Indiana	258	185	443	67
Iowa	360	155	515	78
Kansas	364	154	518	78
Kentucky	188	199	387	58
Louisiana	190	199	389	59
Maine	341	160	501	76
Maryland	295	182	477	72
Massachusetts	379	149	528	80
Michigan				
Washtenaw County	445	129	574	87
Wayne County	418	137	555	84
Minnesota	500	113	613	93
Mississippi	96	199	295	45
Missouri	261	184	445	67
Montana	332	163	495	75
Nebraska	350	158	508	77
Nevada	228	194	422	64
New Hampshire	341	160	501	76

Table B.4 *continued*

New Jersey	360	155	515	78
New Mexico	258	185	443	67
New York				
Suffolk County	579	98	677	102
New York City	474	130	604	91
North Carolina	202	199	401	61
North Dakota	357	156	513	78
Ohio	276	180	456	69
Oklahoma	282	178	460	70
Oregon	368	188	556	84
Pennsylvania	350	158	508	77
Rhode Island	462	157	619	94
South Carolina	142	199	341	52
South Dakota	321	166	487	74
Tennessee	127	199	326	49
Texas	148	199	347	52
Utah	362	154	516	78
Vermont	530	104	634	96
Virginia	310	170	480	73
Washington	462	134	596	90
West Virginia	206	199	405	61
Wisconsin	513	109	622	94
Wyoming	325	165	490	74
Guam	265	293	558	84
Puerto Rico	100	151	251	38
Virgin Islands	209	243	452	68
Median AFDC State	321	166	487	74

Source: US Congress, House, Committee on Ways and Means, *Background Material and Data on Programs Within the Jurisdiction of the Committee on Ways and Means*, 98th Cong., 2nd sess., February 21, 1984, pp. 299–300

Table B.5 United States: marriage and divorce rates, 1940–1984

	Marriage rate	Divorce rate	
	per 1,000 women 15 years and over	per 1,000 women 15 years and over	per 1,000 children under 18 years of age
1940	82.8	8.8	
1941	88.5	9.4	
1942	93.0	10.1	
1943	83.0	11.0	
1944	76.5	12.0	
1945	83.6	14.4	
1946	118.1	17.9	
1947	106.2	13.6	
1948	98.5	11.2	
1949	86.7	10.6	
1950	90.2	10.3	6.3
1951	86.6	9.9	6.1
1952	83.2	10.1	6.2
1953	83.7	9.9	6.4
1954	79.8	9.5	6.4
1955	80.9	9.3	6.3
1956	82.4	9.4	6.3
1957	78.0	9.2	6.4
1958	72.0	8.9	6.5
1959	73.6	9.3	7.5
1960	73.5	9.2	7.2
1961	72.2	9.6	7.8
1962	71.2	9.4	7.9
1963	73.4	9.6	8.2
1964	74.6	10.0	8.7
1965	75.0	10.6	8.9
1966	75.6	10.9	9.5
1967	76.4	11.2	9.9
1968	79.1	12.5	11.1
1969	80.0	13.4	11.9
1970	76.5	14.9	12.5
1971	76.2	15.8	13.6
1972	77.9	17.0	14.7
1973	76.0	18.2	15.7
1974	72.0	19.3	16.2
1975	66.9	20.3	16.7
1976	65.2	21.1	16.9
1977	63.6	21.1	16.7
1978	64.1	21.9	17.7
1979	63.6	22.8	18.4
1980	61.4	22.6	17.3
1981	61.7	22.6	18.7
1982	61.4	21.7	17.6
1983	59.9	21.3	17.4
1984		21.5	17.2

Sources: US Department of Health and Human Services, *Monthly Vital Statistics Report*, vol. XXXV, no. 1, supplement, May 2, 1986, p. 5; no. 6, supplement, September 25, 1986, pp. 5, 7

Table B.6 United States: births to unmarried women, 1940–1984 (ratio per 1,000 live births)[a]

	White	All other	
		Total	Black[b]
1940	19.5	168.3	
1941	19.0	174.5	
1942	16.9	169.2	
1943	16.5	162.8	
1944	20.2	163.4	
1945	23.6	179.3	
1946	21.1	170.1	
1947	18.5	168.0	
1948	17.8	164.7	
1949	17.3	167.5	
1950	17.5	179.6	
1951	16.3	182.8	
1952	16.3	183.4	
1953	16.9	191.1	
1954	18.2	198.5	
1955	18.6	202.4	
1956	19.0	204.0	
1957	19.6	206.7	
1958	20.9	212.3	
1959	22.1	218.0	
1960	22.9	215.8	
1961	25.3	223.4	
1962	27.0	227.8	
1963	30.4	235.5	
1964	33.9	245.0	
1965	39.5	263.2	
1966	44.4	276.5	
1967	48.7	293.8	
1968	53.3	312.0	
1969	54.7	325.1	348.7
1970	56.6	349.3	375.8
1971	56.1	373.3	405.3
1972	60.4	402.6	439.1
1973	63.9	416.9	457.5
1974	65.4	427.3	470.9
1975	73.0	441.7	487.9
1976	76.8	451.5	503.0
1977	81.8	464.9	517.4
1978	87.1	475.6	532.0
1979	93.6	488.1	546.5
1980	101.5	489.5	554.6
1981	115.9	485.1	559.5
1982	120.7	487.5	566.8
1983	127.7	499.5	582.0
1984	134.1	507.5	592.0

[a] Data for 1940–1980, "estimated"; for 1981–4 "reported/inferred."
[b] Data for "Black" not available prior to 1969.

Sources: US Department of Health and Human Services, *Vital Statistics of the United States, 1982* (Hyattsville, MD: National Center for Health Statistics, 1986), vol. I, *Natality*, table 1–31, p. 53, and *Monthly Vital Statistics Report*, vol. XXXIV, no. 6, supplement, September 20, 1985, table 16, p. 30; vol. XXXV, no. 4, supplement, July 18, 1986, table 16, p. 30

Table B.7 Monthly welfare benefits in Pennsylvania for a single parent with two children

Earned income ($)	AFDC payment ($)	Food stamps ($)	Net taxes[a] ($)	Disposable income[b] ($)	Implicit marginal tax rate[c] (%)
0	318	138	0	456	0
100	224	140	6	458	98
200	130	142	12	460	98
300	35	144	17	462	98
400	0	119	23	496	66
500	0	81	44	537	59
600	0	54	83	571	66
700	0	0	110	590	81
800	0	0	138	664	26
900	0	0	176	724	40
1,000	0	0	208	792	32

[a] Includes earned-income credit and $40 allowance for transportation expenses.
[b] Disposable income equals gross earnings plus food stamps, plus AFDC, minus net taxes (payroll, state, and federal income taxes).
[c] Defined as the percentage of the increase in earned income that is offset by benefit reductions.

Source: Barry P. Bosworth, *Tax Incentives and Economic Growth* (Washington, DC: Brookings Institution, 1984), p. 165

Appendix C

Supplementary Tables for Chapter 13

Table C.1 Selected measures of educational attainment by ethnic or racial group and sex, persons aged 23–35 in 1980

	Mean grades completed		Percentage completing less than grade 9		Percentage high school graduates		Percentage with some college	
	Men	Women	Men	Women	Men	Women	Men	Women
North American Indians	12.1	11.9	8.9	7.7	71.6	71.3	34.3	28.2
Asian Indians	15.9	14.5	2.2	6.4	94.1	84.7	84.6	72.0
Chinese	14.9	14.1	5.3	7.5	90.1	86.9	77.0	67.2
Filipinos	13.7	14.0	3.4	8.0	88.5	84.8	62.3	66.0
Japanese	14.8	14.5	1.1	1.1	96.9	95.4	75.8	71.2
Korean	14.4	12.4	3.0	12.4	93.4	78.5	69.8	42.6
Vietnamese	12.4	11.1	12.9	24.6	79.7	61.5	48.2	31.4
Hispanic	10.4	10.5	29.7	28.1	50.6	51.5	21.2	19.5
Black[a]	12.0	12.2	7.7	6.1	71.6	72.5	30.9	33.7
White[b]	13.4	13.1	4.5	3.3	86.4	85.7	49.9	44.7

[a] "Non-Hispanic black."
[b] "Non-Hispanic white."

Source: Robert D. Mare and Christopher Winship, "Ethnic and racial patterns of educational attainment and school enrollment," Paper presented at conference on Minorities in Poverty, Airlie, VA, November 1986 reproduced in "Conference summary," *Focus*, University of Wisconsin Institute for Research on Poverty, X (Summer 1987), p. 5

Table C.2 Mean income and incidence of poverty by family type, 1984

	White	Black	Hispanic
Composition of families with children (%)			
Two parent	80.2	44.1	70.5
Single parent, male	3.3	4.1	4.0
Single parent, female	16.5	51.8	25.5
	100.0	100.0	100.0
Incidence of poverty (%)			
All families with children	14	39	31
All two-parent families with children	9	19	23
All female-headed families with children	41	61	63
Mean real income (1984 dollars)			
All families with children	31,298	18,504	21,663
All two-parent families with children	34,954	28,096	25,777
All female-headed families with children	14,611	10,522	10,560

Sources: Sheldon Danziger and Peter Gottschalk, "How have families with children been faring?" University of Wisconsin Institute for Research on Poverty Discussion Paper 801–86, January 1986, pp. 10, 24; "The changing economic circumstances of children: families losing ground," *Focus*, University of Wisconsin Institute for Research on Poverty, IX (Spring 1986), p. 7

Table C.3 Differentials in median family income and poverty rates, 1960–1980 (in 1985 dollars)

	Median income[a] ($)		
	Married-couple families	Single-headed families	Absolute poverty rate, all families[b] (%)
Blacks			
1960	11,210	5,092	47.8
1970	19,888	9,328	29.8
1980	24,430	11,084	26.3
Percentage change, 1960–80	+117.9	+117.7	−45.0
Mexicans			
1960	14,809	6,792	37.7
1970	20,370	9,873	28.3
1980	23,195	11,841	21.7
Percentage change, 1960–80	+56.6	+74.3	−42.4
Puerto Ricans			
1960	13,230	8,545	35.8
1970	18,776	8,726	28.8
1980	20,951	7,228	34.9
Percentage change, 1960–80	+58.4	−15.4	−2.5
Other Hispanics			
1960	16,213	7,110	31.7
1970	25,011	13,058	20.7
1980	26,901	13,543	16.1
Percentage change, 1960–80	+65.9	+90.5	−49.2
American Indians			
1960	11,673	5,835	54.2
1970	20,311	7,832	29.5
1980	24,919	10,912	20.5
Percentage change, 1960–80	+113.5	+87.0	−62.2
Whites[c]			
1960	20,569	12,699	14.6
1970	29,291	17,313	8.1
1980	31,978	17,935	6.5
Percentage change, 1960–80	+55.5	+41.2	−55.5

[a] In 1985 dollars.
[b] Using official poverty thresholds, which are based on cash income before taxes.
[c] "Non-Hispanic whites."

Source: Marta Tienda and Leif Jensen, "Poverty and minorities: a quarter century profile of labor and socioeconomic disadvantage," paper presented at conference on Minorities in Poverty, Airlie, VA, November 1986, Tables 3 and 4 (data from Public Use Microdata files of the decenial censuses), reproduced in "The declining economic status of Puerto Ricans," *Focus*, University of Wisconsin Institute for Research on Poverty, X (Summer 1987), p. 26

Table C.4 Percentage distribution of principal type of child care arrangements used by employed mothers 18–44 years old for their youngest child under 5 years: June 1982

| | Total | Age of youngest child | | |
		Less than 1	1–2 years old	3–4 years old
Number of mothers (thousands)[a]	5,086	1,116	2,284	1,644
Total (percent)	100.0	100.0	100.0	100.0
Care in child's home	30.5	34.3	33.3	24.6
By father	13.9	13.9	15.8	11.0
By grandparent	5.9	8.9	6.3	3.6
By other relative	5.2	5.1	5.0	5.7
By nonrelative	5.5	6.4	6.2	4.3
Care in another home	40.2	42.7	43.0	35.4
By grandparent	11.3	13.5	10.5	11.0
By other relative	6.9	6.2	7.3	7.1
By nonrelative	22.0	23.0	25.2	17.3
Group care center	14.8	5.3	11.7	25.8
Nursery school	5.6	1.7	3.2	11.7
Day care center	9.2	3.6	8.5	14.1
Mother cares for child[b]	9.1	9.2	8.6	9.9
Other arrangements[c]	0.2	–	0.2	0.4
Don't know/No answer	5.1	8.6	3.3	3.9

[a] The total number of mothers includes women who did not report the age of their youngest child.
[b] Includes mother working at home or outside the home.
[c] Includes child taking care of self.

Source: US Department of Commerce, "Child care arrangements of working mothers: June 1982," *Current Population Reports*, Special Studies, Series P–23, no. 129, November 1983, table 2

Appendix D

The Marginal Productivity Theory of Factor Pricing

The Marginal Productivity Theory of Wages: An Agrarian Example

Economics has a long-standing tradition of illustrating complex phenomena with oversimplified examples, the simplicity designed to show the basic causal forces at work in everyday economic transactions. Following in those footsteps, let us imagine a farmer in a fairly primitive setting – say, upstate New York of the 1850s – who is wondering how many workers to employ on his newly acquired farm of 1,000 acres. Standing on his front porch are several youths with husky builds and high expectations of being hired. If the farmer is considering adding only one hired hand he would presumably ask himself: What would that one add to total farm output? Assume that the prospective crop is corn and the answer to the question is estimated by the farmer to be 400 bushels. (In the jargon of economics, 400 bushels is the worker's marginal physical product: "physical product," because that is what the worker would create; "marginal," because it is the addition to total output from adding one extra laborer.) A second question follows logically from the first. If one extra worker is expected to add 400 bushels, how much will that corn sell for? Again assume that the farmer can make a tolerably accurate estimate, and the estimate in this case is $2 a bushel. The farmer can then solve one problem, but must immediately face a second. The dollar amount the first worker hired will add to farm receipts is $800 (400 bushels × $2), or again in the jargon of economics, the worker's marginal physical product times the price of the output, with the resulting value termed, unsurprisingly, the value of the worker's marginal product. If unskilled farm labor is available in the area for $360 a year, clearly the farmer should hire one of the youths standing on his front porch at that wage. The expected addition to his revenue will be $800, the extra cost will be $360, and the gain in net receipts will be the difference between the two, or $440. But should the farmer also hire a second worker? As more workers are added, each one will work with (or "cooperate" with) less and less land, given the size of the farm is fixed at 1,000 acres. This is the law of diminishing returns, familiar to all farmers (or all who hope to continue farming) and to all beginning students of economics (or all who hope to pass the course). The law concerns the relationship between increments of physical units: outputs (in this case, corn) and inputs (in this case, labor). The central idea is that when one input is held constant (in our example, the amount of land is held constant at 1000 acres) then as each additional worker is added, the resulting increment in corn output attributable to the efforts of that extra worker (the marginal physical product of labor) will begin to decline in size after some point. The phrase "after some point" acknowledges the possibility that when the first few workers are added, the second *may* add more to total output than the first because the second (acting with the first) is able to initiate highly productive cooperation or specialization in different farm activities that was not possible before the second was added. The law of diminishing returns therefore may or may not set in when the first few workers are added to a fixed amount of land, but it certainly will set in if workers continue to be added.

To keep our example simple, assume that this law sets in immediately. If it only sets in after a number of workers were added, none of the main points about to be made would be affected. Assume further (economists are never daunted by assuming further) that the farm owner estimates how much each extra worker would add to total output, for each of ten prospective workers, and the results of that estimation are as documented in table D.1.

Table D.1 1850 corn farm of 1,000 acres: hypothetical relationship between workers hired and output created

I	*II*	*III*	*IV*
		Corn output added by last worker hired	
Total no. of workers hired	*Resulting total corn output (bushels)*	*Quantity*	*Value (corn prices; $2/bushels) ($)*
1	400	400	800
2	720	320	640
3	970	250	500
4	1,170	200	400
5	1,340	170	340
6	1,475	135	270
7	1,565	90	180
8	1,610	45	90
9	1,640	30	60
10	1,655	15	30

Notice three features of this table.

1   The first and second columns express an estimated relationship between two physical units, namely, number of laborers hired and resulting bushels of corn. To estimate such a relationship is crucial for any business that would maximize profits, although making such an estimate may be more difficult for some than for others.

2   The second column (total output) defines the third (marginal output); that is, each entry in the third column is just the difference between two successive total output figures in the second column.

3   The fourth column (the value of the worker's marginal product) is simply the third column (the worker's marginal physical output) multiplied by the price per bushel that corn is expected to fetch in the market place ($2.00).

This oversimplified example and associated numerical assumptions enable us to reach several important conclusions. One concerns the question noted earlier: How many workers should the farm owner hire? Table D.1 provides the answer. If the farmer wants to maximize net receipts, he will keep adding workers until the value of what the last one contributes to receipts barely exceeds (or is just equal to) the wage that must be paid to hire that particular worker. In our example, each farm laborer costs $360 per year; to hire a fourth worker would add $400 to total revenues; to hire a fifth would add only $340; accordingly, four workers are hired, but not the fifth.

At this point the reader unfamiliar with economics should be bothered by several unanswered questions. The first is: Why pay each farm hand the same wage? If the first worker adds $800 to total receipts, should not that worker be paid more than the "going wage" of $360? Alternatively, why not cut the wage offered to the fifth worker to something less than the value of his marginal product ($340) and hire that worker too? The answer to all three questions concerns how a labor market works. Each worker in that market is assumed to be no more and no less skilled than any other worker. (The question of differential skills will be considered later on; here, the key assumption in the jargon of economics is that all the laborers in the market are homogeneous.) The farm owner is therefore indifferent as to which four workers he hires. Further – and crucial to the argument – all workers in this labor market compete with one another for available jobs. That is what the word "market" implies. Although it is true that the first worker hired adds more to total receipts than the fourth, the farm owner pays both workers the same wage, namely, the going wage ($360), because that is all he must pay to hire workers. Similarly, if the farm owner tried to hire the fifth worker for something less than the going wage, that worker would turn him down and seek employment elsewhere.

Another question that the reader should be puzzled about is how that wage rate of $360 became established in the first place. A satisfactory answer requires a theory of wage determination. If such a theory can be constructed using marginal productivity analysis, and the same theory generalized to all factors of production (a theory of wages, by itself, explains only the payments made to one factor, namely, labor), then that generalized theory will constitute a theory of income distribution. And lest the point be lost in the details of our example, the primary concern was not to learn about nineteenth century corn farming, but to understand how one simple concept – marginal productivity – can be used to generate a theory of income distribution.

The first step, as noted, is to construct a theory of wages. Conventional economic analysis approaches such a problem by noting that the wage rate is simply a price (the price of labor), and like any other price, tends to be established by the forces of supply and demand operating in a competitive market (in this case, the labor market). The problem therefore reduces to specifying what the forces of supply and demand are in that market. As illustrated in the previous example, the demand for labor by a single producer is determined by that producer's estimates of the value of the marginal productivity of labor to him. The point can be made initially for one producer, and then collectively for all producers. In our example, the data in the fourth column of table D.1 indicated, for a particular corn farmer in upstate New York, what the value of the marginal product was expected to be for successive workers added to his farm. But those same data also indicated how many workers that corn farmer would want to hire (or be willing to demand) at different posible wage rates: at a wage rate of $800, he would want only one worker; at $640, two workers; at $500, three; and so on.

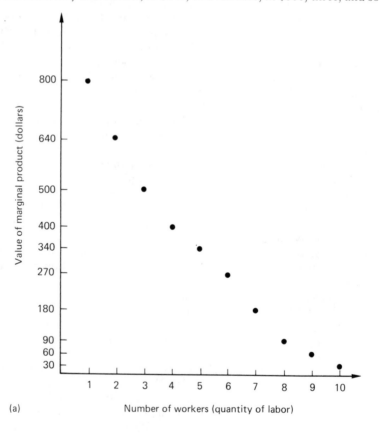

(a)   Number of workers (quantity of labor)

Figure D.1 (a) Value of worker's marginal product.

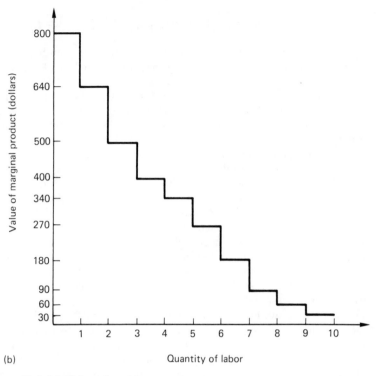

(b)

Figure D.1 (b) Value of worker's marginal product.

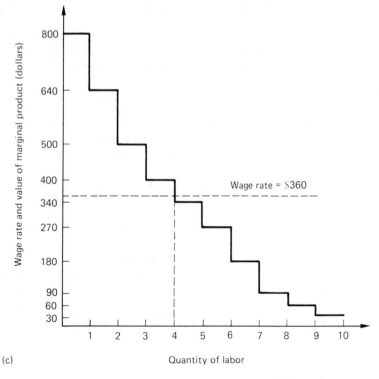

(c)

Figure D.1 (c) Wage rate and value of worker's marginal product.

This information could be plotted on a graph, where the number of workers is measured on the horizontal axis, and the value of each worker's marginal product is measured on the vertical axis, as in figure D.1(a). Each dot indicates, as workers are added to the farm, what the last one hired is expected to add to farm receipts (or the value of that particular worker's marginal product). The dots can then be joined to make a kind of step-function, as in figure D.1(b), with the declining steps indicating how the value of the marginal product of labor falls as workers are added to the farm.

This step-function can be viewed in two different ways. From one perspective, it portrays the value of labor's marginal product to a particular producer. From another perspective, precisely because the function portrays the value of labor's marginal product it can be viewed as that producer's demand curve for labor. For each possible wage, the step-function indicates how many workers that producer will want to hire. If the wage rate is, say, $360 per year, this can be represented by a horizontal straight line, as in figure D.1(c). The point where this horizontal line intersects the step-function will then indicate how many workers the farmer will want to hire at a price of $360 per worker.

The reader unfamiliar with economics will probably wonder why this excursion into two-dimensional geometry in pursuit of a theory of wages. The answer is that such geometry tends to be, for most individuals, a helpful way of illustrating the basic mechanics of a market. Two further steps are still required. The first is to construct an aggregate demand curve; the second, to construct an aggregate supply curve. The intersection of supply and demand will then indicate the price for labor that will tend to be established in our market.

First, the matter of aggregate demand. Within an area defined as "the labor market" will be a number of producers who will compete with each other for the available supply of workers. Each of those producers faces the same question as our original corn farmer: How many should I hire? To answer that question, each producer will do what the corn farmer did: attempt to estimate what the value of the marginal product will be as successive units of labor are added to his work force. The results of those estimates (as previously) can be plotted as a step-function, and each step-function (as previously) will portray the demand curve for labor of the producer who made the estimates. (No two of these step-functions, of course, will necessarily look the same.) Finally, all these numerical estimates can be added together and the results plotted to give an aggregate demand curve for labor, or what amounts to the same thing, all the individual step-functions can be added together to give an aggregate demand curve. (Geometrically, all that is required is to add all curves horizontally.) In either case, the resulting curve would indicate, for each possible wage rate, how many workers would be demanded by *all* potential users of labor in this particular labor market, as in figure D.2.

Notice two features of figure D.2. One is that the step-like appearance has disappeared (or almost disappeared) because with many would-be de-

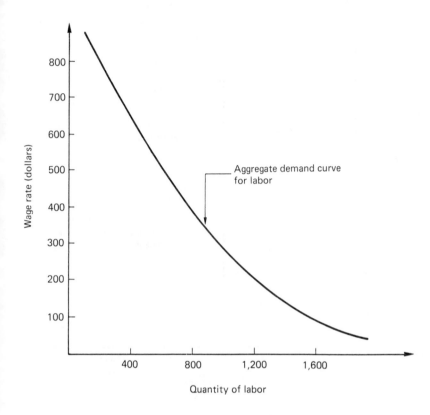

Figure D.2 Aggregate demand curve for labor.

manders in the market, the demand for workers will probably change for every small reduction in the wage rate. Secondly, while the scaling of the vertical axis remains unchanged, the scaling of the horizontal axis has been altered dramatically because now, for a given wage rate, hundreds of workers are demanded by many producers instead of a few workers demanded by one producer.

Finally, to issues of aggregate supply. One approach – the simplest one – is to assume that each potential worker in the area must work to survive, lacks alternative opportunities outside this particular labor market, and accordingly is willing to work whether the wage rate is high or low. If the area has, say, 843 workers, this willingness to work irrespective of variations in the wage rate would be portrayed by a vertical line at 843 laborers, as in figure D.3(a). The vertical line S in figure D.3(a) is the aggregate supply curve: it indicates, for each possible wage, how many workers will be willing

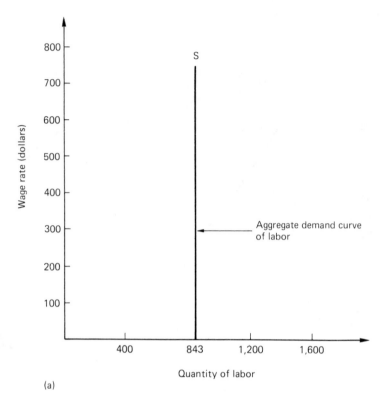

Figure D.3 (a) Aggregate supply curve of labor: no supply response to wage change.

to work. In this special case, that number is always 843 irrespective of whether the wage rate is high or low.

To alter this assumption is to change the curve. Workers in upstate New York might migrate to other states when wages in upstate New York become depressed. In addition, when local wages fall, some youths might simply withdraw from the work force, for example to continue their education (although such a possibility is undoubtedly more important in the 1990s than it was in the 1850s). For these and other reasons,[1] the aggregate supply curve will probably not be vertical, but instead will slope upward to the right, as in figure D.3(b), indicating that as wages rise, more labor will be supplied, and as wages fall, less labor will be supplied.

The remaining task is to bring together aggregate supply and aggregate demand, or to combine figure D.2 and figure D.3(b), as in figure D.4. If the aggregate demand curve D indicates, for each wage, how many workers will

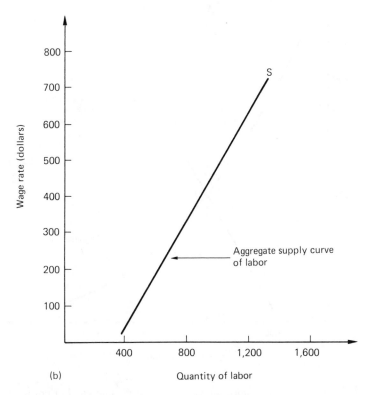

Figure D.3 (b) Aggregate supply curve of labor: supply changes as wages change.

be demanded by all producers in the market, and if the aggregate supply curve S indicates, for each wage, how many workers will offer themselves for hire, then the only wage where the number of workers demanded will equal the number of workers supplied is where the two curves intersect (E), or where 821 workers are hired at a price of $360 per worker per year.

Some readers may suspect that the geometry has been rigged to make these two curves intersect at the wage rate previously cited of $360, and so it has. But that numerical result is incidental to our example. The main point – which is true of any competitive market – is that where the aggregate demand curve intersects the aggregate supply curve, the price (in this case, the wage) is such that the quantity demanded (at that price) equals the quantity supplied (at that price) and thus the market clears. At a higher price – say, $400 per worker – the number of workers wanting to be hired would exceed the number demanded, and thus the wage rate would fall. At a lower price – say, $325 per worker – the demand for workers would exceed supply and thus the wage would rise.

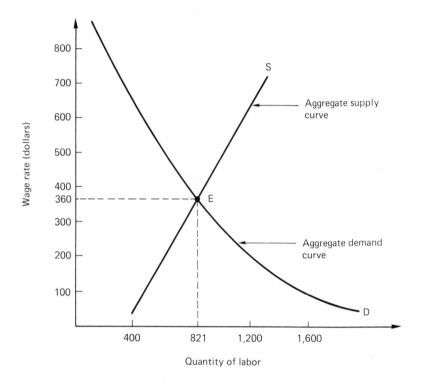

Figure D.4 Labor market: supply curve, demand curve, and equilibrium wage rate.

Recall that a demand curve and a supply curve are constructed to summarize graphically a variety of forces operating in a market, and where the two intersect, the resulting wage (in this instance $360) is necessarily an equilibrium wage; that is, it will not be pressured by market forces to move up or down. If market forces shift – for example, the price of corn falls steeply – the value of each worker to corn producers will decline, the demand for workers by corn producers will accordingly be cut back, and the aggregate demand curve will shift to the left, as in figure D.5. How much the demand curve will shift to the left will depend upon whether corn producers constitute a large or small percentage of those demanding the services of labor in this market. In figure D.5, the new reduced demand curve for labor D_2 intersects the old supply curve S at a lower wage ($300), where fewer workers are demanded (770) and fewer workers are supplied (770). This newly established lower wage, under changed market conditions (a cutback in demand), is now the equilibrium wage: it is under no pressure to move

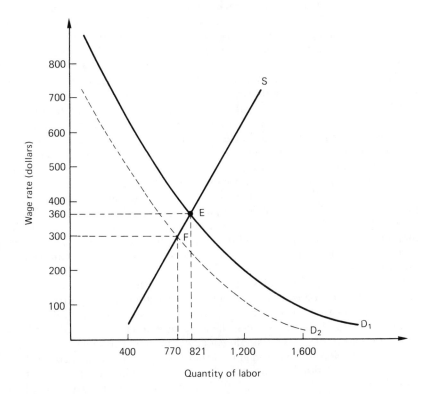

Figure D.5 Labor market: response of wage rate to a drop in aggregate demand.

either up or down unless market forces – summarized in the two curves of supply and demand – shift once more. If they do, yet another equilibrium wage will be established.

One final point. Consider again the geometry of figure D.4 and the market forces summarized by that geometry leading to an equilibrium wage of $360. As stressed repeatedly above, this notion of equilibrium implies a tendency not to move: in this case, a tendency of the wage rate not to move, because at $360 the number of workers demanded equals the number of workers supplied. Equilibrium, however, has a second implication which, for our purposes, is more important than the stability of the wage rate. If the focus is not shifted away from the market at large and back to the individual producer, an obvious point is easily missed. Our particular corn farmer achieved an equilibrium in the number of workers he hired by making sure that the value of the marginal product of the last worker hired exceeded the wage rate established in the market of $360. But this should be true of every single demander of labor in this market; that is, for each producer using hired labor, what the last worker hired adds to production (the value of that worker's marginal product) either equals or slightly exceeds the going wage. (The more the step-function of figure D.1(b) approaches a smooth curve, the smaller will be the gap between the wage rate and value of what the marginal worker adds.) The critical implication for a theory of income distribution is that, within a given labor market, *every* worker is receiving a wage ($360) roughly equal to the value of labor's marginal product in *every* productive activity using labor. Or put another way, and more in the jargon of economics, equilibrium conditions in a labor market imply an approximate equality between (a) the wage rate, or the price paid for the factor of production "labor," and (b) the value of labor's marginal product to all users of that factor of production. How rough or exact this equality will be depends mainly upon (a) the extent to which the step-function of each producer permits that producer to achieve equality between the wage rate and the value added by the last worker hired, and (b) the rapidity with which the market adjusts to changing conditions of supply and demand; that is, once market forces shift, does the wage rate move toward the new equilibrium quickly or slowly?

To review: the above analysis has developed a theory of wages (they are the product of the forces of supply and demand acting in labor markets) and a crucial implication of that theory (labor tends to be paid the value of its marginal product). In the process, the analysis demonstrated (with the help of a simple example) how a single concept – marginal productivity – could be used to develop the demand side of that theory, and to demonstrate that, with the demand side developed in this way, in equilibrium the wage rate should be roughly the value of labor's marginal product. Below we shall explore how this type of theory can be generalized to cover all factor payments (notably, the payments to the factors "land," "capital," and "enterprise"). This result – the generalized theory – will provide what we have been seeking from the outset in this appendix; namely, a theory of income distribution which explains the payments made to each factor of production in a competitive market. At this point, however, several traps have been laid. They all concern the assumptions in the previous example.

Assumptions, Hidden and Explicit

Does a labor market really work this way? Or to return one final time to our example, in upstate New York of the 1850s, would the wage rate for unskilled labor have been established by the processes described above? The answer to both questions is the same: yes, provided the reality being analyzed closely approximates the crucial assumptions of the theory. But that answer merely shifts the question. Which assumptions are "crucial," and how "closely" must those assumptions approximate reality to be "close enough"?

The beginning assumptions of the theory seem eminently reasonable: a producer surely prefers more profits to less, and thus when hiring labor, that producer will attempt to estimate what each additional worker will add to profits, adding workers until prospective profit increments threaten to turn negative. All of neoclassical microeconomics is built upon a similar assumption; that is, profit-maximizing behavior by all producers in the economic system. This behavioral assumption, in turn, gives to any theory which employs it considerable common-sense appeal.

The appeal is further strengthened in the above analysis by recourse to an agrarian example. Every producer, according to marginal productivity theory, will estimate, for each prospective worker, the value of that worker's marginal product. Our corn farmer's estimation problems were deliberately made to appear relatively simple: how many bushels of corn would a prospective worker add, and what would that corn be selling for when it was brought to market. If such numbers cannot be estimated with complete accuracy, surely they can be estimated with "tolerable" accuracy, the hidden implication seems to be. A second implicit argument supports the first. If the farmer makes a mistake, he can correct for that mistake (and thus improve his profits) by hiring or firing workers as the actual harvest and the market price realized for that harvest indicate whether initial estimates were wide of the mark. Finally, if the farmer refuses to correct for past mistakes, he will end up making losses, and repeated losses will drive him out of the farming business. In this Darwinian landscape, then, survivors do a tolerable job of making estimates and correcting for past mistakes, because that behavior is a condition of survival. The crucial questions, to be considered in detail in appendix E, are therefore:

1 Do businesses try to maximize profits, and is the ability to achieve maximum profits a condition of survival?
2 In contemporary America, can most businesses estimate with reasonable accuracy the value of a factor's marginal product, and do they try to make such estimates?

A third assumption raises a third question. (The first two were profit-maximizing behavior and its corollary: estimating for each factor of production the value of its marginal product.) The market in which the wage rate for our unskilled workers was established was assumed to be like a competitive auction market: many workers (all of them with similar skills) compete with each other for available jobs, and the producers seeking to hire labor are so numerous that each is a "price-taker;" that is, each views himself as responding to a wage rate set by impersonal market forces, and no producer is large enough to view his own bids for labor as directly affecting the market wage. Notice that allowing for several grades of labor skill is easily incorporated into the theory. The result would be, say, three different markets for three grades of labor – perhaps "unskilled," "semi-skilled," and "skilled" – but in each market the wage rate would be determined by the forces of supply and demand as described above. At least one major difficulty, however, is buried in the above description. The labor market is portrayed as a highly competitive auction involving only small-scale price-takers. To put the difficulty as a question:

3   How well does that portrayal (that is, the assumption of a highly competitive market) square with the facts of contemporary American labor markets, which include large-scale unions and giant corporations seeking to establish wages through collective bargaining?

To these three questions and related issues the discussion will return in appendix E. What matters at this point is to note the questions that in later analysis will have a crucial bearing on the adequacy of the theory outlined above. That theory as developed thus far is merely a theory of wages. The final assignment of this appendix is to explain how such a theory can be easily extended to explain not just wages, but the prices paid to all factors of production.

The Theory Generalized

The concept of marginal product can be used to construct a demand curve for labor or for any other factor of production. In the corn production example used above, the farmer was assumed to have a fixed amount of land and to vary labor inputs.[2] His economic problem was accordingly portrayed as deciding how much labor to hire, and his demand curve for hired workers was built up from estimates of the value of each prospective worker's marginal product.

Suppose instead that the would-be corn farmer is assumed to begin with a fixed supply of labor – say, three strapping sons plus himself – and his decision-making focuses on how much land to combine with that labor. Acres can be rented, but as the size of rented acreage increases, the fixed supply of four workers will be spread ever more thinly over soil that needs to be tilled and weeded. Each additional acre rented will therefore add some corn to total output, but after some point, the amount of corn added for each new acre rented will begin to decline. This is yet another illustration of the law of diminishing returns. (In the previous example where land was fixed and labor varied, the extra output added by extra laborers declined after some point.) Just as before, the farmer estimates how much extra corn will be added to total output by each additional acre rented; this extra amount of corn (the marginal physical product of land) is multiplied by an expected price for corn; and the resulting series of estimates indicates the value of the marginal product for acres rented. And just as before, this series of estimates gives the demand curve for land for this particular farmer; all potential users of land make similar estimates; and all these individual estimates, when added together, give the aggregate demand curve for land. The supply of land in our upstate region might be considered to be fixed (particularly in the short run; in the longer run, land clearing can change supply). The aggregate supply curve would therefore be a vertical line, as in figure D.3(a), and the rental rate for land would be established by the intersection of this supply curve with the aggregate demand curve built up from individual estimates of the value of the marginal product of land to different possible users of land. This equilibrium price – the rental rate per acre of land – will tend to remain stable until market forces shift supply or demand. More importantly – and again, just as before – at this equilibrium price, the rental rate of land equals (or roughly equals) the value of the marginal product of land in every use to which this land is put.

Notice that the analysis is not threatened by the existence of land ownership. Each owner should think of owned acres as having an imputed rent equal to the going rental rate. If the market rental rate exceeds the value of the marginal product of these particular acres to their owner, that land should be rented out. Alternatively, if acres can be rented for a rate below the value of the marginal product of those acres to a farm owner, he should rent the additional acres and expand his operation.

Notice finally that various grades of land are easily incorporated into the analysis (just as various grades of labor were), and that more fertile land (like more highly skilled labor) will command a higher price because the value of its marginal product will be higher.

In sum, as long as the assumptions made for a labor market can also be made for a land market (producers want to maximize profits, marginal productivity can be estimated, and prices are established in a competitive market), then similar reasoning leads to a similar conclusion: the price established in the market for a factor of production (in this case, the rental rate for land) will tend to equal the value of that factor's marginal product to all producers using it. Further, if land and labor were the only two factors of production, all producers would juggle the amount of each they wanted to employ until (in equilibrium) *each* factor would receive the value of its marginal product.

Land and labor are, of course, not the only factors of production. The many inputs that contribute to production not considered so far are usually lumped by economists under two broad headings: "capital" and "enterprise."[3] The first of these, "capital," raises a number of complex issue, but fortunately almost none of them are particularly relevant in an elementary exploration of income distribution theory. Once again, the objective is to show that in a competitive market, this factor of production will tend to be paid the value of its marginal product. One difficulty concerns the appropriate definition of "capital." To keep the analysis simple, assume that our corn farmer has a fixed supply of labor and land, and that to this fixed supply he is contemplating adding various kinds of capital equipment, such as hoes, plows, harrows, and rakes. For each prospective piece of capital equipment, he will (as before) attempt to estimate the value of its marginal product. To acquire this equipment, assume that he must borrow the necessary dollars. The cost of borrowing dollars is the rate of interest, which might be viewed as the rental rate of dollars. With the aim of maximizing his profits, the farmer will borrow dollars and add capital equipment until the prospective return from the last dollar borrowed is (roughly) equal to the rate of interest. As was true for the case of land, ownership of dollars does not complicate the analysis. If the prospective return in his own farming operation for dollars owned is lower than the market rate of interest, the farmer should lend them out. If the prospective return is higher, he should use those dollars to acquire capital equipment and increase his own production.

At this point, some economists would view the list of general factors of production as complete, lumping all available factors under the three headings "labor," "land," and "capital." Others prefer to single out a particular kind of human service for business organizers and term that service "enterprise." Providers of this service, or entrepreneurs, can be hired to act as a senior executive of a company, or they can be self-employed. In both cases, the service they provide is managing the business and taking risks, and in either case (if this service is bought and sold in a market), they should tend to receive the value of the marginal product of that service when applied to various business ventures. Our upstate farmer, for example, could either operate a farm himself or rent his entrepreneurial skills to others. As long as our familiar assumptions can be applied to this particular factor of production (including (a) the marginal productivity of the factor, entrepreneurship, can be estimated, and (b) the price of this particular factor is also determined in a competitive market), the farmer, as entrepreneur, should tend to receive the value of his market product. In addition, he may, of course, also receive a return on land he owns or on capital he owns, or a payment for his services as a worker in the fields (a laborer's wage), as distinct from his services as manager and risk-taker.

The theory is almost complete. All factors of production available for productive use can be viewed as belonging to one of four categories: land (or natural resources), labor, capital, and enterprise. If the assumptions noted hold, each should tend to receive a price equal to the value of its marginal product. Finally – a new point, and of critical importance to complete the theory – if *all* factors of production are paid the value of their marginal product, the sum total paid to all factors (land, labor, capital, and enterprise) will just equal the value of the output created by those factors of production. Or put differently, the value paid out to all factors will just equal the value of goods and services created by all factors. The reasons for this need not concern us here.[4] Our main objective in this appendix was to develop a theory of income distribution based upon the concept of marginal productivity, and that goal has now been achieved. Income is distributed to factors of production in payment for services provided by those factors in the productive processes of the economy. Payments are explained as the price for a factor; those prices are established in a competitive market by the forces of supply and demand; and the demand side of that market is determined by estimates of marginal productivity. Each factor of production (such as land or labor) is paid a price (such as rent or wages) which tends to reflect the contribution to total production resulting from the application of the last, or marginal, unit of that factor in every productive activity in which that factor is employed.[5]

How Good a Theory?

Additions Needed to Complete the Theory as a Theory

The purpose of this section is not to develop a fully articulated marginal productivity theory of income distribution, but merely to point out that if the above analysis were to achieve completeness as a theory, several loose ends would need to be tidied up. Or these, two are particularly important. One concerns supply. In the case of the factor "labor," for example, the marginal productivity of workers determines demand, but what determines how much work laborers are willing to supply at different wage levels? Advocates of marginal productivity theory usually attempt to answer that question by employing behavioral assumptions similar to those used for producers. Producers are assumed to want to maximize profits, and thus to make predictable tradeoffs when choosing the number and type of factors of production to employ. In a similar vein, workers are assumed to want to maximize their own utility, and to make work–leisure tradeoffs as they strive to achieve the greatest utility (or personal satisfaction) possible. Potential suppliers of capital also confront a tradeoff: between consuming income now, or forgoing consumption and earning money on savings supplied to the capital market, with the extra money thereby earned permitting a higher level of consumption later on.

Once supply problems have been adequately solved (and the foregoing only hints at the solution), the other obvious gap in marginal productivity theory, as a theory, concerns the determinants of output prices. At first glance, this gap may not appear to be a gap at all. Marginal productivity theory concerns income distribution, that distribution is determined by factor prices, and thus only factor prices seem to need to be explained by the theory. But factor prices are themselves determined by the value of each factor's marginal product, and this value is the result of the multiplication of two numbers: (a) the extra physical output that the factor adds to production (its marginal physical product), and (b) the price that output is selling for in the market. Thus the original objective of explaining factor prices inevitably raises the problem of explaining the prices of what those factors are creating, or output prices. Here, too, the requisite analysis need not detain us, because fortunately it is not central to issues that lie ahead.[6]

Nature of the Resulting Theory as a Theory of Income Distribution

If all loose ends can be successfully tied up (and many American economists believe that they can), will the resulting theory do what it is supposed to do, namely, explain the distribution of income in a market economy? The answer is yes, although the resulting explanation is a special kind of income theory. It focuses upon payments to factors of production, not upon the incomes received by particular individuals. To establish what a given individual will receive as total income one must therefore know how much of each factor of production that individual controls: how much land and capital are owned, and what labor skills (including entrepreneurial skills) that individual possesses. But if individual incomes are a function of property owned and skills possessed, a "complete" theory of income distribution, it might be argued, must also explain how property and skills are acquired. Marginal productivity ignores the latter challenge. It is, at least as usually articulated, a theory of factor payments, taking property ownership and existing skills as given.

This theory (with that limitation) has proved to be enormously appealing to American economists.[7] To a significant degree, this popularity can be attributed to several features of the theory which mesh well with widely shared premises of neoclassical economics as practised and taught within the United States. The portrayal of an economic world dominated by the maximizing motivations of rational participants who interact within the institutional framework of a competitive market – a market in which all prices are established by the forces of supply and demand: this *is* the paradigm of the neoclassical approach to explaining prices in any market. Marginal productivity theory is thus appropriately viewed as a logical extension of neoclassical price theory to factor markets. The subsequent use of the same theory to explain income distribution is viewed by many economists as a somewhat derivative finding. The central issue is to explain prices, and the majority of American economists assume that the neoclassical approach explains prices very well, or at least explains prices better than any of the competing theories of price determination. To put the matter as a negative proposition, if marginal productivity theory were challenged as an inadequate explanation of how factor prices are determined, and if at the heart of that challenge was a questioning of the legitimacy of the underlying assumptions, that challenge when logically pursued would threaten nothing less than the neoclassical paradigm itself, which in turn is the very bedrock upon which most of microeconomics is constructed in the United States. Small wonder, then, that many American economists readily accept marginal productivity theory as an explanation of American income distribution. Even those who challenge some of its assumptions, as we have seen in chapter 5, are reluctant to pursue that challenge to a wholesale rejection of the theory.

Appraising a Theory: What Does "Good" Mean?

Fashionability among economists is of course no guarantee of the validity of the theory that is fashionable. (The repeated shifts in what is popular in the economics profession would seem convincing proof of that.) But what criteria might be used to determine whether a given theory is an apt description of the forces at work in the economic world which the theory is attempting to analyze and explain? In particular, how might we judge the aptness of marginal productivity theory as a description of the forces determining income distribution within a market economy such as that of present-day America?

If the issue is whether or not a particular theory deserves to be labeled "good," the criteria that immediately come to mind for the theoretician are such properties as completeness and internal consistency. These properties, as important as they are, nevertheless seem of secondary importance to the layman. What matters to that audience is not so much whether the theory is admirable as a theory, but whether that theory is an "apt" or "good" description of the forces determining results in the economic world as that world actually functions.

The test normally applied for "goodness" in this sense, at least by social scientists, is whether the theory predicts well or badly. At first glance, marginal productivity theory appears to have formidable prediction capabilities. If receipts for televising baseball games rise sharply, baseball salaries will also tend to rise. If demand for haircuts suddenly falls because of a change in fashion, the wages paid to barbers will also tend to fall. Cotton prices soar, and growers of cotton seek more land to cultivate; steel prices plummet, and steel companies lay off workers, just as the theory predicts. Those who endorse a marginal productivity explanation of economic facts, such as economist Tibor Scitovsky, therefore seem justified in their reliance upon a theory

that stresses merely that the rates of remuneration of productive factors are market prices determined by supply and demand, and influencing in turn the quantities and proportions in which individual entrepreneurs demand the services of the productive factors.[8]

The reader at this point is in danger of being hoodwinked. Marginal productivity theory makes primarily two kinds of predictions. One concerns directional tendencies of the sort just noted. Market forces are represented by supply and demand curves which determine an equilibrium price, shifts in market forces are accordingly portrayed as causing a shift in one or both of these curves, and that shift will indicate the *direction* in which factor prices will move (up or down) and *the directional change* in factor quantities employed (more or less). All the examples in the previous paragraph are of this sort.

The other kind of prediction of marginal productivity theory is perhaps too easily forgotten in the triumphs of the sort just noted. The second kind is far more crucial for our purposes. At issue is *not* the directional tendencies of factor prices and quantities employed in response to shifts in market forces, but rather the achievement of a particular equilibrium condition after all the shifting is completed. The claim of the theory – and a crucial claim it is – concerns the achievement of an equality between (a) the price paid to each factor of production and (b) the value of that factor's marginal product in *all* productive uses of that factor. Most economists will be quick to protest that exact equality is never promised by the theory, but only a "tendency to equality." That concession, however, could ultimately imperil the usefulness of marginal productivity as a theory of income distribution. The obvious question is whether the tendency to equality is strong or weak, and whether movements toward equality are prompt or sluggish. The weaker the tendency and the more sluggish the movements, the wider the gap is likely to be between the value of a factor's marginal product and the actual market price of that factor. The wider the gap, the less the theory explains about what determines observed factor prices in a real market. And the less the theory explains about these prices, the less it tells us about what determines income distribution in the economy as it actually functions.

In sum, to claim that marginal productivity theory predicts tolerably well the directional changes in prices and quantities as market forces shift in factor markets is *not* to establish that the equilibrium conditions hypothesized by that theory will be achieved, or even approximately achieved, in those markets as they actually function. And the achievement of a particular equilibrium condition is vital to marginal productivity theory if it is to claim a special place as a theory of income distribution. The key empirical issue is therefore how well factor markets function to bring about equality between what a factor is paid and what that factor is adding to production. About these issues – the functioning of factor markets and the achievement of equality as postulated by the theory – even staunch advocates of marginal productivity admit to certain doubts. To quote again from Tibor Scitovsky, market forces operating in factor markets, he notes,

may be much weaker and much more sluggish than is generally supposed; and for all we know they may, in some respects, operate quite differently from those that operate in the market for bread.[9]

Appendix E

Are Factors of Production Paid the Value of Their Marginal Product?

The agrarian example used in chapter 3 and appendix D follows a well-established pattern in economics. Most textbooks, when elaborating neoclassical distribution theory, rely exclusively upon examples chosen from agriculture. The reader tends to find the imagery both simple and intuitively appealing: the unskilled laborer trudging up to some small-scale farm; the owner of the farm responding to a request for a job by sizing up the worker's likely contribution to farm output and then estimating what that extra output might be sold for in the local marketplace. Much of the intuitive appeal is undermined, however, if this picture of bucolic simplicity is supplanted by some variant of contemporary agribusiness, where the worker's prospective tasks might include operating and repairing the machinery on some sprawling wheat farm in the Midwest, or alternatively managing a "milking parlor" at an up-to-date dairy farm where capital investment can easily exceed half a million dollars. The complexity of the implied calculations for the would-be employer foreshadows a larger problem. Not all American farms are large-scale and highly specialized, but even if the vast majority resembled the simple small-scale units portrayed in economic examples, the agriculture sector in present-day America employs less than 3 percent of the labor force.[1] What of the 97 percent? How does an employer estimate the value of the marginal product for, say, a research chemist at Du Pont or a vice-president in charge of sales at General Motors? To put the point in a general way, as the skills of the labor force become more specialized and more diverse and their assigned tasks become less obviously linked to increments in firm output, assessments by employers of the kind hypothesized by marginal productivity theory appear increasingly far-fetched. For most of the workers in America today, employers surely do not know what the value of their marginal product is, and few employers are interested in estimating such a number. To do so would be costly, and the final figure would be regarded in most cases as such a tentative approximation to the truth that its impact upon firm decision-making would be minimal.

To the charge that most employers simply do not know what marginal productivity is, the neoclassical economist has a standard rebuttal which amounts to a shift in basic assumptions. Wages will still *tend* to equal the value of the worker's marginal product, the argument runs, provided that labor markets are highly competitive and that employers try to maximize profits and can see some observable linkage between changes in the work force and resulting changes in profits. If, for example, the manager of a firm hires a worker and the wage paid is less than the value of that worker's marginal product, then profits will rise. If the wage paid is more, profits will fall. Accordingly, the manager will continue to juggle the size of his work force in response to observed changes in profits (while knowing nothing about the actual value of the marginal product of any worker), and each juggling should tend to narrow the gap between wages paid and the value of the marginal product created by the last worker hired or fired.

As noted at the outset, the neoclassical economist in this attempted rebuttal has merely replaced one assumption with another. Gone is the assumption that each employer actually knows what each prospective worker will add to total output.[2] In its stead is a set of assumptions, some of which are old, and one of which is new. The old assumptions are those required for neoclassical distribution theory as elaborated in chapter 3; namely,

1   that the employer's only motivation is to maximize profits, and
2   that all workers are hired and fired in a highly competitive labor market characterized by many participants and highly flexible wages.

The new assumption compensates for the lack of knowledge about what marginal product actually is, namely,

3   that an employer can identify those variations in profits caused by increases or decreases in his work force (as opposed to profit variations attributable to other causes).

But surely, many will object, in the modern corporation where profits are a function of so many variables, the kind of knowledge hypothesized by assumption (3) is also far too unrealistic to support a theory of income distribution. The neoclassical economist has two replies, one relevant and the other not. The irrelevant reply is to point out that this particular assumption holds *ceteris paribus* or "other things being equal," which amounts to little more than an effort to redeem a dubious assumption with a bit of Latin. Such a ploy will not do, precisely because other things are not equal; that is, the problem at issue is that a multitude of forces affect profits and often the employer has no precise way of identifying only those profit changes caused by the last worker hired. The neoclassical economist is therefore reduced to one last response – one final line of intellectual defense which must withstand attack if his theory of income distribution is to survive. That response amounts to replacing assumption (3) with:

4   that employers do not know what marginal product actually is for workers hired, nor do they know the exact linkages between variations in employment and variations in profits, but (4a) only those employers who somehow manage roughly to equate wage payments with the value of their workers' marginal products will maximize profits, and (4b) only those employers who maximize profits will tend to survive.

Neoclassical theory revised in this way concerns not an exact equality but a tendency: the tendency for the wage rate to equal the value of the worker's marginal product, now viewed as a somewhat weaker tendency operating "in the long run." (The theorist would also want to add that all of the above assumptions, couched in terms of the single factor of production "labor," apply with equal force to all the other factors of production, notably, "capital," "enterprise," and "land" or "natural resources.")

Notice what has happened, and what is at stake. A crucial assumption was challenged as being far too unrealistic to support a theory of how income distribution actually is determined in America. The response was to replace the implausible assumption with another. Will the revised set (assumptions (1), (2), and (4)) prove vulnerable to a similar charge? If they are and these assumptions must also be jettisoned, then with them goes the one theory of income distribution widely supported by the American economics profession. That profession therefore has a vested interest in the theory and its assumptions surviving unscathed. What are the charges, and what is the evidence in support of those charges?

The assumption that employers maximize profits has been repeatedly challenged on many counts, but three criticisms tend to dominate the economics literature.[3] One retains the behavioral postulate of maximization, but proposes a revision in what tends to be maximized. In the large-scale modern corporation where the owners (the stockholders) are usually a separate group from those who manage the company, the pay and prestige of top executives will tend to increase as the firm becomes larger, as will the odds of those executives having access to such perquisites as chauffeur-driven limousines and private company aircraft. Accordingly, those who make the key decisions for the firm may be concerned not just with profits or – a more extreme version of the hypothesis – even primarily with profits, but rather with trying to maximize the sales or the growth of the firm.[4] A second criticism of the profit-maximization assumption challenges the notion that all participants in the company will always do their best, thus enabling the maximum to be achieved. If effort varies with motivation, and motivation varies for a single worker over time, and among various workers at any point in time, the achievement of maximum profits will be the limiting case, rarely even approximated in a complex production unit with many human actors.[5] A third criticism, usually termed "a behavioral theory of the firm," pursues the methodology of the second criticism to its logical conclusion.[6] The key to understanding what firms actually do, the argument runs, is not to hypothesize a motivation (profit maximization) and then infer behavior from that hypothesis, but rather to observe what determines decision-making within actual firms, and then construct a theory of the firm from those observations. The advocates of this approach accordingly play down the possibility of a single-minded pursuit of a single goal, and emphasize instead the diffuse nature of decision-making in a business world fraught with uncertainty, within complex business units where personalities, differing judgments, conflicting goals and administrative structure all play an important part.

Notice how each of the above three criticisms undermines the key assertion of neoclassical theory that is the focus of this appendix: that employers will pay each factor of production the value of that factor's marginal product. This assertion was derived from the postulate of profit-maximizing behavior. To the extent that top executives attempt to maximize sales or growth instead of profits[7] (criticism 1), or the participants within a firm seldom perform near their maximum because they lack the motivation to do so (criticism 2)[8], or decision-making within the firm is the result of a complicated bargaining process in which judgments and objectives are many and outcomes are uncertain (criticism 3), then the results can hardly be assumed to be exactly those hypothesized by the neoclassical model. But might not the results be "close" to those hypothesized? That is a question which seems at first glance to depend on how closely the actual behavior of present-day American firms corresponds to profit maximization or to the kind of behavior suggested by the critics of profit maximization.

First impressions suggest that the bulk of the evidence favors the critics. One point on which all firm surveys agree is that no conscious effort is made by businessmen to achieve the kind of profit-maximizing conditions hypothesized by neoclassical theory, including the condition that all factors of production be paid the value of their marginal product.[9] What is less clear, however, is how far actual practice strays from this ideal. Case studies have indicated that in large-scale firms in which ownership is divorced from control, revenue-maximizing or sales-maximizing behavior is more prevalent[10], as is the tendency for substantial and prolonged over-investment (which is consistent with the sales-maximizing hypothesis, but not with the profit-maximizing hypothesis).[11] Such firms have also been found to have lower profit rates than firms where ownership and control are not separated.[12] As for the tendency of profit maximization to be undercut by defective motivation and insufficient effort, the leading exponent of this viewpoint claims that "inertia, slothfulness, lack of concentration and attentiveness, friction between peers, and friction between those at different hierarchical levels, are ubiquitous elements in normal productive units."[13] Case studies also lend support to the idea, originating with behavioral theories of the firm, that decision-making within the business corporation is often based upon rules of thumb, and that these rules bear no necessary relationship to those rules the firm should follow if its goal were to maximize profit.[14]

In sum: an overwhelming body of evidence suggests that firms neither pursue nor achieve the kind of profit maximizing hypothesized by neoclassical theory. How far actual behavior diverges from this ideal remains an open question to which the discussion will subsequently return.

The second key assumption of neoclassical theory, as previously noted, is that all workers are hired in highly competitive labor markets characterized by many participants and flexible wages. As was true with profit maximization, this assumption has been attacked as being widely at variance with the facts. Again the attacks can be grouped under three major headings.

The first notes what is little more than common knowledge: that most wages in America are not flexible, but instead are notoriously "sticky" on the down side; that is, when demand for labor slumps, few wages fall immediately, and most are slow to fall even after a considerable lag (even when that lag is accompanied by widespread unemployment).[15] This suggests that the economic reality to be explained is rather more complicated than the simple supply-and-demand world encountered in the early chapters of introductory textbooks, in which the price (in this case, the wage rate) rapidly adjusts to clear the market. Even exponents of the neoclassical model concede the need to modify that model when the topic of analysis is the American labor market.

We must emphasize that labor is definitely not bought and sold in competitive auction markets of the kind we see for grain and common stocks. You can grade wheat into neat market categories, but you cannot do that with human beings. No auctioneer allocates workers to the highest bidder.[16]

But in what kind of markets is labor bought and sold? Critics of neoclassical theory usually focus upon two kinds of market situations and a single characteristic common to both: bargaining power. If a single employer is the only purchaser of labor – or the only purchaser of consequence in close proximity, as can happen in the so-called "company" town – the market power resulting from the employer's monopoly position (what economists call "monopsony") will result in workers' wages being less than would otherwise be the case.[17] Workers may, of course, combine into their own union to achieve what John Kenneth Galbraith has termed "countervailing power,"[18] but if they do, a second problem arises for neoclassical distribution theory which is more troublesome that the first. If an employer is a monopsonist, wages will be depressed, but neoclassical theory can at least specify how those wages will be determined. If a single large union confronts a single large employer (or an association of large employers), the result will be collective bargaining over wages in which personalities and market power will play important roles and – the crucial point – the final outcome will be *indeterminate* according to conventional neoclassical theory.[19] In short, the economist has a theory to predict the results of the first situation (monopsony) but not the second (bilateral monopoly). If the results are indeterminate, will the actual outcome of collective bargaining yield wages similar to, or very different from, those hypothesized by neoclassical theory, in which all workers are assumed to receive the value of their marginal product? The more bargaining power influences the outcome of wage negotiations, the more pressing that question becomes. But are such problems typical of American labor markets?

The charge that employers have monopoly power and use that power to depress wages is as old as industrialization within America, and is still much in evidence today. In their recent pastoral letter, for example, the Catholic bishops expressed concern because "employers frequently possess greater bargaining power than do employees in the negotiation of wage agreements."[20] Particular instances can be found to support the claim that employers have "undue power" and use such power to depress wages. Nurses and public school teachers outside metropolitan areas, for example, both frequently seem to be at a disadvantage when negotiating with their employers.[21] Surprisingly, however, the number of documented cases remains relatively small and – perhaps more surprising still – almost no general studies have been undertaken to establish how pervasive monopsony power is in different American labor markets, and whether that power, where it does exist, has been used to depress wages "a little" or "a lot." One notable exception to this general neglect is a study of the immediate postwar era, which found few labor markets dominated by a handful of employers, and in the few that were, the monopsony power implicit in the situation appeared to be largely unexploited.[22]

Examples of big unions confronting large-scale employers are more readily found, but the effect of resulting power struggles on wages remains unclear. Only about a quarter of the American work force belongs to a union,[23] but the influence of unions is more pervasive than this number might suggest, in part because of the tendency of nonunion wages to be influenced by wage settlements achieved by comparable workers in the unionized sector of the economy.[24] As for the prevalence of large-scale firms, slightly more than half the American work force is employed by enterprises with 500 employees or more.[25] The presence of large firms can complicate the analysis of resulting wages in three different ways. First, as previously noted, in situations of bilateral monopoly in which a single large union confronts a single large employer, the wage rate, according to neoclassical analysis, is indeterminate. Second, whether or not unions are present to affect the bargaining, large firms tend to have "internal labor markets;" that is, markets which operate internal to the firm in which higher-level jobs are primarily or exclusively filled by applicants from within the company's own ranks. Here, too, the resulting wage rate remains theoretically indeterminate.[26] Third, and perhaps least important, the salaries of executives in large-scale corporations have an indeterminacy of their own. According to critics of the neoclassical approach, these salaries are little influenced by what the executives actually contribute to the firm, and instead are "a function . . . of tradition, hierarchical position and bureaucratic power."[27]

In sum, large-scale business units pervade the American economy, and how wages are established within such units cannot be determined by neoclassical theory. The possibility nevertheless still exists that actual wages (however they are determined) will be roughly what neoclassical theory says they will be. Even if unions tend to raise wages above competitive market levels – and the evidence suggests that they do[28] – employers of unionized workers could respond by cutting back on the number hired until the value of the marginal product of workers retained roughly equaled the higher union wage. But does the American economy actually function this way? Do employers of both union and nonunion workers somehow grope their way toward the neoclassical solution?

Evidence bearing on this crucial question is exceedingly sparse, but what little there is suggests the following. First, although worker productivity varies with motivation, the nature of most wage contracts and the limitations of information available on day-to-day productivity severely restrict the employer's ability to modify wages in response to changes in worker productivity.[29] Second, although much of this problem might be solved by a piece-rate payments scheme, over 85 percent of American workers are paid for hours worked, not output created during work.[30] Third, across the same class of workers, unions tend to emphasize rewarding seniority more than rewarding variations in productivity, and the evidence from both union and nonunion wage data indicates less dispersion and more bunching than considerations of productivity alone would warrant.[31] Fourth, fragmentary evidence (and relevant evidence is fragmentary in the extreme) suggests that at least in some cases, as seniority increases and wages rise, worker productivity actually declines.[32] The reasons for that decline are far from clear, but at least one problem is declining motivation, consistent with the first point made above. To quote from a case study of 2,500 design and development engineers, "An older engineer often views the future with pessimism. He expects little positive reward, even if he does put forth greater effort."[33]

All that the discussion has accomplished to this point is to raise a troubling suspicion, namely, that neoclassical distribution theory may not fit the facts of the American economy very well and the wages of the country's workers may differ markedly from the value of their marginal product.[34] As noted earlier, however, the neoclassical economist has an argument designed to counter such suspicions: if employers did not pay factors of production (including workers) the value of their marginal product (or "roughly" the value of their marginal product), their firm would not maximize profits; if their firm did not maximize profits, it would go out of business; therefore, any firm surviving for any length of time must be behaving as neoclassical theory hypothesizes, whether that behavior is the result of a conscious effort to maximize profit or the result of some other set of decision rules. Advocates of this argument often drive the point home with the aid of a billiard-playing analogy. The expert billiard player, they note, almost surely does not make a multitude of precise geometric calculations each time before he shoots, and yet that expert plays *as if* he were making such calculations. Only if the balls follow a specified geometric path on the billiard table will they collide, and only if they collide repeatedly will the expert survive in competition and earn a reputation as an "expert." Similarly, the argument runs, the businessman must operate his firm *as if* he were making all the hypothetical calculations of neoclassical theory (such as equating marginal revenue with marginal cost and paying each factor of production the value of its marginal product), because only if the businessman somehow manages to achieve the result implied by those calculations (profit maximization) will his firm survive in the competition of the marketplace. The implied mechanism is Darwinian. The incompetent will be weeded out, leaving only the competent as survivors.

> The process of "natural selection" thus helps to validate the hypothesis [the neoclassical theory of the firm] – or, rather, given natural selection, acceptance of the hypothesis can be based largely on the judgment that it summarizes appropriately the conditions for survival.[35]

But does it? The implication of this analogy is that the margin for error is quite small if the player is to survive the rigors of competition. But is that a fair description of how the American business community functions? To modify the game only slightly – from billiards to pocket pool – consider the problem of making one pool ball strike another so that the second drops into a designated pocket. Here too the expert player will perform as if he were making geometric calculations to a very fine tolerance. But is making enough profit to survive in business analogous to sinking pool balls, or is it more like kicking a football between two goal posts set quite far apart? In the first instance, the margin for error is small; in the second, it is fairly wide. Which one better describes the survival conditions for the American business firm is an empirical issue – and one that remains largely unexplored by the neoclassical theorist who usually settles for arguing by analogy instead of arguing from the facts.[36]

To be fair to the neoclassical advocates, one should concede at the outset that available evidence bearing on this question is far from satisfactory. Among the relevant bits and pieces are the following.

1   The annual failure rate of American business firms appears to vary between 30 and 50 per 10,000 firms.[37] The annual rate thus averages less than half of 1 percent, implying (as a rough approximation) that less than 5 percent of all business establishments will fail within a decade.
2   Of the firms that fail, the vast majority are small-scale. Over 95 percent employ fewer than 50 workers; over 80 percent employ fewer than 20.[38]
3   Business failures are heavily concentrated in retail trade and construction, which together account for more than half of all failures and bankruptcies.[39]
4   About half of American business firms that fail have been in business for five years or less; about 80 percent, for ten years or less.[40]

The above evidence, fragmentary though it is, does not suggest a business world rife with Darwinian carnage. To fail is clearly the exception and survival is the rule. This propensity to survive, however, could still be explained by two quite different hypotheses. Following the neoclassical line of argument, one would claim that such evidence merely indicates that the vast majority of firms, precisely because they continue to survive, must be continually maximizing profits. A second line of argument would contradict the first. According to this interpretation, the evidence disproves the claim that the profit needed for survival is narrowly defined (that is, that special limiting case where profit is maximized) and instead supports the view that profits can be anywhere within a band, with the overwhelming dominance of survivors over failures indicating that this band must be very broad indeed. Two competing hypotheses are thus consistent with the same evidence. The only way to decide which one better fits the facts is, unsurprisingly, to add more facts.

The facts of obvious relevance are those presented previously in the discussion of the challenges to the neoclassical assumptions that (a) employers maximize profits and (b) wages are determined in highly competitive labor markets. The evidence presented there suggests a business world fraught with imprecision and uncertainties: a world of rules of thumb and conflicting business goals; a world of variable motivation and variable effort; of higher profit rates for firms in which ownership is not separated from control; of big unions bargaining collectively with giant corporations with the results of that bargaining theoretically indeterminate. Such a pattern of evidence would seem to make highly improbable the claim (hypothesis 1 above) that most American business firms most of the time hit a narrow target called maximum profits. But if they seldom (if ever) hit it exactly, on the average how close do they come? And most crucial from the standpoint of this discussion, if they seldom pay a wage exactly equal to the value of a worker's marginal product, on the average how close are actual wages to that ideal?

Notice how the answer will determine the fate of the one distribution theory with widespread popularity in America. If evidence such as that above gives *no* reason for believing that the answer must read "tolerably close to the neoclassical ideal," then the case for accepting neoclassical distribution theory collapses. The discussion has thus arrived by a circuitous route at the critics' basic point. The tradition of a science, and presumably of a social science, is that he who makes an assertion has an obligation to offer proof of that assertion. Neoclassical theorists have an elaborate assertion – the distribution theory outlined in chapter 3 – and yet those theorists offer no convincing evidence (or no evidence convincing to the critics) as to why their particular theory describes with tolerable accuracy how wages are actually determined in the American economy (or how any other payments are determined for other factors of production).[41] Nor is this dilemma resolved by the oft-repeated claim that neoclassical theory postulates only a tendency: a tendency of factor payments to move toward equality with the value of each factor's marginal product. If a theory is to be a useful guide for prediction and explanation, the key empirical issue is whether that tendency is strong or weak.[42] The weaker the tendency, the wider the gap is likely to be between what wages are and what, according to the theory, wages are supposed to be. And the wider the gap, the more the issue remains in doubt as to the actual forces causing the observed pattern of factor payments in America today. Or to return to the question posed at the beginning of this appendix – Are factors of production paid the value of their marginal product? – not only have advocates of marginal productivity theory failed to marshal evidence that they are, but those advocates leave totally unclear the extent to which the tendencies they postulate to be at work result in large or small gaps between their theoretical ideal and actual factor payments in contemporary America.

Appendix F

The Market Defended: Two Dubious Defenders Favored by George Stigler

One of the best known and most respected economists of the so-called "Chicago School," George Stigler[1] has long been an advocate of the free market as an efficient means for resource allocation. When shifting from questions of the efficiency of the market to those concerned with the intrinsic justice of that allocation system, Stigler restricts himself to an indirect endorsement of "the view that the value of the marginal product of a person [is] the just rate of his remuneration."[2] Rather than boldly nailing his own colors to this particular mast, he notes the widespread appeal of this idea for the American public,[3] and cites with evident approval the opinions of two other economists who, he claims, did endorse what we have termed "marginal productivity justice," John Bates Clark and Thomas Nixon Carver.[4] Given Stigler's prominence as a Nobel laureate and his reputation as a vigorous defender of the market, his reliance upon these two raises the expectation that from them (if not from Stigler) will come a carefully reasoned explanation of why paying factors of production the value of their marginal product is fair or just.

John Bates Clark

That expectation, in the case of Clark, is doomed to disappointment. Not only is his justification for paying factors the value of their marginal product sparse in the extreme, but Clark never argues that such a payments scheme is "just."

One of the founders of the American Economics Association and its third president, John Bates Clark was one of the pioneers in expounding the doctrine explained in chapter 3: that in a competitive market system, factors of production will tend to be paid the value of their marginal product.[5] When Clark shifted from explaining income distribution to offering a justification for the results, his discussion is little better than a two-page aside in a book devoted to elaborating marginal productivity theory.[6] That theory was couched in terms that did encourage the type of ethical inference outlined in chapter 3. Factors were paid "what they created"; or as Clark put it:

. . . where natural laws have their way, the share of income that attaches to any productive function is gauged by the actual product of it. In other words, free competition tends to give to labor what labor creates, to capitalists what capital creates, and to *entrepreneurs* what the coordinating function creates.[7]

As his son later explained, this part of Clark's research was motivated in part by the Marxian claim that workers were "exploited."[8] If, through the mechanisms of the market, labor tends to be paid "what labor creates," that charge would seem unwarranted.[9] Expanding on this theme of nonexploitation, Clark suggested that a system which "gives to every man his own" is an "honest system," and there he let the matter rest.[10] "Honesty" is not of course synonymous with "justice," as Clark well knew. Later in his book – and again as an aside in what was basically a treatise on economic theory – he pointed out the difference between the two concepts, and then dismissed related puzzles as "a matter of pure ethics" and thus not appropriately pursued in a book devoted to describing how pricing was established in factor markets.

We might raise the question, whether a rule that gives to each man his product is, in the highest sense, just. Certain socialists have, indeed, contended that such a rule cannot attain justice. Work according to ability and pay according to need, is a familiar formula, which expresses a certain ideal of equity in distribution. This rule would require the taking from some men of a part of their product, in order to bestow it on others who might be more necessitous. It would violate what is ordinarily regarded as a property right. The entire question whether this is just or not lies outside of our inquiry, for it is a matter of pure ethics.[11]

In pointing out the linkage between standards of economic justice and property rights, Clark noted a theme which others would develop into a full-blown defense of the income distribution generated by the market. But exploring such issues was never attempted by Clark himself.

The other author cited by George Stigler does provide what Clark omits: a full-blown defense of market payments as "just" or "right." What Stigler never makes clear is that the defense in question would strike most contemporary Americans as bizarre.

Thomas Nixon Carver

A single quotation from Carver is reproduced in some detail by Stigler, but nowhere in either the quotation or in Stigler's commentary on it is there any indication of why Carver believes that an income distribution based upon marginal productivity payments is a just distribution. This failure to clarify Carver's position may be partly explained by the peculiar nature of Carver's arguments.

An Iowa farmer who became, by the beginning of the present century, a professor of economics at Harvard University, Thomas Nixon Carver followed the lead of his contemporary, John Bates Clark, in two senses: he endorsed and publicized Clark's marginal productivity theory explaining how income was distributed, and (unlike Clark) he attempted to pursue the question of why the resulting factor payments scheme was fair or just. Both men recognized that such a pursuit must ultimately confront the intellectual quagmires of "pure ethics" (Clark's phrase), but Carver was not deterred by that prospect. The intrinsic justice of factor payments generated by a market system, he believed, could be convincingly defended by a combination of economic theory, Christian theology, and the Darwinian principle of natural selection. That defense, although not well explained in the Carver book cited by Stigler,[12] is laid out simply and candidly in an earlier work by Carver: *The Religion Worth Having*.[13]

Although the argument is straightforward, the concepts and terminology used by Carver may strike contemporary readers as somewhat odd. For this reason, several steps in the argument are followed by quotations in which Carver makes the same point in his own terms.

The first (and more fundamental) part of a two-stage argument is totally divorced from economics and heavily dependent upon Carver's views of Christian metaphysics and Darwinian theory about the natural world. Carver begins with a basic Christian premise, which then leads to economic issues in four quick steps.

1 The obligation of every Christian is to obey the divine will. This is the foundation upon which all of Carver's other arguments are built – that fundamental premise which is considered to be self-evident.

2 The central problem for a Christian is thus to discover the divine will. This can be accomplished, Carver believes, by studying the laws of nature, because that will is manifest in those laws ("the observed uniformities commonly called natural laws are merely the observed uniformities of the operation of the divine will"[14]).

3 One of the most discernible of all natural laws is natural selection, and thus the results of natural selection (as well as the law itself) are expressions of the divine will ("the laws of natural selection are merely God's regular methods of expressing his choice and approval"[15]).

4 Christians should therefore follow the imperatives evident in the laws of natural selection; that is, they should struggle to compete and flourish within the world with the express intention of dominating the world ("That nation, or that people, whose average individual character and conduct and whose social institutions and customs are such as to make them strong in competition with other peoples, and able to spread over the earth and subdue it and have dominion over it, becomes, by that very fact, the chosen people"[16]).

In sum, the objective is to "win the world," and anything that contributes to that goal is, in the language previously used, an instrumental good. Carver then turns to economics to show (or try to show) which economic practices and institutions will best contribute to that winning. He argues:

5 the key to winning is economic power;

6 the key to economic power is maximizing efficiency and growth;

7 these two objectives are best pursued within the context of a free-market system; including

8 the distribution mechanisms of that system; namely, paying factors of production the value of their marginal product.

The economic reasoning linking (6), (7), and (8) is never well worked out by Carver. This shortcoming is understandable, given that in Carver's day the full-blown neoclassical model had yet to be developed with all its implications for why a competitive market tends to maximize the efficient use of economic resources.[17] Carver's arguments reduce to little more than noting how the effective use of resources is encouraged by economic freedom and equality of opportunity, and how the incentive system of paying factors according to their marginal product will increase effort and therefore output.[18]

For all the lack of rigor in Carver's economic reasoning, the ethical implications of that reasoning plus arguments (1) through (5) are readily apparent. A "moral" or "right" action or institution is anything that enables society "to grow and flourish and hold its own in competition with other societies."[19] "Just" principles are those which contribute to that same goal, and thus paying factors of production the value of their marginal product, which also contributes to this goal, is also "just" or "right."[20] The implied ruthlessness toward the economically unfit is not only admitted but vigorously endorsed:

> . . . distribution according to worth, usefulness or service is the system which would most facilitate the process of human adaptation, [in part by exercising] a beneficial selective influence upon the stock or race, because the useful members would survive and perpetuate their kind and the useless and criminal members would be exterminated.[21]

The case of Carver illustrates how clarifying premises can sometimes make comparatively easy the dismissal of a well-reasoned argument. In Carver's case, once the structure of the argument is made clear, its limited appeal becomes apparent. Most Americans would balk at points (2), (3), and (4) above, particularly the identification of the divine will with the processes of natural selection, and the making of natural selection principles the touchstones for determining what counts as moral behavior in human societies. Carver's approach to economic justice is also flawed at a more fundamental level. It is unacceptable not merely because of values it endorses but also because of all that it ignores, notably, all those other values that matter to most Americans, some of which often conflict with values advocated by Carver. In short, this is a classic example of the philosopher's general approach to ethics being applied to the particular topic of economic justice. As such, it founders on the difficulties outlined in chapter 1. *Any* effort to construct from a handful of premises a logical system that claims to determine appropriate judgments about economic justice in every concrete situation will yield inferences in many situations that will strike the majority of the populace as wrong. At the core of that negative reaction are usually concerns for values ignored by the system in question, the clashes of ignored values with those featured by the system, and the inability to specify an appropriate resolution independent of the details of the concrete situation.

One puzzle remains. Why should an economist as distinguished as George Stigler choose to defend marginal productivity justice indirectly by citing with approval two authors, one of whom offers no defense of any consequence, while the other provides a carefully developed set of arguments that even Stigler is surely reluctant to endorse?

Appendix G

The Market Defended: The Lack of Logic in the Arguments of Irving Kristol

The title of this appendix should not mislead the reader about the general capabilities of Irving Kristol. He is widely regarded as one of the most thoughtful and least contentious of contemporary writers of the right, and that reputation is well deserved. His defense of the market system, however, is more than a little curious.[1]

Kristol begins by pointing out that the approach to economic justice of arch-conservatives such as Friedrich Hayek has the effect of putting two basic American values, freedom and justice, at odds with one another. A free society, according to Hayek, cannot also be a just society – or at least not a society in which the distribution of income is popularly perceived as being "fair" or "just." And for Americans, Kristol notes, to be asked to choose between the two is not merely repugnant, but to insist upon a choice that most citizens simply refuse to acknowledge must be made.[2] They want instead a fusion of both values – freedom and economic justice – in their larger concept of what their society is and what it ought to be. Kristol therefore sets himself the task of reconstructing such a fusion while remaining true to his conservative beliefs.

He begins by resurrecting the nineteenth century premises outlined in chapter 2. The freedom of the individual pursuing his own goals in a competitive marketplace, according to this older view, was consistent with economic justice, and that consistency, Kristol notes, was achieved by arguing that income was received as the reward for meritorious behavior, specifically for the exercise of such old-fashioned virtues as "honesty, sobriety, diligence and thrift."[3] Moreover, Kristol adds, this fusion in the popular imagination of individual freedom and virtuous behavior earning its "just" reward was encouraged by a Protestant theology that imbued American life with a sense of purpose and a sense of values.[4]

The reader can anticipate the problems Kristol will encounter as he attempts to understand why a fusion of similar ideas is more difficult to achieve in present-day America. The expectation is that all the arguments of chapter 3 will be reviewed again: arguments that undercut the easy linkage between merit and reward by noting the role of luck as a determinant of income payments. That expectation, however, proves incorrect, and for reasons that are not easy to follow.

Kristol glosses over dilemmas raised because accidental circumstances of heredity and environment and supply and demand can lead to gains or losses in the marketplace quite unrelated to meritorious behavior.[5] Accordingly, "it is still believed, *and it is still reasonable to believe*, that worldly success . . . has a definite connection with personal virtues such as diligence, rectitude, sobriety [and] honest ambition."[6] Or more cautiously, this belief is still justified for "the lower socioeconomic levels," which are defined as "the working class, lower-middle class, and even [the] middle class."[7] The single difficulty is with the upper income class, which Kristol discusses only in the context of executives' salaries. The problem here, he claims, is that executives of large corporations are "nameless and faceless," and "one really has no way of knowing what they are doing 'up there'."[8] What is not clear, therefore, is whether "up there" worldly success also has "a definite connection" with personal virtues, and proving that it does can be a complicated task.[9]

The missing perspective in these assertions, as previously noted, is that worldly success (or income received) also has a definite connection with luck, and the ignored dilemma is which matters and how much: luck or the exercise of personal virtues. What has been salvaged by this omission – or at least would seem reasonably intact – is the nineteenth century linkage between reward and merit, at least for the vast majority of income recipients.

Kristol is nevertheless not sanguine about preserving such a fusion, particularly when his first problem (a lack of knowledge about what executives actually do) is compounded by a second. Here the difficulty is not the linking of reward to merit, but the erosion of popular agreement about what merit is. The old Protestant ethic – what Kristol terms "the bourgeois ethos" – extolling the virtues of "probity, diligence, thrift, self-reliance, self-respect, candor, [and] fair dealing"[10] has lost much of its moral force because the religious beliefs extolling such virtues no longer pervade society as they once did. The threat, for Kristol, is that within this society of waning religious beliefs, economic success may become "severed from its moral moorings," and the pursuit of self-fulfillment in a free society may degenerate in the marketplace to the pursuit of gain for reasons no more dignified than greed.[11]

For such reasons Kristol feels compelled to beat a retreat: to find alternative arguments to justify the income payments generated by a market system that make no reference to merit earning its "just" reward. Here too the reader is inclined to form an expectation as to which direction that retreat will take on the basis of the arguments of chapter 4. This time that expectation will prove correct, as Kristol chooses a path already traveled by Milton Friedman and many other writers of the right.

Although the argument, in broad outline, is predictable, the final series of inferences is not.

1 Kristol begins by quoting Aristotle: that a "just" society is one in which inequalities (including inequalities of income) "are generally perceived by the citizenry as necessary for the common good."[12]
2 Within American society, the common good is commonly conceived to include both individual freedom and economic growth (the latter charac-

terized by Kristol as "the improvement of the material conditions of life"[13]).

3   For Kristol (as for Friedman), individual liberty is the most important goal.[14]

4   For Kristol (as for Friedman) the importance of economic growth per se is secondary. What Kristol underscores is the role growth plays in promoting the all-important goal of freedom. Growth, he points out, has made possible "a huge expansion of the property-owning middle classes," and that in turn is "a necessary . . . condition for a liberal society in which individual rights are respected."[15]

5   Another "necessary condition" for a free society (other than economic growth) is a free-market system, because of "the connection between economic liberty and all our other liberties."[16] (Unlike Friedman, Kristol does not explain in any detail what those connections are.)

The final steps in the argument Kristol makes in an odd way.

6a   A "liberal society," he argues, is characterized by widespread support for the priority of economic growth, and a tolerant attitude toward "capitalist transactions between consulting adults," partly because those transactions are presumed to be to the mutual benefit of those involved, and partly because a free-market system of voluntary exchanges should maximize gross national product, a development that is "to everyone's material advantage."[17]

6b   These assertions, Kristol evidently believes, lead *directly* to an endorsement of marginal productivity justice. Hard on the heels of the previous reasoning he adds: "And, consequently, a liberal society will think it reasonable and 'fair' that income should, on the whole, be distributed according to one's productive input into the economy, as this is measured by the marketplace and the transactions which occur there."[18]

6c   A second inference follows from the first. In the sentence following the one just quoted, Kristol concludes: "In sum, the distribution of income under liberal capitalism is 'fair' if, and only if, you think that liberty is, or ought to be, the most important political value. If not, then not."[19]

The reader at this point may feel somewhat lost because successive statements do not seem to follow, one from the other, in any rigorous way. But that would seem to reflect more a failing in Kristol's reasoning than in the understanding of his audience. One thing is clear. Although beginning with the problem of merit and reward, Kristol ultimately beats a retreat to the same redoubt chosen by Friedman. The ultimate goal is individual freedom; one instrumental good (now a necessary condition) for achieving that goal is a market system; and thus the income generated by the market must be accepted as part of an economic system required for the realization of this ultimate goal of freedom. But for reasons such as these, does that income distribution deserve to be labelled "fair"?

Kristol seems to believe that it does. His argument, somewhat compressed, is that (a) a "just" society is one in which inequalities are generally perceived as necessary for the common good; (b) the market system, with the income distribution that it generates, is required for furthering the common good (the latter encompassing liberty and economic growth); thus (c) the income distribution of the market is accordingly to be considered "fair." But notice the shift in adjectives and the changing nouns they modify. One proceeds from a definition of a "just society" to conclusions about a "fair income distribution." Even if all of Kristol's arguments are accepted, the income distribution of the market hardly seems to warrant the label "fair." "Necessary," to be sure – here, necessary for the preservation of freedom, and for that reason perhaps "right" for society. But surely not "fair." As Kristol himself points out, for most Americans, the concept of fairness when applied to income distribution requires some linkage with the notion of merit earning its just reward. And this linkage, Kristol claims (although for reasons that seen somewhat secondary), can no longer be easily presumed within modern society.

Notice finally that Kristol raises and then fails to address (as Milton Friedman raises and then fails to address) two related problems. If liberty or freedom is to be the ultimate goal – and the *only* ultimate goal[20] – (a) What justification can be given for ignoring so many other values important to Americans in deciding issues involving economic justice? and (b) Even if freedom is the only goal, how should freedom be defined?

Notes

Introduction: The problem

1 David R. Henderson, "A liberal economist's case," *Fortune*, CXVI (November 9, 1987), p. 185.
2 Ibid., p. 188.
3 Subsequent discussion will ignore the distinction between "distributive justice" and "corrective justice," which is not important for our purposes. See Nicholas Rescher, *Distributive Justice* (New York: University Press of America, 1966), pp. 5–6.
4 Discussions of economic justice commonly shift – as this one has just shifted – from examining the distribution of economic goods and services to examining the distribution of incomes needed to acquire those goods and services.
5 Rescher, *Distributive Justice*, p. 89.
6 The term "social justice" can be used to encompass much more than the justice of the distribution of economic goods and services within society. One might, for example, include the justice of the legal or the political system under such a general heading. When writers use this phrase in works cited in this study, however, they tend to use it as a synonym for "economic justice." The popular tendency to equate "fair" and "just" can also be challenged by the advocates of rigorous reasoning for reasons put concisely by the philosopher Nicholas Rescher. "There is *justice in the narrower sense of fairness*, on the one hand, and on the other, *justice in a wider sense, taking account of the general good*. These two types of justice are distinct, and can even come into conflict with one another." Consider, suggests Rescher, two possible distributions: the first, in which equals are treated equally and all receive an equal share of a small bundle of goods and services (or, if you will, a small "pie"), and the second, in which equals are treated unequally in the distribution of a much larger bundle of goods and services, but because that bundle is larger, even the smallest share exceeds the evenly distributed shares of the first situation. The procedures of the second are clearly "unfair" (equals are treated unequally), but the end result may still be judged as "just . . . taking account of the general good," where the general or common good in this case includes all participants achieving a higher standard of living. (Rescher, *Distributive Justice*, pp. 90–2.
7 Rescher, *Distributive Justice*, p. 7.
8 Bernard Williams, *Ethics and the Limits of Philosophy* (Cambridge, MA: Harvard University Press, 1985).
9 This phrasing glosses over the problem of defining precisely what an ethical theory is or ought to be. Williams, for reasons associated with the objectives of his book, offers "a rather complex" definition: "An ethical theory is a theoretical account of what ethical thought and practice are, which account either implies a

general test for the correctness of basic ethical beliefs and principles or else implies that there cannot be such a test" (ibid., p. 72). What philosophers seem to want is "unity and system" in their efforts "to impose on ethical thought . . . [a] structure of discursive rationality and impersonal principle" (H.L.A. Hart, "Who can tell right from wrong?" (review of Williams's book), *New York Review of Books*, XXXIII (July 17, 1986), p. 49).

10 For examples of this process in action, see Williams's criticisms of (among others) Kant, John Rawls, and R. M. Hare in Williams, *Ethics and the Limits of Philosophy*.
11 Ibid., p. 4.
12 In his review of Williams's book, *Journal of Philosophy*, LXXXIII (June 1986), p. 351.
13 Isaiah Berlin, "On the pursuit of the ideal," *New York Review of Books*, XXV (March 17, 1988), p. 15.
14 Ibid., p. 18.
15 Rescher, *Distributive Justice*, p. 7.

1 The approach

1 Clifford Geertz, *The Interpretation of Cultures: Selected Essays* (New York: Basic Books, 1973), p. 194.
2 Albert Jay Nock, *Our Enemy, The State* (New York: William Morrow, 1935), p. 26.
3 Henry George, *Progress and Poverty* (New York: Robert Schalkenbach Foundation, 1975), p. 303.
4 "How is it," Samuel Johnson asked of the colonists, "we hear the loudest yelps for liberty among the drivers of negroes?" This particular propensity has a long history.
5 Lionel Trilling, *The Liberal Imagination* (New York: Viking, 1950), p. 9.
6 Our focus will be on income, not on wealth, because the former tends to be the popular American focus. The two are obviously linked, given that wealth at any point in time is a function of income previously received and saved. The tempting inference is that if the annual distribution of income is "just," whatever wealth is subsequently accumulated will also be "just" (or "reasonably just"). Such an inference ignores a host of problems, including those associated with a "just" sytem of inheritance, but (as we shall see) Americans in general are not given to agonizing about such problems.
7 See especially Richard Hofstadter, *The American Political Tradition* (New York: Alfred A. Knopf, 1948), pp. v–xi.
8 Louis Hartz, *The Liberal Tradition in America* (New York: Harcourt, Brace & World, 1955), p. 134.
9 Herbert Stein, "How to be a conservative," *Fortune*, CXIV (November 10, 1986), p. 198.
10 One might expect from another branch of the discipline, "welfare economics," a range of insights useful for discussions of economic justice. The literature of this branch, however, is characterized by rigorous reasoning to conclusions of little or no relevance for the making of distributional judgments of the sort typically required in conjunction with policy debates. For an economist's views concerning the limited usefulness of welfare economics for discussions of economic justice, see Amartya Sen, *On Economic Inequality* (New York: W. W. Norton, 1973), especially pp. 6, 23; for those of a philosopher, see Nicholas Rescher, *Distributive Justice* (New York: University Press of America, 1966), pp. 12–18.

11 Isaiah Berlin, "On the pursuit of the ideal," *New York Review of Books*, XXXV (March 17, 1988), p. 11.
12 For a recent review of the history of this lack of popularity among even the poor in America, see Jennifer L. Hochschild, *What's Fair?* (Cambridge, MA: Harvard University Press, 1981), ch. 1.

2 Economic justice in historical perspective

1 The puzzle of explaining why Americans hold the views they do concerning economic justice has been addressed in literature attempting to answer a question initially posed in the title of a book by Werner Sombart: Why is there no socialism in the United States? (The original German version was published in 1906 with the title *Warum gibt es in den Vereinigten Staaten keinen Sozialismus?*) Much of this literature is summarized in John H. M. Laslett and Seymour M. Lipset (eds), *Failure of a Dream?* (Garden City, NY: Doubleday, 1974); and Seymour Martin Lipset, "Why no socialism in the United States?", in Seweryn Bialer and Sophia Sluzar (eds), *Radicalism in the Contemporary Age* (Boulder, CO: Westview Press, 1977), vol. I, pp. 31–149. Sociologists and social psychologists have also attempted to explain Americans' conceptions of distributive justice, but as they themselves are quick to emphasize, these efforts have achieved limited success. A review of some of these efforts is provided by Karol Edward Soltan, "Empirical studies of distributive justice," *Ethics*, XCII (July 1982), pp. 673–91; and Karen S. Cook and Karen A. Hegtvedt, "Distributive justice, equity, and equality," *Annual Review of Sociology*, IX (1983), pp. 217–41.
2 Bernard Mayo (ed.), *Jefferson Himself* (Charlottesville, VA: University of Virginia Press, 1976), p. 323. For a discussion of early tensions between popular notions of virtue and political and social attitudes toward economic activity, and conflicting views of how and when those tensions were resolved, see Joyce Appleby, "The social origins of American revolutionary ideology," *Journal of American History*, LXIV (March 1978), pp. 935–58; J. G. A. Pocock, "Virtue and commerce in the eighteenth century," *Journal of Interdisciplinary History*, III (Summer 1972), pp. 119–34; Robert E. Shalhope, "Republicanism and early American historiography," *William and Mary Quarterly*, XXXIX (January 1982), pp. 334–56.
3 Roy P. Basler (ed.), *The Collected Works of Abraham Lincoln* (New Brunswick, NJ: Rutgers University Press, 1953), vol. VII, p. 301.
4 Robert C. Winthrop (ed.), *Memoir of the Hon. Nathan Appleton, LL.D.* (Boston, MA: John Wilson, 1861), p. 59.
5 Ralph Waldo Emerson, *The Conduct of Life* (Boston, MA: Ticknor and Fields, 1860), p. 86.
6 Ibid., p. 78.
7 See ibid., pp. 71–110; also Ralph Waldo Emerson, *Nature, Addresses, and Lectures* (Boston, MA: Houghton Mifflin, 1895), pp. 20, 47.
8 Emerson, *Conduct of Life*, pp. 82–3.
9 Reginald L. Cook (ed.), *Ralph Waldo Emerson: Selected Prose and Poetry* (New York: Holt, Rinehart & Winston, 1969), p. 550.
10 Rev. H. W. Bellows, "The moral significance of the Crystal Palace: A Sermon, preached first to his own Congregation, and repeated in the Church of the Messiah, on Sunday Evening, October 30, 1853," *North American Review*, LXXIX (July 1854), p. 2.

11 Thomas Ewbank, *The World a Workshop* (New York: Appleton, 1855), p. 141.

12 Ibid., p. 14.

13 Ibid., p. 18.

14 Ibid., p. 15.

15 "The Way to Wealth, etc.," in Donald Mackintosh (ed.), *Mackintosh's Collection of Gaelic Proverbs and Familiar Phrases* (Edinburgh: Charles Stewart, 1819), p. 222.

16 Howard Mumford Jones, *O Strange New World* (New York: Viking, 1964), p. 338. The James quotation is included in Howard Mumford Jones's discussion, but no source is given.

17 *An Address to the Assembly of the Friends of American Manufactures . . . the 9th of August, 1787* (Philadelphia, PA: Aitken, 1787), pp. 29–30.

18 Nathan Appleton, "Labor, its relations, in Europe and the United States, compared," *[Hunt's] Merchants' Magazine*, XI (September 1844), p. 218.

19 Willard Phillips, *A Manual of Political Economy, with Particular Reference to the Institutions, Resources, and Condition of the United States* (Boston, MA: Hilliard, Gray, Little, and Wilkins, 1828), p. 153.

20 Davy Crockett, *An Account of Col. Crockett's Tour of the North and Down East* (Philadelphia, PA: E. L. Carey and A. Hart, 1835), p. 92.

21 Harriet Farley, "Editorial," *Lowell Offering*, V (March 1845), p. 72.

22 "American genius and enterprise," *Scientific American*, XI (September 4, 1847), p. 397.

23 Chauncey M. Depew, *Address of the Hon. Chauncey M. Depew, LL.D., at the Unveiling of the Statue of Cornelius Vanderbilt, at the Vanderbilt University, Nashville, Tennessee, October 11th, 1897*, p. 2. Depew's original address used "forecast" in place of "foresight."

24 "Defense of mechanical philosophy," *North American Review*, XXXIII (July 1831), p. 134.

25 Quoted in Perry Miller, "The responsibility of mind in a civilization of machines," *American Scholar*, XXXI (Winter 1961–2), p. 60.

26 William Ellery Channing, "Remarks on national literature" (1830), reprinted in Clarence Arthur Brown (ed.), *The Achievement of American Criticism* (New York: Ronald Press, 1954), p. 140.

27 "What is the Golden Age?" *Scientific American*, V (December 22, 1849), p. 109.

28 Daniel Webster, *Writings and Speeches of Daniel Webster* (Boston, MA: Little, Brown, 1903), vol. IV, p. 117.

29 Louis Hartz, *The Liberal Tradition in America* (New York: Harcourt, Brace & World, 1955), p. 62.

30 Lucy Larcom, "Among Lowell mill-girls: a reminiscence," *Atlantic Monthly*, XLVIII (November 1881), p. 611.

31 "What Benefit can accrue to the publick . . . to take Boys and Girls from the low and necessary Employments of Life, make them impatient of the Condition they were born to, and in which they would have thought themselves happy, to be Seamstresses, Footmen, and Servant Maids, and teach them to read Ballads?" John Trenchard (ed.), *The Third and Last Collection of Cato's Letters, in the British Journal* (London: T. Woodward, 1723), p. 41.

32 Louis Auguste Felix Beaujour, *Sketch of the United States of North America, at the Commencement of the Nineteenth Century, from 1800 to 1810*, trans. William Walton (London: J. Booth, 1814), p. 146.

33 Edward Everett, *Orations and Speeches* (Boston, MA: Little, Brown, 1878), vol. II, p. 294.

34 Karl Marx and Frederick Engels, *Selected Works* (New York: International Publishers, 1974), p. 104.

35 Basler (ed.), *Works of Abraham Lincoln*, vol. III, p. 462.

36 Ibid., vol. IV, p. 24. In the same speech at New Haven, Connecticut, Lincoln added: "I take it that it is best for all to leave each man free to acquire property as fast as he can. Some will get wealthy. I don't believe in a law to prevent a man from getting rich; it would do more harm than good. So while we do not propose any war upon capital, we do wish to allow the humblest man an equal chance to get rich with everybody else. [Applause.]"

37 Few visitors to nineteenth century America were more impressed by the pervasiveness of equality than Alexis de Tocqueville. The very first words of his classic, *Democracy in America*, ed. Richard D. Heffner (New York: New American Library (Mentor Books), 1956), indicate how impressed he was:

> Amongst the novel objects that attracted my attention during my stay in the United States, nothing struck me more forcibly than the general equality of condition among the people. I readily discovered the prodigious influence which this primary fact exercises on the whole course of society; it gives a peculiar direction to public opinion, and a peculiar tenor to the laws; it imparts new maxims to the governing authorities, and peculiar habits to the governed.
>
> I soon perceived that the influence of this fact extends far beyond the political character and the laws of the country, and that it has no less empire over civil society than over the government; it creates opinions, gives birth to new sentiments, founds novel customs, and modifies whatever it does not produce. The more I advanced in the study of American society, the more I perceived that this equality of condition is the fundamental fact from which all others seem to be derived, and the central point at which all my observations constantly terminated.

38 J. Hector S. John Crèvecoeur, *Letters from an American Farmer* (New York: Fox, Duffield, 1904), p. 79.

39 Ibid.

40 See for example Jon C. Teaford, *The Municipal Revolution in America* (Chicago, IL: University of Chicago Press, 1975), especially chs 2, 4, 7.

41 American colonists, to be sure, had experienced many attempts by the British to regulate the manufacturing and commerce of British North America. The evidence suggests, however, that manufacturing regulations were seldom effective, and the regulations of foreign trade – with a few notable exceptions, such as the tobacco trade – did not inflict a perceptible burden of any great significance on any group of colonial participants in the marketplace. See for example Peter D. McClelland, "The cost to America of British Imperial policy," *American Economic Review*, LIX (May 1969), pp. 370–81.

42 Charles Dickens, *Pictures from Italy and American Notes* (New York: Thomas Y. Crowell, undated), p. 270.

43 Ibid., p. 271.

44 "The spirit of discontent," *Lowell Offering*, I (April 1841), p. 112.

45 "We wished to imply no mock humility – nothing like the idea that we were worms, and other people stars, but that our situations were lowly, and our aims high" (Farley, "Editorial").

46 Quoted in John F. Kasson, *Civilizing the Machine* (New York: Grossman, 1976), p. 60.

47 Emerson, *Conduct of Life*, p. 79.

48 Noah Webster, *An American Dictionary of the English Language* (New York: S. Converse, 1828); Samuel Johnson, *A Dictionary of the English Language* (London: J. Johnson, G. Dilly, 1799). In both dictionaries, this meaning of the word "station" is the eighth definition given. Not surprisingly, condensed American dictionaries of the period tended to omit this definition altogether. See, for example, Joseph Hamilton (ed.), *Johnson's Dictionary of the English Language* (Boston, MA: West & Blake, 1810).

49 Charles Francis Adams, *The Works of John Adams* (Boston, MA: Charles C. Little and James Brown, 1851), vol. IV, p. 633.

50 Phillips, *Political Economy*, p. 152.

51 Francis Bowen, *The Principles of Political Economy* (Boston, MA: Little, Brown, 1856), p. 125.

52 For example, Francis Bowen speculates that even among "savages," when each reaps the fruits of his own labor, savings and investment are encouraged ("a wigwam well stocked with implements of war and the chase, and a store of food for future use"). Accordingly the entire community benefits ("the whole community profits by his savings; they operate to some extent as an insurance to them all against famine"), because that stock, while privately owned, is available for purchase or to repay a debt or in exchange for honors. (Bowen, *Political Economy*, p. 127.)

53 See for example Stephen Thernstrom, *Poverty and Progress* (Cambridge, MA: Harvard University Press, 1964), pp. 63–8. For other secondary sources on the same point, see ibid., p. 251, n. 4.

54 Ewbank, *World A Workshop*, p. 139.

55 Bowen, *Political Economy*, p. 127 (emphasis added).

56 Emerson, *Conduct of Life*, p. 91.

57 For a recent example, see Sean Wilentz, *Chants Democratic: New York City and the Rise of the American Working Class, 1788–1850* (New York: Oxford University Press, 1984), especially ch. 6.

58 For a brief outline of these movements and related documents, see John R. Commons et al. (eds), *A Documentary History of American Industrial Society* (New York: Russell & Russell, 1958), vol. VII, part II. The distinction between "productive" and "unproductive" labor (or classes) did persist in collective statements made by important union movements. When read in context, however, those statements did not imply (as radical usage of the same words did imply) that only labor or "productive" labor was deserving of reward. What was usually demanded in the name of productive labor was the restoration of fairness in the market system of the sort discussed below, not a new economic system. See also Maurice F. Neufeld, "The persistence of ideas in the American labor movement; the heritage of the 1830's," *Industrial and Labor Relations Review*, XXXV (January 1982), pp. 209–10.

59 For a careful refutation of Edward Pessen's claim that "in the Jacksonian period, anticapitalist thought was characteristic not of the fringe but of the central leadership of the American labor movement," see Maurice F. Neufeld, "Critique of Edward Pessen's *Most Uncommon Jacksonians: The Radical Leaders of the Early Labor Movement*," unpublished paper, Cornell University, 1982.

60 Commons et al., *Documentary History*, vol. V, pp. 87, 157, 160, 209, 212, 292–3, 308; vol. VI, pp. 184–6; vol. VII, pp. 113, 118–24, 129, 309; vol. VIII, pp. 235, 298; see also Wilentz, *Chants Democratic*, pp. 242, 252, 374.

61 Commons et al., *Documentary History*, vol. VI, p. 96.

62 Commons et al., *Documentary History*, vol. VIII, p. 130. See also ibid., vol. V, pp. 87–8; vol. VII, p. 113, 118; New-England Association of Farmers, Mechanics, and Other Working Men, *Preamble to 1831 Constitution*, reproduced in Knights of Labor, *Official Hand Book of the Rhode Island District Assembly 99* (District Executive Board, 1894), pp. 40–1.

63 Recommendations for limiting hours (usually to a maximum of ten) occur repeatedly in Commons et al., *Documentary History*, vols. V–VIII. For proposals to restrict apprentices, see ibid., vol. VI, pp. 167, 326; vol. VII, pp. 125–6.

64 Commons et al., *Documentary History*, vol. V, pp. 93, 150–2, 163, 258, 287–8, 301, 362, 367–8; vol. VI, pp. 25, 125, 165–6, 206; vol. VIII, pp. 94, 101; see also Neufeld, "Persistence of ideas," pp. 212–13. Another common "monopoly" concern of labor at this time was "monopoly of the soil." See for example Commons et al., *Documentary History*, vol. VIII, part V.

65 Commons et al., *Documentary History*, vol. V, p. 213; vol. VI, pp. 24, 26–7, 31, 55, 70, 117–18, 203, 206, 252, 294; vol. VIII, p. 96; also Wilentz, *Chants Democratic*, p. 247.

66 Commons et al., *Documentary History*, vol. VI, p. 252.

67 Commons et al., *Documentary History*, vol. VI, p. 27 (emphasis added).

68 *Voice of Industry*, July 3, 1845; reproduced in Norman Ware, *The Industrial Worker, 1840–1860* (Chicago, IL: Quadrangle, 1964), p. 210.

69 Ibid., pp. 209, 210. (The reporter ("an outsider") who gave the above account considered the plan advanced "one of the greatest pieces of folly I ever heard propounded by a man out of a mad-house" (ibid., p. 210).)

70 Commons et al., *Documentary History*, vol. V, pp. 93, 98–100, 158, 161, 174–7, 188, 195–9; vol. VI, pp. 201, 206–9, 256, 275; vol. VIII, p. 101; see also Neufeld, "Persistence of ideas," pp. 214–16.

71 Commons et al., *Documentary History*, vol. V, pp. 53–6; vol. VI, pp. 201, 236, 243–4; vol. VIII, pp. 225, 322–3.

72 The above quotations appear in Commons et al., *Documentary History*, vol. VI, pp. 85, 246–7. As further evidence of their moderate approach, and despite their distrust of political parties as too influenced by elites in general and employers in particular, labor organizations continually exhorted their members to use regular channels to elected officials to press their claims, and expressed confidence in "the constitutional and safe antidote of the ballot box" to "unequal legislation." (Ibid., vol. V, pp. 321–2; see also vol. VIII, pp. 99–101, 327–9.)

73 Written by T. V. Powderly, reproduced in *Labor: Its Rights and Wrongs* (Washington, DC: Labor Publishing Company, 1886), p. 71. For an example of the moderate tone that informed the Knights of Labor approach to strikes, see Knights of Labor, General Assembly, *Ninth Regular Session*, Hamilton, Ontario, October 6, 1885, pp. 89–90. For an illustration of how supply and demand analysis informed some of their policy positions, see the position taken on the merits of restricting immigration, ibid., pp. 121, 163.

74 Commons et al., *Documentary History*, vol. IX, p. 124.

75 Commons et al., *Documentary History*, vol. IX, pp. 247–51.

76 Commons et al., *Documentary History*, vol. X, p. 40.

77 Commons et al., *Documentary History*, vol. X, pp. 100–3.

78 Industrial Workers of the World, *Preamble and Constitution* (Chicago, IL: IWW General Headquarters, 1911), pp. 3–4. For an earlier example expressing similar sentiments in less strident language, see "Platform of the Social Democratic

Party," *Labor: Its Rights and Wrongs*, pp. 167–8.

79 For details of the various platforms framed at various national conventions (Ocala, 1890; Omaha, 1891; Cincinnati, 1891; St. Louis, 1892; Omaha again, 1892), see Fred A. Shannon (ed.), *American Farmers' Movements* (Princeton, NJ: Van Nostrand, 1957), pp. 151–61. For a sketch of post Civil War developments leading to these demands, see Commons et al., *Documentary History*, "Introduction to Volumes IX and X," vol. IX, pp. 19–51; for documents anticipating some of these demands, see ibid., vols. IX and X.

80 For an earlier example of a labor union tracing many of the nation's economic ills to a defective system of currency and credit, see Knights of Labor, General Assembly, *Ninth Regular Session*, pp. 118–19, 132, 164.

81 Earlier versions of this demand viewed government ownership as a last resort, as for example at the Populist's Cincinnati Convention (1891), which included in its platform: "We demand the most rigid, honest and just national control and supervision of the means of public communication and transportation, and if this control and supervision does not remove the abuses now existing we demand the government ownership of such means of communication and transportation."

82 See for example Lawrence Goodwyn, *The Populist Movement* (New York: Oxford University Press, 1978), pp. 293–319. Cooperative and communal ambtions also informed a large number of labor movements in powerful ways. This makes the widespread failure of cooperatives all the more puzzling. Although the details are still a subject of debate, the failure of a large number of cooperatives at bottom was an economic failure: they could not offer, over a sustained period of time, similar goods and services to those provided by private enterprises at prices that remained competitive. A question seldom asked is why cooperative prices had to be competitive. If belonging to a cooperative venture yielded high utility to participants, such ventures should have been able to survive while charging higher prices, with the incremental charge a measure of the utility to cooperative participants. The absence of such price differentials over sustained periods suggests that, whatever the utility from belonging, it did not translate into a very high monetary value.

83 With respect to taxation and its desired effects on income distribution, for example, the Populists did not want taxation, "National or State [to be] used to build up one interest or class at the expense of another." They did favor "a just and equitable system of graduated tax on incomes," but wanted the resulting revenue to be used not for income transfer programs, but for "the reduction of the burden of taxation now levied upon the domestic industries of this country." (Shannon, *American Farmers' Movements*, pp. 152, 154, 160.)

84 See Louis M. Hacker, *The Course of American Economic Growth and Development* (New York: Wiley, 1970), p. 265.

85 John L. Thomas, *Alternative America: Henry George, Edward Bellamy, Henry Demarest Lloyd and the Adversary Tradition* (Cambridge, MA: Belknap, 1983), p. 310.

86 Ibid., p. 331. The conventional nature of popular responses to perceived defects of the economic sytem during this period is illustrated by two other developments. Federal legislation crafted to combat monopolies did not attack bigness per se – a policy with far-reaching implications – but chose the narrow course of trying to define and outlaw certain "unfair competitive practices," such as price discrimination and exclusive-dealing arrangements. The Progressive Movement – a summary label for a variety of causes and a variety of actors – did address a wide

range of defects in the economic system, but that movement, as even writers of the extreme left concede, "had no cohesive body of doctrine or theoretical criticism of society." (Hacker, *American Economic Growth*, p. 259.)

87 Labor organizations did exist that were dominated by socialist, communist, or anarchist ideas. But even liberal historians concede that such groups existed only "along the edges of the labor movement, appealing especially to embattled miners, isolated lumberjacks, and outcast migratory workers in the West . . . ." (Robert H. Wiebe, *The Search For Order 1877–1920* (New York: Hill and Wang, 1967), p. 204.)

88 Ewbank, *World A Workshop*, pp. 171–2.

89 Bowen, *Political Economy*, p. 126.

90 Allen Thorndike Rice (ed.), *Reminiscences of Abraham Lincoln* (New York: North American Review, 1888), p. 297.

91 William M. Gouge, *A Short History of Paper-Money and Banking in the United States* (New York: B. & S. Collins, 1835), p. 30.

92 See for example John Patrick Diggins, *The Lost Soul of American Politics* (New York: Basic Books, 1984), p. 147; Rush Welter, *The Mind of America, 1820–1860* (New York: Columbia University Press, 1975), pp. 132–4.

93 *Federalist* (New York: Tudor, 1937), no. X, p. 70.

3 Economic justice and marginal productivity theory

1 For reasons why this difficulty cannot be satisfactorily circumvented by referring to directional changes in quantity and price in factor markets in response to shifts in demand or supply, see appendix E.

2 The position that the realism of assumptions is irrelevant for testing a theory is often incorrectly associated with the name of Milton Friedman. For a discussion of why such a position is highly suspect and not endorsed even by Friedman, see Peter D. McClelland, *Causal Explanation and Model Building in History, Economics, and the New Economic History* (Ithaca, NY: Cornell University Press, 1975), pp. 136–43.

3 Harvey Leibenstein, "More on X-efficiency: comment," *Quarterly Journal of Economics*, LXXXVI (May 1972), p. 330.

4 For a review of the main alternatives, see Martin Bronfenbrenner, "Neo-classical macro-distribution theory," in Jean Marchal and Bernard Ducros (eds), *The Distribution of National Income* (New York: Macmillan, 1968), pp. 476–501, and "Ten issues in distribution theory," in Sidney Weintraub (ed.), *Modern Economic Thought* (Philadelphia, PA: University of Pennsylvania Press, 1977), pp. 395–419.

5 The wide divergence between the premises of chapter 2 and the facts of contemporary English social and economic life may also help to explain why the principal attacks on marginal productivity theory – at least within the English-speaking world – have come from economists residing in Britain. These attacks have taken two main forms. One criticizes the assumptions of marginal productivity theory. The other attempts to develop an alternative theory of income distribution, which itself has been roundly criticized or largely ignored by American economists. This alternative theory makes distribution a function of decisions to save and to invest. In its simplest form, it assumes two classes of savers (property owners and workers), both with stable propensities to save from income (where income consists of profits and wages, and property owners are assumed to have the larger propensity to save). Income distribution (in equili-

brium) is therefore that distribution required to make total desired savings (the sum of savings by the two different groups) equal to desired investment. Thus the propensity to save and the propensity to invest become the key variables determining income distribution. For an outline of the theory and discussion of some of its flaws, see J. A. Kregel, "Some post-Keynesian distribution theory," in Weintraub (ed.), *Modern Economic Thought*, pp. 421–38. The Kregel survey also includes a helpful "Bibliographical note," pp. 437–8.

6 *Webster's Third New International Dictionary* (1981 edn).

7 P. T. Bauer, "Discussion," in Michael Novak and John W. Cooper (eds), *The Corporation: A Theological Inquiry* (Washington, DC: American Enterprise Institute, 1981), p. 101.

8 Henry Hazlitt, *The Foundations of Morality* (New York: Van Nostrand, 1964), p. 262. See also Irving Kristol, *Two Cheers for Capitalism* (New York: New American Library (Mentor Book), 1979), p. 172; Milton Friedman, *Capitalism and Freedom* (Chicago, IL: University of Chicago Press (Phoenix Books), 1965), pp. 164–6.

9 In some cases, the likelihood of continuing on to college was more than twice as great. See data on enrollment of 1968 high school graduates at senior and junior colleges in *Toward Equal Opportunity for Higher Education, Report of the Panel on Financing Low-Income and Minority Students in Higher Education* (New York: College Entrance Examination Board, 1973), p. 12.

10 Paul A. Samuelson, *Economics*, 11th edn, revised (New York: McGraw-Hill, 1980), p. 759. "The same relative scarcity of children of working-class families at state universities is found in Europe and in the Third World" (ibid.).

11 With respect to reading achievement, for example, "When the population of a school comes from homes in which the parents are themselves well educated, economically advantaged, and able to provide an environment in which reading materials and communications media are available, the school shows a generally superior level of reading achievement"; whereas "it must be admitted that [this] study provides very little evidence of the impact of the school or of specific school factors on the progress of students in reading"; both of which support the conclusion that "the home is the primary and continuing influence on a child . . . ." (Richard L. Thorndike, *Reading Comprehension Education in Fifteen Countries: An Empirical Study* (Stockholm: Almquist & Wiksell, 1973), pp. 177–9.) For a more recent study reaching similar conclusions, see Joyce L. Epstein, "Longitudinal effects of family–school–person interactions on student outcomes," *Research in Sociology of Education and Socialization*, IV (1983), 101–27.

12 Walter Lippmann, *Essays in the Public Philosophy* (New York: Mentor Book, 1955), p. 74.

13 Russell H. Conwell, *Acres of Diamonds* (New York: Harper & Brothers, 1915), p. 21.

14 Edward C. Banfield, *The Unheavenly City Revisited* (Boston, MA: Little, Brown, 1974), p. 235.

15 Michael Harrington, *The Other America: Poverty in the United States* (Baltimore, MD: Penguin, 1963), p. 131.

16 James Baldwin et al., "Liberalism and the Negro: a round-table discussion," *Commentary*, XXXVII (March 1964), p. 32.

17 A different and perhaps complementary explanation from that of constrained opportunity has occasionally been emphasized by writers of both left and right. Given (a) low income and (b) diminishing marginal utility of money, one would expect to find among low-income recipients a stronger than average preference for present gratification (what economists label "a higher marginal time preference").

See for example Kristol, *Two Cheers for Capitalism*, p. 213; Arthur M. Okun, *Equality and Efficiency: The Big Tradeoff* (Washington, DC: Brookings Institution, 1975), p. 80.

18 Thomas Sowell, *Race and Economics* (New York: Longman, 1975), p. 234. Sowell advances the argument as "anti-Malthusian," and not necessarily his.

19 Ibid.; see also p. 135.

20 The conservative Edward Banfield cited previously (see note 14) does not deny this possibility, but neither is he willing to endorse it as established fact. See Banfield, *Unheavenly City Revisited*, pp. 56, 61. Liberal economists sometimes bypass complex issues of behaviorism, but still suggest the poor (by and large) are not responsible for their poverty by noting the vicious circle an absence of money can perpetuate. See for example Robert Heilbroner and Lester Thurow, *Understanding Macroeconomics*, 8th edn (Englewood Cliffs, NJ: Prentice-Hall, 1984), p. 38.

21 Henry George, *Progress and Poverty* (New York: Robert Schalkenback Foundation, 1975), p. 309.

22 James Boswell, *The Life of Samuel Johnson* (London: George Bell, 1884), vol. III, p. 273; letter to James Boswell, December 7, 1782.

23 See, for example, Harrington, *The Other America*, pp. 21–3; Sowell, *Race and Economics*, pp. 225–38.

24 George Bernard Shaw, "On Mr. Mallock's proposed trumpet performance (A rejoinder)," *Fortnightly Review*, LXI (April 1, 1884), p. 478.

25 Paul A. Samuelson, *Economics from the Heart: A Samuelson Sampler*, ed. Maryann O. Keating (Sun Lakes, AZ: Thomas Horton and Daughters, 1983), p. 5.

26 The list would tend to be different for different factors of production. Entrepreneurs in pursuit of profits, for example, would be rewarded for such attributes as creativity and risk-taking.

27 William E. Simon, *A Time for Truth* (New York: McGraw-Hill, 1978), p. 199. Simon at this juncture is referring to the beliefs of the Founding Fathers, but he quickly adds "That is the quintessentially American philosophy" (ibid.).

28 Giovanni Sartori, *Democratic Theory* (Detroit, MI: Wayne State University Press, 1962), p. 327; quoted with approval by David Spitz, "A grammar of equality," *Dissent*, XXI (Winter 1974), p. 66.

29 See, for example, Friedrich A. Hayek, *The Constitution of Liberty* (Chicago, IL: University of Chicago Press, 1960), pp. 89, 388; Friedman, *Capitalism and Freedom*, pp. 165–6; Kristol, *Two Cheers for Capitalism*, p. 176; Michael Novak, *The American Vision: An Essay on the Future of Democratic Capitalism* (Washington, DC: American Enterprise Institute, 1978), pp. 24–5; Thomas Sowell, *The Economics and Politics of Race* (New York: William Morrow, 1983), p. 255; George F. Will, *Statecraft as Soulcraft* (New York: Simon & Schuster, 1983), pp. 130–1.

4 The market defended: confusions of the right

1 See for example Thomas Sowell, *Markets and Minorities* (New York: Basic Books, 1981), p. 45; Murray N. Rothbard, *Power and Market: Government and the Economy* (Kansas City, KS: Sheed Andrews and McMeel, 1977), ch. 3; Lay Commission on Catholic Social Teaching and the US Economy, *Toward the Future* (New York: Lay Commission on Catholic Social Teaching and the US Economy, 1984), p. 42; Irving Kristol, *Two Cheers for Capitalism*, (New York: New American Library (Mentor Book), 1979), p. 102.

2 Alan Truscott, "Chance steps in," *New York Times* (January 12, 1986), p. H38.
3 Friedrich A. Hayek, *The Constitution of Liberty* (Chicago, IL: University of Chicago Press, 1960), pp. 89–90; *The Road to Serfdom* (Chicago, IL: University of Chicago Press, 1960), p. 122; *Law, Legislation and Liberty* (Chicago, IL: University of Chicago Press, 1976), vol. 2, pp. 10, 71–3, 84–5, 87, 127; *New Studies in Philosophy, Politics, Economics and the History of Ideas* (Chicago, IL: University of Chicago Press, 1978), pp. 60, 141.
4 Hayek, *Constitution of Liberty*, pp. 88, 96–100; *New Studies in Philosophy*, pp. 57, 62–5, 140; *Road to Serfdom*, pp. 56, 58–9, 75, 79, 102–5, 124–5; *Law, Legislation and Liberty*, pp. 69–78, 83–5, 92, 94, 99.
5 More recently Hayek has modified, but only in a trivial way, his earlier assertions that any interference by the government in the workings of the market system would tend to lead to totalitarianism. While admitting "these fears so far have not materialized," and that since World War II "developments . . . in Britain as well as in the rest of the Western world have gone much less in the direction which the prevalent collectivist doctrines seemed to suggest was likely," he nevertheless has "never felt so pessimistic about the chances of preserving a functioning market economy as I do at this moment – and this means also of the prospects of preserving a free political order." The main threat he now views to be "the striving after this mirage of social justice." (Hayek, *New Studies in Philosophy*, pp. 105–6, 111.)
6 Herbert Clark Hoover, "The miracle of America," *Woman's Home Companion*, LXXV (November 1948), pp. 32–3.
7 Hayek, *New Studies in Philosophy*, p. 105.
8 A number of writers have tried to argue that Hayek did not make such dire forecasts. Hayek's own statement on the topic reads as follows: "Thirty years ago I wrote a book which, in a manner which many regarded as unduly alarmist, described the dangers that the then visible collectivist tendencies created for personal freedom. I am glad that these fears so far have not materialized, but I do not think this has proved me wrong. In the first instance I did not, as many misunderstood me, contend that if government interfered at all with economic affairs it was bound to go the whole way to a totalitarian system. I was trying to argue rather what in more homely terms is expressed by saying 'if you don't mend your principles you will go to the devil'." (*New Studies in Philosophy*, p. 105.) How such statements undercut the claim of making dire forecasts is unclear. George Stigler has argued that Hayek was not advancing a historical proposition but rather an analytical proposition "that totalitarian systems are an extreme form of, not a different type from, the democratic welfare states . . . ." (Stigler, *The Citizen and the State* (Chicago, IL: University of Chicago Press, 1975), p. 17.) But that analytical proposition was couched in terms that implied a high probability of a shift toward the extreme, and that tendency, in turn, is of little interest if it is presumed to have no grounding in historical fact.
9 Hayek, *Constitution of Liberty*, p. 99.
10 Hayek, *Law, Legislation and Liberty*, vol. 2, p. 83. "The attribute of justice may thus be predicated about the intended results of human action but not about circumstances which have not deliberately been brought about by men" (ibid., p. 70).
11 Conservative Irving Kristol has suggested an answer to this particular puzzle that is less than flattering to Hayek: " . . . I conclude, despite Professor Hayek's ingenious analysis, that men cannot accept the historical accidents of the marketplace – seen merely as accidents – as the basis for an enduring and

legitimate entitlement to power, privilege, and property. And, in actual fact, Professor Hayek's rationale for modern capitalism is never used outside a small academic enclave; I even suspect it cannot be believed except by those whose minds have been shaped by overlong exposure to scholasticism." (Kristol, *Two Cheers for Capitalism*, p. 247.)

12 The reader can find a similar reliance upon universal propositions to develop conclusions about economic justice in the writings of T. N. Carver, as explained in appendix F. One difference between these two writers is the intellectual progression evident in their work. Carver moved from general philosophical considerations in an earlier book to their economic implications in a later one. Rothbard appears to have begun with economic issues, and only gradually evolved a philosophical position to defend his economic policies. The sequence of his major books is *Man, Economy and State: A Treatise on Economic Principles* (Loss Angeles, CA: Nash, 1962); *Power and Market* (1970); *For a New Liberty* (New York: Macmillan, 1973); *The Ethics of Liberty* (Atlantic Highlands, NJ: Humanities Press, 1982).

13 Here Rothbard is quoting with approval the psychologist Leonard Carmichael (Rothbard, *Ethics of Liberty*, p. 11).

14 Ibid., p. 10.

15 Ibid.

16 Ibid., p. 6.

17 Ibid., p. 7, n. 2.

18 Rothbard discusses some of these philosophers in ibid., pp. 12–13, 15 n. 15.

19 Ibid., p. 10.

20 Ibid., pp. 4–5.

21 Rothbard, *For a New Liberty*, p. 26.

22 Ibid.

23 See for example Rothbard, *For a New Liberty*, pp. 26, 30, 31; *Ethics of Liberty*, pp. 31, 35.

24 Rothbard, *For a New Liberty*, p. 30.

25 The issue of rewarding the deserving traits of the producer also sems to be lurking in passages such as the following: "What is more inherent in an individual, more uniquely *his own*, than his inherited ability? If he is not to reap the reward from this, conjoined with his own willed effort, what *should* he reap a reward from? And why, then, should *someone else* reap a reward from *his* unique ability? Why, in short, should the able be consistently penalized, and the unable consistently subsidized?" (Rothbard, *Power and Market*, p. 187.) At other times Rothbard writes as if the claim to the fruits of one's labors is based upon the facts of causation. For example, he quotes approvingly the statement of a French laissez-faire economist who writes with respect to goods produced from "Nature": "This property is legitimate; it constitutes a right as sacred for man as is the free exercise of his faculties. It is his because it has come *entirely* from himself, and is in no way anything but an emanation from his being." (Rothbard, *For a New Liberty*, p. 36; emphasis added.)

26 Rothbard, *For a New Liberty*, p. 35.

27 Rothbard, *Ethics of Liberty*, p. 42.

28 See Rothbard, *Power and Market*, pp. 159, 169; also *Ethics of Liberty*, ch. 28, in which Rothbard challenges Friedrich Hayek's definition of "absence of coercion."

29 Here Rothbard is quoting James Sadowsky's "cogent and trenchant" definition (Rothbard, *Ethics of Liberty*, p. 23).

30 Rothbard, *Power and Market*, pp. 11, 66.

31 Ibid., p. 13.

32 Ibid., p. 101.

33 Rothbard, *For a New Liberty*, p. 41.

34 See, for example, Rothbard, *Power and Market*, pp. 108, 110, 120, 157. Occasionally – and only occasionally – statements are made suggesting that markets may not function all that well (see ibid., p. 172).

35 Ibid., p. 185; Rothbard, *Man, Economy, and State*, vol. I, ch. 7.

36 Stanley I. Kutler, *The Supreme Court and the Constitution: Readings in American Constitutional History* (Boston, MA: Houghton Mifflin, 1969), pp. 328–9.

37 "In the profoundest sense," Rothbard writes, "there *are* no rights but property rights" because "alleged 'human rights' can be boiled down to property rights . . ." (Rothbard, *Power and Market*, p. 176). For Rothbard's explanation of why the latter can be boiled down to the former, see ibid., pp. 176–7.

38 Even the noted conservative, Friedrich Hayek, has a broader and more complex definition than this, and for that reason is criticized by Rothbard (see *Ethics of Liberty*, ch. 28). The question of how freedom should be defined will be taken up in chapter 6.

39 For example, Rothbard claims that because perfect equality of opportunity can never be achieved, that goal should never be pursued (Rothbard, *Power and Market*, pp. 158–9).

40 Although his views are largely neglected by conservatives, another author of the right who defends marginal productivity justice is Henry Hazlitt. Like Rothbard, Hazlitt derives an "ought" from an "is," but without relying upon natural law. His argument in outline is that (a) happiness is the ultimate good, (b) social cooperation promotes happiness, (c) the market furthers social cooperation, and (d) paying factors the value of their marginal product is an integral part of the market system. Thus (a) is the intrinsic good, (b) and (c) are instrumental goods leading to (a), and (d) is an integral part of (c). See Henry Hazlitt, *The Foundations of Morality* (New York: Van Nostrand, 1964), passim; also *Man vs. The Welfare State* (New Rochelle, NY: Arlington House, 1969), pp. 116–22; *The Conquest of Poverty* (New Rochelle, NY: Arlington House, 1973), pp. 43–53, 56–8, 113–24.

41 Milton Friedman, *Capitalism and Freedom* (Chicago, IL: University of Chicago Press (Phoenix Books), 1965), p. 5. This is Friedman's landmark work on questions of freedom, justice, and the market sytem, with later writings elaborating or repeating points emphasized in this book. For other comments about freedom as the "ultimate goal," see ibid., pp. 4, 12, 195. Friedman's later works include *There's No Such Thing as a Free Lunch* (LaSalle, IL: Open Court, 1975); *From Galbraith to Economic Freedom*, Occasional Paper 49, Institute of Economic Affairs (Lancing, West Sussex: Gordon Pro-Print, 1977); *Bright Promises, Dismal Performance* (New York: Harcourt Brace Jovanovich, 1983); Milton Friedman and Rose Friedman, *Free to Choose* (New York: Harcourt Brace Jovanovich, 1980).

42 Friedman, *Capitalism and Freedom*, p. 2.

43 Ibid., pp. 2–3.

44 Ibid., p. 13.

45 Ibid., p. 8.

46 Ibid., p. 15. For a general discussion of the above points, see ibid., pp. 4–10, 13, 168; *There's No Such Thing as a Free Lunch*, pp. 131, 206.

47 If concentration of economic power results from the monopolistic practices of labor unions or big business, Friedman argues, the solution is to pass laws inhibiting those practices. See for example Friedman, *Capitalism and Freedom*, ch. 8.

48 Ibid., p. 4; see also pp. 5–16.
49 Friedman, *Bright Promises*, p. 101.
50 Friedman and Friedman, *Free to Choose*, pp. 133, 138. Friedman also notes the added bonus that the market, by providing an economic game of chance, contributes to the satisfaction (or utility) of those with a taste for uncertainty or games of chance (ibid., pp. 136–7; Friedman, *Capitalism and Freedom*, pp. 162–3).
51 See Milton Friedman, *Price Theory: A Provisional Text*, revised edn, (Chicago, IL: Aldine, 1970), chs. 9, 10; see also Friedman, *Capitalism and Freedom*, pp. 161–8.
52 Friedman, *Capitalism and Freedom*, pp. 163–6; *Bright Promises*, p. 101; Friedman and Friedman, *Free to Choose*, p. 136.
53 Friedman and Friedman, *Free to Choose*, pp. 134–5; Friedman, *Bright Promises*, pp. 92, 100–1.
54 Friedman and Friedman, *Free to Choose*, p. 134.
55 Ibid., p. 135.
56 Friedman, *Capitalism and Freedom*, p. 174.
57 Kristol, *Two Cheers for Capitalism*, p. 62; see below, chapter 11.
58 Friedman and Friedman, *Free to Choose*, p. 66.
59 Ibid., pp. 134–5; Friedman, *Bright Promises*, p. 92.

5 Redistribution defended: confusions of the left

1 See for example Paul A. Samuelson, *Economics*, 11th edn, revised (New York: McGraw-Hill, 1980), chs. 27–31. In a moment of candor, Samuelson has acknowledged, " . . .I fear that when the economic theorist turns to the general problem of wage determination and labor economics, his voice becomes muted and his speech halting. If he is honest with himself, he must confess to a tremendous amount of uncertainty and self-doubt concerning even the most basic and elementary parts of the subject." (Joseph E. Stiglitz, *Collected Scientific Papers of Paul A. Samuelson* (Cambridge, MA: MIT Press, 1966), vol. II, p. 1556.)
2 See for example Arthur M. Okun, *Equality and Efficiency: The Big Tradeoff* (Washington, DC: Brookings Institution, 1975), p. 42; Lester C. Thurow, "Toward a definition of economic justice," *Public Interest*, XXXI (Spring 1973), pp. 70–1, and *The Zero-Sum Society* (New York: Penguin 1981), pp. 56–7. Although not always appearing in the context of considering the worth of marginal productivity theory, the assumptions of that theory are often vigorously attacked as part of a larger dissatisfaction with neoclassical theory. See for example John Kenneth Galbraith, *The New Industrial State*, 2nd edn, revised (Boston, MA: Houghton Mifflin, 1971), pp. 124–35 (the assumption that employers maximize profits); "First draft of the U.S. bishops' Pastoral Letter on Catholic social teaching and the U.S. economy," *Origins*, XIV (November 15, 1984), pp. 352–3 (the assumption that labor markets are highly competitive).
3 Even many writers far to the left of center indicate a bias for preserving marginal productivity theory in some form. See for example Robert Heilbroner, *The Limits of American Capitalism* (New York: Harper & Row (Harper Torchbooks), 1967), p. 77; Branko Horvat, *The Political Economy of Socialism* (Armonk, NY: M. E. Sharpe, 1982), p. 275; Robert Lekachman, *National Income and The Public Welfare* (New York: Random House, 1972), p. 82.
4 Edward Nell, "Two books on the theory of income distribution: a review article," *Journal of Economic Literature*, X (June 1972), p. 444.

5 Again the reader is reminded of the point made earlier: "the left" examined here consists of those American writers left of center but right of more radical solutions, such as socialism and communism.

6 Irving Kristol, *Two Cheers for Capitalism*, (New York: New American Library (Mentor Book), 1979), p. 161.

7 Okun, *Equality and Efficiency*, p. 47. The reader might compare this justification for redistribution with the more narrow and less eloquent justification based upon the diminishing marginal utility of income that formed the core of Alan Blinder's case encountered in chapter 1.

8 See Okun, *Equality and Efficiency*, pp. 35–40.

9 Ibid., p. 37.

10 Ibid., p. 61.

11 See for example Kenneth J. Arrow, "A case for redistributing income: taxation and democratic values," *New Republic*, CLXXI (November 2, 1974), p. 25; Thurow, "Definition of economic justice," p. 80; James Tobin, "On limiting the domain of inequality," *Journal of Law and Economics*, XIII (October 1970), p. 276; Alan S. Blinder, *Hard Heads, Soft Hearts: Tough-Minded Economics for a Just Society* (Reading, MA: Addison-Wesley, 1987), pp. 23–6.

12 This concern for efficiency is sometimes explained in terms of the claim of neoclassical theory that a competitive equilibrium is a Pareto optimum; that is, in equilibrium, no one can be made better off without making someone else worse off (see for example Allen Buchanan, *Ethics, Efficiency and the Market* (Totowa, NJ: Rowman & Allanheld, 1985), chs. 1 and 2). But whether any economy has ever approximated the assumptions of the competitive model – and thus approximated a competitive equilibrium – is highly dubious (see Peter D. McClelland, *Causal Explanation and Model Building in History, Economics, and the New Economic History* (Ithaca, NY: Cornell University Press, 1975) pp. 117–25). All that is required for the purposes of this discussion is that *some* tradeoff exists: that as income is redistributed to achieve greater income equality, the effect on incentives and therefore on effort has a negative impact on total output. How that negative impact will work through a perfectly competitive market can be traced in detail by neoclassical theory, but that level of detail would not seem crucial to understanding the simple causal connections postulated here.

13 Exceptions can be found, but none would seem to have major status among the American economics profession. For examples of economists well to the left of center who do support this reasoning, see Robert Heilbroner, *Between Capitalism and Socialism* (New York: Vintage, 1970), pp. 94–7; Thomas E. Weisskopf, "Capitalism and equality," in Richard C. Edwards, Michael Reich, and Thomas E. Weisskopf (eds), *The Capitalist System* (Englewood Cliffs, NJ: Prentice-Hall, 1972), p. 128.

14 The reader should not infer that these are the only determinants of economic growth. As discussed below, the causes of growth remain, at best, poorly understood, but clearly involve such noneconomic factors as cultural values and political institutions (see chapter 10, pp. 188–94).

15 The classic statement of this presumed linkage is still A. C. Pigou, *The Economics of Welfare*, 4th edn (London: Macmillan, 1960), chs. 1, 7. For a compact review of Pigou's contributions to this idea and some of the lurking economic problems, see Harry Landreth, *History of Economic Thought* (Boston, MA: Houghton Mifflin, 1976), pp. 404–8.

16 Irving Kristol, *Reflections of a Neoconservative* (New York: Basic Books, 1983), p. 193.

17 This argument resonates with the concerns of T. N. Carver noted in appendix F, but can be found in such contemporary writers as Thomas Sowell, *The Economics and Politics of Race* (New York: William Morrow, 1983), pp. 136–7.

18 See for example Jack Kemp, *An American Renaissance* (New York: Berkley Books, 1981), ch. 2; Reginald H. Jones, "The transnational enterprise and world economic development," in Michael Novak and John W. Cooper (eds), *The Corporation: A Theological Inquiry* (Washington, DC: American Enterprise Institute, 1981), p. 139; Kristol, *Reflections of a Neoconservative*, p. 322; Michael Novak, *The Spirit of Democratic Capitalism* (New York: Simon and Schuster, 1982), pp. 272–6; Lay Commission on Catholic Social Teaching and the US Economy, *Toward the Future* (New York: Lay Commission on Catholic Social Teaching and the US Economy, 1984), pp. 23, 50, 70.

19 Walter W. Heller, *New Dimensions of Political Economy* (Cambridge, MA: Harvard University Press, 1967), pp. 12–13. For similar opinions emphasizing the same idea, see Alan S. Blinder, "A 7% jobless rate is just not good enough," *Business Week* (February 3, 1986), p. 16; Robert L. Heilbroner, *Business Civilization in Decline* (New York: W. W. Norton, 1976), p. 109.

20 John Rawls, *A Theory of Justice* (Cambridge, MA: Harvard University Press, 1971), p. 303 (emphasis added). The literature criticizing Rawls is voluminous, and ranges far beyond his positions on economic issues. Some of the more incisive of these writings are Robert Nozick, *Anarchy, State, and Utopia* (New York: Basic Books, 1974), pp. 183–231; Thomas Nagel, "Rawls on justice," *Philosophical Review* LXXXII (April 1973), pp. 220–34; R. M. Hare, "Rawls': A Theory of Justice," Parts I and II, *Philosophical Quarterly*, XXIII (April 1973), pp.144–55, and (July 1973), pp. 241–52.

21 An objection from philosopher David Lyons should be noted at this point. While he agrees that this assertion is a popular interpretation of Rawls's position, he believes it to be an incorrect interpretation. According to Lyons, "Although there are textual grounds for supposing that [Rawls] favors 'transfers' to improve the lot of the least advantaged, these are misleading because his principles apply only to the 'basic structure' (e.g., the basic economic institutions) and thus do not apply to (e.g.) legislative or administrative acts" (David Lyons, personal communication, July 19, 1988). When questioned on this point, Rawls replied: "The matter is quite complicated, but I should have thought that at least in a *general* way the two principles of justice do apply to legislation and administration, to their *overall* tendency. Whether a system of transfer payments is best (or an idea of Milton Friedman's [concerning] negative income taxes, now not much in favor) is another question, and perhaps rather doubtful" (John Rawls, personal communication, December 1988).

22 In their first draft, the bishops write that "The right to have a share of earthly goods sufficient for oneself and one's family belongs to everyone." This right, in turn, "establishes a strong presumption against inequality of income or wealth as long as there are poor, hungry and homeless people in our midst. . . . This presumption can be overcome only if an absolute scarcity of resources makes the fulfillment of the basic needs of all strictly impossible or if unequal distribution stimulates productivity in a way that truly benefits the poor." ("First draft of the U.S. bishops' Pastoral Letter," p. 352, para. 99.) This would not seem to be markedly different from Rawls's position, which the bishops evidently concede (ibid., p. 378, n. 23).

23 "Second draft of the U.S. bishops' Pastoral Letter on Catholic social teaching and the U.S. economy," *Origins*, XV (October 10, 1985), pp. 266–7, 275.

24 See for example Okun, *Equality and Efficiency*, p. 93; Joseph A. Pechman (ed.), *Economics for Policymaking: Selected Essays of Arthur M. Okun* (Cambridge, MA: MIT Press, 1983), pp. 610–11; Thurow, "Definition of economic justice," p. 62. Thurow (ibid.) also notes the further problem that the Rawlsian position would tend to favor a policy adding a small amount to the incomes of the poor while making the wealthiest 100 people twice as rich, a possibility that he finds objectionable.

25 John Kenneth Galbraith, *Economics and the Public Purpose* (Boston, MA: Houghton Mifflin, 1973), p. 266.

26 Thurow, *Zero-Sum Society*, p. 201.

27 Ibid.

28 Ibid.; see also Thurow, "Definition of economic justice," p. 79.

29 Thurow, *Zero-Sum Society*, p. 201. Thurow is quick to add that this particular distribution is not advanced as being ideal, but rather an "interim equity goal" (ibid., p. 202). For other related distribution policies advocated by Thurow, see ibid., p. 211.

30 Thurow, "Definition of economic justice," p. 78.

31 John Stuart Mill, *Principles of Political Economy* (London: Longmans, Green, 1902), p. 422. Thurow's pursuit of this possibility to the policy recommendation noted is foreshadowed in his earlier work *Generating Inequality: Mechanisms of Distribution in the U.S. Economy* (New York: Basic Books, 1975), pp. 48–9.

32 See for example Winifred Bell, Robert Lekachman, and Alvin L. Schorr, *Public Policy and Income Distribution* (New York: Center for Studies in Income Maintenance Policy, 1974), pp. 3–4; "Second draft of the U.S. bishops' Pastoral Letter," p. 275; Michael Harrington, *Decade of Decision: The Crisis of the American System* (New York: Simon and Schuster (Touchstone Book), 1980), p. 152n; Robert Lekachman, *Greed Is Not Enough* (New York: Pantheon, 1982), p. 207; Marcus G. Raskin, "Programmatic notes: progressive liberalism for the '80's," *Nation*, CCXXX (May 17, 1980), p. 590; Paul A. Samuelson, *Economics from the Heart*, ed. Maryann O. Keating (Sun Lakes, AZ: Thomas Horton and Daughters, 1983), p. 220.

33 Irving Kristol, "The high cost of equality," *Fortune*, XCII (November 1975), p. 199.

34 Okun, *Equality and Efficiency*, pp. 91–106.

35 Ibid., pp. 94–5.

36 Ibid.

37 Frank H. Knight, *The Ethics of Competition* (London: George Allen & Unwin, 1935), p. 56n. For a similar emphasis on "conscientious" and/or "productive" effort, see Herbert J. Gans, "Some problems of equality," *Dissent*, XX (Fall 1973), p. 413.

38 R. H. Tawney, *The Acquisitive Society* (New York: Harcourt Brace Jovanovich (Harvest Book), 1948), p. 179. In defense of this criterion, Tawney adds: "If a man has important work, and enough leisure and income to enable him to do it properly, he is in possession of as much happiness as is good for any of the children of Adam" (ibid.).

39 William A. Banner, "Distributive justice and welfare claims," *Social Research*, XLVII (Summer 1980), pp. 392–3. For a discussion of the lack of precision in Catholic church pronouncements on these matters prior to the bishops' Pastoral Letter cited earlier, see Hans J. Morgenthau, "On trying to be just," *Commentary*, XXXV (May 1963), pp. 421–2.

40 See for example Philip M. Crane, *The Sum of Good Government* (Ottawa, IL: Green

Hill, 1976), p. 35; Kristol, *Two Cheers for Capitalism*, pp. 26, 165–71, 208–9; Ayn Rand (ed.), *Capitalism: The Unknown Ideal* (New York: New American Library (Signet Book), 1967), pp. 193–4, 210; William E. Simon, *A Time for Truth* (New York: McGraw-Hill, 1978), p. 142.

41 See for example Ken Auletta, *The Underclass* (New York: Random House, 1982), p. xvi; Philip Green, *The Pursuit of Inequality* (New York: Pantheon, 1981), p. 217; Tom Hayden, *The American Future: New Visions Beyond Old Frontiers* (Boston, MA: South End Press, 1980), p. 178; Samuelson, *Economics from the Heart*, p. 21; Tawney, *Acquisitive Society*, p. 28; Thurow, *Zero-Sum Society*, p. 23.

6 On freedom

1 US Congress, Senate, Joint Committee on Atomic Energy, *Hearings on Confirmation of the Atomic Energy Commission and the General Manager*, 80th Cong., 1st sess., February 4, 1947, p. 131.

2 Isaiah Berlin, *Four Essays on Liberty* (revised edn) (New York: Oxford University Press, 1979), p. 121.

3 A compact survey of the history and various uses of both definitions is given by P. H. Partridge, "Freedom," in Paul Edwards (ed.), *Encyclopedia of Philosophy* (New York: Macmillan, 1967), vol. III, pp. 221–5.

4 With the aid of reasoning that would strike most Americans as convoluted, one can even defend the premise that the best way to make a people free is to have them submit to the will of a dictator (see Berlin, *Four Essays*, pp. 145–66). The very curiosity of this reasoning – which is not curious at all to many Europeans – is one more indication of how narrow the American spectrum of political ideology is compared with that of western Europe.

5 Partridge, "Freedom," p. 222.

6 Even within this seemingly narrow definition of freedom there is room for considerable disagreement as to what should count as "coercion." See, for example, Murray Rothbard's attack on Friedrich Hayek's notion of coercion in Rothbard, *The Ethics of Liberty* (Atlantic Highlands, NJ: Humanities Press, 1972), ch. 28.

7 *Federalist* (New York: Tudor, 1937), no. XV, p. 110.

8 "First inaugural address, 1801," in Saul K. Padover (ed.), *The Complete Thomas Jefferson* (New York: Tudor Publishing, 1943), p. 386. It should perhaps be added that Jefferson and Hamilton had different ideas about how frugal a government should be.

9 John Locke, *Two Treatises of Government*, ed. Peter Laslett (New York: New American Library, 1965), vol. II, para. 22, p. 324.

10 Modern interpretations of colonial concerns are dominated by Bernard Bailyn, *The Ideological Origins of the American Revolution* (Cambridge, MA: Harvard University Press, 1967). For recent reviews of related literature, see Joyce Appleby, "Introduction: republicanism and ideology," *American Quarterly*, XXXVII (Fall 1985), pp. 461–73; Linda K. Kerber, "The republican ideology of the revolutionary generation," *American Quarterly*, XXXVII (Fall 1985), pp. 474–95.

11 Quoted in Adrienne Koch, *Power, Morals and the Founding Fathers* (Ithaca, NY: Cornell University Press, 1961), p. 82.

12 Popular ideas for controlling the abuse of power by governments within America are, of course, not limited to those related to checks and balances. Others include

the Lockean notion that the right to govern rests on the consent of the governed, and the associated right to replace (or overthrow) a government that abuses the rights of the people. Also of crucial importance is the right to representative assemblies and to widespread suffrage. At bottom, all these ideas reflect the ideological foundations noted at the outset of this chapter: the dignity and integrity of the individual, and the associated belief that the state exists to serve the individual, and not vice versa.

13 Adam Smith, *The Wealth of Nations*, ed. Edwin Cannan (Chicago, IL: University of Chicago Press, 1976), vol. II, pp. 208–9 (vol. II, book IV, ch. 9).

14 Milton Friedman and Rose Friedman, *Free to Choose* (New York: Harcourt Brace Jovanovich, 1980), p. 20. For other examples of a similar endorsement of the minimal state, see Howard E. Kershner, *Dividing the Wealth* (Old Greenwich, CT: Devin-Adair, 1971), pp. 64–6; Ayn Rand, "The nature of government," in Ayn Rand (ed.), *Capitalism: The Unknown Ideal* (New York: New American Library (Signet Book), 1967), pp. 329–37; Rothbard, *Ethics of Liberty*, part III.

15 From Reagan's 1976 campaign for the presidential nomination, quoted in George F. Will, *Statecraft as Soulcraft* (New York: Simon and Schuster, 1983), p. 123.

16 Apart from minimizing the functions of government, conservatives also tend to favor diffusing the resulting power in America as widely as possible: from the federal government to the states and from the states to the localities. An additional benefit perceived to flow from such diffusion of power is making government less prone to waste and more responsive to the citizens' needs.

17 "Property" here means property in material things or revenues. For a brief account of how this narrow modern definition contrasts with older and broader definitions of property, see C. B. Macpherson, "Human rights as property rights," *Dissent*, XXIV (Winter 1977), pp. 72–3.

18 Edmund Burke, *Reflections on the Revolution in France*, ed. Conor Cruise O'Brien (New York: Penguin, 1981), p. 245.

19 *Federalist*, no. LXXIX, p. 472. Hamilton here is not arguing the case for property in general but for fixed salaries for judges in order to assure an independent judiciary.

20 "Freedom first," *Time* (June 16, 1986), p. 26.

21 A distinction should be noted in this context between (a) the strength of a right, and (b) the scope of a right. My property right to exclude trespassers may be "inviolable," or it may be a conditional right, subject to violation in times of national emergencies. But even if that particular right (to exclude trespassers) admits of no exceptions, the scope of my property rights may still be limited; for example, I may not have the right to use my property in ways that inflict damage on your property – say, by building downstream dams that flood your upstream acres. Rothbard seems to favor both the broadest possible scope, and the inviolability of rights covered within that scope.

22 John Stuart Mill, *Principles of Political Economy* (London: Longmans, Green, 1902), vol. I, book II, ch. 2, p. 278.

23 If monopoly power and its potential for coercive acts are generated in the private sector, the state should intervene to restore competition in the marketplace, or as a last resort, regulate a monopoly that cannot be avoided.

24 Michael Novak, *The Spirit of Democratic Capitalism* (New York: Simon and Schuster, 1982), p. 79.

25 See for example William F. Buckley, Jr, *Up From Liberalism* (New York: Stein and Day, 1984), p. 207; Philip M. Crane, *The Sum of Good Government* (Ottawa, IL: Green Hill, 1976), p. 13; Lay Commission on Catholic Social Teaching and the

US Economy, *Toward the Future* (New York: Lay Commission on Catholic Social Teaching and the US Economy, 1984), p. 48.

26 Milton Friedman, *Capitalism and Freedom* (Chicago, IL: University of Chicago Press (Phoenix Books), 1965), p. 4; Friedrich A. Hayek, *The Road to Serfdom* (Chicago, IL: University of Chicago Press, 1976), p. 100; Irving Kristol, *Two Cheers for Capitalism* (New York: New American Library (Mentor Book), 1979), p. xi; Novak, *Spirit of Democratic Capitalism*, p. 14; William E. Simon, "Big government or freedom – the line of economic freedom leads to slavery," *Vital Speeches of the Day*, XXXI (April 15, 1975), p. 389; Ludwig von Mises, *The Anti-Capitalist Mentality* (Princeton, NJ: Princeton University Press, 1956), p. 112.

27 Smith, *Wealth of Nations*, vol. I, book IV, ch. 2, p. 477.

28 Total output and total income generated in the creation of that output are merely two ways of aggregating the results of the same production process.

29 For a summary of the history of English ideas that came to link individual freedom, the minimal state, property rights, and freedom in the marketplace, see C. B. Macpherson, *The Political Theory of Possessive Individualism: Hobbes to Locke* (New York: Oxford University Press, 1979), ch. 6.

30 Charles Anderson, *The Political Economy of Social Class* (Englewood Cliffs, NJ: Prentice-Hall, 1974), p. 325.

31 Friedrich A. Hayek, *The Constitution of Liberty* (Chicago, IL: University of Chicago Press (Phoenix Books), 1978), pp. 20–1. Not all members of the right or left accept an identical definition of coercion, but Hayek's definition represents the opinion of many on both sides. For Hayek's disagreement with conservative Murray Rothbard on this point, see note 6.

32 Samuel Bowles and Herbert Gintis, *Schooling in Capitalist America* (New York: Basic Books, 1976), p. 54.

33 Philip Green, *The Pursuit of Inequality* (New York: Pantheon Books, 1981), p. 237.

34 See for example Anderson, *Political Economy of Social Class*, pp. 96, 299, 316.

35 Quoted in Ken Auletta, *The Underclass* (New York: Random House, 1982), p. 310; see also Bowles and Gintis, *Schooling in Capitalist America*, p. 37.

36 R. H. Tawney, *Equality* (Totowa, NJ: Barnes & Noble, 1980), p. 228. With imagery that is at once more colorful and more strained, Tawney makes the same point as "freedom for the pike is death for the minnows" (ibid., p. 164).

37 Bowles and Gintis, *Schooling in Capitalist America*, p. 10.

38 Karl Marx and Friedrich Engels, *The German Ideology*, ed. R. Pascal (New York: International Publishers, 1939), p. 59.

39 Martin Carnoy and Derek Sheaner, *Economic Democracy: The Challenge of the 1980's* (New York: M. E. Sharpe, 1980), p. 345; also ibid., pp. 17, 327.

40 Anderson, *Political Economy of Social Class*, p. 250.

41 Barry Goldwater, *The Conscience of a Conservative* (Shepherdsville, KY: Victor, 1960), p. 14 (emphasis in original).

42 "Second fireside chat of 1934, September 30," in Kenneth D. Yielding and Paul H. Carlson (eds), *Ah That Voice: The Fireside Chats of Franklin Delano Roosevelt* (Odessa, TX: John Ben Shepperd, Jr, Library of the Presidents, 1976), p. 48.

43 See for example Isaac Kramnick, "Equal opportunity and 'the race of life'," *Dissent*, XXVIII (Spring 1981), p. 183; Maurice Cranston, "Liberalism: English liberalism," in Paul Edwards (ed.), *Encyclopedia of Philosophy* (New York: Macmillan, 1967), vol. IV, p. 458.

44 US Congress, House, *Message to Congress, January 6, 1941*, 77th Cong., 1st sess., 1941, *Congressional Record*, 46.

45 The question of what a "right" means in this context will be taken up in chapter 9.

46 US Congress, House, *S.380 Debated in House*, 79th Cong., 1st sess., December 13, 1945, *Congressional Record*, 91, 12015.

47 John Locke, *An Essay Concerning Human Understanding*, ed. John W. Yolton (New York: Dutton, 1978), vol. I, book II, ch. 21, section 15, p. 200.

48 See Partridge, "Freedom," p. 222.

49 For a brief summary of those complexities, see ibid., pp. 221–5.

7 On equality

1 Isaiah Berlin, "Equality," *Proceedings of the Aristotelian Society*, new series, LVI (1955–6), p. 301.

2 "Mesh" does not imply that one idea logically entails the other, but rather, as Berlin points out, that the linkage is "more historical and psychological than logical" (Berlin, "Equality," p. 302).

3 Both claims, the secular and the theological, are, as Bernard Williams notes, "equally metaphysical" (Bernard Williams, "The idea of equality," in Peter Laslett and W. G. Runciman (eds), *Philosophy, Politics and Society* (Oxford: Basil Blackwell, 1962), 2nd series, p. 116).

4 Philosophers can offer a somewhat sterile derivation of the same point: sterile in the sense that while the logical linkage is more precise, the emotional appeal for Americans tends to be far less compelling. For example, "the 'naturalness' of the idea of equality seems to derive from the dual assumption that (a) men are all members of one species, of a simple class of objects (i.e., human beings) and (b) all members of a class should be treated uniformly unless there is good and sufficient reason not to do so" (Irving Kristol, "Equality as an ideal," in David L. Sills (ed.), *International Encyclopedia of the Social Sciences* (New York: Macmillan, 1968), vol. V, p. 108).

5 Cited in Jack Beatty, "The partriotism of values," *New Republic*, CLXXXV (July 4 and 11, 1981), p. 20.

6 Mario Cuomo, "Your one life can make a difference," speech delivered at Harvard Class Day, Cambridge, MA, July 5, 1985, *Vital Speeches of the Day*, LI (July 15, 1986), p. 584.

7 John Winthrop, "A model of Christian charity," *Collections of the Massachusetts Historical Society*, 3rd series, VII, p. 37.

8 Quoted from "Revised typescript for *The Swimmers*," in Matthew J. Bruccoli, *Some Sort of Epic Grandeur: The Life of F. Scott Fitzgerald* (New York: Harcourt Brace Jovanovich, 1981), p. 280.

9 See Max Lerner, *Tocqueville and American Civilization* (New York: Harper & Row (Harper Colophon Books), 1969), p. 20.

10 "One thinks first of the Americans' generosity. This trait distinguishes them from almost every other society on earth." Quoted in "To see ourselves as others see us," *Time* (June 16, 1986), p. 52.

11 Quoted in William Broyles, Jr, "The promise of America," *US News & World Report* (July 7, 1985), p. 28.

12 See for example US Congress, House, *Economic Opportunity Act of 1964 – Remarks on House Bill H.R. 11377*, 88th Cong., 2nd sess., August 7, 1964, *Congressional Record*, 18590; ibid., Subcommittee of the War on Poverty Program of the Committee on Education and Labor, *Hearings, Economic Opportunity Act of 1964*, 88th Cong., 2nd sess., 1964, pp. 189, 604; ibid., Senate, Select Committee on Poverty of the

Committee on Labor and Public Welfare, *Hearings, Economic Opportunity Act of 1964*, 88th Cong., 2nd sess., 1964, p. 265; ibid., House, *Social Security Act – Remarks in House*, 89th Cong., 1st sess., April 8, 1965, *Congressional Record*, 7373; ibid., Senate, *Social Security Act – Remarks in the Senate on Medical Care for the Aged H.R. 6675*, 89th Cong., 1st sess., July 8, 1965, *Congressional Record*, 15969; ibid., July 28, 1965, *Congressional Record*, 18512.

13 Richard Hofstadter, *The American Political Tradition* (New York: Alfred A. Knopf, 1948), p. viii.

14 Jacques Barzun, *God's Country and Mine* (Boston, MA: Little, Brown, 1954), p. 106.

15 Berlin, "Equality," pp. 302–5.

16 Ibid., pp. 302–3.

17 See W. D. Ross (ed.), *The Student's Oxford Aristotle* (London: Oxford Press, 1942), book VII, ch. 14, p. 1332b; Stanley I. Benn, "Justice," in Paul Edwards (ed.), *Encyclopedia of Philosophy* (New York: Macmillan, 1967), vol. IV, pp. 298–9.

18 This tendency to defend equality by striking down rather than building up would seem to be the norm. "Egalitarianism might be said not so much to assert equality as to deny the justice of some existing inequality of treatment based on some allegedly irrelevant differences of quality or circumstances" (Stanley I. Benn, "Equality, moral and social," in Edwards (ed.), *Encyclopedia of Philosophy*, vol. III, p. 40). In the case of American socialism, for example, "the inner core of the socialist critique," according to Robert Heilbroner, "has always been simple. It has attacked the institutions of society that have permitted the accumulation of private wealth, because it has identified wealth . . . with injustice" (Robert Heilbroner, *Between Capitalism and Socialism* (New York: Vintage Books, 1970), p. 35). This identification generally proceeds by attempting to knock down all of the arguments advanced by others to show that unequal distribution of wealth is just.

19 See for example Nicholas Rescher, *Distributive Justice* (New York: University Press of America, 1982), p. 74, including footnote 2; Heilbroner, *Between Capitalism and Socialism*, pp. 94–5. This reluctance of liberals to advocate perfect equality would seem to make largely irrelevant conservative attacks on this ideal as impossible to achieve (see for example Murray Rothbard, *Power and Market: Government and the Economy* (Kansas City, KS: Sheed Andrews and McMeel, 1970), pp. 212–16).

20 Arthur M. Okun, *Equality and Efficiency: The Big Tradeoff* (Washington, DC: Brookings Institution, 1975), p. 102; Henry C. Simons, *Personal Income Taxation* (Chicago, IL: University of Chicago Press, 1938), pp. 18–19. Both Okun and Simons support this claim in part by denying that prevailing inequalities have any justification in terms of desert. For other arguments by noted economists in favor of income redistribution, see Kenneth J. Arrow, "A case for redistributing income: taxation and democratic values," *New Republic*, CLXXI (November 2, 1974), pp. 23–5; James Tobin, "On limiting the domain of inequality," *Journal of Law and Economics*, XIII (October 1970), pp. 263–77.

21 Okun, *Equality and Efficiency*, p. 47. Other grounds have sometimes been offered by liberal economists in defense of income equality, in particular the twin assumptions of (a) identical utility functions across all individuals and (b) diminishing marginal utility of money (see for example Jan Tinbergen, *Income Distribution: Analysis and Policy* (Amsterdam: North-Holland, 1975), p. 129; Benjamin I. Page, "Utilitarian arguments for equality," unpublished Discussion Paper DP547-79, Institute for Research on Poverty, University of Wisconsin-Madison, pp. 14–15.) However, the latter kind of argument has never had widespread appeal as a foundation on which to base egalitarian claims. Indeed, it does not appeal to Okun (see Okun, *Equality and Efficiency*, p. 47, n. 22).

22 The example of cake dividing is much used to illustrate the point that the norm is equality of shares and inequality of shares requires justification. But almost never is this example accompanied by any discussion of how production conditions might provide the requisite justification for inequality of shares. See for example Berlin, "Equality," p. 305; Ian Bowen, *Acceptable Inequalities: An Essay on the Distribution of Income* (London: George Allen & Unwin, 1970), p. 97; Rescher, *Distributive Justice*, passim.

23 Okun, *Equality and Efficiency*, p. 33.

24 For evidence that worker rejection of McGovern's proposal went far beyond rubber workers, see Michael Harrington, *Decade of Decision* (New York: Simon and Schuster (Touchstone Book), 1980), p. 167.

25 Okun, *Equality and Efficiency*, p. 34.

26 Occasionally liberals will hint at a mismatch between their equality ideals and the ideals of most Americans. Robert Lekachman, for example, speaks of a particular negative income tax scheme he favors as appealing only to "a very few equality freaks like myself . . ." (Robert Lekachman, *Greed is Not Enough* (New York: Pantheon Books, 1982), p. 94). But almost never do they candidly admit that, for most Americans, income inequality per se is *not* unlovely.

8 Equality and freedom in the economic race: the modern perspective

1 Rarely do conservatives oppose free universal education as a policy goal. (Opponents, however, are not impossible to find; for example, Ludwig von Mises, *The Free and Prosperous Commonwealth; An Exposition of the Ideas of Classical Liberalism* (Princeton, NJ: Van Nostrand, 1962), p. 115.) The idea of education vouchers made popular by Milton Friedman, while constituting a radical revision in the way that public education would be supplied, is merely a variant of making that education free through the provision of vouchers (see Milton Friedman, *Capitalism and Freedom* (Chicago, IL: University of Chicago Press (Phoenix Books), 1965), ch. VI).

2 For evidence on education categories in which America leads other countries, see Sidney Verba and Gary R. Orren, *Equality in America: The View from the Top* (Cambridge, MA: Harvard University Press, 1985), p. 12, and the sources they cite on p. 302, n. 16.

3 R. H. Tawney, *Equality* (Totowa, NJ: Barnes & Noble, 1980), p. 145.

4 Brown v. Board of Education of Topeka, 347 U.S. 483, 494–5, 1954.

5 John Dewey, *Democracy and Education* (New York: Macmillan, 1916), p. 24. James Coleman, author of the much discussed Coleman Report of the mid-1960s, summarized his findings of this complex topic this way: "The finding is that students do better when they are in schools where their fellow students come from backgrounds strong in educational motivation and resources. The results might be paraphrased by the statement that the educational resources provided by a child's fellow students are more important for his achievement than are the resources provided by the school board. This effect appears to be particularly great for students who themselves come from educationally-deprived backgrounds. For example, it is about twice as great for Negroes as for whites." ("Toward open schools," *Public Interest*, IX (Fall 1967), p. 21.)

6 US Congress, Senate, Select Committee on Poverty of the Committee on Labor and Public Welfare, *Hearings, Economic Opportunity Act of 1964*, 88th Cong., 2nd sess., 1964, p. 109.

7　For a concise review of the history of federal action and a discussion of some of the limitations of federal programs as they currently exist, see Sandra R. Baum and Saul Schwartz, "The fairness test for student-aid cuts," *Challenge*, XXVIII (May–June, 1985), pp. 39–46.

8　Aside from egalitarian issues, imperfections in the capital market are also a commonly cited reason by economists to justify government support of student loans. See for example Charles L. Schultze, *The Public Use of Private Interest* (Washington, DC: Brookings Institution, 1977), p. 40.

9　US Congress, House, *Economic Opportunity Act of 1964, Remarks in House on Bill (H.R. 11377) to enact*, 88th Cong., 2nd sess., August 7, 1964, *Congressional Record*, 18591.

10　US Congress, Senate, Select Committee on Poverty of the Committee on Labor and Public Welfare, *Hearings, Economic Opportunity Act of 1964*, 88th Cong., 2nd sess., 1964, p. 98.

11　Congressman Roman C. Pucinski of Illinois, quoting from an editorial in the Chicago *Sun–Times*; US Congress, House, *Economic Opportunity Act of 1964, Remarks in House on Bill (H.R. 11377) to enact*, 88th Cong., 2nd sess., August 7, 1964, *Congressional Record*, 18592.

12　US Congress, House, *Economic Opportunity Act of 1964, Remarks in House on Bill (H.R. 11377) to enact*, 88th Cong., 2nd sess., August 5, 1964, *Congressional Record*, 18208.

13　*Preamble to the Economic Opportunity Act*, US Congress, Senate, Select Committee on Poverty of the Committee on Labor and Public Welfare, *Hearings, Economic Opportunity Act of 1964*, 88th Cong., 2nd sess., 1964, p. 3.

14　One public program, the Job Corps, was designed as an alternative to classroom training. Established under the Economic Opportunity Act of 1964, it provided the equivalent of boarding schools designed to remove low-income youth from the allegedly undesirable influences of economically deprived neighborhoods. Costs were accordingly high and participation limited. Thus the program, while offering benefits to those involved, has reached only a small percentage of the disadvantaged.

15　For a concise review of the main public and private programs provided and the evidence concerning their limited success, see Gary Burtless, "Manpower policies for the disadvantaged: what works?" *Brookings Review*, III (Fall 1984), pp. 18–22.

16　Robert Kuttner, "A great American tradition: government opening opportunity," *Challenge*, XXIX (March–April 1986), p. 23.

17　David Jay (ed.), *The Kennedy Reader* (New York: Bobbs-Merrill, 1967), p. 8.

18　Robert Rhodes (ed.), *Winston S. Churchill: His Complete Speeches, 1897–1963* (New York: Chelsea House, 1974), vol. II, p. 1317.

19　See note 10.

20　Economists commonly distinguish between having monopoly power as a seller (simply called "monopoly") and having monopoly power as a buyer (or "monopsony"), where the latter case can exist, for example, in the "company town" of only one employer.

21　Generations of economists have quoted the Scotsman's pessimistic expectations on this point: "People of the same trade seldom meet together, even for merriment and diversion, but the conversation ends in a conspiracy against the public, or in some contrivance to raise prices" (Adam Smith, *The Wealth of Nations*, ed. Edwin Cannan (Chicago, IL: University of Chicago Press, 1976), book I, ch. 10, part II, p. 144).

22　Theodore Roosevelt, *Address of President Roosevelt on the Occasion of the Laying of the Corner Stone of the Pilgrim Memorial Monument, Provincetown, Massachusetts, August 20, 1907* (Washington, DC: Government Printing Office, 1907), p. 47.

23 Franklin D. Roosevelt, "Acceptance of the Renomination for the Presidency, Philadelphia, Pa., June 27, 1936," in Samuel I, Rosenman (ed.), *The Public Papers and Addresses of Franklin D. Roosevelt* (New York: Random House, 1938), vol. V, p. 233.

24 The economist's attack on monopoly focuses upon issues of efficiency, not on issues of fairness. But the issue for most Americans has always been fairness first, with efficiency a distant second.

25 See for example Milton Friedman, *There's No Such Thing As A Free Lunch* (LaSalle, IL: Open Court, 1975), p. 35; Friedrich Hayek, *The Constitution of Liberty* (Chicago, IL: University of Chicago Press (Phoenix Books), 1978), ch. 18; Henry Hazlitt, *The Conquest of Poverty* (New Rochelle, NY: Arlington House, 1973), p. 142; Sylvester Petro, "Labor-service agencies in a free society," in *Champions of Freedom*, Ludwig von Mises Lecture Series (Hillsdale, MI: Hillsdale College Press, 1974), pp. 93–109; Murray Rothbard, *Man, Economy and State: A Treatise on Economic Principles* (Los Angeles, CA: Nash, 1962), pp. 620–32.

26 John Kenneth Galbraith, *American Capitalism: The Concept of Countervailing Power* (Boston, MA: Houghton Mifflin, 1956); for a summary of policies advocated, see Galbraith, *Economics and the Public Purpose* (Boston, MA: Houghton Mifflin, 1973), p. 263.

27 US Congress, House, Subcommittee on the War of Poverty Program of the Committee on Education and Labor, *Hearings, Economic Opportunity Act of 1964*, 88th Cong., 2nd sess., 1964, p. 438.

28 Ibid., p. 429.

29 Mark R. Disler, Deputy Assistant Attorney General, Civil Rights Division, Justice Department, letter to the *New York Times* (August 2, 1986), p. 22.

30 Ibid.

31 See for example Friedman, *Capitalism and Freedom*, pp. 111–15.

32 See for example Michael Harrington and Irving Howe, *The Seventies: Problems and Proposals* (New York: Harper & Row, 1972), pp. 282, 338; Sar A. Levitan and Clifford M. Johnson, *Beyond the Safety Net: Reviving the Promise of Opportunity in America* (Cambridge, MA: Ballinger, 1984), p. 168; Rudy Oswald, "The economy and workers' jobs, the living wage and a voice," in John W. Houck and Oliver F. Williams (eds), *Catholic Social Teaching and The United States Economy* (Washington, DC: University Press of America, 1984), pp. 83–4; Lester C. Thurow, *The Zero-Sum Society* (New York: Penguin, 1981), pp. 204–6.

33 Advocates of a steep inheritance tax are not impossible to find; for example, it is mentioned as something of an aside in Kenneth J. Arrow, "A case for redistributing income: taxation and democratic values," *New Republic*, CCXXI (November 2, 1974), p. 25, and vigorously advocated in Michael Harrington, *Decade of Decision* (New York: Simon and Schuster (Touchstone Book), 1980), pp. 174–6. The position of most American liberals, however, would seem closer to that of Arthur Okun, who underscores the efficiency costs and questions the benefits of using very high income taxes or steep inheritance taxes to limit the political power of the wealthy (Okun, *Equality and Efficiency: The Big Tradeoff* (Washington, DC: Brookings Institution, 1975), pp. 22–31, 94).

34 Even when someone as influential as newly elected Speaker of the House Jim Wright proposed in December 1986 that the tax rate for the wealthy be revised slightly upward from the top rate enacted by the sweeping tax reform bill of that year, the responses in Congress on both sides of the aisle "ranged from skepticism to outright hostility." The Wright proposal was therefore quickly scrapped (*New York Times* (December 10, 1986), pp. A1, D2).

35 Disabled persons were, according to Aristotle, entitled to "a grant for food at the public expense at the rate of 2 obols a day each" (Aristotle, *The Athenian Constitution*, trans. H. Rackham (Cambridge, MA: Harvard University Press, 1971), vol. XX, pp. 137, 139).

36 "The welfare state and its neoconservative critics." *Dissent*, XX (Fall 1973), p. 453.

37 Okun, *Equality and Efficiency*, p. 17.

38 Following the American Civil War, a comprehensive pension scheme for veterans and their dependents was introduced in America. But the introduction of this program obviously was not symptomatic of a widespread desire to pioneer social welfare programs, as subsequent developments demonstrated repeatedly.

39 Rosenman (ed.), *Public Papers and Addresses of Franklin D. Roosevelt*, vol. I, p. 458.

40 "Message to the Congress on Social Security, January 17, 1935," in ibid., p. 46.

41 Testimony of Bernard J. Sheil, Auxiliary Bishop of Chicago, in US Congress, Senate, Subcommittee of the Committee on Banking and Currency, *Hearings, Full Employment Act of 1945*, 79th Cong., 1st sess., 1945, p. 839.

42 Ibid., p. 1016.

43 The social security system of old-age benefits actually introduced was never, strictly speaking, an insurance scheme even at the outset, although the popular view and the popular debates tended to emphasize this aspect. The linkage between payments made and benefits received was never ironclad, even at the beginning, and through successive amendments was gradually made even less so over time.

44 Rosenman (ed.), *Public Papers and Addresses of Franklin D. Roosevelt*, vol. IV, p. 19.

45 Ibid., p. 20.

46 See George H. Gallup, *The Gallup Polls, 1935–1971* (New York: Random House, 1972), vol. I: *1935–1948*, pp. 61, 84, 155, 173; Michael E. Schiltz, *Public Attitudes Toward Social Security, 1935–1965* (Washington, DC: US Government Printing Office, 1970), pp. 115–17, 156.

47 US Congress, Senate, *Remarks in Senate on Bill (H.R. 6000) to enact*, 81st Cong., 2nd sess., June 19, 1950, *Congressional Record*, 8803.

48 Ibid., 8789.

49 "Income maintenance including financing of health costs from the White House Conference of Aging," reproduced in US Congress, Senate, *Remarks in Senate on Bill (H.R. 10606) to enact*, 87th Cong., 2nd sess., July 17, 1962, *Congressional Record*, 13838.

50 US Congress, House, *Remarks in House on Bill (H.R. 6675) to enact*, 89th Cong., 1st sess., April 8, 1965, *Congressional Record*, 7369.

51 Senator Hiram L. Fong, in US Congress, Senate, *Remarks in Senate on Bill (H.R. 6675) to enact*, 89th Cong., 1st sess., July 28, 1965, *Congressional Record*, 18512.

52 For a discussion of the origins of this phrase and the popularity of the idea, see James T. Patterson, *America's Struggle Against Poverty, 1900–1980* (Cambridge, MA: Harvard University Press, 1981) ch. 12.

53 For a brief description and evaluation of these training programs, see pp. 128–9.

54 "Office of Economic Opportunity during the Administration of President Lyndon B. Johnson, Nov. 1963–Jan. 1969: an administrative history," vol. I, p. 33, Lyndon Johnson Library, Austin, TX; quoted in Patterson, *America's Struggle Against Poverty*, p. 135.

55 Edward Kosner, Jacquin Sandels and Frank Trippet, "Poverty U.S.A.," *Newsweek* (February 17, 1964), p. 38.

56 Quoted in "Around the Capitol," *Congressional Quarterly Weekly Report*, XXII (March 27, 1964), p. 632.

57 Patterson, *America's Struggle Against Poverty*, p. 164.

58 The decline in unemployment insurance spending in constant dollar terms between 1975 and 1983 – two years in which unemployment hovered in the 9 percent range – reflects to a significant degree a drop in the percentage of jobless workers collecting benefits. According to a Labor Department official, 67.2 percent of all jobless workers collected such benefits in May 1975 compared with 28.5 percent in September 1986. Observed Jane L. Norwood, Commissioner of Labor Statistics, "we really don't know" the reasons for this decline, but she "guesses that it primarily relates to actions to tighten eligibility requirements, most of them by individual states, in the Carter and Reagan years." (Quoted in Robert D. Hershey, Jr, "High, but stable, U.S. unemployment is gaining acceptance," *New York Times* (October 14, 1986), p. A28.)

59 In constant (1967) dollar terms, from $157 in 1970 to $136 in 1975 to $105 in 1983. Average monthly payment per family from US Department of Commerce, *Statistical Abstract of the United States: 1981* (Washington, DC: US Government Printing Office, 1981), p. 345; *Statistical Abstract of the United States: 1986* (Washington, DC: US Government Printing Office, 1986), p. 381. Data deflated by consumer price index (CPI-U series) in US Department of Commerce, *Business Statistics: 1984* (Washington, DC: US Government Printing Office, 1985), p. 24.

60 Here "public welfare" was defined as "education," "health," and "income maintenance expenditure." See Organization for Economic Co-operation and Development (OECD), "Public expenditure trends," *Studies in Resource Allocation*, no. 5 (Paris: OECD, 1978), p. 25. (Percentages calculated for gross domestic product rather than gross national product).

61 Ibid. Such rankings can be criticized for their failure to correct for the relative needs of the respective populations. See, for example, Neil Gilbert, "How to rate a social-welfare system," *Wall Street Journal* (January 13, 1987), p. 28. But these corrections, even if they could be made in generally accepted ways, would be unlikely to challenge the central point of this and other evidence – that American treatment of its disadvantaged is markedly different from that of most other advanced industrial nations.

62 The plan called for a minimum of $500 per adult and $300 per child per year, or $1600 for a two-parent family of four.

63 All adult recipients except the aged, disabled, and mothers with preschool children had to accept training or work or forfeit their subsidies. Families could keep the first $60 per month of income earned without giving up any aid, and beyond that amount relief payments would go down as income earnings increased (up to a specified maximum), but reductions in the first were significantly less than gains in the second.

64 For a summary of this resistance plus a list of sources on the in-fighting, see Patterson, *America's Struggle Against Poverty*, pp. 192–8; James Welsh, "Welfare reform: born, Aug. 8, 1969; died, Oct. 4, 1972 – a sad case study of the American political process," *New York Times Magazine* (January 7, 1973), pp. 14–17, 21–3; Theodore R. Marmor and Martin Rein, "Reforming the 'welfare mess': the fate of the family assistance plan, 1969–72," in Allan P. Sindler (ed.), *Policy and Politics in America* (Boston, MA: Little, Brown, 1973), pp. 2–28.

65 Mitchell Ginsberg, "An indefatigable lobbyist for the FAP approach," quoted in James Welsh, "Welfare reform," p. 23.

66 Patterson, *America's Struggle Against Poverty*, p. 99.
67 Ibid., p. 209. For a similar characterization based upon comparisons with other advanced industrial nations, see Robert Kuttner, *The Economic Illusion* (Boston, MA: Houghton Mifflin, 1984), pp. 238–58.

9 On rights

1 US Congress, House, Committee on Expenditures in the Executive Departments, *Hearings, Full Employment Act of 1945*, 79th Cong., 1st sess., 1945, p. 1.
2 US Congress, Senate, *Full Employment Act of 1945, Remarks in Senate on Bill (S. 380) to enact*, 79th Cong., 1st sess., September 25, 1945, *Congressional Record*, 8958.
3 See for example US Congress, House, Committee on Expenditures in the Executive Departments, *Full Employment Act of 1945*, 79th Cong., 1st sess., 1945, p. 619.
4 For a short review of these issues, see Stanley I. Benn, "Rights," in Paul Edwards (ed.), *The Encyclopedia of Philosophy* (New York: Macmillan, 1967), vol. VII, pp. 195–9; for a longer review, see A. I. Melden, *Rights and Right Conduct* (Oxford: Basil Blackwell, 1959).
5 Benn, "Rights," p. 196.
6 Adam Smith, *The Theory of Moral Sentiments* (Indianapolis, IN: Liberty Classics, 1976), p. 158.
7 Herbert Spencer, *The Man Versus The State* (Indianapolis, IN: Liberty Classics, 1981), p. 187.
8 Ayn Rand, "Man's rights," in Ayn Rand (ed.), *The Virtue of Selfishness* (New York: New American Library (Signet Book), 1964), p. 95.
9 David Hume, *A Treatise of Human Nature*, ed. L. A. Selby-Bigge (Oxford: Clarendon Press, 1975), book III, part II, section VI, p. 526.
10 Samuel I. Rosenman (ed.), *The Public Papers and Addresses of Franklin D. Roosevelt* (New York: Harper, 1950), vol. XIII, p. 41.
11 *The Impact of the Universal Declaration of Human Rights* (New York: United Nations Department of Social Affairs, 1951), p. 40.
12 Rights advocated by the Pope are outlined and discussed in "First draft of the U.S. bishops' Pastoral Letter on Catholic social teaching and the U.S. economy," *Origins*, XIV (November 15, 1984), p. 350.
13 Democratic Congressman Estes Kefauver, in US Congress, House, *Full Employment Act of 1945, Remarks in House on Bill (S. 380) to enact*, 79th Cong., 1st sess., December 13, 1945, *Congressional Record*, 12015.
14 US Congress, Senate, *Full Employment Act of 1945, Remarks in Senate on Bill (S. 380) to exact*, 79th Cong., 1st sess., September 28, 1945, *Congressional Record*, 9116.
15 Ibid., September 27, 1945, *Congressional Record*, 9065.
16 Section 3(d) of the proposed act read in part:

> . . . the Federal Government shall, in cooperation with industry, agriculture, labor, State and local governments, and others, develop and pursue a consistent and carefully planned economic program with respect to, but not limited to, taxation; banking, credit, and currency; monopoly and monopolistic practices; wages, hours, and working conditions; foreign trade and investment; agriculture; education; housing; social security; natural resources; the provision of public services, works, and research; and other revenue, investment, expenditure, service, or regulatory activities of the Federal Government. Such program shall, among other things –

(1) stimulate, encourage, and assist private enterprises to provide, through an expanding production and distribution of goods and services, the largest feasible volume of employment opportunities;

(2) stimulate, encourage, and assist State and local governments, through the exercise of their respective functions, to make their most effective contribution to assuring continuing full employment . . . .

(ibid., September 20, 1945, *Congressional Record*, 8917).

17 The act did state that "to the extent that continuing full employment cannot otherwise be assured, [the Federal Government shall] provide such volume of Federal investment and expenditure as may be needed, in addition to the investment and expenditure by private enterprises, consumers, and State and local governments, to assure continuing full employment" (ibid.). But Keynesian theory justifying such action was little understood by American legislators in 1945, and the associated Keynesian countercyclical policies were never deliberately implemented until the 1960s.

18 US Congress, Senate, Subcommittee of the Committee on Banking and Currency, *Hearings, Full Employment Act of 1945*, 79th Cong., 1st sess., 1945, p. 1008; testimony of Rt Rev. Msgr John O'Grady, Secretary, National Conference of Catholic Charities.

19 George F. Will, *The Pursuit of Virtue and Other Tory Notions* (New York: Simon and Schuster, 1982), p. 92.

20 Edmund Fuller, in a review of Robert Nisbet's *Prejudices: A Philosophical Dictionary* in *Wall Street Journal* (October 4, 1982), p. 32. For a recent and pointed statement on rights reflecting the deep division between liberals and conservatives within the Catholic Church concerning the appropriate usage of this term, see Lay Commission on Catholic Social Teaching and the U.S. Economy, "LIBERTY and justice for all," Report on the final draft (June 1986) of the US Catholic bishops' Pastoral Letter "Economic justice for all," November 5, 1986, pp. 10–12.

21 Chamber of Commerce of the United States, *Proceedings of the National Symposium on Guaranteed Income*, Washington, DC, December 9, 1966, p. 13.

22 "We will need to adopt the concept of an absolute constitutional right to an income. This would guarantee to every citizen of the United States, and to every person who has resided within the United States for a period of five consecutive years, the right to an income from the federal government sufficient to enable him to live with dignity. No government agency, judicial body, or other organization whatsoever should have the power to suspend or limit any payments assured by these guarantees" (Robert Theobold (ed.), *The Guaranteed Income: Next Step in Economic Evolution* (Garden City, NY: Doubleday, 1966), p. 229).

23 Tom Hayden, *The American Future: New Visions Beyond Old Frontiers* (Boston, MA: South End Press, 1980), p. 307.

24 Walter F. Heller, *New Dimensions of Political Economy* (Cambridge, MA: Harvard University Press, 1967), p. 59.

25 David Spitz, "A grammar of equality," *Dissent*, XXI (Winter 1974), p. 76.

26 US Congress, Senate, Subcommittee of the Committee on Banking and Currency, *Hearings, Full Employment Act of 1945*, 79th Cong., 1st sess., 1945, p. 121.

10 Four questions of fact

1 William F. Buckley, Jr, *Up From Liberalism* (New York: Stein and Day, 1984), p. 211.

2 Lay Commission on Catholic Social Teaching and the US Economy, *Toward the Future* (New York: Lay Commission on Catholic Social Teaching and the US Economy, 1984), p. 50. The Commission here is speaking of the causes of "the wealth of nations," but present wealth is a function of past growth.

3 Daniel Patrick Moynihan, *Family and Nation* (New York: Harcourt Brace Jovanovich, 1986), p. 143; Charles Murray, *Losing Ground: American Social Policy 1950–1980* (New York: Basic Books, 1984), pp. 227–8, and "No, welfare isn't really the problem," *Public Interest* LXXXIV (Summer 1986), pp. 6–8. (The title of the latter is misleading: for Murray, welfare is at the heart of the problem.)

4 "First draft of the U.S. bishops' Pastoral Letter on Catholic social teaching and the U.S. economy," *Origins*, XIV (November 15, 1984), pp. 337–83.

5 Lay Commission, *Toward the Future.*

6 One exception to this propensity of economists to ignore broad causal forces in narrowly circumscribed growth models is the recent work of Gary Becker, whose "preliminary results confirm the evidence from several other studies that per capita income growth is *positively* related to the degree of political democracy" (Gary S. Becker, "An environment for economic growth," *Wall Street Journal* (January 1, 1989), p. A8). The key issue, however, is whether such institutions contribute a lot or a little; to estimate that contribution requires a model; and contribution estimates of even simple growth models are highly suspect, as subsequent discussion attempts to demonstrate.

7 Quoted in Robert Kuttner, "It's dismal, all right – but is it a science?" *Business Week* (January 30, 1989), p. 16.

8 Murray, "No, welfare isn't really the problem," p. 7.

9 For a recent review of some of the main findings of child psychologists, see Urie Bronfenbrenner, "Ecological systems theory," in Rose Vasta (ed.), *Six Theories of Child Development: Revised Formulations and Current Issues* (Greenwich, CT: JAI Press, 1989), Annals of Child Development VI, pp. 187–249.

10 Quoted in Philip M. Crane, *The Sum of Good Government* (Ottawa, IL: Green Hill, 1976), p. 113. Congressman Crane writes that this quotation "stemmed from days I was researching for my Ph.D.," but his staff were unable to find the original, as was I (Philip M. Crane, personal communication, July 31, 1987). Close approximation to these sentiments can be found in a number of Hoover's statements including Herbert Hoover, *Addresses Upon The American Road: 1933–1938* (New York: Scribner's Sons, 1938), p. 67, and *Addresses Upon The American Road: 1950–1955* (Stanford, CA: Stanford University Press, 1955), pp. 76–7.

11 Adam Smith, *The Theory of Moral Sentiments* (Indianapolis, IN: Liberty Classics, 1969), pp. 380–1.

12 Olmstead v. United States, 227 U.S. 479, 957 (1928).

13 See for example US Congress, House, *Full Employment Act of 1945, Remarks in House on Bill (S. 380) to enact,* 79th Cong., 1st sess., December 13, 1945, *Congressional Record,* 11982; Senate, ibid., September 26, 1945, 9034; ibid., September 28, 1945, 9133; Senate, Subcommittee of the Committee on Banking and Currency, *Hearings, Full Employment Act of 1945,* 79th Cong., 1st sess., 1945,

pp. 173, 276, 340, 361, 893; House, Committee on Expenditures in the Executive Departments, *Hearings, Full Employment Act of 1945*, 79th cong., 1st sess., 1945, pp. 658, 754.

14 Ashbrook, a Republican, is quoting from an article compiled by an employee of the Republican congressional committee, US Congress, House, *Economic Opportunity Act of 1964, Remarks in House on Bill (H. R. 11377) to enact*, 88th Cong., 2nd sess., July 2, 1964, *Congressional Record*, 15949. For further complaints of a similar nature, see ibid., August 5, 1964, 18199, 18211.

15 See, for example, Buckley, *Up From Liberalism*, p. 211; Milton Friedman, *There's No Such Thing As A Free Lunch* (LaSalle, IL: Open Court, 1975), p. 294; Milton Friedman and Rose Friedman, *Free to Choose* (New York: Avon, 1979), p. 56; Howard E. Kershner, *Dividing The Wealth* (Old Greenwich, CT: Devin-Adair, 1971), pp. 64–5; Robert A. Nisbet, "The fatal ambivalence of an idea: equal freemen or equal serfs?" *Encounter*, LXVII (December 1976), p. 21; Ayn Rand, *The Virtue of Selfishness* (New York: New American Library (Signet Book), 1964), pp. 68–9, 114; Murray N. Rothbard, *Power and Market: Government and the Economy* (Kansas City, KS: Sheed Andrews & McMeel, 1970), p. 264.

16 George Stigler, *The Citizen and the State* (Chicago, IL: University of Chicago Press, 1975), p. 14.

17 For Stigler's views, see ibid., pp. 3–19. For an example of failing to confront directly the critical issue of lack of evidence, see Peter L. Berger, *The Capitalist Revolution* (New York: Basic Books, 1986), pp. 82, 88–9.

18 See, for example, the national accounts of OECD countries in Organization for Economic Co-operation and Development (OECD), "Public expenditure trends," *Studies in Resource Allocation*, no. 5 (Paris: OECD, 1978), p. 16.

19 Current data from US Department of Commerce, *Statistical Abstract of the United States: 1986* (Washington, DC: US Government Printing Office, 1985), pp. 264, 431; historical data from US Department of Commerce, *Historical Statistics of the United States* (Washington, DC: US Government Printing Office, 1975), vol. I, p. 224, vol. II, p. 1120.

20 Ronald Max Hartwell, "Capitalism and the historians," in Fritz Machlup (ed.), *Essays on Hayek* (New York: New York University Press, 1976), p. 85.

21 See, for example, Stigler, *The Citizen and the State*, p. 17; Hartwell, "Capitalism and the historians," pp. 76–7.

22 Friedrich A. Hayek, *The Road to Serfdom* (Chicago, IL: University of Chicago Press, 1976), p. xiv.

23 Ibid., 1976 Preface, p. xxi; see also Hayek, *New Studies in Philosophy, Politics, Economics and the History of Ideas* (Chicago, IL: University of Chicago Press, 1978), p. 105.

24 Hayek, *Road to Serfdom*, 1976 edn, p. vii; see also Hayek, *The Constitution of Liberty* (Chicago, IL: University of Chicago Press (Phoenix Books), 1978), pp. 254–5.

25 Hayek, *New Studies in Philosophy*, pp. 111, 140–1; *Constitution of Liberty*, p. 289.

26 Hayek, *New Studies in Philosophy*, p. 106.

27 Hayek, *Constitution of Liberty*, p. 255.

28 See, for example, Stigler, *The Citizen and The State*, pp. 5, 16–17.

29 Buckley, *Up From Liberalism*, p. 211.

30 Herbert Stein, *Presidential Economics* (New York: Simon and Schuster, 1984), p. 74.

31 "Final text of the U.S. bishops' economy Pastoral: economic justice for all; Catholic social teaching and the U.S. economy," *Origins*, XVI (November 27, 1986), p. 409.

32 "The Lay Commission was formed in 1984 to encourage debate and discussion of these issues, following the announcement by the U.S. Catholic Bishops that a Pastoral Letter would be written on the U.S. economy. The Commission was chaired by Mr. Simon, former Secretary of the Treasury, and Mr. Novak, writer and theologian, and consisted of 27 other prominent American Catholics from the fields of public service, business, education, labor, law, and journalism" ("Statement by William E. Simon and Michael Novak, Co-chairmen, Lay Commission on Catholic Social Teaching and the U.S. Economy," Press Release, November 5, 1986, pp. 3–4).

33 The bishops issued three drafts of their Pastoral Letter plus a final approved version. These were "First draft of the U.S. bishops' Pastoral Letter on Catholic social teaching and the U.S. economy," *Origins*, XIV (November 15, 1984), pp. 337–83; "Second draft of the U.S. bishops' Pastoral Letter on Catholic social teaching and the U.S. economy," *Origins*, XV (October 10, 1985), 257–96; "Third draft of the U.S. bishops' economy Pastoral: economic justice for all, Catholic social teachings and the U.S. economy," *Origins*, XVI (June 5, 1986), pp. 33–76; "Final text of the U.S. bishops' economy Pastoral: economic justice for all; Catholic social teaching and the U.S. economy," *Origins*, XVI (November 27, 1986), pp. 409–55. The Lay Commission on Catholic Social Teaching and the US Economy published *Toward the Future: Catholic Social Thought and the U.S. Economy – A Lay Letter* (New York: American Catholic Committee, 1984) in response to the bishops' first draft and in response to the final draft issued a press release ("Statement by William E. Simon and Michael Novak, Co-chairmen, Lay Commission on Catholic Social Teaching and the U.S. Economy," November 5, 1986) plus a 23-page statement by Simon and Novak, "LIBERTY and justice for all," Report on the final draft (June 1986) of the US Catholic bishops' Pastoral Letter "Economic justice for all," November 5, 1986.

34 "Final text of the U.S. bishops' economy Pastoral," p. 422, para. 90. This wording first appeared in the second draft, and remained unchanged in the third draft (*Origins*, XV, p. 274, para. 169; ibid., XVI, p. 42, para. 89). As noted above, this constituted a substantial shift from the position taken in the first draft, in which fulfillment of the basic needs of the poor was made the single dominant priority (note 33).

35 Lay Commission, "LIBERTY and justice for all," p. 4.

36 Lay Commission, *Toward the Future*, p. 58. Elsewhere in the same document the Lay Commission made a similar point in more theological terms: "It is of profound human and Christian concern to uplift the poor universally" (ibid., p. 46).

37 For a brief review of the assumptions and the challenges written for noneconomists, see Peter D. McClelland, *Causal Explanation and Model Building in History, Economics, and the New Economic History* (Ithaca, NY: Cornell University Press, 1975), pp. 117–25.

38 For an elementary discussion of the model and the mathematics, see ibid., pp. 194–201.

39 See William J. Baumol and Kenneth McLennan (eds), *Productivity Growth and U.S. Competitiveness* (New York: Oxford University Press, 1985), p. 8 and ch. 2. The authors cite the range for capital's contribution as 20–50 percent, but concede in a footnote that Edward Denison, one of the leading experts in the field, gives no significance to changes in capital investment (ibid., p. 27, n. 4). See also Barry P. Bosworth, *Tax Incentives and Economic Growth* (Washington, DC: Brookings Institution, 1984), ch. 2. For a recent survey of related problems, see

the papers in "Symposium: The Slowdown in Productivity Growth," *Journal of Economic Perspectives*, II (Fall 1988), pp. 3–97. As summarized by Stanley Fisher, these papers further support "the overall impression . . . that economists are as yet unable to pin down the relative contributions of the potential causes of the productivity slowdown" (ibid., p. 6).

40 Ronald D. Utt and William Orzechowski, "International perspectives on economic growth," *Cato Policy Report*, VII (July–August 1985), p. 11. For a brief and more balanced view of this same evidence, see John Kendrick, "How to produce economic growth," *Cato Policy Report*, VII (May–June 1985), pp. 8–9.

41 See Herbert Stein, "Should growth be a priority of national policy?" *Challenge*, XXIX (March–April 1986), p. 16.

42 These and subsequent arguments are woven throughout the two major publications of the Lay Commission; thus, subsequent citations refer only to a subset of those possible. For the argument cited, see especially *Toward the Future*, pp. xii, 7, 15, 27, 47–8, 54–6; "LIBERTY and justice for all," p. 9.

43 See especially Lay Commission, *Toward the Future*, pp. 27, 37–40, 46, 51, 77; "LIBERTY and justice for all," pp. 3, 7–10.

44 The Lay Commission also emphasizes a "massive commitment to universal education," but that commitment is not peculiar to capitalist countries (Lay Commission, "LIBERTY and justice for all." p. 7).

45 Lay Commission, *Toward the Future*, p. 47.

46 Ibid., p. 48.

47 Ibid., p. 3.

48 Ibid., p. 50.

49 Many American conservatives have argued what the Catholic Lay Commission argues: that the key to helping the poor is economic growth, and the crucial variable for achieving economic growth is "the free-market system." These conservatives also almost invariably make the same two mistakes made by the Lay Commission: (a) they assume that "the free-market system" is a well-defined entity, and (b) they assume that we have sufficient knowledge to gauge the relative contribution of that ill-defined entity to the processes of economic growth. See for example Berger, *The Capitalist Revolution*, pp. 36–7; Friedman and Friedman, *Free to Choose*, pp. 3, 55–6, 137; Irving Kristol, *Two Cheers for Capitalism* (New York: New American Library (Mentor Book, 1979), pp. 224–7; Bertel M. Sparks, "Retreat from contract to status," in Barbara J. Smith (ed.), *Champions of Freedom* (Hillsdale, MI: Hillsdale College Press, 1975), vol. II, pp. 73–4; George J. Stigler, *The Pleasures and Pains of Modern Capitalism* (Albuquerque, NM: Transatlantic Arts, 1982), pp. 13–14.

50 "Final text of the U.S. bishops' economy Pastoral," pp. 428–32.

51 Lay Commission, "LIBERTY and justice for all," p. 8.

52 Various refinements can be added to this mechanism linking tax cuts to increased demand, including the tendency of initial consumer spending to stimulate increases in output, thus raising incomes paid out by producers, thereby fostering further rounds of consumer spending (the Keynesian multiplier sequence), and the tendency of investment spending to receive a favorable stimulus as total output and total income in the nation rise.

53 Will Durant and Ariel Durant, *The Lessons of History* (New York: Simon and Schuster, 1968), p. 61.

54 For a readable account for noneconomists of the historical roots of ideas currently fashionable with supply-side advocates traced in considerable detail, see Robert E. Keleher and William P. Orzechowski, "Supply-side effects of fiscal

policy: some historical perspectives," Federal Reserve Bank of Atlanta, Working Paper Series, August 1980.

55 See for example Jack Kemp, *American Renaissance* (New York: Berkeley Books, 1981), p. 9; Irving Kristol, *Reflections of a Neoconservative* (New York: Basic Books, 1983), p. 244; William E. Simon, *Reforming the Income Tax System* (Washington, DC: American Enterprise Institute, 1981), p. 25; Ronald Reagan, "State of the Union, 1982," *Vital Speeches of the Day*, XLVIII (February 15, 1982), p. 260; Utt and Orzechowski, "International perspectives on economic growth," p. 12.

56 Supply-side advocates have other concerns besides these principal concerns, including the tendency of high taxes to foster tax evasion through exploiting loopholes in the tax law and through outright cheating (see for example Kemp, *American Renaissance*, pp. 48–50). Here as elsewhere the crucial question is the sensitivity of behavior (in this case tax avoidance behavior) to changes in tax levies.

57 Kemp, *American Renaissance*, p. 39.

58 In the jargon of economics, the first involves a substitution effect (of work for leisure because the opportunity cost of leisure has increased), and the second involves an income effect (prompting the individual, who now has more income, to "buy" more leisure, provided leisure is not an "inferior" good).

59 For a recent and comprehensive review of this literature, see Bosworth, *Tax Incentives and Economic Growth*. Somewhat more dated is US Congress, Congressional Budget Office, *An Analysis of the Roth–Kemp Tax Cut Proposal*, October 1978.

60 Simon, *Reforming the Income Tax System*, p. 31.

61 Bosworth, *Tax Incentives and Economic Growth*, p. 186. Bosworth goes on to point out the important qualification that this sensitivity to taxes is significantly greater if the total tax burden remains little changed but the marginal tax rate is varied. Or as he puts the point, "changes in the structure of the tax system that alter the marginal tax rate . . . without altering the average tax rate . . . will have a more substantial influence on labor supply decisions" (ibid.).

62 For a review of some of this evidence, see US Congress, Congressional Budget Office, *Analysis of the Roth–Kemp Tax Cut Proposal*, p. 13; Michael Harrington, *Decade of Decision* (New York: Simon and Schuster (Touchstone Book), 1980), pp. 165–6; Lester Thurow, "Toward a definition of economic justice," *Public Interest*, XXI (Spring 1973), p. 76.

63 Bosworth, *Tax Incentives and Economic Growth*, p. 143, citing the findings of Don Fullerton, "On the possibility of an inverse relationship between tax rates and government revenues," *Journal of Public Economics*, XIX (October 1982), pp. 16–19. For another aggregation effort in the same range, see US Congress Congressional Budget Office, *Analysis of the Roth–Kemp Tax Cut Proposal*, p. 14.

64 Kershner, *Dividing the Wealth*, pp. 32–3.

65 Economists instinctively will want to add to this assertion "other things being equal" to rule out such possibilities as a dramatic reduction in other factor supplies.

66 A rise in savings, if accompanied by a slump in aggregate demand, could cause short-run problems of recession, but the focus of this analysis is primarily long-run and the problems of fostering secular growth. This discussion also ignores problems of international capital flows, thereby ignoring the possibility that has developed for America in recent years of augmenting domestic savings with foreign capital inflows. (For a compact and nontechnical description of this latter process, see Joseph Bisignano, "Impervious saving behavior," *Federal Reserve Bank of San Francisco Weekly Letter* (September 28, 1984), pp. 1–3.)

67 Intuition suggests that the poor save a lower percentage of total income received than do the rich, and thus any tax change that significantly redistributes income from rich to poor will lower total saving. The facts, however, do not support that intuition. More specifically, the evidence suggests that the proportion saved from income increments (in economics jargon, the marginal propensity to save) is not markedly different for different income groups. See for example the sources quoted in Bosworth, *Tax Incentives and Economic Growth*, p. 86. For similar findings of older studies, see Henry C. Wallich, "Inequality and growth," in Edward C. Budd (ed.), *Inequality and Poverty* (New York: W. W. Norton, 1967), p. 23.

68 This stability is the product of largely offsetting movements in the two components of the gross private saving rate: personal saving and business saving. For a review of the postwar trends in the aggregate rate and its components, see Bisignano, "Impervious saving behavior," pp. 1–3.

69 Bosworth, *Tax Incentives and Economic Growth*, p. 84. The agnostic tone of such surveys has not changed much over time. See for example Richard A. Musgrave and Peggy B. Musgrave, *Public Finance in Theory and Practice* (New York: McGraw-Hill, 1973), p. 478.

70 Subsequent discussion will ignore many of the complexities of theories of investment behavior not germane to this discussion, incuding the distinction between decision rules based upon present value and those based upon the expected rate of return of a proposed investment.

71 Richard W. Kopcke, "Investment spending and the federal taxation of business income," Federal Reserve Bank of Boston *New England Economic Review* (September–October 1985), p. 32, n. 2.

72 Ibid., p. 12. Understanding why accelerating depreciation write-offs can stimulate investment is also not a simple task, as Kopcke notes (ibid.):

> Accelerated depreciation fosters capital formation by permitting investors to claim allowances sooner, thereby increasing the present value of cash flow for eligible projects. Unlike an investment tax credit, the ratio of the present value of deductions to the purchase price of an asset will vary from project to project depending on asset life, the tax rate, the businesses's relevant after-tax discount rate, and other factors. At a 15 percent discount rate, the switch to accelerated depreciation is worth 3.3 cents per dollar of capital expenditure for a five-year investment project. . . . For a 10-year project, this acceleration of allowances is worth 5.6 cents per dollar of capital expenditure. At a 7.5 percent discount rate, however, accelerated deductions are worth only 1.9 cents per dollar of investment spending for a project with a five-year lifetime. Therefore, accelerated allowances tend to be most valuable for profitable businesses that use high discount rates and invest in long-lived capital assets.

73 Bosworth, *Tax Incentives and Economic Growth*, p. 185.

74 Bosworth, quoted in Marc Levinson, "The shaky case for aiding investment," *Dun's Business Month*, CXXVII (March 1986), p. 23.

75 In the technical language familiar to economists, these estimates of the elasticity of substitution range from close to zero to close to unity. For a concise summary of this long-standing debate intelligible to the layman, see Bosworth, *Tax Incentives and Economic Growth*, pp. 106–10.

76 Illustrative of this extensive and contentious literature are Robert S. Chirinko, "The ineffectiveness of effective tax rates on business investment," Hoover Institution Working Papers in Economics E-85-20, Stanford University, August 1985; Levinson, "The shaky case for aiding investment," pp. 22–4; Robert S. McIntyre and Dean C. Tipps, "Exploding the investment-incentive myth,"

Challenge, XXVIII (May–June 1985), pp. 47–52; Murray L. Weidenbaum, "Do tax incentives for investment work?" Contemporary Issues Series 20, Center for the Study of American Business, Washington University, St. Louis, MO, June 1986.

77 See for example Levinson, "The shaky case for aiding investment," p. 22.

78 Lay Commission, *Toward the Future*, pp. 32, 58–66; "LIBERTY and justice for all," pp. 12, 20.

79 Lay Commission, "LIBERTY and justice for all," p. 8 (emphasis added).

80 Lay Commission, *Toward the Future*, pp. 58, 65; "LIBERTY and justice for all," p. 7.

81 "From the beginning, these [poverty programs] were intended to enhance 'the integrity and preservation of the family unit.' This generous aim . . . has scarcely been achieved; quite the opposite." (Lay Commission, *Toward the Future*, p. 59.) Symptomatic of this caution are the observations of Michael Novak, a principal author of *Toward the Future*, when interviewed by a national magazine about poverty, dependency, and family structure:

> On welfare policy, the problem that has developed in recent years is that a disproportionately high share of the new poverty is caused by males abandoning their family responsibilities. Whether because of broken marriages or unwed motherhood, hundreds of thousands of women have been left alone to raise small children. The present welfare system *may* encourage this pattern because it focuses on the individual. The woman gets a check and may be better off financially than the male who abandoned her. A better approach, which we *hint of* in our letter, might be to give the check to a church or other local organization, where the young woman could go for meals, day care, training and counseling ("A Catholic's reply to bishops: poor nations can learn from U.S.," *U.S. News & World Report* (November 26, 1984), pp. 61–2; emphasis added).

82 See for example Martin Anderson, *Welfare: The Political Economy of Welfare Reform in the United States* (Stanford, CA: Hoover Institution Press, 1978), p. 56; Crane, *Sum of Good Government*, pp. 29–30, 207; Barry Goldwater, *The Conscience of a Conservative* (Shepherdsville, KY: Victor, 1960), p. 73; Kristol, *Two Cheers for Capitalism*, pp. 204, 220; Dwight R. Lee, "The politics of poverty and the poverty of politics," *Cato Journal*, V (Spring–Summer 1985), pp. 32–5. In a radio broadcast of December 1983, Ronald Reagan expressed similar sentiments: "There is no question that many well-intentioned Great Society type programs contributed to family break-ups, welfare dependency and a large increase in births out of wedlock" (quoted in Richard P. Nathan, "The missing link in applied social science," *Society*, XXII (January–February 1985), p. 71).

83 Rothbard, *Power and Market*, p. 172. Here Rothbard is quoting with approval from Thomas Mackay, *Methods of Social Reform* (London: John Murray, 1896), p. 210.

84 George Gilder, "The disease of government," *National Review*, XXXII (December 31, 1980), pp. 1566–7.

85 See for example Kristol, *Two Cheers for Capitalism*, p. 204; Friedman and Friedman, *No Such Thing As A Free Lunch*, pp. 28, 217; Edward C. Banfield. *The Unheavenly City Revisited* (Boston, MA: Little, Brown, 1974), p. 140. A recent report by a Reagan Administration panel on the family expressed similar sentiments: "welfare contributes to the failure to form the family in the first place," it concluded, and "easy availability of welfare in all of its forms has become a powerful force for destruction of family life through perpetuation of the welfare culture" (quoted in Leslie Maitland Werner, "U.S. Report asserts

administration halted liberal 'anti-family agenda'," *New York Times* (November 14, 1986), p. A12).

86 See George Gilder, *Wealth and Poverty* (New York: Basic Books, 1981), pp. 117–18.

87 Murray, *Losing Ground*, pp. 227–8.

88 Willard Phillips, *A Manual of Political Economy* (Boston, MA: Hilliard, Gray, Little, and Wilkins, 1828), p. 147.

89 In-kind benefits, such as Food Stamps, housing assistance, and medical care are not counted as income for purposes of defining poverty, and their impact on the poor is accordingly not reflected in figure 10.1. If post-transfer poverty rates are plotted, however, the shape of the resulting line is substantially the same as that appearing in figure 10.1, although the plateau of the 1970s occurs at a somewhat lower aggregate rate. See "Poverty in the United States: where do we stand now?" *Focus*, University of Wisconsin Institute of Poverty, VII (Winter 1984), p. 2. This leveling off in the aggregate poverty rate in the 1970s also holds for the poverty rates of separate races. See New York (State) Task Force on Poverty and Welfare, "A new social contract," Report submitted to Governor Mario M. Cuomo, December 1986, p. 4.

90 Friedman and Friedman, *Free To Choose*, p. 98.

91 That is, the father had either left or had never been a part of the family unit.

92 US Congress, House, Committee on Ways and Means, *Public Welfare Amendments of 1962, Report to accompany H.R. 10616*, 87th Cong., 2nd sess., Report No. 1414, March 10, 1962, p. 3.

93 In 1967 the Work Incentive Program (WIN) was introduced, whereby working AFDC recipients could retain each month the first $30 they earned plus one-third of the rest of their earned income. In addition, "allowable work expenses" did not reduce AFDC benefits. Prior to that time, a dollar of benefits was lost for each dollar earned.

94 In 1981, the Omnibus Budget Reconciliation Act (a) lowered the countable resource limit from $2,000 per family member to $1,000 per family, (b) disqualified from AFDC students (upon their eighteenth birthday), strikers, and unborn children before the third trimester of the mother's pregnancy, and (c) required a portion of step-parent income to be counted. In 1982, the Tax Equity and Fiscal Responsibility Act "permitted states to prorate the shelter and utilities portion of benefits for shared households; eliminated parental absence for uniformed service as grounds for AFDC eligibility; permitted States to require job search of AFDC applicants; required States to prorate initial benefits to date of application and to round benefits down to the nearest dollar." Further details on changing requirements and the history of the program can be found in US Congress, House, Committee on Ways and Means, *Children in Poverty*, 99th Cong., 1st sess., May 22, 1985, appendix A, pp. 463–73. (The quotation just noted is from ibid., p. 464.)

95 The relevant numbers can be found in appendix B, table B.1. In the 1980s real benefit levels per recipient (as opposed to per family) had fallen to the $106–107 range, which was close to what those benefits were in the mid-1960s before the War on Poverty began (again, see appendix B, table B.1).

96 A sense of the underlying complexity can be gained from the following:

Each state determined AFDC eligibility by comparing family circumstances to its own need standard. Whereas Georgia and Michigan determine basic needs by considering only the costs of food, shelter, clothing, utilities, and personal care items, Connecticut considers 20 cost items, including educational expenses, dry-cleaning bills, insurance premiums, and summer camp fees. Thus, a family with a given set of circumstances is eligible in some states, not in others. Further complexity is added since the states vary in the proportion of the need standard that they will pay to recipients. Only 18 states pay up to the level of the need standard they determined was necessary in the first place. In addition, the states have the discretion to include or exclude several optional components of the overall AFDC program. About half the states provide the unemployed parent option, half do not (Janet E. Kodras, "The spatial perspective in welfare analysis," *Cato Journal*, VI (Spring–Summer 1986), p. 80).

97 In order to retain eligibility, unemployed or partially employed able-bodied adult household members must register for, seek, and accept "suitable employment" if offered. For a summary of other eligibility rules, see US Congress, House, *Children in Poverty*, pp. 475–6.

98 Part A of the Medicare law (available to all) is designed to cover hospitalization costs for the elderly through funds accumulated in the Social Security Fund. Part B (available on a voluntary basis) is designed to cover a percentage of other medical costs, with part of the funds generated by individual contributions by participants in the program and the rest of the funds contributed by the federal government.

99 To qualify, a state had to provide at least five basic services by July 1, 1967: inpatient hospital services, outpatient hospital care, laboratory and X-ray care, nursing home benefits, and physicians' services. The optional services are (1) clinic services, (2) prescribed drugs, (3) dental services, (4) prosthetic devices, (5) eyeglasses, (6) private-duty nursing, (7) physical therapy and related services, (8) other diagnostic, screening, preventive, and rehabilitation services, (9) emergency hospital services, (10) skilled nursing facility services for patients under 21, (11) optometrists' services, (12) podiatrists' services, (13) chiropractors' services, (14) care for patients 65 or older in institutions for mental diseases, (15) care for patients 65 or older in institutions for tuberculosis, (16) care for patients under 21 in psychiatric hospitals, and (17) institutional services in intermediate care facilities.

100 For a brief review of the program as it currently operates, see US Congress, House, *Children in Poverty*, pp. 476–87.

101 US Department of Commerce, *Statistical Abstract: 1986*, p. 382

102 See for example Morley D. Glicken, "Transgenerational welfare dependency," *Journal of Contemporary Studies*, IV (Summer 1981), pp. 33–4.

103 Economists will notice that in both instances individuals can be viewed as choosing rationally and maximizing utility at any point in time, but that in the second case the preference functions are assumed to change over time. The other relevant aside to economists is to note that (unlike the case of taxes) the income and substitution effects generally operate in the same direction for transfer payments, namely, to encourage the increased use of welfare payments.

104 Murray, *Losing Ground*, pp. 75–80.

105 Across all age cohorts, the evidence suggests that this decline in black male participation in the labor force was most pronounced for the least educated. See James P. Smith and Finis R. Welch, *Closing the Gap: Forty Years of Economic Progress for Blacks* (Santa Monica, CA: Rand Corporation, 1986), pp. 81–2.

106 See Murray, *Losing Ground*, pp. 78–80; David T. Ellwood and Lawrence H. Summers, "Is welfare really the problem?" *Public Interest*, LXXXIII (Spring 1986), pp. 74–6; Sara McLanahan et al., "*Losing Ground*: a critique," University of Wisconsin Institute for Research on Poverty, Special Report Series no. 38,

August 1985, pp. 15–23; Reynolds Farley, "Assessing black progress: employment, occupation, earnings, income, poverty," *Economic Outlook USA*, XIII (Third Quarter 1986), p. 14.

107 See for example Richard R. Freeman, "Cutting black youth unemployment: create jobs that pay as well as crime," *New York Times* (July 20, 1986), p. 2F; Moynihan, *Family and Nation*, p. 99.

108 Ken Auletta, *The Underclass* (New York: Random House, 1982), p. 267.

109 This high rate of effective taxation is inevitable in any welfare system that attempts to distribute the majority of benefits to the poor. That priority implies a rapid phase-out as earnings approach the threshold of eligibility. The more rapid the phase-out, the higher will be the effective rate of taxation on dollars earned.

110 The following estimates of marginal tax rates, which represent an effort to summarize the findings of a variety of recent estimation efforts, are taken from James Gwartney and Richard Stroup, "Transfers, equality, and the limits of public policy," *Cato Journal*, VI (Spring–Summer 1986), p. 128. The effective tax rates, of course, will be lower to the extent that welfare recipients do not report all income earned, a possibility stressed in many studies of this problem (see for example Bosworth, *Tax Incentives and Economic Growth*, p. 166).

111 Legislation passed in the 1980s has made the marginal tax rate for AFDC recipients even more pronounced. The resulting policy for counting monthly earned income is as follows: the first $75 is disregarded for work expenses, child care costs of $160 per month per child are deducted, and then a standard $30 deduction for 12 months followed by a deduction of one-third of remaining earnings for four months.

112 See for example Gilder, *Wealth and Poverty*, p. 120; Murray, *Losing Ground*, pp. 151–3.

113 The sites were New Jersey and Pennsylvania (1968–72), rural areas of North Carolina and Iowa (1970–2), Seattle and Denver (1970–8), and Gary, Indiana (1971–4).

114 The population was divided into two groups – an "experimental" group and a "control" group – with the former receiving NIT benefits and the latter not. The effect of the experiment was then measured as the average difference in work effort between the two groups.

115 US Congress, Senate, Committee on Finance, *Hearings, Welfare Reform Proposals, Testimony of Robert G. Spiegelman, Director, Center for the Study of Welfare Policy, Menlo Park, CA*, 95th Cong., 2nd sess., May 1, 1978, p. 1050. The labor supply effects of these studies are briefly reviewed in Robert A. Moffitt, "The negative income tax: would it discourage work?" *Monthly Labor Review*, CIV (April 1981), pp. 23–7, and more extensively reviewed in SRI International, *Final Report of the Seattle–Denver Income Maintenance Experiment*, Volume 1, *Design and Results* (Washington, DC: US Government Printing Office May 1983), part III, pp. 91–198.

116 See US Congress, House, *Children In Poverty*, p. 157; Elizabeth Evanson, "Employment programs for the poor: Government in the labor market," *Focus*, University of Wisconsin Institute for Research on Poverty, VII (Fall 1984), 4; "Are we *Losing Ground?*" ibid., VIII (Fall and Winter 1985), p. 5; McLanahan et al., "*Losing Ground*: a critique," pp. 23–7.

117 See Moffitt, "The negative income tax," p. 24.

118 The results of some of these studies are summarized in Sheldon Danziger and Peter Gottschalk, "The poverty of *Losing Ground*," *Challenge*, XXVIII (May–June 1985), p. 37; June O'Neill, "Transfers and poverty: cause and/or effect?" *Cato*

Journal, VI (Spring–Summer 1986), p. 70; Eugene Smolensky, "Is a golden age in poverty policy right around the corner?" *Focus*, University of Wisconsin Institute for Research on Poverty, VIII (Spring 1985), p. 10.

119 Sheldon Danziger, Robert Haveman, and Robert Plotnick, "How income transfer programs affect work, savings, and the income distribution: a critical review," *Journal of Economic Literature*, XIX (September 1981), p. 1020. For a more recent opinion emphasizing a similar uncertainty, see Bosworth, *Tax Incentives and Economic Growth*, p. 167.

120 Sources of recent estimates and a summary of the findings of these studies can be found in James Gwartney and Thomas S. McCaleb, "Have antipoverty programs increased poverty?" *Cato Journal*, V (Spring–Summer 1985), pp. 7–8; Greg J. Duncan and Saul D. Hoffman, "Welfare dynamics and the nature of need," *Cato Journal*, VI (Spring–Summer 1986), pp. 36–42.

121 The results are summarized in Greg J. Duncan et al., *Years of Poverty, Years of Plenty* (Ann Arbor, MI: Institute for Social Research, University of Michigan, 1984), especially pp. 41, 75.

122 One recent study of AFDC recipients indicated that about half received this form of welfare on a continuous basis for more than one year, 16–18 percent received it for five or more years, and 5 to 7 percent received it for ten or more years. See Gwartney and McCaleb, "Have antipoverty programs increased poverty?" p. 8 (summarizing the results in June A. O'Neill et al., *Analysis of Time on Welfare* (Washington, DC: Urban Institute, 1984)). Duncan estimates based upon the University of Michigan Panel Study (see note 121) indicate that in the period 1969–78, of those who received welfare payments, 25 percent received them for one or more years; 8 percent, for five or more years; and 2 percent, for all ten years (Duncan et al., *Years of Poverty*, p. 75). All of these estimates refer to one spell of continuous welfare receipts. The question of multiple spells is discussed in note 128 below. A more recent study using PSID data but more sophisticated modeling techniques than Duncan has yielded essentially the same two basic conclusions about many being poor for a brief period and a few being poor for long periods. See May Jo Bane and David T. Ellwood, "Slipping into and out of poverty: the dynamics of spells," *Journal of Human Resources*, XXI (Winter 1986), pp. 1–23.

123 Duncan and Hoffman, "Welfare dynamics," p. 49.

124 Ibid., p. 35 (summarizing the results of Bane and Ellwood, "Slipping into and out of poverty").

125 Charles Murray, "*Losing Ground* two years later," *Cato Journal*, VI (Spring–Summer 1986), p. 19 (citing the study by Mary Jo Bane and David Ellwood, "The dynamics of dependence: the routes to self-sufficiency," Department of Health and Human Services Contract Report (Cambridge, MA: Urban Systems Research and Engineering Inc., 1983), table 1, p. 11). Readers may wonder how the two statements can both be true: (a) at any point in time, half of those receiving AFDC are in the midst of a welfare spell that will last eight years or more, and (b) between half and two-thirds of all welfare spells last only one or two years. This seeming paradox is explained by Bane and Ellwood, using an example difficult to improve upon: "Consider a 13-bed hospital in which 12 beds are occupied for an entire year by 12 chronically ill patients, while the other bed is used by 52 patients, each of whom stays exactly one week. On any given day, a hospital census would find that about 85 percent of patients (12 of the 13) were in the midst of long spells of hospitalization. Nevertheless, viewed over the course of

a year, short-term use clearly dominates: Out of the 64 patients using hospital services, about 80 percent (52 of the 64) spent only one week in the hospital" (reproduced in Duncan and Hoffman, "Welfare dynamics," p. 40).

126 Bane and Ellwood, "The dynamics of dependence," p. 30.

127 These findings are reviewed in Robert Pear, "Young mothers said to be on welfare longer," *New York Times* (September 10, 1986), p. A28. One of those most expert on the data base used by Murray conceded that Murray's numbers were "essentially correct" (ibid.). Murray's findings are elaborated in Charles Murray, "According to age: longitudinal profiles of AFDC recipients and the poor by age group," paper prepared for the Working Seminar on the Family and American Welfare Policy, Institute for Family Studies, Marquette University, September 1986.

128 All the evidence pertains to a single continuous stay on welfare, and leaves unanswered questions about recurring use of welfare, even by those who use it only for a brief period of time. Data limitations complicate any attempt to construct reliable estimates of total lifetime welfare participation. The best of recent efforts of this sort suggest (a) that 30–40 percent of welfare spells are followed by subsequent spells and (b) that about half of women beginning an AFDC spell will accumulate five years or more on welfare, while roughly one-quarter will accumulate ten years or more (Duncan and Hoffman, "Welfare dynamics," p. 41; O'Neill, "Transfers and poverty," p. 65, summarizing the findings of David T. Ellwood, "Targeting 'would-be' long-term recipients of AFDC," Contract No. 100-84-0059, US Department of Health and Human Services, OS/ASPE, January 1986, and Mary Jo Bane and David T. Ellwood "The impact of AFDC: structure and living arrangements," *Report to the US Department of Health and Human Services*, Harvard University, 1984). The extent to which recurring use is symptomatic of dependency is a hotly debated topic (see, for example, Rebecca M. Blank, "How important is welfare dependence?" Working Paper 2026, National Bureau of Economic Research, September 1986, pp. 3–4).

129 "Once the culture of poverty has come into existence it tends to perpetuate itself. By the time slum children are six or seven they have usually absorbed the basic attitudes and values of their subculture. Thereafter they are psychologically unready to take full advantage of changing conditions or improving opportunities that may develop in their lifetime" (Oscar Lewis, "The culture of poverty," *Scientific American*, CCVI (October 1966), p. 21).

130 Martha S. Hill et al., "Final report of the project: 'Motivation and Economic Mobility of the Poor'; Part 1: Intergenerational and short-run dynamic analyses," Institute for Social Research, University of Michigan, Survey Research Center Working Paper, August 3, 1983, p. 6; quoted in Glen G. Cain, "The economics of discrimination: Part 1," *Focus*, University of Wisconsin Institute for Research on Poverty, VII (Summer 1984), p. 16.

131 Martha S. Hill and Michael Ponza, "Poverty and welfare dependence across generations," *Economic Outlook USA*, X (Summer 1983), pp. 61–4; "The dynamics of dependency: family background, family structure, and poverty," *Focus*, University of Wisconsin Institute for Research on Poverty, VII (Summer 1984), pp. 14–17; Duncan and Hoffman, "Welfare dynamics," pp. 42–5; Martin Rein and Lee Rainwater, "Patterns of welfare use," *Social Service Review*, LII (December 1978), pp. 318–19. The test results have suggested minimal intergenerational dependence for all races, with indications of a somewhat more pronounced

(if still weak) relationship for whites. In the more formal language of a survey of these tests, "The only evidence of welfare dependence transmission was observed for whites, and then only for very high levels of parental welfare dependence, based on a small number of observations, and with effects that were not consistent across all models tested" (Duncan and Hoffman, "Welfare dynamics," p. 43). More recent evidence, suggesting daughters from "highly dependent homes"'" are more likely to become "highly dependent" themselves, is summarized in Greg J. Duncan, Martha S. Hill, and Saul D. Hoffman, "Welfare dependence within and across generations," *Science*, CCXXXIX (January 1988), pp. 469–70.

132 Edward M. Gramlich, "The main themes," in Sheldon H. Danziger and Daniel H. Weinberg (eds), *Fighting Poverty* (Cambridge, MA: Harvard University Press, 1986), p. 342.

133 See "The dynamics of dependency," p. 15; "Welfare in America: is it a flop?" *U.S. News & World Report* (December 24, 1984), p. 41.

134 Children growing up in mother-only families, relative to those growing up in two-parent (husband–wife) families "are more likely to drop out of school, to give birth out of wedlock, to divorce or separate, and to become dependent on welfare" (Irwin Garfinkel and Sara S. McLanahan, *Single Mothers and Their Children: A New American Dilemma* (Washington, DC: Urban Institute, 1986), pp. 1–2). Although Garfinkel and McLanahan repeatedly emphasize the associations just noted (for example, see ibid., pp. 11–12, 28–31, 41–2, 165), their conclusion echoes the agnosticism of this section (ibid., p. 170): "The question is, does the provision of welfare increase or reduce the extent to which subsequent generations will be poor and dependent? The answer is, we do not know."

135 For a recent review of these trends, including evidence that remarriage after divorce is becoming less frequent and that more women will never marry at all, see Arthur J. Norton and Jeanne E. Moorman, "Current trends in marriage and divorce among American women," *Journal of Marriage and the Family*, XLIX (February 1987), pp. 3–14.

136 More subtle variants of this argument can be made linking increased welfare support to either the breaking up of families or the failure to establish two-parent families. The psychological propensities discussed above can be discussed again, in which increased welfare is viewed as undermining a sense of personal responsibility, but now the sense of responsibility in question is that for one's own offspring (especially on the part of those who father illegitimate children). A quite different line of reasoning from the same starting point is to emphasize how increased welfare support undermines male authority and a sense of self-worth within established families. (For example, see Gilder, *Wealth and Poverty*, pp. 114–15.) But this latter kind of argument is more appropriately considered under the possibilities raised by Charles Murray (see below).

137 To the extent that such calculations are made, the relevant comparison would be between (a) the cost of rearing a child in a low-income family (estimated by the US Department of Agriculture) and (b) the cash and food-stamp benefits available per poor child. What these data show for the late 1970s "is that the average of these two forms of welfare benefits exceeds the additional cost of rearing a child up to about age 12" (Richard Vedder and Lowell Gallaway, "AFDC and the Laffer principle," *Wall Street Journal* (March 26, 1986), p. 30).

138 What disqualifies a family from receiving welfare is the presence of both natural parents, whether married or unmarried, whereas the presence of a stepfather need not disqualify the family from receiving assistance.

139 The breakdown for 1982 is as follows (percentage distribution of AFDC recipient families on the basis of eligibility):

Father:	deceased	0.9%
	incapacitated	3.5%
	unemployed	6.0%
	absent from home	
	divorced	20.6%
	separated	19.0%
	not married to mother	46.5%
	other	2.2%
Mother:	absent from home	1.3%

(US Department of Commerce, *Statistical Abstract: 1986*, p. 382).

140 The results of all four income maintenance experiments are summarized in SRI International, *Final Report of the Seattle–Denver Income Maintenance Experiment*, vol. I. For comments on these results and other studies of the results, see US Congress, House, *Children in Poverty*, 1985, pp. 13, 120; William Julius Wilson and Kathryn M. Neckerman, "Poverty and family structure: the widening gap between evidence and public policy issues," in Sheldon H. Danziger and Daniel H. Weinberg (eds), *Fighting Poverty* (Cambridge, MA: Harvard University Press, 1986), pp. 249–51.

141 See Henry J. Aaron, "Six welfare questions still searching for answers," *Brookings Review*, III (Fall 1984), p. 17, n. 8; "New work underway," *Focus*, University of Wisconsin Institute for Research on Poverty, IX (Spring 1986), p. 23. For a recent attempt to show that when the effects of counseling and training are factored out, the impact of the "pure" NIT program on marriages is not statistically significant, see Glen G. Cain and Douglas A. Wissoker, "Do income maintenance programs break up marriages? A reevaluation of SIME-DIME," *Focus*, University of Wisconsin Institute for Research on Poverty, X (Winter 1987–8), pp. 1–15.

142 Aaron, "Six welfare questions," p. 15.

143 Ellwood and Bane, "The impact of AFDC on family structure." Their techniques have been summarized as follows:

> The Ellwood and Bane analysis is the most complete to date of the effects of the existing welfare system on family structure. Their conclusions are based on three separate analytic techniques: (1) "over time comparisons" of state differences in changing family structure and benefit payments, (2) "eligible vs. ineligible comparisons" both of divorce rates for women with and without children and of birth rates of married and unmarried women, and (3) "likely vs. unlikely recipient comparisons" of divorce and unmarried birth rates of women who are more likely recipients of welfare to the rates of women who are less likely recipients. They note that their findings were highly consistent regardless of the methodologies used (US Congress, House, *Children in Poverty*, p. 120).

144 See for example Moynihan, *Family and Nation*, p. 136; Sylvia Nasar, "America's poor: how big a problem?" *Fortune*, CXIII (May 26, 1986), p. 78; Danziger and Gottschalk, "The poverty of *Losing Ground*," p. 36.

145 The results of these studies are reviewed in US Congress, House, *Children in Poverty*, pp. 118–23; Wilson and Neckerman, "Poverty and family structure," pp. 247–52; O'Neill, "Transfers and poverty," pp. 62–9; Duncan and Hoffman, "Welfare dynamics," pp. 20–3; Garfinkel and McLanahan, *Single Mothers and*

Their Children, pp. 55–63, 141–2, 150–1, 166–7. A more dated review of earlier literature can be found in Maurice Macdonald and Isabel V. Sawhill, "Welfare policy and the family," *Public Policy*, XXVI (Winter 1978), pp. 105–19.

146 Gilder, "The disease of government," p. 1567.

147 Murray, *Losing Ground*, p. 227.

148 Murray, "No, welfare isn't really the problem," pp. 6–7. The title is misleading, as will become clear below.

149 Ibid., p. 7.

150 Ibid.

151 Ibid., p. 11.

152 Ibid., pp. 7–8.

153 Ibid., p. 9. On the issue of illegitimacy, Murray describes one variant of the threshold model as follows:

> At some very low level, welfare benefits have no causal effect on poor single women having and keeping babies. At some high level (higher than any existing package), welfare benefits would make having a baby so economically beneficial for a poor person that it would be in itself a "cause" of such behavior. Between those two extremes, a break point exists at which the level of welfare benefits is sufficiently large that it permits an alternative to not having (or not keeping) the baby that would otherwise not exist. Once this break point is passed, welfare benefits become an enabling factor: they do not cause single women to decide to have a baby, but they enable women who are pregnant to make the decision to keep the baby. If in all states the package of benefits is already large enough to have passed the break point for a large proportion of the potential single mothers, then the effects on increases in the welfare package as measured by Ellwood and Bane will be very small. ("Have the poor been 'Losing Ground'?" *Political Science Quarterly*, C (Fall 1985), p. 441).

154 Murray has been attacked repeatedly on factual matters, such as the representativeness and accuracy of the calculations in his Harold and Phyllis example. (See Robert Greenstein, "Losing faith in 'Losing Ground'," *New Republic*, CXCII (March 25, 1985), pp. 12–14; "Are we *Losing Ground?*" pp. 6–7.) But even if this particular attack carries the day, Murray's central hypothesis would be left virtually unscathed.

155 At one point Murray seems to argue that the main reason illegitimacy rates did not jump in the 1960s is that "women's threshold definitions are different but bunched within a relatively small range . . ." (Murray, "No, welfare isn't really the problem," p. 5). But this would seem to ignore some of the more subtle and dynamic aspects of his own model that also imply a change in behavioral response will take time.

156 The reader may be puzzled, as I was, at the lower incidence of poverty among "Nonwhites, never married" than among "Nonwhites, married" in table 10.6. Sandra Danziger, who constructed the table, explains: "The lower proportion of never-married who live in poverty reflect that most (over 83%) of these young women live as subfamilies in larger households with other adults who contribute to total household income" (Sandra Danziger, personal communication, June 25, 1987).

157 Indicative of such problems is the following from a recent survey:

> Murray and Richard Vedder and Lowell Gallaway . . . also claim that the nature of income support programs, especially AFDC, promote teen pregnancy and divorce, both proximate causes of the growth in female-headed familes. Female headship, in its turn,

correlates strongly with poverty status. We examined this proposition in detail . . . and found no correspondence between the magnitude of transfer payments and growth in female-headed families among blacks using post-1950 time-series data. Fertility and family formation among low-income black women did not prove to be terribly sensitive to variations in the magnitude of transfer payments. Of course, our use of standard regression techniques did not enable us to address causal processes that feature cumulative, sleeper, and/or threshold effects (William A. Darity, Jr, and Samuel L. Myers, Jr, "Do transfer payments keep the poor in poverty?" *American Economic Review*, LXXVII (May 1987), p. 219).

158 See for example Wilson and Neckerman, "Poverty and family structure," p. 248; Gramlich, "The main themes," p. 341; O'Neill, "Transfers and poverty" p. 68; Duncan and Hoffman, "Welfare dynamics," p. 52; William A. Darity, Jr, and Samuel L. Myers, Jr, "Welfare and work: microeconomics vs macroeconomics considerations," *Cato Journal*, VI (Spring–Summer 1986) p. 246; Arland Thornton, "The changing American family: living arrangements and relationships with kin," *Economic Outlook USA*, XII (Second Quarter 1985), p. 37; Saul D. Hoffman and Greg J. Duncan, "A choice-based analysis of remarriage and welfare decisions of divorced women," paper prepared for the Annual Meetings of the Population Association of America, San Francisco, CA, April 1986, pp. 4–7; Working Seminar on Family and American Welfare Policy, *The New Consensus on Family and Welfare* (Washington, DC: American Enterprise Intitute, 1987), p. 56; Catherine Foster Alter, "Preventing family dependency," *Society*, XXIV (March–April 1987), p. 13; Institute for Poverty Research, "Conference Summary. Poverty and Social Policy: The Minority Experience," Special Report Series 43, February 1987, pp. iv, 21, 32.

159 For examples of other statements about causation that seem to claim more than is justified by the evidence, see Gary S. Becker, *A Treatise on the Family* (Cambridge, MA: Harvard University Press, 1981), p. 252; Gwartney and McCaleb, "Have antipoverty programs increased poverty?" p. 14; Gary L. Bauer, Undersecretary of Education, quoted in Jane Mayer, "What's behind divorce, teen-age pregnancies? Head of White House Policy Team blames welfare," *Wall Street Journal* (June 13, 1986), p. 48; Sara McLanahan, "Charles Murray and the family," in Sara McLanahan et al., "*Losing Ground*: a critique," University of Wisconsin Institute for Research on Poverty, Special Report Series 38, August 1985, p. 6.

160 Moynihan, *Family and Nation*, p. 143. Elsewhere Moynihan has claimed that studies "show conclusively that differences in welfare-benefit levels are not the primary cause of variations in family structure" ("We can't avoid family policy much longer," *Challenge*, XXVIII (September–October 1985), p. 16).

161 Glenn C. Loury, "The family, the nation, and Senator Moynihan," *Commentary*, LXXXI (June 1986), p. 26.

11 Dilemmas few confront

1 Adam Smith, *The Theory of Moral Sentiments* (Indianapolis, IN: Liberty Classics, 1976), p. 135.

2 For recent examples of this reasoning, see William Ryan, *Equality* (New York: Pantheon, 1981), ch. 1; Philip Green, *The Pursuit of Inequality* (New York: Pantheon, 1981), ch. 6.

3 Michael Harrington, *The Twilight of Capitalism* (New York: Simon and Schuster (Touchstone Book), 1976), p. 320.

4 Thomas Sowell, *A Conflict of Visions* (New York: William Morrow, 1987), pp. 191–2.

5 See for example Lay Commission on Catholic Social Teaching and the US Economy, *Toward the Future* (New York: Lay Commission on Catholic Social Teaching and the US Economy, 1984), p. 12; Milton Friedman, *Capitalism and Freedom* (Chicago, IL: University of Chicago Press (Phoenix Books), 1965), p. 167; Friedrich Hayek, *The Constitution of Liberty* (Chicago, IL: University of Chicago Press (Phoenix Books), 1978), p. 93; Michael Novak, *The American Vision: An Essay on the Future of Democratic Capitalism* (Washington, DC: American Enterprise Institute for Public Policy Research, 1978), p. 24.

6 See for example Lay Commission, *Toward the Future*, p. 37; William E. Simon, *A Time for Truth* (New York: McGraw-Hill, 1978), pp. 199–200; Novak, *The American Vision*, pp. 24–5; Jack Kemp, *An American Renaissance* (New York: Harper & Row (Berkley Book), 1981), pp. 1, 10, 14, 29.

7 Thornton W. Burgess, *Mother West Wind "How" Stories* (New York: Grosset & Dunlap, 1944), p. 74.

8 If state action has been progressively endorsed to alleviate the worst effects of misfortune, Americans have evidenced little interest in state action designed to penalize those who become extremely wealthy because of luck. The general lack of interest in imposing a maximum on winnings has been discussed in chapter 8. Here one might merely note a related reluctance to reduce in any major way largesse clearly attributable to good fortune, as evidenced for example by the absence of support for heavy taxes on large winnings in state lotteries.

9 See for example Ian Bowen, *Acceptable Inequalities: An Essay on the Distribution of Income* (London: George Allen & Unwin, 1970), p. 47; Antony Flew, "The Procrustean ideal: libertarians vs. egalitarians," *Encounter*, L (March 1978), p. 74; Murray N. Rothbard, *Power and Market: Government and the Economy* (Kansas City, KS: Sheed Andrews and McMeel, 1970), pp. 214–15. After noting that equality of opportunity would require "the abolition of the family" and "the communal rearing of chldren," Rothbard concludes that the goal of equality of opportunity is "conceptually unrealizable and . . . therefore absurd. Any drive to achieve [it] is *ipso facto* absurd as well."

10 Mario Cuomo, "Abraham Lincoln and our 'unfinished work'," address before the Abraham Lincoln Association, Springfield, IL, February 12, 1986, p. 19.

11 Quoted in US Congress, Senate, Select Committee on Poverty of the Committee on Labor and Public Welfare, *Hearings, Economic Opportunity Act of 1964*, 88th Cong., 2nd sess., June 1964, p. 253.

12 US Congress, House, Committee on Expenditures in the Executive Departments, *Hearings, Full Employment Act of 1945*, 79th Cong., 1st sess., 1945, p. 971.

13 Aristotle, *The "Art" of Rhetoric*, trans. John Henry Freese (Cambridge, MA: Harvard University Press, 1967), p. 259. To this Aristotle added: "In a word, the character of the rich man is that of a fool favored by fortune."

14 Horace, *The Third Book of Horace's Odes*, trans. Gordon Williams (Oxford: Clarendon Press, 1969), p. 125.

15 V. Adoratsky (ed.), *Karl Marx: Selected Works* (New York: International Publishers, 1936), vol. I, p. 268.

16 Thomas H. Johnson (ed.), *The Poems of Emily Dickinson* (Cambridge, MA: Belknap Press, 1955), vol. III, p. 858. Reprinted by permission of the publishers and the Trustees of Amherst College from *The Poems of Emily Dickinson*, edited by Thomas H. Johnson, Cambridge, Mass.: The Belknap Press of Harvard

University Press, copyright 1951, © 1955, 1979, 1983, by the President and Fellows of Harvard College.

17 Daniel Patrick Moynihan, *Family and Nation* (New York: Harcourt Brace Jovanovich, 1986), p. 38.

18 Ken Auletta, *The Underclass* (New York: Random House, 1982), p. 98.

19 Recall from the previous chapter the distinction between (a) a welfare system that leaves individual personalities unchanged, and by presenting new options alters observed (maximizing) behavior, and (b) a welfare system that shifts the utility functions of recipients so they are more prone to prefer welfare in the future. The second would seem to be the central mechanism at issue in the kind of environmental–personality arguments discussed here.

20 Irving Kristol, *Two Cheers for Capitalism* (New York: New American Library (Mentor Book), 1979), p. 225.

21 Thomas Sowell, *The Economics and Politics of Race* (New York: William Morrow, 1983), pp. 135–43, and *Race and Economics* (New York: Longman, 1975), pp 225–38.

22 Friedrich Hayek, *The Road to Serfdom* (Chicago, IL: University of Chicago Press, 1976), p. xi.

23 Irving Kristol, *Reflections of a Neoconservative* (New York: Basic Books, 1983), pp. 76–7.

24 As something of a side issue in this more general debate, the more successfully one attacks the notion that consumer preferences are fixed and independent by insisting that consumer preferences are highly malleable and deliberately molded by those wishing to sell goods and services, the more one undermines one of the assumptions needed by neoclassical economics for its demonstration that a competitive equilibrium is a Pareto optimum. See for example John Kenneth Galbraith, *The New Industrial State*, 2nd edn, revised (Boston, MA: Houghton Mifflin, 1971), pp. 6–7.

25 Michael Harrington, *The Other America: Poverty in the United States* (Baltimore, MD: Penguin, 1963), p. 123.

26 Gunnar Myrdal, *An American Dilemma: The Negro Problem and Modern Democracy* (New York: Harper & Row, 1962), p. 75.

27 See Joan Robinson, *Freedom and Necessity* (London: George Allen & Unwin, 1971), p. 121; Robert L. Heilbroner, *Between Capitalism and Socialism* (New York: Vintage, 1970), p. 106.

28 For a discussion of some of the philosophical questions involved and citations to some of the relevant literature, see Isaiah Berlin, *Four Essays on Liberty*, revised edition (New York: Oxford University Press, 1979), pp. xxxvii–xliii.

29 Joel Feinberg, *Social Philosophy* (Englewood Cliffs, NJ: Prentice-Hall, 1973), p. 13.

30 Ibid., p. 7.

31 Ibid., p. 9.

32 Sowell, *Conflict of Visions*, p. 91.

33 Ibid., pp. 91–2.

34 One might note in passing the obvious inconsistency between (a) insisting upon the limitations of human knowledge as a reason for nonintervention and (b) insisting, as Charles Murray does, that the welfare system be abandoned because we know enough to identify the detrimental effects of that system on the personality traits of the poor.

35 Harald Ofstad, *An Inquiry into the Freedom of Decision* (London: George Allen & Unwin, 1961), p. 279.

36 Kristol, *Two Cheers for Capitalism*, p. 178.

37 John Stuart Mill, *On Liberty* (New York: Penguin, 1981), p. 72.
38 In the evolution of Anglo-American law, the question of a defendant's legal (as distinct from moral) responsibility for homicidal acts came to turn crucially upon the issue of "criminal insanity," with the latter depending upon the "M'Naghten Rule" dating from an English case of 1843. The judges in that case affirmed that "to establish a defence on the ground of insanity it must be clearly proved that, at the time of committing the act, the party accused was labouring under such a defect of *reason,* from disease of the mind, as not to know the *nature and quality of the act he was doing,* or, if he did know it, that he did not *know he was doing what was wrong* . . . . The question has generally been, whether the accused at the time of doing the act *knew the difference between right and wrong.*" (Emphasis added.) (Quoted in Arnold S. Kaufman, "Responsibility, moral and legal," in Paul Edwards (ed.), *Encyclopedia of Philosophy* (New York: Macmillan, 1967), vol. VII, p. 187.)
39 Ibid., p. 183.
40 Charles Murray, "Helping the poor: a few modest proposals," *Commentary,* LXXIX (May 1985), p. 28.
41 Barry Goldwater, *The Conscience of a Conservative* (Shepherdsville, KY: Victor, 1960), p. 12.
42 George F. Will, *Statecraft as Soulcraft* (New York: Simon and Schuster, 1983), p. 60.
43 Daniel Bell, "Meritocracy and equality," *Public Interest,* XXIX (Fall 1972), p. 40.
44 Lay Commission, *Toward the Future,* p. 44.
45 Hayek, *Road to Serfdom,* p. 119.
46 Quoted in Auletta, *The Underclass,* p. 38.
47 Ibid., p. 156.
48 Daniel Goldman, "Feeling of control viewed as central in mental health," *New York Times* (October 7, 1986), p. C-11.
49 Roy P. Basler (ed.), *The Collected Works of Abraham Lincoln* (New Brunswick, NJ: Rutgers Press, 1953), vol. IV, p. 169.
50 Quoted in Auletta, *The Underclass,* p. 156.
51 Ibid., pp. 65–6.
52 Paul Mariani, "Renewing the symbolic contract," *Imprimis,* XV (December 1986), p. 6.
53 Robin M. Williams, Jr, "The concept of values," in David L. Sills (ed.), *International Encyclopedia of the Social Sciences* (New York: Macmillan, 1968), vol. XVI, p. 283. To indicate the multiplicity of uses to which the word is put in the social sciences, Williams adds:

> Psychologists have employed an array of related terms: attitudes, needs, sentiments, dispositions, interests, preferences, motives, cathexes, valences . . . . Anthropologists have spoken of obligation, . . . ethos, culture pattern, themes, and life style. Sociologists and political scientists have referred to interests, ethics, ideologies, mores, norms, attitudes, aspirations, obligations, rights, and sanctions (ibid., p. 284).

54 "What's wrong?" *Time* (May 25, 1987), pp. 14–17.
55 Myron Magnet, "The decline and fall of business ethics," *Fortune,* CXIV (December 8, 1986), pp. 65–6, 68, 72, and "The money society," *Fortune,* CXVI (July 6, 1987), pp. 26–31.
56 Magnet, "The money society," p. 26.
57 James Baldwin et al., "Liberalism and the Negro: a round-table discussion," *Commentary,* XXXVII (March 1964), p. 28.

58 Samuel Ricard, *Traité général du commerce* (Amsterdam: Chez E. van Harrevelt et Soeters, 1781), p. 463; translated and quoted in Albert O. Hirschman, *Rival Views of Market Society* (New York: Viking, 1986), p. 108.

59 Arthur Shenfield, "Capitalism under the tests of ethics," in John Andrews (ed.), *Champions of Freedom* (Hillsdale, MI: Hillsdale College Press, 1982), vol. IX, p. 30.

60 Alan Greenspan, "The assault on integrity," in Ayn Rand (ed.), *Capitalism: The Unknown Ideal* (New York: New American Library (Signet Book), 1967), p. 121.

61 Michael Novak, *The Spirit of Democratic Capitalism* (New York: Simon and Schuster, 1982), p. 347.

62 Heilbroner, *Between Capitalism and Socialism*, p. 40.

63 Esmond Wright, "Life, liberty, and the pursuit of excellence," in Barbara J. Smith (ed.), *Champions of Freedom* (Hillsdale, MI: Hillsdale College Press, 1976), vol. III, p. 10.

64 Shenfield, "Capitalism under the tests of ethics," p. 33.

65 Frank S. Mead (ed.), *The Encyclopedia of Religious Quotations* (Westwood, NJ: Fleming H. Revell, 1965), p. 193. Other variants include "Surely it is the maxim of loving-kindness: Do not unto others that you would not have them do unto you" (Confucianism) and "Do naught unto others which would cause you pain if done to you" (Brahamanism) (ibid., pp. 191–2).

66 Claude Koch, "The unwritten texts," *Imprimis*, XV (October 1986), pp. 4–5.

67 Nathaniel Branden, "Alienation," in Ayn Rand (ed.), *Capitalism: The Unknown Ideal* (New York: New American Library (Signet Book), 1967), p. 286.

68 Arthur M. Okun, *Equality and Efficiency: The Big Tradeoff* (Washington, DC: The Brookings Institution, 1975), p. 47.

69 Green, *Pursuit of Inequality*, p. 7.

70 Albert Hofstadter, "The career open to personality: the meaning of equality of opportunity for an ethics for our time," in Lyman Bryson (ed.), *Aspects of Human Equality* (New York: Harper & Brothers, 1956), p. 119.

71 Novak, *Spirit of Democratic Capitalism*, p. 353. In the King James version of The Bible *agapē* is translated "charity" when a noun and "love" when a verb.

72 Thus Erich Fromm, a one-time favorite target of conservatives, emphasizes in his notion of love not distance and distinctiveness but "union" and "uniting," the experience of "sharing," of "communion," of "human solidarity": "the active and creative relatedness of man to his fellow man." With union comes knowledge: "If I love . . . I know him, I have penetrated through his surface to the core of his being, and related myself to him from my core, from the center . . . of my being." (Erich Fromm, *The Sane Society* (New York: Rinehart, 1955), pp. 30–3.)

73 Green, *Pursuit of Inequality*, p. 245.

74 Fromm, *The Sane Society*, p. 139. For a vigorous attack on Fromm from the right, see Branden, "Alienation," pp. 273–88.

75 Kemp, *American Renaissance*, p. 25.

76 Kristol, *Two Cheers for Capitalism*, p. x.

77 Milton Friedman, *There's No Such Thing As A Free Lunch* (LaSalle, IL: Open Court, 1975), p. 31.

78 Kristol, *Two Cheers for Capitalism*, p. xi.

79 Novak, *Spirit of Democratic Capitalism*, p. 137.

80 Ibid., p. 139.

81 Ibid., p. 137.

82 Ibid.

83 Ibid., pp. 137–8.

84 Ibid., p. 138.

85 An issue typically glossed over in this writing is whether the word "freedom" takes on, for purposes of this discrediting, a meaning well beyond the conventional conservative bounds, confined as the latter are to the absence of violence and the threat of violence.

86 Ayn Rand, *The Fountainhead* (New York: Bobbs-Merrill, 1968), quoted with enthusiasm in Branden, "Alienation," p. 284.

87 Will, *Statecraft as Soulcraft*, p. 165.

88 Beth Brophy, "Ethics 101: can the good guys win?" *U.S. News & World Report* (April 13, 1987), p. 54.

89 Kathleen Teltsch, "Corporate pressures slowing gifts to charity," *New York Times* (July 8, 1987), p. D2.

90 Vernon E. Jordan, Jr, "The free enterprise system," *Vital Speeches of the Day*, LIII (May 15, 1987), p. 467.

91 Teltsch, "Corporate pressures," p. A1.

92 Ibid., p. D2.

93 Cited in Magnet, "The money society," p. 26.

94 "Harvard's $30 million windfall for ethics 101," *Business Week* (April 13, 1987), p. 40.

95 See for example "The end of corporate loyalty?" *Business Week* (August 4, 1986), pp. 42–5, 48–9, including the survey results, p. 49.

96 Ibid., p. 43.

97 Ibid., p. 44.

98 Magnet, "Decline and fall of business ethics," p. 66.

99 Magnet, "The money society," p. 29.

100 "Quotes of the week," *U.S. News & World Report* (June 1, 1987), p. 9.

101 Alison Leigh Cowan, "Harvard to get $30 million ethics gift," *New York Times* (March 31, 1987), p. D1.

102 Quoted in Magnet, "Decline and fall of business ethics," p. 65.

103 Ibid.

104 See for example *Federalist* (New York: Tudor, 1937), No. IL, p. 348; No. LV, p. 383.

105 Shirley R. Letwin, "The morality of the free man," in Barbara J. Smith (ed.), *Champions of Freedom* (Hillsdale, MI: Hillsdale College Press, 1976), vol. III, p. 151.

106 "Ethics: what's wrong?" *Time* (May 25, 1987), p. 15.

107 Alexander Cockburn, "Social Darwinism on the big and small screens," *Wall Street Journal* (June 11, 1987), p. 25.

108 "Morality among the supply-siders," *Time* (May 25, 1987), p. 18.

109 Will, *Statecraft as Soulcraft*, pp. 19–20.

110 Ibid., pp. 69–70. "Would those people who deny that law should seek to shape morals also deny that morals shape law? Given that the law is shaped as well as shaping, is it not reasonable that law should be concerned with its social and cultural roots? Have they all been mistaken, all the philosophers and statesmen from Plato to the present, who have argued that particular forms of government have social and cultural prerequisites, including shared ideas, values and character traits in the citizenry? If a society wills just laws, should it not will the means – the moral prerequisites – to the end?" (Ibid., pp. 83–4.)

111 As of 1986. See "How the states regulate sex," *Newsweek* (July 14, 1986), p. 37.

112 "Pornography: a poll," *Time* (July 21, 1986), p. 22. The wording of the poll is not entirely clear, the agreement being "at least in part" to the wording noted. Comparable figures for females polled were 67 percent and 44 percent respectively.

113 George Will, "Conservatism with a kindly face? In defense of the welfare state," *New Republic*, CLXXXVIII (May 9, 1983), p. 20.

114 The passage and subsequent repeal of the Volstead Act illustrates that views can change about which values to include in this list.

115 Ronald Dworkin, "Liberalism," in Stuart Hampshire (ed.), *Public and Private Morality* (Cambridge, England: Cambridge University Press, 1978), p. 127.

116 Ibid.

117 Lester C. Thurow, *The Impact of Taxes on the American Economy* (New York: Praeger, 1971), p. 147.

118 Ibid., pp. 146–8, 163.

119 Some liberals (such as Thurow in the passage just noted) do occasionally write as if all values were of the second sort; that is, a matter of personal preference and nothing more (including those values associated with equality). But this line of reasoning, if pressed, would lead to ethical relativism, and as such, would deny the writer any moral base from which to advocate or criticize values.

120 The discussion at this point could be accused of confusing (a) promoting laws to promote values and (b) using values to decide the terms of legislation quite unrelated to the promotion of values. In practice, the line between the two tends to be blurred, if for no other reason than activity (b), when the values are trumpeted as a reason for the legislation in question, serves to promote the importance of those values with the public.

121 Kai Nielsen, "Ethics, problems of," in Paul Edwards (ed.), *The Encyclopedia of Philosophy* (New York: Macmillan, 1967), vol. III, p. 125; see also Richard B. Brandt, "Ethical relativism," ibid., pp. 75–8.

122 Stephen Hart, "Ethical relativism, left-wing politics," *Dissent*, XXIX (October 1, 1982), p. 484.

123 "Who is to say what's right in teaching about ethics?" *New York Times* (April 19, 1987), p. E. 18.

124 "A government in the bedroom," *Newsweek* (July 14, 1986), p. 38.

125 "Now, a few words from the wise," *Time* (June 22, 1987), p. 69.

126 Jeffrey Schmalz, "Cuomo says Reagan government lacks respect for the rule of law," *New York Times* (July 29, 1987), p. A16.

127 See, for example, George C. Roche III, "The relevance of Friedrich A. Hayek," in Fritz Machlup (ed), *Essays on Hayek* (New York: New York University Press, 1976), pp. 9–11; Viktor Vanberg, "Cultural evolution vs. rationalism in Hayek's thought," *Cato Policy Report*, VII (January–February 1985), p. 3. Hayek's views on the centrality of spontaneous order to "liberalism" are outlined in Hayek, *Studies in Philosophy, Politics and Economics* (Chicago; IL: University of Chicago Press, 1967), ch. 11, especially p. 162.

128 Hayek, *Constitution of Liberty*, p. 160; quoting Michael Polanyi, *The Logic of Liberty* (London: Routledge & Kegan Paul, 1951), p. 159.

129 For a layman's guide to both, see Peter D. McClelland, *Causal Explanation and Model Building in History, Economics, and the New Economic History* (Ithaca, NY: Cornell University Press, 1975), pp. 117–25.

130 " . . . the term 'rule' is used for a staement by which a regularity of the conduct of individuals can be described, irrespective of whether such a rule is 'known' to the

individuals in any other sense than that they normally act in accordance with it" (Hayek, *Studies in Philosophy*, p. 67).

131 Norman P. Barry, *Hayek's Social and Economic Philosophy* (London:Macmillan, 1979), p. 80.

132 Ibid., p. 60. In more muted language, conservative Thomas Sowell writes of the belief that selfishness is "an unchangeable part of human nature" as being an integral part of what Sowell terms the "constrained vision" popular with conservatives (Sowell, *Conflict of Visions*, p. 85).

133 Hayek, *Constitution of Liberty*, p. 27.

134 "Freedom was made possible by the gradual evolution of the *discipline of civilization which is at the same time the discipline of freedom*. It protects him by impersonal abstract rules against arbitrary violence of others and enables each individual to try and build for himself a protected domain with which nobody else is allowed to interfere and within which he can use his own knowledge for his own purposes" (Hayek, *The Three Sources of Human Values* (London: London School of Economics and Political Science, 1978), p. 16).

135 Perhaps the most concise and candid statement of Hayek's views on these processes can be found in Chiaki Nishiyama and Kurt R. Leube (eds), *The Essence of Hayek* (Stanford, CA: Hoover Institution, 1984), ch. 17. The same ideas are developed in Hayek, *Studies in Philosophy*, ch. 4 and *Law, Legislation and Liberty*, vol. I, *Rules and Order* (Chicago, IL: University of Chicago Press, 1973), chs 1, 2, 4, 5.

136 Samuel Brittan, "Hayek, the New Right, and the crisis of social democracy," *Encounter*, LIV (January 1980), pp. 33–4, A similar framework can be applied to English common law (as distinct from moral rules in general), the structure of that law being "characterized by unplanned growth yet . . . nevertheless [providing] a coherent framework of rules within which individuals may behave reasonably predictably toward one another. The essential point is that the total structure is not the product of will"; that is, "not the product of a design or deliberate plan . . . " (Barry, *Hayek's Social and Economic Philosophy*, p. 85).

137 Hayek, *Constitution of Liberty*, p. 161.

138 Ibid., p. 27.

139 At one point in his earlier writing, Hayek quotes Alexander Carr-Saunders that "Those groups practising the most advantageous customs will have an advantage in the constant struggle with adjacent groups" (Hayek, *Studies in Philosophy*, p. 67, n. 3). Elsewhere in his own words Hayek argues:

These rules of conduct have thus not developed as the recognized conditions for the achievement of a known purpose, but have evolved because the groups who practised them were more successful and displaced others. They were rules which, given the kind of environment in which man lived, secured that a greater number of the groups or individuals practising them would survive. (Hayek, *Law, Legislation and Liberty*, vol. I, p. 18).

Later in the same work he adds:

The reason why such rules will tend to develop is that the groups which happen to have adopted rules conducive to a more effective order of actions will tend to prevail over other groups with a less effective order. The rules that will spread will be those governing the practice or customs existing in different groups which make some groups stronger than others. And certain rules will predominate by more successfully guiding expectations in relation to other persons who act independently (ibid., p. 99).

140 On rare occasions, Hayek will acknowledge the problem. For example:

> I have so far carefully avoided saying that evolution is identical with progress, but when it becomes clear that it was the evolution of a tradition which made civilization possible, we may at least say that spontaneous evolution is a necessary if not a sufficient condition of progress. And though it clearly also produces much that we did not foresee and do not like when we see it, it does bring to ever increasing numbers what they have been mainly striving for (*The Three Sources of Human Values*, p. 21).

Here the only accomplishment beyond survival is allowing the many to realize "what they have been mainly striving for" – an observation that raises problems to be taken up below. In most of Hayek's writing, however, the emphasis is exclusively upon survival.

141 Edmund Burke, *Reflections on the Revolution in France*, ed. Conor Cruise O'Brien (New York: Penguin, 1981), p. 91.

142 This darker vision of humanity is evident in the conservative belief that all power tends to corrupt and absolute power corrupts absolutely. But this unflattering view of dangerous tendencies ranges far beyond the likely human response to political power. Thus, for example, Thomas Sowell writes of "a tragic vision of the human condition" (Sowell, *Conflict of Visions*, p. 33), Hayek writes of "man's more primitive and ferocious instincts" (Hayek, *Constitution of Liberty*, p. 60), and Bernard Murchland interprets The Bible as asserting "the human heart is deceitful above all things, and exceedingly corrupt," adding his own judgment that "We are fallible and imperfect creatures, driven by passion and self-interest, misled by our illusions, divided in our loyalties, forever tortured and tempted by the world, the flesh, and the devil" (Bernard Murchland, "The socialist critique of the corporation," in Michael Novak and John W. Cooper (eds), *The Corporation: A Theological Inquiry* (Washington, DC: American Enterprise Institute for Public Policy Research, 1981), p. 161).

143 Kristol, *Two Cheers for Capitalism*, p. 251.

144 Ibid.

145 "While there is nothing a theory of cultural evolution can tell us about the appropriateness of our institutions apart from their 'evolutionary success,' throughout the tradition of classical liberalism a fundamental criterion of appropriateness *has* been stressed: Those rules and institutions are considered appropriate that are conducive to a social order in which people, as much and as effectively as possible, are allowed to pursue their own purposes" (Vanberg, "Cultural evolution," p. 5).

146 "It is neither the striving for beauty, nor for justice, nor any other foreseen or intended aim of human evolution, which can perform the necessary function that alone selectively evoked morals can perform, namely to enhance the production of, or to maintain, more lives" (Nishiyama and Leube (eds), *Essence of Hayek*, p. 325). Or again: " . . . the fundamental function of morals [is] to keep alive that part of mankind which we feed only through the constant adaptation to incessant unforeseeable changes which enabled us to raise them in the first instance. Morals are not a matter of taste. They are very necessary but most unwelcome restraints telling us which of the things we would instinctively like to do we must not do if we are to preserve an order on which most of us depend for our survival but which we have neither made nor learnt to understand" (ibid., p. 328).

147 Friedman notes, for example, "that reliance on the freedom of people to control their own lives in accordance with their own values is the surest way to achieve

the full potential of a great society" (Milton Friedman and Rose Friedman, *Free to Choose* (New York: Harcourt Brace Jovanovich, 1980), p. 297). But the meaning of "great" in "great society" remains unclear, as does the meaning of "full potential."

148 Kristol, *Two Cheers for Capitalism*, p. 62.
149 Ibid., pp. 62–3.
150 Felix Rohatyn, quoted in Magnet, "Decline and fall of business ethics," p. 72.
151 Ira Michael Heyman, "Trapped in an 'athletics arms race'," *U.S. News & World Report* (July 20, 1987), p. 7.
152 Friedrich Hayek, *Knowledge, Evolution, and Society* (London: Butler & Tanner, 1983), p. 50.
153 Ibid., pp. 50–1.Elsewhere Hayek makes a similar concession, although couched in the form of an "if . . . then" statement.

> It has, of course, never been denied that the existence of norms in a given group of men is a fact. What has been questioned is that from the circumstance that the norms are in fact obeyed the conclusion could be drawn that they ought to be obeyed. The conclusion is of course possible only if it is tacitly assumed that the continued existence of the group is desired. But if such continued existence is regarded as desirable, or even the further existence of the group as an entity with a certain order is presupposed as a fact, then it follows that certain rules of conduct (not necessarily all those which are now observed) will have to be followed by its members (Hayek, *Law, Legislation and Liberty*, vol. I, p. 81).

Hayek recognizes the close affinity of his approach with ethical relativism, but repeatedly retreats into tying the "rightness" or "goodness" of evolving moral rules to the priority of survival. Thus:

> Nor can we, for the purpose of maintaining our society, accept all moral beliefs which are held with equal conviction as equally legitimate, and recognize a right to blood feud or infanticide or even theft, or any other moral beliefs contrary to those on which the working of our society rests. What makes an individual a member of society and gives him claims is that he obeys its rules. Wholly contradictory views may give him rights in other societies but not in ours. For the science of anthropology all cultures or morals may be equally good, but we maintain our society by treating others as less so (ibid., vol. III, p. 172).

154 For a general discussion of the many limitations in Hayek's ethical views, see Graham Walker, *The Ethics of Friedrich Hayek* (Geneva: Institut Universitaire de Hautes Etudes Internationales, 1984), particularly chs 4 and 7.
155 Sowell, *Conflict of Visions*, p. 86.
156 Ibid., p. 100.
157 Ibid. See also ibid., pp. 70, 90, 202–3 and, for the traditional conservative endorsement of material progress, pp. 86, 127, 130.
158 Will, *Statecraft as Soulcraft*, p. 23.
159 Kristol, *Two Cheers for Capitalism*, p. 251.
160 Occasionally Sowell writes of other values as if they were "desirable" or "good" – such as "humane feelings," "self-discipline," and "consideration for others" – but how their realization is linked to his larger utilitarian aim is never explored in any detail (see Sowell, *Conflict of Visions*, pp. 147, 150).
161 Sowell's position on preference realization also complements the traditional conservative emphasis on the absence of a commonly agreed upon hierarchy of values. In one of the best summaries of both points, Hayek writes:

[The philosophy of individualism] does not assume, as is often asserted, that man is egoistic or selfish or ought to be. It merely starts from the indisputable fact that the limits of our powers of imagination make it impossible to include in our scale of values more than a sector of the needs of the whole society, and that, since, strictly speaking, scales of value can exist only in individual minds, nothing but partial scales of values exist – scales which are inevitably different and often inconsistent with each other. From this the individualist concludes that the individuals should be allowed, within defined limits, to follow their own values and preferences rather than somebody else's; that within these spheres the individual's system of ends should be supreme and not subject to any dictation by others. It is this recognition of the individual as the ultimate judge of his ends, the belief that as far as possible his own views ought to govern his actions, that forms the essence of the individualist position (Hayek, *Road to Serfdom*, p. 59).

162 J. J. C. Smart, "Utilitarianism," in Paul Edwards (ed.), *The Encyclopedia of Philosophy* (New York: Macmillan, 1967), vol. VIII, p. 209.
163 The priority of preference realization is also the normative centerpiece of "constitutional economics," a relatively new field in economics concerned with the choice of constraints (or choosing among alternative sets of rules) rather than with choice within constraints. For a concise summary of the main assumptions, analytical techniques, and findings, see James M. Buchanan, "Constitutional economics," in John Eatwell et al. (eds), *The New Palgrave: A Dictionary of Economics* (New York: Stockton, 1987), vol. I, pp. 585–8. As an explanation for the choice of rules actually made, such an approach in many instances has demonstrated predictive value. As a guide for which rules should be chosen in the name of economic justice, such an approach fails, not in a small way but in a major way, and for the same reasons that Sowell fails: the single goal of preference realization will not do for the vast majority of Americans as a guide to what is "right" or "just."

12 Summing up: a personal perspective

1 Edwin R. A. Seligman, "Is the income tax constitutional and just?" *Forum*, XIX (March 1895), p. 49; reproduced in Edith M. Phelps (ed.), *Selected Articles on the Income Tax* (Minneapolis, MN: H. H. Wilson, 1911), p. 65.
2 Tom Hayden, *The American Future: New Visions Beyond Old Frontiers* (Boston, MA: South End, 1980), p. 76.
3 By one estimate, the total killed by civil and international wars in this century is 36 million, and by governments wreaking havoc on their own people, 119 million (R. J. Rummel, "War isn't this century's biggest killer," *Wall Street Journal* (July 7, 1986), p. 12).
4 Sidney Verba et al., *Elites and the Idea of Equality* (Cambridge, MA: Harvard University Press, 1987), pp. 130–1.
5 Robert Kuttner, *The Economic Illusion* (Boston, MA: Houghton Mifflin, 1984), pp. 276, 277.
6 See for example Benjamin Barber, "A new language for the left: translating the conservative discourse," *Harper's Magazine*, CCLXXIII (November 1986), pp. 47–52.
7 Lionel Trilling, *The Liberal Imagination* (New York: Viking, 1950), p. 9.
8 Clifford Geertz, *The Interpretation of Cultures: Selected Essays* (New York: Basic Books, 1973), p. 127.

9 George Bernard Shaw, letter to *The New Republic*, February 12, 1936; reproduced in Edwin McDowell, "Book Notes," *New York Times* (July 27, 1988), p. C19.
10 Walter Lippmann, *A Preface to Politics* (Ann Arbor, MI: University of Michigan Press (Ann Arbor Paperbacks), 1962), p. 170.
11 Ibid., p. 159.
12 This does not rule out the possibility of a better understanding of human nature leading to refinements in what counts as discriminatory behavior, or counts as the unfair use of undue power.

13 The American dream and present-day America

1 John Gunther, *Inside U.S.A.* (London: Hamish Hamilton, 1945), p. ix.
2 John G. Nicolay and John Hay, *Abraham Lincoln: Complete Works* (New York: Century, 1907), vol. I, p. 655.
3 See for example the discussion of "loner" in Harold Wentworth and Stuart Berg Flexner (eds), *Dictionary of American Slang* (New York: Thomas Y. Crowell, 1975), p. 323.
4 Michael Novak, *The Spirit of Democratic Capitalism* (New York: Simon and Schuster, 1982), p. 347.
5 "New prospects, old values," *Time* (June 17, 1985), p. 68.
6 Ibid., p. 69.
7 Louis Filler, *The President Speaks* (New York: G.P. Putnam's Sons, 1964), p. 27.
8 For labor force participation rates for women ages 20–64 see Council of Economic Advisors, *1987 Annual Report*, p. 211. The rise in the labor force participation of *all* women has been slightly less dramatic, from 20 percent at the turn of the century to 55 percent in 1986. For estimates of both participation rates from 1870 to the present, see Barbara R. Bergmann, *The Economic Emergence of Women* (New York: Basic Books, 1986), p. 21.
9 William McKinley, *Speeches and Addresses: From his Election to Congress to the Present Time* (New York: D. Appleton, 1893), pp. 78–9.
10 In a recent survey of 532 companies, 51 percent of "large companies" had female board members, and 43 percent of all companies responding had female board members. (Amanda Bennett, "Losing ground? Surveyed firms report fewer women directors," *Wall Street Journal* (July 17, 1987), p. 21. The "loss of ground" referred to in the article is a decline in the percentage of "all companies" having female board members from 45 percent in 1985 to 43 percent in 1986.) Women are also represented on 44 percent of the boards of the "Fortune 1000" as of 1986 (see Sara E. Rix (ed.), *The American Woman, 1987–88*, Women's Research & Education Institute of the Congressional Caucus for Women's Issues (New York: Norton, 1987), p. 314).
11 Rix (ed.), *The American Woman, 1987–88*, p. 197.
12 Quoted in Donald Lambro, *Land of Opportunity* (Boston, MA: Little, Brown, 1986), p. 128.
13 The second percentages, for 1984, are dentistry 19.6 percent, medicine 28.2 percent, and law 36.8 percent. (US Department of Commerce, *Statistical Abstract of the United States: 1987* (Washington, DC: US Government Printing Office 1987), p. 148. Data on other degrees from ibid., p. 146.)
14 Quoted in Anne B. Fisher, "Where women are succeeding," *Fortune*, CXVI (August 3, 1987), p. 80.

15 Gunnar Myrdal, *An American Dilemma: The Negro Problem and Modern Democracy* (New York: Harper & Brothers, 1944), p. 203.

16 For modern data on the earnings gap that still persists between black males and black females, see Bergmann, *Economic Emergence of Women*, p. 69.

17 All estimates based upon data from the 1940 Census. See James P. Smith and Finis R. Welch, *Closing the Gap: Forty Years of Economic Progress for Blacks* (Santa Monica, CA: Rand, 1986), pp. viii, 6, 23, 29.

18 For sources of this and previous numbers cited, see Smith and Welch, *Closing the Gap*, pp. viii, ix, xxviii, 5, 12, 27; and appendix C, table C.1. The black–white gap in average yearly earnings is larger than the gap in weekly earnings because, on the average, blacks work fewer hours per year. Thus, by one estimate, average hourly earnings of black males are 74 percent of those for whites, whereas their average yearly earnings are only 66 percent. See Reynolds Farley, "Assessing black progress: employment, occupation, earnings, income, poverty," *Economic Outlook USA*, XIII (Third quarter 1986), p. 16.

19 For recent estimates of this gap, see Bergmann, *Economic Emergence of Women*, p. 69; Farley, "Assessing black progress," pp. 16–17; Council of Economic Advisors, *1987 Annual Report*, p. 224.

20 Data from Smith and Welch, *Closing the Gap*, pp. xxiv, 103. This comparison of black–white family income differentials ignores the difficulties associated with the rise of single-parent families, to be taken up below.

21 "Strike one and you're out," *U.S. News & World Report*, (July 27, 1987), p. 54.

22 Charles C. Moskos, "Success story: blacks in the army," *The Atlantic*, CCLVII (May 1986), p. 64.

23 Data for 1963 from US Bureau of Labor Statistics, *Employment and Earnings*, X (January 1964), p. 10; for 1986, from ibid., XXXIV (January 1987), p. 36.

24 For 1964 data, see James E. Conyers and Walter L. Wallace, *Black Elected Officials* (New York: Russell Sage Foundation, 1976), p. 2; for more recent data, see US Department of Commerce, *Statistical Abstract: 1987*, p. 240.

25 Franklin D. Roosevelt, "Annual message to the Congress, January 6, 1941," in Samuel I. Rosenman (ed.), *The Public Papers and Addresses of Franklin D. Roosevelt* (New York: Macmillan, 1941), 1940 volume, p. 671.

26 Average female earnings relative to that of males remained stubbornly in the 60 percent range from the mid-1960s to the early 1980s, and recently have risen slightly to about 64 percent (comparisons made between median wage or salary income of year-round full-time, civilian workers; see Council of Economic Advisers, *1987 Annual Report*, p. 221).

27 For discussion of this divergence and supporting data, see Bergmann, *Economic Emergence of Women*, pp. 67–9.

28 Patricia B. Reuss, lobbyist for the Women's Equity Action League, quoted in Robert Pear, "Women reduce lag in earnings but disparities with men remain," *New York Times* (September 4, 1987), p. A1.

29 See for example the discussion and sources cited in Francine D. Blau and Marianne A. Ferber, "Discrimination: empirical evidence from the United States," *American Economic Review*, LXXVII (May 1987), pp. 316–20; Bergmann, *Economic Emergence of Women*, pp. 67–82; Earl F. Mellor, "Investigating the differences in weekly earnings of men and women," *Monthly Labor Review*, CVII (June 1984), pp. 17–28.

30 Rix (ed.), *The American Woman, 1987–88*, p. 118.

31 US Department of Commerce, *Statistical Abstract: 1987*, pp. 385–6.

32 Elizabeth Ehrlich, "What the boss is really like," *Business Week* (October 23, 1987), p. 40.
33 Rix (ed.), *The American Woman, 1987–88*, p. 313.
34 Data from the National Assessment of Educational Progress reading tests, cited in National Governors' Association Center for Policy Research, *Making America Work: Bringing Down the Barriers* (Washington, DC: National Governors' Association, 1987), p. 37.
35 See Edward B. Fiske, "Steady gains achieved by blacks on college admission test scores," *New York Times* (September 23, 1987), p. A1. The averages reported were:

	White		Black	
Year	Verbal	Math	Verbal	Math
1977	448	489	330	357
1987	447	489	351	377

36 The one notable exception by age group is that the unemployment rate for black male youths has significantly worsened compared with that of white male youths. See, for example, Smith and Welch, *Closing the Gap*, p. xxvii.
37 For example, Barbara Bergmann estimates that the weekly earnings of black males were, on the average, 77 percent of white earnings in 1975, and 73 percent in 1985 (Bergmann, *Economic Emergence of Women*, p. 69). Comparisons are for weekly earnings of full-time wage and salary workers. Inferences from the gap in wages to a gap in average earnings for the adult population must be tempered by the fact that more black than white adult males have dropped out of the labor force in recent years. See Smith and Welch, *Closing the Gap*, pp. 79–81; Sheldon Danziger and Peter Gottschalk, "Earnings inequality, the spatial concentration of poverty, and the underclass," *American Economic Review*, LXXVII (May 1987), pp. 211–15.
38 For a recent survey of estimates of the magnitude of this "unexplained" gap in the average wages of black and white males, see Blau and Ferber, "Discrimination," pp. 316–20.
39 Smith and Welch, *Closing the Gap*, p. 7. In addition to being paid less than their white counterparts, black males also work fewer hours per year, but the extent to which this is caused by discrimination is unclear. See, for example, Reynolds Farley, *Blacks and Whites: Narrowing the Gap?* (Cambridge, MA: Harvard University Press, 1984), p. 195.
40 For comparisons of education levels and median income by family type, see appendix C, tables C.1 and C.3. For data on male earnings relative to those of white males, see "The socioeconomic status of native Americans: a special policy problem," *Focus*, University of Wisconsin Institute for Research on Poverty, IX (Spring 1986), p. 25. For a discussion of the reasons for the gap in male wages relative to whites, see Gary D. Sandefur and Wilbur J. Scott, "Minority group status and the wages of Indian and black males," *Social Science Research*, XII (1983), pp. 44–68, and "A sociological analysis of white, black and American Indian male labor force activities," University of Wisconsin Institute for Research on Povert, Discussion Paper 765–84, November 1984.

41 "The *past* discrimination experienced by American Indians has placed them in isolated regions of the country, with few opportunities to work in core industries or nonmanual occupations, has promoted poor health, and has led to inadequate educational opportunities. So it is the internal colonization and past discrimination experienced by American Indians . . . that help explain their lower wages" (Sandefur and Scott, "White, black, and American Indian male labor force activities," p. 33).

42 For median income levels, see appendix C, table C.3. For poverty rates see US Department of Commerce, "The Hispanic population in the United States: March 1986 and 1987," *Current Population Reports*, series P-20, no. 416 (August 1987), p. 7; ibid., "Money income and poverty status of families and persons in the United States: 1986," *Current Population Reports*, series P-60, no. 157 (July 1987), p. 26. For a discussion of some of the possible reasons for such high poverty rates and low incomes among Puerto Ricans, see Marta Tienda, "The Puerto Rican worker: current labor market status and future prospects," *Journal of Hispanic Politics*, I (1985), pp. 27–51.

43 For a list of some of these reports and a discussion of their findings, see Physician Task Force on Hunger in America, *Hunger Reaches Blue Collar America: An Unbalanced Recovery in a Service Economy* (Boston, MA: Harvard School of Public Health, 1987), pp. 53–8.

44 All of the following examples are from Physician Task Force on Hunger in America, *Hunger in America: The Growing Epidemic* (Boston, MA: Harvard School of Public Health, 1985). More recent examples from the same research group can be found in *Hunger Reaches Blue Collar America*.

45 Ibid., p. 30.

46 Ibid., p. 40.

47 Quoted in Jeffrey Schmalz, "2,000 Catholics lobby leaders in Albany visit," *New York Times* (March 10, 1987), p. A1.

48 Quoted in "Mayors seek federal aid to curb poverty in cities," *New York Times* (December 19, 1986), p. A23.

49 "Study says families with children swell ranks of homeless," *New York Times* (March 31, 1987), p. A16. Families with children are now estimated to comprise "35 percent of the homeless population, making families the largest group within the homeless population, according to . . . the president of the Partnership for the Homeless and author of a report on the survey" (ibid.).

50 Lydia Chavez, "Welfare hotel children: tomorrow's poor," *New York Times* (July 16, 1987), p. B1.

51 Dr Steve Himmelstein, quoted in ibid.

52 Tom Wolfe, *The Kandy-Kolored Tangerine-Flake Streamlined Baby* (New York: Farrar, Straus, and Giroux, 1965), p. 176.

53 For a brief survey of proposals on workfare and a listing of the major recent welfare reports, see Robert D. Reischauer, "Welfare reform: will consensus be enough?" *Brookings Review*, V (Summer 1987), pp. 3–8.

54 One objection to the official measure of poverty is that it fails to include under income in-kind welfare benefits, such as food stamps and school lunches. Estimates of income that do include such benefits indicate that, of the children now officially counted as poor, counting such benefits would lift one in four above the poverty line but still leave the other three below it. See, for example, US Congress, House, Committee on Ways and Means, *Children in Poverty*, 99th Cong., 1st sess., May 22, 1985, pp. 25–6; Sheldon H. Danziger, Robert H.

Haveman, and Robert D. Plotnick, "Antipoverty policy: effects on the poor and the nonpoor," in Sheldon H. Danziger and Daniel H. Weinberg (eds), *Fighting Poverty* (Cambridge, MA: Harvard University Press, 1986), pp. 55–6.

55 See US Congress, House, *Children in Poverty*, p. 6. The evidence also suggests that not only are minority children more likely to be poor relative to white children at any point in time, but that minority children are more likely to be poor for a much larger number of their total childhood years than are white children. See Greg J. Duncan and Willard L. Rodgers, "The prevalence of childhood poverty," unpublished paper, University of Michigan Survey Research Center, March 25, 1986, p. 17 and table 1.

56 Mark R. Rosenweig, "Who receives medical care? Income, implicit prices and the distribution of medical services among pregnant women in the United States," Yale University Economic Growth Center, Discussion Paper 522, November 1986, p. 1.

57 William S. Woodside, "Health care for the poor: how to pay for it," *Wall Street Journal* (May 29, 1987), p. 26.

58 For various recent estimates of day care costs, see Elizabeth Ehrlich, "Child care: the private sector can't do it alone," *Business Week* (October 6, 1986), p. 52; "The child-care dilemma," *Time* (June 22, 1987), pp. 57–8.

59 Physician Task Force on Hunger, *Hunger Reaches Blue Collar America*, p. 34.

60 See for example Miriam Horn, "The burgeoning educational underclass," *U.S. News & World Report* (May 18, 1987), pp. 66–7.

61 Andrew Hahn and Jacqueline Danzberger, *Dropouts in America* (Washington DC: Institute for Educational Leadership, 1987), pp. 2–3.

62 Of all children living in single-parent families, three out of four are living in poverty if the mother has never been married, and two out of four if the mother is separated or divorced. (US Congress, House, *Children In Poverty*, pp. 6, 35.)

63 John E. Jacob, "A society that is just and fair," *Vital Speeches of the Day*, LIII (September 15, 1987), p. 733.

64 Neil Gilbert, "The unfinished business of welfare reform," *Society*, XXIV (March–April 1987), p. 6.

65 Franklin D. Roosevelt, "Second Inaugural Address, January 20, 1937," in Rosenman (ed.), *The Public Papers and Addresses of Franklin D. Roosevelt*, 1937 volume, p. 5.

66 Physician Task Force on Hunger in America, *Hunger in America*, pp. 97–9. "Cuts imposed in the school meal programs were brought about by lowering federal meal subsidies, altering income criteria by which eligibility is determined, making many low-income families pay more for each meal, and by making the application process more cumbersome" (ibid., p. 97).

67 For a summary of these developments, see Paul Starr, "Health care for the poor: the past twenty years," in Sheldon H. Danziger and Daniel H. Weinberg (eds), *Fighting Poverty* (Cambridge, MA: Harvard University Press, 1986), pp. 106–32.

68 Peter D. Salins, "Can we ensure that all Americans are well housed?" in *Housing America's Poor* (Chapel Hill, NC: University of North Carolina Press, 1987), p. 177. For less comprehensive surveys of the problem, see John Herbers, "Outlook for sheltering the poor growing even bleaker," *New York Times* (March 8, 1987), p. E5; William Celis III, "Crumbling projects: public-housing units are rapidly decaying, causing many to close," *Wall Street Journal* (December 15, 1986), p. 1.

69 Sheldon Danziger and Peter Gottschalk, "How have families with children been

faring?" University of Wisconsin Institute for Research on Poverty, Discussion Paper 801–86, January 1986, pp. 29–31.

70 For sources of these calculations, see Physician Task Force on Hunger in America, *Hunger Reaches Blue Collar America*, pp. 47, 75.

71 "The child-care dilemma," p. 55.

72 Quoted in ibid., p. 59.

73 Ibid., p. 58.

74 Quoted in Martin O'Connell and David E. Bloom, "Cutting the apron strings: women in the labor force in the 1980's," Harvard Institute of Economic Research, Discussion Paper 1297, January 1987, p. 23.

75 C. Turner, US Department of Health and Human Services, personal communication, December 1987. (The numerator for this calculation is total Head Start enrollment – 446,508 in late 1987 – and the denominator is the total number of three-, four-, and five-year-olds who are officially classified as poor.)

76 "Welfare that works," *New Republic*, CIIIC (August 24, 1987), p. 7.

77 "Back to basics," *Newsweek* (September 21, 1987), p. 54.

78 National Governors' Association, *Making America Work*, p. 79.

79 Ibid., p. 80.

80 "Back to basics," p. 54.

81 For a brief review of the history of these programs, see Laurie J. Bassi and Orley Ashenfelter, "The effect of direct job creation and training programs on low-skilled workers," in Sheldon H. Danziger and Daniel H. Weinberg (eds), *Fighting Poverty* (Cambridge, MA: Harvard University Press, 1986), pp. 133–51.

82 The programs are Job Corps, adult education, JTPA, Work Incentive program (WIN), and public service employment; the cut in total funding in constant dollar terms was from $8 billion to $2.8 billion. See Sar A. Levitan and Isaac Shapiro, "What's missing in welfare reform," *Challenge*, XXX (July–August 1987), p. 45; see also Bassi and Ashenfelter, "Effects of direct job creation," pp. 137, 147.

83 Bassi and Ashenfelter, "Effects of direct job creation," pp. 149–50.

84 For a review of some of the difficulties in resolving this debate, see ibid., pp. 138–51; Gary Burtless, "Manpower policies for the disadvantaged: what works?" *Brookings Review*, III (Fall 1984), pp. 18–22.

85 Committee on Youth Employment Programs, *Youth Employment and Training Programs: The YEDPA Years* (Washington, DC: National Academy Press, 1985), p. 33.

86 Quoted in Hahn and Danzberger, *Dropouts in America*, p. 51.

87 US Congress, Senate, Select Committee on Poverty, *Hearings, Economic Opportunity Act of 1964*, 88th Cong., 2nd sess., 1964, pp. 207–8.

88 George F. Will, *Statecraft as Soulcraft* (New York: Simon and Schuster, 1983), pp. 130–1.

89 National Governors' Association, *Making America Work*, p. 25.

90 All of the following are from US Department of Health and Human Services, "Head Start: a child development program," Washington, DC, 1986.

91 Research and Policy Committee of the Committee for Economic Development, *Children in Need: Investment Strategies for the Educationally Disadvantaged* (Washington, DC: Committee for Economic Development, 1987), p. 25.

92 Robert Reinhold, "California tries caring for its growing ranks of latchkey children," *New York Times* (October 25, 1987), p. E4.

93 Hahn and Danzberger, *Dropouts in America*, p. 35.

94 Natalie de Combray, "Volunteering in America," *American Demographics*, IX (March 1987), p. 50.

95 For a recent and brief review of the Boston COMPACT structure and its successes in a comparative framework, see William J. Spring, "Youth unemployment and the transtion from school to work: programs in Boston, Frankfurt, and London," Federal Reserve Bank of Boston *New England Economic Review* (March–April 1987), pp. 3–16.

96 Hahn and Danzberger, *Dropouts in America*, p. 35.

97 The present system of financial aid for students wishing to attend college has achieved considerable success in making such educational opportunities available to students from low-income families. For a review of the legislative history and of the evidence of success, see "Financial aid for college students: have the barriers to opportunity been lowered?" *Focus*, University of Wisconsin Institute for Research on Poverty, X (Fall 1987), pp. 6–9.

98 George Marshall, "Address at Harvard University, June 5, 1947," *By These Words: Great Documents of American Liberty*, ed. Paul M. Angle (New York: Rand McNally, 1954), p. 527.

99 The comparison with Marshall's plan for the rehabilitation of Europe is easily overstrained, but several other thoughts from his Harvard commencement speech are worth noting: "the remedy lies in . . . restoring the confidence of the European people in the economic future"; "assistance . . . must not be on a piecemeal basis as various crises develop"; "an essential part of any successful action . . . is an understanding on the part of the people of America of the character of the problem and the remedies to be applied"; and finally – an extemporaneous sentence added to his text – "I cannot overstate the importance to this country of facing up to the opportunity that confronts us" (ibid., pp. 524–8).

100 Richard B. Freeman, "Cutting black youth unemployment: create jobs that pay as well as crime," *New York Times* (July 20, 1986), p. F2.

101 The proposed program of Liberty Scholarships "will guarantee seventh grade students from families within 130% of the poverty level that if they persevere, graduate from high school and are accepted at a New York college or university, the State will provide them with additional funding beyond their other State and federal grants to cover their full costs of attendance for up to four years at the State University or City University, or to apply that same amount toward their attendance at an independent sector institution" (New York (State), Governor, *Annual Message to the Legislature*, January 6, 1988, p. 13).

102 National Governors' Association, *Making America Work*, p. 19.

103 For a concise review of many of these difficulties, see Bassi and Ashenfelter, "Effects of direct job creation," pp. 138–51; Nathan Glazer, "Education and training programs and poverty," in Sheldon H. Danziger and Daniel H. Weinberg (eds), *Fighting Poverty* (Cambridge, MA: Harvard University Press, 1986), pp. 152–73.

104 Isabel V. Sawhill, "Anti-poverty strategies for the next decade," in Ben W. Heineman, Jr, et al., *Work and Welfare: The Case for New Directions in National Policy* (Washington, DC: Center for National Policy, 1987), pp. 23–5.

105 All examples are from Janice C. Simpson, "Firm steps: a shallow labor pool spurs business to act to bolster education," *Wall Street Journal* (September 28, 1987), p. 1.

106 National Governors' Association, *Making America Work*, p. 79; see also ibid., pp. 37, 86.

107 Allan L. Otten, "Poor will find many jobs will be out of reach as labor market shrinks, demands for skills rise," *Wall Street Journal* (May 27, 1987), p. 6; Leonard Silk, "Changes in labor by the year 2000," *New York Times* (January 6, 1988), p. D2.

108 See National Governors' Association, *Making America Work*, p. 37; Hahn and Danzberger, *Dropouts in America*, pp. 48–50.

109 Robert Pear, "Increasingly, those who have jobs are poor, too," *New York Times* (December 27, 1987), p. E5; "America's hidden poor," *U.S. News & World Report* (January 11, 1988), pp. 18–24.

110 "State prisons were estimated to be operating between 106 percent and 124 percent of their capacities while the Federal prisons were operating at about 127 percent to 159 percent of their capacities" ("A record prison census," *New York Times* (May 17, 1987), p. E4). Since 1980, the inmate population of federal prisons has almost doubled to a total of 44,000 as of September 1987. According to a Justice Department forecast, that population could reach 72,000–79,000 by 1992, and go as high as 118,000 by 1997 (Peter Kerr, "War on drugs puts strain on prisons, U.S. officials say," *New York Times* (September 25, 1987), p. A1).

111 D. Michael Stewart, "Poor laws and pauper policies," *Vital Speeches of the Day*, LIII (February 1, 1987), p. 246.

112 Adrienne Koch and William Peden (eds), *The Selected Writings of John and John Quincy Adams* (New York: Alfred A. Knopf, 1946), p. 47.

113 Bernard Mayo (ed.), *Jefferson Himself* (Charlottesville, VA: University Press of Virginia, 1976), p. 89. Here Jefferson is speaking on behalf of a bill "to provide an education adapted to the years, to the capacity, and the condition of everyone . . ." (ibid., p. 88).

114 Paul Leicester Ford (ed.), *The Writings of Thomas Jefferson* (New York: G. P. Putnam's Sons, 1899), vol. X, p. 161.

115 *The Texas Declaration of Independence: An Exact Facsimile* (Houston, TX: Anson Jones, 1943), p. 5.

116 John F. Kennedy, "Inaugural Address, January 20, 1961," *The Inaugural Addresses of The American Presidents*, ed. Davis Newton Lott (New York: Holt, Rinehart & Winston, 1961), p. 270.

117 Quoted in US Congress, Senate, *Full Employment Act of 1945, Remarks in Senate on Bill (S.380) to enact*, 79th Cong., 1st sess., September 27, 1945, *Congressional Record*, 9054.

118 Langston Hughes, "Harlem," in *Montage Of A Dream Deferred* (New York: Henry Holt, 1951), p. 71. Copyright 1951 by Langston Hughes. Reprinted from *Selected Poems of Langston Hughes*, by permission of Alfred A. Knopf, Inc.

Appendix A American opinion polls and economic justice

1 Sidney Verba and Kay Lehman Schlozman, "Unemployment, class consciousness, and radical politics," *Journal of Politics*, XXXIX (May 1977), p. 302, and *Injury to Insult* (Cambridge, MA: Harvard University Press, 1979), pp. 202–21; Herbert McCloskey and John Zaller, *The American Ethos* (Cambridge, MA: Harvard University Press, 1984), pp. 110, 119, 120, 122, 134–5; George H. Gallup, *The Gallup Poll: Public Opinion 1972–1977* (Wilmington, DE: Scholarly Resources Inc., 1978), pp. 1004–7.

2 Joe R. Feagin, "Poverty: we still believe that God helps those who help themselves," *Psychology Today*, VI (November 1972), p. 110; McClosky and Zaller, *American Ethos*, pp. 71, 84.

3 Wayne M. Alves and Peter H. Rossi, "Who should get what? Fairness judgments of the distribution of earnings," *American Journal of Sociology*, LXXXIV (November 1978), p. 547.

4 See, for example, George Gallup, Jr, *The Gallup Poll: Public Opinion 1985* (Wilmington, DE: Scholarly Resources Inc., 1986), pp. 41–2; Hugh Heclo, "The political foundations of antipoverty policy," in Sheldon H. Danziger and Daniel H. Weinberg, *Fighting Poverty* (Cambridge, MA: Harvard University Press, 1986), p. 328.

5 "*Fortune* quarterly survey: X," *Fortune*, XVI (October 1937), p. 154; "*Fortune* survey: XXII," *Fortune*, XIX (June 1939), pp. 68–9; Verba and Schlozman, "Unemployment, class consciousness," p. 302, and *Injury to Insult*, pp. 202–3, 220.

6 "*Fortune* survey: XXVIII," *Fortune*, XXI (March 1940), p. 98; McClosky and Zaller, *American Ethos*, p. 120; Verba and Schlozman, "Unemployment, class consciousness," p. 302, and *Injury to Insult*, pp. 202, 221.

7 Michael E. Schiltz, *Public Attitudes Toward Social Security* (Washington, DC: US Government Printing Office, 1970), pp. 114–17, 158–61; George H. Gallup, *The Gallup Polls, 1935–1971* (New York: Random House, 1972), vol. I, *1935–1948*, pp. 61, 84, 155, 173, and *The Gallup Poll: Public Opinion 1979* (Wilmington, DE: Scholarly Resources Inc., 1980), pp. 67–9; Gallup, Jr, *Gallup Poll: Public Opinion 1985*, pp. 278–80; Feagin, "Poverty," p. 110; Verba and Schlozman, "Unemployment, class consciousness," p. 302.

8 Feagin, "Poverty," p. 107; Schiltz, *Public Attitudes Toward Social Security*, pp. 155–8; Gallup, *Gallup Poll: Public Opinion 1979*, p. 66. For a brief historical review tracing these ideas from colonial times to the present, see Neil Betten, "American attitudes toward the poor: a historical overview," *Current History*, LXV (July 1973), pp. 1–5.

9 "*Fortune* survey: XXII," pp. 68–9; Verba and Schlozman, "Unemployment, class consciousness," p. 302; Schiltz, *Public Attitudes Toward Social Security*, pp. 111, 159; Heclo, "Political foundations of antipoverty policy," p. 331.

10 Feagin, "Poverty," p. 107; Heclo, "Political foundations of antipoverty policy," p. 330; Schiltz, *Public Attitudes Toward Social Security*, p. 152.

11 See Schiltz, *Public Attitudes Toward Social Security*, p. 154; Heclo, "Political foundations of antipoverty policy," p. 328.

12 Schiltz, *Public Attitudes Toward Social Security*, p. 160; Gallup, Jr, *Gallup Poll: Public Opinion 1985*, pp. 43–4.

13 Feagin, "Poverty," p. 101–4; McClosky and Zaller, *American Ethos*, p. 92.

14 See McClosky and Zaller, *American Ethos* (on "Influentials"); recent Gallup polls (sometimes by income groups, sometimes by sex, ethnic background, education, or geographical location); Verba and Schlozman, *Injury to Insult* (by age, education, and employment status); Sidney Verba and Gary R. Orren, *Equality in America: The View from the Top* (Cambridge, MA: Harvard University Press, 1985), chs 4, 8 ("leaders from significant sectors of American society"); Robert E. Lane, *Political Ideology: Why the American Common Man Believes What He Does* (New York: Free Press of Glencoe, 1962), ch. 4 (small sample of workers).

Appendix D The marginal productivity theory of factor pricing

1 Economists will realize that the first influence – the out-migration of labor – might be portrayed as a shift to the left of a still vertical short-run curve. For purposes of this analysis, the distinction between short- and long-run adjustments is less crucial than it is in a conventional discussion of price theory.

2 To present the theory in its modern guise would require a number of refinements, including the relaxation of this assumption about other factor supplies being fixed. See for example MIlton Friedman, *Price Theory* (Chicago, IL: Aldine, 1962), pp. 176–8, 187.

3 The term "land" is generally used by economists to refer not just to acres of soil but to all natural resources, including minerals and timber.

4 For a discussion of marginal productivity theory using a limited amount of calculus and culminating with a proof that paying factors the value of their marginal product will exhaust total output (provided that production is subject to constant returns to scale), see Donald N. McClosky, *The Applied Theory of Price*, 2nd edn (New York: Macmillan, 1985), pp. 448–75. For an introductory analysis of some of the more subtle problems with the theory employing no calculus, see Milton Friedman, *Price Theory: A Provisional Text*, revised edition (Chicago, IL: Aldine, 1970), chs 9, 10.

5 In addition, the total quantity of each factor employed is such that the ratio between "effectiveness" of any two factors (the ratio between the values of their marginal products) equals the ratio between their respective unit costs (the ratio between the prices of those two factors). For a commentary on the history of this latter optimizing condition, see Syed N. Alam, "The marginal productivity theory of distribution – a survey," *Indian Economic Journal*, XVIII (October–December 1970), p. 230.

6 Were the analysis to attempt to develop a fully articulated theory, the usual route would involve constructing a production function for the entire economy (an aggregate production function) linking total output to total supplies of labor and capital (or labor, capital, and natural resources), with distribution to any type of factor determined by the nature of that aggregate function. For an outline of this approach and some indication of the storm of protest that it has produced (primarily in England under the caustic leadership of Joan Robinson), see M. Bronfenbrenner, "Neoclassical macro-distribution theory," in Jean Marchal and Bernard Ducros (eds), *The Distribution of National Income* (New York: St Martin's, 1968), pp. 476–87; M. J. C. Surrey, *Macroeconomic Themes* (Oxford: Oxford University Press, 1976), ch. 8.

7 The claim that one theory tends to dominate a profession is not easily documented, particularly in a profession as divided as economics often is. Within the American economic community, however, a belief in a marginal productivity theory of income distribution does seem to dominate, irrespective of position in the ideological spectrum (provided that position is to the right of extreme left-wing ideologies of limited popularity in America, namely, socialism, communism, and variants of Marxism). See for example Syed N. Alam, "Marginal productivity theory," p. 248; Kenneth E. Boulding, "Puzzles over distribution," *Challenge*, XXVIII (November–December 1985), p. 5; Bronfenbrenner, "Neoclassical macro-distribution theory," p. 476; William J. Fellner, "Significance and limitations of contemporary distribution theory," *American Economic Review*, XLIII (May

1953), p. 484; C. E. Ferguson, "Two books on the theory of income distribution: a review article," *Journal of Economic Literature*, X (June 1972), p. 438; Irving B. Kravis, "Income distribution: functional share," in David L. Sills (ed.), *International Encyclopedia of the Social Sciences* (New York: Macmillan, 1968), vol. VII, p. 140; Assar Lindbeck, *The Political Economy of the New Left*, 2nd edn (New York: Harper & Row, 1977), p. 10; Lester Thurow, "Toward a definition of economic justice," *Public Interest*, XXXI (Spring 1973), p. 71.

8 Tibor Scitovsky, "A survey of some theories of income distribution," in National Bureau of Economic Research, *The Behavior of Income Shares, Studies in Income and Wealth* (Princeton, NJ: Princeton University Press, 1964), vol. XXVII, p. 22.

9 Ibid., p. 25.

Appendix E Are factors of production paid the value of their marginal product?

1 See US Department of Commerce, *Statistical Abstract of the United States: 1985* (Washington, DC: US Government Printing Office, 1984), p. 400.

2 More rigorously, the assumption now relaxed concerns the employer's knowledge of marginal physical product and what that product can be sold for, for all factors of production.

3 A classic, if somewhat dated, survey of this dispute is Fritz Machlup, "Theories of the firm: marginalist, behavioral, managerial," *American Economic Review*, LVII (March 1967), pp. 1–33. More recent citations can be found in the references cited in Yakov Amihud and Jacob Kamin, "Revenue vs. profit maximization: differences in behavior by the type of control and by market power," *Southern Economic Journal*, XLV (January 1979), p. 846; Patrick J. Welch, "On the compatibility of profit maximization and other goals of the firm," *Review of Social Economy*, XXXVIII (April 1980), p. 74.

4 This approach is usually associated with William Baumol (see for example Amihud and Kamin, "Revenue vs. profit maximization," p. 838), but John Kenneth Galbraith has noted the marked similarity of Baumol's conclusions about the nature of firm decision-making to his own. See John Kenneth Galbraith, *The New Industrial State* (Boston, MA: Houghton Mifflin, 1971), ch. 15, especially p. 171, n. 6.

5 The most formidable critic under this heading has been Harvey Leibenstein. See for example Leibenstein, "Microeconomics and X-efficiency theory: if there is no crisis, there ought to be," in Daniel Bell and Irving Kristol (eds), *The Crisis in Economic Theory* (New York: Basic Books, 1981), pp. 97–110.

6 The pioneers of this approach were R. M. Cyert and J. G. March, and their pioneering work was *Behavioral Theory of the Firm* (Englewood Cliffs, NJ: Prentice-Hall, 1963). For other citations, see the references in note 5. Historically, the work of Cyert and March preceded that of Leibenstein.

7 Here the distribution assertion noted might hold, to the extent that executives still minimized costs.

8 The associated premise is that wages will not vary as much as effort because the employer lacks the information to make such adjustments.

9 The pioneering survey was done by R. L. Hall and C. J. Hitch, "Price theory and business behavior," *Oxford Economic Papers*, II (May 1939), pp. 12–45. For a review of subsequent investigations, see Machlup, "Theories of the firm."

10 See for example Amihud and Kamin, "Revenue vs. profit maximization," pp. 838–46.

11 John R. Hiller, "Long-run profit maximization: an empirical test," *Kyklos*, XXXI, Fasc. 3 (1978), pp. 475–90.

12 R. Joseph Monsen, John S. Chiu, and David E. Cooley, "The effect of separation of ownership and control on the performance of large firms," *Quarterly Journal of Economics*, LXXXII (August 1968), pp. 435–51.

13 Harvey Leibenstein, "More on X-efficiency: comment," *Quarterly Journal of Economics*, LXXXVI (May 1972), p. 330.

14 See for example William J. Baumol and Maco Stewart, "On the behavioral theory of the firm," in Robin Marris and Adrian Wood (eds), *The Corporate Economy* (Cambridge, MA: Harvard University Press, 1971), pp. 118–43.

15 This assertion applies to nominal wages, not to real wages (that is, actual wages corrected for inflation). For a comment on the pervasiveness of sticky nominal wages and the limited ability of economists to explain that stickiness, see Charles L. Schultze, "Microeconomic efficiency and nominal wage stickiness," *American Economic Review*, LXXV (March 1985), pp. 1–15. A rapid fall in real wages can, in theory, be caused by rapid inflation if nominal wages remain relatively stable. In practice such rapid erosion has not been a common feature of American labor markets.

16 Paul A. Samuelson and William D. Nordhaus, *Economics*, 12th edn (New York: McGraw-Hill, 1985), p. 640.

17 For a neoclassical demonstration of this result, see Ronald G. Ehrenberg and Robert S. Smith, *Modern Labor Economics*, 2nd edn, revised (Glenview, IL: Scott, Foresman, 1985), pp. 64–6.

18 John Kenneth Galbraith, *American Capitalism: A Theory of Countervailing Power* (Boston, MA: Houghton Mifflin, 1956).

19 For a discussion why the results, in principle, are indeterminate, see Samuelson and Nordhaus, *Economics*, p. 644.

20 "First draft of the U.S. bishops' Pastoral Letter on Catholic social teaching and the U.S. economy," *Origins*, XIV (November 15, 1984), p. 353.

21 See Richard Hurd, "Equilibrium vacancies in a labor market dominated by non-profit firms: the 'shortage' of nurses," *Review of Economics and Statistics*, LV (May 1973), pp. 234–40; Roger Feldman and Richard Scheffler, "The union impact on hospital wages and fringe benefits," *Industrial and Labor Relations Review*, XXXV (January 1982), pp. 190–206; C. R. Link and J. H. Landon, "Monopsony and union power in the market for nurses," *Southern Economic Journal*, XLI (April 1975), pp. 649–59; Ronald G. Ehrenberg and Gerald Goldstein, "A model of public sector wage determination," *Journal of Urban Economics*, II (April 1975), pp. 223–45; Robert N. Baird and John H. Landon, "The effect of collective bargaining on public school teachers' salaries," *Industrial and Labor Relations Review*, XXV (April 1972), pp. 410–16.

22 Robert L. Bunting, *Employer Concentration in Local Labor Markets* (Chapel Hill, NC: University of North Carolina Press, 1962).

23 In 1980, the percentage was 25.2 (US Department of Commerce, *Statistical Abstract: 1985*, p. 424).

24 For example, see Ehrenberg and Smith, *Modern Labor Economics*, pp. 379–80.

25 The percentages employed by "all industries" with 500 or more are as follows: 1976, 54.4%; 1978, 59.1%; 1980, 54.2%; 1982, 52.2% (Small Business Administration, *The State of Small Business: A Report of the President, Transmitted to the Congress,*

March 1984 (Washington, DC: US Government Printing Office, 1984), p. 74). These figures should be distinguished from those for "establishments," which are by separate location, whether or not the "establishment" is part of a larger "enterprise" (that is, "establishment" is the smallest unit of observation for business units). The similar employment percentages for "establishments" are about half those for "enterprises"; that is, about 25 percent of the total labor force works for "establishments" with 500 or more employees. See Small Business Administration, *The State of Small Business: A Report of the President, Transmitted to the Congress, March 1983* (Washington, DC: US Government Printing Office, 1983), pp. 208, 210.

26 See for example Peter B. Doeringer and Michael J. Piore, *Internal Labor Markets and Manpower Analysis* (Lexington, MA: D. C. Heath, 1971), p. 90. For a recent review of relevant literature, see Harry J. Holzer, "Hiring procedures in the firm: their economic determinants and outcomes," National Bureau of Economic Research Working Paper 2185, March 1987, pp. 4–8.

27 John Kenneth Galbraith, *Economics and the Public Purpose* (Boston, MA: Houghton Mifflin, 1973), p. 269.

28 Union workers appear to receive a wage 10–20 percent above comparable workers not in unions. For a summary of the evidence and source citations, see Ehrenberg and Smith, *Modern Labor Economics*, pp. 395–8, 422–3.

29 The technical terminology is that contracts for labor are "incomplete" and not all inputs are marketed, or, if marketed, are not available "on equal terms to all buyers." See Harvey Leibenstein's seminal article "Allocative efficiency vs. X-efficiency," *American Economic Review*, LVI (June 1966), pp. 392–415.

30 See Ehrenberg and Smith, *Modern Labor Economics*,. p. 349. For a description of the practical problems involved in paying workers according to their productivity, see "Back to piecework: many companies now base workers' raises on their productivity," *Wall Street Journal* (November 15, 1985), pp. 1, 15.

31 For evidence on union wages, see Ehrenberg and Smith, *Modern Labor Economics*, p. 396. For evidence that wage dispersion is less than productivity considerations would seem to warrant among nonunion employees, see Robert H. Frank, "Are workers paid their marginal products?" *American Economic Review*, LXXIV (September 1984), pp. 549–71. See also John Bishop, "The recognition and reward of employee performance," *Journal of Labor Economics*, V (October 1987), part 2, pp. S36–S56.

32 Three case studies of white male mangerial and professional employees in three large US manufacturing corporations found either no association or a negative association between experience (and wages) on the one hand, and rated performance on the other (see James L. Medoff and Katherine G. Abraham, "Experience, performance, and earnings," *Quarterly Journal of Economics*, XCV (December 1980), pp. 703–36, and "Are those paid more really more productive?" *Journal of Human Resources*, XVI (Spring 1981), pp. 186–216). A study of 2,500 design and development engineers in six organizations ("three . . . primarily in the aerospace industry and three . . . in other representative, technology-based commercial industries") found that performance tended to peak in the middle to late thirties and then decline, while salaries continued to climb until the early forties before leveling off (see Gene W. Dalton and Paul H. Thompson, "Accelerating obsolescence of older engineers," *Harvard Business Review*, XLIX (September–October 1971), pp. 57–67). For recent efforts by neoclassical theorists to explain this phenomenon, see Andrew Weiss and Henry Landau, "On the

negative correlation between performance and experience and education," National Bureau of Economic Research Working Paper 1613, April 1985. (The Weiss and Landau explanation fails to account for rising salaries of workers not promoted, unless combined with some type of lifetime contracting theory.)

33 Dalton and Thompson, "Accelerating obsolescence," p. 63.

34 Many labor economists would object that, while evidence of the sort noted above is inconsistent with the hypothesis that workers receive the value of their marginal product (VMP) at any point in time (or a person's "spot wage" equals the value of that person's marginal product), it is not necessarily inconsistent with a more complex hypothesis postulating that over an extended period of time workers do tend to receive the VMP. This would be the case, for example, if during a lifetime of employment with one firm the worker received less than VMP wages early in his career and more than VMP wages in later years, but for the period of employment as a whole, the two variables (wages and VMP) did tend to be roughly equal. (For a recent review of related literature and unresolved puzzles, see Robert M. Hutchens, "Seniority, wages, and productivity," unpublished paper, New York State School of Industrial and Labor Relations, Cornell University, January 1988.) But this assumes that equality is established between two variables (wages and VMP) over a long period of time (the duration of employment with a given employer), despite the evidence that employers at any point in time neither seek nor have information about the two variables in question.

35 The originator of this comparison appears to be Milton Friedman (quoted above) in his *Essays in Positive Economics* (Chicago, IL: University of Chicago Press, 1953), pp. 21–2. For evidence of how the related imagery influences the thinking of neoclassical economists concerned with explaining factor markets, see Ehrenberg and Smith, *Modern Labor Economics*, pp. 57–8. For an indication of the continuing popularity of the billiard-playing analogy among economists, see Robert Kuttner, "The poverty of economics," *Atlantic Monthly*, CCLV (February 1985), p. 79.

36 Milton Friedman, for example, urges the reader to consider the evidence but then offers no evidence whatsoever:

> Confidence in the maximization-of-returns hypothesis is justified by evidence of a very different character. This evidence is in part similar to that adduced on behalf of the billiard-player hypothesis – unless the behavior of businessmen in some way or other approximated behavior consistent with the maximization of returns, it seems unlikely that they would remain in business for long. Let the apparent immediate determinant of business behavior be anything at all – habitual reaction, random chance, or whatnot. Whenever this determinant happens to lead to behavior consistent with rational and informed maximization of returns, the business will prosper and acquire resources with which to expand; whenever it does not, the business will tend to lose resources and can be kept in existence only by the addition of resources from outside. The process of "natural selection" thus helps to validate the hypothesis – or, rather, given natural selection, acceptance of the hypothesis can be based largely on the judgment that it summarizes appropriately the conditions for survival (Friedman, *Positive Economics*, p. 22).

37 See Small Business Administration, *The State of Small Business, March 1983*, p. 158; *The State of Small Business: A Report of the President, Transmitted to the Congress, March 1985* (Washington, DC: US Government Printing Office, 1985), p. 13; US Department of Commerce, *Historical Statistics of the United States: Colonial Times to 1970* (Washington, DC: US Government Printing Office, 1975), vol. II, p. 912.

For evidence on the declining failure rate since the early 1960s and an assessment of the weaknesses in the underlying data, see Julius W. Allen and Mark Jickling, "Business failure: a review of the concept and its significance in the American economy," *Report 81–195E*, Congressional Research Service, September 1981.

38 These data are based on failures in three states (California, Florida, and Illinois) in the period 1981–2 (see Small Business Administration, *The State of Small Business, March 1983*, p. 161.) According to an official of the Small Business Administration, national data are not available. For data on failure by firms with liabilities of less than $100,000 – a less reliable indicator than employment because of inflation – see US Department of Commerce, *Historical Statistics of the United States*, vol. II, p. 912.

39 Small Business Administration, *The State of Small Business, March 1983*, p. 156; for data on bankruptcy by industry, see ibid., pp. 156, 264.

Failure and bankruptcy statistics are not comparable. Part of the difference between the failure data and the bankruptcy series is attributable to counting bankruptcy cases filed in the court system, rather than the number of businesses themselves. For example, when a partnership files a bankruptcy petition, the court assigns each partner a case number. Consequently, this may result in several bankruptcy petitions but only one business failure (ibid., p. 153, n. 27).

See also ibid., p. 154, n. 30.

40 Small Business Administration, *The State of Small Business, March 1983*, p. 238; see also ibid., pp. 263–4. Inferences about the average longevity of firms cannot be made from such data, insofar as "approximately 90 percent of . . . dissolutions are voluntary, e.g., retirement of the owner or the desire of an entrepreneur to shift to a more profitable field. The remaining 10 percent cease operations for financial reasons; these are the business failures" (ibid., p. 148). See also Candee S. Harris, "Icebergs and business statistics: a comparison of data for failures and dissolutions," paper prepared for the Office of Advocacy of The Small Business Administration (Contract No. SBA 2641 OA 79), January 1984, p. 32.

41 One variation of neoclassical distribution theory should be noted in passing. While the evidence indicates that many workers experience a rapid turnover of employers (the median length of employment is less than four years for the entire labor force), some workers continue with the same employer for long periods of time. The neoclassical theorist has hypothesized that in the latter case, what will tend to be equalized is the present value of the worker's career-long marginal product and the present value of the worker's career earnings stream. In support of this hypothesis, the theorist can cite evidence that workers and employers do behave as if long-run considerations are affecting the wage-bargaining process, but not a shred of evidence has been offered as to why the results of that bargaining should closely approximate the equality noted. (The evidence considered previously suggests that the achievement of this complex equality is even less likely than the simple equalization of wages with the value of the worker's marginal product where both are calculated not for an entire career but rather for a brief period of time such as a month or a year.) For discussion of this variant of neoclassical distribution theory, see Ehrenberg and Smith, *Modern Labor Economics*, pp. 134–5, 258; for evidence on multiple-period bargaining, see Robert E. Hall, "The importance of lifetime jobs in the U.S. economy," *American Economic Review*, LXXII (September 1982), pp. 716–24; Edward Lazear, "Why is there mandatory retirement?" *Journal of Political Economy*, LXXXVII (December 1979), pp.

1261–84; Martin Feldstein, "Temporary layoffs in the theory of unemployment," *Journal of Political Economy*, LXXXIV (October 1976), pp. 937–57. Other sources can be found in Ehrenberg and Smith, p. 355, n. 28.

42 George Stigler, for example, discounts Frank Knight's criticisms of neoclassical theory, noting "Knight made a series of the most sweeping and confident empirical judgments . . . for which he could not have even a cupful of supporting evidence," but Stigler offers no convincing evidence himself for believing that the tendencies postulated by neoclassical distribution theory are strong tendencies (George Stigler, *The Economist as Preacher and Other Essays* (Chicago, IL: University of Chicago Press, 1982), p. 19 and passim). Similarly, in his classic defense of the usefulness of the neoclassical theory of the firm, Fritz Machlup repeatedly focuses on questions of predicting directional changes in price and quantity and glosses over the question of the extent to which the marginal equivalences postulated by neoclassical theory are actually approximated, given the many divergences between neoclassical assumptions and real world evidence which he is examining (Machlup, "Theories of the firm").

Appendix F The market defended: two dubious defenders favored by George Stigler

1 For many years, Stigler taught at the University of Chicago, and is presently an editor of that Universty's best known economics journal, the *Journal of Political Economy*, and the Charles R. Walgreen Distinguished Service Professor Emeritus in the Department of Economics and in the Graduate School of Business.

2 George Stigler, *The Economist as Preacher and Other Essays* (Chicago, IL: University of Chicago Press, 1982), p. 17.

3 Ibid., pp. 17, 19.

4 Ibid., pp. 17–18. Although Stigler promises to "have more to say about acceptable ethical positions shortly" (ibid., p. 19), he never gives any coherent defense of his own for marginal productivity justice. He does note what Nathan Appleton and others emphasized in the nineteenth century (see above, pp. 28–31): that participation in the market fosters certain virtues among the participants, such as "candor," "responsibility," and "honesty" (ibid., p. 24).

5 This idea was also developed independently at roughly the same time by two other economists: Philip Wicksteed, an Englishman, and Knut Wicksell, a Swede.

6 John Bates Clark, *The Distribution of Wealth: A Theory of Wages, Interest and Profits* (New York: Macmillan, 1902) (first published in 1899).

7 Ibid., p. 3 (emphasis in original).

8 John Maurice Clark, "J. M. Clark on J. B. Clark," in Henry W. Spiegel (ed.), *The Development of Economic Thought: Great Economists in Perspective* (New York: Wiley, 1952), p. 610. J. B. Clark also acknowledged that his development of marginal productivity theory was partly in response to issues raised by the American, Henry George, and in particular, George's claim that the return on land was unearned income. See J. B. Clark, *The Distribution of Wealth*, pp. viii, 84–5.

9 "If we are to test the charge, however, we must enter the realm of production. We must resolve the product of social industry into its component elements, in order to see whether the natural effect of competition is or is not to give to each producer the amount of wealth that he specifically brings into existence" (ibid., p. 4).

10 Ibid., pp. 4–5.

11 Ibid., p. 8.

12 Thomas Nixon Carver, *Essays in Social Justice* (Cambridge, MA: Harvard University Press, 1915).

13 Thomas Nixon Carver, *The Religion Worth Having* (New York: Houghton Mifflin, 1912).

14 Ibid., p. 85.

15 Ibid., p. 88.

16 Ibid., pp. 88–9.

17 In the jargon of economics, the key insight, yet to be fully developed in Carver's time, was that a competitive equilibrium was also a Pareto optimum, the latter referring to a situation where no one can be made better off without making someone else worse off. Those familiar with the relevant economic theory should note a hidden problem: that while this condition has clear implications for efficiency (getting the largest pie possible from existing resources and technology), it has no clear implications for maximizing economic growth (getting the largest increase in the size of the pie over time).

18 Carver, *Essays in Social Justice*, pp. 81, 155, 165–8, 201.

19 Ibid., p. 25.

20 Carver, *The Religion Worth Having*, p. 84; *Essays in Social Justice*, pp. 25, 35, 160–1, 168, 171.

21 Carver, *Essays in Social Justice*, pp. 168–9.

Appendix G The market defended: the lack of logic in the arguments of Irving Kristol

1 Although Kristol is among the best of the conservative writers on philosophical issues, he largely ignores the related economic issues. The question of what factors actually receive is never addressed directly, nor is the related puzzle of how satisfactory marginal productivity theory is. As will be spelled out below, he does appear to endorse the belief that factors *ought* to receive whatever they tend to be paid in a well-functioning market. See Irving Kristol, *Two Cheers for Capitalism* (New York: New American Library (Mentor Book), 1979), pp. 176–8.

2 Ibid., pp. 60, 246–7.

3 Ibid., p. 60.

4 Ibid., pp. 60, 234.

5 At times Kristol does acknowledge that luck affects income, but his concept of luck is little more than "being in the right place at the right time" (ibid., p. 176; see also Kristol, *Reflections of a Neoconservative* (New York: Basic Books, 1983), p. 197).

6 Kristol, *Two Cheers for Capitalism*, p. 247 (emphasis added).

7 Ibid., p. 247.

8 Ibid., p. 170.

9 Ibid., pp. 169–70, 248.

10 Ibid., p. 81.

11 Ibid., pp. 174, 234–8, 246.

12 Ibid., p. 162. ("I do not see that this definition has ever been improved on . . . " (ibid).)

13 Ibid., p. 178; see also pp. 166–8.

14 Ibid., p. 178.

15 Kristol, *Reflections of a Neoconservative*, p. 193; see also p. 76.

16 Kristol, *Two Cheers for Capitalism*, p. xiii.
17 Ibid., p. 178.
18 Ibid.
19 Ibid.
20 As noted above, Kristol expresses this point as "liberty is, or ought to be, the most important political value" (ibid, p. 178). One might argue this does not imply that liberty is the only ultimate goal. But if that is the case, the questions that come immediately to mind are: (1) What are the other goals? and (2) If these goals clash with liberty, how should that conflict be resolved? Neither kind of question is featured in Kristol's writing, which suggests that, for him, freedom is rightly treated as the only ultimate goal.

Works Cited

Aaron, Henry. "Six welfare questions still searching for answers," *Brookings Review*, III (Fall 1984), 12–17.

Adams, Charles Francis. *The Works of John Adams* (Boston, MA: Charles C. Little and James Brown, 1851).

Adoratsky, V. (ed.) *Karl Marx: Selected Works* (New York: International Publishers, 1936).

Alam, Syed N. "The marginal productivity theory of distribution – a survey," *Indian Economic Journal*, XVIII (October–December 1970), 230–50.

Allen, Julius W. and Mark Jickling. "Business failure: a review of the concept and its significance in the American economy," *Report No. 81-195E*, Congressional Research Service, September 1981.

Alter, Catherine Foster. "Preventing family dependency," *Society*, XXIV (March–April 1987), 12–16.

Alves, Wayne M. and Peter H. Rossi. "Who should get what? Fairness judgments of the distribution of earnings," *American Journal of Sociology*, LXXXIV (November 1978), 541–64.

"American genius and enterprise," *Scientific American*, XI (September 4, 1847), 397.

"America's hidden poor," *US News & World Report* (January 11, 1988), 18–24.

Amihud, Yakov and Jacob Kamin. "Revenue vs. profit maximization: differences in behavior by the type of control and by market power," *Southern Economic Journal*, XLV (January 1979), 838–46.

Anderson, Charles. *The Political Economy of Social Class* (Englewood Cliffs, NJ: Prentice-Hall, 1974).

Anderson, Martin. *Welfare: The Political Economy of Welfare Reform in the United States* (Stanford, CA: Hoover Institution Press, 1978).

Appleby, Joyce. "Introduction: republicanism and ideology," *American Quarterly*, XXXVII (Fall 1985), 461–73.

——"The social origins of American revolutionary ideology," *Journal of American History*, LXIV (March 1978), 935–58.

Appleton, Nathan. "Labor, its relations, in Europe and the United States, compared," *[Hunt's] Merchants' Magazine*, XI (September 1844), 217–23.

"Are we *Losing Ground?*" *Focus*, University of Wisconsin Institute for Research on Poverty, VIII (Fall and Winter 1985), 1–12.

Aristotle. *The "Art" of Rhetoric*, trans. John Henry Freese (Cambridge, MA: Harvard University Press, 1967).

——*The Athenian Consitution*, trans. H. Rackham (Cambridge, MA: Harvard University Press, 1971).

"Around the Capitol," *Congressional Quarterly Weekly Report*, XXII (March 27, 1964), 632.

Arrow, Kenneth J. "A case for redistributing income: taxation and democratic values," *New Republic*, CLXXI (November 2, 1974), 23–5.

Auletta, Ken. *The Underclass* (New York: Random House, 1982).

"Back to basics," *Newsweek* (September 21, 1987), 54–57.

"Back to piecework: many companies now base workers' raises on their productivity," *Wall Street Journal* (November 15, 1985), 1, 15.

Bailyn, Bernard. *The Ideological Origins of the American Revolution* (Cambridge, MA: Harvard University Press, 1967).

Baird, Robert N. and John H. Landon. "The effect of collective bargaining on public school teachers' salaries," *Industrial and Labor Relations Review*, XXV (April 1972), 410–16.

Baldwin, James, Nathan Glazer, Sidney Hook and Gunnar Myrdal. "Liberalism and the Negro: a round-table discussion," *Commentary*, XXXVII (March 1964), 25–42.

Bane, Mary Jo and David T. Ellwood. "The dynamics of dependence: the routes to self-sufficiency," *Department of Health and Human Services Contract Report* (Cambridge, MA: Urban Systems Research and Engineering Inc., 1983).

——"The impact of AFDC: structure and living arrangements," *Report to the US Department of Health and Human Services*, Harvard University, 1984.

——"Slipping into and out of poverty: the dynamics of spells," *Journal of Human Resources*, XXI (Winter 1986), 1–23.

Banfield, Edward C. *The Unheavenly City* (Boston, MA: Little, Brown, 1974).

——*The Unheavenly City Revisited* (Boston, MA: Little, Brown, 1974).

Banner, William A. "Distributive justice and welfare claims," *Social Research*, XLVII (Summer 1980), 383–98.

Barber, Benjamin. "A new language for the left: translating the conservative discourse," *Harper's Magazine*, CCLXXIII (November 1986), 47–52.

Barnes, John S. *A Stone, A Leaf, A Door: Poems by Thomas Wolfe* (New York: Charles Scribner's Sons, 1945).

Barry, Norman P. *Hayek's Social and Economic Philosophy* (London: Macmillan, 1979).

Barzun, Jacques. *God's Country and Mine* (Boston, MA: Little, Brown, 1954).

Basler, Roy (ed.) *The Collected Works of Abraham Lincoln* (New Brunswick, NJ: Rutgers University Press, 1953).

Bassi, Laurie J. and Orley Ashenfelter. "The effects of direct job creation and training programs on low-skilled workers," in Sheldon H. Danziger and Daniel H. Weinberg (eds), *Fighting Poverty* (Cambridge, MA: Harvard University Press, 1986), pp. 133–51.

Bauer, P. T. "Discussion," in Michael Novak and John W. Cooper (eds), *The Corporation: A Theological Inquiry* (Washington, DC: American Enterprise Institute, 1981), p. 101.

Baum, Sandra R. and Saul Schwartz. "The fairness test for student-aid cuts," *Challenge*, XXVIII (May–June 1985), 39–46.

Baumol, William J. and Kenneth McLennan (eds). *Productivity Growth and U.S. Competitiveness* (New York: Oxford University Press, 1985).

——and Maco Stewart. "On the behavioral theory of the firm," in Robin Marris and Adrian Wood (eds), *The Corporate Economy* (Cambridge, MA: Harvard University Press, 1971), pp. 118–43.

Beatty, Jack. "The patriotism of values," *New Republic*, CLXXXV (July 4 and 11 1981), 18–20.

Beaujour, Louis Auguste Felix. *Sketch of the United States of North America, at the Commencement of the Nineteenth Century, from 1800 to 1810*, trans. William Walton (London: J. Booth, 1814).

Becker, Gary S. "An environment for economic growth," *Wall Street Journal* (January 19, 1989), A8.

——*A Treatise on the Family* (Cambridge, MA: Harvard University Press, 1981).

Bell, Daniel. "Meritocracy and equality," *Public Interest*, XXIX (Fall 1972), 29–68.

Bell, Winifred, Robert Lekachman and Alvin L. Schorr. *Public Policy and Income Distribution* (New York: Center for Studies in Income Maintenance Policy, 1974).

Bellows, Rev. H. W. "The moral significance of the Crystal Palace: a sermon, preached first to his own congregation, and repeated in the Church of the Messiah, on Sunday evening, October 30, 1853," *North American Review*, LXXIX (July 1854), 1–30.

Benn, Stanley I. "Equality, moral and social," in Paul Edwards (ed.), *Encyclopedia of Philosophy* (New York: Macmillan, 1967), vol. III, pp. 38–42.

——"Justice," in Paul Edwards (ed.), *Encyclopedia of Philosophy* (New York: Macmillan, 1967), vol. IV pp., 298–302.

——"Rights," in Paul Edwards (ed.), *Encyclopedia of Philosophy* (New York: Macmillan, 1967), vol. VII, pp. 195–9.

Bennett, Amanda. "Losing ground? Surveyed firms report fewer women directors," *Wall Street Journal* (July 17, 1987), 21.

Berger, Peter L. *The Capitalist Revolution* (New York: Basic Books, 1986).

Bergmann, Barbara R. *The Economic Emergence of Women* (New York: Basic Books, 1986).

Berlin, Isaiah. "Equality," *Proceedings of the Aristotelian Society* (new series), LVI (1955–6), 301–26.

——*Four Essays on Liberty*, revised edition (New York: Oxford University Press, 1979).

——"On the pursuit of the ideal," *New York Review of Books*, XXV (March 17, 1988), 11–18.

Betten, Neil. "American attitudes toward the poor: a historical overview," *Current History*, LXV (July 1973), 1–5.

Bishop, John. "The recognition and reward of employee performance," *Journal of Labor Economics*, V (October 1987), part 2, S36–S56.

Bisignano, Joseph. "Impervious saving behavior," Federal Reserve Bank of San Francisco *Weekly Letter* (September 28, 1984), 1–3.

Blank, Rebecca M. "How important is welfare dependence?" National Bureau of Economic Research Working Paper 2026, September 1986.

Blau, Francine D. and Marianne A. Ferber. "Discrimination: empirical evidence from the United States," *American Economic Review*, LXXVII (May 1987), 316–20.

Blinder, Alan S. *Hard Heads, Soft Hearts: Tough-Minded Economics for a Just Society* (New York: Addison-Wesley, 1987).

——"A 7% jobless rate is just not good enough," *Business Week* (February 3, 1986), 16.

Boswell, James. *The Life of Samuel Johnson* (London: George Bell and Sons, 1884).

Bosworth, Barry P. *Tax Incentives and Economic Growth* (Washington, DC: Brookings Institution, 1984).

Boulding, Kenneth E. "Puzzles over distribution," *Challenge*, XXVIII (November–December 1985), 4–10.

Bowen, Francis. *The Principles of Political Economy* (Boston, MA: Little, Brown, 1856).

Bowen, Ian. *Acceptable Inequalities: An Essay on the Distribuion of Income* (London: George Allen & Unwin, 1970).

Bowles, Samuel and Herbert Gintis. *Schooling in Capitalist America*. (New York: Basic Books, 1976).

Branden, Nathaniel. "Alienation," in Ayn Rand (ed.), *Capitalism: The Unknown Ideal* (New York: New American Library (Signet Book), 1967), pp. 270–96.

Brandt, Richard B. "Ethical relativism," in Paul Edwards (ed.), *Encyclopedia of Philosophy* (New York: Macmillan, 1967), vol. III, pp. 75–8.

Brittan, Samuel. "Hayek, the New Right, and the crisis of social democracy," *Encounter*, LIV (January 1980), 30–46.

Bronfenbrenner, Martin. "Neo-classical macro-distribution theory," in Jean Marchal and Bernard Ducros (eds), *The Distribution of National Income* (New York: Macmillan, 1968), pp. 476–501.

——"Ten issues in distribution theory," in Sidney Weintraub (ed.), *Modern Economic Thought* (Philadelphia, PA: University of Pennsylvania Press, 1977), pp. 395–419.

Bronfenbrenner, Urie. "Ecological systems theory," in Ross Vasta (ed.), *Six Theories of Child Development: Revised Formulations and Current Issues*, Annals of Child Development VI (Greenwich, CT: JAI Press, 1989), pp. 187–249.

Brophy, Beth. "Ethics 101: can the good guys win?" *U.S. News & World Report* (April 13, 1987), 54.

Brown v. Board of Education of Topeka, 347 U.S. 483, 1954.

Broyles, William, Jr. "The promise of America," *U.S. News & World Report* (July 7, 1985), 25–9.

Bruccoli, Matthew J. *Some Sort of Epic Grandeur: The Life of F. Scott Fitzgerald* (New York: Harcourt Brace Jovanovich, 1981).

Buchanan, Allen. *Ethics, Efficiency and the Market* (Totowa, NJ: Rowman & Allanheld, 1985).

Buchanan, James M. "Constitutional economics," in John Eatwell et al. (eds), *The New Palgrave: A Dictionary of Economics* (New York: Stockton, 1987), vol. I, pp. 585–8.

Buckley, William F., Jr. *Up From Liberalism* (New York: Stein and Day, 1984).

Bunting, Robert L. *Employer Concentration in Local Labor Markets* (Chapel Hill, NC: University of North Carolina Press, 1962).

Burgess, Thornton W. *Mother West Wind "How" Stories* (New York: Grosset & Dunlap, 1944).

Burke, Edmund. *Reflections on the Revolution in France*, ed. Conor Cruise O'Brien (New York: Penguin Books, 1981).

Burtless, Gary. "Inequality in America: where do we stand?" *Brookings Review*, V (Summer 1987), 9–16.

——"Manpower policies for the disadvantaged: what works?" *Brookings Review*, III (Fall 1984), 18–22.

Cain, Glen G. "The economics of discrimination: part 1," *Focus*, University of Wisconsin Institute for Research on Poverty, VII (Summer 1984), 1–11.

——and Douglas A. Wissoker. "Do income maintenance programs break up marriages? A reevaluation of SIME-DIME," *Focus*, University of Wisconsin Institute for Research on Poverty, X (Winter 1987–8), 1–15.

Carnoy, Martin and Derek Sheaner. *Economic Democracy: The Challenge of the 1980's* (New York: M. E. Sharpe, 1980).

Carver, Thomas Nixon. *Essays in Social Justice* (Cambridge, MA: Harvard University Press, 1915).

——*The Religion Worth Having* (New York: Houghton Mifflin, 1912).

Celis, William, III. "Crumbling projects: public-housing units are rapidly decaying, causing many to close," *Wall Street Journal* (December 15, 1986), 1.

Chamber of Commerce of the United States. *Proceedings of the National Symposium on Guaranteed Income, Washington, DC, December, 1966.*

"The changing economic circumstances of children: families losing ground," *Focus*,

University of Wisconsin Institute for Research on Poverty, IX (Spring 1986), 6–10.

Channing, William Ellery. "Remarks on national literature," in Clarence Arthur Brown (ed.), *The Achievement of American Criticism* (New York: Ronald Press, 1954), pp. 126–45.

Chavez, Lydia. "Welfare hotel children: tomorrow's poor," *New York Times* (July 16, 1987), B1.

"The child-care dilemma," *Time* (June 22, 1987), 54–60.

Chirinko, Robert S. "The ineffectiveness of effective tax rates on business investment," Hoover Institution Working Papers in Economics E-85-20, Stanford University, August 1985.

Clark, John Bates. *The Distribuion of Wealth: A Theory of Wages, Interest and Profits* (New York: Macmillan, 1902).

Clark, John Maurice. "J. M. Clark on J. B. Clark," in Henry W. Spiegel (ed.), *The Development of Economic Thought: Great Economists in Perspective* (New York: Wiley, 1952), pp. 592–612.

Cockburn, Alexander. "Social Darwinism on the big and small screens," *Wall Street Journal* (June 11, 1987), 25.

Coleman, James. "Toward open schools," *Public Interest*, IX (Fall 1967), 20–7.

de Combray, Natalie. "Volunteering in America," *American Demographics*, IX (March 1987), 50–2.

Committee on Youth Employment Programs. *Youth Employment and Training Programs: The YEDPA Years* (Washington, DC: National Academy Press, 1985).

Commons, John R. et al. (eds) *A Documentary History of American Industrial Society* (New York: Russell & Russell, 1958).

"Conference summary," *Focus*, University of Wisconsin Institute for Research on Poverty, X (Summer 1987), 1–10.

Congressional Budget Office, *An Analysis of the Roth–Kemp Tax Cut Proposal*, October 1978.

Conwell, Russell H. *Acres of Diamonds* (New York: Harper & Brothers, 1915).

Conyers, James E. and Walter L. Wallace. *Black Elected Officials* (New York: Russell Sage Foundation, 1976).

Cook, Karen S. and Karen A. Hegtvedt. "Distributive justice, equity, and equality," *Annual Review of Sociology*, IX (1983), 217–41.

Cook, Reginald L. (ed.) *Ralph Waldo Emerson: Selected Prose and Poetry* (New York: Holt, Rinehart & Winston, 1969).

Council of Economic Advisers, *1987 Annual Report.*

Cowan, Alison Leigh. "Harvard to get $30 million ethics gift," *New York Times* (March 31, 1987), D1.

Coxe, Tenche. *An Address to the Assembly of the Friends of American Manufactures . . . the 9th of August, 1787* (Philadelphia, PA: Aitken, 1787).

Crane, Philip M. *The Sum of Good Government* (Ottawa, IL: Green Hill, 1976).

Cranston, Maurice. "Liberalism: English liberalism," in Paul Edwards (ed.), *Encyclopedia of Philosophy* (New York: Macmillan, 1967), vol. IV, pp. 458–61.

Crèvecoeur, J. Hector S. John. *Letters from an American Farmer* (New York: Fox, Duffield, 1904).

Crockett, Davy. *An Account of Col. Crockett's Tour of the North and Down East* (Philadelphia, PA: E. L. Carey and A. Hart, 1835).

Cuomo, Mario. "Abraham Lincoln and Our 'Unfinished Work'," address before the Abraham Lincoln Association, Springfield, Illinois, February 12, 1986.

——"Your one life can make a difference," *Vital Speeches of the Day*, LI (July 15, 1985), 581–4.

Cyert, R. M. and J. G. March. *Behavioral Theory of the Firm* (Englewood Cliffs, NJ: Prentice-Hall, 1963).

Dalton, Gene W. and Paul H. Thompson. "Accelerating obsolescence of older engineers," *Harvard Business Review*, XLIX (September–October 1971), 57–67.

Danziger, Sheldon H. "Breaking the chains," University of Wisconsin Institute for Research on Poverty Discussion Paper 825–86.

——and Peter Gottschalk. "Earnings inequality, the spatial concentration of poverty, and the underclass," *American Economic Review*, LXXVII (May 1987), 211–15.

——"How have families with children been faring?" University of Wisconsin Institute for Research on Poverty Discussion Paper 801–86, January 1986.

——"The poverty of *Losing Ground*," *Challenge*, XXVIII (May–June 1985), 32–8.

——,Robert H. Haveman and Robert D. Plotnick. "Antipoverty policy: effects on the poor and the nonpoor," in Sheldon H. Danziger and Daniel H. Weinberg (eds), *Fighting Poverty* (Cambridge, MA: Harvard University Press, 1986), pp. 50–77.

——"How income transfer programs affect work, savings, and the income distribution: a critical review," *Journal of Economic Literature*, XIX (September 1981), 975–1028.

Darity, William A., Jr. and Samuel L. Myers, Jr. "Do transfer payments keep the poor in poverty?" *American Economic Review*, LXXVII (May 1987), 216–22.

——"Welfare and work: microeconomics vs. macroeconomic considerations," *Cato Journal*, VI (Spring–Summer 1986), 245–50.

"The declining economic status of Puerto Ricans," *Focus*, University of Wisconsin Institute for Research on Poverty, X (Summer 1987), 25–7.

"Defense of mechanical philosophy," *North American Review*, XXXIII (July 1831), 134.

Depew, Chauncey M. Address of the Hon. Chauncey M. Depew, LL.D., at the Unveiling of the Statue of Cornelius Vanderbilt, at the Vanderbilt University, Nashville, Tennessee, October 11th, 1897.

Dewey, John. *Democracy and Education* (New York: Macmillan, 1916).

Dickens, Charles. *Pictures from Italy and American Notes* (New York: Thomas Y. Crowell, undated).

Diggins, John Patrick. *The Lost Soul of American Politics* (New York: Basic Books, 1984).

Doeringer, Peter B. and Michael J. Piore. *Internal Labor Markets and Manpower Analysis* (Lexington, MA: D.C. Heath, 1971).

Duncan, Greg J., Martha S. Hill and Saul D. Hoffman, "Welfare dependence within and across generations," *Science*, CCXXXIX (January 29, 1988), 467–71.

——and Saul D. Hoffman. "Welfare dynamics and the nature of need," *Cato Journal*, VI (Spring–Summer 1986), 36–42.

——and Willard L. Rodgers. "The prevalence of childhood poverty," Unpublished paper, University of Michigan Survey Research Center, March 25, 1986.

——et al. *Years of Poverty, Years of Plenty* (Ann Arbor, MI: Institute for Social Research, University of Michigan, 1984).

Durant, Will and Ariel Durant. *The Lessons of History* (New York: Simon and Schuster, 1968).

Dworkin, Ronald. "Liberalism," in Stuart Hampshire (ed.), *Public and Private Morality* (Cambridge: Cambridge University Press, 1978), pp. 113–43.

"The dynamics of dependency: family background, family structure, and poverty," *Focus*, University of Wisconsin Institute for Research on Poverty, VII (Summer 1984), 14–17.

Ehrenberg, Ronald G. and Gerald Goldstein. "A model of public sector wage determination." *Journal of Urban Economics*, II (April 1975), 223–45.

——and Robert S. Smith. *Modern Labor Economics*, 2nd edn, revised (Glenview, IL: Scott, Foresman, 1985).

Ehrlich, Elizabeth. "Child care: the private sector can't do it alone," *Business Week* (October 6, 1986), 52–3.

——"What the boss is really like," *Business Week* (October 23, 1987), 37–44.

Ellwood, David T. *Targeting "Would-be" Long-Term Recipients of AFDC*, Contract No. 100-84-0059, US Department of Health and Human Services, OS/ASPE, January 1986.

——and Mary Jo Bane. "The impact of AFDC on family structure and living arrangements," in Ronald G. Ehrenberg (ed.), *Research on Labor Economics* (Greenwich, CT: JAI Press, 1985), vol. VII, pp. 137–207.

——and Lawrence H. Summers. "Is welfare really the problem?" *Public Interest*, LXXXIII (Spring 1986), 57–78.

Emerson, Ralph Waldo. *The Conduct of Life* (Boston, MA: Ticknor and Fields, 1860).

——*Nature, Addresses and Lectures* (Boston, MA: Houghton Mifflin, 1895).

Employment and Training Report of the President, Transmitted to the Congress, 1981.

"The end of corporate loyalty?" *Business Week* (August 4, 1986), 42–5, 48–9.

Epstein, Joyce L. "Longitudinal effects of family–school–person interactions on student outcomes," *Research in Sociology of Education and Socialization*, IV (1983), 101–27.

"Ethics: what's wrong?" *Time* (May 25, 1987), 14–17.

Evanson, Elizabeth. "Employment programs for the poor: government in the labor market." *Focus*, University of Wisconsin Institute for Research on Poverty, VII (Fall 1984), 1–7.

Everett, Edward. *Orations and Speeches* (Boston, MA: Little, Brown, 1878).

Ewbank, Thomas. *The World A Workshop* (New York: D. Appleton, 1855).

Farley, Harriet. "Editorial," *Lowell Offering*, V (March 1845), 72.

Farley, Reynolds. "Assessing black progress: employment, occupation, earnings, income, poverty," *Economic Outlook USA*, XIII (Third Quarter 1986), 14–19.

——*Blacks and Whites: Narrowing the Gap?* (Cambridge, MA: Harvard University Press, 1984).

Feagin, Joe R. "Poverty: we still believe that God helps those who help themselves," *Psychology Today*, VI (November 1972), 101–10, 129.

The Federalist (New York: Tudor, 1937).

Feinberg, Joel. *Social Philosophy* (Englewood Cliffs, NJ: Prentice-Hall, 1973).

Feldman, Roger and Richard Scheffler. "The union impact on hospital wages and fringe benefits," *Industrial and Labor Relations Review*, XXXV (January 1982), 190–206.

Feldstein, Martin. "Temporary layoffs in the theory of unemployment," *Journal of Political Economy*, LXXXIV (October 1976), 937–57.

Fellner, William J. "Significance and limitations of contemporary distribution theory," *American Economic Review*, XLIII (May 1953), 484–94.

Ferguson, C. E. "Two books on the theory of income distribution," *Journal of Economic Literature*, X (June 1972), 437–42.

Filler, Louis. *The President Speaks* (New York: G. P. Putnam's Sons, 1964).

"Final text of the U.S. bishops' economy Pastoral: economic justice for all, Catholic social teaching and the U.S. economy," *Origins*, XVI (November 27, 1986), 409–55.

"Financial aid for college students: have the barriers to opportunity been lowered?" *Focus*, University of Wisconsin Institute for Research on Poverty, X (Fall 1987), 6–9.

"First draft of the U.S. bishops' Pastoral Letter on Catholic social teaching and the U.S. economy," *Origins*, XIV (November 15, 1984), 337–83.

Fisher, Anne B. "Where women are succeeding," *Fortune*, CXVI (August 3, 1987), 78–86.

Fiske, Edward B. "Steady gains achieved by blacks on college admission test scores," *New York Times* (September 23, 1987), A1, D30.

Flew, Antony. "The Procrustean ideal: libertarians vs. egalitarians," *Encounter*, L (March 1978), 70–9.

Flora, Peter and Arnold J. Heidenheimer (eds) *The Development of Welfare States in Europe and America* (New Brunswick, NJ: Transaction Books, 1981).

Ford, Paul Leicester (ed.) *The Writings of Thomas Jefferson* (New York: G. P. Putnam's Sons, 1899).

"FORTUNE quarterly survey: X," *Fortune*, XVI (October 1937), 154.

"FORTUNE survey: XXII," *Fortune*, XIX (June 1939), 68–9.

"FORTUNE survey: XXVIII," *Fortune*, XXI (March 1940), 98.

Frank, Robert H. "Are workers paid their marginal product?" *American Economic Review*, LXXIV (September 1984), 549–71.

"Freedom first," *Time* (June 16, 1986), 26–32.

Freeman, Richard B. "Cutting black youth unemployment: create jobs that pay as well as crime," *New York Times* (July 20, 1986), F2.

Friedman, Milton. *Bright Promises, Dismal Performance* (New York: Harcourt Brace Jovanovich, 1983).

——*Capitalism and Freedom* (Chicago, IL: University of Chicago Press (Phoenix Books), 1965).

——*Essays in Positive Economics* (Chicago, IL: University of Chicago Press, 1953).

——*From Galbraith to Economic Freedom*, Occasional Paper 49, Institute of Economic Affairs (Lancing, West Sussex: Gordon Pro-Print, 1977).

——*Price Theory: A Provisional Text*, revised edition (Chicago, IL: Aldine, 1970).

——*There's No Such Thing as a Free Lunch* (LaSalle, IL: Open Court, 1975).

——and Rose Friedman. *Free to Choose* (New York: Harcourt Brace Jovanovich, 1980).

Fromm, Erich. *The Sane Society* (New York: Rinehart, 1955).

Fuller, Edmund. "Review of Robert Nisbet's prejudices: a philosophical dictionary," *Wall Street Journal* (October 4, 1982), 32.

Fullerton, Don. "On the possibility of an inverse relationship between tax rates and government revenues," *Journal of Public Economics*, XIX (October 1982), 16–19.

Galbraith, John Kenneth. *American Capitalism: The Concept of Countervailing Power* (Boston, MA: Houghton Mifflin, 1956).

——*Economics and the Public Purpose* (Boston, MA: Houghton Mifflin, 1973).

——*The New Industrial State*, 2nd edn, revised (Boston, MA: Houghton Mifflin, 1971).

Gallup, George H. *The Gallup Poll: Public Opinion, 1972–1977* (Wilmington, DE: Scholarly Resources Inc., 1978).

——*The Gallup Poll: Public Opinion 1979* (Wilmington, DE: Scholarly Resources Inc., 1980).

——*The Gallup Polls, 1935–1971* (New York: Random House, 1972).

Gallup, George, Jr. *The Gallup Poll: Public Opinion 1985* (Wilmington, DE: Scholarly Resources Inc., 1986).

Gans, Herbert J. "Some problems of equality," *Dissent*, XX (Fall 1973), 409–14.

Garfinkel, Irwin and Sara S. McLanahan. *Single Mothers and Their Children: A New American Dilemma* (Washington, DC: Urban Institute, 1986).

Geertz, Clifford. *The Interpretation of Cultures: Selected Essays* (New York: Basic Books, 1973).

George, Henry. *Progress and Poverty* (New York: Robert Schalkenbach Foundation, 1975).

Gilbert, Neil. "How to rate a social-welfare system," *Wall Street Journal* (January 13, 1987), 28.

——"The unfinished business of welfare reform," *Society*, XXIV (March–April 1987), 5–11.

Gilder, George. "The disease of government," *National Review*, XXXII (December 31, 1980), 1566–70.

——*Wealth and Poverty* (New York: Basic Books, 1981).

Glazer, Nathan. "Education and training programs and poverty," in Sheldon H. Danziger and Daniel H. Weinberg (eds), *Fighting Poverty* (Cambridge, MA: Harvard University Press, 1986), pp. 152–73.

Glicken, Morley D. "Transgenerational welfare dependency," *Journal of Contemporary Studies*, IV (Summer 1981), 31–41.

Goldman, Daniel. "Feeling of control viewed as central in mental health," *New York Times* (October 7, 1986), C11.

Goldwater, Barry. *The Conscience of a Conservative* (Shepherdsville, KY: Victor Publishing, 1960).

Goodwyn, Lawrence. *The Populist Movement* (New York: Oxford University Press, 1978).

Gouge, William M. *A Short History of Paper-Money and Banking in the United States* (New York: B. & S. Collins, 1835).

"A government in the bedroom," *Newsweek* (July 14, 1986), 38.

Gramlich, Edward M. "The main themes," in Sheldon H. Danziger and Daniel H. Weinberg (eds), *Fighting Poverty* (Cambridge, MA: Harvard University Press, 1986), pp. 341–47.

Green, Philip. *The Pursuit of Inequality* (New York: Pantheon, 1981).

Greenspan, Alan. "The assault on integrity," in Ayn Rand (ed.), *Capitalism: The Unknown Ideal* (New York: New American Library (Signet Book), 1967), pp. 118–21.

Greenstein, Robert. "Losing faith in 'Losing Ground'," *New Republic*, CXCII (March 25, 1985), 12–17.

Gunther, John. *Inside U.S.A.* (London: Hamish Hamilton, 1945).

Gwartney, James and Thomas S. McCaleb. "Have anti-poverty programs increased poverty?" *Cato Journal*, V (Spring–Summer 1985), 1–16.

——and Richard Stroup. "Transfers, equality, and the limits of public policy," *Cato Journal*, VI (Spring–Summer 1986), 111–37.

Hacker, Louis M. *The Course of American Economic Growth and Development* (New York: Wiley, 1970).

Hahn, Andrew and Jacqueline Danzberger. *Dropouts In America* (Washington, DC: Institute for Educational Leadership, 1987).

Hall, Robert, E. "The importance of lifetime jobs in the U.S. economy," *American Economic Review*, LXXII (September 1982), 716–24.

Hall, R. L. and C. J. Hitch. "Price theory and business behavior," *Oxford Economic Papers*, II (May 1939), 12–45.

Hamilton, Joseph (ed.) *Johnson's Dictionary of the English Language* (Boston, MA: West & Blake, 1810).

Hare, R. M. "Rawls': a theory of justice, Parts I and II" *Philosophical Quarterly*, XXIII (April 1973), 144–55; (July 1973), 241–52.

Harrington, Michael. *Decade of Decision: The Crisis of the American System* (New York: Simon and Schuster (Touchstone Books), 1980).

——*The Other America: Poverty in the United States* (Baltimore, MD: Penguin, 1963).

——*The Twilight of Capitalism* (New York: Simon and Schuster (Touchstone Books), 1976).

——"The welfare state and its neoconservative critics," *Dissent*, XX (Fall 1973), 435–54.

——and Irving Howe. *The Seventies: Problems and Proposals* (New York: Harper & Row, 1972).

Harris, Candee S. "Icebergs and business statistics: a comparison of data for failures and dissolutions," Paper prepared for the Office of Advocacy of The Small Business Administration, Contract No. SBA 2641 OA 79, January 1984.

Hart, H. L. A. "Who can tell right from wrong?" *New York Review of Books*, XXXIII (July 17, 1986), 49–52.

Hart, Stephen. "Ethical relativism, left-wing politics," *Dissent*, XXIX (October 1, 1982), 483–6.

Hartwell, Ronald Max. "Capitalism and the historians," in Fritz Machlup (ed.), *Essays on Hayek* (New York: New York University Press, 1976), pp. 73–93.

Hartz, Louis. *The Liberal Tradition in America* (New York: Harcourt, Brace & World, 1955).

"Harvard's $30 million windfall for ethics 101," *Business Week* (April 13, 1987), 40.

Hayden, Tom. *The American Future: New Visions Beyond Old Frontiers* (Boston, MA: South End, 1980).

Hayek, Friedrich A. *The Constitution of Liberty* (Chicago, IL: University of Chicago Press, 1960; Phoenix Edition, 1978).

——*Knowledge, Evolution, and Society* (London: Butler & Tanner, 1983).

——*Law, Legislation and Liberty* (Chicago, IL: University of Chicago Press, 1976).

——*New Studies in Philosophy, Politics, Economics and the History of Ideas* (Chicago, IL: University of Chicago Press, 1978).

——*The Road to Serfdom* (Chicago, IL: University of Chicago Press, 1976).

——*Studies in Philosophy, Politics and Economics* (Chicago, IL: University of Chicago Press, 1967).

——*The Three Sources of Human Values* (London: London School of Economics and Political Science, 1978).

Hazlitt, Henry. *The Conquest of Poverty* (New Rochelle, NY: Arlington House, 1973).

——*The Foundations of Morality* (New York: Van Nostrand, 1964).

——*Man vs. The Welfare State* (New Rochelle, NY: Arlington House, 1969).

Heclo, Hugh. "The political foundation of antipoverty policy," in Sheldon H. Danziger and Daniel H. Weinberg (eds), *Fighting Poverty* (Cambridge, MA: Harvard University Press, 1986), pp. 312–40.

Heilbroner, Robert L. *Between Capitalism and Socialism* (New York: Vintage, 1970).

——*Business Civilization in Decline* (New York: W. W. Norton, 1976).

——*The Limits of American Capitalism* (New York: Harper & Row (Harper Torchbook), 1967).

——and Lester C. Thurow. *Understanding Macroeconomics*, 8th edn (Englewood Cliffs, NJ: Prentice-Hall , 1984).

Heller, Walter F. *New Dimensions of Political Economy* (Cambridge, MA: Harvard University Press, 1967).

Henderson, David R. "A liberal economist's case," *Fortune*, CXVI (November 9, 1987), 187–8.

Herbers, John. "Outlook for sheltering the poor growing even bleaker," *New York*

Times (March 8, 1987), E5.

Hershey, Robert D., Jr. "High, but stable, U.S. unemployment is gaining acceptance," *New York Times* (October 14, 1986), A28.

Heyman, Ira Michael. "Trapped in an 'athletics arms race'," *U.S. News & World Report* (July 20, 1987), 7.

Hill, Martha S. et al. "Final report of the project: 'Motivation and Economic Mobility of the Poor'; Part 1: Intergenerational and short-run dynamic analysis," Institute for Social Research, University of Michigan, Survey Research Center Working Paper, August 3, 1983.

——and Michael Ponza. "Poverty and welfare dependence across generations," *Economic Outlook USA*, X (Summer 1983), 61–4.

Hiller, John R. "Long-run profit maximization: an empirical test," *Kyklos*, XXXI, Fasc. 3 (1978), 475–90.

Hirschman, Albert O. *Rival Views of Market Society* (New York: Viking, 1986).

Hochschild, Jennifer L. *What's Fair?* (Cambridge, MA: Harvard University Press, 1981).

Hoffman, Saul D. and Greg J. Duncan. "A choice-based analysis of remarriage and welfare decisions of divorced women." Paper prepared for the annual meetings of the Population Association of America, San Francisco, California, April 1986.

Hofstadter, Albert. "The career open to personality: The meaning of equality of opportunity for an ethics for our time," in Lyman Bryson (ed.), *Aspects of Human Equality* (New York: Harper & Brothers, 1956), pp. 111–42.

Hofstadter, Richard. *The American Political Tradition* (New York: Alfred A. Knopf, 1948).

Holzer, Harry J. "Hiring procedures in the firm: their economic determinants and outcomes," National Bureau of Economic Research Working Paper 2185, March 1987.

Hoover, Herbert Clark. *Addresses Upon The American Road: 1933–1938* (New York: Scribner's Sons, 1938).

——*Addresses Upon The American Road: 1950–1955* (Stanford, CA: Stanford University Press, 1955).

——"The miracle of America," *Woman's Home Companion*, LXXV (November 1948), 32–3.

Horace. *The Third Book of Horace's Odes*, trans. Gordon Williams (Oxford: Clarendon Press, 1969).

Horn, Miriam. "The burgeoning educational underclass," *U.S. News & World Report* (May 18, 1987), 66–7.

Horvat, Branko. *The Political Economy of Socialism* (Armonk, NY: M. E. Sharpe, 1982).

"How the states regulate sex," *Newsweek* (July 14, 1986), 37.

Hughes, Langston. *Montage Of A Dream Deferred* (New York: Henry Holt, 1951).

Hume, David. *A Treatise of Human Nature*, ed. L. A. Selby-Bigge (Oxford: Clarendon Press, 1975).

Hurd, Richard. "Equilibrium vacancies in a labor market dominated by non-profit firms: the 'shortage' of nurses," *Review of Economics and Statistics*, LV (May 1973), 234–40.

Hutchens, Robert M. "Seniority, wages, and productivity," Unpublished paper, New York State School of Industrial and Labor Relations, Cornell University, January 1988.

The Impact of the Universal Declaration of Human Rights (New York: United Nations Department of Social Affairs, 1951).

Industrial Workers of the World. Preamble and Constitution (Chicago, IL: IWW General Headquarters, 1911).

Institute for Poverty Research. "CONFERENCE SUMMARY. Poverty and social policy: the minority experience," Special Report Series 43, February 1987.

Jacob, John E. "A society that is just and fair," *Vital Speeches of the Day*, LIII (September 15, 1987), 733–6.

Jay, David (ed.) *The Kennedy Reader* (New York: Bobbs-Merrill, 1967).

Jensen, Orla. *Social Welfare in Denmark* (Copenhagen: Det Danske Selskab, 1961).

Johnson, Samuel. *A Dictionary of the English Language* (London: J. Johnson, G. Dilly, 1799).

Johnson, Thomas H. (ed.) *The Poems of Emily Dickinson* (Cambridge, MA: Belknap Press, 1955).

Jones, Howard Mumford. *O Strange New World* (New York: Viking, 1964).

Jones, Reginald H. "The transnational enterprise and world economic development," in Michael Novak and John W. Cooper (eds), *The Corporation: A Theological Inquiry* (Washington, DC: American Enterprise Institute, 1981), pp. 129–41.

Jordan, Vernon E. Jr. "The free enterprise system," *Vital Speeches of the Day*, LIII (May 15, 1987), 466–8.

Kasson, John F. *Civilizing the Machine* (New York: Grossman, 1976).

Kaufman, Arnold S. "Responsibility, moral and legal," in Paul Edwards (ed.), *Encyclopedia of Philosophy* (New York: Macmillan, 1967), vol. VII, pp. 183–8.

Keleher, Robert E. and William P. Orzechowski. "Supply-side effects of fiscal policy: some historical perspectives," Federal Reserve Bank of Atlanta Working Paper Series, August 1980.

Kemp, Jack. *An American Renaissance* (New York: Berkley Books, 1981).

Kendrick, John. "How to produce economic growth," *Cato Policy Report*, VII (May/June 1985), 8–9.

Kerber, Linda K. "The Republican ideology of the revolutionary generation," *American Quarterly*, XXXVII (Fall 1985), 474–95.

Kerr, Peter. "War on drugs puts strain on prisons, U.S. officials say," *New York Times* (September 25, 1987), A1, A40.

Kershner, Howard E. *Dividing the Wealth* (Old Greenwich, CT: Devin-Adair, 1971).

Keynes, John Maynard. *Essays in Persuasion* (New York: W. W. Norton, 1963).

Knight, Frank H. *The Ethics of Competition* (London: George Allen & Unwin, 1935).

Knights of Labor, General Assembly, Ninth Regular Session, Hamilton, Ontario, October 6, 1885.

——Official Hand Book of the Rhode Island District Assembly 99, District Executive Board, 1894.

Koch, Adrienne. *Power, Morals and the Founding Fathers* (Ithaca, NY: Cornell University Press, 1961).

——and William Peden (eds). *The Selected Writings of John and John Quincy Adams* (New York: Alfred A. Knopf, 1946).

Koch, Claude. "The unwritten texts," *Imprimis*, XV (October 1986), 1–8.

Kodras, Janet E. "The spatial perspective in welfare analysis," *Cato Journal*, VI (Spring–Summer 1986), 77–83.

Kohler, Peter A. and Hans F. Zacker. *The Evolution of Social Insurance 1881–1981* (New York: St Martin's, 1982).

Kopcke, Richard W. "Investment spending and the federal taxation of business income," Federal Reserve Bank of Boston *New England Economic Review* (September–October, 1985), 9–33.

Kosner, Edward, Jacquin Sandels and Frank Trippet. "Poverty U.S.A.," *Newsweek* (February 17, 1964), 19–38.

Kramnick, Isaac. "Equal opportunity and 'The Race of Life'," *Dissent*, XXVIII (Spring 1981), 178–87.

Kravis, Irving B. "Income distribution: functional share," in David L. Sills (ed.) *International Encyclopedia of the Social Sciences* (New York: Macmillan, 1968), vol. VII, pp. 132–45.

Kregel, J. A. "Some post-Keynesian distribution theory," in Sidney Weintraub (ed.), *Modern Economic Thought* (Philadelphia, PA: University of Pennsylvania Press, 1977), pp. 421–38.

Kristol, Irving. "Equality as an ideal," in David L. Sills (ed.), *International Encyclopedia of the Social Sciences* (New York: Macmillan, 1968), vol. V, pp. 108–11.

——"The high cost of equality," *Fortune*, XCII (November 1975), 199–200.

——*Reflections of a Neoconservative* (New York: Basic Books, 1983).

——*Two Cheers for Capitalism* (New York: New American Library (Mentor Book), 1979).

Kutler, Stanley I. *The Supreme Court and the Constitution: Readings in American Constitutional History* (Boston, MA: Houghton Mifflin, 1969).

Kuttner, Robert. *The Economic Illusion* (Boston, MA: Houghton Mifflin, 1984).

——"A great American tradition: government opening opportunity," *Challenge*, XXIX (March–April 1986), 18–25.

——"It's dismal, all right – but is it a science?" *Business Week* (January 30, 1989), 16.

——"The poverty of economics," *Atlantic Monthly*, CCLV (February 1985), 74–84.

Labor: Its Rights and Wrongs (Washington, DC: Labor Publishing Company, 1886).

Lambro, Donald. *Land of Opportunity* (Boston, MA: Little, Brown, 1986).

Landreth, Harry. *History of Economic Thought* (Boston, MA: Houghton Mifflin, 1976).

Lane, Robert E. *Political Ideology: Why the American Common Man Believes What He Does* (New York: Free Press of Glencoe, 1962).

Larcom, Lucy. "Among Lowell mill-girls: a reminiscence," *Atlantic Monthly*, XLVIII (November 1881), 611.

Laslett, John H. M. and Seymour M. Lipset (eds) *Failure of a Dream?* (Garden City, NY: Doubleday, 1974).

Lay Commission on Catholic Social Teaching and the US Economy. "LIBERTY and justice for all," Report on the final draft (June 1986) of the US Catholic bishops' Pastoral Letter "Economic justice for all," November 5, 1986.

——*Toward the Future* (New York: Lay Commission on Catholic Social Teaching and the US Economy, 1984).

Lazear, Edward. "Why is there mandatory retirement?" *Journal of Political Economy*, LXXXVII (December 1979), 1261–84.

Lee, Dwight R. "The politics of poverty and the poverty of politics," *Cato Journal*, V (Spring–Summer 1985), 32–5.

Leibenstein, Harvey. "Allocative efficiency vs. X-efficiency," *American Economic Review*, LVI (June 1966), 392–415.

——"Microeconomics and X-efficiency theory: if there is no crisis, there ought to be," in Daniel Bell and Irving Kristol (eds), *The Crisis in Economic Theory* (New York: Basic Books, 1981), pp. 97–110.

——"More on X-efficiency: comment," *Quarterly Journal of Economics*, LXXXVI (May 1972), 327–31.

Leiby, James. *A History of Social Welfare and Social Work in the United States* (New York: Columbia University Press, 1978).

Lekachman, Robert. *Greed Is Not Enough* (New York: Pantheon, 1982).

——*National Income and The Public Welfare* (New York: Random House, 1972).

Lerner, Max. *Tocqueville and American Civilization* (New York: Harper & Row (Harper Colophon Books), 1969).

Letwin, Shirley R. "The morality of the free man," in Barbara J. Smith (ed.), *Champions of Freedom*, Ludwig von Mises Lecture Series (Hillsdale, MI: Hillsdale College Press, 1976), vol. III, pp. 131–54.

Levinson, Marc. "The shaky case for aiding investment," *Dun's Business Month*, CXXVII (March 1986), 22–4.

Levitan, Sar A. and Clifford M. Johnson. *Beyond the Safety Net: Reviving the Promise of Opportunity in America* (Cambridge, MA: Ballinger, 1984).

——and Isaac Shapiro. "What's missing in welfare reform," *Challenge*, XXX (July–August 1987), 41–8.

Lewis, Oscar. "The culture of poverty," *Scientific American*, CCVI (October 1966), 19–25.

Lindbeck Assar. *The Political Economy of the New Left*, 2nd edn (New York: Harper & Row, 1977).

Link, C. R. and J. H. Landon. "Monopsony and union power in the market for nurses," *Southern Economic Journal*, XLI (April 1975), 649–59.

Lippmann, Walter. *Essays in The Public Philosophy* (New York: Mentor Book, 1955).

——*A Preface to Politics* (Ann Arbor, MI: University of Michigan, 1962).

Lipset, Seymour Martin. "Why no socialism in the United States?" in Seweryn Bialer and Sophia Sluzar (eds), *Radicalism in the Contemporary Age* (Boulder, CO: Westview Press, 1977), vol. I, pp. 31–149.

Locke, John. *An Essay Concerning Human Understanding*, ed. John W. Yolton (New York: Dutton, 1978).

——*Two Treatises of Government*, ed. Peter Laslett (New York: New American Library, 1965).

Lott, David Newton (ed.) *The Inaugural Addresses of the American Presidents* (New York: Holt, Rinehart & Winston, 1961).

Loury, Glenn C. "The family, the nation, and Senator Moynihan," *Commentary*, LXXXI (June 1986), 21–6.

McClelland, Peter D. *Causal Explanation and Model Building in History, Economics, and The New Economic History* (Ithaca, NY: Cornell University Press, 1975).

——"The cost to America of British Imperial policy," *American Economic Review*, LIX (May 1969), 370–81.

McCloskey, Donald N. *The Applied Theory of Price*, 2nd edn (New York: Macmillan, 1985).

McClosky, Herbert and John Zaller. *The American Ethos* (Cambridge, MA: Harvard University Press, 1984).

Macdonald, Maurice and Isabel V. Sawhill. "Welfare policy and the family," *Public Policy*, XXVI (Winter 1978), 105–19.

McDowell, Edwin. "Book notes," *New York Times* (July 27, 1988), C19.

Machlup, Fritz. "Theories of the firm: marginalist, behavioral, managerial," *American Economic Review*, LVII (March 1967), 1–33.

McIntyre, Robert S. and Dean C. Tipps. "Exploding the investment-incentive myth," *Challenge*, XXVIII (May–June 1985), 47–52.

Mackay, Thomas. *Methods of Social Reform* (London: John Murray, 1896).

McKinley, William. *Speeches and Addresses: From his Election to Congress to the Present Time* (New York: D. Appleton, 1893).

Mackintosh, Donald (ed.) *Mackintosh's Collection of Gaelic Proverbs and Familiar Phrases* (Edinburgh: Charles Stewart, 1819).

McLanahan, Sara. "Charles Murray and the family," in Sara McLanahan et al., "LOSING GROUND: a critique," University of Wisconsin Institute for Research on Poverty, Special Report Series 38, August 1985.

——et al. "LOSING GROUND: a critique," Univerity of Wisconsin Institute for Research on Poverty, Special Report Series 38, August 1985.

Macpherson, C. B. "Human rights as property rights," *Dissent*, XXIV (Winter 1977), 72–7.

——*The Political Theory of Possessive Individualism: Hobbes to Locke* (New York: Oxford University Press, 1976).

Magnet, Myron. "The decline and fall of business ethics," *Fortune*, CXIV (December 8, 1986), 65–6, 68, 72.

——"The money society," *Fortune*, CXVI (July 6, 1987), 26–31.

Marcussen Ernst. *Social Welfare in Denmark* (Copenhagen: Det Danske Selskab, 1980).

Mare, Robert D. and Christopher Winship. "Ethnic and racial patterns of educational attainment and school enrollment." Paper presented at Conference on Minorities in Poverty, Airlie, Virginia, November 1986.

Mariani, Paul. "Renewing the symbolic contract," *Imprimis*, XV (December 1986), 1–8.

Marmor, Theodore R. and Martin Rein. "Reforming the 'welfare mess': the fate of the Family Assistance Plan, 1969–72," in Allan P. Sindler (ed.), *Policy and Politics in America* (Boston, MA: Little, Brown, 1973), pp. 2–28.

Marshall, George. "Address at Harvard University, June 5, 1947," in Paul M. Angle (ed.), *By These Words: Great Documents of American Liberty* (New York: Rand McNally, 1954), pp. 224–8.

Marx, Karl and Friedrich Engels. *The German Ideology*, ed. R. Pascal (New York: International Publishers, 1939).

——*Selected Works* (New York: International Publishers, 1974).

Mayer, Jane. "What's behind divorce, teen-age pregnancies? Head of White House policy team blames welfare," *Wall Street Journal* (June 13, 1986), 48.

Mayo, Bernard (ed.) *Jefferson Himself* (Charlottesville, VA: University Press of Virginia, 1976).

"Mayors seek federal aid to curb poverty in cities," *New York Times* (December 19, 1986), A23.

Mead, Frank S. (ed.) *The Encyclopedia of Religious Quotations* (Westwood, NJ: Fleming H. Revell, 1965).

Mead, Lawrence M. *Beyond Entitlement* (New York: Free Press, 1986).

Medoff, James L. and Katherine G. Abraham. "Are those paid more really more productive?" *Journal of Human Resources*, XVI (Spring 1981), 186–216.

——"Experience, performance, and earnings," *Quarterly Journal of Economics*, XCV (December 1980), 703–36.

Melden, A. I. *Rights and Right Conduct* (Oxford: Basil Blackwell, 1959).

Mellor, Earl F. "Investigating the differences in weekly earnings of men and women," *Monthly Labor Review*, CVII (June 1984), 17–28.

Mill, John Stuart. *On Liberty* (New York: Penguin, 1981).

——*Principles of Political Economy* (London: Longmans, Green, 1902).

Miller, Perry. "The responsibility of mind in a civilization of machines," *American Scholar*, XXXI (Winter 1961–2), 51–69.

von Mises, Ludwig. *The Anti-Capitalist Mentality* (Princeton, NJ: Princeton University

Press, 1956).

——*The Free and Prosperous Commonwealth; An Exposition of the Ideas of Classical Liberalism* (Princeton, NJ: Van Nostrand, 1962).

Moffitt, Robert A. "The negative income tax: would it discourage work?" *Monthly Labor Review*, CIV (April 1981), 23–7.

Monsen, R. Joseph, John S. Chiu, and David E. Cooley, "The effect of separation of ownership and control on the performance of large firms," *Quarterly Journal of Economics*, LXXXII (August 1968), 435–51.

"Morality among the supply-siders," *Time* (May 25, 1987), 18–20.

Morgenthau, Hans J. "On trying to be just," *Commentary*, XXXV (May 1963), 420–3.

Moskos, Charles C. "Success story: blacks in the army," *Atlantic Monthly*, CCLVII (May 1986), 64–72.

Moynihan, Daniel Patrick. *Family and Nation* (New York: Harcourt Brace Jovanovich, 1986).

——"We can't avoid family policy much longer," *Challenge*, XXVIII (September–October 1985), 9–17.

Murchland, Bernard. "The socialist critique of the corporation," in Michael Novak and John W. Cooper (eds), *The Corporation: A Theological Inquiry* (Washington, DC: American Enterprise Institute, 1981), pp. 156–71.

Murray, Charles. "According to age: longitudinal profiles of AFDC recipients and the poor by age group." Paper prepared for the Working Seminar on the Family and American Welfare Policy, Institute for Family Studies, Marquette University, September 1986.

——"Have the poor been 'Losing Ground'?" *Political Science Quarterly*, C (Fall 1985), 427–45.

——"Helping the poor: a few modest proposals," *Commentary*, LXXIX (May 1985), 27–34.

——*Losing Ground: American Social Policy, 1950–1980* (New York: Basic Books, 1984).

——"*Losing Ground* two years later," *Cato Journal*, VI (Spring–Summer 1986), 19–29.

——"No, welfare isn't really the problem," *Public Interest*, LXXXIV (Summer 1986), 3–11.

Musgrave, Richard A. and Peggy B. Musgrave. *Public Finance In Theory and Practice* (New York: McGraw-Hill, 1973).

Myrdal, Gunnar. *An American Dilemma: The Negro Problem and Modern Democracy* (New York: Harper & Brothers, 1944).

Nagel, Thomas. "Rawls on justice," *Philosophical Review*, LXXXII (April 1973), 220–34.

Nasar, Sylvia. "America's poor: how big a problem?" *Fortune*, CXIII (May 26, 1986), 74–80.

Nathan, Richard P. "The missing link in applied social science," *Society*, XXII (January–February 1985), 71–7.

National Governors' Association. *Making America Work: Bringing Down The Barriers* (Washington, DC: National Governors' Association, 1987).

Nell, Edward. "Two books on the theory of income distribution: a review article," *Journal of Economic Literature*, X (June 1972), 442–53.

Neufeld, Maurice F. "Critique of Edward Pessen's *Most Uncommon Jacksonians: The Radical Leaders of the Early Labor Movement*." Unpublished paper, Cornell University, 1982.

——"The persistence of ideas in the American labor movement; the heritage of the 1830's," *Industrial and Labor Relations Review*, XXXV (January 1982), 207–20.

"New prospects, old values," *Time* (June 17, 1985), 68–9.

"New work under way," *Focus*, University of Wisconsin Institute for Research on Poverty, IX (Spring 1986), 21–4.

New York (State), Governor, Annual Message to the Legislature, January 6, 1988.

New York (State), Task Force on Poverty and Welfare, "A new social contract," Report submitted to Governor Mario M. Cuomo, December 1986.

Nicolay, John G. and John Hay. *Abraham Lincoln: Complete Works* (New York: Century, 1907).

Nielsen, Kai. "Ethics, problems of," in Paul Edwards (ed.), *Encyclopedia of Philosophy* (New York: Macmillan, 1967), vol. III, pp. 117–34.

Nisbet, Robert A. "The fatal ambivalence of an idea: equal freemen or equal serfs?" *Encounter*, LXVII (December 1976), 10–21.

Nishiyama, Chiaki and Kurt R. Leube (eds) *The Essence of Hayek* (Stanford, CA: Hoover Institution, 1984).

Nock, Albert Jay. *Our Enemy, The State* (New York: William Morrow, 1935).

Norton, Arthur J. and Jeanne E. Moorman. "Current trends in marriage and divorce among American women," *Journal of Marriage and the Family*, XLIX (February 1987), 3–14.

Novak, Michael. *The American Vision: An Essay on the Future of Democratic Capitalism* (Washington, DC: American Enterprise Institute, 1978).

——"A Catholic's reply to bishops: poor nations can learn from U.S.," *U.S. News & World Report* (November 26, 1984), 61–2.

——*The Spirit of Democratic Capitalism* (New York: Simon and Schuster, 1982).

"Now, a few words from the wise," *Time* (June 22, 1987), 69.

Nozick, Robert. *Anarchy, State, and Utopia* (New York: Basic Books, 1974).

O'Connell, Martin and David E. Bloom. "Cutting the apron strings: women in the labor force in the 1980's," Harvard Institute of Economic Research Discussion Paper 1297, January 1987.

Ofstad, Harald. *An Inquiry into the Freedom of Decision* (London: George Allen & Unwin, 1961).

Okun, Arthur M. *Equality and Efficiency: The Big Tradeoff* (Washington, DC: Brookings Institution, 1975).

O'Neill, June. "Transfers and poverty: cause and/or effect?" *Cato Journal*, VI (Spring–Summer 1986), 62–9.

——et al. *Analysis of Time on Welfare* (Washington, DC: Urban Institute, 1984).

Organization for Economic Co-Operation and Development. "Public expenditure trends," *Studies in Resource Allocation Number 5* (Paris: OECD, 1978).

Oswald, Rudy. "The economy and workers' jobs, the living wage and a voice," in John W. Houck and Oliver F. Williams (eds), *Catholic Social Teaching and The United States Economy* (Washington, DC: University Press of America, 1984), pp. 77–89.

Otten, Alan L. "Poor will find many jobs will be out of reach as labor market shrinks, demands for skills rise," *Wall Street Journal* (May 27, 1987), 6.

Padover, Saul K. *The Complete Thomas Jefferson* (New York: Tudor Publishing, 1943).

Page, Benjamin I. "Utilitarian arguments for equality." Unpublished Discussion Paper DP547-79, Institute for Research on Poverty, University of Wisconsin-Madison.

Partridge, P. H. "Freedom," in Paul Edwards (ed.), *Encyclopedia of Philosophy* (New York: Macmillan, 1967), vol. III, pp. 221–5.

Patterson, James T. *America's Struggle Against Poverty, 1900–1980* (Cambridge, MA: Harvard University Press, 1981).

Pear, Robert. "Increasingly, those who have jobs are poor, too," *New York Times* (December 27, 1987), E5.

——"Women reduce lag in earnings but disparities with men remain," *New York Times* (September 4, 1987), A1.

——"Young mothers said to be on welfare longer," *New York Times* (September 10, 1986), A28.

Pechman, Joseph A. (ed.) *Economics for Policymaking: Selected Essays of Arthur M. Okun* (Cambridge, MA: MIT Press, 1983).

Petro, Sylvester. "Labor-service agencies in a free society," in *Champions of Freedom*, Ludwig von Mises Lecture Series (Hillsdale, MI: Hillsdale College Press, 1974), vol. I, pp. 93–109.

Phelps, Edith M. (ed.) *Selected Articles on the Income Tax* (Minneapolis, MN: H. W. Wilson, 1911).

Phillips, Willard. *A Manual of Political Economy, with Particular Reference to the Institutions, Resources, and Condition of the United States* (Boston, MA: Hilliard, Gray, Little, and Wilkins, 1828).

Physician Task Force on Hunger in America. *Hunger in America: A Growing Epidemic* (Boston, MA: Harvard School of Public Health, 1985).

——*Hunger Reaches Blue Collar America: An Unbalanced Recovery in a Service Economy* (Boston, MA: Harvard School of Public Health, 1987).

Pigou, A. C. *The Economics of Welfare*, 4th edn (London: Macmillan, 1960).

Plamenatz, John. *The English Utilitarians* (Oxford: Basil Blackwell, 1949).

Pocock, J. G. A. "Virtue and commerce in the eighteenth century," *Journal of Interdisciplinary History*, III (Summer 1972), 119–34.

Polanyi, Michael. *The Logic of Liberty* (London: Routledge & Kegan Paul, 1951).

"Pornography: a poll," *Time* (July 21, 1986), 22.

"Poverty in the United States: where do we stand now?" *Focus*, University of Wisconsin Institute of Poverty, VII (Winter 1984), 1–13.

"Quotes of the week," *U.S. News & World Report* (June 1, 1987), 9.

Rand, Ayn (ed.) *Capitalism: The Unknown Ideal* (New York: New American Library (Signet Book), 1967).

——*The Fountainhead* (New York: Bobbs-Merrill, 1968).

——(ed.) *The Virtue of Selfishness* (New York: New American Library (Signet Book), 1964).

Raskin, Marcus G. "Programmatic notes: progressive liberalism for the '80s," *Nation*, CCXXX (May 17, 1980), 577, 587–91.

Rawls, John. *A Theory of Justice* (Cambridge, MA: Harvard University Press, 1971).

Reagan, Ronald. "State of the Union, 1982," *Vital Speeches of the Day*, XLVIII (February 15, 1982), 258–62.

"A record prison census," *New York Times* (May 17, 1987), E4.

Rein, Martin and Lee Rainwater. "Patterns of welfare use," *Social Service Review*, LII (December 1978), 511–34.

Reinhold, Robert. "California tries caring for its growing ranks of latchkey children," *New York Times* (October 25, 1987), E4.

Reischauer, Robert D. "Welfare reform: will consensus be enough?" *Brookings Review*, V (Summer 1987), 3–8.

Rescher, Nicholas. *Distributive Justice* (New York: University Press of America, 1966).

Research and Policy Committee of the Committee for Economic Development. *Children In Need: Investment Strategies for the Educationally Disadvantaged* (Washington, DC: Committee for Economic Development, 1987).

Rhodes, Robert (ed.) *Winston S. Churchill: His Complete Speeches, 1897–1963* (New York: Chelsea House, 1974).

Rice, Allen Thorndike (ed.) *Reminiscences of Abraham Lincoln* (New York: North American Review, 1888).

Rimlinger, Gaston V. *Welfare Policy and Industrialization in Europe, America, and Russia* (New York: Wiley, 1971).

Rix, Sara E. *The American Woman, 1987–88*, Women's Research and Education Institute of the Congressional Caucus for Women's Issues (New York: Norton, 1987).

Robinson, Joan. *Freedom and Necessity* (London: George Allen & Unwin, 1971).

Roche, George C., III. "The relevance of Friedrich A. Hayek," in Fritz Machlup (ed.), *Essay on Hayek* (New York: New York University Press, 1976), pp. 1–11.

Roosevelt, Theodore. *Address of President Roosevelt on the Occasion of the Laying of the Corner Stone of the Pilgrim Memorial Monument, Provincetown, Massachusetts, August 20, 1907* (Washington, DC: US Government Printing Office, 1907).

Rosenman, Samuel I. (ed.) *The Public Papers and Addresses of Franklin D. Roosevelt* (New York: Random House, 1938).

——(ed.) *The Public Papers and Addresses of Franklin D. Roosevelt* (New York: Macmillan, 1941).

——(ed.) *The Public Papers and Addresses of Franklin D. Roosevelt* (New York: Harper, 1950), vol. XIII.

Rosenweig, Mark R. "Who receives medical care? Income, implicit prices and the distribution of medical services among pregnant women in the United States," Yale University Growth Center Discussion Paper 522, November 1986.

Ross, W. D. (ed.) *The Student's Oxford Aristotle* (London: Oxford University Press, 1942).

Rothbard, Murray N. *The Ethics of Liberty* (Atlantic Highlands, NJ: Humanities Press, 1982).

——*For a New Liberty* (New York: Macmillan, 1973).

——*Man, Economy and State: A Treatise on Economic Principles* (Los Angeles, CA: Nash Publishing, 1962).

——*Power and Market: Government and the Economy* (Kansas City, KS: Sheed Andrews and McMeel, 1970).

Rummel, R. J. "War isn't this century's biggest killer," *Wall Street Journal* (July 7, 1986), 12.

Ryan, William. *Equality* (New York: Pantheon, 1981).

Salins, Peter D. *Housing America's Poor* (Chapel Hill, NC: University of North Carolina Press, 1987).

Samuelson, Paul A. *Economics*, 11th edn, revised (New York: McGraw-Hill, 1980).

——*Economics from the Heart: A Samuelson Sampler*, ed. Maryann O. Keating (Sun Lakes, AZ: Thomas Horton and Daughters, 1983).

——and William D. Nordhaus. *Economics*, 12th edn (New York: McGraw-Hill, 1985).

Sandefur, Gary D. and Wilbur J. Scott. "Minority group status and the wages of Indian and black males," *Social Science Research*, XII (1983), 44–68.

——"A sociological analysis of white, black and American Indian male labor force activities," University of Wisconsin Institute for Research on Poverty Discussion Paper 765–84, November 1984.

Sartori, Giovanni. *Democratic Theory* (Detroit, MI: Wayne State University Press, 1962).

Sawhill, Isabel V. "Anti-poverty strategies for the next decade," in Ben W.

Heineman, Jr. et al., *Work and Welfare: The Case for New Directions in National Policy* (Washington, DC: Center for National Policy, 1987), pp. 21–34.

Schiltz, Michael E. *Public Attitudes Toward Social Security, 1935–1965* (Washington, DC: US Government Printing Office, 1970).

Schmalz, Jeffrey. "Cuomo says Reagan government lacks respect for the rule of law," *New York Times* (July 29, 1987), A16.

——"2,000 Catholics lobby leaders in Albany visit," *New York Times* (March 10, 1987), A1.

Schultze, Charles L. "Microeconomic efficiency and nominal wage stickiness," *American Economic Review*, LXXV (March 1985), 1–15.

——*The Public Use of Private Interest* (Washington, DC: Brookings Institution, 1977).

Scitovsky, Tibor. "A survey of some theories of income distribution," in National Bureau of Economic Research, *The Behavior of Income Shares. Studies in Income and Wealth* (Princeton, NJ: Princeton University Press, 1964), vol. XXVII, pp. 15–31.

"Second draft of the U.S. bishops' Pastoral Letter on Catholic social teaching and the U.S. economy," *Origins*, XV (October 10, 1985), 257–96.

Sen, Amartya. *On Economic Inequality* (New York: W. W. Norton, 1973).

Shalhope, Robert E. "Republicanism and early American historiography," *William and Mary Quarterly*, XXXIX (January 1982), 334–56.

Shannon, Fred A. (ed.) *American Farmers' Movements* (Princeton, NJ: Van Nostrand, 1957).

Shaw, George Bernard. "On Mr. Mallock's proposed trumpet performance. (A rejoinder)," *The Fortnightly Review*, LV, New Series (April 1, 1884), 470–93.

Shenfield, Arthur. "Capitalism under the tests of ethics," in John Andrews (ed.), *Champions of Freedom*, Ludwig von Mises Lecture Series (Hillsdale, MI: Hillsdale College, 1982), vol. IX, pp. 17–34.

Silk, Leonard. "Changes in labor by the year 2000," *New York Times* (January 6, 1988), D2.

Simon, William E. "Big government or freedom – the line of economic freedom leads to slavery," *Vital Speeches of the Day*, XXXI (April 15, 1975), 386–9.

——*Reforming the Income Tax System* (Washington, DC: American Enterprise Institute, 1981).

——*A Time for Truth* (New York: McGraw-Hill, 1978).

Simons, Henry C. *Personal Income Taxation* (Chicago, IL: University of Chicago Press, 1938).

Simpson, Janice C. "Firm steps: a shallow labor pool spurs business to act to bolster education," *Wall Street Journal* (September 28, 1987), 1.

Small Business Administration. *The State of Small Business: A Report of the President, Transmitted to the Congress*, various dates (Washington, DC: US Government Printing Office).

Smart, J. J. C. "Utilitarianism," in Paul Edwards (ed.), *Encyclopedia of Philosophy* (New York: Macmillan, 1967), vol. VIII, pp. 206–12.

Smeeding, Timothy, Barbara Boyle Torrey and Martin Rein. "Comparative well-being of children and elderly," *Contemporary Policy Issues*, V (April 1987), 57–71.

Smith, Adam. *The Theory of Moral Sentiments* (Indianapolis, IN: Liberty Classics, 1976).

——*The Wealth of Nations*, ed. Edwin Cannan (Chicago, IL: University of Chicago Press, 1976).

Smith, James P. and Finis R. Welch. *Closing the Gap: Forty Years of Economic Progress for Blacks* (Santa Monica, CA: Rand Corporation, 1986).

Smolensky, Eugene. "Is a golden age in poverty policy right around the corner?" *Focus*, University of Wisconsin Institute for Research on Poverty, VIII (Spring 1985), 9–11, 18.

Social Welfare Board. *Social Sweden* (Stockholm: Gernandts Boktryckeri, 1952).

"The socioeconomic status of native Americans: a special policy problem," *Focus*, University of Wisconsin Institute for Research on Poverty, IX (Spring 1986), 25–6.

Soltan, Karol Edward. "Empirical studies in distributive justice," *Ethics*, XCII (July 1982), 673–91.

Sowell, Thomas. *A Conflict of Visions* (New York: William Morrow, 1987).

——*The Economics and Politics of Race* (New York: William Morrow, 1983).

——*Markets and Minorities* (New York: Basic Books, 1981).

——*Race and Economics* (New York: Longman, 1975).

Sparks, Bertel M. "Retreat from contract to status," in Barbara J. Smith (ed.), *Champions of Freedom*, Ludwig von Mises Lecture Series (Hillsdale, MI: Hillsdale College Press, 1975), vol. II, pp. 59–82.

Spencer, Herbert. *The Man Versus The State* (Indianapolis, IN: Liberty Classics, 1981).

"The spirit of discontent," *Lowell Offering*, I (April 1841), 111–14.

Spitz, David. "A grammar of equality," *Dissent*, XXI (Winter 1974), 63–78.

Spring, William J. "Youth unemployment and the transition from school to work: programs in Boston, Frankfurt, and London," Federal Reserve Bank of Boston *New England Economic Review* (March–April 1987) 3–16.

Sraffa, Piero (ed.) *The Works and Correspondence of David Ricardo* (Cambridge: Cambridge University Press, 1951).

SRI International. *Final Report of the Seattle–Denver Income Maintenance Experiment*, vol I, *Design and Result* (Washington, DC: US Government Printing Office, 1983).

Starr, Paul. "Health care for the poor: the past twenty years," in Sheldon H. Danziger and Daniel H. Weinberg (eds), *Fighting Poverty* (Cambridge, MA: Harvard University Press, 1986), pp. 106–32.

Stein, Herbert. "How to be a conservative," *Fortune*, CXIV (November 10, 1986), 197–8.

——*Presidential Economics* (New York: Simon and Schuster, 1984).

——"Should growth be a priority of national policy?" *Challenge*, XXIX (March–April 1986), 11–17.

Stewart, D. Michael. "Poor laws and pauper policies," *Vital Speeches of the Day*, LIII (February 1, 1987), 245–8.

Stigler, George J. *The Citizen and the State* (Chicago, IL: University of Chicago Press, 1975).

——*The Economist as Preacher and Other Essays* (Chicago, IL: University of Chicago Press, 1982).

——*The Pleasures and Pains of Modern Capitalism* (Albuquerque, NM: Transatlantic Arts, 1982).

Stiglitz, Joseph E. *Collected Scientific Papers of Paul A. Samuelson* (Cambridge, MA: MIT Press, 1966).

"Strike one and you're out," *U.S. News & World Report* (July 27, 1987), 52–7.

"Study says families with children swell ranks of homeless," *New York Times* (March 31, 1987), A16.

Surrey, M. J. C. *Macroeconomic Themes* (Oxford: Oxford University Press, 1976).

"Symposium: the slowdown in productivity growth," *Journal of Economic Perspectives*, II (Fall 1988), 3–97.

Tawney, R. H. *The Acquisitive Society* (New York: Harcourt Brace Jovanovich (Harvest Book), 1948).

——*Equality* (Totowa, NJ: Barnes & Noble, 1980).

Teaford, Jon C. *The Municipal Revolution in America* (Chicago, IL: University of Chicago Press, 1975).

Teltsch, Kathleen. "Corporate pressures slowing gifts to charity," *New York Times* (July 8, 1987), A1, D2.

The Texas Declaration of Independence: An Exact Facsimile (Houston, TX: Anson Jones, 1943).

Theobold, Robert (ed.) *The Guaranteed Income: Next Step in Economic Evolution* (Garden City, NJ: Doubleday, 1966).

Thernstrom, Stephen. *Poverty and Progress* (Cambridge, MA: Harvard University Press, 1964).

"Third draft of the U.S. bishops' economy Pastoral: Economic justice for all, Catholic social teaching and the U.S. economy," *Origins*, XVI (June 5, 1986), 33–76.

Thomas, John L. *Alternative America: Henry George, Edward Bellamy, Henry Demarest Lloyd and the Adversary Tradition* (Cambridge, MA: Belknap, 1983).

Thorndike, Richard L. *Reading Comprehension Education in Fifteen Countries: An Empirical Study* (Stockholm: Almquist & Wiksell, 1973).

Thornton, Arland. "The changing American family: living arrangements and relationships with kin," *Economic Outlook USA*, XII (Second quarter 1985), 34–8.

Thurow, Lester C. *Generating Inequality: Mechanisms of Distribution in the U.S. Economy* (New York: Basic Books, 1975).

——*The Impact of Taxes on the American Economy* (New York: Praeger, 1971).

——"Toward a definition of economic justice," *Public Interest*, XXXI (Spring 1973), 56–80.

——*The Zero-Sum Society* (New York: Basic Books, 1980).

Tienda, Marta. "The Puerto Rican worker: Current labor market status and future prospects," *Journal of Hispanic Politics*, I (1985), 27–51.

Tinbergen, Jan. *Income Distribution: Analysis and Policy* (Amsterdam: North-Holland, 1975).

Tobin, James. "On limiting the domain of inequality," *Journal of Law and Economics*, XIII (October 1970), 263–77.

de Tocqueville, Alexis. *Democracy in America*, ed. Richard D. Heffner (New York: New American Library (Mentor Book), 1956).

"To see ourselves as others see us," *Time* (June 16, 1986), 52–3.

Toward Equal Opportunity for Higher Education. *Report of the Panel on Financing Low-Income and Minority Students in Higher Education* (New York: College Entrance Examination Board, 1973).

Trenchard, John (ed.) *The Third and Last Collection of Cato's Letters, in the British Journal* (London: T. Woodward, 1723).

Trilling, Lionel. *The Liberal Imagination* (New York: Viking, 1950).

Truscott, Alan. "Chance steps in," *New York Times* (January 12, 1986), H38.

US Bureau of Labor Statistics. *Employment and Earnings*.

US Congress. Congressional Budget Office. *An Analysis of the Roth–Kemp Tax Cut Proposal*, October 1978.

US Congress. House. Committee on Expenditures in the Executive Departments. *Hearings, Full Employment Act of 1945*. 79th Cong., 1st sess., 1945.

——Committee on Ways and Means. *Background Material and Data on Programs Within the Jurisdiction of the Committee on Ways and Means*. 98th Cong., 2nd sess., February 1984.

——Committee on Ways and Means. *Children in Poverty*. 99th Cong., 1st sess., May 22, 1985.

——Committee on Ways and Means. *Public Welfare Amendments of 1962. Report to accompany H. R. 10616*. 87th Cong., 2nd sess., Report No. 1414, March 10, 1962.

——*Congressional Record*.

——Subcommittee of the War on Poverty Program of the Committee on Education and Labor. *Hearings, Economic Opportunity Act of 1964*. 88th Cong., 2nd sess., 1964.

US Congress. Senate. Committee on Finance. *Hearings, Welfare Reform Proposals*. 95th Cong., 2nd sess., 1978.

——Joint Committee on Atomic Energy. *Hearings on Confirmation of the Atomic Energy Commission and the General Manager*. 80th Cong., 1st sess., February 4, 1947.

——Select Committee on Poverty of the Committee on Labor and Public Welfare. *Hearings, Economic Opportunity Act of 1964*. 88th Cong., 2nd sess., June 1964.

——Subcommittee of the Committee on Banking and Currency. *Hearings, Full Employment Act of 1945*. 79th Cong., 1st sess., 1945.

US Department of Commerce. *Business Statistics 1984* (Washington, DC: US Government Printing Office, 1985).

——"Characteristics of the low-income population: 1972," *Current Population Reports*, Series P-60, no. 91, December 1973.

——"Characteristics of the population below the poverty level: 1981," *Current Population Reports*, Series P-60, no. 138, March 1983.

——"Child care arrangements of working mothers: June, 1982," *Current Population Reports*, Special Studies, Series P-23, no. 129, November 1983.

——*Current Population Reports*, Series P-20.

——*Current Population Reports*, Series P-60.

——*Historical Statistics of the United States: Colonial Times to 1970* (Washington, DC: US Government Printing Office, 1975).

——"Money income and poverty status of families and persons in the United States: 1985," *Current Population Reports*, Series P-60, no. 154, August 1986.

——*Statistical Abstract of the United States* (Washington, DC: US Government Printing Office).

US Department of Health and Human Services. "Head Start: a child development program" (Washington, DC, 1986).

——*Monthly Vital Statistics Report*.

——*Vital Statistics of the United States*.

Utt, Ronald D. and William Orzechowski. "International perspectives on economic growth," *Cato Policy Report*, VII (July–August 1985), 8–12.

Vanberg, Viktor. "Cultural evolution vs. rationalism in Hayek's thought," *Cato Policy Report*, VII (January–February 1985), 1, 3–5.

Vedder, Richard and Lowell Gallaway. "AFDC and the Laffer principle," *Wall Street Journal* (March 26, 1986), 30.

Verba, Sidney and Gary R. Orren. *Equality in America: The View from the Top* (Cambridge, MA: Harvard University Press, 1985).

——and Kay Lehman Schlozman. *Injury to Insult* (Cambridge, MA: Harvard University Press, 1979).

——"Unemployment, class consciousness, and radical politics," *Journal of Politics*, XXXIX (May 1977), 291–323.

——et al. *Elites and the Idea of Equality* (Cambridge, MA: Harvard University Press, 1987).

Walker, Graham. *The Ethics of Friedrich Hayek* (Geneva: Institut Universitaire Hautes Etudes Internationales, 1984).

Wallich, Henry C. "Inequality and growth," in Edward C. Budd (ed.), *Inequality and Poverty* (New York: W. W. Norton, 1967), pp. 14–26.

Ware, Norman. *The Industrial Worker, 1840–1860* (Chicago, IL: Quadrangle, 1964).

Webster, Daniel. *The Writings and Speeches of Daniel Webster* (Boston, MA: Little, Brown, 1903).

Webster, Noah. *An American Dictionary of the English Language* (New York: S. Converse, 1828).

Weicher, John C. "The 'safety net' and the 'fairness' issue," *AEI Economist* (August 1984), 1–12.

Weidenbaum, Murray L. "Do tax incentives for investment work?" Contemporary Issue Series 20, Center for the Study of American Business, Washington University, St. Louis, June 1986.

Weiss, Andrew and Henry Landau. "On the negative correlation between performance and experience and education," National Bureau of Economic Research Working Paper 1613, April 1985.

Weisskopf, Thomas E. "Capitalism and inequality," in Richard C. Edwards, Michael Reich, and Thomas E. Weisskopf (eds), *The Capitalist System* (Englewood Cliffs, NJ: Prentice-Hall, 1972), pp. 125–32.

Welch, Patrick J. "On the compatibility of profit maximization and other goals of the firm," *Review of Social Economy*, XXXVIII (April 1980), 65–74.

"Welfare in America: is it a flop?" *U.S. News & World Report* (December 24, 1984), 38–43.

"Welfare that works," *New Republic*, XCVII (August 24, 1987), 7–9.

Welsh, James. "Welfare reform: born, Aug. 8, 1969; Died, Oct. 4, 1972 – A sad case study of the American political process," *New York Times Magazine* (January 7, 1973), 14–17, 21–3.

Welter, Rush. *The Mind of America, 1820–1860* (New York: Columbia Univerity Press, 1975).

Wentworth, Harold and Stuart Berg Flexner (eds). *Dictionary of American Slang* (New York: Thomas Y. Crowell, 1975).

Werner, Leslie Maitland. "U.S. report asserts administration halted liberal 'Anti-Family Agenda'," *New York Times* (November 14, 1986), A12.

"What is the Golden Age?" *Scientific American*, V (December 22, 1849), 109.

"What's wrong? Hypocrisy, betrayal and greed unsettle the nation's soul," *Time* (May 25, 1987), 14–17.

"Who is to say what's right in teaching about ethics?" *New York Times* (April 19, 1987), E18.

Wiebe, Robert H. *The Search for Order, 1877–1920* (New York: Hill and Wange, 1967).

Wilentz, Sean. *Chants Democratic: New York City and the Rise of the American Working Class, 1788–1850* (New York: Oxford University Press, 1984).

Will, George F. "Conservatism with a kindly face? In defense of the welfare state," *New Republic*, CLXXXVIII (May 9, 1983), 20–1, 24–5.

——*The Pursuit of Virtue and Other Tory Notions* (New York: Simon and Schuster, 1982).

——*Statecraft as Soulcraft* (New York: Simon and Schuster, 1983).

Williams, Bernard. *Ethics and the Limits of Philosophy* (Cambridge, MA: Harvard

University Press, 1985).

——"The idea of equality," in Peter Laslett and W. G. Runciman (eds), *Philosophy, Politics and Society* (Oxford: Basil Blackwell, 1962), pp. 110–31.

Williams, Robin M., Jr. "The concept of value," in David L. Sills (ed.), *International Encyclopedia of the Social Sciences* (New York: Macmillan, 1968), vol. XVI, pp. 283–7.

Wilson, William Julius and Kathryn M. Neckerman. "Poverty and family structure: the widening gap between evidence and public policy issues," in Sheldon H. Danziger and Daniel H. Weinberg (eds), *Fighting Poverty* (Cambridge, MA: Harvard University Press, 1986), pp. 232–59.

Winthrop, John. "A model of Christian charity," *Collections of the Massachusetts Historical Society, 3rd series*, VII, 33–48.

Winthrop, Robert C. (ed.) *Memoir of the Hon. Nathan Appleton, LL.D.* (Boston, MA: John Wilson, 1861).

Wolfe, Tom. *The Kandy-Kolored Tangerine-Flake Streamlined Baby* (New York: Farrar, Straus, and Giroux, 1965).

Woodside, William. "Health care for the poor: how to pay for it," *Wall Street Journal* (May 29, 1987), 26.

Working Seminar on Family and American Welfare Policy. *The New Consensus on Family and Welfare* (Washington, DC: American Enterprise Institute, 1987).

Wright, Esmond. "Life, liberty, and the pursuit of excellence," in Barbara J. Smith (ed.), *Champions of Freedom*, Ludwig von Mises Lecture Series (Hillsdale, MI: Hillsdale College Press, 1976), vol. III, pp. 1–33.

Yielding, Kenneth D. and Paul H. Carlson (eds) *Ah That Voice: The Fireside Chats of Franklin Delano Roosevelt* (Odessa, TX: John Ben Shepperd, Jr., Library of the Presidents, 1976).

Index